Lecture Notes in Computer Science 6461

Commenced Publication in 1973
Founding and Former Series Editors:
Gerhard Goos, Juris Hartmanis, and Jan van I

Editorial Board

Kazunori Ueda (Ed.)

Programming Languages and Systems

8th Asian Symposium, APLAS 2010
Shanghai, China, November 28 - December 1, 2010
Proceedings

Springer

Volume Editor

Kazunori Ueda
Dept. of Computer Science and Engineering
Waseda University
3-4-1, Okubo, Shinjuku-ku, Tokyo, 169-8555, Japan
E-mail: ueda@ueda.info.waseda.ac.jp

Library of Congress Control Number: 2010939049

CR Subject Classification (1998): D.3, D.2, F.3, D.4, D.1, F.4.1, C.2

LNCS Sublibrary: SL 2 – Programming and Software Engineering

ISSN	0302-9743
ISBN-10	3-642-17163-X Springer Berlin Heidelberg New York
ISBN-13	978-3-642-17163-5 Springer Berlin Heidelberg New York

springer.com

Printed in Germany

Typesetting: Camera-ready by author, data conversion by Scientific Publishing Services, Chennai, India
Printed on acid-free paper 06/3180

Preface

This volume contains the papers presented at APLAS 2010, the eighth Asian Symposium on Programming Languages and Systems, held from November 28 to December 1, 2010, in Shanghai, China. The symposium was sponsored by the Asian Association for Foundation of Software (AAFS) and Shanghai Jiao Tong University.

APLAS is a premiere forum for the discussion of programming languages, based in Asia and serving the worldwide research community. The past APLAS symposia were successfully held in Seoul (2009), Bangalore (2008), Singapore (2007), Sydney (2006), Tsukuba (2005), Taipei (2004), and Beijing (2003), after three well-attended workshops held in Shanghai (2002), Daejeon (2001), and Singapore (2000). Proceedings of the past symposia were published in Springer's LNCS volumes 2895, 3302, 3780, 4279, 4807, 5356, and 5904.

APLAS 2010 solicited submissions in two categories, *regular research papers* and *system and tool presentations*. Ninety-five abstracts were submitted, of which 75 (70 regular research papers and 5 system and tool presentations from 21 countries) were followed by their full versions. Each submission was reviewed by at least three Program Committee members with the help of external reviewers. The Program Committee meeting was conducted electronically over a period of two weeks in July/August 2010. The Program Committee decided to accept 23 regular research papers (33%) and 2 system and tool presentations (40%). Seven of them were accepted conditionally, with specific requirements of necessary improvements; then the revised papers and the accompanying replies to the reviewers' comments were checked (and further shepherded for some papers) by the Program Committee before they were finally accepted. I would like to thank all the Program Committee members for their hard work dedicated to reviews and discussions, and all the external reviewers for their invaluable contributions.

The volume also contains the full papers and extended abstracts of four distinguished invited speakers: Gerwin Klein (National ICT Australia), Dale Miller (INRIA Saclay – Ile-de-France), Mingsheng Ying (Tsinghua University and University of Technology Sydney), and Chaochen Zhou (Chinese Academy of Sciences). It also contains a paper for a tutorial delivered by Aquinas Hobor (National University of Singapore) and Robert Dockins (Princeton University). I would like to thank all of these speakers for accepting our invitation and contributing papers.

I am grateful to Yuxi Fu, General Chair, for the invaluable support and guidance that made our symposium in Shanghai possible and enjoyable. I am also indebted to Xiaoju Dong, Local Arrangement Chair, for her effort in organizing and publicizing the meeting. I would like to thank Guoqiang Li for serving as the

Poster Chair. EasyChair made the handling of submissions and the production of the proceedings extremely smooth and efficient. Last but not least, I would like to thank the members of the AAFS Executive Committee and Zhenjiang Hu, the Program Chair of the last APLAS, for their advice.

December 2010 Kazunori Ueda

Organization

General Chair

Yuxi Fu	Shanghai Jiao Tong University, China

Program Chair

Kazunori Ueda	Waseda University, Japan

Program Committee

Roberto Amadio	Université Paris Diderot, France
Lennart Beringer	Princeton University, USA
Dino Distefano	Queen Mary, University of London, UK
Yuxi Fu	Shanghai Jiao Tong University, China
Joxan Jaffar	National University of Singapore, Singapore
Yukiyoshi Kameyama	University of Tsukuba, Japan
Gabriele Keller	University of New South Wales, Australia
Ralf Lämmel	University of Koblenz-Landau, Germany
Aditya V. Nori	Microsoft Research India, India
Sungwoo Park	Pohang University of Science and Technology, South Korea
Sanjiva Prasad	Indian Institute of Technology Delhi, India
Christian Schulte	Royal Institute of Technology, Sweden
Eijiro Sumii	Tohoku University, Japan
Alwen Tiu	Australian National University, Australia
Yih-Kuen Tsay	National Taiwan University, Taiwan
Kazunori Ueda	Waseda University, Japan
Hongwei Xi	Boston University, USA
Jian Zhang	Chinese Academy of Sciences, China

Local Arrangements Chair

Xiaoju Dong	Shanghai Jiao Tong University, China

Poster Chair

Guoqiang Li	Shanghai Jiao Tong University, China

External Reviewers

Andreas Abel
Luca Aceto
Kento Aida
S. Arun-Kumar
Nicolas Ayache
David Baelde
Josh Berdine
K.K. Biswas
Kirill Bogdanov
Filippo Bonchi
Matko Botincan
Michele Bugliesi
Xiaojuan Cai
Manuel Chakravarty
Kung Chen
Liqian Chen
Shikun Chen
Yu-Fang Chen
Yuting Chen
Wei-Ngan Chin
Olivier Danvy
Jeremy Dawson
Yuxin Deng
Mike Dodds
Daniel Dougherty
Matthew Fluet
Andrew Gacek
Jacques Garrigue
Stéphane Glondu
Jens Chr. Godskesen
Robert Grabowski
Radu Grigore
Torsten Grust
Bhargav Gulavani
Ashutosh Gupta
Makoto Hamana
Duc Hiep
Thomas Hildebrandt
Daniel Hirschkoff
Petra Hofstedt
Atsushi Igarashi
Hyeonseung Im
Kazuhiro Inaba
Oleg Kiselyov
Jean Krivine
Akash Lal
Rasmus Lerchedahl Petersen
Roman Leshchinskiy
Guoqiang Li
Zhaopeng Li
Ben Lippmeier
Hans-Wolfgang Loidl
Huan Long
Etienne Lozes
Kenneth MacKenzie
Antoine Madet
Stephen Magill
Luc Maranget
Hidehiko Masuhara
Trevor McDonell
Yasuhiko Minamide
Virgile Mogbil
Alberto Momigliano
Jean-Yves Moyen
Shin-Cheng Mu
Rasmus Ejlers Møgelberg
Peter Müller
Shin Nakajima
Jorge Navas
Vivek Nigam
Gustavo Petri
Stefan M. Petters
Christian Queinnec
Zhilei Ren
Arend Rensink
John Reppy
Dulma Rodriguez
Kristoffer Rose
Jan Rutten
Andrew Santosa
Mark Schellhase
Ulrich Schöpp
Sam Staton
Peter Stuckey
Purui Su
Jun Sun
Guido Tack
Ming-Hsien Tsai
Viktor Vafeiadis
Stephan van Staden
Kapil Vaswani
Dimitrios Vytiniotis
Philip Wadler
Ting Wang
Yongji Wang
Simon Winwood
Hui Wu
Zhongxing Xu
Yu Yang
Roland Yap
Masahiro Yasugi
Taiichi Yuasa
Ian Zerny
Chenyi Zhang
Neng-Fa Zhou
Dengping Zhu
Florian Zuleger

Table of Contents

Invited Talks

Session 1

Session 2

Session 3

Session 4

Session 5

Session 6

Session 7

Session 8

Session 9

Tutorial

A Calculus for Hybrid CSP*

Jiang Liu[1], Jidong Lv[2], Zhao Quan[1], Naijun Zhan[1], Hengjun Zhao[1], Chaochen Zhou[1], and Liang Zou[1]

[1] State Key Lab. of Computer Science, Institute of Software, CAS
[2] State Key Lab. of Rail Traffic Control and Safety, Beijing Jiaotong University

Abstract. Hybrid Communicating Sequential Processes (HCSP) is an extension of CSP allowing continuous dynamics. We are interested in applying HCSP to model and verify hybrid systems. This paper is to present a calculus for a subset of HCSP as a part of our efforts in modelling and verifying hybrid systems. The calculus consists of two parts. To deal with continuous dynamics, the calculus adopts differential invariants. A brief introduction to a complete algorithm for generating polynomial differential invariants is presented, which applies DISCOVERER, a symbolic computation tool for semi-algebraic systems. The other part of the calculus is a logic to reason about HCSP process, which involves communication, parallelism, real-time as well as continuous dynamics. This logic is named as Hybrid Hoare Logic. Its assertions consist of traditional pre- and post-conditions, and also Duration Calculus formulas to record execution history of HCSP process.

Keywords: Chinese Train Control System, Differential Invariant, DISCOVERER, Duration Calculus, Hoare Logic, Hybrid CSP, Hybrid Logic.

1 Introduction

We are interested in modelling and verifying hybrid systems, and take the Level 3 of Chinese Train Control System (CTCS-3) [17] as a case study, which is an informal specification of Chinese high speed train control system that ensures safety and high throughput of trains. There are many reasons to guarantee the high throughput. But our case study only focuses on the analysis and verification of the safety of CTCS-3.

In CTCS-3, there are specifications of 14 scenarios. For example, one of the 14 scenarios specifies that trains are only allowed to move within their current *movement authorities* (MAs) which are determined and updated by *Radio Block Center* (RBC). Hence, the train controller should restrict the movement of the train to ensure that it always runs within its MA with a speed in the scope predefined by the MA. In this scenario, there are continuous dynamics of trains that are described by differential equations, communications between train and RBC, real-time aspects of the movement, etc.

* This work is supported in part by the projects NSFC-60721061, NSFC-90718041, NSFC-60736017, NSFC-60970031, NSFC-60634010 and RCS2008K001.

K. Ueda (Ed.): APLAS 2010, LNCS 6461, pp. 1–15, 2010.

In order to verify the safety of scenarios, we have to first give a formal model of the scenarios. CSP is a good candidate for modelling communication and parallelism among trains and RBCs. However CSP lacks of mechanisms to describe continuous dynamics of train. In [4,16], a Hybrid CSP (HCSP) is proposed to model hybrid systems. HCSP introduces into CSP continuous variables, differential equations, and interruptions by events including timeout, communicating, boundary reaching etc. Our experience in using HCSP to model CTCS-3 is quite satisfactory, and the details will be reported in another paper.

This paper is to present a calculus to verify the safety of HCSP process. The calculus consists of two parts. One is to reason about differential equations. We adopt *differential invariants* [10,12,11,3]. In their papers, the authors respectively demonstrate different sufficient conditions to generate/check a differential invariant with respect to a given differential equation. These conditions are useful, but too restrictive to generate some of invariants for our verification of CTCS-3. In [5], we develop an algorithm, which is *complete* in the sense that, if the differential equation is given in polynomials and it has a polynomial inequality (equality) as its invariant, then this algorithm can guarantee the generation of this polynomial invariant. The generation of polynomial differential invariant by this algorithm is supported by a symbolic computation tool for semi-algebraic systems, DISCOVERER [13,14,15]. This paper gives a brief introduction to this algorithm. Details of the algorithm can be referred to [5].

The other part of the calculus to verify an HCSP process is a logic to deal with communications, parallelism, differential equations, interruptions, timing, etc. In the literature, the Differential Algebraic Dynamic Logic [8] can deal with differential equations through differential invariants. However it does not take into account communication, parallelism, interruption, etc. In this paper we propose a logic which can handle all these issues. Its sequential part is similar to Hoare Logic. For parallel part, since HCSP (like CSP) does not allow memory sharing, we follow the interleaving model for concurrency except communicating. Therefore comparison between sequential processes of a parallel system does not make sense unless synchronization (i.e. communication) happens. Hence, we separate pre- and post-condition for each sequential subsystem of a parallel system, although literally mixing them up is not difficult. A similar idea can be found in [1]. When communication happens, the logic must consider the timing issue of two involved parties. So, in addition to pre- and post-condition, we introduce into Hoare Logic a history formula, which is a Duration Calculus formula[1]. It can treat timing issue and record changes of variable values. The history formula can also help in dealing with interruptions. By interruption we mean a sudden stopping of a process followed by a transition to another one. Reasoning about interruption is really difficult. The paper demonstrates our first attempt to tackle this problem. This logic is based on Hoare Logic, Duration Calculus and Differential Invariants. Thus, we call it Hybrid Hoare Logic.

[1] In [7], Duration Calculus is also used to prove safety critical property for European railways.

2 Hybrid CSP

Hybrid CSP is a modelling language for hybrid systems [4,16]. HCSP is an extension of CSP, which introduces into CSP differential equations, time constructs, interruptions, etc. It can be used for describing continuous, communicating and real-time behaviour of hybrid systems.

The vocabulary of HCSP includes:

- **Var** is a countable set of discrete variables.
- **Continuous** is a countable set of continuous variables, which are interpreted as continuous functions from time (non-negative reals) to reals. We use **VC** to stand for **Var** ∪ **Continuous**.
- **Chan** is a countable set of channels. We use $ch_1, ch_2, \ldots$ to range over channels, and $ch?$ to stand for input, while $ch!$ for output.

Thus, a process of HCSP is defined according to the following grammar:[2]

$$\begin{aligned} P ::= & \ \mathbf{stop} \mid \mathbf{skip} \mid v := e \mid ch?x \mid ch!e \mid \langle F(\dot{s}, s) = 0 \wedge B \rangle \mid \\ & P; Q \mid B \rightarrow P \mid P \trianglerighteq_d Q \mid P \trianglerighteq \|_{i \in I}(io_i \rightarrow Q_i) \mid P^* \\ S ::= & \ P \mid P \parallel S \end{aligned}$$

where B is a first order formula over **VC**, and $d > 0$. Intuitively, the above constructs can be understood as follows:

- **stop** does nothing but keeps idle for ever.
- **skip** terminates immediately and does nothing.
- $v := e$ is to assign the value of the expression e to v and then terminates.
- $ch?x$ receives a value to x through the channel ch.
- $ch!e$ sends the value of e to the channel ch, and e is an arithmetic expression of **VC**.
- $\langle F(\dot{s}, s) = 0 \wedge B \rangle$[3] is a continuous statement. It defines an evolution by a differential equation over s. In fact, s could be a vector of continuous variables, and F be a group of differential equations. B is a first order formula of s, which defines a domain of s in the sense that, if the evolution of s is beyond B, the statement terminates. Otherwise it goes forward.[4]
- $P; Q$ behaves like P first and then behaves like Q after P terminates.
- $B \rightarrow P$ behaves like P if B is true. Otherwise it terminates.
- $P \trianglerighteq_d Q$ behaves like P if P can terminate within d time units. Otherwise, after d time units, it will behave like Q. Here we assume that both P and Q do not contain communications. A **wait** statement, which postpones process behaviour for d time units, can be defined as

$$\mathbf{wait}\ d \mathrel{\widehat{=}} \mathbf{stop} \trianglerighteq_d \mathbf{skip}$$

[2] This is only a subset of HCSP in [4,16].

[3] This notation is from [9], but here it is interpreted a little differently.

[4] This is written as $\langle F(\dot{s}, s) = 0 \rangle \rightarrow \neg B$ in [4,16].

- $P \trianglerighteq \|_{i\in I}(io_i \rightarrow Q_i)$ behaves like P until a communication in the following context appears. Then it behaves like Q_i immediately after communication io_i occurs. Here I is a non-empty finite set of indices, and $\{io_i \mid i \in I\}$ are input and output statements. We also assume that P does not contain any communications. Furthermore, the *external choice* of CSP can be defined as

$$\|_{i\in I}(io_i \rightarrow Q_i) \mathrel{\widehat{=}} \mathbf{stop} \trianglerighteq \|_{i\in I}(io_i \rightarrow Q_i).$$

- P^* means the execution of P can be repeated arbitrarily finitely many times.
- $P \parallel Q$ behaves as if P and Q are executed independently except that all communications along the common channels between P and Q are to be synchronized. In order to guarantee P and Q having no shared continuous nor discrete variables, and neither shared input nor output channels, we give the following syntactical constraints:

$$\begin{aligned}(\mathbf{VC}(P) \cap \mathbf{VC}(Q)) &= \emptyset\\ (\mathbf{InChan}(P) \cap \mathbf{InChan}(Q)) &= \emptyset\\ (\mathbf{OutChan}(P) \cap \mathbf{OutChan}(Q)) &= \emptyset,\end{aligned}$$

where $\mathbf{VC}(P)$ stands for the set of discrete and continuous variables that indeed appear in P, $\mathbf{InChan}(P)$ ($\mathbf{OutChan}(P)$ for input (output) channels of P.

Examples

1. Plant Controller: A plant is sensed by a computer periodically (say every d time units), and receives a control (u) from the computer soon after the sensing.

$$((\langle F(u,s,\dot{s})=0\rangle \trianglerighteq (c_{p2c}!s \rightarrow \mathbf{skip})); c_{c2p}?u)^* \parallel (\mathbf{wait}\ d; c_{p2c}?x; c_{c2p}!e(x))^*$$

where $\langle F(u,s,\dot{s})=0\rangle$ (i.e. $\langle F(u,s,\dot{s})=0 \wedge \mathit{true}\rangle$ describes the behaviour of the plant. We refer this HCSP process as *PLC* in the rest of the paper.
2. Emergency Brake: A train is moving at an acceleration a until the train reaches an Emergency Brake Intervention speed. Then, it will take an emergency deceleration ($a = -lb$) to return to safe velocity (v_s). During its moving, the train always listens to RBC, if it receives from RBC a message of emergency brake, it decelerates with $-lb$ until it stops. This only shows what a piece of HCSP process joining in the models of CTCS-3 scenarios looks like.

$$\begin{aligned}&(\langle(\dot{s}=v,\dot{v}=a)\wedge(v<v_{ebi})\rangle;\langle(\dot{s}=v,\dot{v}=-lb)\wedge(v\geq v_s)\rangle;...)\\ &\trianglerighteq c_{r2t}?x \rightarrow (x=EB \rightarrow \langle(\dot{s}=v,\dot{v}=-lb)\wedge(v>0)\rangle);...\\ &\parallel \mathbf{wait}\ d; (c_{r2t}!EB \rightarrow ...\|...)\end{aligned}$$

3 Differential Invariants

Verification of HCSP process consists of two parts: an algorithm to generate or check differential invariants and a logic to reason about assertions of the process.

A differential invariant of a differential equation

$$\langle F(s, \dot{s}) = 0 \wedge B \rangle$$

for given initial values of s is a first order formula of s, which is satisfied by the initial values and also by all the values within the area defined by B and reachable by the trajectory of s defined by the differential equation.

In [10], Platzer and Clarke proposed a sufficient condition to check a differential invariant. For differential equation and its domain written as

$$\langle (\dot{s}_1 = f_1, ..., \dot{s}_n = f_n) \wedge B \rangle,$$

$e \leq g$ is a differential invariant of the above differential equations with given initial values of $s_1, ..., s_n$, if the initial values satisfy $e \leq g$, and the first order Lie derivative of e is less than g's, i.e.

$$\sum_{i=1}^{n} \frac{\partial e}{\partial s_i} f_i \leq \sum_{i=1}^{n} \frac{\partial g}{\partial s_i} f_i$$

This condition is useful, but quite rough in checking a differential invariant. For example, $v \leq v_{ebi}$ is a differential invariant of

$$\langle (\dot{s} = v, \dot{v} = a) \wedge v < v_{ebi} \rangle.$$

But it cannot be proved through this sufficient condition unless $a \leq 0$.

When f_js are polynomials in s_i ($i = 1, ..., n$), and B is a conjunction of polynomial equations and inequalities, the above differential equation is called *semi-algebraic* differential equation. In fact, suppose $\mathbf{s}(t)$ is the trajectory of the above semi-algebraic differential equation starting from a point on the boundary of $e \leq g$, i.e. $e = g$, then the first non-zero higher order Lie derivative of $e(\mathbf{s}(t)) - g(\mathbf{s}(t))$ with respect to t at $t = 0$ provides full information about the evolution tendency of $\mathbf{s}(t)$ with respect to $e \leq g$. If it is less than 0, $\mathbf{s}(t)$ will meet $e \leq g$ as t increases, i.e. $e \leq g$ is an invariant; otherwise, $e \leq g$ will be violated.

Using the above observation, in [5], we proposed a sound and complete method on generating polynomial differential invariants for the semi-algebraic differential equations. The basic idea is to suppose a template of differential invariant $p(s_1, \cdots, s_n, u_1, \cdots, u_m) \sim 0$ first, where p is a polynomial in continuous variables $s_1, \cdots, s_n$ and parameters $u_1, \cdots, u_m$, and $\sim \in \{\geq, >, \leq, <, =, \neq\}$; and then repeatedly compute p's Lie derivative of different order and derive constraints on the parameters according to the signs of the computed derivatives. The hardest part of our method is how to guarantee the termination of the above procedure. By applying some fundamental theories in algebraic geometry, we show that the above procedure of computing derivatives will never be endless. Thus, it is proved that the existence of differential invariants of the predefined template is equivalent to the existence of the solutions of the resulted constraints. Furthermore, the solutions of the constraints construct coefficients of the differential invariant.

Using our method to check the differential invariant of the above example, it amounts to check the validity of

$$\forall v. \begin{pmatrix} (v = v_{ebi} \wedge a \leq 0) \Rightarrow a \leq 0 \wedge \\ (v = v_{ebi} \wedge v < v_{ebi}) \Rightarrow a \leq 0) \end{pmatrix},$$

which is obvious.

In order to generate and solve constraints on the parameters of a template of a differential invariant, we can apply DISCOVERER [13,14,15], a tool for symbolic computation of semi-algebraic systems, as well as for quantifier elimination [2].

Compared with the existing work on this topic [10,12,11,3], our method is the first sound and complete one to generate polynomial differential invariants for semi-algebraic differential equations. Details are referred to [5].

4 Hybrid Hoare Logic

HCSP adopts message passing communications but rejects memory sharing paradigm. Comparison between variables of different sequential processes of a parallel program makes sense only if they are synchronized. We therefore restrict assertions to formulas of **VC** of each sequential process, although it is not difficult to literally mix them up.

HCSP employs sequential composition of statements, and we follow the traditional pre- and post- conditions of Hoare Logic to deal with sequential composition. A pre-condition specifies the **VC** values right before an execution of a statement, while a post-condition specifies the values immediately after the execution of the statement if it terminates. We use first order formulas of **VC** to express pre- and post- conditions.

However HCSP also includes interruptions by reaching a boundary, by timeout or by a communication. Hence, we need a record of the history of process execution, so that we can retreat to the place where the interruption happens. We take a subset of Duration Calculus (DC) formulas [19,18] to record an execution history of a process. That is a sequence of DC states over intervals linked together by the modality ($\frown$). It must be very tedious to remember all details of a history, and we need abstraction to develop a simple logic. Computer computation and continuous evolution of plant have different time granularity, and we adopt *super dense computation* [6] to assume computer computation consuming zero time. This agrees with the abstraction of DC: a state being present over an interval means that the state holds *almost everywhere* in the interval. This abstraction has many advantages. But in some cases it may damage the connection after an interruption. So, through DC events [18], history can still remember the points where value changes do happen, although it may neglect the particular values at those points.

4.1 Subset of DC Formulas

As indicated before, we will use a subset of DC formulas to record execution history of HCSP process. The formula in this subset is denoted as *HF* (*history formula*) and given as follows.

$$\begin{aligned} HF ::= & \ l < T \mid l = T \mid l > T \mid \uparrow_X \mid \lceil S \rceil \\ & \mid HF^\frown HF \mid HF \wedge HF \mid HF \vee HF \end{aligned}$$

where l stands for interval length, X is a subset of **VC**, S is a first order formula of **VC**, and $T \geq 0$.

$\uparrow_X$ is an event to mean changes of variables in X taking place at a time point. The axioms and rules can be copied from the event calculus in [18]. But in order to maintain this information unaltered during deductions, we only list two of them as axioms. The others can be used as antecedence when needed. These two axioms are

$$\begin{aligned} \uparrow_\emptyset &\Leftrightarrow (l = 0) \\ \uparrow_X {}^\frown \uparrow_Y &\Leftrightarrow \uparrow_{X \cup Y} \end{aligned}$$

$\lceil S \rceil$ means S true almost everywhere over an interval. It follows all the theorems of $\lceil S \rceil$ in [18], such as

$$\begin{aligned} \lceil S \rceil^\frown \lceil S \rceil &\Leftrightarrow \lceil S \rceil, \\ \lceil S \rceil^\frown (l = 0) &\Leftrightarrow \lceil S \rceil, \\ \text{etc.} \end{aligned}$$

All proofs for *HF* are given in DC (plus the above two axioms for $\uparrow_X$), and will not be explicitly indicated. For example, we can prove in DC:

$$\begin{aligned} \mathit{false} &\Leftrightarrow (l < 0) \\ \mathit{true} &\Leftrightarrow (l = 0) \vee (l > 0) \end{aligned}$$

Since an interruption may occur at any time during process execution, to locate it we define prefix closure of *HF* and denote it as $HF^<$.

$$\begin{aligned}
(l < T)^< &=_{df} (l < T) \\
(l = T)^< &=_{df} (l \leq T) \\
(l > T)^< &=_{df} \mathit{true} \\
(\uparrow_X)^< &=_{df} \bigvee_{Y \subseteq X} \uparrow_Y \\
\lceil S \rceil^< &=_{df} (l = 0) \vee \lceil S \rceil \\
(HF_1{}^\frown HF_2)^< &=_{df} \begin{cases} \mathit{false} & \text{if } HF_2 \Rightarrow \mathit{false} \\ (HF_1)^< \vee HF_1{}^\frown (HF_2)^< & \text{otherwise} \end{cases} \\
(HF_1 \wedge HF_2)^< &=_{df} \begin{cases} \mathit{false} & \text{if } HF_1 \wedge HF_2 \Rightarrow \mathit{false} \\ (HF_1)^< \wedge (HF_2)^< & \text{otherwise} \end{cases} \\
(HF_1 \vee HF_2)^< &=_{df} (HF_1)^< \vee (HF_2)^<
\end{aligned}$$

It is obvious that the prefix closure of any formula of the subset still belongs to it. From the above definition, we can prove

$$\begin{aligned} \mathit{true}^< &\Leftrightarrow \mathit{true} \\ \mathit{false}^< &\Leftrightarrow \mathit{false} \end{aligned}$$

4.2 Assertions

An assertion of Hybrid Hoare Logic consists of four parts: precondition, process, postcondition and history, written as

$$\{Pre\}P\{Post; HF\}$$

where *Pre* specifies values of $\mathbf{VC}(P)$ before an execution of P, *Post* specifies $\mathbf{VC}(P)$ values when it terminates, and *HF* is a formula of $\mathbf{VC}(P)$ from the DC subset to describe the execution history of P, which includes differential invariants of P. In Hoare Logic, a loop invariant joins in postcondition of the loop, so does in this Hybrid Hoare Logic. HCSP has three kinds of interruptions: boundary interruption, e.g. $\langle F(\dot{s}, s) = 0 \wedge B\rangle$, timeout interruption, e.g. $P \trianglerighteq_d Q$ and communication interruption, e.g. $P \trianglerighteq \|_{i \in I}(io_i \rightarrow Q_i)$. For these three kinds of interruptions, *HF* has to join in reasoning. In *HF*, $\uparrow_X$ indicates that the changes of variables in X may take place at this point, and reasoning about assertions at this point should not rely on these variables.

For a parallel process, say $P_1 \| ... \| P_n$, the assertion becomes

$$\{Pre_1, ..., Pre_n\}P_1 \| ... \| P_n\{Post_1, ..., Post_n; HF_1, ..., HF_n\}$$

where $Pre_i, Post_i, HF_i$ are (first order or DC) formulas of $\mathbf{VC}(P_i)$ $(i = 1, ..., n)$.

Another role of *HF* is to specify real-time (continuous) property of an HCSP process, while *Pre* and *Post* can only describe its discrete behaviour. *HF* therefore bridges up the gap between discrete and continuous behaviour of the process. For example, we may want the plant controller example (*PLC*) in Section 2 stable after T time units, i.e. after T time units the distance between the trajectory of s and its target s_{targ} must be small. This can be specified through the following assertion.

$$\begin{array}{l}\{s = s_0 \wedge u = u_0 \wedge Ctrl(u_0, s_0), Pre_2\}PLC \\ \quad \{Post_1, Post_2; (l = T)^\frown\lceil | s - s_{targ} | \leq \epsilon\rceil, HF_2\}\end{array}$$

where $Ctrl(u, s)$ may express a controllable property, and the other formulas are not elaborated here.

4.3 Axioms and Rules

We do not list all axioms and rules for all HCSP processes, but explain our idea how to establish this logic. Say, in this subsection we only use a parallel process consisting of two sequential ones to demonstrate the logic.

1. **Monotonicity**

$$\begin{array}{l}\text{If } \{Pre_1, Pre_2\}P_1 \| P_2\{Post_1, Post_2; HF_1, HF_2\}, \\ \text{and } Pre_i' \Rightarrow Pre_i, Post_i \Rightarrow Post_i', HF_i \Rightarrow HF_i' (i = 1, 2), \\ \text{then } \{Pre_1', Pre_2'\}P_1 \| P_2\{Post_1', Post_2'; HF_1', HF_2'\}\end{array}$$

where we use first order logic to reason $Pre_i' \Rightarrow Pre_i$ and $Post_i \Rightarrow Post_i'$, but use DC (plus the two axioms for $\uparrow_X$) to reason $HF_i \Rightarrow HF_i'$. From now on we will not repeatedly mention this.

2. **Case Analysis**

$$\text{If } \{Pre_{1i}, Pre_2\}P_1 \parallel P_2\{Post_1, Post_2; HF_1, HF_2\} \ (i = 1, 2),$$
$$\text{then } \{Pre_{11} \vee Pre_{12}, Pre_2\}P_1 \parallel P_2\{Post_1, Post_2; HF_1, HF_2\}$$

Symmetrically,

$$\text{If } \{Pre_1, Pre_{2i}\}P_1 \parallel P_2\{Post_1, Post_2; HF_1, HF_2\} \ (i = 1, 2),$$
$$\text{then } \{Pre_1, Pre_{21} \vee Pre_{22}\}P_1 \parallel P_2\{Post_1, Post_2; HF_1, HF_2\}$$

3. **Parallel vs. Sequential**
These two rules show a simple relation between assertions of a parallel process and its sequential components that can ease a proof.

$$\text{If } \{Pre_1, Pre_2\}P_1 \parallel P_2\{Post_1, Post_2; HF_1, HF_2\}$$
$$\text{then } \{Pre_i\}P_i\{Post_i; HF_i\} \ (i = 1, 2)$$

and

$$\text{If } \{Pre_i\}P_i\{Post_i; HF_i\} \ (i = 1, 2),$$
$$\text{and } P_i \ (i = 1, 2) \text{ do not contain communication,}$$
$$\text{then } \{Pre_1, Pre_2\}P_1 \parallel P_2\{Post_1, Post_2; HF_1, HF_2\}$$

4. **Stop**
stop does nothing, and never terminates. So, **stop** will keep any precondition true for ever. Hence, for any $r \geq 0$,

$$\{Pre\}\mathbf{stop}\{Pre; \lceil Pre \rceil \wedge (l > r)\}$$

5. **Skip**

$$\{Pre\}\mathbf{skip}\{Pre; l = 0\},$$

where by $l = 0$ we assume that, in comparison with physical device, computation takes no time (i.e. *supper dense computation* [6])

6. **Assignment**

$$\{Pre[e/x]\}x := e\{Pre, \uparrow_x\}$$

The precondition and postcondition are copied from Hoare Logic. Here we use $\uparrow_x$ as its history to indicate that, a change of x takes place at this time point, although the history does not record the values of x before and after the change.

7. **Communication**
Since HCSP rejects variable sharing, a communication looks like the output party $(P_1; ch!e)$ assigning to variable x of the input one $(P_2; ch?x)$ a value (e). Besides, in order to synchronize both parties, one may have to wait for another. During the waiting of P_i, $Post_i$ must stay true ($i = 1$ or 2).

Furthermore, when we conclude range of the waiting time, we need to reduce $\uparrow_X$ to $(l=0)$.

If $\{Pre_1, Pre_2\}P_1 \parallel P_2\{Post_1, Post_2; HF_1, HF_2\}$,
$Post_1 \Rightarrow G(e)$,
and $\Box(\bigwedge_{X\subseteq \mathbf{VC}} \uparrow_X \Rightarrow (l=0)) \wedge (((HF_1^\frown(\lceil Post_1\rceil)^<) \wedge HF_2) \vee (HF_1 \wedge (HF_2^\frown(\lceil Post_2\rceil)^<))) \Rightarrow Rg(l)$
where $Rg(l)$ is a box constraint (HF formula) of l to define its range
then $\{Pre_1, Pre_2\}(P_1; ch!e) \parallel (P_2; ch?x)$
$\{Post_1, G(x) \wedge \exists x Post_2; HF_1^\frown(\lceil Post_1\rceil)^< \wedge Rg(l), (HF_2^\frown(\lceil Post_2\rceil)^< \wedge Rg(l))^\frown \uparrow_x\}$

Example
If

$$\{Pre_1, Pre_2\}P_1 \parallel P_2$$
$$\{y=3, x=1; (\lceil y=0\rceil \wedge (l=3))^\frown \uparrow_y, \lceil x=0\rceil \wedge (l=5)^\frown \uparrow_x\},$$

we want to deduce through this rule

$$\{Pre_1, Pre_2\}P_1; ch!y \parallel P_2; ch?x\{Post_3, Post_4; HF_3, HF_4\}.$$

Since $(y=3) \Rightarrow (3=3)$ and

$$\Box \bigwedge_{X\subseteq\{x,y\}}(\uparrow_X \Rightarrow (l=0)) \wedge$$
$$(((\lceil y=0\rceil \wedge (l=3))^\frown \uparrow_y^\frown ((l=0) \vee \lceil y=3\rceil)) \wedge ((\lceil x=0\rceil \wedge (l=5))^\frown \uparrow_x)$$
$$\Rightarrow (l=5),$$

we can conclude that $Post_3$ is $y=3$, $Post_4$ is $x=3$,
HF_3 is

$$((\lceil y=0\rceil \wedge (l=3))^\frown \uparrow_y^\frown \lceil y=3\rceil) \wedge (l=5),$$

and HF_4 is

$$(l=5)^\frown \uparrow_x^\frown \uparrow_x$$

which is equivalent to

$$(l=5)^\frown \uparrow_x$$

by the axioms of $\uparrow_X$.

8. **Continuous**
This is about $\langle F(\dot{s}, s)=0 \wedge B\rangle$, where s can be a vector and F be a group of differential equations, such as

$$\langle(\dot{s}_1 = f_1, ..., \dot{s}_n = f_n) \wedge B\rangle.$$

As indicated in Section 3, in this paper we only deal with *semi-algebraic* differential equations and polynomial differential invariants. That is, f_js are polynomials in s_i $(i=1,...,n)$, B is a conjunction of polynomial equations and inequalities of s_i $(i = 1, ..., n)$, and differential invariants are also restricted to polynomial equations and inequalities.

We have two rules for semi-algebraic differential equations. The first one is about differential invariant. Given a polynomial differential invariant *Inv* of $\langle F(\dot{s}, s) = 0 \wedge B\rangle$ with initial values satisfying *Init*

$$\begin{array}{l} \text{If } \mathit{Init} \Rightarrow \mathit{Inv}, \\ \text{then } \{\mathit{Init} \wedge \mathit{Pre}\}\langle F(\dot{s}, s) = 0 \wedge B\rangle\{\mathit{Pre} \wedge \mathbf{Close}(\mathit{Inv}) \wedge \mathbf{Close}(\neg B); \\ \qquad (l = 0) \vee \lceil \mathit{Inv} \wedge \mathit{Pre} \wedge B\rceil\} \end{array}$$

where *Pre* does not contain s, **Close**(G) stands for the *closure* of G, [5] and $(l = 0)$ in the history is to record the behaviour when the initial values satisfy $\neg B$ at very beginning.

The second rule is about explicit time.

$$\begin{array}{l} \text{If } \{\mathit{Pre}\}\langle F(\dot{s}, s) = 0 \wedge B\rangle\{\mathit{Post}; \mathit{HF}\} \\ \text{and } \{\mathit{Pre} \wedge t = 0\}\langle (F(\dot{s}, s) = 0, \dot{t} = 1) \wedge B\rangle\{\mathit{Rg}(t); \mathit{HF}'\}, \\ \text{then } \{\mathit{Pre}\}\langle F(\dot{s}, s) = 0 \wedge B\rangle\{\mathit{Post}; \mathit{HF} \wedge \mathit{Rg}(l)\} \end{array}$$

where t is a clock to count the time, and $\mathit{Rg}(t)$ is a box constraint as explained in the rule for communication.

Example

We know from Section 3 that $v \leq v_{ebi}$ is an invariant of

$$\langle (\dot{s} = v, \dot{v} = a) \wedge v < v_{ebi}\rangle.$$

Thus, by the first rule

$$\begin{array}{l} \{(v = v_0 \leq v_{ebi})\}\langle (\dot{s} = v, \dot{v} = a) \wedge v < v_{ebi}\rangle \\ \quad \{(v \leq v_{ebi}) \wedge (v \geq v_{ebi}); (l = 0) \vee \lceil (v \leq v_{ebi}) \wedge (v < v_{ebi})\rceil\} \end{array}$$

In addition, we can prove that, if the initial values are $v = v_0$ and $t = 0$, and we assume $p \geq a \geq w$, then

$$((v_0 + wt) \leq v \leq (v_0 + pt)) \wedge (v \leq v_{ebi})$$

is an invariant of $\langle (\dot{s} = v, \dot{v} = a, \dot{t} = 1) \wedge v < v_{ebi}\rangle$. So under the assumption $(p \geq a \geq w)$

$$\begin{array}{l} \{(v = v_0 \leq v_{ebi}) \wedge (t = 0)\}\langle (\dot{s} = v, \dot{v} = a, \dot{t} = 1) \wedge v < v_{ebi}\rangle \\ \quad \{(v = v_{ebi}) \wedge ((v_0 + wt) \leq v \leq (v_0 + pt)); \\ \quad\quad (l = 0) \vee \lceil (v < v_{ebi}) \wedge ((v_0 + wt) \leq v \leq (v_0 + pt))\rceil\} \\ \{(v = v_0 \leq v_{ebi}) \wedge (t = 0)\}\langle (\dot{s} = v, \dot{v} = a, \dot{t} = 1) \wedge v < v_{ebi}\rangle \\ \quad \{\frac{v_{ebi} - v_0}{w} \geq t \geq \frac{v_{ebi} - v_0}{p}; \mathit{true}\} \end{array}$$

Therefore assuming $(p \geq a \geq w)$ we can have

$$\begin{array}{l} \{(v = v_0 \leq v_{ebi})\}\langle (\dot{s} = v, \dot{v} = a) \wedge v < v_{ebi}\rangle \\ \quad \{(v = v_{ebi}); \lceil (v < v_{ebi})\rceil \wedge (\frac{v_{ebi} - v_0}{w} \geq l \geq \frac{v_{ebi} - v_0}{p})\} \end{array}$$

[5] When G is constructed by polynomial inequalities through $\wedge$ and $\vee$, **Close**(G) can be obtained from G by replacing $<$ (and $>$) with $\leq$ (and $\geq$) in G.

9. **Sequential**

   If $\{Pre_1, Pre_2\}P_1 \parallel P_2\{Post_1, Post_2; HF_1, HF_2\}$,
   $\{Post_i\}P_{i+2}\{Post_{i+2}; HF_{i+2}\}$ $(i = 1, 2)$,
   and both P_3 and P_4 do not contain communication,
   then $\{Pre_1, Pre_2\}P_1; P_3 \parallel P_2; P_4\{Post_3, Post_4; HF_1^\frown HF_3, HF_2^\frown HF_4\}$.

10. **Timeout**

    We have two rules for $P_1 \trianglerighteq_d P_2$. One is for the case when P_1 terminates before d time units. Another is for the timeout. The first one is

$$\begin{array}{l}\text{If } \{Pre\}P_1\{Post; HF\}\\ \text{and } (\Box(\bigwedge_{X\subseteq \mathbf{VC}} \uparrow_X \Rightarrow (l = 0)) \wedge HF) \Rightarrow (l < d)\\ \text{then } \{Pre\}P_1 \trianglerighteq_d P_2\{Post; HF\}\end{array}$$

The second one is more complicated. The execution of P_1 is interrupted after d time units, and then P_2 starts its execution. Therefore the postcondition of P_1 cannot be used for this transition, and we have to use its history at time d.

$$\begin{array}{l}\text{If } \{Pre_1\}P_1\{Post_1; HF_1\},\\ \quad \{Pre_2\}P_2\{Post_2; HF_2\},\\ \quad (\Box(\wedge_{X\subseteq \mathbf{VC}} \uparrow_X \Rightarrow (l = 0)) \wedge HF_1) \Rightarrow (l \geq d)\\ \text{and } G \;\Rightarrow\; Pre_2\\ \text{then } \;\{Pre_1\}P_1 \trianglerighteq_d P_2\{Post_2; HF^{*\frown} HF_2\}\end{array}$$

where G and HF^* are constructed as follows. Choose an HF^* in the form of

$$\bigvee_{i=1}^{n} HF_i^{*\frown}(\lceil G_i \wedge F_i\rceil \wedge Rg_i(l))^\frown \uparrow_{X_i}$$

according to the following two criteria. If no variable of G_i is included in X_i $(i = 1, ..., n)$, then we let G be $\bigvee_{i=1}^{n} G_i$.

The first criterion to choose HF^* is to guarantee that HF^* does not lose any $\uparrow_X$ in HF_1. That is, we have to prove

$$\begin{array}{l}HF^* \;\Rightarrow\; HF_1^{\leq}, \text{ and}\\ \Box(\bigwedge_{((X\neq Y)\wedge X,Y\subseteq \mathbf{VC})} \neg(\uparrow_X \wedge \uparrow_Y))\\ \quad \Rightarrow\; \bigwedge_{i=1}^{n} \neg((HF_i^{*\frown}(\lceil G_i \wedge F_i\rceil \wedge Rg_i(l))^\frown \uparrow_{Y_i}) \wedge HF_1^{\leq})\end{array}$$

for any $Y_i \supset X_i$.

The second criterion is about the length of HF^* and another direction of the implication between HF_1 and HF^*. That is

$$\begin{array}{l}\Box(\bigwedge_{X\subseteq \mathbf{VC}} \uparrow_X \Rightarrow (l = 0)) \wedge HF^* \;\Rightarrow\; (l = d), \text{ and}\\ \Box(\bigwedge_{X\subseteq \mathbf{VC}} \uparrow_X \Rightarrow (l = 0)) \wedge HF_1^{\leq} \wedge (l = d) \;\Rightarrow\; HF^*\end{array}$$

In summary, HF^* is a part of $(HF_1^{\leq} \wedge (l = d))$ that includes all information about variable changes at time points until d (inclusive), and G therefore catches the last states of $(HF_1^{\leq} \wedge (l = d))$, which do not change at time d.

Examples

(a) **wait** d $(d > 0)$

$$\{Pre\}\mathbf{wait}\ d\{Pre; \lceil Pre \rceil \wedge (l = d)\}$$

where **wait** d is defined as $\mathbf{stop} \trianglerighteq_d \mathbf{skip}$. Its proof can be given as follows. Since

$\{Pre\}\mathbf{stop}\{Pre; \lceil Pre \rceil \wedge (l > d)\}$,
$\{Pre\}\mathbf{skip}\{Pre; (l = 0)\}$,
$(l > d) \ \Rightarrow\ (l \geq d)$,
and we can choose HF^* as $(\lceil Pre \rceil \wedge (l = d))$, and hence, G as Pre,

we can conclude

$$\{Pre\}\mathbf{stop} \trianglerighteq_d \mathbf{skip}\{Pre; (\lceil Pre \rceil \wedge (l = d))^\frown (l = 0)\}.$$

That is

$$\{Pre\}\mathbf{wait}\ d\{Pre; \lceil Pre \rceil \wedge (l = d)\}.$$

(b) Let P be

$$z := 0; \mathbf{wait}\ 3; y := 3; \mathbf{wait}\ 2$$

and we can prove

$$\begin{array}{l}\{y = 1, z = 2\}P\{(z = 0) \wedge (y = 3); \\ \quad \uparrow_z^\frown (\lceil (y = 1) \wedge (z = 0) \rceil \wedge (l = 3))^\frown \uparrow_y \\ \quad {}^\frown(\lceil (z = 0) \wedge (y = 3) \rceil \wedge (l = 2))\}\end{array}$$

and denote the history formula of P as $HF(P)$. For $P \trianglerighteq_3 Q$, P is interrupted after being executed 3 time unit. Let HF^* be

$$\uparrow_z^\frown (\lceil (y = 1) \wedge (z = 0) \rceil \wedge (l = 3))^\frown \uparrow_y$$

We can prove

$$\begin{array}{l} HF^* \ \Rightarrow\ HF(P)^<, \\ \Box \bigwedge_{(x \neq y)} \neg(\uparrow_{\{x,y\}} \wedge \uparrow_y) \\ \quad \Rightarrow\ \neg((\uparrow_z^\frown (\lceil (y = 1) \wedge (z = 0) \rceil \wedge (l = 3))^\frown \uparrow_{\{x,y\}}) \wedge HF(P)^<), \\ \Box(((\uparrow_y \vee \uparrow_z) \Rightarrow (l = 0)) \wedge HF^*) \ \Rightarrow\ (l = 3), \text{ and} \\ \Box((\uparrow_y \vee \uparrow_z) \Rightarrow (l = 0)) \wedge HF(P)^< \wedge (l = 3) \ \Rightarrow\ HF^*. \end{array}$$

So, G is $(z = 0)$ (and $(y = 1)$ is not involved), and $(z = 0)$ can therefore be used as a precondition of Q.

11. **Choice**
This is about inference rule for $(P \trianglerighteq \|_{i \in I}(io_i \rightarrow Q_i))$. It involves communication interruption which happens randomly, and must be difficult to deal with. If we assume that from one party of the communication we can derive a range of the interruption time, then we can use the history to support the reasoning. Of course we also have to take into account the waiting time of two parties. But all those ideas have been explained before. Thus we omit them here.

12. **Repetition**
    We can pick up rules from the literature for the repetition. Here we only show a rule which ends off an assertion reasoning.

    If $\{Pre_1, Pre_2\}P_1 \parallel P_2\{Pre_1, Pre_2; HF_1, HF_2\}$,
    $((\Box \bigwedge_{X \subseteq \mathbf{VC}}(\uparrow_X \Rightarrow (l = 0))) \wedge HF_i) \;\Rightarrow\; (D_i \wedge (l = T))\; (i = 1, 2,\; T > 0)$,
    and $D_i^\frown D_i \;\Rightarrow\; D_i$,
    then $\{Pre_1, Pre_2\}P_1^* \parallel P_2^*\{Pre_1, Pre_2; D_1, D_2\}$

    where T is the time consumed by both P_1 and P_2 that can guarantee the synchronisation of the starting point of each repetition.

5 Conclusion

This paper sketches part of our on-going efforts in formally modelling and verifying hybrid systems. We choose a subset of HCSP for modelling, and explain our idea to develop a calculus for this subset, including an improvement of generating and checking differential invariants. So far we are not sure whether this subset is good enough to model interesting hybrid systems, say CTCS-3, and neither the calculus is powerful enough in verifying its safety. Although this is a subset of HCSP, it is quite complicated already in terms of verification. In particular, it includes random interruptions which are hard to handle. Our idea is to use history of execution which records the continuous evolution of process as well as the discrete change of its variables. The calculus tries to leave details as far as we can. Its soundness is not trivial. For this, we need formal semantics of HCSP. A DC-based denotational semantics for HCSP has been established in [16]. Recently, we defined an operational semantics for HCSP, and will check the soundness of the logic against the semantics formally as a future work.

References

1. Apt, K., de Boer, F., Olderog, E.-R.: Verfication of Sequential and Concurrent Programs. Springer, Heidelberg (2009) ISBN 978-1-184882-744-8
2. Collins, G.E.: Quantifier elimination for real closed fields by cylindrical algebraic decomposition. In: Brakhage, H. (ed.) GI-Fachtagung 1975. LNCS, vol. 33, pp. 134–183. Springer, Heidelberg (1975)
3. Gulwani, S., Tiwari, A.: Constraint-based approach for analysis of hybrid systems. In: Gupta, A., Malik, S. (eds.) CAV 2008. LNCS, vol. 5123, pp. 190–203. Springer, Heidelberg (2008)
4. He, J.: From CSP to hybrid systems. In: The Proc. of A Classical Mind: Essays in Honour of C. A. R. Hoare. International Series In Computer Science, pp. 171–189. Prentice-Hall, Englewood Cliffs (1994) ISBN:0-13-294844-3
5. Liu, J., Zhan, N., Zhao, H.: A complete method for generating polynomial differential invariants. Technical Report of State Key Lab. of Comp. Sci., ISCAS-LCS-10-15 (2010)
6. Manna, Z., Pnueli, A.: Models of reactitivity. Acta Informatica 30(7), 609–678 (1993)

7. Olderog, R.-R., Dierks, H.: Real-Time Systems: Formal Secification and Automatic Verification. Cambridge University Press, Cambridge (2008)
8. Platzer, A.: Differential-algebraic dynamic logic for differential-algebraic programs. J. of Logic and Computation 20(1), 309–352 (2010)
9. Platzer, A.: Differential dynamic logic for hybrid systems. J. of Automated Reasoning 41, 143–189 (2007)
10. Platzer, A., Clarke, E.M.: Computing differential invariants of hybrid systems as fixedpoints. In: Gupta, A., Malik, S. (eds.) CAV 2008. LNCS, vol. 5123, pp. 176–189. Springer, Heidelberg (2008)
11. Prajna, S., Jadbabaie, A.: Safety verification of hybrid systems using barrier certificates. In: Alur, R., Pappas, G.J. (eds.) HSCC 2004. LNCS, vol. 2993, pp. 477–492. Springer, Heidelberg (2004)
12. Sankaranarayanan, S., Sipma, H.B., Manna, Z.: Constructing invariants for hybrid systems. In: Alur, R., Pappas, G.J. (eds.) HSCC 2004. LNCS, vol. 2993, pp. 539–554. Springer, Heidelberg (2004)
13. Xia, B.: DISCOVERER: A tool for solving semi-algebraic systems. In: Software Demo at ISSAC 2007, Waterloo (July 30, 2007), Also: ACM SIGSAM Bulletin 41(3),102–103 (September 2007)
14. Yang, L.: Recent advances on determining the number of real roots of parametric polynomials. J. Symbolic Computation 28, 225–242 (1999)
15. Yang, L., Hou, X., Zeng, Z.: A complete discrimination system for polynomials. Science in China (Ser. E) 39, 628–646 (1996)
16. Zhou, C., Wang, J., Ravn, A.: A formal description of hybrid systems. In: Alur, R., Sontag, E.D., Henzinger, T.A. (eds.) HS 1995. LNCS, vol. 1066, pp. 511–530. Springer, Heidelberg (1996)
17. Zhang, S.: The General Technical Solutions to Chinese Train Control System at Level 3 (CTCS-3). China Railway Publisher (2008)
18. Zhou, C., Hansen, M.: Duration Calculus: A Formal Approach to Real-Time Systems. Springer, Heidelberg (2004) ISBN 3-540-40823-1
19. Zhou, C., Hoare, C.A.R., Ravn, A.: A calculus of durations. Information Processing Letters 40(5), 269–276 (1991)

Foundations of Quantum Programming (Extended Abstract)

Mingsheng Ying*

Center for Quantum Computation and Intelligent Systems,
University of Technology, Sydney, Australia
and
State Key Laboratory of Intelligent Technology and Systems,
Tsinghua University, Beijing, China

Keywords: Quantum computation; loop programs; predicate transformer semantics; Floyd-Hoare logic.

Progress in the techniques of quantum devices has made people widely believe that large-scale and functional quantum computers will be eventually built. By then, super-powered quantum computer will solve many problems affecting economic and social life that cannot be addressed by classical computing. However, our experiences with classical computing suggest that once quantum computers become available in the future, quantum software will play a key role in exploiting their power, and quantum software market will even be much larger than quantum hardware market. Unfortunately, today's software development techniques are not suited to quantum computers due to the essential differences between the nature of the classical world and that of the quantum world. To lay a solid foundation for tomorrow's quantum software industry, it is critically essential to pursue systematic research into quantum programming methodology and techniques.

Intensive research on quantum programming has been conducted in the last 15 years, and many exciting results have been reported. The existing research can be roughly classified into the following categories.

- Design of quantum programming languages [1], [11], [13], [14], [15], [23].
- Semantics of quantum programming languages [5].
- Verification of quantum programs [2], [3], [4], [6].
- Quantum software architecture [17].
- Quantum compilers [25], [12]
- Concurrent quantum programming and quantum process algebras [7], [9], [10], [21], [24]

There are already two excellent survey papers of quantum programming [8], [16]. This talk mainly summarizes the author and his collaborators' work in the foundations of quantum programming.

* This work was partly supported by the National Foundation of Natural Sciences of China (Grant No: 60736011).

K. Ueda (Ed.): APLAS 2010, LNCS 6461, pp. 16–20, 2010.

1 Quantum Loop Programs [22]

Loops are a powerful program construct in classical computation. Some high-level control features such as loop and recursion are provided in Selinger's functional quantum programming language QFC [15]. The power of quantum loop programs is yet to be further exploited. The exploitation of such power requires a deep understanding of the mechanism of quantum loops. The author and Yuan Feng examined thoroughly the behaviors of quantum loops in a language-independent way and found some convenient criteria for deciding termination of a general quantum loop on a given input in the case of finite-dimensional state spaces. More precisely, in [22], a general scheme of quantum loop programs was introduced, the computational process of a quantum loop was described, and the essential difference between quantum loops and classical loops was analyzed. In addition, we introduced the notions of termination and almost termination of a quantum loop. The function computed by a quantum loop was also defined. Quantum walks were considered to show the expressive power of quantum loops. Then we found a necessary and sufficient condition under which a quantum loop program terminates on a given mixed input state. A similar condition is given for almost termination. Furthermore, we proved that a quantum loop is almost terminating if and only if it is uniformly almost terminating, and a small disturbance either on the unitary transformation in the loop body or on the measurement in the loop guard can make any quantum loop (almost) terminating, provided that some dimension restriction is satisfied. A representation of the function computed by a quantum loop was presented in terms of finite summations of complex matrices.

2 Predicate Transformer Semantics of Quantum Programs [20], [19]

Since it provides a goal-directed program development strategy and nondeterminacy can be accommodated well in it, predicate transformer semantics has a very wide influence in classical programming methodology. There have been already two approaches to predicate transformer semantics of quantum programs in the literature. The first approach was proposed by Sanders and Zuliani [14] in designing qGCL, a quantum extension of the guarded-command language. In this approach, quantum computation is reduced to probabilistic computation by the observation (measurement) procedure. Thus, predicate transformer semantics developed for probabilistic programs can be conveniently used for quantum programs. The second approach was proposed by D'Hondt and Panangaden [5], where the notion of a predicate is directly taken from quantum mechanics; that is, a quantum predicate is defined to be an observable (a Hermitian operator) with eigenvalues within the unit interval. In this approach, forward operational semantics of quantum programs is described by super-operators according to Selinger [15], and a beautiful Stone-type duality between state-transformer (forwards) and predicate-transformer (backwards) semantics of quantum programs can be established by employing the Kraus representation theorem for super-operators.

To further develop the second approach, we have to tackle some problems that would not arise in the realm of classical and probabilistic programming. One of such problems is the commutativity of quantum weakest preconditions. Various logical operations of quantum weakest preconditions such as conjunction and disjunction will be needed in reasoning about complicated quantum programs, but defining these operations requires commutativity between the involved quantum predicates. However, the author and his collaborators [19] noticed that the weakest preconditions of two commutative quantum predicates do not necessarily commute. This is an obvious obstacle in the further development of predicate transformer semantics for quantum programs, and it seems to be very difficult to overcome in the general setting. The author and his collaborators [20] decided to focus their attention on a special class of quantum predicates, namely projection operators. One reason for this decision is conceptual, and it comes from the following observation: the quantum predicates dealt with in [5] are Hermitian operators whose eigenvalues are within the unit interval, and in a sense, they can be envisaged as quantization of probabilistic predicates. On the other hand, projection operators are Hermitian operators with 0 or 1 as their eigenvalues, and they should be thought of as quantization of classical (Boolean) predicates. Physically, the simplest type of measuring instrument is one performing so-called yes-no measurement. Only a single change may be triggered on such an instrument, and it is often called an effect by physicists. Another reason is technical: there is a bijective correspondence between the projection operators in a Hilbert space and the closed subspaces of this space. The set of closed subspaces of a Hilbert space was recognized by Birkhoff and von Neumann as (the algebraic counterpart) of the logic of quantum mechanics, and its structure has been thoroughly investigated in the development of quantum logic for over 70 years. Thus, we are able to exploit the power of quantum logic in our research on predicate transformer semantics of quantum logic.

The author and his collaborators [20] developed a quite complete predicate transformer semantics of quantum programs by employing some powerful mathematical tools developed in Birkhoff-von Neumann quantum logic. In particular, they proved universal conjunctivity, termination law and Hoare's induction rule for quantum programs. The proof of termination law requires an essential application of Takeuti's technique of strong commutator introduced in his studies of quantum set theory.

3 Floyd-Hoare Logic for Quantum Programs [18]

The fact that human intuition is much better adapted to the classical world than the quantum world is one of the major reasons that it is difficult to find efficient quantum algorithms. It also implies that programmers will commit much more faults in designing programs for quantum computers than programming classical computers. Thus, it is even more critical than in classical computing to provide formal methods for reasoning about correctness of quantum programs. Indeed, several proof systems for verification of quantum programs and quantum communication protocols have been proposed in the recent literature. For example, Baltag and Smets [2] presented a dynamic logic formalism of information flows in quantum systems, which is capable of describing various quantum operations such as unitary evolutions and quantum measurements, and particularly entanglements in multi-partite quantum systems. Brunet and Jorrand [3] introduced a way of applying Birkhoff and von Neumann's quantum logic to the study of quantum programs by expanding the usual propositional languages with new primitives representing unitary transformations and quantum measurements. In [4], Chadha, Mateus and Sernadas proposed a Floyd-Hoare-style proof system for reasoning about imperative quantum programs using a quantitative state logic, but only bounded iterations are allowed in their programming language. Feng et al. [6] found some useful proof rules for reasoning about quantum loops, generalizing several effective proof rules for probabilistic loops.

Recently, the author [18] established of a full-fledged Floyd-Hoare logic for deterministic quantum programs based on Selinger's idea [15] of modeling quantum programs as super-operators and D'Hondt and Panangaden's notion of quantum predicate as an Hermitian operator [5]. This logic includes a proof system for partial correctness and a proof system for total correctness of deterministic quantum programs. In particular, we are able to prove its (relative) completeness by exploiting the power of weakest preconditions and weakest liberal preconditions for quantum programs. It is worth mentioning that the proof of the (relative) completeness requires techniques quite different from those for classical programs and tools from analytic (continuous) mathematics.

References

1. Altenkirch, T., Grattage, J.: A functional quantum programming language. In: Proceedings of the 20th Annual IEEE Symposium on Logic in Computer Science (LICS), pp. 249–258 (2005)
2. Baltag, A., Smets, S.: LQP: the dynamic logic of quantum information. Mathematical Structures in Computer Science 16, 491–525 (2006)
3. Brunet, O., Jorrand, P.: Dynamic quantum logic for quantum programs. International Journal of Quantum Information 2, 45–54 (2004)
4. Chadha, R., Mateus, P., Sernadas, A.: Reasoning about imperative quantum programs. Electronic Notes in Theoretical Computer Science 158, 19–39 (2006)
5. D'Hondt, E., Panangaden, P.: Quantum weakest preconditions. Mathematical Structures in Computer Science 16, 429–451 (2006)
6. Feng, Y., Duan, R.Y., Ji, Z.F., Ying, M.S.: Proof rules for the correctness of quantum programs. Theoretical Computer Science 386, 151–166 (2007)
7. Feng, Y., Duan, R.Y., Ji, Z.F., Ying, M.S.: Probabilistic bisimulations for quantum processes. Information and Computation 205, 1608–1639 (2007)
8. Gay, S.J.: Quantum programming languages: survey and bibliography. Mathematical Structures in Computer Science 16, 581–600 (2006)
9. Gay, S.J., Nagarajan, R.: Communicating quantum processes. In: Proceedings of the 32nd ACM Symposium on Principles of Programming Languages, Long Beach, California, USA, pp. 145–157. ACM Press, New York (2005)

10. Jorrand, P., Lalire, M.: Toward a quantum process algebra. In: Proceedings of the 1st ACM Conference on Computing Frontiers, Ischia, Italy, pp. 111–119. ACM Press, New York (2005)
11. Knill, E.H.: Conventions for quantum pseudocode, Technical Report LAUR-96-2724, Los Alamos National Laboratory (1996)
12. Nagarajan, R., Papanikolaou, N., Williams, D.: Simulating and compiling code for the sequential quantum random access machine. Electronic Notes in Theoretical Computer Science 170, 101–124 (2007)
13. Ömer, B.: Structural quantum programming, Ph.D. Thesis. Technical University of Vienna (2003)
14. Sanders, J.W., Zuliani, P.: Quantum programming. In: Backhouse, R., Oliveira, J.N. (eds.) MPC 2000. LNCS, vol. 1837, pp. 88–99. Springer, Heidelberg (2000)
15. Selinger, P.: Towards a quantum programming language. Mathematical Structures in Computer Science 14, 527–586 (2004)
16. Selinger, P.: A brief survey of quantum programming languages. In: Kameyama, Y., Stuckey, P.J. (eds.) FLOPS 2004. LNCS, vol. 2998, pp. 1–6. Springer, Heidelberg (2004)
17. Svore, K.M., Aho, A.V., Cross, A.W., Chuang, I.L., Markov, I.L.: A layered software architecture for quantum computing design tools. IEEE Computer 39, 74–83 (2006)
18. Ying, M.S.: Hoare logic for quantum programs, `http://xxx.lanl.gov/abs/0906.4586`
19. Ying, M.S., Chen, J.X., Feng, Y., Duan, R.Y.: Commutativity of quantum weakest preconditions. Information Processing Letters 104, 152–158 (2007)
20. Ying, M.S., Duan, R.Y., Feng, Y., Ji, Z.F.: Predicate transformer semantics of quantum programs. In: Mackie, I., Gay, S. (eds.) Semantic Techniques in Quantum Computation, pp. 311–360. Cambridge University Press, Cambridge (2010)
21. Ying, M.S., Feng, Y.: An algebraic language for distributed quantum computing. IEEE Transactions on Computers 58, 728–743 (2009)
22. Ying, M.S., Feng, Y.: Quantum loop programs. Acta Informatica 47, 221–250 (2010)
23. Ying, M.S., Feng, Y.: A flowchart language for quantum programming. (submitted)
24. Ying, M.S., Feng, Y., Duan, R.Y., Ji, Z.F.: An algebra of quantum processes. ACM Transactions on Computational Logic 10, 19 (2009)
25. Zuliani, P.: Compiling quantum programs. Acta Informatica 41, 435–473 (2005)
26. Zuliani, P.: Reasoning about faulty quantum programs. Acta Informatica 46, 403–432 (2009)

From a Verified Kernel towards Verified Systems

Gerwin Klein

[1] NICTA, Australia

[2] School of Computer Science and Engineering, UNSW, Sydney, Australia
gerwin.klein@nicta.com.au

Abstract. The L4.verified project has produced a formal, machine-checked Isabelle/HOL proof that the C code of the seL4 OS microkernel correctly implements its abstract implementation. This paper briefly summarises the proof, its main implications and assumptions, reports on the experience in conducting such a large-scale verification, and finally lays out a vision how this formally verified kernel may be used for gaining formal, code-level assurance about safety and security properties of systems on the order of a million lines of code.

1 L4.Verified

In previous work [13], we reported on the result of the L4.verified project: a machine-checked, formal verification of the seL4 operating system microkernel from a high-level model in Higher-Order logic down to low-level C code.

To the best of our knowledge, this is the first complete code-level proof of any general-purpose OS kernel, and in particular the first machine-checked such proof of full functional correctness.

Early pioneering attempts at formal OS verification like UCLA Secure Unix [20] or PSOS [9] did not proceed substantially over the specification phase. In the late 1980s, Bevier's KIT [2] is the first code-level proof of an OS kernel, albeit only a very simple one. There have been a number of formal verifications of either functional correctness, temporal, or information flow properties of OS kernels, recently for instance the Common Criteria EAL6+ certified INTEGRITY kernel [18]. None of these, however, truly formally verified the code-level implementation of the kernel. Instead, what is verified is usually a formal model of the code, which can range from very precise as in the INTEGRITY example to design-level or more abstract models. Correspondence between C code as seen by the compiler and the formal model is established by other means. In the L4.verified project, this critical missing step is for the first time formal and machine-checked.

Contemporary OS verification projects include Verisoft, Verisoft XT, and Verve. The Verisoft project has not yet fully completed all parts of its OS kernel proof, but it has conclusively demonstrated that formal verification of OS code can be driven down to verified hardware — similarly to the verified CLI stack [3] from the 1980s, but going up to a verified C0 compiler with support for inline assembly and up to substantial scale. The Verisoft XT project [7] has

K. Ueda (Ed.): APLAS 2010, LNCS 6461, pp. 21–33, 2010.

demonstrated that the technology exists to deal with concurrent C at a scale of tens of thousands lines of code. The Verve kernel [22] shows that type and memory safety properties can be established on the assembly level via type systems and therefore with much lower cost. Verve contains a formally verified runtime system, in particular a garbage collector that the type system relies on. Even though it only shows type safety, not functional correctness, the smaller cost of verification makes the approach attractive for larger code bases if full functional correctness is not required or too expensive to obtain.

The formal proof for the seL4 kernel establishes a classical functional correctness result: all possible behaviours of the C implementation are already contained in the behaviours of its abstract specification. In the L4.verified project, this proof was conducted in two stages in the interactive theorem prover Isabelle/HOL [17]. The first stage is comparable to other detailed model-level kernel verifications. It connects an abstract, operational specification with an executable design specification of the kernel. This design specification is low-level enough to clearly see a direct one-to-one correspondence to C code for the large majority of the code. The second step in the proof was to show that the C code implements this low-level design. The result is one concise overall theorem in Isabelle/HOL stating that the behaviour of the C code as specified by its operational semantics is contained in the behaviours of the specification.

Like any proof, this verification has assumptions. For the correctness of a running seL4 system on real hardware we need to assume correctness of the C compiler and linker, assembly code, hardware, correct use of low-level TLB and cache-flushing instructions, and correct boot code. The verification target was the ARM11 uniprocessor version of seL4. There also exists an (unverified) x86 port of seL4 with optional multi-processor and IOMMU support.

The key benefit of a functional correctness proof is that proofs about the C implementation of the kernel can now be reduced to proofs about the specification if the property under investigation is preserved by refinement. Additionally, our proof has a number of implications, some of them desirable direct security properties. If the assumptions of the verification hold, we have mathematical proof that, among other properties, the seL4 kernel is free of buffer overflows, NULL pointer dereferences, memory leaks, and undefined execution. There are other properties that are not implied, for instance general security without further definition of what security is or information flow guaranties that would provide strict secrecy of protected data. A more in-depth description of high-level implications and limitations has appeared elsewhere [12,11].

2 What Have We Learned?

To be able to successfully complete this verification, we have contributed to the state of the art in theorem proving and programming languages on a number of occasions, including tool development [16], memory models [19], and scalable refinement frameworks [6,21]. These are published and do not need to be repeated in detail here. Other interesting aspects of the project concern lessons that are harder to measure such as proof engineering, teaching theorem proving to new team members, close collaboration between the kernel and verification teams, and a prototyping methodology for kernel development.

On a higher level, the main unique aspects of this project were its scale and level of detail in the proof. Neither would have been achievable without a mechanical proof assistant. The proof, about 200,000 lines of Isabelle script, was too large for any one person in the team to fully keep in their head, and much too large and technically involved to manually check and have any degree of confidence in the result. Software verifications like this are only possible with the help of tools.

The cost of the verification was around 25 person years counting all parts of the project, including exploratory work and models that were later not used in the verification. About twelve of these person years pertain to the kernel verification itself. Most of the rest was spent on developing frameworks, tools, proof libraries, and the C verification framework, including a precise memory model [19] and a C to Isabelle/HOL parser [21].

This means, we have demonstrated that proving functional correctness of low-level C code is possible and feasible at a scale of about 10,000 lines of code, but the cost is substantial. Clearly, we have to conclude that currently this approach does not lend itself to casual software development.

The story is different for high-assurance systems. It is currently very expensive to build truly trustworthy systems and to provide substantial assurance that they will indeed behave as expected. It is hard to get useful numbers for such comparisons, but one data point that is close enough, and where some experience and cost estimates are available, are Common Criteria (CC) security evaluations. CC on high evaluation levels prescribe the use of formal specifications and proofs down to the design level. Correspondence of models to code is established by testing and inspection.

L4.verified spent about $700 per line of code (loc) for the verification if we take the whole 25 person years, and less than $350/loc if we take the 12 actually spent on the kernel. We estimate that, with the experience gained and with the tools and libraries available now, the cost could be further reduced to 10, maybe 8 person years for a similar code base verified by the same team, i.e. about $230/loc. Even assuming $350/loc, the verification compares favourably with the quoted cost for CC EAL6 evaluation at $1000/loc [10]. EAL7 (the highest CC level) which arguably still provides less assurance than formal code-level proof, can safely be assumed to be more costly still. The comparison is not entirely fair, since the Common Criteria mostly address security properties and not functional correctness, and because the verification aspect is only one of the aspects of the certification process. On the other hand one can argue that general functional correctness is at least as hard to prove as a specific security property and that while verification is not the only aspect, it is the most expensive one. We believe that formal, code-level verification is cost attractive for the vendor as well as for the certification authority, while increasing assurance at the same time.

For the certification authority, risk is reduced. Since the proof is machine-checked, only the high-level specification and its properties as well as the bottom-level model need to be scrutinised manually and with care to trust the system. Validating the high-level properties is the same as in the current evaluation scheme. The bottom-level model, however, is different. In the current scheme, the bottom level model is different for each certification and needs to be connected to code by careful validation, testing and inspection which is expensive to conduct and hard to check. In our case, the model does not depend on the certification artefact: it is just the semantics of our subset of C. Once validated, this could be re-used over many certifications and amortised to gain even higher assurance than what would otherwise be cost effective.

Our result of feasible but high-cost verification at about 10,000 loc does not mean that formal verification could not scale further. In fact, microkernels such as seL4 typically lack two properties that make formal verification scale better: modularity and strong internal abstractions. We would expect application-level code and even user-level OS code to be much better targets for scalable, compositional verification techniques.

However, even with nicely structured code, it appears infeasible at this stage to formally verify the functional correctness of systems with millions of lines of code. The field is making progress in scaling automated techniques for reasonably simple properties to such systems, but complex safety or security properties or properties that critically rely on functional correctness of at least parts of the system still appear without our reach.

3 A Secure System with Large Untrusted Components

This section presents a vision of how assurance even of complex safety properties could nevertheless be feasibly be achieved within (or close to) the current state of the art in code-level formal proof.

The key idea is the original microkernel idea that is also explored in the MILS (multiple independent levels of security and safety) space [4]: using system architectures that ensure security by construction, relying on basic kernel mechanisms to separate trusted from untrusted code. Security in these systems is not an additional feature or requirement, but fundamentally determines the core architecture of how the system is laid out, designed, and implemented.

This application space was one of the targets in the design of the seL4 kernel. Exploiting the verified properties of seL4, we should be able to architect systems such that the trusted computing base for the desired property is small and amenable to formal verification, and that the untrusted code base of the system provably cannot affect overall security.

The basic process for building a system in this vision could be summarised as follows:

1. Architect the system on a high level such that the trusted computing base is as small as possible for the security property of interest.

2. Map the architecture to a low-level design that preserves the security property and that is directly implementable on the underlying kernel.
3. Formalise the system, preferably on the architecture level.
4. Analyse, preferably formally prove, that it enforces the security property. This analysis formally identifies the trusted computing base.
5. Implement the system, with focus for high assurance on the trusted components.
6. Prove that the behaviour of the trusted components assumed in the security analysis is the behaviour that was implemented.

The key property of the underlying kernel that can make the security analysis feasible is the ability to reduce the overall security of the system to the security mechanisms of the kernel and the behaviour of the trusted components only. Untrusted components will be assumed to do anything in their power to subvert the system. They are constrained only by the kernel and they can be as big and complex as they need to be. Components that need further constraints on their behaviour in the security analysis need to be trusted to follow these constraints. They form the trusted components of the system. Ideally these components are small, simple, and few.

In the following subsections I demonstrate how such an analysis works on an example system, briefly summarise initial progress we have made in modelling, designing, formally analysing, and implementing the system, and summarise the steps that are left to gain high assurance of overall system security. A more detailed account is available elsewhere [1].

The case study system is a secure access controller (SAC) with the sole purpose of connecting one front-end terminal to either of two back-end networks one at a time. The back-end networks A and B are assumed to be of different classification levels (e.g. top secret and secret), potentially hostile and collaborating. The property the SAC should enforce is that no information may flow through it between A and B.

3.1 Architecture

Figure 1 shows the high-level architecture of the system. The boxes stand for software components, the arrows for memory or communication channel access. The main components of the SAC are the SAC Controller (SAC-C), the Router (R), and the Router Manager (RM). The Router Manager is the only trusted user-level component in the system. The system is implemented on top of seL4 and started up by a user-level booter component. The SAC Controller is an embedded Linux instance with a web-server interface to the front-end control network where a user may request to be connected to network A or B. After authenticating and interpreting such requests, the SAC Controller passes them on as simple messages to the Router Manager. The Router Manager receives such switching messages. If, for example, the SAC is currently connected to A, there will be a Router instance running with access to only the front-end data network card and the network card for A. Router instances are again embedded Linuxes

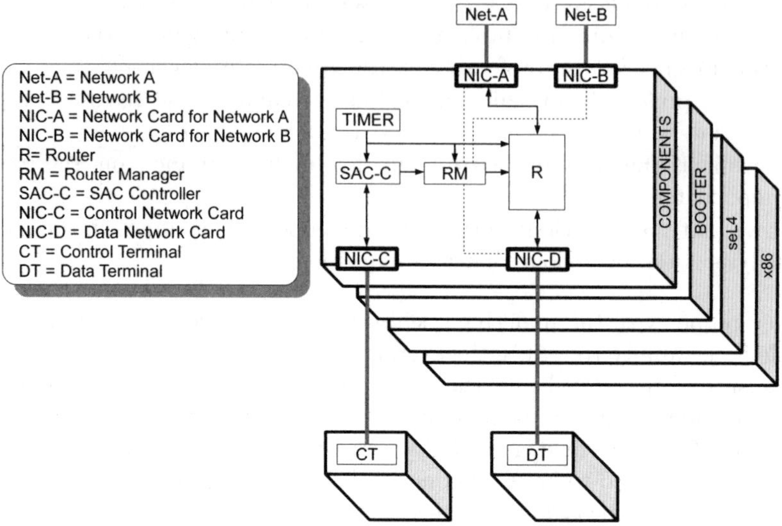

Fig. 1. SAC Architecture

with a suitable implementation of TCP/IP, routing etc. If the user requests a switch to network B, the Router Manager will tear down the current A-connected Linux instance, flush all network cards, create a new Router Linux and give it access to network B and the front end only.

The claim is that this architecture enforces the information flow property. Each Router instance is only ever connected to one back-end network and all storage it may have had access to is wiped when switching. The Linux instances are large, untrusted components in the order of a million lines of code each. The trusted Router Manager is small, about 2,000 lines of C.

For this architecture to work, there is an important non-functional requirement on the Linux instances: we must be able to tear down and boot Linux in acceptable time (less than 1-2 seconds). The requirement is not security-critical, so it does not need to be part of the analysis, but it determines if the system is practical. Our implementation achieves this.

So far, we have found an architecture of the system that we think enforces the security property. The next sections explore design/implementation and analysis.

3.2 Design and Implementation

The main task of the low-level design is to take the high-level architecture and map it to seL4 kernel concepts. The seL4 kernel supports a number of objects for threads, virtual memory, communication endpoints, etc. Sets of these map to components in the architecture. Access to these objects is controlled by capabilities: pointers with associated access rights. For a thread to invoke any operation on an object, it must first present a valid capability with sufficient rights to that object.

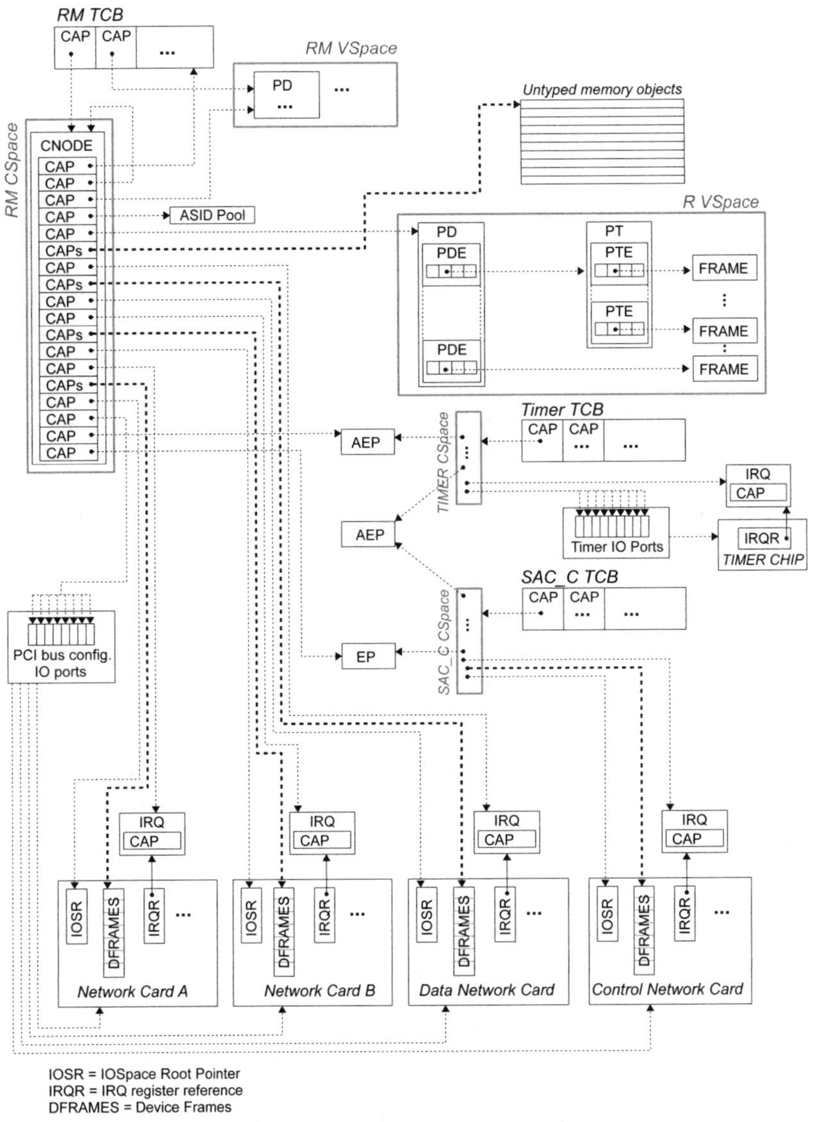

Fig. 2. Low-Level Design

Figure 2 shows a simplified diagram of the SAC low-level design as it is implemented on seL4. The boxes in the picture stand for seL4 kernel objects, the arrows for seL4 capabilities. The main message of this diagram is that it is significantly more complex than the architecture-level picture we started out with. For the system to run on an x86 system with IOMMU (which is necessary to achieve untrusted device access), a large number of details have to be taken care of. Access to hardware resources has to be carefully divided, large software components will be implemented by sets of seL4 kernel objects with further internal access control structure, communications channels and shared access need to be mapped to seL4 capabilities, and so forth.

The traditional way to implement a picture such as the one in Figure 2 is by writing C code that contains the right sequence of seL4 kernel calls to create the required objects, to configure them with the right initial parameters, and to connect them with the right seL4 capabilities with the correct access rights. The resulting code is tedious to write, full of specific constants, and not easy to get right. Yet, this code is crucial: it provides the known-good initial capability state of the system that the security analysis is later reduced to.

To simplify and aid this task, we have developed the small formal domain-specific language capDL [15] (capability distribution language) that can be used to concisely describe capability and kernel object distributions such as Figure 2. A binary representation of this description is the input for a user-level library in the initial root task of the system and can be used to fully automatically set up the initial set of objects and capabilities. Since capDL has a formal semantics in Isabelle/HOL, the same description can be used as the basis of the security analysis. It can also be used to debug, inspect and visualise the capability state of a running system.

For further assurance, we plan to formally verify the user-level library that translates the static capDL description into a sequence of seL4 system calls. Its main correctness theorem will be that after the sequence of calls has executed, the global capability distribution is the one specified in the original description. This will result in a system with a known, fully controlled capability distribution, formally verified at the C code level.

For system architectures that do not rely on known behaviour of trusted components, such as a classic, static separation kernel setup or guest OS virtualisation with complete separation, this will already provide a very strong security argument.

The tool above will automatically instantiate the low-level structure and access-control design into implementation-level C code. What is missing is providing the behaviour of each of the components in the system. Currently, components are implemented in C, and capDL is rich enough to provide a mapping between threads and the respective code segments that implement their behaviour. If the behaviour of any of these components needs to be trusted, this code needs to be verified — either formally, or otherwise to the required level of assurance. There is no reason component behaviour has to be described in C — higher-level languages such as Java or Haskell are being ported to seL4 and may well be better suited for providing assurance.

4 Security Analysis

Next to the conceptual security architecture of the SAC, we have at this stage of the exposition a low-level design mapping the architecture to the underlying platform (seL4), and an implementation in C. The implementation is running and the system seems to perform as expected. This section now explores how we can gain confidence that the SAC enforces its security property.

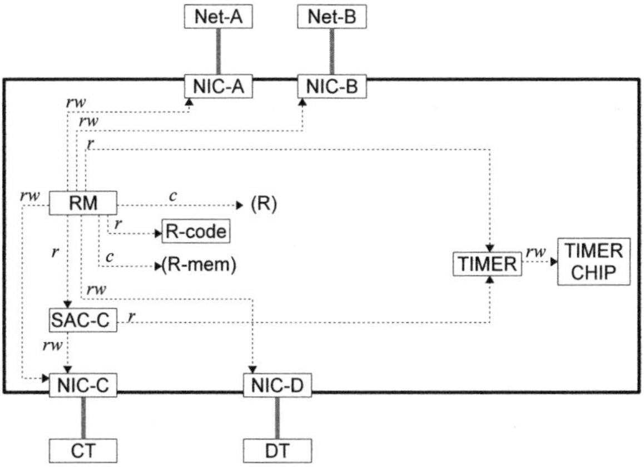

Fig. 3. SAC Abstraction

The capDL specification corresponding to Figure 2 is too detailed for this analysis. Instead, we would like to conduct the analysis on a more abstract level, closer to the architecture picture that we initially used to describe the SAC.

In previous work, we have investigated different high-level access control models of seL4 that abstract from the specifics of the kernel and reduce the system state to a graph where kernel objects are the nodes and capabilities are the edges, labelled with access rights [8,5]. We can draw a simple formal relationship between capDL specifications and such models, abstracting from seL4 capabilities into general access rights. We can further abstract by grouping multiple kernel objects together and computing the capability edges between these sets of objects as the union of the access rights between the elements of the sets. With suitable grouping of objects, this process results in Figure 3 for the SAC. The figure shows the initial system state after boot, the objects in parentheses (R) and (R-mem) are areas of memory which will later be turned into the main Router thread and its memory frames using the *create* operation, an abstraction of the seL4 system call that will create the underlying objects.

This picture now describes an abstract version of the design. We have currently not formally proved the connection between this model and the capDL specification, neither have we formally proved that the grouping of components is a correct abstraction, but it is reasonably clear that both are possible in principle.

For a formal security analysis, we first need to express the behaviour of RM in some way. In this case, we have chosen a small machine-like language with conditionals, jumps, and seL4 kernel calls as primitive operations. For all other components, we specify that at each system step, they may nondeterministically attempt any operation — it is the job of the kernel configured to the capability distribution in Figure 3 to prevent unwanted accesses.

To express the final information flow property, we choose a label-based security approach in this example and give each component an additional bit of state: it is set if the component potentially has had access to data from NIC A. It is easy to determine which effect each system operation has on this state bit. The property is then simple: in no execution of the system can this bit ever be set for NIC B.

Given the behaviour of the trusted component, the initial capability distribution, and the behaviour of the kernel, we can formally define the possible behaviours of the overall system and formally verify that the above property is true. This verification took a 3-4 weeks in Isabelle/HOL and less than a week to conduct in SPIN, although we had to further abstract and simplify the model to make it work in SPIN.

A more detailed description of this analysis has appeared elsewhere [1].

5 What Is Missing?

With the analysis described so far, we do not yet have a high-assurance system. This section explores what would be needed to achieve one.

The main missing piece is to show that the behaviour we have described in a toy machine language for the security analysis is actually implemented by the 2,000 lines of C code of the Router Manager component. Most of these 2,000 lines are not security critical. They deal with setting up Linux instances, providing them with enough information and memory, keeping track of memory used etc. Getting them wrong will make the system unusable, because Linux will fail to boot, but it will not make it break the security property. The main critical parts are the possible sequence of seL4 kernel calls that the Router Manager generates to provide the Linux Router instance with the necessary capabilities to access network cards and memory. Classic refinement as we have used it to prove correctness of seL4 could be used to show correctness of the Router Manager.

Even with this done, there are a number of issues left that I have glossed over in the description so far. Some of these are:

- The SAC uses the unverified x86/IOMMU version of seL4, not the verified ARM version. Our kernel correctness proof would need to be ported first.
- We need to formally show that the security property is preserved by the existing refinement.
- We need to formally connect capDL and access control models. This includes extending the refinement chain of seL4 upwards to the levels of capDL and access control model.
- We need to formally prove that the grouping of components is a correct, security preserving abstraction.
- We need to formally prove that the user-level root task sets up the initial capability distribution correctly and according to the capDL specification of the system.
- We need to formally prove that the information flow abstraction used in the analysis is a faithful representation of what happens in the system. This is

essentially an information flow analysis of the kernel: if we formalise in the analysis that a Read operation only transports data from A to B, we need to show that the kernel respects this and that there are no other channels in the system by which additional information may travel. The results of our correctness proof can potentially be used for this, but it goes beyond the properties we have proved so far.

6 Conclusion

We have demonstrated that formal code verification at a scale of about 10,000 lines of code is possible and feasible. We have argued that, for high-assurance systems, it is also cost-effective. There are no real barriers to conducting verifications like this routinely.

The bad news is that while these techniques may optimistically scale in the next few years up to 100,000s lines of code for nicely structured, appropriate code bases, realistic systems beyond that size still seem out of reach for the near future. Modern embedded systems frequently comprise millions of lines of code. None of these large systems are high-assurance systems yet, but a clear trend towards larger and more complex systems is observable even in this space, and some of these large systems, e.g. automobile code, should become high-assurance systems, because current practices are unsatisfactory [14].

Even though we may not be able to prove full functional correctness of such systems in the near future, our thesis is that it is nevertheless possible to provide formal, code-level proof of specific safety and security properties of systems in the millions of lines of code. We plan to achieve this by exploiting formally verified microkernel isolation properties, suitable security architectures, and code-level formal proofs for the small trusted computing base of such systems.

Acknowledgements. NICTA is funded by the Australian Government as represented by the Department of Broadband, Communications and the Digital Economy and the Australian Research Council through the ICT Centre of Excellence program.

This material is in part based on research sponsored by the Air Force Research Laboratory, under agreement number FA2386-09-1-4160. The U.S. Government is authorised to reproduce and distribute reprints for Governmental purposes notwithstanding any copyright notation thereon. The views and conclusions contained herein are those of the authors and should not be interpreted as necessarily representing the official policies or endorsements, either expressed or implied, of the Air Force Research Laboratory or the U.S. Government.

References

1. Andronick, J., Greenaway, D., Elphinstone, K.: Towards proving security in the presence of large untrusted components. In: Klein, G., Huuck, R., Schlich, B. (eds.) Proceedings of the 5th Workshop on Systems Software Verification, Vancouver, Canada. USENIX (October 2010)

2. Bevier, W.R.: Kit: A study in operating system verification. IEEE Transactions on Software Engineering 15(11), 1382–1396 (1989)
3. Bevier, W.R., Hunt, W.A., Moore, J.S., Young, W.D.: An approach to systems verification. Journal of Automated Reasoning 5(4), 411–428 (1989)
4. Boettcher, C., DeLong, R., Rushby, J., Sifre, W.: The MILS component integration approach to secure information sharing. In: 27th IEEE/AIAA Digital Avionics Systems Conference (DASC), St. Paul, MN (October 2008)
5. Boyton, A.: A verified shared capability model. In: Klein, G., Huuck, R., Schlich, B. (eds.) Proceedings of the 4th Workshop on Systems Software Verification, Aachen, Germany. Electronic Notes in Computer Science, vol. 254, pp. 25–44. Elsevier, Amsterdam (2009)
6. Cock, D., Klein, G., Sewell, T.: Secure microkernels, state monads and scalable refinement. In: Mohamed, O.A., Muñoz, C., Tahar, S. (eds.) TPHOLs 2008. LNCS, vol. 5170, pp. 167–182. Springer, Heidelberg (2008)
7. Cohen, E., Dahlweid, M., Hillebrand, M., Leinenbach, D., Moskal, M., Santen, T., Schulte, W., Tobies, S.: VCC: A practical system for verifying concurrent C. In: Berghofer, S., Nipkow, T., Urban, C., Wenzel, M. (eds.) Theorem Proving in Higher Order Logics. LNCS, vol. 5674, pp. 23–42. Springer, Heidelberg (2009)
8. Elkaduwe, D., Klein, G., Elphinstone, K.: Verified protection model of the seL4 microkernel. Technical Report NRL-1474, NICTA (October 2007), `http://ertos.nicta.com.au/publications/papers/Elkaduwe_GE_07.pdf`
9. Feiertag, R.J., Neumann, P.G.: The foundations of a provably secure operating system (PSOS). In: AFIPS Conference Proceedings, 1979 National Computer Conference, New York, NY, USA, pp. 329–334 (June 1979)
10. Hart, B.: SDR security threats in an open source world. In: Software Defined Radia Conference, Phoenix, AZ, USA, pp. 3.5–3 1–4 (November 2004)
11. Klein, G.: Correct OS kernel? proof? done! USENIX;login: 34(6), 28–34 (2009)
12. Klein, G., Andronick, J., Elphinstone, K., Heiser, G., Cock, D., Derrin, P., Elkaduwe, D., Engelhardt, K., Kolanski, R., Norrish, M., Sewell, T., Tuch, H., Winwood, S.: seL4: Formal verification of an OS kernel. Communications of the ACM 53(6), 107–115 (2010)
13. Klein, G., Elphinstone, K., Heiser, G., Andronick, J., Cock, D., Derrin, P., Elkaduwe, D., Engelhardt, K., Kolanski, R., Norrish, M., Sewell, T., Tuch, H., Winwood, S.: seL4: Formal verification of an OS kernel. In: Proceedings of the 22nd ACM Symposium on Operating Systems Principles, Big Sky, MT, USA, pp. 207–220. ACM, New York (2009)
14. Koscher, K., Czeskis, A., Roesner, F., Patel, S., Kohno, T., Checkoway, S., McCoy, D., Kantor, B., Anderson, D., Shacham, H., Savage, S.: Experimental security analysis of a modern automobile. In: Proceedings of the IEEE Symposium on Security and Privacy, Oakland, CA, USA, pp. 447–462 (May 2010)
15. Kuz, I., Klein, G., Lewis, C., Walker, A.: capDL: A language for describing capability-based systems. In: Proceedings of the 1st Asia-Pacific Workshop on Systems, New Delhi, India (to appear, August 2010)
16. Meng, J., Paulson, L.C., Klein, G.: A termination checker for Isabelle Hoare logic. In: Beckert, B. (ed.) Proceedings of the 4th International Verification Workshop, Bremen, Germany. CEUR Workshop Proceedings, vol. 259, pp. 104–118 (July 2007)
17. Nipkow, T., Paulson, L., Wenzel, M.: Isabelle/HOL. LNCS, vol. 2283. Springer, Heidelberg (2002)

18. Richards, R.J.: Modeling and security analysis of a commercial real-time operating system kernel. In: Hardin, D.S. (ed.) Design and Verification of Microprocessor Systems for High-Assurance Applications, pp. 301–322. Springer, Heidelberg (2010)
19. Tuch, H., Klein, G., Norrish, M.: Types, bytes, and separation logic. In: Hofmann, M., Felleisen, M. (eds.) Proceedings of the 34th ACM SIGPLAN-SIGACT Symposium on Principles of Programming Languages, Nice, France, pp. 97–108 (January 2007)
20. Walker, B.J., Kemmerer, R.A., Popek, G.J.: Specification and verification of the UCLA Unix security kernel. Communications of the ACM 23(2), 118–131 (1980)
21. Winwood, S., Klein, G., Sewell, T., Andronick, J., Cock, D., Norrish, M.: Mind the gap: A verification framework for low-level C. In: Berghofer, S., Nipkow, T., Urban, C., Wenzel, M. (eds.) Theorem Proving in Higher Order Logics. LNCS, vol. 5674, pp. 500–515. Springer, Heidelberg (2009)
22. Yang, J., Hawblitzel, C.: Safe to the last instruction: automated verification of a type-safe operating system. In: Proceedings of the 2010 ACM SIGPLAN Conference on Programming Language Design and Implementation, Toronto, Ontario, Canada, pp. 99–110. ACM, New York (June 2010)

Reasoning about Computations Using Two-Levels of Logic

Dale Miller

INRIA Saclay & LIX, École Polytechnique
Palaiseau, France

Abstract. We describe an approach to using one logic to reason about specifications written in a second logic. One level of logic, called the "reasoning logic", is used to state theorems about computational specifications. This logic is classical or intuitionistic and should contain strong proof principles such as induction and co-induction. The second level of logic, called the "specification logic", is used to specify computation. While computation can be specified using a number of formal techniques—*e.g.*, Petri nets, process calculus, and state machines—we shall illustrate the merits and challenges of using logic programming-like specifications of computation.

1 Introduction

When choosing a formalism to use to specify computation (say, structured operational semantics, Petri nets, finite state machines, abstract machines, λ-calculus, or π-calculus), one needs that specification framework to be not only expressive but also amenable to various kinds of reasoning techniques. Typical kinds of reasoning techniques are algebraic, inductive, co-inductive, and category theoretical.

Logic, in the form of logic programming, has often been used to specify computation. For example, Horn clauses are a natural setting for formalizing structured operational semantics specifications and finite state machines; hereditary Harrop formulas are a natural choice for specifying typing judgments given their support for hypothetical and generic reasoning; and linear logic is a natural choice for the specification of stateful and concurrent computations. (See [27] for an overview of how operational semantics have been specified using the logic programming paradigm.) The fact that logic generally has a rich and deep meta-theory (soundness and completeness theorems, cut-elimination theorems, *etc*) should provide logic with powerful means to help in reasoning about computational specifications.

The activities of specifying computation and reasoning about those specifications are, of course, closely related activities. If we choose logic to formulate both of these activities, then it seems we must also choose between using one logic for both activities and using two different logics, one for each activity. While both approaches are possible, we shall focus on the challenges and merits of treating

K. Ueda (Ed.): APLAS 2010, LNCS 6461, pp. 34–46, 2010.

these two logics as different. In particular, we shall assume that our "reasoning logic" formalizes some basic mathematical inferences, including inductive and co-inductive reasoning. On the other hand, we shall assume that our "specification logic" is more limited and designed to describe the evolution (unfolding) of computations. Speaking roughly, the reasoning logic will be a formalization of a part of mathematical reasoning while the specification logic will be a logic programming language.

This paper is a summary of some existing papers (particularly [16]) and is structured as follows. Section 2 presents a specific reasoning language $\mathcal{G}$ and Section 3 presents a specific specification logic hH^2. Section 4 describes how hH^2 is encoded in $\mathcal{G}$. Section 5 describes a few implemented systems that have been used to help explore and validate the intended uses of hH^2 and $\mathcal{G}$. Section 6 presents an overview of the various key ingredients of these two logics as well as suggesting other possibilities for them. Finally, Section 7 describes some related work.

2 The Reasoning Logic

Our reasoning logic, which we call $\mathcal{G}$ (following [14]) is a higher-order logic similar to Church's Simple Theory of Types [9] (axioms 1 - 6) but with the following differences.

Intuitionistic vs classical logic. Our reasoning logic is based on intuitionistic logic instead of Church's choice of classical logic. While defaulting to a constructive approach to proving theorems about computation is certainly sensible, this choice is not essential and the sequent calculus proof system used to describe the intuitionistic reasoning logic can easily be modified to capture the classical variant. The choice between intuitionistic and classical logic can have, however, surprising consequences that are not immediately related to the familiar distinction between constructive and non-constructive logic. In particular, Tiu & Miller [44] have shown that, for a certain declarative treatment of binding in the π-calculus, provability of the bisimulation formula yields "open" bisimulation when the reasoning logic is intuitionistic and late ("closed") bisimulation if that logic is classical.

Variables of higher-order type. Following Church, we used the type o to denote formulas: thus, a variable of type $\tau_1 \to \cdots \to \tau_n \to o$ (for some $n \geq 0$) is a variable at "predicate type." In what follows, we shall not use such higher-order variables within formulas. We shall use variables of higher-order type that are not predicate types: in particular, we shall quantify over variables of type $\tau_1 \to \cdots \to \tau_n \to \tau_0$ (for some $n \geq 0$) where $\tau_0, \ldots, \tau_n$ are all primitive types. Removing restrictions on predicate quantification should be possible but, for the kind of project we intend here, it seems to be an unnecessary complication.

Generic quantification. We include in $\mathcal{G}$ the ∇-quantifier [30] and the associated notion of *nominal abstraction* [14] so that the "generic" reasoning associated with eigenvariables in the specification logic can be modeled directly and declaratively in $\mathcal{G}$. While ∇ is a genuine departure from Church's original logic, it is a weak addition to the logic and is only relevant to the treatment of bindings in syntax (it enriches the possibilities of *binder mobility* [26]). If one is not treating bindings in syntax expressions of the specification logic, this quantifier plays no role.

Induction and co-induction. A reasoning logic must certainly be powerful enough to support induction and co-induction. The logic $\mathcal{G}$ allows for the direct specification of recursive predicate definitions and to interpret them either as a least and or greatest fixed point in the sense of [2,5,22,31]. The rules for induction and co-induction use higher-order predicate schema variables in their premises in order to range over possible pre- and post-fixed points. For example, the recursive definitions (written like logic programming clauses)

$$\begin{array}{rcl} \mathit{nat}\ z & \stackrel{\mu}{=} & \top \\ \mathit{nat}\ (s\ N) & \stackrel{\mu}{=} & \mathit{nat}\ N \end{array} \qquad \begin{array}{rcl} \mathit{member}\ B\ (B :: L) & \stackrel{\mu}{=} & \top \\ \mathit{member}\ B\ (C :: L) & \stackrel{\mu}{=} & \mathit{member}\ B\ L \end{array}$$

are admitted to $\mathcal{G}$ as the following fixed point expressions:

$$\begin{array}{rcl} \mathit{nat} & = & \mu(\lambda p \lambda x.(x = 0) \vee (\exists y.(s\ y) = x \wedge p\ y)) \\ \mathit{member} & = & \mu(\lambda m \lambda x \lambda l.(\exists k.\ l = (x :: k)) \vee (\exists k \exists y.\ l = (y :: k) \wedge m\ x\ k)) \end{array}$$

In order to support induction and co-induction, the *closed world assumption* must be made: that is, we need to know the complete specification of a predicate in order to state the induction and co-induction rule for that predicate. Thus, the reasoning logic will assume the closed world assumption. On the other hand, computing with λ-tree syntax [25] uses the higher-order judgments of GENERIC and AUGMENT. Since these two judgments only make sense assuming the *open world assumption*, the specification logic will make that assumption. The next two sections contain a description of the specification logic and its encoding in the reasoning logic.

3 The Specification Logic

For our purposes here, we shall use the intuitionistic theory of hereditary Harrop formulas [28] restricted to second order as the specification logic. In particular, formulas in hH^2 are of two kinds. The *goal formulas* are given by:

$$G = \top \mid A \mid G \wedge G \mid A \supset G \mid \forall_\tau x.G,$$

where A denotes atomic formulas and τ ranges over types that do not themselves contain the type o of formulas. The *definite clauses* are formulas of the form $\forall x_1 \ldots \forall x_n.(G_1 \supset \cdots \supset G_m \supset A)$, where $n, m \geq 0$ and where quantification is, again, over variables whose types do not contain o. This restricted set of formulas is "second-order" in that to the left of an implication in a definite formula one finds goal formulas and to the left of an implication in a goal formula, one finds only atomic formulas.

$$\frac{}{\Sigma : \Delta \vdash \top}\ \text{TRUE} \qquad \frac{\Sigma : \Delta \vdash G_1 \quad \Sigma : \Delta \vdash G_2}{\Sigma : \Delta \vdash G_1 \wedge G_2}\ \text{AND}$$

$$\frac{\Sigma : \Delta, A \vdash G}{\Sigma : \Delta \vdash A \supset G}\ \text{AUGMENT} \qquad \frac{\Sigma \cup \{c : \tau\} : \Delta \vdash G[c/x]}{\Sigma : \Delta \vdash \forall_\tau x.G}\ \text{GENERIC}$$

$$\frac{\Sigma : \Delta \vdash G_1[\bar{t}/\bar{x}] \quad \cdots \quad \Sigma : \Delta \vdash G_n[\bar{t}/\bar{x}]}{\Sigma : \Delta \vdash A}\ \text{BACKCHAIN}$$

where $\forall \bar{x}.(G_1 \supset \ldots \supset G_n \supset A') \in \Delta$ and $A'[\bar{t}/\bar{x}]$ λ-*conv* A

Fig. 1. Derivation rules for the hH^2 logic

Provability in hH^2 is formalized by a sequent calculus proof system in which sequents are of the form $\Sigma : \Delta \vdash G$, where Δ is a list of definite clauses, G is a goal formula, and Σ is a set of eigenvariables. The inference rules for hH^2 are presented in Figure 1: these rules are shown in [28] to be complete for the intuitionistic theory of hH^2. The GENERIC rule introduces an eigenvariable (reading rules from conclusion to premise) and has the usual freshness side-condition: c is not in Σ. In the BACKCHAIN rule, for each term t_i in the list $\bar{t}$, we require that $\Sigma \vdash t_i : \tau_i$ holds, where τ_i is the type of the quantified variable x_i. An important property to note about these rules is that if we use them to search for a proof of the sequent $\Sigma : \Delta \vdash G$, then all the intermediate sequents that we will encounter will have the form $\Sigma' : \Delta, \mathcal{L} \vdash G'$ for some Σ' with $\Sigma \subseteq \Sigma'$, some goal formula G', and some set of atomic formulas $\mathcal{L}$. Thus the initial context Δ is *global*: changes occur only in the set of atoms on the left and the goal formula on the right. In presenting sequents, we will elide the signature when it is inessential to the discussion.

The logic hH^2 is a subset of the logic programming language λProlog [32] and is given an effective implementation by Teyjus implementation of λProlog [33]. This logic has also been used to formally specify a wide range of operational semantic specifications and static (typing) judgments [15,27,23].

An example: a typing judgment. We briefly illustrate the ease with which type assignment for the simply typed λ-calculus can be encoded in hH^2. There are two classes of objects in this domain: types and terms. Types are built from a single base type called i and the arrow constructor for forming function types. Terms can be variables x, applications $(m\ n)$ where m and n are terms, and typed abstractions $(\lambda x : a.r)$ where r is a term and a is the type of x. The standard rules for assigning types to terms are given as the following inference rules.

$$\frac{x : a \in \Gamma}{\Gamma \vdash x : a} \qquad \frac{\Gamma \vdash m : (a \to b) \quad \Gamma \vdash n : a}{\Gamma \vdash m\ n : b} \qquad \frac{\Gamma, x : a \vdash r : b}{\Gamma \vdash (\lambda x{:}a.r) : (a \to b)}\ x \text{ not in } \Gamma$$

Object-level simple types and untyped λ-terms can be encoded in a simply typed (meta-level) λ-calculus as follows. We assume the types ty and tm for representing object-level simple types and untyped λ-terms. The simple types are built from the two constructors $i : ty$ and $arr : ty \to ty \to ty$ and terms are built using the two constructors $app : tm \to tm \to tm$ and $lam : ty \to (tm \to tm) \to tm$. Note that the bound variables in an object-level abstraction are encoded by an explicit, specification logic abstraction: for example, the object-level term $(\lambda f : i \to i.(\lambda x : i.(f\ x)))$ will be represented by the specification logic term $lam\ (arr\ i\ i)\ (\lambda f. lam\ i\ (\lambda x.app\ f\ x))$. Given this encoding of the untyped λ-calculus and simple types, the standard inference rules for the typing judgment can be specified by the following theory describing the binary predicate *of*.

$$\forall m, n, a, b.(of\ m\ (arr\ a\ b) \supset of\ n\ a\ \supset\ of\ (app\ m\ n)\ b)$$
$$\forall r, a, b.(\forall x.(of\ x\ a \supset of\ (r\ x)\ b) \supset of\ (lam\ a\ r)\ (arr\ a\ b))$$

This specification in hH^2 does not maintain an explicit context for typing assumptions but uses hypothetical judgments instead. Also, the explicit side-condition in the rule for typing abstractions is not needed since it is captured by the freshness side-condition of the GENERIC rule in hH^2.

4 Encoding Provability of the Specification Logic

The definitional clauses in Figure 2 encode hH^2 provability in $\mathcal{G}$; this encoding is based on ideas taken from [23]. Formulas in hH^2 are represented in this setting by terms of type *form* and we reuse the symbols $\wedge$, $\vee$, $\supset$, $\top$, and $\forall$ for constants involving this type in $\mathcal{G}$; we assume that the context will make clear which reading of these symbols is meant. The constructor $\langle\cdot\rangle$ is used to inject atomic formulas in hH^2 into the type *form* in $\mathcal{G}$. As we have seen earlier, provability in hH^2 is about deriving sequents of the form $\Delta, \mathcal{L} \vdash G$, where Δ is a fixed list of definite clauses and $\mathcal{L}$ is a varying list of atomic formulas. Our encoding uses the $\mathcal{G}$ predicate *prog* to represent the definite clauses in Δ. In particular, the definite clause $\forall \bar{x}.[G_1 \supset \cdots \supset G_n \supset A]$ is encoded as the clause $\forall \bar{x}.prog\ A\ (G_1 \wedge \cdots \wedge G_n) \stackrel{\mu}{=} \top$ and a set of such hH^2 definite clauses is encoded as a set of *prog* clauses. (The descriptions of *prog* above and of *seq* in Figure 2 use the symbol $\stackrel{\mu}{=}$ to indicate that these names are to be associated with fixed point definitions.) Sequents in hH^2 are represented in $\mathcal{G}$ by formulas of the form $seq_N\ L\ G$ where L is a list encoding the atomic formulas in $\mathcal{L}$ and where G encodes the goal formula. The provability of such sequents in hH^2, given by the rules in Figure 1, leads to the clauses that define *seq* in Figure 2. The argument N that is written as a subscript in the expression $seq_N\ L\ G$ encodes an upper bound on the height of the corresponding hH^2 derivation and is used to formalize proofs by induction on the height of proofs. This argument has type *nt* for which there are two constructors: *z* of type *nt* and *s* of type $nt \to nt$. Similarly, the type of the non-empty list constructor :: is $atm \to lst \to lst$, where *atm* denotes the type of atomic formulas and *lst* denotes the type of a list of atomic formulas.

Notice the following points about this specification of provability. First, the ∇-quantifier is used in the reasoning logic to capture the "generic" reasoning

$$
\begin{array}{lcl}
seq_{(s\ N)}\ L\ \top & \stackrel{\mu}{=} & \top \\
seq_{(s\ N)}\ L\ (B \wedge C) & \stackrel{\mu}{=} & seq_N\ L\ B \wedge seq_N\ L\ C \\
seq_{(s\ N)}\ L\ (A \supset B) & \stackrel{\mu}{=} & seq_N\ (A :: L)\ B \\
seq_{(s\ N)}\ L\ (\forall B) & \stackrel{\mu}{=} & \nabla x. seq_N\ L\ (B\ x) \\
seq_{(s\ N)}\ L\ \langle A \rangle & \stackrel{\mu}{=} & member\ A\ L \\
seq_{(s\ N)}\ L\ \langle A \rangle & \stackrel{\mu}{=} & \exists b. prog\ A\ b \wedge seq_N\ L\ b
\end{array}
$$

Fig. 2. Encoding provability of hH^2 in $\mathcal{G}$

involved with using eigenvariables in specifying the provability of the specification logic universal quantifier. Second, the *seq* predicate contains an explicit list of atomic formulas and this is augmented by an atomic assumption whenever the proof of an implication is attempted. Third, the last clause for *seq* specifies backchaining over a given hH^2 definite clauses stored as *prog* clauses. The matching of atomic judgments to heads of clauses is handled by the treatment of definitions in the logic $\mathcal{G}$; thus the last rule for *seq* simply performs this matching and makes a recursive call on the corresponding clause body. Finally, the natural number (subscript) argument to *seq* is used to measure the height of specification logic proofs.

Since we have encoded derivability in hH^2, we can prove general properties about it in $\mathcal{G}$. For example, the following theorem in $\mathcal{G}$ states that the judgment $seq_n\ \ell\ g$ is not affected by permuting, contracting, or weakening the context ℓ.

$$\forall n, \ell_1, \ell_2, g.(seq_n\ \ell_1\ g) \wedge (\forall e.member\ e\ \ell_1 \supset member\ e\ \ell_2) \supset (seq_n\ \ell_2\ g)$$

Using this theorem with the encoding of typing judgments for the simply typed λ-calculus, for example, we immediately obtain that permuting, contracting, or weakening the typing context of a typing judgment does not invalidate that judgment.

Two additional $\mathcal{G}$ theorems are called the *instantiation* and *cut* properties. To state these properties, we use the following definition to abstract away from proof sizes.

$$seq\ \ell\ g \stackrel{\mu}{=} \exists n.nat\ n \wedge seq_n\ \ell\ g.$$

The *instantiation property* states that if a sequent judgment is proved generically (using ∇) then, in fact, it holds universally (that is, for all substitution instances). The exact property is

$$\forall \ell, g.(\nabla x.\ seq\ (\ell\ x)\ (g\ x)) \supset (\forall t.\ seq\ (\ell\ t)\ (g\ t)).$$

The *cut property* allows us to remove hypothetical judgments using a proof of such judgments. This property is stated as the $\mathcal{G}$ theorem

$$\forall \ell, a, g.(seq\ \ell\ \langle a \rangle) \wedge (seq\ (a :: \ell)\ g) \supset seq\ \ell\ g,$$

To demonstrate the usefulness of the instantiation and cut properties, note that using them together with our encoding of typing for the simply typed λ-calculus leads to an easy proof of the type substitution property, *i.e.*, if $\Gamma, x : a \vdash m : b$ and $\Gamma \vdash n : a$ then $\Gamma \vdash m[x := n] : b$.

5 Various Implemented Systems

Various systems and prototypes have been built to test and exploit the concepts of λ-tree syntax, higher-order judgments, and two-level logic. We overview these systems here.

5.1 Teyjus

Nadathur and his students and colleagues have developed the Teyjus compiler and run-time system [33] for λProlog. Although Teyjus is designed to compile and execute a rich subset of higher-order intuitionistic logic, it provides an effective environment for developing and animating the more restricted logic of hH^2.

5.2 Bedwyr

Baelde *et. al.* have implemented the Bedwyr model checker [4] which automates deduction for a subset of $\mathcal{G}$. The core logic engine in Bedwyr implements a sequent calculus prover that unfolds fixed points on both sides of sequents. As a result, it is able to perform standard model checking operations such as reachability, simulation, and winning strategies. Since unfolding is the only rule used with fixed points, such unfoldings must terminate in order to guarantee termination of the model checker. Bedwyr also provides the ∇-quantifier so model checking problems can directly express problems involving bindings. A particularly successful application of Bedwyr is on determining (open) simulation for the finite π-calculus [43,44].

5.3 Abella

Gacek has built the Abella interactive theorem prover [12] for proving theorems in $\mathcal{G}$. The two level logic approach is built into Abella and the cut and instantiation properties of Section 4 are available as reasoning steps (tactics). Abella accepts hH^2 specifications written as λProlog programs. Reasoning level predicates can then be defined inductively or co-inductively: these can also refer to provability of hH^2 specifications. Examples of theorems proved in Abella: precongruence of open bisimulation for the finite π-calculus; POPLmark challenge problems 1a and 2a; the Church-Rosser property and standardization theorems for the λ-calculus; and a number of properties related to the specification of the static and dynamic semantics of programming languages (type preservation, progress, and determinacy).

5.4 Tac

Baelde *et. al.* [7] have built an automated theorem prover for a fragment of $\mathcal{G}$. This prototype prover was developed to test various theorem prover designs that are motivated by the theory of focused proofs for fixed points [6]. This prover is able to automatically prove a number of simple theorems about relational specifications. Currently, Tac does not have convenient support for treating two-level logic although there is no particular problem with having such support added.

6 Various Aspects of Logic

There have been a number of papers and a number of logics that have been proposed during the past several years that shaped our understanding of the two-level logic approach to specifying and reasoning about computation. In this section, I briefly overview the key ingredients to that understanding.

6.1 Abstract Syntax as λ-Tree Syntax

The λProlog programming language [32] was the first programming language to support what was later called "higher-order abstract syntax" [35]. This later term referred to the encoding practice of using "meta-level" binding in a programming language to encode the "object-level" bindings in syntactic objects. Unfortunately, the meta-level bindings available in functional programming (which build functions) and logic programming (which build syntactic expressions with bindings) are quite different. Since using the term "higher-order abstract syntax" to refer to both styles of encoding is confusing, the term *λ-tree syntax* was introduced in [25] to denote the treatment of syntax using weak equality (such as α, β, and η on simply typed λ-terms). A key ingredient to the manipulation of λ-tree syntax involves the unification of λ-terms [19,24].

6.2 Fixed Points

Schroeder-Heister [39,40] and Girard [17] independently proposed a proof-theoretic approach to the closed-world assumption. The key development was the shift from viewing a logic program as a theory that provided *some* of the meaning of *undefined* predicates to viewing logic programs as recursive *definitions* that *completely* describe predicates. In this later case, it is easy to view predicates then as only convenient names for fixed point expressions. The proof theoretic treatment of such fixed points involves the first-order unification of eigenvariables. It was straightforward to extend that unification to also involve the unification of simply typed λ-terms and, as a result, this treatment of fixed points could be extended to the treatment of λ-tree syntax [21,22].

6.3 ∇-Quantification

The ∇-quantifier was introduced by Miller & Tiu [29,30] in order to help complete the picture of fixed point reasoning with λ-tree syntax. To provide a quick motivation for this new quantifier, consider the usual inference rule for proving the equality of two λ-abstracted terms.

$$(\zeta) \qquad \text{if } M = N \text{ then } \lambda x.M = \lambda x.N$$

In a formalized meta-theory, the quantification of x in the premise equation must be resolved and the universal quantification of x is a natural candidate. This choice leads to accepting the equivalence

$$(\forall x.M = N) \equiv (\lambda x.M = \lambda x.N).$$

This equivalence is, however, problematic when negation is involved. For example, since there is no (capture-avoiding) substitution for the variable w that makes the two (simply typed) term $\lambda x.w$ and $\lambda x.x$ equal (modulo λ-conversion), one would expect that our reasoning logic is strong enough to prove $\forall w.\neg(\lambda x.x = \lambda x.w)$. Using the equivalence above, however, this is equivalent to $\forall w.\neg\forall x.x = w$. Unfortunately, this formula should not be provable since it is true if the domain of quantification is a singleton. The ∇-quantifier is designed to be the proper quantifier to match the λ-binder: in fact, the formula $\forall w.\neg\nabla x.x = w$ has a simple proof in the proof systems for ∇. (As this example suggests, it is probably challenging to find a model-theory semantics for ∇.)

Two variants of ∇ appear in the literature and they differ on whether or not they accept the following *exchange* and *strengthening* equivalences:

$$\nabla x \nabla y.Bxy \equiv \nabla y \nabla x.Bxy \qquad\qquad \nabla x_\tau.B \equiv B \quad (x \text{ not free in } B)$$

While the first equivalence is often admissible, accepting the second rule is significant since it forces the domain of quantification for x (the type τ) to be infinite: that is, the formula

$$\exists_\tau x_1 \ldots \exists_\tau x_n. \left[\bigwedge_{1\leq i,j\leq n, i\neq j} x_i \neq x_j \right]$$

is provable for any $n \geq 1$. The *minimal generic quantification* of Baelde [3] rejects these as proof principle in part because there are times when a specification logic might need to allow possibly empty types: accepting these principles in the reasoning logic would force types using ∇-quantification to have infinite extent. On the other hand, the *nominal generic quantification* of Gacek *et. al.* [13,14] accepts these two additional equivalences.

6.4 Induction and Co-induction

The earlier work on fixed points only allowed for the unfolding of fixed points: as a result, it was not possible to reason specifically about the least or the greatest fixed point. In the series of PhD thesis, McDowell [21], Tiu [42], Baelde [2], and Gacek [13] developed numerous enrichments to our understanding of induction and co-induction: the last three of these theses have also been concerned with the interaction of the ∇-quantifier and fixed point reasoning.

6.5 Two-Level Logic

The force behind developing a two-level logic approach to reasoning about logic specifications is the necessity to treat both induction (and co-induction) and higher-order judgments (AUGMENT and GENERIC in Figure 1). These latter judgments only make sense when the "open world assumption" is in force: that is, atoms are undefined and we can always add more clauses describing their meaning. On the other hand, induction and co-induction only makes sense when the "close world assumption" is in force: that is, we can only induct when we have completely defined a predicate. It seems that we are at an impasse: in order to reason about logic specifications employing higher-order judgments, we need to have a logic that does not have higher-order judgments. To get around this impasse, McDowell & Miller [21,22] proposed using two logics: the reasoning logic assumes the closed world assumption and contains the principles for induction and co-induction while the specification logic assumes the open-world assumption and allows for higher-order judgments. The interface between these two logics has two parts. First, the term structures (including those treating binding) are shared between the two logics, and, second, provability of the specification logic is encoded as a predicate in the reasoning logic (as in Figure 2).

There are, of course, choices in the selection of not only the specification logic but also the proof system used to encode that logic. For example, extending hH^2 to allow the linear logic implication $\multimap$ was considered in [21,22]: the linear specification logic allowed for natural specifications of the operational semantics of a number of imperative programming features. There are also choices in how one describes specification logic provability: while two different proof systems should describe the same notion of provability, the form of that definition plays a large role in theorems involving provability. For example, the proof system in Figure 1 describes the *uniform proofs* of [28], which, in the terminology of focused proofs systems for intuitionistic logic [20], arises from assigning the *negative polarity* to all atomic formulas. The resulting "goal-directed" ("top-down") proofs mimic the head-normal form of typed λ-terms. Thus, induction over the *seq* judgment corresponds closely to induction over head-normal form. It is also possible to consider a proof system for *seq* in which all atoms are assigned a positive polarity. The resulting proofs would be "bottom-up": such proofs would naturally encode terms that contains explicit sharing. There may be domains where an induction principle over such bottom-up proofs would be more natural and revealing than for top-down proofs.

7 Related Work

This paper provides an overview of a multi-year effort to develop a logic and its proof theory that treats binding and fixed point together. It is common, however, that these two aspects of logic have been treated separately, as we describe below.

Many systems for reasoning about computations start with established inductive logic theorem provers such as Coq [10,8] and Isabelle/HOL [34], and then use those systems to build approaches to binding and substitution. Three such notable approaches are the locally nameless representation [1], the Nominal package for Isabelle/HOL [45], and Hybrid [11].

On the other hand, there are a variety of systems for specifying computations which take binding as a primitive notion and then attempt to define separately notions of induction. Many of these systems start with the LF logical framework [18], a dependently typed λ-calculus with a direct treatment of variable binding. While the LF type system can directly treat λ-tree syntax, it does not include a notion of induction. Twelf [36] is able to establish that various recursively defined relations on LF-typed terms are, in fact, determinate (*i.e.*, functional) and/or total. These conclusions can be used in concert with the dependently typed λ-terms to conclude a wide range of properties of the original LF specification. Similar functional approaches have been developed starting with $\mathcal{M}_2^+$ [41], a simple meta-logic for reasoning over LF representations where proof terms are represented as recursive functions. More recent work includes the Delphin [38] and Beluga [37] functional languages which can be used in the same spirit as $\mathcal{M}_2^+$. In all of these approaches, however, side-conditions for termination and coverage are required and algorithms have been devised to check for such properties. Since termination and coverage are in general undecidable, such algorithms are necessarily incomplete.

Acknowledgments. I thank Andrew Gacek and Alwen Tiu for their comments on this paper.

References

1. Aydemir, B., Charguéraud, A., Pierce, B.C., Pollack, R., Weirich, S.: Engineering formal metatheory. In: 35th ACM Symp. on Principles of Programming Languages, pp. 3–15. ACM, New York (January 2008)
2. Baelde, D.: A linear approach to the proof-theory of least and greatest fixed points. PhD thesis, Ecole Polytechnique (December 2008)
3. Baelde, D.: On the expressivity of minimal generic quantification. In: Abel, A., Urban, C. (eds.) International Workshop on Logical Frameworks and Meta-Languages: Theory and Practice (LFMTP 2008). ENTCS, vol. 228, pp. 3–19 (2008)
4. Baelde, D., Gacek, A., Miller, D., Nadathur, G., Tiu, A.: The bedwyr system for model checking over syntactic expressions. In: Pfenning, F. (ed.) CADE 2007. LNCS (LNAI), vol. 4603, pp. 391–397. Springer, Heidelberg (2007)
5. Baelde, D., Miller, D.: Least and greatest fixed points in linear logic. In: Dershowitz, N., Voronkov, A. (eds.) LPAR 2007. LNCS (LNAI), vol. 4790, pp. 92–106. Springer, Heidelberg (2007)
6. Baelde, D., Miller, D., Snow, Z.: Focused inductive theorem proving. In: Giesl, J., Hähnle, R. (eds.) Automated Reasoning. LNCS, vol. 6173, pp. 278–292. Springer, Heidelberg (2010)
7. Baelde, D., Miller, D., Snow, Z., Viel, A.: Tac: A generic and adaptable interactive theorem prover (2009), `http://slimmer.gforge.inria.fr/tac/`
8. Bertot, Y., Castéran, P.: Interactive Theorem Proving and Program Development. Coq'Art: The Calculus of Inductive Constructions. Texts in Theoretical Computer Science. Springer, Heidelberg (2004)
9. Church, A.: A formulation of the simple theory of types. J. of Symbolic Logic 5, 56–68 (1940)
10. Coquand, T., Paulin, C.: Inductively defined types. In: Martin-Löf, P., Mints, G. (eds.) COLOG 1988. LNCS, vol. 417, pp. 50–66. Springer, Heidelberg (1990)

11. Felty, A., Momigliano, A.: Hybrid: A definitional two-level approach to reasoning with higher-order abstract syntax. To appear in the J. of Automated Reasoning
12. Gacek, A.: The Abella interactive theorem prover (system description). In: Armando, A., Baumgartner, P., Dowek, G. (eds.) IJCAR 2008. LNCS (LNAI), vol. 5195, pp. 154–161. Springer, Heidelberg (2008)
13. Gacek, A.: A Framework for Specifying, Prototyping, and Reasoning about Computational Systems. PhD thesis, University of Minnesota (2009)
14. Gacek, A., Miller, D., Nadathur, G.: Combining generic judgments with recursive definitions. In: Pfenning, F. (ed.) 23th Symp. on Logic in Computer Science, pp. 33–44. IEEE Computer Society Press, Los Alamitos (2008)
15. Gacek, A., Miller, D., Nadathur, G.: Reasoning in Abella about structural operational semantics specifications. In: Abel, A., Urban, C. (eds.) International Workshop on Logical Frameworks and Meta-Languages: Theory and Practice (LFMTP 2008). ENTCS, vol. 228, pp. 85–100 (2008)
16. Gacek, A., Miller, D., Nadathur, G.: A two-level logic approach to reasoning about computations (November 16, 2009) (submitted)
17. Girard, J.-Y.: A fixpoint theorem in linear logic. An email posting to the mailing list linear@cs.stanford.edu (February 1992)
18. Harper, R., Honsell, F., Plotkin, G.: A framework for defining logics. J. of the ACM 40(1), 143–184 (1993)
19. Huet, G.: A unification algorithm for typed λ-calculus. Theoretical Computer Science 1, 27–57 (1975)
20. Liang, C., Miller, D.: Focusing and polarization in linear, intuitionistic, and classical logics. Theoretical Computer Science 410(46), 4747–4768 (2009)
21. McDowell, R.: Reasoning in a Logic with Definitions and Induction. PhD thesis, University of Pennsylvania (December 1997)
22. McDowell, R., Miller, D.: Cut-elimination for a logic with definitions and induction. Theoretical Computer Science 232, 91–119 (2000)
23. McDowell, R., Miller, D.: Reasoning with higher-order abstract syntax in a logical framework. ACM Trans. on Computational Logic 3(1), 80–136 (2002)
24. Miller, D.: A logic programming language with lambda-abstraction, function variables, and simple unification. J. of Logic and Computation 1(4), 497–536 (1991)
25. Miller, D.: Abstract syntax for variable binders: An overview. In: Lloyd, J., et al. (eds.) CL 2000. LNCS (LNAI), vol. 1861, pp. 239–253. Springer, Heidelberg (2000)
26. Miller, D.: Bindings, mobility of bindings, and the ∇-quantifier. In: Marcinkowski, J., Tarlecki, A. (eds.) CSL 2004. LNCS, vol. 3210, p. 24. Springer, Heidelberg (2004)
27. Miller, D.: Formalizing operational semantic specifications in logic. Concurrency Column of the Bulletin of the EATCS (October 2008)
28. Miller, D., Nadathur, G., Pfenning, F., Scedrov, A.: Uniform proofs as a foundation for logic programming. Annals of Pure and Applied Logic 51, 125–157 (1991)
29. Miller, D., Tiu, A.: A proof theory for generic judgments: An extended abstract. In: Kolaitis, P. (ed.) 18th Symp. on Logic in Computer Science, pp. 118–127. IEEE, Los Alamitos (June 2003)
30. Miller, D., Tiu, A.: A proof theory for generic judgments. ACM Trans. on Computational Logic 6(4), 749–783 (2005)
31. Momigliano, A., Tiu, A.: Induction and co-induction in sequent calculus. In: Coppo, M., Berardi, S., Damiani, F. (eds.) TYPES 2003. LNCS, vol. 3085, pp. 293–308. Springer, Heidelberg (2004)

32. Nadathur, G., Miller, D.: An Overview of λProlog. In: Fifth International Logic Programming Conference, Seattle, pp. 810–827. MIT Press, Cambridge (August 1988)
33. Nadathur, G., Mitchell, D.J.: System description: Teyjus — A compiler and abstract machine based implementation of λProlog. In: Ganzinger, H. (ed.) CADE 1999. LNCS (LNAI), vol. 1632, pp. 287–291. Springer, Heidelberg (1999)
34. Nipkow, T., Paulson, L.C., Wenzel, M.: Isabelle/HOL: A Proof Assistant for Higher-Order Logic. LNCS, vol. 2283. Springer, Heidelberg (2002)
35. Pfenning, F., Elliott, C.: Higher-order abstract syntax. In: Proceedings of the ACM-SIGPLAN Conference on Programming Language Design and Implementation, pp. 199–208. ACM Press, New York (1988)
36. Pfenning, F., Schürmann, C.: System description: Twelf — A meta-logical framework for deductive systems. In: Ganzinger, H. (ed.) CADE 1999. LNCS (LNAI), vol. 1632, pp. 202–206. Springer, Heidelberg (1999)
37. Pientka, B.: A type-theoretic foundation for programming with higher-order abstract syntax and first-class substitutions. In: 35th Annual ACM Symposium on Principles of Programming Languages (POPL 2008), pp. 371–382. ACM, New York (2008)
38. Poswolsky, A., Schürmann, C.: System description: Delphin - A functional programming language for deductive systems. In: Abel, A., Urban, C. (eds.) International Workshop on Logical Frameworks and Meta-Languages: Theory and Practice (LFMTP 2008), vol. 228, pp. 113–120 (2008)
39. Schroeder-Heister, P.: Cut-elimination in logics with definitional reflection. In: Pearce, D., Wansing, H. (eds.) All-Berlin 1990. LNCS, vol. 619, Springer, Heidelberg (1992)
40. Schroeder-Heister, P.: Rules of definitional reflection. In: Vardi, M. (ed.) Eighth Annual Symposium on Logic in Computer Science, pp. 222–232. IEEE Computer Society Press, Los Alamitos (June 1993)
41. Schürmann, C.: Automating the Meta Theory of Deductive Systems. PhD thesis, Carnegie Mellon University (October 2000) CMU-CS-00-146
42. Tiu, A.: A Logical Framework for Reasoning about Logical Specifications. PhD thesis, Pennsylvania State University (May 2004)
43. Tiu, A.: Model checking for π-calculus using proof search. In: Abadi, M., de Alfaro, L. (eds.) CONCUR 2005. LNCS, vol. 3653, pp. 36–50. Springer, Heidelberg (2005)
44. Tiu, A., Miller, D.: Proof search specifications of bisimulation and modal logics for the π-calculus. ACM Trans. on Computational Logic 11(2) (2010)
45. Urban, C.: Nominal reasoning techniques in Isabelle/HOL. J. of Automated Reasoning 40(4), 327–356 (2008)

Typechecking Higher-Order Security Libraries

Karthik Bhargavan[1,3], Cédric Fournet[1,2], and Nataliya Guts[1]

[1] MSR-INRIA Joint Centre
[2] Microsoft Research
[3] INRIA

Abstract. We propose a flexible method for verifying the security of ML programs that use cryptography and recursive data structures. Our main applications are X.509 certificate chains, secure logs for multi-party games, and XML digital signatures. These applications are beyond the reach of automated cryptographic verifiers such as ProVerif, since they require some form of induction. They can be verified using refinement types (that is, types with embedded logical formulas, tracking security events). However, this entails replicating higher-order library functions and annotating each instance with its own logical pre- and post-conditions. Instead, we equip higher-order functions with precise, yet reusable types that can refer to the pre- and post-conditions of their functional arguments, using generic logical predicates. We implement our method by extending the F7 typechecker with automated support for these predicates. We evaluate our approach experimentally by verifying a series of security libraries and protocols.

1 Security Verification by Typing

We intend to verify the security of programs that implement protocols and applications (rather than their abstract models). Operating at the level of source code ensures that both design and implementation flaws will be caught, and also facilitates the adoption of verification tools by programmers. In this work, we rely on F7 [3, 6], an SMT-based typechecker developed for the modular verification of security protocols and their cryptographic operations written in ML.

Suppose that Bob hosts a web application and Alice is one of his clients. Alice sends a request to Bob, who must authenticate Alice's request before delivering a response. Bob programs in ML, so he can use the F7 typechecker to validate that his code enforces his security policy. Depending on the control- and data-flow of the protocol between Alice and Bob, typechecking essentially checks that the program obeys the logical pre- and post-conditions specified in the interfaces of the protocol and the cryptographic and communications libraries. The programmer provides a few protocol-specific type annotations (for instance when accepting a message or allocating a key). The rest of the verification is automated.

In practice, protocol implementations involve various data structures, and thus the need for type annotations extends to various library functions that manipulate this data. Although F7 supports polymorphism à la ML, it is difficult to give these library functions precise, yet polymorphic refinement types. In particular, recursive data processing involves higher-order functions, and the programmer must often provide a refinement type each time he uses these functions. Pragmatically, this involves replicating the code

K. Ueda (Ed.): APLAS 2010, LNCS 6461, pp. 47–62, 2010.

for these functions (and some of the functions they call); annotating each replica with its *ad hoc* type; and letting F7 typecheck the replica for each particular usage.

Suppose that the message format used by Alice and Bob is under development and changes often. Each change trickles down the protocol data flow, demanding many changes to logical annotations, and possibly further code replication. This hinders code modularity. Can we write less code and annotations, and focus on the security properties of our program? In this work we show how using automatic predicates for pre- and post-conditions allows us to write more flexible and reusable types.

Example. F7 is based on a typed call-by-value lambda calculus, called RCF, described in more detail in Section 2. Expressions are written in a subset of F#, a dialect of ML. Types are F# types refined with first-order formulas on ML values. For instance, the refinement type $v : int\ \{v > 5\}$ is the type of integers greater than 5. More precisely, this type can be given to any expression such that, whenever it returns, its value is greater than 5. RCF defines judgements for assigning types to expressions and for checking whether one type is a subtype of another. For instance, $v : int\ \{v > 5\}$ is a subtype of *int*. Functions can also be given precise refinement types. For instance, the dependent function type $v{:}int \rightarrow w{:}int\ \{w{>}v\}$, a subtype of $int \rightarrow int$, represents functions that, when called with an integer v, may return only an integer greater than v.

Consider the type $\alpha\ option$, which is part of the standard ML library. Its instance *int option* is the type of optional integers: its values range over *None* and *Some n*, where n is an integer. Using option types, we can, for example, program protocols that have optional fields in their messages. To manipulate a message field of type *int option*, it is convenient to use the higher-order library function *map*:

```
val map: (int → int) → int option → int option
let map f x = match x with
  | None → None
  | Some(v) → let w = f v in Some(w)
```

This function can be applied to any function whose type is a subtype of $int \rightarrow int$, of the form $x{:}int \rightarrow y{:}int\{C(x,y)\}$ for some formula C that can refer to both x and y. Suppose that we compute a value using *map* over a function *f* with type $v : int \rightarrow w : int\ \{w{>}v\}$:

```
let y = map f (Some(0))
```

We would like to give *y* a type that records the post-condition of f:

val $y{:}int\ option\{\exists w.\ y = Some(w) \wedge w > 0\}$

What type must *map* have in order for *y* to have this type? Within RCF, the most precise type we can give is

val $map{:}\ f{:}(int \rightarrow int) \rightarrow x{:}(int\ option) \rightarrow y{:}(int\ option)$
$\{\ (x = None \wedge y = None) \vee (\exists v,w.\ x = Some(v) \wedge y = Some(w))\}$

This type accounts for the various cases (*None* vs *Some*) of the argument, but not for the post-condition of f. In RCF, terms in formulas range over ML values, such as *Some*(*w*), but not expressions, such as *f x*, since their evaluation may cause and depend on side-effects. Thus, the only way to check that *y* has its desired type is to copy the definition of the *map* function just for *f* and to annotate and typecheck it again:

val map_copy: f:(v:int $\rightarrow$ w:int $\{w>v\}$) $\rightarrow$ x:(int $option$) $\rightarrow$ y:(int $option$)
$\{ (x = None \wedge y = None) \vee (\exists v,w.\ x = Some(v) \wedge y = Some(w) \wedge w > v)\}$

Our main idea is to let the F7 typechecker automatically inject and check annotations for pre- and post-conditions. This yields precise, generic types for higher-order functions, thereby preventing the need for manual code duplication and annotation. To this end, we introduce predicates *Pre* and *Post* within the types of higher-order functions to refer to the pre- and post-conditions of their functional arguments. For instance, the formula $Post(f,v,w)$ can refer to the post-condition of a function parameter f applied to v returning w, and we can give *map* the type:

val map: f:($int \rightarrow int$) $\rightarrow$ x:int $option$ $\rightarrow$ y:int $option$
$\{(x = None \wedge y = None) \vee (\exists v,w.\ x = Some(v) \wedge y = Some(w) \wedge Post(f,v,w))\}$

Whenever *map* is called (say within the definition of y above), the actual post-condition of f is statically known ($w>v$) and can be used instead of $Post(f,v,w)$. Hence, y can be given its desired type without loss of modularity.

More generally, we show how to use *Pre* and *Post* predicates to give precise reusable types to a library of recursive higher-order functions for list processing, and use the library to verify protocol implementations using lists. Verifying such implementations is beyond the reach of typical security verification tools, since their proof requires some form of induction. For example, FS2PV [4] compiles F# into the applied pi calculus, for analysis with ProVerif [8], a state-of-the-art domain-specific prover. Although FS2PV and ProVerif are able to prove complex XML-based cryptographic protocol code, they do so by bounding lists to a constant length and then inlining and re-verifying the list processing code at each call site.

Contributions. We present extensions of the RCF type system and the F7 typechecker to automatically support pre- and post-condition predicates. We study three different semantics for these predicates and we illustrate their use. We design precise and modular APIs for lists and for several cryptographic protocol implementations using lists, such as X.509 certificates, XML digital signatures, and auditable multi-party protocols.

Contents. Section 2 recalls the syntax, semantics and main results for F7. Section 3 explains our extension of F7 for pre- and post-conditions, presenting different design choices. Section 4 illustrates the use of pre- and post-conditions to verify a basic authentication protocol. Section 5 illustrates their use to give reusable types to a library for lists. Section 6 describes and evaluates larger verification case studies of cryptographic protocol implementations. Section 7 discusses related work.

This work is part of a long-term effort to develop a refinement type-based security verification framework for F# code. We extend the type system, implementation, and cryptographic libraries developed in earlier work [3, 6]. Additional details, including source code and the full version of this paper, are available online [7].

2 Refinement Types for ML (Review)

We review the syntax and semantics of our core calculus, RCF, and its implementation in the F7 typechecker; we refer to Bengtson et al. [3] for a detailed description.

RCF consists of the standard Fixpoint Calculus [18] augmented with local names and message-passing concurrency (as in the pi calculus) and with refinement types. (Our syntax slightly deviates from Bengtson et al.; the main difference is that we have recursive functions, as in F7, instead of a fold constructor; we also use explicit type annotations, and demand that all function values be annotated.)

The source programs described in this paper are written in an extended ML-like syntax treated as syntactic sugar for core RCF values and expressions. Values M include unit, pairs, constructed terms, and (possibly recursive) functions. Expressions e are in A-normal form: they include values, function application, pattern matching, let-bindings for sequential composition, fork for parallel composition, and message passing over channels. The concurrency and message passing constructs do not appear in source programs; they are used to symbolically model run-time processes (e.g. principals running a cryptographic protocol and their adversary) and network-based communications.

For specification purposes, RCF includes constructs for assuming and asserting first-order logic formulas. Formally, as an RCF expression executes, it maintains an abstract log of formulas that have been assumed so far. The expression **assume** C adds a formula C to the log, and the expression **assert** C *succeeds* if C can be logically derived from the log. We use assumes and asserts to specify correctness and security properties—concretely, these two primitives and all formulas are erased after verification. We say that an expression is *safe* when all of its **assert**s succeed in every run.

To statically verify the safety of RCF expressions, we equip it with a refinement type system. Type environments E keep track of the log of assumed formulas, and type-checking ensures that every asserted formula logically holds in the current environment. Pretypes P are ML-like types extended with dependent functions, written $x\!:\!T_1 \rightarrow T_2$, and dependent pairs. A refinement type T, of the form $x\!:\!P\{C\}$, is the type of expressions that return values M of pretype P such that the formula $C[M/x]$ can be derived from the log of assumed formulas. Hence, a function type can be fully written out as $x : (x : P\{C\}) \rightarrow y : P'\{C'\}$, where its argument has pretype P and must satisfy the precondition C, and its return value has pretype P' and is guaranteed to satisfy the postcondition C'. We usually omit the second binder x for brevity, and write function types as $x\!:\!P\{C\} \rightarrow y\!:\!P'\{C'\}$.

The type system has the following judgments.

$E \vdash \diamond$	environment E is well-formed
$E \vdash C$	formula C holds in environment E
$E \vdash T <: T'$	T is a subtype of T' in environment E
$E \vdash e : T$	expression e has type T in environment E

An environment is well-formed if all the variables in it are well-scoped. A formula holds in an environment if it can be deduced from the formulas in the environment. A refinement type $x\!:\!P\{C\}$ is a subtype of $x\!:\!P'\{C'\}$ in environment E when P is a subtype of P' in E and $E \vdash C \Rightarrow C'$. The rest of the subtyping rules are straightforward.

To illustrate expression typing, we recall four typing rules, those for **assume**s and **assert**s, and those for functions and applications:

$$\frac{E \vdash \diamond \quad fv(C) \subseteq dom(E)}{E \vdash \textbf{assume}\ C :\ \ \_\!:\!unit\{C\}} \qquad \frac{E \vdash C}{E \vdash \textbf{assert}\ C :\ \ \_\!:\!unit\{C\}}$$

$$\frac{T = x{:}T_1 \to T_2 \quad E, f : T, x : T_1 \vdash e : T_2}{E \vdash \mathbf{rec}\ f : T.(\mathbf{fun}\ x \to e)\ :\ T} \qquad \frac{E \vdash M : x{:}T_1 \to T_2 \quad E \vdash N : T_1}{E \vdash (M\,N) :\ T_2\{N/x\}}$$

An expression **assume** C returns a value with postcondition C, while **assert** C requires C to hold in the environment. A recursive function annotated with T of the form $x{:}T_1 \to T_2$ can be given type T if its body has type T_2 in an environment extended for f and x. An application $M\ N$ has type $T_2\{N/x\}$ if M has the function type type $x : T_1 \to T_2$ and N has a type which is a subtype of T_1.

Type safety. We rely on the main result of Bengtson et al. [3]: if a program is well-typed, then it is safe. Moreover, if a program is well-typed in an empty environment, then it is *robustly safe*, that is, it is safe when composed with any expression that has no **asserts**. Robust safety is useful for protocol security: it states that the properties of the program hold even when composed with an arbitrary active adversary that is given access to the public interface of the program.

F7 implementation. Our prototype typechecker, F7, is an implementation of the RCF type system that supports a significant subset of F#. In particular, it supports programs that contain type- and value- parametered types, records, polymorphism, mutual recursion, match expressions and mutable references, but it does not, for example, support classes or objects. The typechecker takes two kinds of input files

- F# implementation files (e.g. file.fs) that mention only F# types; and
- F7 interfaces (e.g. file.fs7) with logical assumptions and RCF type annotations.

The typechecker then verifies whether an implementation is well-typed against its interface. To verify the validity of logical formulas (judgment $E \vdash C$), the typechecker can call out to any first-order logic theorem prover. We currently use a leading SMT solver, Z3 to discharge our proof obligations. First-order logic validity is undecidable, so Z3 may fail to prove or disprove some formulas. In these cases, we require additional assumptions (with semi-automated proofs) to verify the program.

3 Refinements for Pre- and Post-Conditions

Classically, for a given function application, a pair of formulas (C_1, C_2) is a valid pair of pre- and post-conditions when, if C_1 holds just before calling the function, then C_2 holds just after the function completes. Hoare [16] originally proposed them for arbitrary programs. More recently, for example, Spec# [2] and Code Contracts [12] let function definitions be annotated with contracts (formulas) expressing intended pre- and post-conditions, which may be checked statically or dynamically. F7 naturally supports pre- and post-conditions for functions as refinements of their argument and return types. For instance, if an F7 function has type $x_1 : P_1\{C_1\} \to x_2 : P_2\{C_2\}$, then asserting C_1 before the function call and C_2 after the function returns is always safe.

In this section we show how to explicitly refer to pre- and post-conditions of functions using generic predicates indexed by function value. There are at least three ways to define the semantics of these predicates. When considering a program with verification annotations, the pre- and post-condition of a function can refer either to the formulas declared with that function, or to the formulas available at the call site, or to events tracking run-time calls and returns. For each semantics, we introduce a pair of generic predicates, informally explain their use, and then give (1) a formal code transformation; and (2) a patch to the F7 typing rules to implement and validate this semantics.

Event-based semantics. Pre- and post-conditions can be seen as events marking the beginning and the end of a function execution. We systematically record them by assuming facts for two predicates *Call* and *Return*: the fact *Call*(M,N) means that M is a function that has been applied to the argument N; *Return*(M,N,O) means that M is a function that has been applied to N and has returned the value O. Formally, this yields a concrete, extensional, finite model, for each partial run of a whole program.

We can use *Call* and *Return* to reason about run-time events, instead of introducing *ad hoc* predicates for that purpose. For instance, if a function *send* parameterized by m assumes a "begin event" *Send*(m) before signing a message with payload m, we can remove this assume and use instead the generic event *Call*$(send,m)$ in security specifications. Similarly, suppose that keys are represented as bitstrings, but that the keys in use should be generated only by a designated algorithm *genKey*. We can assign to keys the refinement type k : *bytes* { *Return*$(genKey,(),k)$ }. This pattern frequently applies to cryptographic materials such as nonces, initialization vectors, and tags.

To preserve consistency of the assumed formulas, we rely on a standard notion of positive and negative positions in types and formulas. In the program before the transformation, we forbid positive occurrences of *Call* and *Return* in assumed formulas.

Code transformation. We specify the event-based semantics by translating every syntactic function and every function application

$$[\![\, \textbf{rec}\, f\!: T.\ \textbf{fun}\ x \to e]\!]_E \triangleq \textbf{rec}\, f\!: T.\ \textbf{fun}\ x \to \textbf{assume}\ Call(f,x); [\![e]\!]_E$$
$$[\![\, M\ N]\!]_E \triangleq \textbf{let}\ r = [\![M]\!]_E\ [\![N]\!]_E \textbf{in assume}\ Return(M,N,r);\ r$$

(where r is fresh in M,T, and N) and letting $[\![]\!]_E$ be a homomorphism for all other expressions. Thus, we bracket each call with events before and after the call.

Modifying the typechecker. We achieve the same effect as the transformation by directly injecting formulas when typechecking functions and applications. We modify two typing rules, given below, and let RCF$_E$ be the resulting type system.

$$\frac{T = x{:}T_1 \to T_2 \qquad E, f : T, x : T_1, Call(f,x) \vdash e : T_2}{E \vdash (\textbf{rec}\ f : T.\textbf{fun}\ x \to e) : T} \qquad \frac{E \vdash M : x{:}T_1 \to r{:}P\{C\} \quad E \vdash N : T_1 \quad T_2 = r{:}P\{C \wedge Return(M,x,r)\}}{E \vdash (M\ N) : T_2\{N/x\}}$$

Results. We check that our transformation does not affect the operational behaviour, safety, and well-typedness of programs that do not use *Call* and *Return*, and that the code transformation and the modified typing rules yield the same typing judgements. Let e be a closed program. Let $e \Downarrow M$ denote evaluation of the expression e ($e \longrightarrow^* \nu\tilde{a}.e' \upharpoonright M$ where e' consists of assumptions and auxiliary threads).

Lemma 1. *Suppose that Call and Return do not occur in e.*

- Evaluation: *for any value M, $e \Downarrow M$ if and only if $[\![e]\!]_E \Downarrow [\![M]\!]_E$;*
- Safety: *e is safe if and only if $[\![e]\!]_E$ is safe; and*
- Typing: *e is well-typed in RCF if and only if $[\![e]\!]_E$ is well-typed in RCF.*

Lemma 2. *$[\![e]\!]_E$ is well-typed in RCF if and only if e is well-typed in RCF$_E$.*

Macro-expansion semantics. Pre- and post-conditions may also be seen as pure syntactic sugar, abbreviations that refer to concrete formulas in the types of functions in scope (similar to the *pre* and *post* projections of Régis-Gianas and Pottier [19]). It is useful to refer to the pre- or post-condition of a known and fully annotated function to avoid copying a formula which is big or likely to change during the verification process.

To denote such macro-definitions, we introduce generic predicates *#Pre* and *#Post*. They may occur anywhere in the program or its interface, provided that their first argument is a variable name that has a declared function type in their scope. *Before typechecking,* we replace each of their occurrences with a concrete formula read off the environment without breaking well-formedness.

Implementation. If $E(f) = x_1 : P_1\{C_1\} \rightarrow x_2 : P_2\{C_2\}$, then we replace $\#Pre(f, M)$ with $C_1[M/x_1]$, and $\#Post(f, M, N)$ with $C_2[M/x_1, N/x_2]$. If the lookup fails, or the returned type is not a function type, preprocessing fails—the macro-definition is ill-formed.

Subtyping-based semantics. As opposed to the type annotations of function definitions, the declared types of function arguments in higher-order functions are in general only supertypes of the argument types actually used at their call sites, themselves supertypes of the functional types verified at the function definitions. Thus, as we type the higher-order function, the actual refinements for its argument are unknown, and we cannot just rely on macro-expansion. We refer to these refinements using predicates *Pre* and *Post*.

- We use them parametrically when typing higher-order functions, as if each function argument f had a type of the form $x_1 : P_1\{Pre(f, x_1)\} \rightarrow x_2 : P_2\{Post(f, x_1, x_2)\}$.
- We define their logical model as follows: for each closed function value, of the form

$$M = \textbf{rec}\ f : x_1 : P_1^\circ\{C_1^\circ\} \rightarrow x_2 : P_2^\circ\{C_2^\circ\}.\textbf{fun}\ x_1 \rightarrow e$$

  - $Pre(M,M_1)$ if and only if $C_1^\circ[M_1/x_1]$ and
  - $Post(M,M_1,M_2)$ if and only if $C_1^\circ[M_1/x_1] \Rightarrow C_2^\circ[M_1/x_1, M_2/x_2]$.
- When applying a function parameter f of type $T = x_1{:}P_1\{C_1\} \rightarrow x_2{:}P_2\{C_2\}$ at the call site, for any runtime instance M of f of the form above, we have $\forall x_1.\ C_1 \Rightarrow C_1^\circ$ and $\forall x_1,x_2.\ C_1 \wedge C_2^\circ \Rightarrow C_2$ by type safety and subtyping. Accordingly, for relating C_1 and C_2 to the (unknown) parametric pre- and post-conditions of f during typechecking, we automatically assume the formula

$$\phi_{f:T} = \forall x_1.\ C_1 \Rightarrow Pre(f,x_1) \wedge \forall x_1,x_2.\ (C_1 \wedge Post(f,x_1,x_2)) \Rightarrow C_2$$

Relation to the event-based semantics. Within the body of a higher-order function with function argument f, whenever f is applied to a value N, the event $Call(f, N)$ records this application, and typing requires that the predicate $Pre(f, N)$ holds. At runtime, for each instance M of f, the actual pre-condition of M holds (by typing) and implies the formal precondition of f (by assumption) so we have $\forall f,x.\ Call(f,x) \Rightarrow Pre(f,x)$.

Similarly, when f returns, we have $Return(f, N, O)$, and its formal post-condition $Post(f, N, O)$ implies the actual post-condition for any instance M of f (by assumption) so we have $\forall f,x,y.\ Return(f,x,y) \Rightarrow Post(f,x,y)$. We thus assume both of these formulas for typechecking.

Code transformation. To support *Pre* and *Post*, we rely on events, so we first apply the event-based code transformation, then we transform every binding whose expression has a function type annotation and apply $[\![]\!]_S$ homomorphically to other expressions. In particular, we transform every function let binding (since they are always annotated) and every syntactic function definition, ensuring that all functional arguments are annotated in higher-order functions. Let T abbreviate $x_1{:}P_1\{C_1\} \to x_2{:}P_2\{C_2\}$.

$$[\![\, \textbf{let}\, f = e : (f : T)\, \{C_f\})\ \textbf{in}\ e' \,]\!]_S \triangleq \textbf{let}\, f = [\![e]\!]_S\ \textbf{in assume}\ \phi_{f:T};\ [\![e']\!]_S$$
$$[\![\, \textbf{rec}\, f{:}\ T.\ \textbf{fun}\ x \to\ e \,]\!]_S \triangleq \textbf{rec}\, f{:}\ T.\ \textbf{fun}\ x \to [\![\textbf{let}\ x = (x : T_1)\ \textbf{in}\ e]\!]_S$$

Modifying the typechecker. We modify F7 to support *Pre* and *Post* by modifying insertions of variables entries with function types into the typing environment. Hence, E extended with $f : T$ is now written $E \oplus f : T$, and defined by pattern matching on T. If T is a function type, it is of the form $f{:}(x_1{:}P_1\{C_1\} \to x_2{:}P_2\{C_2\})\{C_f\}$ and we let

$$E \oplus f : T \triangleq E, f : T, \phi_{f:x_1:P_1\{C_1\} \to x_2:P_2\{C_2\}}$$

Otherwise $E \oplus f : T$ is just $E, f : T$. We call the modified type system RCF_S. To maintain logical consistency, we forbid positive occurrences of *Pre* and *Post* in assumed formulas.

Results. We obtain a variant of Lemma 1 for the subtyping semantics: we have a similar Evaluation property. The proof of Safety involves showing the logical consistency of the injected assumptions. We also prove two flavours of Correctness: we have a variant of Lemma 2 that relates typing with RCF_S and the specification $[\![]\!]_S$. Besides, we show a simple pattern such that *Pre* and *Post* can be eliminated by replicating the code of a higher-order functions at each call site and annotating each replica with an *ad hoc* type.

Lemma 3 (Inlining). *Let* e_0 = ***let*** *h = H* ***in*** *e be a well-typed expression in* RCF_S *such that* H *is a function with type* $T = g{:}(x{:}T_1 \to T_2) \to T_3$, h *only occurs in applicative position and Pre and Post occur only in* T_3 *and always have* g *as first argument.*

Let e_1 *be* e_0 *after replacing each subexpression of the form* $(h\ f) : T'$ *in* e *with* $(H_f\ f){:}T'$, *where* H_f *is* H *after replacing each Pre(g,M) and Post(g,M,N) with #Pre(f,M) and #Post(f,M,N), respectively. Then* e_1 *is also well-typed in* RCF_S.

Functions with multiple arguments. Our definitions above assume curried functions. For convenience, we have also implemented typechecking support for functions with multiple arguments, recorded as a list in our predicates. For example, the function call *M a b* assumes the event *Call(M,[a;b])*.

4 Example: A MAC-Based Authentication Protocol

We first recast a simple client-server authentication protocol, to recall protocol verification using F7, and to illustrate our event-based semantics.

$$a \longrightarrow b : m \mid (\texttt{mac}\ k_{ab}\ m)$$

(The symbol | represents an invertible concatenation of bytestrings.) When a principal a wants to send a message m to principal b, it also sends a MAC over m computed with a key k_{ab} known only to a and b. This MAC protects message integrity and authenticates both sender and intended receiver.

This simple protocol can be implemented in ML as follows, for example:

```
let mkKey a b = hmac_keygen()
let client a b k m =
    let c = Net.connect p in
    let h = hmac k m in
    let w = concat m h in
    Net.send c w

let server a b k =
    let c = Net.listen p in
    let w = Net.recv c in
    let (m,h) = iconcat w in
     hmac_verify k m h;
     m
```

The function *mkKey* generates a fresh MAC key for use with messages sent from *a* to *b*. (Messages in the reverse direction rely on a separate key.) The function *client* uses a key *k* to protect a message *m* that *a* wishes to send to *b* over the public network. The function *server* receives a message over this network and uses a key to verify its MAC.

This protocol code runs in a hostile environment where an attacker may use the public interfaces of the protocol and the libraries to interfere with the protocol. The attacker may call the networking functions *send*, *recv* on any TCP connection to intercept and interject messages of his choice. He may construct and verify MACs by calling *hmac* and *hmac_verify* with keys that he already knows. He may also start any number of copies of the client and server and get them to communicate with each other.

The authentication goal for the protocol is that, if the *server* function returns *m* when called with *a*, *b*, and a key *k* generated by the *mkKey* function, then the client function was called with *a*, *b*, and *m*. In particular, an adversary who does not know a key generated for *a* and *b* cannot fool *b* into accepting a message that was not sent by *a*.

We express this security goal within the refinement types for these functions:

```
val mkKey: a:str → b:str → k:key
val client:
    a:str → b:str →
    k:key{Return(mkKey,[a;b],k)} →
    m:bytespub → unit

val server:
    a:str → b:str →
    k:key{Return(mkKey,[a;b],k)} →
    m:bytespub{Call(client,[a;b;k;m])}
```

To verify that the code actually meets these types, we rely on the unforgeability of MACs, expressed as types for the cryptographic library [6]. In particular, the function *hmac* has a precondition *MACSays(k,m)*, representing the conditions under which the key *k* may be used to MAC *m*. Every protocol that uses MACs must specify *MACSays* for the keys that it uses. The function *hmac_verify* has a post-condition that it returns a value *m* only if either *MACSays(k,m)* or if the key *k* is *public*, that is, known to the attacker.

For the keys in our authentication protocol, we use *MACSays* to specify that a key k generated for a and b using *mkKey* will only be used to MAC a message m after *client* has been called with a, b, k, and m:

assume $\forall a,b,k.\ Return(mkKey,[a;b],k) \Rightarrow (MACSays(k,m) \Leftrightarrow Call(client,[a;b;k;m]))$

We then verify that this assumption is adequate to typecheck our protocol code against the cryptographic and networking library, and thus, by the type safety theorem of RCF, that it is secure against any attacker in our model.

Comparison with other methods. Many symbolic verification tools can handle the simple protocol above. Tools such as ProVerif [8] can even automatically infer the logical assumption on *MACSays*, thus requiring almost no annotations. In comparison to earlier work on F7, our type specification above uses the events *Call* and *Return*. In their absence, the programmer would have to define his own predicates corresponding to these events and enforce their relationship to the function calls by assuming them within protocol code. Here, these events are declared and managed automatically.

5 Example: A Reusable Typed Interface for Lists

Lists are perhaps the most commonly-used data structures in functional programs. The F# *List* library provides efficient implementations of recursive list processing functions; for generality, these functions are typically higher-order and polymorphic. Our goal is to give this library a reusable refinement typed interface, using our *Pre* and *Post* predicates and their subtyping-based semantics. The full interface is available online [7].

We detail our approach on the function *List.fold*, the general iterator on lists (also called *fold_left*). Its ML type is $(\alpha \rightarrow \beta \rightarrow \alpha) \rightarrow \alpha \rightarrow \beta\ list \rightarrow \alpha$. It takes as argument a function *f*, an initial *accumulator a*, a list *l* and traverses the list *l*, applying *f* to the current accumulator and the next value in the list to obtain the next accumulator; when it reaches the end of the list, it returns the accumulator. For example, *fold* (+) 0 [1;2;3;4] computes the sum of the elements in the list.

First attempt: Using Recursive Predicates. Let us define two predicates *PreFold* and *PostFold* to represent the pre- and post-condition of *fold*. By inspecting the code for *fold* (on the left below) we can define these predicates as shown:

```
let rec                    assume ∀f,acc,l.              assume ∀f,acc,l,r.
  fold f acc l =           PreFold(f,acc,l)              PostFold(f,acc,l,r)
  match l with             ⇔                             ⇔
   | [] → acc               (l=[]                          ((l=[] ∧ r=acc)
                            ∨                              ∨
   | hd :: tl →             (∃hd,tl. l=hd::tl ∧            (∃hd,tl. l=hd::tl ∧
     let acc' = f acc hd in  Pre(f,[acc;hd]) ∧
                             (∀acc'. Post(f,[acc;hd],acc')  (∃acc'. Post(f,[acc;hd],acc')
     fold f acc' tl                ⇒ PreFold(f,acc',tl))))  ∧ PostFold(f,acc',tl,r))))
```

The definition for *PreFold* can be read as follows. If the list is empty, there is no pre-condition. Otherwise, the pre-condition of the argument *f* must hold for the head of the list and the current accumulator, and if *f* terminates and returns a new accumulator, *PreFold* must hold for the tail of the list and this new accumulator. *PostFold* is defined similarly. The resulting type for *fold*

val *fold*: $f{:}(\alpha \rightarrow \beta \rightarrow \alpha) \rightarrow acc{:}\alpha \rightarrow l{:}\beta\ list\{PreFold(f,acc,l)\} \rightarrow r{:}\alpha\ \{PostFold(f,acc,l,r)\}$

is precise and easy to typecheck against the code of *fold*, yet difficult to use at call sites. Indeed, even for a function with no pre-condition ($\forall x.\ Pre(f,x)$), proving *PreFold(f,acc,l)* requires the use of induction, which is generally beyond the reach of the SMT solver Z3 that underlies F7. Can we use a non-recursive predicate to specify *fold*?

Second attempt: Using Invariants. In our second approach, we adopt the style of Régis-Gianas and Pottier [19] for specifying higher-order iterators, such as *fold*. We introduce a generic predicate *Inv* that is used to define logical *invariants* for functions that may be used as an argument to *fold*. The formula *Inv(f,aux,acc,l)* is an invariant that holds when the function f is being applied to a list of elements: l is the remainder of the list, acc is the intermediate result of the computation, and aux contains function-specific auxiliary information about the initial arguments to the *fold*.

As an example, consider the function *fmem* that can be used with *fold* to search for an element in a list; its code, refinement type, and invariant are as follows:

let *fmem v*	**val** *fmem*: $v{:}\alpha \rightarrow$	$(\forall v,f.\ Post(fmem,v,f) \Rightarrow$
acc	$acc{:}bool \rightarrow$	$(\forall iv,acc,l.\ Inv(f,iv,acc,l) \Leftrightarrow$
n	$n{:}\alpha\ a \rightarrow$	$(\exists x,linit.\ iv{=}(x,linit) \wedge x = v$
=	$found{:}bool\{$	$\wedge (\forall y.\ Mem(y,l) \Rightarrow Mem(y,linit))$
if $v = n$	$(v = n$	$\wedge ((\ Mem(x,linit)$
then true	$\wedge found = \mathbf{true})$	$\wedge\ acc{=}\mathbf{true})$
else *acc*	$\vee (found = acc)\}$	$\vee\ acc = \mathbf{false}\ ))))$

The function *fmem* takes an element v to search for, an accumulator *acc* and an integer n, and returns true if either $v = n$ or *acc* is true. The invariant for the function obtained by the partial application *fmem v* is defined on the right; its auxiliary argument *aux* is a pair consisting of the searched element v and the initial list *linit*. Its auxiliary argument is a pair consisting of the integer v to search for, and the initial list *linit*. The invariant says that the remaining list l contains a subset of the elements in *linit*, and that the accumulator is true only if v is a member of *linit*.

The next step, following Régis-Gianas and Pottier, is to prove that the invariant is *hereditary*, namely that the invariant of each function f is at least as strong as its pre-condition, and that the invariant is preserved by function application. We define a predicate *Hereditary* that captures this notion and use it to give a type to *fold* as shown below; note that to use this style we need to add an additional argument *aux* to *fold*.

let rec *fold v f acc l* =	**assume** $(\forall f.\ Hereditary(f)$
match *l* **with**	$\Leftrightarrow$
$\mid [] \rightarrow acc$	
$\mid hd :: tl \rightarrow$	$(\ \forall v,acc,h,t.\ Inv(f,v,acc,hd{::}tl) \Rightarrow$
let *acc' = f acc hd* **in**	$(Pre(f,[acc;hd])$
fold v f acc' tl	$\wedge (\forall r.\ Post(f,[acc;hd],r) \Rightarrow Inv(f,v,r,tl)))))$

$$\mathbf{val}\ fold{:}\ v{:}\ \gamma \rightarrow f{:}(\alpha \rightarrow \beta \rightarrow \alpha)\ \{Hereditary(f)\} \rightarrow acc{:}\alpha \rightarrow xs{:}\beta\ list\ \{Inv(f,v,acc,xs)\}$$
$$\rightarrow r{:}\alpha\ \{\ (xs = [] \wedge r{=}acc) \vee Inv(f,v,r,[])\ \}$$

The type of *List.fold* requires that (1) the invariant of the iterated function is hereditary; and that (2) the invariant holds for the initial accumulator. The post-condition states that the invariant holds for the final accumulator.

For example, to check that the application *fold* (v,l) *(fmem v)* **false** l can be given the type $b{:}bool\ \{b = \mathbf{true} \Rightarrow Mem(v,l)\}$ we must prove that $\forall v,f.\ Post(fmem,v,f) \Rightarrow Hereditary(f)$, and that the invariant of *fmem v* holds for the initial values (**false**,l). For a simple function like *fmem* this can be proved automatically, but for more complex functions *Hereditary* may have to be proved by hand. The rest of the typechecking is fully automatic.

6 Case Studies: Cryptographic Protocol Implementations

We can use our new types for lists to verify more realistic cryptographic applications. We present three case studies of programs previously verified using F7 and how our extensions help reduce the number of annotations required for typechecking.

XML digital signatures. The XML digital signature standard specifies cryptographic mechanisms to provide integrity, message authentication, and signer authentication for arbitrary XML data [11]. These mechanisms are used within web services security protocols to protect messages, and processing each message involves tree and list processing. For example, consider a single-message protocol, where the principal a uses an XML signature to protect $n \geq 1$ XML elements $m_1, \ldots, m_n$ located at URIs #1, ..., #n within the message, using the MAC key k_{ab}. The main security goal for this protocol is that the list $[m_1; \cdots; m_n]$ be authenticated; the protocol is often used as a component within a larger protocol that enforces more abstract security properties. The protocol with a slightly simplified message format can be written as follows:

$a \longrightarrow b$: ⟨Message⟩
    $m_1\ m_2\ \ldots\ m_n$
    ⟨Signature⟩
     ⟨SignatureInfo⟩
      ⟨Reference⟩base64 (sha1 m_1)) ⟨/Reference⟩
      ...
      ⟨Reference⟩base64 (sha1 m_n)) ⟨/Reference⟩
     ⟨/SignatureInfo⟩
     ⟨SignatureValue⟩
      base64 (mac k_{ab} (⟨SignatureInfo⟩ ··· (*as above*) ··· ⟨/SignatureInfo⟩))
     ⟨/SignatureValue⟩
    ⟨/Signature⟩
   ⟨/Message⟩

In previous work, Bhargavan et al. [6] used F7 to program and verify a library for manipulating such XML signatures. Now we can use *List.map* to improve this library and ease its verification. Consider the following excerpt of the library interface and implementation.

val *mkRef*: *m*:*item* → *r*:*item*{*Ref*(*m*,*r*)}

val *xml_sign*: *a*:*str* → *b*:*str* →
 k:*key*{*Return*(*mkXmlKey*,[*a*;*b*],*k*)} →
 ml:*item list* → *dsig*:*item*

val *xml_verify*: *a*:*str* → *b*:*str* →
 k:*key*{*Return*(*mkXmlKey*,[*a*;*b*],*k*)} →
 ml:*item list* → *dsig*:*item* →
 unit{*Call*(*xml_sign*,[*a*;*b*;*k*;*ml*])}

let *xml_sign a b k ml* =
  let *rl* = *map mkRef ml* **in**
  let *si* = *Xn*(*signatureInfo*,[],*rl*) **in**
  let *h* = *hmac k* (*ditem2bytes si*) **in**
  Xn(*signature*,[],[*si*;*Xn*(*sigValue*,[],[*txt h*])])

assume ∀*a*,*b*,*k*. *Return*(*mkKey*,[*a*;*b*],*k*) ⇒
 (∀*si*. *MACSays*(*k*,*si*) ⇔
  (∃*ml*. *Call*(*xml_sign*,[*a*;*b*;*k*;*ml*]) ∧
   SigInfo(*si*,*ml*)))

The type *item* represents XML elements; its constructor *Xn*(*q*,*al*,*il*) corresponds to an XML element of the form `<q al>`*il*`</q>`, where q is a qualified name, such as `Signature`, *al* is a list of XML attributes, and *il* is a list of XML items.

The function *mkRef* generates a *sha1* cryptographic hash of its argument and returns it within a `<Reference>` element. The function *xml_sign* generates an XML signature over a list of XML elements; it uses *map* over *mkRef* to generate a list of references, encapsulates them within a `<SignatureInfo>` element, and MACs it with the given key *k*. The function *xml_verify* parses and verifies XML signature. Its post-condition guarantees that the signature must have been generated using *xml_sign* by a valid client (as part of an authenticated message).

The use of *List.map* avoids the need to inline the recursive code for *map* in the code for *xml_sign* and *xml_verify*. In our previous verification of the full library, there were four instances where we needed to inline list-processing functions and define new type annotations for each instance. These are no longer necessary, reducing the annotation burden significantly.

X.509 certification paths. The X.509 recommendation [17] defines a standard format and processing procedure for public-key certificates. Each certificate contains at least a principal name, a public-key belonging to that principal, an issuer, and a signature of the certificate using the private key of the issuer.

On receiving a certificate, the recipient first checks that the issuer is a trusted certification authority and then verifies the signature on the certificate before accepting that the given principal has the given public key. To account for situations where the certification authority may not be known to the recipient, the certificate may itself contain a *certification path*: an ordered sequence of public-key certificates that begins with a certificate issued by a trusted certification authority and ends with a certificate for the desired principal. The X.509 sub-protocol for verifying certification paths can be written as follows:

$$\begin{aligned} a \longrightarrow b : & \ \texttt{Certificate}(a_1 \mid pk_{a_1} \mid \textbf{rsa\_sign}\ sk_{CA}\ (a_1 \mid pk_{a_1})) \\ & \ \texttt{Certificate}(a_2 \mid pk_{a_2} \mid \textbf{rsa\_sign}\ sk_{a_1}\ (a_2 \mid pk_{a_2})) \\ & \ \ldots \\ & \ \texttt{Certificate}(a \mid pk_a \mid \textbf{rsa\_sign}\ sk_{a_{n-1}}\ (a \mid pk_a)) \end{aligned}$$

We write and verify a new library for manipulating X.509 certificates. The code for certificate verification uses *List.fold* to iterate through a certification path:

```
val verify:
    x:cert{Certificate(x)} → b:bytes →
    r:cert {Certifies(x,r) ∧ Certificate(r)}
val verify_all:
  x:cert{Certificate(x)} → l: bytes list →
  r:cert {Certifies(x,r)}
```

```
let verify_all ca path =
  fold ca verify ca path

assume ∀ca,x,h,l.
  Inv(verify,ca,x,l) ⇔
    (Certificate(x) ∧ Certifies(ca,x))
```

The predicate *Certifies(x,y)* specifies that there is some sequence of certificates starting with *x* and ending with *y*, $x{=}x_0, x_1, \ldots, x_n{=}y$, such that the principal mentioned in each x_i has issued the certificate x_{i+1}; hence if every principal mentioned in this sequence is honest, then we can trust that the public-key in the final certificate *y* indeed belongs to the principal mentioned in *y*. The function *verify_all* takes as argument a certificate *ca* for a trusted certification authority and it accepts only those certification paths that begin with certificates issued with *ca*'s public-key. To typecheck *verify_all* we define the *fold* invariant for *verify* as the property that the accumulator *x* always has a valid certificate (*Certificate*(*x*)) and a valid certification path from *ca* to *x* (*Certifies*(*ca*,*x*)).

The use of *List.fold* in *verify_all* is the natural way of writing this code in ML. We could copy the code for *List.fold* and redo the work of annotating and typechecking it for this protocol, but reusing the types and formulas in *List* is more modular, and we believe, the right way of developing proofs for such cryptographic applications.

Compact types for audit. F7 has also been used to verify security properties beyond authentication. Guts et al. [15] show how to use refinement types to specify and verify auditability in protocol implementations. Informally, a program collecting cryptographic evidence has an auditable property if this property can be checked by the program (immediately) and by a third-party judge (*a posteriori*) using the evidence.

For example, consider the authentication protocol in Section 4. We may require that the server be able to convince a judge that a valid client sent him a given message. The server may consider presenting the message and its MAC as evidence for this property. However, such evidence does not suffice to convince the judge: since the MAC is based on a shared key known to both parties, the judge cannot decide whether the client or the server created the MAC. Hence, this property is not auditable in this program.

To achieve auditability, the parties can use public-key signatures instead of MACs: a client signs the message using its private key so that the server—or any third party who has access to the public key—can check the signature to authenticate the message.

To verify that the new program is indeed auditable, we first define a judge function that checks the evidence for an instance of the audited property. All verification functions used by the judge must be total, terminating and deterministic, and may use additional, trusted data (such as public keys) only as agreed on beforehand by all protocol participants. Then, the audited program is annotated with *audit* requests where the property is expected to be auditable: that is, if the judge was called at this program point with the same arguments as evidence, it would concur.

In the example of Section 4, suppose we add an audit request for client authentication in the code of the server function, using the verified signature as evidence. The judge function for this property would be:

```
let judge a b k m s = rsa_verify k m s
```

The judge simply calls the signature verification function *rsa_verify*, which never throws exceptions and returns **true** if and only if the message has been signed using the public key. (The full interface for public-key signature functions is available online [7].) Hence, the type of the judge is:

```
val judge: a:str → b:str →
  k:key{∃sk. Return(mkKey,[a;b],(k,sk))} → m:bytes → s:bytes →
  t:bool { t=true ⇔ (∃sk. Return(mkKey,[a;b],(k,sk)) ∧ IsSignature(s,sk,m))}
```

To formally check the auditability of this protocol, first we need to show that the judge is *correct*: whenever it returns **true**, the audited property holds:

$\forall a,b,k,k,m,s.\ \#Post(judge,[a;b;k;m;s]) \Rightarrow (\exists sk.\ PubPrivKeyPair(k,sk) \wedge Call(client,[a;b;k;m]))$

Then, to check that at every audit request the judge would have returned **true**, we set the precondition of the *audit* primitive to *#Post* of the judge:

val *audit*: *a*:*str* $\rightarrow$ *b*:*str* $\rightarrow$ *k*:*key*$\{\exists$*sk*. *Return*(*mkKey*,[*a*;*b*],(*k*,*sk*))$\}$ $\rightarrow$ *m*:*bytes* $\rightarrow$
s:*bytes* $\{$*#Post*(*judge*,[*a*;*b*;*k*;*m*;*s*])$\}$ $\rightarrow$ *unit*

The use of the macro-expansion predicate *#Post* here is a convenient way of making this type dependent on the type of judge, hence avoiding the the need to rewrite it when the protocol or the judge change. Note that we cannot use the *Return* event or the *Post* predicate here (instead of *#Post*) because both rely on a function having been called; here the call to *audit* must be typable without actually calling the judge function.

An auditable multi-party protocol. We have also applied the three semantics for pre- and postconditions to verify an auditable multi-party protocol implementation for on-line games between n players and a server [15]. In this protocol, the participants make minimal trust assumptions on the other players and the server, and shield themselves from various attacks.

Since the number of the players is a run-time parameter of the protocol, the participants have to manipulate lists of cryptographic evidence. For instance, the function *List.forall* is used for three different series of checks, so in the original F7 implementation the function code had to be replicated and equipped with different *ad hoc* types. Using the subtyping-based semantics, the same library function *List.forall* is used at all call sites, which makes the code more compact and more readable.

7 Related Work

Pre- and post-condition checking is supported by many program verification tools [e.g. 2, 13, 22]. Our approach is most closely related to that of Régis-Gianas and Pottier [19], who show how to use Hoare-style annotations to check programs written in a call-by-value language with recursive higher-order functions and polymorphic types. However, their system only uses declared types (*#Pre*,*#Post*), and disregards subtyping and events.

Symbolic methods for verifying the security of protocol implementations utilize a variety of techniques, such as static analysis [14], model-checking [9], and cryptographic theorem-proving [4]. The RCF type system is the first to use refinement types for verifying protocol implementations [3]. Its implementation in the F7 typechecker has been successfully used to verify complex cryptographic applications [1, 5, 6]. F7 requires programmer intervention in the form of type annotations, whereas some of the other verification tools are fully automated. However, these other tools generally do not apply to programs with recursive data structures. Besides, whole-program analysis techniques seldom scales as well as modular ones, such as typechecking.

Fine [21, 10] is another extension of F# with refinement types. It also supports affine types and proof-carrying bytecode verification. Its type system has a notion of predicate polymorphism that captures some of the benefits of our pre- and post-condition predicates. To use them, the programmer declares predicate parameters for higher-order types and functions, and explicitly instantiates these predicates at each call site. In contrast, our approach is able to verify legacy programs written purely in F# by automatically injecting pre- and post-condition predicates.

By relying on standard verification techniques, we hope to benefit from their recent progress. For example, Liquid Types [20] have been proposed as a technique for inferring refinement types for ML programs. The types inferred by Liquid Types are quite adequate for verifying simple safety properties of a program, but not for the security types in this paper. As future work, we plan to adapt such inference techniques to reduce F7 annotations even further.

References

[1] Backes, M., Hriţcu, C., Maffei, M., Tarrach, T.: Type-checking implementations of protocols based on zero-knowledge proofs. In: FCS (2009)
[2] Barnett, M., Leino, M., Schulte, W.: The Spec# programming system: An overview. In: CASSIS, pp. 49–69 (January 2005)
[3] Bengtson, J., Bhargavan, K., Fournet, C., Gordon, A.D., Maffeis, S.: Refinement types for secure implementations. In: CSF, pp. 17–32 (2008)
[4] Bhargavan, K., Fournet, C., Gordon, A.D., Tse, S.: Verified interoperable implementations of security protocols. ACM TOPLAS 31, 5:1–5:61 (2008)
[5] Bhargavan, K., Corin, R., Deniélou, P., Fournet, C., Leifer, J.: Cryptographic protocol synthesis and verification for multiparty sessions. In: CSF, pp. 124–140 (2009)
[6] Bhargavan, K., Fournet, C., Gordon, A.D.: Modular verification of security protocol code by typing. In: POPL, pp. 445–456 (2010)
[7] Bhargavan, K., Fournet, C., Guts, N.: Typechecking higher-order security libraries. Technical Report (2010), `http://msr-inria.inria.fr/Projects/sec/infer`
[8] Blanchet, B.: An efficient cryptographic protocol verifier based on Prolog rules. In: CSFW, pp. 82–96 (2001)
[9] Chaki, S., Datta, A.: ASPIER: An automated framework for verifying security protocol implementations. In: CSF, pp. 172–185 (2009)
[10] Chen, J., Chugh, R., Swamy, N.: Type-preserving compilation for end-to-end verification of security enforcement. In: PLDI, pp. 412–423 (June 2010)
[11] Eastlake, D., Reagle, J., Solo, D., Bartel, M., Boyer, J., Fox, B., LaMacchia, B., Simon, E.: XML-Signature Syntax and Processing. W3C Recommendation (2002)
[12] Fähndrich, M., Barnett, M., Logozzo, F.: Embedded Contract Languages. In: SAC OOPS (2010)
[13] Flanagan, C., Leino, K.R.M., Lillibridge, M., Nelson, G., Saxe, J.B., Stata, R.: Extended static checking for Java. SIGPLAN Not. 37(5), 234–245 (2002)
[14] Goubault-Larrecq, J., Parrennes, F.: Cryptographic protocol analysis on real C code. In: Cousot, R. (ed.) VMCAI 2005. LNCS, vol. 3385, pp. 363–379. Springer, Heidelberg (2005)
[15] Guts, N., Fournet, C., Zappa Nardelli, F.: Reliable evidence: Auditability by typing. In: Backes, M., Ning, P. (eds.) ESORICS 2009. LNCS, vol. 5789, pp. 168–183. Springer, Heidelberg (2009)
[16] Hoare, C.: An axiomatic basis for computer programming. Communications of the ACM (1969)
[17] Recommendation X.509 (1997 E): Information Technology - Open Systems Interconnection - The Directory: Authentication Framework. ITU-T (June 1997)
[18] Plotkin, G.D.: Denotational semantics with partial functions. Unpublished lecture notes, CSLI, Stanford University (July 1985)
[19] Régis-Gianas, Y., Pottier, F.: A Hoare logic for call-by-value functional programs. In: Audebaud, P., Paulin-Mohring, C. (eds.) MPC 2008. LNCS, vol. 5133, pp. 305–335. Springer, Heidelberg (2008)
[20] Rondon, P., Kawaguci, M., Jhala, R.: Liquid types. In: PLDI, pp. 159–169 (2008)
[21] Swamy, N., Chen, J., Chugh, R.: Enforcing stateful authorization and information flow policies in fine. In: Gordon, A.D. (ed.) ESOP 2010. LNCS, vol. 6012, pp. 529–549. Springer, Heidelberg (2010)
[22] Xu, D.N.: Extended static checking for Haskell. In: Haskell, pp. 48–59 (2006)

Towards Deriving Type Systems and Implementations for Coroutines

Konrad Anton and Peter Thiemann

Institut für Informatik, Universität Freiburg
{anton,thiemann}@informatik.uni-freiburg.de

Abstract. Starting from reduction semantics for several styles of coroutines from the literature, we apply Danvy's method to obtain equivalent functional implementations (definitional interpreters) for them. By applying existing type systems for programs with continuations, we obtain sound type systems for coroutines through the translation. The resulting type systems are similar to earlier hand-crafted ones. As a side product, we obtain implementations for these styles of coroutines in OCaml.

1 Introduction

Coroutines are an old programming construct, dating back to the 1960s [5]. They have been neglected for a while, but are currently enjoying a renaissance (e.g. in Lua [12]), sometimes in the limited form of generators (Python [20], C# [17]) and sometimes under different names (e.g., fibers in .NET).

Type systems for coroutines have not been considered in the past. Coroutines without parameters and return values (Simula, Modula 2 [21]), coroutine operations whose effects are tied to the static structure of the program (ACL, [16]), or coroutines lexically limited to the body of one function (C#), could be integrated into said languages without special support in the type system.

In an earlier paper [1], we developed the first type system for a simply-typed λ-calculus with coroutines. This development was done in an ad-hoc style for a feature-rich calculus and resulted in a type and effect system with a simple notion of subeffecting to capture the control effects of coroutine operations.

In this paper, we follow a different course and rigorously derive a type system for a simple core calculus. The derivation starts with a reduction semantics from the literature [11]. To this reduction semantics, we apply Danvy's method [6] to obtain a denotational semantics after several semantics-preserving transformation steps. Then we further transform the semantics to a denotational implementation (a combinator implementation) using methods developed by one of the authors [19]. This combinator implementation of the coroutine operations is directly and practically usable. It is available for OCaml on the web.

The denotational implementation also provides good grounds for constructing a type system that is aware of coroutines. As the combinators contains control operators, we apply a type system for (the control operators) shift and reset [7,2] to them and abstract from the types to obtain the desired system. This approach

K. Ueda (Ed.): APLAS 2010, LNCS 6461, pp. 63–79, 2010.

allows us to construct a variety of type systems. We provide a type soundness proof for one of them by specifying a typed translation to cps augmented with a reader monad. This translation is *not ad-hoc* either, because we fork it off from an intermediate transformation result of Danvy's method.

In summary, the contributions of this paper are:

- Systematically derived implementation of coroutine library for OCaml.
- Systematically derived monomorphic type system for coroutines.
- Type soundness proof via a typed translation to a standard monomorphic lambda calculus with references.

Major intermediate steps of the transformation are available on the web along with the OCaml implementation.[1]

Overview. Sec. 2 recalls an operational semantics for coroutines from the literature. Sec. 3 applies Danvy's method to the operationals semantics. Sec. 4 applies Thiemann's method to the resulting interpreter to obtain a denotational implementation. Sec. 5 performs the derivation of the type system and Sec. 6 considers type soundness.

2 Reduction Semantics for Coroutines

In their paper "Revisiting Coroutines" (henceforth abbreviated RC), Moura and Ierusalimschy [11] define a core calculus that can be extended to cover various styles and features of coroutines. They consider two styles of coroutines, symmetric and asymmetric. In the symmetric setting, a coroutine passes control by explicitly invoking another coroutine. In the asymmetric setting, there are two ways of passing control. Either a coroutine can explicitly invoke another coroutine, in which case it establishes a parent-child relationship to the next coroutine, or it can pass control to the implicit parent coroutine. In each case, the coroutine that passes control suspends itself. As a final variation, not considered in RC, a coroutine implementation may support both styles of control passing [1, 14].

The base calculus is a call-by-value lambda calculus with assignment, locations, equality, and a conditional. Evaluation proceeds from right to left. Fig. 1 defines its syntax and its reduction rules. The latter work on a configuration that consists of an expression e, a store $\theta \in (\mathit{Var} \cup \mathit{Loc}) \to \mathit{Value}$ that maps variables and locations to values, and a location $l \in \mathit{Loc}$. Here, *Var* is a set of variables and *Loc* is a set of store locations. The base calculus does not use the third location component, but the symmetric coroutine operations do.

The calculus models beta reduction in Scheme style by renaming the bound variable to a fresh variable z and assigning the substituted value to that variable. These fresh variables serve as locations and facilitate a straightforward implementation of the assignment operation.

[1] `http://proglang.informatik.uni-freiburg.de/projects/coroutines/`

$$
\begin{array}{lll}
\text{Expressions} & e & ::= l \mid x \mid \lambda x.e \mid e\,e \mid x := e \mid \textbf{if}\ e\ \textbf{then}\ e\ \textbf{else}\ e \mid e = e \mid \textbf{nil} \\
\text{Values} & v & ::= l \mid \lambda x.e \mid \textbf{nil} \\
\text{Ev. contexts} & C & ::= \Box \mid e\,C \mid C\,v \mid x := C \mid \textbf{if}\ C\ \textbf{then}\ e\ \textbf{else}\ e \mid e = C \mid C = v
\end{array}
$$

$$
\begin{array}{lll}
(C[x], \theta, l_0) & \Rightarrow & (C[\theta(x)], \theta, l_0) \\
(C[(\lambda x.e)\,v], \theta, l_0) & \Rightarrow & (C[e[z/x]], \theta[z \mapsto v], l_0) \text{ where } z \text{ is fresh} \\
(C[x := v], \theta, l_0) & \Rightarrow & (C[v], \theta[x \mapsto v], l_0) \\
(C[\textbf{if nil then}\ e_2\ \textbf{else}\ e_3], \theta, l_0) & \Rightarrow & (C[e_3], \theta, l_0) \\
(C[\textbf{if}\ v\ \textbf{then}\ e_2\ \textbf{else}\ e_3], \theta, l_0) & \Rightarrow & (C[e_2], \theta, l_0) \text{ if } v \neq \textbf{nil} \\
(C[l = l], \theta, l_0) & \Rightarrow & (C[l], \theta, l_0) \\
(C[l_1 = l_2], \theta, l_0) & \Rightarrow & (C[\textbf{nil}], \theta, l_0) \text{ if } l_1 \neq l_2
\end{array}
$$

Fig. 1. Syntax and reductions of the base calculus

2.1 Symmetric Coroutines

The symmetric coroutine calculus extends the base calculus with operations to create a coroutine and to transfer control to a coroutine. Moreover, there is an operation to obtain the identity of the currently running coroutine.

Fig. 2 defines the extended syntax as well as the additional evaluation contexts and reduction rules. For simplicity, it differs from the calculus in RC in that it does not have the notion of a main coroutine, to which execution falls back if a coroutine just terminates without passing on control. The equivalence proof of symmetric and asymmetric coroutines in RC relies on this feature.

This calculus (as well as the following ones) models coroutines exclusively as storable values in the sense of the EOPL book [13]. Thus, an expression never denotes a coroutine directly, but only via a store location.

The definition of the **transfer** operation implements the convention that an active coroutine is not represented in the store. Creating a coroutine obtains an unused store location and assigns it a procedure. Transferring control to a coroutine sets its location to **nil** and suspending the coroutine overwrites it with a new procedure (the continuation that arises as the context of the **transfer**). The second reduction rule for **transfer** implements the special case that a coroutine transfers control to itself.

$$
\begin{array}{lll}
\text{Expressions} & e & ::= \cdots \mid \textbf{create}\ e \mid \textbf{transfer}\ e\ e \mid \textbf{current} \\
\text{Ev. contexts} & C & ::= \cdots \mid \textbf{create}\ C \mid \textbf{transfer}\ e\ C \mid \textbf{transfer}\ C\ v
\end{array}
$$

$$
\begin{array}{lll}
(C[\textbf{create}\ v], \theta, l_0) & \Rightarrow & (C[l], \theta[l \mapsto v], l_0) \text{ where } l \notin \text{dom}(\theta) \\
(C[\textbf{transfer}\ l\ v], \theta, l_0) & \Rightarrow & (\theta(l)\,v, \theta[l \mapsto \textbf{nil}, l_0 \mapsto \lambda x.C[x]], l) \text{ where } l \neq l_0 \\
(C[\textbf{transfer}\ l_0\ v], \theta, l_0) & \Rightarrow & (C[v], \theta, l_0) \\
(C[\textbf{current}], \theta, l_0) & \Rightarrow & (C[l_0], \theta, l_0)
\end{array}
$$

Fig. 2. Syntax and reductions of the calculus with symmetric coroutines

2.2 Asymmetric Coroutines

The asymmetric calculus is slightly more complicated. To the base calculus, it adds operations to create a coroutine, to resume another coroutine (establishing the parent-child relationship mentioned at the beginning), and to yield to the parent coroutine.

$$\begin{array}{lll} \text{Expressions} & e ::= \cdots \mid \textbf{create}\ e \mid \textbf{resume}\ e\ e \mid \textbf{yield}\ e \mid l : e \\ \text{Ev. contexts} & C ::= \cdots \mid \textbf{create}\ C \mid \textbf{resume}\ e\ C \mid \textbf{resume}\ C\ v \mid \textbf{yield}\ C \\ \text{Ev. contexts II} & D ::= \Box \mid C[l : D] \end{array}$$

$$\begin{array}{lll} (D[C[\textbf{create}\ v]], \theta, l_0) & \Rightarrow & (D[C[l]], \theta[l \mapsto v], l_0) \text{ where } l \notin \text{dom}(\theta) \\ (D[C[\textbf{resume}\ l\ v]], \theta, l_0) & \Rightarrow & (D[C[l_0 : \theta(l)\ v]], \theta[l \mapsto \textbf{nil}], l) \text{ where } l \neq l_0 \\ (D[C[\textbf{resume}\ l_0\ v]], \theta, l_0) & \Rightarrow & (D[C[v]], \theta, l_0) \\ (D[C[l : C_0[\textbf{yield}\ v]]], \theta, l_0) & \Rightarrow & (D[C[v]], \theta[l_0 \mapsto \lambda x.C_0[x]], l) \\ (D[C[l : v]], \theta, l_0) & \Rightarrow & (D[C[v]], \theta, l) \end{array}$$

Fig. 3. Syntax and reductions of the calculus with asymmetric coroutines

Fig. 3 shows the extended syntax, evaluation contexts, and reductions. Deviating from the presentation in RC, the configuration keeps the current coroutine l_0 in the third component and the evaluation context has been split in an inner evaluation context C and an outer evaluation context D. The D contexts structure the evaluation contexts in pieces between the newly introduced labeled expressions $l : \ldots$. The latter denote return points for the **yield** operation and they keep and restore the identity l of the parent coroutine if a coroutine terminates without yielding. The reductions imported from the base calculus are all lifted to work in context $D[C[\ldots]]$ instead of just plain $C[\ldots]$.

In this calculus, a coroutine may terminate sensibly. If it finishes with a value, it implicitly yields to its parent or, at the top-level, it concludes the computation. There is again a special case for a coroutine to resume to itself.

2.3 Dahl-Hoare Style Coroutines

Dahl-Hoare style coroutines combine the features of the symmetric and the asymmetric calculus as suggested by Haynes and coworkers [14]. Fig. 4 extends the syntax and semantics of the asymmetric calculus with the straightforward adaptation of the **transfer** rules to nested evaluation contexts of the form $D[C[\ldots]]$. It is noteworthy that **transfer** still captures only the innermost C-continuation.

$$\begin{array}{ll} \text{Expressions} & e ::= \cdots \mid \textbf{transfer}\ e\ e \\ \text{Ev. contexts} & C ::= \cdots \mid \textbf{transfer}\ e\ C \mid \textbf{transfer}\ C\ v \end{array}$$

$$\begin{array}{lll} (D[C[\textbf{transfer}\ l\ v]], \theta, l_0) & \Rightarrow & (D[\theta(l)\ v], \theta[l \mapsto \textbf{nil}, l_0 \mapsto \lambda x.C[x]], l) \text{ if } l \neq l_0 \\ (D[C[\textbf{transfer}\ l_0\ v]], \theta, l_0) & \Rightarrow & (D[C[v]], \theta, l_0) \end{array}$$

Fig. 4. Extension of the asymmetric calculus with Dahl-Hoare style coroutines

3 From Reduction Semantics to Denotational Implementation

In a series of papers, Danvy developed a systematic method to interconvert different styles of semantic artifacts while preserving their meaning. Here, we are interested in the route from reduction semantics to a definitional interpreter as spelt out in Danvy's invited presentation at ICFP 2008 [6]. We follow that route exactly for the three reduction semantics from Sec. 2 to obtain three equivalent definitional interpreters.

In each case, the sequence of semantic artifacts starts with an ML program that implements the respective reduction semantics. The first step converts the reduction semantics to a small-step abstract machine by applying refocusing [10]. The result is fused with an iteration function to obtain a tail-recursive evaluation function. Inlining the reduction function and then applying transition compression (function unrolling on known arguments and simplification) results in a tail-recursive interpreter that still manipulates a syntactic representation of the evaluation context. The next step is to refunctionalize this evaluation context to a continuation resulting in an interpreter with continuations [9]. The interpreter can be converted to direct style and subjected to closure unconversion to obtain a "natural looking" interpreter that represents values no longer syntactically.

As the intermediate steps are amply demonstrated in the work of Danvy and coworkers (e.g., [6]), we refrain from going through them in detail.[2] However, it is important that each transformation step establishes a semantic equivalence in the sense that an expression evaluates to a value if and only if the transformed expression evaluates to a suitably related value. We only comment on special steps that need to be taken for the calculi with the asymmetric coroutine operators and show the essential parts of the final results, in particular omitting the standard lambda calculus parts.

3.1 Symmetric Coroutines

The direct-style version of the interpreter in Fig. 5 is equivalent to the reduction semantics in Fig. 2 because it has been constructed from the latter using a sequence of semantics-preserving transformations. As a final step, we have transformed the store and the currently executed coroutine into two global variables, after observing that they are passed in a single-threaded way.

Most of the code should be self-explanatory. The operations `shift` and `push_prompt` (and `new_prompt`) are from Kiselyov's implementation [15] of the control operators shift and reset [8] that arise from the transformation to direct style. The code avoids separate code for the case where a coroutine transfers control to itself by choosing the right ordering for the reads and writes of the store.

As a fine point, Kiselyov's implementation is typed, but it does not allow the answer type variation of the Danvy/Filinski type system for delimited continuations (see Sec. 5). However, this variation is not needed as long as the

[2] The curious reader may consult `http://proglang.informatik.uni-freiburg.de/projects/coroutines/`

```
(* universal value type *)
type value =
 | VLoc of location
 | VFun of (value -> value)
 | VNil

let pp : value prompt =
 new_prompt ()

let rec evaldu_expr e =
 match e with
 | ...
 | Create e ->
    let v = evaldu_expr e in
    let newl = fresh_loc () in
    upd_loc newl v;
    VLoc newl
 | Transfer (e1, e2) ->
    let v2 = evaldu_expr e2 in
    let VLoc l1 = evaldu_expr e1 in
    let l = !cur_coroutine in
    shift pp (fun ec ->
     upd_loc l (VFun ec);
     let VFun cor = lkup_loc l1 in
     upd_loc l1 VNil;
     cur_coroutine := l1;
     push_prompt pp (fun () ->
      cor v2))
 | Current ->
    let l = !cur_coroutine in
    VLoc l
```

Fig. 5. Definitional interpreter with symmetric coroutines (excerpt)

```
type value = (* as before *)

let pp : value prompt =
 new_prompt ()

let rec evaldg_expr e =
 match e with
 | ...
 | Create e -> (* as before *)
 | Resume (e1, e2) ->
    let v2 = evaldg_expr e2 in
    let VLoc l1 = evaldg_expr e1 in
    let VFun cor = lkup_loc l1 in
    upd_loc l1 VNil;
    let lc = !cur_coroutine in
    let v =
     push_prompt pp
      (fun () ->
        cur_coroutine := l1;
        cor v2)
    in cur_coroutine := lc;
    v
 | Yield e ->
    let v = evaldg_expr e in
    let lc = !cur_coroutine in
    shift pp (fun ec ->
     upd_loc lc (VFun ec);
     v)
```

Fig. 6. Definitional interpreter with asymmetric coroutines (excerpt)

implementation encodes all data in the universal `value` type (see Fig. 5): all argument, return, and answer types are fixed to `value`!

Close scrutiny of the code reveals that `push_prompt` is only called when the evaluation context is empty (which is in fact quite obvious when studying the intermediate results of the transformation). Thus, `push_prompt` need only be placed once at the top-level and `shift` could be replaced by `call/cc` because it would be an error if the call to `cor v2` ever returned. Applying this transformation yields in principle the implementation of coroutines given by Haynes, Friedman, and Wand [14]. Their implementation looks more complicated at first glance because they represent a coroutine by a function and because they abstract the coroutine body over the **transfer** function. But disentangling their implementation of **create** and **transfer** leads to the code in Fig. 5 with `call/cc` in place of `shift`.

3.2 Asymmetric Coroutines

The calculus with asymmetric coroutines requires some extra transformation steps. These extra steps are caused by the second level of evaluation contexts named D in Fig. 3. After the initial transformation steps, the intermediate result is a tail-recursive interpreter with two arguments that hold evaluation contexts, corresponding to the $D[C[\dots]]$ in the reduction semantics. Both of them are then refunctionalized, giving rise to an interpreter with two levels of continuations, and then transformed to direct style two times to obtain the code in Fig. 6. As before, the direct-style transformation introduces the control operators `shift` and `reset`.

The interpreter reuses the same type of values. It merges the two cases for **resume** by choosing the correct ordering for the reads and writes to the store. The `shift` operation in **yield** abstracts the context up to the prompt set in the parent coroutine's **resume** instruction. The variable `lc` in the code for **resume** implements the labeled expression $lc, \cdots :$ and the assignment `current_coroutine := lc` implements its reduction.

3.3 Dahl-Hoare Style Coroutines

To obtain a definitional interpreter with Dahl-Hoare style coroutines, it is sufficient to merge the code from Fig. 5 and Fig. 6. Thanks to the shared configuration, the code fits together without change.

3.4 Correctness

The chain of transformations according to Danvy's recipe preserves the semantics in the following sense. The proof is by appeal to the correctness of each transformation step.

Proposition 1. *Let e be a closed expression and $\stackrel{*}{\Rightarrow}$ be the reflexive transitive closure of $\Rightarrow$. It holds that $(e, \theta_0, l_0) \stackrel{*}{\Rightarrow} (v, \theta, l)$ if and only if* `eval_expr` *e with store $\lceil \theta_0 \rceil$ and* `!current_coroutine` = *l_0 evaluates to $\lceil v \rceil$ with store $\lceil \theta \rceil$ and* `!current_coroutine` = *l with $\lceil \cdot \rceil$ defined by $\lceil l \rceil =$* `VLoc` *l, $\lceil \lambda x.e \rceil =$* `VFun (fun x -> eval_expr` *$e$*`)`*, and $\lceil$***nil***$\rceil =$* `VNil`.

4 Implementation

In earlier work, we exhibited and proved correct a systematic transformation from an interpreter to a denotational implementation [19]. A denotational implementation specifies the semantics of each single language construct in terms of a combinator. Although the referenced work is posed in the area of program generation, the underlying technique is more generally applicable. In particular, it is applicable to the definitional interpreters constructed in Sec. 3.

As we already have closure un-converted interpreters, it remains to transform binders to a higher-order abstract syntax representation and to extract the combinators. Fig. 7 shows the combinators extracted from Fig. 5 and Fig. 6.

```
(*
definitions used

returns fresh location in store
fresh_loc : () -> int =

updates a location with a value
upd_loc : int -> value -> ()

looks up a location in store
lkup_loc : int -> value

location of current coroutine
cur_coroutine : int ref
*)

let create v =
 let newl = fresh_loc () in
 upd_loc newl v;
 VLoc newl
```

```
let resume (VLoc l1, v2) =
 let VFun cor = lkup_loc l1 in
 upd_loc l1 VNil;
 let lc = !cur_coroutine in
 let v =
  push_prompt pp
   (fun () ->
     cur_coroutine := l1;
     cor v2)
 in cur_coroutine := lc;
 v
let yield v =
 let lc = !cur_coroutine in
 shift pp (fun ec ->
  upd_loc lc (VFun ec);
  v)
let transfer (VLoc l1, v2) =
 shift pp (fun ec ->
  let lc = !cur_coroutine in
  let VFun cor = lkup_loc l1 in
  upd_loc l1 VNil;
  upd_loc lc (VFun ec);
  cur_coroutine := l1;
  push_prompt pp
   (fun () -> cor v2))
```

Fig. 7. Combinators extracted from the definitional interpreters

Fortunately, the bytecode implementation of OCaml also performs right-to-left evaluation of function arguments so that it matches the theory perfectly.

The final transformation step in our previous work [19] is tag removal, which gets rid of the `value` type as also advertised by Carette and coworkers [4]. While this step is not essential for deriving a type system, we apply it to obtain a type-safe implementation of coroutines for OCaml. The extended version of the paper contains the code.[3] Space does not permit further discussion of the implementation.

5 Deriving a Type System

The development in Sec. 3 and Sec. 4 shows that coroutines are tightly connected to composable continuations by exhibiting a formally derived implementation of the former with the latter. The results of the RC paper also strongly support this point of view.

To obtain a type system for coroutines, we therefore choose the following strategy. We regard the coroutine operations as abbreviations for the combinators in Fig. 7. As these combinators contain the control operators shift and reset, we

[3] `http://proglang.informatik.uni-freiburg.de/projects/coroutines/`

employ a type system that supports shift and reset to obtain adequate typings for them. Such a system has been proposed by Danvy and Filinski [7] and later extended with polymorphism by Asai and Kameyama [2]. We use that system to informally derive a type system for coroutines and postpone a formal treatment to Sec. 6.

The Danvy/Filinski type system proves judgments of the form $\Gamma; \alpha \vdash e : \tau; \beta$ where the type environment Γ, the expression e, and the resulting type τ are as in a standard type system (e.g., the system of simple types). Here, α and β are answer types and the implicit continuation is a representation of the change of answer type. More precisely, evaluation of the expression e modifies the answer type from α to β. The formal explanation is that the type of e^* is $(\tau^* \to \alpha^*) \to \beta^*$, where * indicates application of the call-by-value CPS transformation to a term or a type. The function type in this system also includes the modification of the answer type of the implicit continuation in its body. We write $\sigma/\alpha \to \tau/\beta$ for a function from σ to τ that modifies the answer type from α to β. For reference, the extended version of the paper contains the typing rules of the monomorphic system in a variant adapted to the right-to-left evaluation order of our calculus.

5.1 Global Variables and the Reader Monad

Another important observation concerns the global variable that contains the current coroutine. Inspection of the interpreter (Fig. 5 and Fig. 6) reveals that the location of the current coroutine does not change while the body of a fixed coroutine executes. For example, the code for **resume** sets the current coroutine to the resumed routine and restores the current coroutine to its previous value when the resumed coroutine terminates or yields. The **transfer** operation overwrites the current coroutine to the called coroutine without remembering the past one.

This observation shows that the current coroutine is essentially stored in a reader monad. Thus, it need not be threaded through the computation, but just passed downwards. Resuming or transferring to another coroutine starts in a freshly initialized reader monad.

A similar observation applies to the global coroutine store θ. Each location of this store either contains a function/continuation or the value **nil**. The value **nil** indicates that the coroutine is either active or suspended by a **resume** operation. With this convention, the semantics enforces that there is only one instance of a coroutine at any time: it is a run-time error to resume or transfer to a coroutine which is currently **nil**.

Analyzing the interpreter shows that the set of coroutine locations that are set to **nil** does not change while the body of a fixed coroutine executes, as long as the **transfer** operation is not used.[4] The code for **resume** overwrites the location of

[4] With **transfer** we could build code that performs the following control transfers. Let l_1, l_2, and l_3 be coroutine locations. At the top-level, first resume to l_1, which in turn resumes l_2. Then transfer to l_3, which yields (to l_1), which in turn transfers to l_2.

When l_2 is first active, l_1 and l_2 are both **nil**. The second time round, only l_2 is **nil**.

the resumed coroutine with **nil** and the corresponding **yield** operation overwrites this location with a captured continuation.

Thus, the information which coroutine must not be invoked (because its location is **nil**) could be stored in a reader monad, but not the actual function or continuation which has to be threaded through the computation.

In the case of (pure) symmetric coroutines, this information does not matter. There is always exactly one active coroutine, the location of which is set to **nil**. According to the semantics, a program can transfer safely to any coroutine without crashing.

5.2 Symmetric Coroutines

If we apply the Danvy/Filinski type system to the **transfer** operator in Fig. 7 and use the standard ML typings for assignment, dereference, and sequencing (extended with threading the answer-type change according to the evaluation order: right-to-left for assignment and left-to-right for sequencing), type-checking the code for **transfer** in Fig. 7 yields the following results.

- The type of a coroutine is a reference to a function type.
- The function type of a coroutine always has the form $\tau/\alpha \rightarrow \alpha/\alpha$.
- Assuming that `current_coroutine` has type $\mathrm{ref}(\tau_1/\alpha_1 \rightarrow \alpha_1/\alpha_1)$, the type of **transfer** is $\mathrm{ref}(\tau_0/\alpha_0 \rightarrow \alpha_0/\alpha_0) \times \tau_0/\alpha_1 \rightarrow \tau_1/\beta_1$.
- Neither the return type of the coroutine type nor its answer types matter because a symmetric coroutine never returns.

$$\sigma, \tau, \alpha, \beta ::= \cdots \mid \sigma \xrightarrow{\alpha} \tau \mid \mathrm{cor}(\beta)$$

$$\frac{\Gamma \vdash e : \sigma \xrightarrow{\sigma} \tau \,\&\, \alpha}{\Gamma \vdash \textbf{create}\ e : \mathrm{cor}(\sigma) \,\&\, \alpha} \qquad \frac{\Gamma \vdash e_1 : \mathrm{cor}(\beta) \,\&\, \alpha \qquad \Gamma \vdash e_2 : \beta \,\&\, \alpha}{\Gamma \vdash \textbf{transfer}\ e_1\ e_2 : \alpha \,\&\, \alpha}$$

$$\Gamma \vdash \textbf{current} : \mathrm{cor}(\alpha) \,\&\, \alpha \qquad \frac{\Gamma, x : \sigma \vdash e : \tau \,\&\, \beta}{\Gamma \vdash \lambda x.e : \sigma \xrightarrow{\beta} \tau \,\&\, \alpha}$$

$$\frac{\Gamma \vdash e_1 : \sigma \xrightarrow{\alpha} \tau \,\&\, \alpha \qquad \Gamma \vdash e_2 : \sigma \,\&\, \alpha}{\Gamma \vdash e_1\ e_2 : \tau \,\&\, \alpha}$$

Fig. 8. Types and relevant typing rules for symmetric coroutines

These findings motivate the abbreviation $\mathrm{cor}(\tau) = \mathrm{ref}(\forall\alpha.\tau/\alpha \rightarrow \alpha/\alpha)$ for the type of a coroutine that accepts a value of type τ. In addition, the type system needs to keep track of the type of the current coroutine, which happens to be stored in a reader monad (Sec. 5.1). This observation leads to an indexed monadic typing judgment of the form $\Gamma \vdash e : \tau \,\&\, \alpha$ where the effect α indicates that the current coroutine has type $\text{cor}(\alpha)$ and function types of the corresponding form $\sigma \xrightarrow{\alpha} \tau$ where α is the expected type of the current coroutine at the call site of the function. Fig. 8 contains the type syntax and the relevant typing rules. These rules are obtained by abstracting the above patterns from the typings of the combinators.

5.3 Asymmetric Coroutines

Again, applying the Danvy/Filinski type system to the **resume** and **yield** operators in Fig. 7, we obtain the following results.

- The type of a coroutine is a reference to a function type.
- The function type of a coroutine always has the form $\tau/\alpha \to \alpha/\alpha$.
- **resume** has type $\text{ref}(\sigma/\tau \to \tau/\tau) \times \sigma/\alpha \to \tau_0/\beta$.
- Assuming that the current coroutine has type $\text{ref}(\sigma/\tau \to \tau/\tau)$, the type of **yield** is $\tau_0/\gamma \to \sigma/\tau_0$.
- If the coroutine also returns normally, then $\tau_0 = \tau$, in which case the types work out to
  - **resume** : $\text{ref}(\sigma/\tau \to \tau/\tau) \times \sigma/\alpha \to \tau/\beta$ and
  - **yield** : $\tau/\gamma \to \sigma/\tau$ (assuming the coroutine was resumed by the above **resume**).

A suitable coroutine type for this constellation is $\text{cor}(\sigma, \tau) = \text{ref}(\sigma/\tau \to \tau/\tau)$ and the corresponding type system is again a monadic system that keeps track of the type of the current coroutine stored in the reader monad. The typing judgment correspondingly reads $\Gamma \vdash e : \tau \,\&\, \alpha \rightsquigarrow \beta$ where the effect $\alpha \rightsquigarrow \beta$ specifies that the current coroutine has type $\text{cor}(\alpha, \beta)$. The function type has the form $\sigma \xrightarrow{\alpha \rightsquigarrow \beta} \tau$ where the current coroutine at the point of the function call is expected to be $\text{cor}(\alpha, \beta)$. Fig. 9 shows the relevant parts of the syntax of types and of the typing rules. The translation in Sec. 6 sheds more light on the relation between the typing of the combinators and the typing rules of the source language.

5.4 Dahl-Hoare Style Coroutines

The Dahl-Hoare style only adds the **transfer** operation to the API for asymmetric coroutines. Thus, it remains to find a typing rule for **transfer** to go along with the system in Sec. 5.3. The rule is similar to the typing of the **resume** operation, but —as it replaces the current coroutine— its return/yield type must be equal to the return type of the current coroutine.

$$\frac{\Gamma \vdash e_1 : \text{cor}(\beta, \delta) \,\&\, \alpha \rightsquigarrow \delta \qquad \Gamma \vdash e_2 : \beta \,\&\, \alpha \rightsquigarrow \delta}{\Gamma \vdash \textbf{transfer}\ e_1\ e_2 : \alpha \,\&\, \alpha \rightsquigarrow \delta} \tag{1}$$

$$\sigma, \tau, \alpha, \beta, \gamma, \delta ::= \cdots \mid \sigma \xrightarrow{\alpha \leadsto \beta} \tau \mid \mathrm{cor}(\alpha, \beta)$$

$$\frac{\Gamma \vdash e : \beta \xrightarrow{\beta \leadsto \gamma} \gamma \,\&\, \alpha \leadsto \delta}{\Gamma \vdash \mathbf{create}\; e : \mathrm{cor}(\beta, \gamma) \,\&\, \alpha \leadsto \delta} \qquad \Gamma \vdash \mathbf{current} : \mathrm{cor}(\alpha, \delta) \,\&\, \alpha \leadsto \delta$$

$$\frac{\Gamma \vdash e_1 : \mathrm{cor}(\beta, \gamma) \,\&\, \alpha \leadsto \delta \qquad \Gamma \vdash e_2 : \beta \,\&\, \alpha \leadsto \delta}{\Gamma \vdash \mathbf{resume}\; e_1\; e_2 : \gamma \,\&\, \alpha \leadsto \delta} \qquad \frac{\Gamma \vdash e : \delta \,\&\, \alpha \leadsto \delta}{\Gamma \vdash \mathbf{yield}\; e : \alpha \,\&\, \alpha \leadsto \delta}$$

$$\frac{\Gamma, x : \sigma \vdash e : \tau \,\&\, \beta \leadsto \gamma}{\Gamma \vdash \lambda x.e : \sigma \xrightarrow{\beta \leadsto \gamma} \tau \,\&\, \alpha \leadsto \delta} \qquad \frac{\Gamma \vdash e_1 : \sigma \xrightarrow{\alpha \leadsto \delta} \tau \,\&\, \alpha \leadsto \delta \qquad \Gamma \vdash e_2 : \sigma \,\&\, \alpha \leadsto \delta}{\Gamma \vdash e_1\; e_2 : \tau \,\&\, \alpha \leadsto \delta}$$

Fig. 9. Types and relevant typing rules for asymmetric coroutines

5.5 Keeping Track of Nil

Up to this point, the type systems do not prevent resuming or transferring to a pending coroutine that waits for a **yield** and has its location set to **nil**. As mentioned in Sec. 5.1, this information could be split from the coroutine store and passed in a reader monad. Reflecting that reader monad in the type system requires a number of changes.

1. There must be a static approximation of the location where the coroutine is stored. We solve that by attaching a source label to each **create** expression using that label.
2. There must be an approximation of the set of locations of pending coroutines. A set of labels is sufficient.
3. The typing judgment must keep track of the additional indexing of the reader monad.
4. The function type and the coroutine type must be extended to accommodate the additional indexing information.

Fig. 10 contains a first draft of a type system that tracks this extra information. The typing judgment extends to $\Gamma; L, l \vdash e : \sigma \,\&\, \alpha \leadsto \delta$ where L is the set of pending labels and $l \in L$ is the label of the currently active coroutine. The function type and the coroutine type carry the same information L, l as indexes. Thus, a coroutine of type $\mathrm{cor}^l_L(\beta, \gamma)$ is stored in location l and, while active, the coroutines in L are pending. A function of type $\sigma \xrightarrow{L,l,\alpha \leadsto \delta} \tau$ can only be called while in coroutine l with pending set L.

The **create** operation transforms a function into a coroutine while preserving its indexes. The **resume** operation checks with $l \notin L'$ that the resumed coroutine is neither active nor in the pending set and demands a suitable pending set $L = L' \cup \{l'\}$ for the resumed coroutine. The **transfer** operation checks similarly that the target coroutine is not in the pending set, but transferring to oneself is permitted. The remaining rules are straightforward.

$$\sigma, \tau, \alpha, \beta, \gamma, \delta ::= \cdots \mid \sigma \overset{L,l,\alpha \rightsquigarrow \beta}{\longrightarrow} \tau \mid \mathrm{cor}^l_L(\alpha, \beta)$$

$$\frac{\Gamma; L', l' \vdash e : \beta \overset{L,l,\beta \rightsquigarrow \gamma}{\longrightarrow} \gamma \,\&\, \alpha \rightsquigarrow \delta}{\Gamma; L', l' \vdash \mathbf{create}^l\ e : \mathrm{cor}^l_L(\beta, \gamma) \,\&\, \alpha \rightsquigarrow \delta} \qquad \Gamma; L, l \vdash \mathbf{current} : \mathrm{cor}^l_L(\alpha, \delta) \,\&\, \alpha \rightsquigarrow \delta$$

$$\frac{\begin{array}{c}\Gamma; L', l' \vdash e_1 : \mathrm{cor}^l_L(\beta, \gamma) \,\&\, \alpha \rightsquigarrow \delta \\ \Gamma; L', l' \vdash e_2 : \beta \,\&\, \alpha \rightsquigarrow \delta \qquad l \notin L' \qquad L = L' \cup \{l'\}\end{array}}{\Gamma; L', l' \vdash \mathbf{resume}^l\ e_1\ e_2 : \gamma \,\&\, \alpha \rightsquigarrow \delta} \qquad \frac{\Gamma; L, l \vdash e : \delta \,\&\, \alpha \rightsquigarrow \delta}{\Gamma; L, l \vdash \mathbf{yield}\ e : \alpha \,\&\, \alpha \rightsquigarrow \delta}$$

$$\frac{\Gamma; L, l' \vdash e_1 : \mathrm{cor}^l_L(\beta, \delta) \,\&\, \alpha \rightsquigarrow \delta \qquad \Gamma; L, l' \vdash e_2 : \beta \,\&\, \alpha \rightsquigarrow \delta \qquad l \notin L \setminus \{l'\}}{\Gamma; L, l' \vdash \mathbf{transfer}^l\ e_1\ e_2 : \alpha \,\&\, \alpha \rightsquigarrow \delta}$$

$$\frac{\Gamma, x : \sigma; L, l \vdash e : \tau \,\&\, \beta \rightsquigarrow \gamma}{\Gamma; L', l' \vdash \lambda x.e : \sigma \overset{L,l,\beta \rightsquigarrow \gamma}{\longrightarrow} \tau \,\&\, \alpha \rightsquigarrow \delta}$$

$$\frac{\Gamma; L, l \vdash e_1 : \sigma \overset{L,l,\alpha \rightsquigarrow \delta}{\longrightarrow} \tau \,\&\, \alpha \rightsquigarrow \delta \qquad \Gamma; L, l \vdash e_2 : \sigma \,\&\, \alpha \rightsquigarrow \delta}{\Gamma; L, l \vdash e_1\ e_2 : \tau \,\&\, \alpha \rightsquigarrow \delta}$$

Fig. 10. Type system for asymmetric coroutines with **nil** tracking

This type system has been constructed systematically from the operational semantics, but it turns out to be quite conservative. First, it disallows a coroutine to resume to itself, which is fine by the operational semantics. However, this restriction is needed to obtain a sound type system.

Suppose we changed the **resume** rule to allow self-resumption. In this case, the constraints in the rule would change to $l \notin L' \setminus \{l'\}$ and $L = L' \setminus \{l'\} \cup \{l\}$. In a program that creates more than one coroutine instance with the same label l, resuming the first of these coroutines and then resuming to coroutine with a different label blocks later resumes to another l-coroutine, which is annoying, but still sound. However, because a coroutine is allowed to resume to itself, the modified type system lets a first instance with label l directly resume to another instance with label l. This instance, in turn could try to resume to the first instance, which is not stopped by the type system but which results in a run-time error. Hence, the system that allows self-resumption would be unsound.

This complication is caused by the procedure-call-like semantics of **resume**. It is not an issue for the **transfer** operation because it replaces the currently running coroutine.

Second, the type system requires subtyping to avoid being overly rigid. Without subtyping, each **resume** operation can only invoke one kind of coroutine, namely the one indexed with the correct l and L. The amendment is to allow multiple **create** operations labeled with the same label and to introduce subtyping with respect to the L index. Fig. 11 contains suitable subtyping rules for the function type and for the coroutine type. When moving to the supertype, both rules admit decreasing the index: a function or coroutine can always be used in a

$$\frac{L \supseteq L' \quad l \notin L'}{\mathrm{cor}^{l}_{L}(\alpha,\beta) \leq \mathrm{cor}^{l}_{L'}(\alpha,\beta)} \qquad \frac{\sigma' \leq \sigma \quad \tau \leq \tau' \quad L \supseteq L' \quad l \notin L'}{\sigma \overset{L,l,\alpha\rightsquigarrow\beta}{\longrightarrow} \tau \leq \sigma' \overset{L',l,\alpha\rightsquigarrow\beta}{\longrightarrow} \tau'}$$

Fig. 11. Subtyping

less restrictive context. The function type is contravariant in the argument and covariant in the result, as usual. The argument and result types of the coroutine need to remain invariant for technical reasons (stored in a reference).

6 Type Soundness

In this section, we consider type soundness of the system in Sec. 5.3 and Sec. 5.4 (Fig. 9 and Equation (1)). That is, we want to show that if a closed expression e is typed then it either performs infinitely many evaluation steps or its evaluation terminates with a value after finitely many steps. However, we wish to avoid the standard technique of proving progress and preservation.

To this end, we propose the following strategy. Danvy and collaborators [6] have proved that each of the transformation steps T (cps transformation, defunctionalization, refocusing, transition compression as well as their inverses) preserve semantic equivalence, in the sense that e evaluates to a value if and only if $T[\![e]\!]$ evaluates to a suitably related value. This statement (for the composition of these transformations) is the essence of Proposition 1.

In particular, this statement also holds for the interpreter shown in Fig. 12, which is forked off an intermediate product of the transformation chain from Sec. 3. In the case of asymmetric coroutines, an intermediate product after refunctionalization was an interpreter with two levels of continuations. According to the observation in Sec. 5.1, we transformed the use of the state monad for the current coroutine in this interpreter into a use of the reader monad. Subsequently, we removed the outer layer of continuations by direct style transformation and moved the interpretation of the lambda from the cases for **resume** and **transfer** into the case for **create**.[5] The consequence of the last transformation step is that a coroutine location *always* contains a continuation, before it could also contain a standard (CPS) function.

With this preparation, we consider the interpreter Fig. 12 in as a translation from the source language to CPS plus reader monad in a lambda calculus with references and read off the accompanying translation on types. As a consequence of Proposition 1, this translation is semantics preserving.

For the purposes of proving type soundness, we switch perspective and regard this translation as actually *defining* the semantics of the original calculus. If we can now prove that the translation preserves typing and there is a type soundness proof for the target type system, then we argue as follows: We *define* that closed expression e diverges iff its translation e^* diverges, similarly e evaluates to a value iff its translation e^* does. Thus, in combination, we obtain type soundness

[5] These steps are documented in the material on the Web.

$$
\begin{aligned}
(\Gamma \vdash e : \tau \,\&\, \alpha \rightsquigarrow \beta)^* &= \Gamma^* \vdash e^* : \mathrm{ref}(\alpha^* \to \beta^*) \to (\tau^* \to \beta^*) \to \beta^* \\
(x_1 : \sigma_1, \ldots, x_n : \sigma_n)^* &= x_1 : \sigma_1^*, \ldots, x_n : \sigma_n^* \\
(\mathrm{cor}(\alpha/\beta))^* &= \mathrm{ref}(\alpha^* \to \beta^*) \\
(\sigma \xrightarrow{\alpha \rightsquigarrow \beta} \tau)^* &= \sigma^* \to \mathrm{ref}(\alpha^* \to \beta^*) \to (\tau^* \to \beta^*) \to \beta^* \\
l^* &= \lambda c.\lambda k.k\, l \\
x^* &= \lambda c.\lambda k.k\, x \\
(\lambda x.e)^* &= \lambda c.\lambda k.k\, (\lambda x.e^*) \\
(e_1\, e_2)^* &= \lambda c.\lambda k.e_2^*\, c\, (\lambda v_2.e_1^*\, c\, (\lambda v_1.v_1\, v_2\, c\, k)) \\
(\textbf{create}\ e_1)^* &= \lambda c.\lambda k.e_1^*\, c(\lambda v_1.\textbf{let}\, l = \mathit{fresh}\, \textbf{in}\, \mathit{update}\, l\, (\lambda v_2.v_1\, v_2\, l\, (\lambda z.z)); k\, l) \\
(\textbf{resume}\ e_1\ e_2)^* &= \lambda c.\lambda k.e_2^*\, c\, (\lambda v_2.e_1^*\, c\, (\lambda v_1.\textbf{let}\, v = \mathit{lookup}\, v_1\, \textbf{in}\, k\, (v\, v_2))) \\
(\textbf{yield}\ e_1)^* &= \lambda c.\lambda k.e_1^*\, c(\lambda v_1.\mathit{update}\, c\, k; v_1) \\
(\textbf{transfer}\ e_1\ e_2)^* &= \lambda c.\lambda k.e_2^*\, c\, (\lambda v_2.e_1^*\, c\, (\lambda v_1.\textbf{let}\, v = \mathit{lookup}\, v_1\, \textbf{in}\, \mathit{update}\, c\, k; v\, v_2))
\end{aligned}
$$

Fig. 12. Translation

"if e is typed, then either e diverges or evaluates to a value" just because type soundness for the target means "if e^* is typed, then either e^* diverges or it evaluates to a value".

There is one final observation to be made for the establishing translation soundness. For the typing to go through, the type of a computation must be polymorphic over the final answer type of the continuation.

Lemma 1. *Suppose that* $\Gamma \vdash e : \tau \,\&\, \alpha \rightsquigarrow \beta$ *in the system of Fig. 9 with the* **transfer** *rule. Then* $\Gamma^* \vdash e^* : \mathit{ref}(\alpha^* \rightsquigarrow \beta^*) \to (\tau^* \to \beta^*) \to \beta^*$ *in a simple type system for call-by-value lambda calculus with references (e.g., [18, Chapter 13]).*

The type soundness of the **nil**-tracking type system in Fig. 10 and Fig. 11 can be shown using a similar translation, but a more expressive type system with set types is needed for the target language. However, space does not permit us to elaborate this translation.

7 Related Work

Language design aspects of coroutines have been explored in the 1970s and 1980s. Coroutines have found entry in some current programming languages (Python [20], Lua [12], C# [17]), but their formal semantics has been neglected.

The exception is the RC paper [11], which rigorously defines small step operational semantics for several styles of coroutines and proves various expressivity results among them and with respect to continuations and subcontinuations. One might also view the Scheme implementation of Haynes and coworkers [14] a formal specification of coroutines.

However, apart from our own work [1], we are not aware of any exploration of type systems tailored to coroutines. The other paper considers a richer calculus inspired by the needs of practical programming and develops its type system in an ad-hoc way. For example, the **resume** operation takes two continuations to distinguish between a yield and a normal return of the invoked coroutine. On the other hand, the system developed in the present paper reveals that the effect in the previous system [1] keeps track of the type of the current continuation which is stored in a reader monad. This insight would not have been possible without the systematic transformation approach.

Blazevic [3] produced a monad-based implementation of symmetric coroutines with session types in Haskell. Our work is based on an eager language, offers asymmetric coroutines, and is derived from a specification.

8 Conclusion

Using the systematic transformation approach advocated by Danvy, we have transformed a small-step reduction semantics for various styles of coroutines to a working, type-safe OCaml implementation. We have further derived a type system for a calculus with coroutines by applying a type system that is aware of control operators to the result of the transformation. Another outcome of the transformation is the translation which is used in constructing a type soundness proof for the type system.

We found that the systematic approach enabled additional insights. An example is the discovery of the use of the reader monad, which leads to the construction of the **nil**-tracking type system. Also the type soundness proof is vastly simplified with the translation that is also derived from an intermediate transformation step. Last but not least, the transformation gave rise to a practically useful, type-safe library implementation.

Acknowledgments. Thanks to the anonymous reviewers for their extensive comments and the ensuing discussion, which served to improve the paper considerably.

References

1. Anton, K., Thiemann, P.: Typing coroutines. In: Page, R., Zsók, V., Horváth, Z. (eds.) Eleventh Symposium on Trends in Functional Programming (draft proceedings), pp. 91–105. University of Oklahoma Printing Services (2010)
2. Asai, K., Kameyama, Y.: Polymorphic delimited continuations. In: Shao, Z. (ed.) APLAS 2007. LNCS, vol. 4807, pp. 239–254. Springer, Heidelberg (2007)
3. Blazevic, M.: monad-coroutine: Coroutine monad transformer for suspending and resuming monadic computations (2010), `http://hackage.haskell.org/package/monad-coroutine`
4. Carette, J., Kiselyov, O., Chieh Shan, C.: Finally tagless, partially evaluated: Tagless staged interpreters for simpler typed languages. J. Funct. Program. 19(5), 509–543 (2009)
5. Conway, M.E.: Design of a separable transition-diagram compiler. ACM Comm. 6(7), 396–408 (1963)

6. Danvy, O.: Defunctionalized interpreters for programming languages, pp. 131–142 (2008)
7. Danvy, O., Filinski, A.: A functional abstraction of typed contexts. Technical Report 89/12, DIKU, University of Copenhagen (July 1989)
8. Danvy, O., Filinski, A.: Abstracting control. In: Proc. 1990 ACM Conference on Lisp and Functional Programming, Nice, France, pp. 151–160. ACM Press, New York (1990)
9. Danvy, O., Millikin, K.: Refunctionalization at work. Science of Computer Programming 74(8), 534–549 (2009)
10. Danvy, O., Nielsen, L.R.: Refocusing in reduction semantics. Research Report BRICS RS-04-26, DAIMI, Department of Computer Science, University of Aarhus, Aarhus, Denmark (November 2004)
11. de Moura, A.L., Ierusalimschy, R.: Revisiting coroutines. ACM Trans. Program. Lang. Syst. 31(2), 1–31 (2009)
12. de Moura, A.L., Rodriguez, N., Ierusalimschy, R.: Coroutines in Lua. Journal of Universal Computer Science 10, 925 (2004)
13. Friedman, D.P., Wand, M.: Essentials of Programming Languages, 3rd edn. MIT Press, McGraw-Hill (2008)
14. Haynes, C.T., Friedman, D.P., Wand, M.: Continuations and coroutines. In: ACM Conference on Lisp and Functional Programming, pp. 293–298 (1984)
15. Kiselyov, O.: Delimited control in OCaml, abstractly and concretely: System description. In: Blume, M., Kobayashi, N., Vidal, G. (eds.) FLOPS 2010. LNCS, vol. 6009, pp. 304–320. Springer, Heidelberg (2010)
16. Marlin, C.D.: Coroutines: a programming methodology, a language design and an implementation. Springer, Heidelberg (1980)
17. Microsoft Corp. C# Version 2.0 Specification (2005), `http://msdn.microsoft.com/en-US/library/618ayhy6v=VS.80.aspx`
18. Pierce, B.C.: Types and Programming Languages. MIT Press, Cambridge (2002)
19. Thiemann, P.: Combinators for program generation. J. Funct. Program. 9(5), 483–525 (1999)
20. Van Rossum, G., Eby, P.: PEP 342 – coroutines via enhanced generators (2005), `http://www.python.org/dev/peps/pep-0342/`
21. Wirth, N.: Programming in Modula-2. Springer, Heidelberg (1982)

Liberal Typing for Functional Logic Programs*

Francisco López-Fraguas, Enrique Martin-Martin, and Juan Rodríguez-Hortalá

Departamento de Sistemas Informáticos y Computación
Universidad Complutense de Madrid, Spain
fraguas@sip.ucm.es, emartinm@fdi.ucm.es, juanrh@fdi.ucm.es

Abstract. We propose a new type system for functional logic programming which is more liberal than the classical Damas-Milner usually adopted, but it is also restrictive enough to ensure type soundness. Starting from Damas-Milner typing of expressions we propose a new notion of well-typed program that adds support for type-indexed functions, existential types, opaque higher-order patterns and generic functions—as shown by an extensive collection of examples that illustrate the possibilities of our proposal. In the negative side, the types of functions must be declared, and therefore types are checked but not inferred. Another consequence is that parametricity is lost, although the impact of this flaw is limited as "free theorems" were already compromised in functional logic programming because of non-determinism.

Keywords: Type systems, functional logic programming, generic functions, type-indexed functions, existential types, higher-order patterns.

1 Introduction

Functional logic programming. Functional logic languages [9] like TOY [19] or Curry [10] have a strong resemblance to lazy functional languages like Haskell [13]. A remarkable difference is that functional logic programs (FLP) can be non-confluent, giving raise to so-called *non-deterministic functions*, for which a *call-time choice* semantics [6] is adopted. The following program is a simple example, using natural numbers given by the constructors z and s—we follow syntactic conventions of some functional logic languages where function and constructor names are lowercased, and variables are uppercased—and assuming a natural definition for *add*: $\{ f\, X \rightarrow X, f\, X \rightarrow s\, X, double\ X \rightarrow add\ X\ X \}$. Here, f is non-deterministic ($f\ z$ evaluates both to z and $s\ z$) and, according to call-time choice, $double\ (f\ z)$ evaluates to z and $s\ (s\ z)$ but not to $s\ z$. Operationally, call-time choice means that all copies of a non-deterministic subexpression ($f\ z$ in the example) created during reduction share the same value.

In the HO-CRWL[1] approach to FLP [7], followed by the TOY system, programs can use *HO-patterns* (essentially, partial applications of symbols to other

* This work has been partially supported by the Spanish projects TIN2008-06622-C03-01, S2009TIC-1465 and UCM-BSCH-GR58/08-910502.

[1] CRWL [6] stands for *Constructor Based Rewriting Logic*; HO-CRWL is a higher order extension of it.

K. Ueda (Ed.): APLAS 2010, LNCS 6461, pp. 80–96, 2010.

patterns) in left hand sides of function definitions. This corresponds to an *intensional* view of functions, i.e., different descriptions of the same 'extensional' function can be distinguished by the semantics. This is not an exoticism: it is known [18] that extensionality is not a valid principle within the combination of HO, non-determinism and call-time choice. It is also known that *HO-patterns* cause some bad interferences with types: [8] and [17] considered that problem, and this paper improves on those results.

All those aspects of FLP play a role in the paper, and Sect. 3 uses a formal setting according to that. However, most of the paper can be read from a functional programming perspective leaving aside the specificities of FLP.

Types, FLP and genericity. FLP languages are typed languages adopting classical Damas-Milner types [5]. However, their treatment of types is very simple, far away from the impressive set of possibilities offered by functional languages like Haskell: type and constructor classes, existential types, GADTs, generic programming, arbitrary-rank polymorphism ... Some exceptions to this fact are some preliminary proposals for type classes in FLP [23,20], where in particular a technical treatment of the type system is absent.

By the term *generic programming* we refer generically to any situation in which a program piece serves for a family of types instead of a single concrete type. Parametric polymorphism as provided by Damas-Milner system is probably the main contribution to genericity in the functional programming setting. However, in a sense it is 'too generic' and leaves out many functions which are generic by nature, like equality. Type classes [26] were invented to deal with those situations. Some further developments of the idea of generic programming [11] are based on type classes, while others [12] have preferred to use simpler extensions of Damas-Milner system, such as GADTs [3,25]. We propose a modification of Damas-Milner type system that accepts natural definitions of intrinsically generic functions like equality. The following example illustrates the main points of our approach.

An introductory example. Consider a program that manipulates Peano natural numbers, booleans and polymorphic lists. Programming a function *size* to compute the number of constructor occurrences in its argument is an easy task in a type-free language with functional syntax:

$$\begin{array}{ll} size\ true \rightarrow s\ z & size\ false \rightarrow s\ z \\ size\ z \rightarrow s\ z & size\ (s\ X) \rightarrow s\ (size\ X) \\ size\ nil \rightarrow s\ z & size\ (cons\ X\ Xs) \rightarrow s\ (add\ (size\ X)\ (size\ Xs)) \end{array}$$

However, as far as *bool*, *nat* and $[\alpha]$ are different types, this program would be rejected as ill-typed in a language using Damas-Milner system, since we obtain contradictory types for different rules of *size*. This is a typical case where one wants some support for genericity. Type classes certainly solve the problem if you define a class *Sizeable* and declare *bool, nat* and $[\alpha]$ as instances of it. GADT-based solutions would add an explicit representation of types to the encoding of *size* converting it into a so-called *type-indexed* function [12]. This kind of encoding is also supported by our system (see the *show* function in

Ex. 1 and *eq* in Fig 4-b later), but the interesting point is that our approach allows also a simpler solution: the program above becomes well-typed in our system simply by declaring *size* to have the type $\forall\alpha.\alpha \rightarrow nat$, of which each rule of *size* gives a more concrete instance. A detailed discussion of the advantages and disadvantages of such liberal declarations appears in Sect. 6 (see also Sect. 4).

The proposed well-typedness criterion requires only a quite simple additional check over usual type inference for expressions, but here 'simple' does not mean 'naive'. Imposing the type of each function rule to be an instance of the declared type is a too weak requirement, leading easily to type unsafety. As an example, consider the rule $f\ X \rightarrow not\ X$ with the assumptions $f : \forall\alpha.\alpha \rightarrow bool$, $not : bool \rightarrow bool$. The type of the rule is $bool \rightarrow bool$, which is an instance of the type declared for f. However, that rule does not preserve the type: the expression $f\ z$ is well-typed according to f's declared type, but reduces to the ill-typed expression $not\ z$. Our notion of well-typedness, roughly explained, requires also that right-hand sides of rules do not restrict the types of variables more than left-hand sides, a condition that is violated in the rule for f above. Def. 1 in Sect. 3.3 states that point with precision, and allows us to prove type soundness for our system.

Contributions. We give now a list of the main contributions of our work, presenting the structure of the paper at the same time:

- After some preliminaries, in Sect. 3 we present a novel notion of well-typed program for FLP that induces a simple and direct way of programming type-indexed and generic functions. The approach supports also existential types, opaque HO-patterns and GADT-like encodings, not available in current FLP systems.
- Sect. 4 is devoted to the properties of our type system. We prove that well-typed programs enjoy *type preservation*, an essential property for a type system; then by introducing *failure* rules to the formal operational calculus, we also are able to ensure the *progress* property of well-typed expressions. Based on those results we state type soundness. Complete proofs can be found in [16].
- In Sect. 5 we give a significant collection of examples showing the interest of the proposal. These examples cover type-indexed functions, existential types, opaque higher-order patterns and generic functions. None of them is supported by existing FLP systems.
- Our well-typedness criterion goes far beyond the solutions given in previous works [8,17] to type-unsoundness problems of the use of *HO-patterns* in function definitions. We can type equality, solving known problems of *opaque decomposition* [8] (Sect. 5.1) and, most remarkably, we can type the *apply* function appearing in the HO-to-FO translation used in standard FLP implementations (Sect. 5.2).
- Finally we discuss in Sect. 6 the strengths and weaknesses of our proposal, and we end up with some conclusions in Sect. 7.

2 Preliminaries

We assume a signature $\Sigma = CS \cup FS$, where CS and FS are two disjoint sets of *data constructor* and *function* symbols resp., all of them with associated arity. We write CS^n (resp. FS^n) for the set of constructor (function) symbols of arity n, and if a symbol h is in CS^n or FS^n we write $ar(h) = n$. We consider a special constructor $\mathit{fail} \in CS^0$ to represent pattern matching failure in programs as it is proposed for GADTs [3,24]. We also assume a denumerable set $\mathcal{DV}$ of *data variables* X. Fig. 1 shows the syntax of *patterns* $\in Pat$—our notion of values—and *expressions* $\in Exp$. We split the set of patterns in two: *first order patterns* $FOPat \ni fot ::= X \mid c\ fot_1 \ldots fot_n$ where $ar(c) = n$, and *higher order patterns* $HOPat = Pat \smallsetminus FOPat$, i.e., patterns containing some partial application of a symbol of the signature. Expressions $c\ e_1 \ldots e_n$ are called *junk* if $n > ar(c)$ and $c \neq \mathit{fail}$, and expressions $f\ e_1 \ldots e_n$ are called *active* if $n \geq ar(f)$. The set of *free variables* of an expression—$fv(e)$—is defined in the usual way. Notice that since our let expressions do not support recursive definitions the binding of the variable only affect e_2: $fv(let\ X = e_1\ in\ e_2) = fv(e_1) \cup (fv(e_2) \smallsetminus \{X\})$. We say that an expression e is *ground* if $fv(e) = \emptyset$. A *one-hole context* is defined as $\mathcal{C} ::= [] \mid \mathcal{C}\ e \mid e\ \mathcal{C} \mid let\ X = \mathcal{C}\ in\ e \mid let\ X = e\ in\ \mathcal{C}$. A *data substitution* θ is a finite mapping from data variables to patterns: $[\overline{X_n/t_n}]$. Substitution application over data variables and expressions is defined in the usual way. The empty substitution is written as id. A *program rule* r is defined as $f\ \overline{t_n} \to e$ where the set of patterns $\overline{t_n}$ is linear (there is not repetition of variables), $ar(f) = n$ and $fv(e) \subseteq \bigcup_{i=1}^{n} var(t_i)$. Therefore, extra variables are not considered in this paper. The constructor *fail* is not supposed to occur in the rules, although it does not produce any technical problem. A program $\mathcal{P}$ is a set of program rules: $\{r_1, \ldots, r_n\}(n \geq 0)$.

For the types we assume a denumerable set $\mathcal{TV}$ of *type variables* α and a countable alphabet $\mathcal{TC} = \bigcup_{n \in \mathbb{N}} \mathcal{TC}^n$ of *type constructors* C. As before, if $C \in \mathcal{TC}^n$ then we write $ar(C) = n$. Fig. 1 shows the syntax of *simple types* and *type-schemes*. The set of *free type variables (ftv)* of a simple type τ is $var(\tau)$, and for type-schemes $ftv(\forall \overline{\alpha_n}.\tau) = ftv(\tau) \smallsetminus \{\overline{\alpha_n}\}$. We say a type-scheme σ is *closed* if $ftv(\sigma) = \emptyset$. A *set of assumptions* $\mathcal{A}$ is $\{\overline{s_n : \sigma_n}\}$, where $s_i \in CS \cup FS \cup \mathcal{DV}$. We require set of assumptions to be *coherent* wrt. CS, i.e., $\mathcal{A}(\mathit{fail}) = \forall \alpha.\alpha$ and for every c in $CS^n \smallsetminus \{\mathit{fail}\}$, $\mathcal{A}(c) = \forall \overline{\alpha}.\tau_1 \to \ldots \to \tau_n \to (C\ \tau'_1 \ldots \tau'_m)$ for some type constructor C with $ar(C) = m$. Therefore the assumptions for constructors must correspond to their arity and, as in [3,24], the constructor *fail* can have any type. The union of sets of assumptions is denoted by $\oplus$: $\mathcal{A} \oplus \mathcal{A}'$ contains all the assumptions in $\mathcal{A}'$ and the assumptions in $\mathcal{A}$ over symbols not appearing in $\mathcal{A}'$. For sets of assumptions $ftv(\{\overline{s_n : \sigma_n}\}) = \bigcup_{i=1}^{n} ftv(\sigma_i)$. Notice that type-schemes for data constructors may be existential, i.e., they can be of the form $\forall \overline{\alpha_n}.\overline{\tau} \to \tau'$ where $(\bigcup_{\tau_i \in \overline{\tau}} ftv(\tau_i)) \smallsetminus ftv(\tau') \neq \emptyset$. If $(s : \sigma) \in \mathcal{A}$ we write $\mathcal{A}(s) = \sigma$. A *type substitution* π is a finite mapping from type variables to simple types $[\overline{\alpha_n/\tau_n}]$. Application of type substitutions to simple types is defined in the natural way and for type-schemes consists in applying the substitution only to their free variables. This notion is extended to set of assumptions in the obvious way. We

Data variables	$X, Y, Z, \ldots$	Patterns	$t ::= X$
Type variables	$\alpha, \beta, \gamma, \ldots$		$\mid c\ t_1 \ldots t_n$ if $n \leq ar(c)$
Data constructors	c		$\mid f\ t_1 \ldots t_n$ if $n < ar(f)$
Type constructors	C	Simple Types	$\tau ::= \alpha$
Function symbols	f		$\mid C\ \tau_1 \ldots \tau_n$ if $ar(C) = n$
			$\mid \tau \rightarrow \tau$
Expressions	$e ::= X \mid c \mid f \mid e\ e$	Type Schemes	$\sigma ::= \forall \overline{\alpha_n}.\tau$
	$\mid$ *let* $X = e$ *in* e	Assumptions	$\mathcal{A} ::= \{s_1 : \sigma_1, \ldots, s_n : \sigma_n\}$
Symbol	$s ::= X \mid c \mid f$	Program rule	$r ::= f\ \overline{t} \rightarrow e$ ($\overline{t}$ linear)
Non variable symbol	$h ::= c \mid f$	Program	$\mathcal{P} ::= \{r_1, \ldots, r_n\}$
Data substitution	$\theta ::= [\overline{X_n/t_n}]$	Type substitution	$\pi ::= [\overline{\alpha_n/\tau_n}]$

Fig. 1. Syntax of expressions and programs

say σ is an *instance* of σ' if $\sigma = \sigma'\pi$ for some π. A simple type τ' is a *generic instance* of $\sigma = \forall\overline{\alpha_n}.\tau$, written $\sigma \succ \tau'$, if $\tau' = \tau[\overline{\alpha_n/\tau_n}]$ for some $\overline{\tau_n}$. Finally, τ' is a *variant* of $\sigma = \forall\overline{\alpha_n}.\tau$, written $\sigma \succ_{var} \tau'$, if $\tau' = \tau[\overline{\alpha_n/\beta_n}]$ and $\overline{\beta_n}$ are fresh type variables.

3 Formal Setup

3.1 Semantics

The operational semantics of our programs is based on *let*-rewriting [18], a high level notion of reduction step devised to express call-time choice. For this paper, we have extended *let*-rewriting with two rules for managing failure of pattern matching (Fig. 2), playing a role similar to the rules for pattern matching failures in GADTs [3,24]. We write $\rightarrow^{lf}$ for the extended relation and $\mathcal{P} \vdash e \rightarrow^{lf} e'$ ($\mathcal{P} \vdash e \twoheadrightarrow^{lf} e'$ resp.) to express one step (zero or more steps resp.) of $\rightarrow^{lf}$ using

(Fapp) $f\ t_1\theta \ldots t_n\theta \rightarrow^{lf} r\theta$, if $(f\ t_1 \ldots t_n \rightarrow r) \in \mathcal{P}$

(Ffail) $f\ t_1 \ldots t_n \rightarrow^{lf}$ *fail*, if $n = ar(f)$ and $\nexists (f\ t'_1 \ldots t'_n \rightarrow r) \in \mathcal{P}$ such that $f\ t'_1 \ldots t'_n$ and $f\ t_1 \ldots t_n$ unify

(FailP) *fail* $e \rightarrow^{lf}$ *fail*

(LetIn) $e_1\ e_2 \rightarrow^{lf}$ *let* $X = e_2$ *in* $e_1\ X$, if e_2 is junk, active, variable application or *let* rooted, for X fresh.

(Bind) *let* $X = t$ *in* $e \rightarrow^{lf} e[X/t]$

(Elim) *let* $X = e_1$ *in* $e_2 \rightarrow^{lf} e_2$, if $X \notin fv(e_2)$

(Flat) *let* $X =$ (*let* $Y = e_1$ *in* e_2) *in* $e_3 \rightarrow^{lf}$ *let* $Y = e_1$ *in* (*let* $X = e_2$ *in* e_3), if $Y \notin fv(e_3)$

(LetAp) (*let* $X = e_1$ *in* e_2) $e_3 \rightarrow^{lf}$ *let* $X = e_1$ *in* $e_2\ e_3$, if $X \notin fv(e_3)$

(Contx) $\mathcal{C}[e] \rightarrow^{lf} \mathcal{C}[e']$, if $\mathcal{C} \neq [\ ]$, $e \rightarrow^{lf} e'$ using any of the previous rules

Fig. 2. Higher Order *let*-rewriting relation with pattern matching failure $\rightarrow^{lf}$

the program $\mathcal{P}$. By $nf_{\mathcal{P}}(e)$ we denote the set of *normal forms* reachable from e, i.e., $nf_{\mathcal{P}}(e) = \{e' \mid \mathcal{P} \vdash e \twoheadrightarrow^{lf} e'$and e' is not $\rightarrow^{lf}$-reducible$\}$.

The new rule (Ffail) generates a failure when no program rule can be used to reduce a function application. Notice the use of unification instead of simple pattern matching to check that the variables of the expression will not be able to match the patterns in the rule. This allows us to perform this failure test locally without having to consider the possible bindings for the free variables in the expression caused by the surrounding context. Otherwise, these should be checked in an additional condition for (Contx). Consider for instance the program $\mathcal{P}_1 = \{true \wedge X \rightarrow X, false \wedge X \rightarrow false\}$ and the expression $let\ Y = true\ in\ (Y \wedge true)$. The application $Y \wedge true$ unifies with the function rule left-hand side $true \wedge X$, so no failure is generated. If we use pattern matching as condition, a failure is incorrectly generated since neither $true \wedge X$ nor $false \wedge X$ match with $Y \wedge true$.

Finally, rule (FailP) is used to propagate the pattern matching failure when *fail* is applied to another expression.

Notice that with the new rules (Ffail) and (FailP) there are still some expressions whose evaluation can get stuck, as happens with *junk expressions* like $true\ z$. As we will see in Sect. 4, this can only happen to ill-typed expressions. We will further discuss there the issues of *fail*-ended and stuck reductions.

3.2 Type Derivation and Inference for Expressions

Both derivation and inference rules are based on those presented in [17]. Our type derivation rules for expressions (Fig. 3-a) correspond to the well-known variation of Damas-Milner's [5] type system with syntax-directed rules, so there is nothing essentially new here—the novelty will come from the notion of well-typed program. $Gen(\tau, \mathcal{A})$ is the closure or generalization of τ wrt. $\mathcal{A}$, which generalizes all the type variables of τ that do not appear free in $\mathcal{A}$. Formally: $Gen(\tau, \mathcal{A}) = \forall\overline{\alpha_n}.\tau\ where\ \{\overline{\alpha_n}\} = ftv(\tau) \setminus ftv(\mathcal{A})$. We say that e is well-typed under $\mathcal{A}$, written $wt_{\mathcal{A}}(e)$, if there exists some τ such that $\mathcal{A} \vdash e : \tau$; otherwise it is ill-typed.

a) Type derivation rules	b) Type inference rules
[ID] $\dfrac{}{\mathcal{A} \vdash s : \tau}$ if $\mathcal{A}(s) \succ \tau$	[iID] $\dfrac{}{\mathcal{A} \Vdash s : \tau \vert id}$ if $\mathcal{A}(s) \succ_{var} \tau$
[APP] $\dfrac{\mathcal{A} \vdash e_1 : \tau_1 \rightarrow \tau \quad \mathcal{A} \vdash e_2 : \tau_1}{\mathcal{A} \vdash e_1\ e_2 : \tau}$	[iAPP] $\dfrac{\mathcal{A} \Vdash e_1 : \tau_1 \vert \pi_1 \quad \mathcal{A}\pi_1 \Vdash e_2 : \tau_2 \vert \pi_2}{\mathcal{A} \Vdash e_1\ e_2 : \alpha\pi \vert \pi_1\pi_2\pi}$ if $\alpha\ fresh\ \wedge$ $\pi = mgu(\tau_1\pi_2, \tau_2 \rightarrow \alpha)$
[LET] $\dfrac{\mathcal{A} \vdash e_1 : \tau_X \quad \mathcal{A} \oplus \{X : Gen(\tau_X, \mathcal{A})\} \vdash e_2 : \tau}{\mathcal{A} \vdash \mathbf{let}\ X = e_1\ \mathbf{in}\ e_2 : \tau}$	[iLET] $\dfrac{\mathcal{A} \Vdash e_1 : \tau_X \vert \pi_X \quad \mathcal{A}\pi_X \oplus \{X : Gen(\tau_X, \mathcal{A}\pi_X)\} \Vdash e_2 : \tau \vert \pi}{\mathcal{A} \Vdash \mathbf{let}\ X = e_1\ \mathbf{in}\ e_2 : \tau \vert \pi_X\pi}$

Fig. 3. Type system

The type inference algorithm $\Vdash$ (Fig. 3-b) follows the same ideas as the algorithm $\mathcal{W}$ [5]. We have given the type inference a relational style to show the similarities with the typing rules. Nevertheless, the inference rules represent an algorithm that fails if no rule can be applied. This algorithm accepts a set of assumptions $\mathcal{A}$ and an expression e, and returns a simple type τ and a type substitution π. Intuitively, τ is the "most general" type which can be given to e, and π is the "most general" substitution we have to apply to $\mathcal{A}$ for deriving any type for e.

3.3 Well-Typed Programs

The next definition—the most important in the paper—establishes the conditions that a program must fulfil to be well-typed in our proposal:

Definition 1 (Well-typed program wrt. $\mathcal{A}$). *The program rule* $f\ t_1 \ldots t_m \to e$ *is* well-typed *wrt. a set of assumptions* $\mathcal{A}$*, written* $wt_{\mathcal{A}}(f\ t_1 \ldots t_m \to e)$*, iff:*

i) $\mathcal{A} \oplus \{\overline{X_n : \alpha_n}\} \Vdash f\ t_1 \ldots t_m : \tau_L | \pi_L$
ii) $\mathcal{A} \oplus \{\overline{X_n : \beta_n}\} \Vdash e : \tau_R | \pi_R$
iii) $\exists \pi.(\tau_L, \overline{\alpha_n \pi_L}) = (\tau_R, \overline{\beta_n \pi_R})\pi$
iv) $\mathcal{A}\pi_L = \mathcal{A}$, $\mathcal{A}\pi_R = \mathcal{A}$, $\mathcal{A}\pi = \mathcal{A}$

where $\{\overline{X_n}\} = var(f\ t_1 \ldots t_m)$ *and* $\{\overline{\alpha_n}\}, \{\overline{\beta_n}\}$ *are fresh type variables. A program* $\mathcal{P}$ *is well-typed wrt.* $\mathcal{A}$*, written* $wt_{\mathcal{A}}(\mathcal{P})$*, iff all its rules are well-typed.*

The first two points check that both right and left hand sides of the rule can have a valid type assigning *some* types for the variables. Furthermore, it obtains the most general types for those variables in both sides. The third point is the most important. It checks that the obtained most general types for the right-hand side and the variables appearing in it are more general than the ones for the left-hand side. This fact guarantees the *type preservation* property (i.e., the expression resulting after a reduction step has the same type as the original one) when applying a program rule. Moreover, this point ensures a correct management of both *skolem* constructors [14] and *opaque variables* [17], either introduced by the presence of existentially quantified constructors or higher order patterns. Finally, the last point guarantees that the set of assumptions is not modified by neither the type inference nor the matching substitution. In practice, this point holds trivially if type assumptions for program functions are closed, as it is usual.

The previous definition presents some similarities with the notion of *typeable* rewrite rule for Curryfied Term Rewriting Systems in [2]. In that paper the key condition is that the *principal type* for the left-hand side allows to derive the same type for the right-hand side. Besides, [2] considers intersection types and it does not provide an effective procedure to check well-typedness.

Example 1 (Well and ill-typed rules and expressions). Let us consider the following assumptions and program:

$\mathcal{A} \equiv \{$ $\mathbf{z} : nat,$ $\mathbf{s} : nat \to nat, \mathbf{true} : bool, \mathbf{false} : bool, \mathbf{cons} : \forall\alpha.\alpha \to [\alpha] \to [\alpha],$
$\mathbf{nil} : \forall\alpha.[\alpha],$ $\mathbf{rnat} : repr\ nat,$ $\mathbf{id} : \forall\alpha.\alpha \to \alpha,$ $\mathbf{snd} : \forall\alpha,\beta.\alpha \to \beta \to \beta,$
$\mathbf{unpack} : \forall\alpha,\beta.(\alpha \to \alpha) \to \beta, \mathbf{eq} : \forall\alpha.\alpha \to \alpha \to bool, \mathbf{showNat} : nat \to [char],$
$\mathbf{show} : \forall\alpha.repr\ \alpha \to \alpha \to [char],$ $\mathbf{f} : \forall\alpha.bool \to \alpha,$ $\mathbf{flist} : \forall\alpha.[\alpha] \to \alpha$ $\}$

$\mathcal{P} \equiv \{$ $id\ X \to X,$ $snd\ X\ Y \to Y,$ $unpack\ (snd\ X) \to X,$ $eq\ (s\ X)\ z \to false,$
$show\ rnat\ X \to showNat\ X,$ $f\ true \to z,$ $f\ true \to false,$
$flist\ (cons\ z\ nil) \to s\ z,$ $flist\ (cons\ true\ nil) \to false$ $\}$

The rules for the functions *id* and *snd* are well-typed. The function *unpack* is taken from [8] as a typical example of the type problems that HO-patterns can produce. According to Def. 1 the rule of *unpack* is not well-typed since the tuple $(\tau_L, \overline{\alpha_n \pi_L})$ inferred for the left-hand side is (γ, δ), which is not matched by the tuple (η, η) inferred as $(\tau_R, \overline{\beta_n \pi_R})$ for the right-hand side. This shows the problem of existential type variables that "escape" from the scope. If that rule was well-typed then type preservation could not be granted anymore—e.g. consider the step $unpack\ (snd\ true) \to^{lf} true$, where the type *nat* can be assigned to $unpack\ (snd\ true)$ but *true* can only have type *bool*. The rule for *eq* is well-typed because the tuple inferred for the right-hand side, $(bool, \gamma)$, matches the one inferred for the left-hand side, $(bool, nat)$. In the rule for *show* the inference obtains $([char], nat)$ for both sides of the rule, so it is well-typed.

The functions f and $flist$ show that our type system cannot be forced to accept an arbitrary function definition by generalizing its type assumption. For instance, the first rule for f is not well-typed since the type *nat* inferred for the right-hand side does not match γ, the type inferred for the left-hand side. The second rule for f is also ill-typed for a similar reason. If these rules were well-typed, type preservation would not hold: consider the step $f\ true \to^{lf} z$; $f\ true$ can have any type, in particular *bool*, but z can only have type *nat*. Concerning $flist$, its type assumption cannot be made more general for its first argument: it can be seen that there is no τ such that the rules for $flist$ remain well-typed under the assumption $flist : \forall\alpha.\alpha \to \tau$.

With the previous assumptions, expressions like $id\ z\ true$ or $snd\ z\ z\ true$ that lead to *junk* are ill-typed, since the symbols *id* and *snd* are applied to more expressions than the arity of their types. Notice also that although our type system accepts more expressions that may produce pattern matching failures than classical Damas-Milner, it still rejects some expressions presenting those situations. Examples of this are $flist\ z$ and $eq\ z\ true$, which are ill-typed since the type of the function prevents the existence of program rules that can be used to rewrite these expressions: $flist$ can only have rules treating lists as argument and *eq* can only have rules handling both arguments of the same type.

Def. 1 is based on the notion of type inference of expressions to stress the fact that it can be implemented easily. For each program rule, conditions *i)* and *ii)* use the algorithm of type inference for expressions, *iii)* is just matching, and *iv*) holds trivially in practice, as we have noticed before. A more declarative alternative to Def. 1 based on type derivations can be found in [16].

We encourage the reader to play with the implementation, made available as a web interface at `http://gpd.sip.ucm.es/LiberalTyping`

In [17] we extended Damas-Milner types with some extra control over HO-patterns, leading to another definition of well-typed programs (we write $wt^{old}_{\mathcal{A}}(\mathcal{P})$ for that). All valid programs in [17] are still valid:

Theorem 1. *If* $wt^{old}_{\mathcal{A}}(\mathcal{P})$ *then* $wt_{\mathcal{A}}(\mathcal{P})$.

To further appreciate the usefulness of the new notion with respect the old one, notice that all the examples in Sect. 5 are rejected as ill-typed by [17].

4 Properties of the Type System

We will follow two alternative approaches for proving type soundness of our system. First, we prove the theorems of *progress* and *type preservation* similar to those that play the main role in the type soundness proof for GADTs [3,24]. After that, we follow a syntactic approach similar to [28].

Theorem 2 (Progress). *If* $wt_{\mathcal{A}}(\mathcal{P})$, $wt_{\mathcal{A}}(e)$ *and* e *is ground, then either* e *is a pattern or* $\exists e'.\ \mathcal{P} \vdash e \to^{lf} e'$.

The *type preservation* result states that in well-typed programs reduction does not change types.

Theorem 3 (Type Preservation). *If* $wt_{\mathcal{A}}(\mathcal{P})$, $\mathcal{A} \vdash e : \tau$ *and* $\mathcal{P} \vdash e \to^{lf} e'$, *then* $\mathcal{A} \vdash e' : \tau$.

In order to follow a syntactic approach similar to [28] we need to define some properties about expressions:

Definition 2. *An expression e is* **stuck** *wrt. a program* $\mathcal{P}$ *if it is a normal form but not a pattern, and is* **faulty** *if it contains a* junk *subexpression.*

Faulty is a pure syntactic property that tries to overapproximate *stuck*. Not all faulty expressions are stuck. For example, $snd\ (z\ z)\ true \to^{lf} true$. However all faulty expressions are ill-typed:

Lemma 1 (Faulty Expressions are ill-typed). *If* e *is faulty then there is no* $\mathcal{A}$ *such that* $wt_{\mathcal{A}}(e)$.

The next theorem states that all finished reductions of well-typed ground expressions do not get stuck but end up in patterns of the same type as the original expression.

Theorem 4 (Syntactic Soundness). *If* $wt_{\mathcal{A}}(\mathcal{P})$, e *is ground and* $\mathcal{A} \vdash e : \tau$ *then: for all* $e' \in nf_{\mathcal{P}}(e)$, e' *is a pattern and* $\mathcal{A} \vdash e' : \tau$.

The following complementary result states that the evaluation of well-typed expressions does not pass through any faulty expression.

Theorem 5. *If* $wt_{\mathcal{A}}(\mathcal{P})$, $wt_{\mathcal{A}}(e)$ *and* e *is ground, then there is no* e' *such that* $\mathcal{P} \vdash e \twoheadrightarrow^{lf} e'$ *and* e' *is faulty.*

We discuss now the strength of our results.

- **Progress and type preservation:** In [22] Milner considered *'a value 'wrong', which corresponds to the detection of a failure at run-time'* to reach his famous lemma *'well-typed programs don't go wrong'*. For this to be true in languages with patterns, like Haskell or ours, not all run-time failures should be seen as wrong, as happens with definitions like *head (cons x xs)* $\rightarrow$ *x*, where there is no rule for *(head nil)*. Otherwise, progress does not hold and some well-typed expressions become stuck. A solution is considering a 'well-typed completion' of the program, adding a rule like *head nil* $\rightarrow$ *error* where *error* is a value accepting any type. With it, *(head nil)* reduces to *error* and is not wrong, but *(head true)*, which is ill-typed, is wrong and its reduction gets stuck. In our setting, completing definitions would be more complex because of HO-patterns that could lead to an infinite number of 'missing' cases. Our *failure* rules in Sect. 2 try to play a similar role. We prefer the word *fail* instead of *error* because, in contrast to FP systems where an attempt to evaluate *(head nil)* results in a run-time error, in FLP systems rather than an error this is a silent failure in a possible space of non-deterministic computations managed by backtracking. Admittedly, in our system the difference between 'wrong' and 'fail' is weaker from the point of view of reduction. Certainly, junk expressions are stuck but, for instance, *(head nil)* and *(head true)* both reduce to *fail*, instead of the ill-typed *(head true)* getting stuck. Since *fail* accepts all types, this might seem a point where ill-typedness comes in hiddenly and then magically disappear by the effect of reduction to *fail*. This cannot happen, however, because *type preservation* holds step-by-step, and then no reduction $e \rightarrow^* fail$ starting with a well-typed e can pass through the ill-typed *(head true)* as intermediate (sub)-expression.
- **Liberality:** In our system the risk of accepting as well-typed some expressions that one might prefer to reject at compile time is higher than in more restrictive languages. Consider the function *size* of Sect. 1. For any well-typed e, *size* e is also well-typed, even if e's type is not considered in the definition of *size*; for instance, *size (true,false)* is a well-typed expression reducing to *fail*. This is consistent with the liberality of our system, since the definition of *size* could perfectly have included a rule for computing sizes of pairs. Hence, for our system, this is a pattern matching failure similar to the case of *(head nil)*. This can be appreciated as a weakness, and is further discussed in Sect. 6 in connection to type classes and GADT's.
- **Syntactic soundness and faulty expressions:** Th. 4 and 5 are easy consequences of progress and type preservation. Th. 5 is indeed a weaker safety criterion, because our faulty expressions only capture the presence of junk, which by no means is the only source of ill-typedness. For instance, the expressions *(head true)* or *(eq true z)* are ill-typed but not faulty. Th. 5 says nothing about

them; it is type preservation who ensures that those expressions will not occur in any reduction starting in a well-typed expression. Still, Th. 5 contains no trivial information. Although checking the presence of junk is trivial (counting arguments suffices for it), the fact that a given expression will not become faulty during reduction is a typically undecidable property approximated by our type system. For example, consider g with type $\forall\alpha,\beta.(\alpha \to \beta) \to \alpha \to \beta$, defined as $g\ H\ X \to H\ X$. The expression *(g true false)* is not faulty but reduces to the faulty *(true false)*. Our type system avoids that because the non-faulty expression *(g true false)* is detected as ill-typed.

5 Examples

In this section we present some examples showing the flexibility achieved by our type system. They are written in two parts: a set of assumptions $\mathcal{A}$ over constructors and functions and a set of program rules $\mathcal{P}$. In the examples we consider the following initial set of assumptions:

$$\mathcal{A}_{basic} \equiv \{\mathbf{true}, \mathbf{false} : bool,\ \mathbf{z} : nat,\ \mathbf{s} : nat \to nat,\ \mathbf{cons} : \forall\alpha.\alpha \to [\alpha] \to [\alpha],\ \mathbf{nil} : \forall\alpha.[\alpha],\ \mathbf{pair} : \forall\alpha,\beta.\alpha \to \beta \to pair\ \alpha\ \beta,\ \mathbf{key} : \forall\alpha.\alpha \to (\alpha \to nat) \to key,\ \wedge, \vee : bool \to bool \to bool,\ \mathbf{snd} : \forall\alpha,\beta.\alpha \to \beta \to \beta, \}$$

5.1 Type-Indexed Functions

Type-indexed functions (in the sense appeared in [12]) are functions that have a particular definition for each type in a certain family. The function *size* of Sect. 1 is an example of such a function. A similar example is given in Fig. 4-a, containing the code for an equality function which only operates with booleans, natural numbers and pairs.

$\mathcal{A} \equiv \mathcal{A}_{basic} \oplus \{\mathbf{eq} : \forall\alpha.\alpha \to \alpha \to bool\}$

$\mathcal{P} \equiv \{$ $eq\ true\ true \to true,$
$eq\ true\ false \to false,$
$eq\ false\ true \to false,$
$eq\ false\ false \to true,$
$eq\ z\ z \to true,$
$eq\ z\ (s\ X) \to false,$
$eq\ (s\ X)\ z \to false,$
$eq\ (s\ X)\ (s\ Y) \to eq\ X\ Y,$
$eq\ (pair\ X_1\ Y_1)\ (pair\ X_2\ Y_2) \to (eq\ X_1\ X_2) \wedge (eq\ Y_1\ Y_2)\ \}$

a) Original program

$\mathcal{A} \equiv \mathcal{A}_{basic} \oplus$
$\{\ \mathbf{eq} : \forall\alpha.repr\ \alpha \to \alpha \to \alpha \to bool,$
$\mathbf{rbool} : repr\ bool, \mathbf{rnat} : repr\ nat,$
$\mathbf{rpair} : \forall\alpha,\beta.repr\ \alpha \to repr\ \beta \to repr\ (pair\ \alpha\ \beta)\ \}$

$\mathcal{P} \equiv \{$ $eq\ rbool\ true\ true \to true,$
$eq\ rbool\ true\ false \to false,$
$eq\ rbool\ false\ true \to false,$
$eq\ rbool\ false\ false \to true,$
$eq\ rnat\ z\ z \to true,$
$eq\ rnat\ z\ (s\ X) \to false,$
$eq\ rnat\ (s\ X)\ z \to false,$
$eq\ rnat\ (s\ X)\ (s\ Y) \to eq\ rnat\ X\ Y,$
$eq\ (rpair\ Ra\ Rb)\ (pair\ X_1\ Y_1)\ (pair\ X_2\ Y_2) \to (eq\ Ra\ X_1\ X_2) \wedge (eq\ Rb\ Y_1\ Y_2)\ \}$

b) Equality using GADTs

Fig. 4. Type-indexed equality

An interesting point is that we do not need a type representation as an extra argument of this function as we would need in a system using GADTs [3,12]. In these systems the pattern matching on the GADT induces a type refinement, allowing the rule to have a more specific type than the type of the function. In our case this flexibility resides in the notion of well-typed rule. Then a type representation is not necessary because the arguments of each rule of *eq* already force the type of the left-hand side and its variables to be more specific (or the same) than the inferred type for the right-hand side. The absence of type representations provides simplicity to rules and programs, since extra arguments imply that all functions using *eq* direct or indirectly must be extended to accept and pass these type representations. In contrast, our rules for *eq* (extended to cover all constructed types) are the standard rules defining strict equality that one can find in FLP papers (see e.g. [9]), but that cannot be written directly in existing systems like TOY or Curry, because they are ill-typed according to Damas-Milner types.

We stress also the fact that the program of Fig. 4-a would be rejected by systems supporting GADTs [3,25], while the encoding of equality using GADTs as type representations in Fig. 4-b is also accepted by our type system.

Another interesting point is that we can handle equality in a quite fine way, much more flexible than in TOY or Curry, where equality is a *built-in* that proceeds structurally as in Fig. 4-a. With our proposed type system programmers can define structural equality as in Fig. 4-a for some types, choose another behavior for others, and omitting the rules for the cases they do not want to handle. Moreover, the type system protects against unsafe definitions, as we explain now: it is known [8] that in the presence of HO-patterns[2] structural equality can lead to the problem of *opaque decomposition*. For example, consider the expression $eq\ (snd\ z)\ (snd\ true)$. It is well-typed, but after a decomposition step using the structural equality we obtain $eq\ z\ true$, which is ill-typed. Different solutions have been proposed [8], but all of them need fully type-annotated expressions at run time, which penalizes efficiency. With the proposed type system that overloading at run time is not necessary since this problem of opaque decomposition is handled statically at compile time: we simply cannot write equality rules leading to opaque decomposition, because they are rejected by the type system. This happens with the rule $eq\ (snd\ X)\ (snd\ Y) \to eq\ X\ Y$, which will produce the previous problematic step. It is rejected because the inferred type for the right-hand side and its variables X and Y is $(bool, \gamma, \gamma)$, which is more specific than the inferred in the left-hand side $(bool, \alpha, \beta)$.

5.2 Existential Types, Opacity and HO Patterns

Existential types [14] appear when type variables in the type of a constructor do not occur in the final type. For example the constructor $key : \forall\alpha.\alpha \to (\alpha \to nat) \to key$ has an existential type, since α does not appear in the final type *key*. In functional logic languages, however, HO-patterns can introduce the same

[2] This situation also appears with first order patterns containing data constructors with existential types.

opacity as constructors with existential type. A prototypical example is $snd\ X$: we know that X has some type, but we cannot know anything about it from the type $\beta \rightarrow \beta$ of the expression. In [17] a type system managing the opacity of HO-patterns is proposed. The program below shows how the system presented here generalizes [17], accepting functions that were rejected there (e.g. $idSnd$) and also supporting constructors with existential type (e.g. $getKey$):

$$\mathcal{A} \equiv \mathcal{A}_{basic} \oplus \{\ \mathbf{getKey} : key \rightarrow nat,\ \mathbf{idSnd} : \forall\alpha,\beta.(\alpha \rightarrow \alpha) \rightarrow (\beta \rightarrow \beta)\ \}$$
$$\mathcal{P} \equiv \{\ getKey\ (key\ X\ F) \rightarrow F\ X,\ idSnd\ (snd\ X) \rightarrow snd\ X\ \}$$

Another remarkable example is given by the well-known translation of higher-order programs to first-order programs often used as a stage of the compilation of functional logic programs (see e.g. [18,1]). In short, this translation introduces a new function symbol @ (‘*apply*’), adds calls to @ in some points in the program and appropriate rules for evaluating it. This latter aspect is interesting here, since the rules are not Damas-Milner typeable. The following program contains the @-rules (written in infix notation) for a concrete example with the constructors *z*, *s*, *nil*, *cons* and the functions *length*, *append* and *snd* with the usual types.

$$\begin{aligned}\mathcal{A} \equiv \mathcal{A}_{basic} \oplus \{\ & \mathbf{length} : \forall\alpha.[\alpha] \rightarrow nat, \mathbf{append} : \forall\alpha.[\alpha] \rightarrow [\alpha] \rightarrow [\alpha], \\ & \mathbf{add} : nat \rightarrow nat \rightarrow nat, @ : \forall\alpha,\beta.(\alpha \rightarrow \beta) \rightarrow \alpha \rightarrow \beta\ \}\end{aligned}$$

$$\begin{aligned}\mathcal{P} \equiv \{\ & s\ @\ X \rightarrow s\ X, cons\ @\ X \rightarrow cons\ X, (cons\ X)\ @\ Y \rightarrow cons\ X\ Y, \\ & append\ @\ X \rightarrow append\ X, (append\ X)\ @\ Y \rightarrow append\ X\ Y, \\ & snd\,@\,X \rightarrow snd\ X, (snd\ X)\,@\,Y \rightarrow snd\ X\ Y, length\,@\,X \rightarrow length\ X\ \}\end{aligned}$$

These rules use HO-patterns, which is a cause of rejection in most systems. Even if HO patterns were allowed, the rules for @ would be rejected by a Damas-Milner type system, no matter if extended to support existential types or GADTs. However using Def. 3.1 they are all well-typed, provided we declare @ to have the type $@ : \forall\alpha,\beta.(\alpha \rightarrow \beta) \rightarrow \alpha \rightarrow \beta$. Because of all this, the @-introduction stage of the FLP compilation process can be considered as a source to source transformation, instead of a hard-wired step.

5.3 Generic Functions

According to a strict view of genericity, the functions *size* and *eq* in Sect. 1 and 5.1 resp. are not truly generic. We have a definition for each type, instead of one ‘canonical’ definition to be used by each concrete type. However we can achieve this by introducing a ‘universal’ data type over which we define the function (we develop the idea for *size*), and then use it for concrete types via a conversion function.

This can be done by using GADTs to represent uniformly the applicative structure of expressions (for instance, the *spines* of [12]), by defining *size* over that uniform representations, and then applying it to concrete types via conversion functions. Again, we can also offer a similar but simpler alternative. A uniform representation of constructed data can be achieved with a data type *data univ* = *c nat [univ]* where the first argument of *c* is for numbering constructors, and the second one is the list of arguments of a constructor application. A universal *size* can be defined as *usize (c _ Xs)* $\rightarrow$ *s (sum (map usize Xs))* using some functions of Haskell's prelude. Now, a generic *size* can be defined as *size* $\rightarrow$ *usize* $\cdot$ *toU*, where *toU* is a conversion function with declared type *toU* : $\forall\alpha.\alpha \rightarrow$ *univ*

toU true $\rightarrow$ *c z []*	*toU false* $\rightarrow$ *c (s z) []*
toU z $\rightarrow$ *c* $(s^2\ z)$ *[]*	*toU (s X)* $\rightarrow$ *c* $(s^3\ z)$ *[toU X]*
toU [] $\rightarrow$ *c* $(s^4\ z)$ *[]*	*toU (X:Xs)* $\rightarrow$ *c* $(s^5\ z)$ *[toU X,toU Xs]*

(s^i abbreviates iterated *s*'s). This *toU* function uses the specific features of our system. It is interesting also to remark that in our system the truly generic rule *size* $\rightarrow$ *usize* $\cdot$ *toU* can coexist with the type-indexed rules for *size* of Sect. 1. This might be useful in practice: one can give specific, more efficient definitions for some concrete types, and a generic default case via *toU* conversion for other types[3].

Admittedly, the type *univ* has less representation power than the spines of [12], which could be a better option in more complex situations. Nevertheless, notice that the GADT-based encoding of spines is also valid in our system.

6 Discussion

We further discuss here some positive and negative aspects of our type system.

Simplicity. Our well-typedness condition, which adds only one simple check for each program rule to standard Damas-Milner inference, is much easier to integrate in existing FLP systems than, for instance, type classes (see [20] for some known problems for the latter).

Liberality (continued from Sect. 4). we recall the example of *size*, where our system accepts as well-typed *(size e)* for any well-typed *e*. Type classes impose more control: *size e* is only accepted if *e* has a type in the class *Sizeable*. There is a burden here: you need a class for each generic function, or at least for each range of types for which a generic function exists; therefore, the number of class instance declarations for a given type can be very high. GADTs are in the middle way. At a first sight, it seems that the types to which *size* can be applied are perfectly controlled because only *representable* types are permitted. The problem, as with classes, comes when considering other functions that are generic but for other ranges of types. Now, there are two options: either you enlarge the family of representable functions, facing up again the possibility of applying *size* to unwanted arguments, or you introduce a new family of representation types, which is a programming overhead, somehow against genericity.

[3] For this to be really practical in FLP systems, where there is not a 'first-fit' policy for pattern matching in case of overlapping rules, a specific syntactic construction for 'default rule' would be needed.

Need of type declarations. In contrast to Damas & Milner system, where principal types exist and can be inferred, our definition of well-typed program (Def. 1) assumes an explicit type declaration for each function. This happens also with other well-known type features, like polymorphic recursion, arbitrary-rank polymorphism or GADTs [3,25]. Moreover, programmers usually declare the types of functions as a way of documenting programs. Notice also that type inference for functions would be a difficult task since functions, unlike expressions, do not have *principal types*. Consider for instance the rule $not\ true \rightarrow false$. All the possible types for the *not* function are $\forall\alpha.\alpha \rightarrow \alpha$, $\forall\alpha.\alpha \rightarrow bool$ and $bool \rightarrow bool$ but none of them is most general.

Loss of parametricity. In [27] one of the most remarkable applications of type systems was developed. The main idea there is to derive "free theorems" about the equivalence of functional expressions by just using the types of some of its constituent functions. These equivalences express different distribution properties, based on Reynold's abstraction theorem there recasted as "the parametricity theorem", which basically exploits the fact that a function cannot inspect the values of argument subexpressions with a polymorphic variable as type. Parametricity was originally developed for the polymorphic λ-calculus, so free theorems have to be weakened with additional conditions in order to accomodate them to practical languages like Haskell, as their original formulations are false in the presence of unbounded recursion, partial functions or impure features like seq [27,13].

With our type system parametricity is lost, because functions are allowed to inspect any argument subexpression, as seen in the *size* function from page 81. This has a limited impact in the FLP setting, since it is known that non-determinism and narrowing—not treated in the present work but standard in FLP systems—not only breaks free theorems but also equational rules for concrete functions that hold for Haskell, like $(filter\ p) \circ (map\ h) \equiv (map\ h) \circ (filter\ (p \circ h))$ [4].

7 Conclusions

Starting from a simple type system, essentially Damas-Milners's one, we have proposed a new notion of well-typed functional logic program that exhibits interesting properties: simplicity; enough expressivity to achieve existential types or GADT-like encodings, and to open new possibilities to genericity; good formal properties (type soundness, protection against unsafe use of HO patterns). Regarding the practical interest of our work, we stress the fact that no existing FLP system supports any of the examples in Sect. 5, in particular the examples of the *equality*—where known problems of *opaque decomposition* [8] can be addressed—and *apply* functions, which play important roles in the FLP setting. Moreover, our work greatly improves our previous results [17] about safe uses of HO patterns. However, considering also the weaknesses discussed in Sect. 6 suggests that a good option in practice could be a partial adoption of our system, not attempting to replace standard type inference, type classes or GADTs, but rather complementing them.

We find suggestive to think of the following future scenario for our system TOY: a typical program will use standard type inference except for some concrete definitions where it is annotated that our new liberal system is adopted instead. In addition, adding type classes to the languages is highly desirable; then the programmer can choose the feature—ordinary types, classes, GADTs or our more direct generic functions—that best fits his needs of genericity and/or control in each specific situation. We have some preliminary work [21] exploring the use of our type-indexed functions to implement type classes in FLP, with some advantages over the classical dictionary-based technology.

Apart from the implementation work, to realize that vision will require further developments of our present work:

- A precise specification of how to mix different typing conditions in the same program and how to translate type classes into our generic functions.
- Despite of the lack of principal types, some work on type inference can be done, in the spirit of [25].
- Combining our genericity with the existence of modules could require adopting *open* types and functions [15].
- Narrowing, which poses specific problems to types, should be also considered.

Acknowledgments. We thank Philip Wadler and the rest of reviewers for their stimulating criticisms and comments.

References

1. Antoy, S., Tolmach, A.P.: Typed higher-order narrowing without higher-order strategies. In: Middeldorp, A. (ed.) FLOPS 1999. LNCS, vol. 1722, pp. 335–353. Springer, Heidelberg (1999)
2. van Bakel, S., Fernández, M.: Normalization Results for Typeable Rewrite Systems. Information and Computation 133(2), 73–116 (1997)
3. Cheney, J., Hinze, R.: First-class phantom types. Tech. Rep. TR2003-1901, Cornell University (2003)
4. Christiansen, J., Seidel, D., Voigtländer, J.: Free theorems for functional logic programs. In: Proc. PLPV 2010, pp. 39–48. ACM, New York (2010)
5. Damas, L., Milner, R.: Principal type-schemes for functional programs. In: Proc. POPL 1982, pp. 207–212. ACM, New York (1982)
6. González-Moreno, J.C., Hortalá-González, T., López-Fraguas, F., Rodríguez-Artalejo, M.: An approach to declarative programming based on a rewriting logic. Journal of Logic Programming 40(1), 47–87 (1999)
7. González-Moreno, J., Hortalá-González, M., Rodríguez-Artalejo, M.: A higher order rewriting logic for functional logic programming. In: Hill, P.M., Warren, D.S. (eds.) Proc. ICLP 1997, pp. 153–167. MIT Press, Cambridge (1997)
8. Gonzalez-Moreno, J.C., Hortala-Gonzalez, M.T., Rodriguez-Artalejo, M.: Polymorphic types in functional logic programming. Journal of Functional and Logic Programming 2001(1) (2001)

9. Hanus, M.: Multi-paradigm declarative languages. In: Dahl, V., Niemelä, I. (eds.) ICLP 2007. LNCS, vol. 4670, pp. 45–75. Springer, Heidelberg (2007)
10. Hanus, M. (ed.): Curry: An integrated functional logic language, version 0.8.2 (2006), `http://www.informatik.uni-kiel.de/~curry/report.html`
11. Hinze, R.: Generics for the masses. J. Funct. Program. 16(4-5), 451–483 (2006)
12. Hinze, R., Löh, A.: Generic programming, now! In: Backhouse, R., Gibbons, J., Hinze, R., Jeuring, J. (eds.) SSDGP 2006. LNCS, vol. 4719, pp. 150–208. Springer, Heidelberg (2007)
13. Hudak, P., Hughes, J., Jones, S.P., Wadler, P.: A History of Haskell: being lazy with class. In: Proc. HOPL III, pp. 12-1–12-55. ACM, New York (2007)
14. Läufer, K., Odersky, M.: Polymorphic type inference and abstract data types. ACM Transactions on Programming Languages and Systems 16. ACM (1994)
15. Löh, A., Hinze, R.: Open data types and open functions. In: Proc. PPDP 2006, pp. 133–144. ACM, New York (2006)
16. López-Fraguas, F.J., Martin-Martin, E., Rodríguez-Hortalá, J.: Liberal Typing for Functional Logic Programs (long version). Tech. Rep. SIC-UCM, Universidad Complutense de Madrid (August 2010), `http://gpd.sip.ucm.es/enrique/publications/liberalTypingFLP/long.pdf`
17. López-Fraguas, F.J., Martin-Martin, E., Rodríguez-Hortalá, J.: New results on type systems for functional logic programming. In: Escobar, S. (ed.) Functional and Constraint Logic Programming. LNCS, vol. 5979, pp. 128–144. Springer, Heidelberg (2010)
18. López-Fraguas, F., Rodríguez-Hortalá, J., Sánchez-Hernández, J.: Rewriting and call-time choice: the HO case. In: Garrigue, J., Hermenegildo, M.V. (eds.) FLOPS 2008. LNCS, vol. 4989, pp. 147–162. Springer, Heidelberg (2008)
19. López-Fraguas, F., Sánchez-Hernández, J.: $\mathcal{TOY}$: A multiparadigm declarative system. In: Narendran, P., Rusinowitch, M. (eds.) RTA 1999. LNCS, vol. 1631, pp. 244–247. Springer, Heidelberg (1999)
20. Lux, W.: Adding haskell-style overloading to curry. In: Workshop of Working Group 2.1.4 of the German Computing Science Association GI, pp. 67–76 (2008)
21. Martin-Martin, E.: Implementing type classes using type-indexed functions. To appear in TPF 2010 (2010), `http://gpd.sip.ucm.es/enrique/publications/implementingTypeClasses/implementingTypeClasses.pdf`
22. Milner, R.: A theory of type polymorphism in programming. Journal of Computer and System Sciences 17, 348–375 (1978)
23. Moreno-Navarro, J.J., Mariño, J., del Pozo-Pietro, A., Herranz-Nieva, Á., García-Martín, J.: Adding type classes to functional-logic languages. In: Proc. APPIA-GULP-PRODE 1996, pp. 427–438 (1996)
24. Peyton Jones, S., Vytiniotis, D., Weirich, S.: Simple unification-based type inference for GADTs. Tech. Rep. MS-CIS-05-22, Univ. Pennsylvania (2006)
25. Schrijvers, T., Peyton Jones, S., Sulzmann, M., Vytiniotis, D.: Complete and decidable type inference for GADTs. In: Proc. ICFP 2009, pp. 341–352. ACM, New York (2009)
26. Wadler, P., Blott, S.: How to make ad-hoc polymorphism less ad hoc. In: Proc. POPL 1989, pp. 60–76. ACM, New York (1989)
27. Wadler, P.: Theorems for free! In: Proc. FPCA 1989, pp. 347–359. ACM, New York (1989)
28. Wright, A.K., Felleisen, M.: A Syntactic Approach to Type Soundness. Information and Computation 115, 38–94 (1992)

A Provably Correct Stackless Intermediate Representation for Java Bytecode

Delphine Demange[1], Thomas Jensen[2], and David Pichardie[2]

[1] ENS Cachan Antenne de Bretagne / IRISA, France
[2] INRIA, Centre Rennes - Bretagne Atlantique, Rennes, France

Abstract. The Java virtual machine executes stack-based bytecode. The intensive use of an operand stack has been identified as a major obstacle for static analysis and it is now common for static analysis tools to manipulate a stackless intermediate representation (IR) of bytecode programs. This paper provides such a bytecode transformation, describes its semantic correctness and evaluates its performance. We provide the semantic foundations for proving that an initial program and its IR behave similarly, in particular with respect to object creation and throwing of exceptions. The correctness of this transformation is proved with respect to a relation on execution traces taking into account that the object allocation order is not preserved by the transformation.

1 Introduction

Several optimization and analysis tools for Java bytecode work on an *intermediate representation* (IR) of the bytecode that makes analyses simpler [3,14]. Using such transformations may simplify the work of the analyser but the overall correctness of the analysis now becomes dependent on the semantics-preserving properties of the transformation. Semantic correctness is particularly crucial when an analysis forms part of the security defense line, as is the case with Java's bytecode verifier (BCV). Surprisingly, the semantic foundations of these bytecode transformations have received little attention. The contribution of this paper is to propose a transformation which at the same time is efficient (in terms of transformation time and produced code) and has a formal correctness proof. The long-term goal motivating this work is to provide a transformation that can be used to integrate other static analyses into an "extended bytecode verifier" akin to the stack map-based lightweight bytecode verifier proposed by Rose [11]. For this to work, the transformation must be efficient so a requirement to our transformation algorithm is that it must work in one pass over the bytecode.

This paper provides a semantically sound, provably correct transformation of bytecode into an intermediate representation (IR). We address in this work three key language features that make a provably correct transformation challenging.

Operand Stack. The Java virtual machine (JVM) is stack-based and the intensive use of the operand stack may make it difficult to adapt standard static analysis techniques that have been first designed for more standard (variable-based) 3-address codes. As noticed by Logozzo and Fähndrich [8], a naive translation from a stack-based code to

K. Ueda (Ed.): APLAS 2010, LNCS 6461, pp. 97–113, 2010.

3-address code may result in an explosion of temporary variables, which in turn may dramatically affect the precision of non-relational static analyses (such as intervals) and render some of the more costly analyses (such as polyhedral analysis) infeasible. The current transformation keeps the number of extra temporary variables at a reasonable level without using auxiliary iterated analyses such as copy propagation.

Splitted Object Creation. The object creation scheme of the JVM is another feature which is difficult to track because it is done in two distinct steps: (i) raw object allocation and (ii) constructor call. References to uninitialized objects are frequently pushed and duplicated on the operand stack, which makes it difficult for an analysis to recover this sequence of actions. The BCV not only enforces type safety of bytecode programs but also a complex object initialization property: an object cannot be used before an adequate constructor has been called on it. The BCV verifies this by tracking aliases of uninitialized objects in the operand stack, but this valuable alias information is lost for subsequent static analyses. The present transformation rebuilds the initialization chain of an object with the instruction `x := new C(arg1, arg2, ...)`. This specific feature puts new constraints on the formalization because object allocation order is no longer preserved.

Exception Throwing Order. A last difficulty for such a bytecode transformation is the wealth of dynamic checks used to ensure intrinsic properties of the Java execution model, such as absence of null-pointer dereferencings, out-of-bounds array accesses, *etc.* The consequence is that many instructions may raise different kinds of exception and any sound transformation must take care to preserve the exception throwing order.

Illustrating Example. Figure 1 presents an example program illustrating these issues. For more readability, we will also refer to Figure 1(a) that gives the corresponding Java source code. Its corresponding bytecode version (Figure 1(c)) shows the JVM object initialization scheme: an expression `new A()` is compiled to the sequence of lines [5; 6; 7]. A new object of class `A` is first allocated in the heap and its address is pushed on top of the operand stack. The address is then duplicated on the stack by the instruction dup and the non-virtual method `A()` is called, consuming the top of the stack. The copy is left on

```
B f(int x, int y) {
  return(new B(x/y, new A()));
}
```

(a) source function

```
B f(x, y);
  0 : t1 := new A();
  1 : t2 := new B(x/y, t1);
  2 : vreturn t2;
```

(b) BIR function (not semantics-preserving)

```
B f(x, y);
  0 : new B
  1 : dup
  2 : load y
  3 : load x
  4 : div
  5 : new A
  6 : dup
  7 : constructor A
  8 : constructor B
  9 : vreturn
```

(c) BC function

```
B f(x, y);
  0 : mayinit B;
  1 : nop;
  2 : nop;
  3 : nop;
  4 : notzero y;
  5 : mayinit A;
  6 : nop;
  7 : t1 := new A();
  8 : t2 := new B(x/y, t1);
  9 : vreturn t2;
```

(d) BIR function (semantics preserving)

Fig. 1. Example of source code, bytecode and two possible transformations

the top of the stack and represents from now on an *initialized* object. This initialization by side-effect is particularly challenging for the BCV [6] which has to keep track of the alias between uninitialized references on the stack. Using a similar approach, we are able to *fold* the two instructions of object allocation and constructor call into a single IR instruction. Figure 1(b) shows a first attempt of such a fusion. However, in this example, side-effect free expressions are generated in a naive way which *changes the semantics* in several ways. First, the program does not respect the *allocation order*. This is unavoidable if we want to keep side-effect free expressions and still re-build object constructions. The allocation order may have a functional impact because of the static initializer `A.⟨clinit⟩` that may be called when reaching an instruction `new A`. In Figure 1(b) this order is not preserved since `A.⟨clinit⟩` may be called before `B.⟨clinit⟩` while the bytecode program follows an inverse order. In Figure 1(d) this problem is solved using a specific instruction `mayinit A` that makes explicit the potential call to a static initializer. The second major semantic problem of the program in Figure 1(b) is that it does not respect the *exception throwing order* of the bytecode version. In Figure 1(b) the call to `A()` may appear before the `DivByZero` exception may be raised when evaluating `x/y`. The program in Figure 1(d) solves this problem using a specific instruction `notzero y` that explicitly checks if `y` is non-zero and raises a `DivByZero` exception if this is not the case.

The algorithm presented in Section 3 and proved correct in Section 4 takes care of these pitfalls. The input (BC) and IR (BIR) languages are presented in Section 2. The transformation demands that input programs pass the BCV and use uninitialized objects in a slightly restricted way (see Section 3). Our algorithm uses the technique of symbolic execution of the input code, which allows dealing simultaneously with the aforesaid challenges, while the main alternative techniques, briefly overviewed in Section 5, proceed in at least two distinct phases on the code: naive code is first generated, it is then optimized in a second phase, using traditional compiler optimization techniques. We believe the symbolic execution scheme gives rise to a rather elegant correctness proof, compared to the one we would obtain by combining correctness proofs of separate phases. This transformation has been implemented for the full Java bytecode language (meeting the same requirements), as part of the SAWJA[1] static analysis framework. Its experimental evaluation [5] of this transformation shows it competes well with other state-of-the-art bytecode transformation tools.

2 Source and Target Languages

Our source language BC is an untyped stack-based Java-like bytecode language with object construction, exceptions and virtual calls. In the formalization part of this work, the main missing feature is multi-threading. Other missing features, e.g. 64 bits values, static elements (static fields and static methods) or method overloading would make the current formalization heavier but do not introduce any new difficulties. The set of bytecodes we consider is given in Figure 2. They are familiar Java bytecodes and will not be explained. In order for the transformation to succeed, additional structural constraints on the bytecode must be satisfied. They are described in the dedicated paragraph *Relative BCV-Completeness* (Section 3).

[1] `http://sawja.inria.fr/`

$\mathbb{C}$ ::= *class names* :	*tvar* ::= *temporary variables:*
C | ...	t | t_1 | t_2 | ...
$\mathbb{F}$ ::= *field names* :	var_{BIR} ::= BIR *variables* :
f | ...	var_{BC} | *tvar*
$\mathbb{M}$ ::= *method names* :	*expr* ::= *side-effect free expressions:*
m | ...	c | null | var_{BIR}
var_{BC} ::= BC *variables* :	| *expr*+*expr* | *expr*/*expr* | *expr*.f
x | x_1 | x_2 | ... this	$instr_{BIR}$ ::= BIR *instructions* :
$instr_{BC}$ ::= BC *instructions* :	nop | mayinit C
nop | push c | pop | dup | add | div	| notnull *expr* | notzero *expr*
| load var_{BC} | store var_{BC}	| var_{BIR}:=*expr* | *expr*.f :=*expr*
| new C | constructor C	| var_{BIR}:= new C(*expr*, ..., *expr*)
| getfield f | putfield f	| *expr*.super (C, *expr*, ..., *expr*)
| invokevirtual C.m	| var_{BIR}:=*expr*.m(C, *expr*, ..., *expr*)
| if pc | goto pc	| *expr*.m(C, *expr*, ..., *expr*)
| vreturn | return	| if *expr* pc | goto pc
	| vreturn *expr* | return

Fig. 2. Instructions of BC and BIR

The BIR target language (Figure 2) provides expressions and instructions for variable and field assignments. BIR distinguishes two kinds of variables: local variables in var_{BC} are identifiers already used at the BC level, while *tvar* is a set of fresh identifiers introduced in BIR. Like BC, BIR is unstructured. What BIR brings here is that conditional jumps now depend on structured expressions.

Object Creation and Initialization. The Java bytecode object creation scheme, as explained in Section 1, forces static analyses to deal with alias information between uninitialized references. But this precise work is already done by the BCV when checking for object initialization. Folding constructor calls into x := new C($e_1, \ldots e_n$) in BIR avoids this redundant task in later static analyses.

Another ambiguous feature of bytecode is that constructor C corresponds to either a constructor or a super-constructor call according to the initialization status of the receiver object. This kind of information is rather costly for static analyses if they need to distinguish both situations. BIR removes this ambiguity by providing a distinct super constructor call instruction (e.super(C′, e_1,. . . ,e_n), where C′ is the super class of C).

Explicit Checks and Class Initialization. The side-effect free expressions requirement sometimes forces the transformation to revert the expression evaluation order, and thus of the exception throwing order. The solution provided by BIR is to use assertions: instructions notzero e and notnull e respectively check if the expression e evaluates to zero or null and raise an exception if the check fails.[2] By the same token, we obtain that

[2] In our formalization, heaps are infinite. Dealing with finite heaps would require preserving OutOfMemory exceptions. BIR would need to be extended with an instruction checkheap C, generated when transforming the BC instruction new C and checking if the heap available space is sufficient to allocate a C object.

the BIR expression evaluation is error-free. As illustrated by the example in the Introduction (Figure 1), folded constructors and side-effect free expressions cause the object allocation order to be modified. Still, preserving the class initialization order must be taken care of, as static class initializers `C.⟨clinit⟩` impact the program semantics. The BIR extra instruction `mayinit C` solves this problem by calling `C.⟨clinit⟩` whenever it is required.

2.1 Semantic Domains of BC and BIR

Our goal is to express in the correctness of the BC2BIR transformation not only the input/output preservation. We want to be as precise as possible, i.e. all what is preserved by BC2BIR should be clearly stated in the theorem. BC and BIR semantics are designed to this end. Semantic domains are given in Figure 3.

One of the subtleties of BC2BIR is that, although the object allocation order is modified, it takes care of preserving a strong relation between objects allocated in the heap, as soon as their initialization has begun. Thus, we attach to objects, seen as functions from fields $\mathbb{F}$ to *Value*, an initialization tag $\in$ *InitTag*. This was first introduced by Freund and Mitchell in [6], but we adapt it to our purpose. Following the Java convention, an object allocated at point pc by `new C` is uninitialized (tagged $\widetilde{\mathtt{C}_{\mathtt{pc}}}$) as long as no constructor has been called on it; an object is tagged C either if its initialization is ongoing (all along the constructor call chain) or completed when the `Object` constructor is called. Note that, unlike [6], *InitTag* does not track intermediate initialization status, but this can be recovered from the observational trace semantics (Section 2.2).

A *normal execution state* consists of a heap, the current method, the next instruction to execute, and the local memory of the method (local variables and operand stack for BC, only local variables, but with more variable names for BIR). We do not model the usual call stack in execution states, but rely on a so-called mostly-small-step semantics (see Section 2.2). In the correctness theorem (Section 4), one BC step is matched by a sequence of BIR steps. The way we define BIR program points avoids awkwardness in this matching by tracking BIR instructions with a pair $(\mathtt{pc}, \ell) \in \mathbb{N} \times instr^*$. A *return state* is made of a heap and a returned value.

We also want the semantic preservation to deal with execution errors. We do not model exception catching in this work but it will not bring much difficulty thanks to the way we define *error states*. These include the method program point of the faulty

$$
\begin{array}{rlrl}
Value = & \mid (Num\ n),\ n \in \mathbb{Z} & InitTag = & \widetilde{\mathbb{C}_{\mathbb{N}}} \cup \mathbb{C} \\
 & \mid (Ref\ r),\ r \in Ref & Object = & (\mathbb{F} \to Value)_{InitTag} \\
 & \mid Null & Heap = & Ref \hookrightarrow Object \\
\overline{Value} = & Value \cup \{Void\} & Error = & \{\ \Omega^{NP}, \Omega^{DZ}\}
\end{array}
$$

$$
\begin{array}{ll}
Stack = Value^* \quad Env_{\mathrm{BC}} = var_{\mathrm{BC}} \hookrightarrow Value & Env_{\mathrm{BIR}} = var_{\mathrm{BIR}} \hookrightarrow Value \\
State_{\mathrm{BC}} = (Heap \times \mathbb{M} \times \mathbb{N} \times Env_{\mathrm{BC}} \times Stack) & State_{\mathrm{BIR}} = (Heap \times \mathbb{M} \times (\mathbb{N} \times instr^*_{\mathrm{BIR}}) \times Env_{\mathrm{BIR}}) \\
\quad \cup \left(Heap \times \overline{Value}\right) & \quad \cup \left(Heap \times \overline{Value}\right) \\
\quad \cup (Error \times \mathbb{M} \times \mathbb{N} \times Env_{\mathrm{BC}} \times Heap) & \quad \cup (Error \times \mathbb{M} \times \mathbb{N} \times Env_{\mathrm{BIR}} \times Heap)
\end{array}
$$

Fig. 3. BC and BIR semantic domains

$$\frac{\begin{array}{c} instrAt_P(m,pc) = \texttt{new C} \\ (Ref\ r) = newObject(C,h) \\ h' = h[r \mapsto (\lambda f.init(f))_t] \quad t = \widetilde{\texttt{C}}_{\texttt{pc}} \end{array}}{\langle h,m,pc,l,s\rangle \xrightarrow{mayinit(\texttt{C})}_0 \langle h',m,pc{+}1,l,(Ref\ r){::}s\rangle}$$

$$\frac{\begin{array}{c} instrAt_P(m,pc) = \texttt{constructor C} \\ V = v_1 :: \cdots :: v_n \quad h(r) = o_{\widetilde{\texttt{C}}_\texttt{j}} \quad h' = h[r \mapsto o_\texttt{C}] \\ \langle h', InitLState(\texttt{C.init}, (Ref\ r) :: V)\rangle \overset{\Lambda}{\Rightarrow}_n \langle h'', Void\rangle \end{array}}{\langle h,m,pc,l,V{::}(Ref\ r){::}s\rangle \xrightarrow{[r\leftarrow \texttt{C.init}(V)].\Lambda_h}_{n+1} \langle h'',m,pc{+}1,l,s\rangle}$$

Fig. 4. BC semantic rules for object allocation and initialization (excerpt)

instruction and the current context (heap and environment), and also keep track of the kind of error: division by zero (Ω^{DZ}) and null pointer dereferencing (Ω^{NP}). BC programs passing the BCV only get stuck in an error or return state of the main method.

2.2 Observational Semantics of BC and BIR

We achieve a fine-grained preservation criterion by using a mostly small-step operational semantics. Indeed, a correctness criterion only stating the preservation of returned values would not bring much information to static analyses dealing with intermediate program points. We push further this approach by labelling transitions with observable events, keeping track of all the program behavior aspects that are preserved by the transformation (even local variable assignments). Observable events are defined as *Evt*, the union of the following sets ($v, v_1, \ldots, v_n \in Value$, $r \in Ref$):

$EvtS ::= x \leftarrow v$ *(local assignment)*	$EvtH ::= r.f \leftarrow v$ *(field assignment)*
	$\mid mayinit(\texttt{C})$ *(class initializer)*
$EvtR ::= return(v)$ *(method return)*	$\mid r.\texttt{C.m}(v_1,\ldots,v_n)$ *(method call)*
$\mid return(Void)$	$\mid r \leftarrow \texttt{C.init}(v_1,\ldots,v_n)$ *(constructor)*
	$\mid r.\texttt{C.init}(v_1,\ldots,v_n)$ *(super constructor)*

Actions irrelevant to the correctness of the transformation are silent transitions labelled with τ. These include expression evaluation steps, as expressions are side-effect and error free. Note that, due to the modification of the object allocation order , the memory effect of the BC instruction new C is kept silent. This is harmless thanks to the strong restrictions imposed by the BCV on the use of uninitialized references [6].

$$\frac{\begin{array}{c} hd(\ell) = x{:=}\texttt{new C}\ (e_1,\ldots,e_n) \\ h,l \models e_i \Downarrow v_i \quad (Ref\ r) = newObject(C,h) \quad h' = h[r \mapsto (\lambda f.init(f))_\texttt{C}] \\ V = v_1 :: \cdots :: v_n \quad \langle h', InitLState(\texttt{C.init}, (Ref\ r) :: V)\rangle \overset{\Lambda}{\Rightarrow}_n \langle h'', Void\rangle \end{array}}{\langle h,m,(pc,\ell),l\rangle \xrightarrow{[r\leftarrow C.init(V)].\Lambda_h.[x\leftarrow (Ref\ r)]}_{n+1} \langle h'',(m,next(pc,\ell)),l[x \mapsto (Ref\ r)]\rangle}$$

Fig. 5. BIR semantic rule for object allocation and initialization (excerpt)

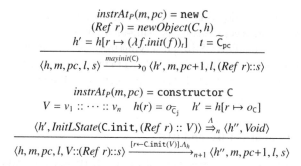

Program execution generates traces of events, which permit expressing sequences of events. We illustrate how event traces are managed intra and inter-procedurally with object allocation and initialization (Figures 4 for BC rules and Figure 5 for BIR rules).

In rule for `new C`, *newObject(C, h)* returns the reference (*Ref r*) freshly allocated in *h*. All object fields are set to their default values (zero for integers and *Null* for references) by the function *init* and the object tag is set to $\widetilde{\mathtt{C}}_{\mathtt{pc}}$, leading to the new heap h'. No "object allocation" event is observed. However, the class initialization order will be preserved[3]: observing *mayinit*(C) in the BC and BIR execution traces (when respectively executing `new C` and `mayinit C`) helps us proving this property. When executing `constructor C` on an object tagged with $\widetilde{\mathtt{C}}_{\mathtt{j}}$ (pointed to by (*Ref r*)), the method `C.init`[4] is entirely executed (in a mostly-small step style) starting from a heap h' where the object tag has been updated to C. The starting local memory *InitLState*(`C.init`, *args*) consists of an empty stack, and local registers (`this` for (*Ref r*) and others registers for arguments). The execution trace of `C.init` restricted to events in *EvtH*, denoted by Λ_h is then exported to the caller (as it contains events related to the heap, which is shared by methods) and appended to the event $r \leftarrow \mathtt{C.init}(V)$. We write $\stackrel{.}{\Rightarrow}$ for the transitive closure of the small-step relation $\stackrel{.}{\rightarrow}$.

In Section 4, we will rely on an inductive reasoning to prove the semantics preservation of the transformation. Therefore, we index transitions with a natural number counting the maximal execution call depth: it is zero whenever no method is called, and incremented each time a method is called.

3 Transformation Algorithm

In this section we describe the BC2BIR algorithm (given in Figure 7) for converting BC code into BIR code. A central feature of our algorithm is the use of a symbolic stack to decompile stack-oriented code into three-address code. In the following we explain how the symbolic stack is used in decompiling BC instructions and how it is managed at control flow join points. Another distinguishing feature of the algorithm is the merging of instructions for object allocation and initialization into one compound BIR instruction which is also performed quite elegantly thanks to the symbolic stack.

The core of the algorithm is the function $\mathrm{BC2BIR}_{instr}$ that maps a BC instruction into a list of BIR instructions and at the same time symbolically executes BC code using an abstract stack of symbolic expressions:

$$\mathrm{BC2BIR}_{instr} : \mathbb{N} \times instr_{\mathrm{BC}} \times AbstrStack \rightarrow \left(instr^*_{\mathrm{BIR}} \times AbstrStack\right) \cup Fail$$
$$AbstrStack = SymbExpr^* \qquad SymbExpr = expr \cup \{UR^{\mathtt{C}}_{\mathtt{pc}} \mid C \in \mathbb{C}, \mathtt{pc} \in \mathbb{N}\}$$

Expressions in *expr* are BC decompiled expressions and $UR^{\mathtt{C}}_{\mathtt{pc}}$ is a placeholder for a reference to an uninitialized object, allocated at point `pc` by the intruction `new C`. $\mathrm{BC2BIR}_{instr}$ is given in Figure 6, where $\mathtt{t}^{\mathtt{i}}_{\mathtt{pc}}$ denote fresh temporary variables introduced at point `pc`. A paragraph at the end of this section describes the failure cases.

---

[3] In order to lighten the formalization, `mayinit C` behaves in the present work as `nop` but raises a specific *mayinit*(C) event.

[4] `C.init` is the JVM conventional name for the C constructors.

Inputs		Outputs	
Instr	Stack	Instrs	Stack
nop	*as*	[nop]	*as*
pop	e::*as*	[nop]	*as*
push c	*as*	[nop]	c::*as*
dup	e::*as*	[nop]	e::e::*as*
load x	*as*	[nop]	x::*as*

Inputs		Outputs	
Instr	Stack	Instrs	Stack
if pc′	e::*as*	[if e pc′]	*as*
goto pc′	*as*	[goto pc′]	*as*
return	*as*	[return]	*as*
vreturn	e::*as*	[return e]	*as*

Inputs		Outputs	
Instr	Stack	Instrs	Stack
add	e_1::e_2::*as*	[nop]	$e_1 + e_2$::*as*
div	e_1::e_2::*as*	[notzero e_2]	e_1/e_2::*as*
new C	*as*	[mayinit C]	UR^{C}_{pc}::*as*
getfield f	e::*as*	[notnull e]	e.f::*as*

Inputs		Outputs		Cond
Instr	Stack	Instrs	Stack	
store x	e::*as*	[x := e]	*as*	$x \notin as$ [a]
		[t^{0}_{pc}:= x; x := e]	$as[t^{0}_{pc}/x]$	$x \in as$ [a]
putfield f	e′::e::*as*	[notnull e; *Fsave*(pc, f, *as*); e.f := e′]	$as[t^{i}_{pc}/e_i]$	[ab]
invokevirtual C.m	$e'_1 \dots e'_n$::e::*as*	[notnull e; *Hsave*(pc, as); t^{0}_{pc} := e.m($e'_1 \dots e'_n$)]	t^{0}_{pc}::$as[t^{j}_{pc}/e_j]$	value return [ac]
		[notnull e; *Hsave*(pc, as); e.m($e'_1 \dots e'_n$)]	$as[t^{j}_{pc}/e_j]$	*Void* return[ac]
constructor C	$e'_1 \dots e'_n$::e_0::*as*	[*Hsave*(pc, as); t^{0}_{pc} := new C($e'_1 \dots e'_n$)]	$as[t^{j}_{pc}/e_j]$	$e_0 = UR^{C}_{pc'}$ [c]
		[notnull e_0; *Hsave*(pc, as); e_0.super(C, $e'_1 \dots e'_n$)]	$as[t^{j}_{pc}/e_j]$	otherwise [a c]

Fig. 6. BC2BIR$_{instr}$ – Transformation of a BC instruction at pc

[a] where for all C and pc', $e \neq UR^{C}_{pc'}$

[b] where $e_i, i = 1 \dots n$ are all the elements of *as* such that $f \in e_i$

[c] where $e_j, j = 1 \dots m$ are all the elements of *as* that read a field

We now explain the main cases of BC2BIR$_{instr}$. For instruction `load x` , the symbolic expression x is pushed on the abstract stack *as* and the BIR instruction nop is generated. We generate nop to make the step-matching easier in the proof of the theorem. Transformations of return and jump instructions are straightforward. Before going into more technicality, we give a simple example of symbolic execution. Successively symbolically executing `load x` and `load y` will lead to the abstract stack y::x::ε. If add were the next instruction to transform, the abstract stack would become (x + y)::ε.

Transforming instructions `store` , `putfield` and `invokevirtual` follows the same principle. However, for semantics preservation issues, we must take care of their memory effect. Their execution might modify the value of local variables or object fields appearing in the expressions of the abstract stack, whose value would be erroneously modified by side effect. We tackle this subtlety by storing in temporary variables (of the form t^{i}_{pc}) each stack element whose value might be modified. In the case of `store x`, it is enough only remembering the old value of x. In the case of `putfield f`, all expressions in *as* accessing an f field are remembered: *Fsave*(pc, f, e_1::e_2::. . .::e_n) generates an assignment $t^{i}_{pc} := e_i$ for all e_i that reads at least once the field f. Finally, in the case of `invokevirtual`, we store the value of each expression accessing the heap, which could be modified by the callee execution: *Hsave*(pc, e_1::e_2::. . .::e_n) generates an assignment $t^{i}_{pc} := e_i$ for all e_i that reads a field.

Object creation and initialization require special attention as this is done by separate (and possibly distant) instructions. Symbolically executing new C at point pc pushes UR^{C}_{pc} (representing the freshly allocated reference) on the stack and generates `mayinit` C for class initialization whenever it is required. Instruction `constructor` C will be transformed differently whether it corresponds to a constructor or a super constructor call. Both cases are distinguished thanks to the symbolic expression on which it is called. We generate a BIR folded constructor call at point pc if the symbolic

```
1  function BC2BIR(P,m) =
2  AS_in[m,0] := nil
3  for (pc = 0, pc ≤ length(m), pc++) do
4    // Compute the entry abstract stack
5    if (pc ∈ jmpTgt^P_m) then
6      if (not C_UR(pc)) then fail end
7      AS_in[m,pc] := newStackJmp(pc, AS_in[m,pc])
8    end
9
10   // Decompile instruction
11   (AS_out[m,pc], code) := BC2BIR_instr(pc, instrAt_P(m,pc), AS_in[m,pc])
12   IR[m,pc] := TAssign(succ(pc) ∩ jmpTgt^P_m, AS_out[m,pc])++code
13
14   // Fail on a non-empty stack backward jump
15   if (AS_out[m,pc] ≠ nil ∧ ∃pc' ∈ succ(pc).pc > pc') then fail end
16
17   // Pass on the output abstract stack
18   if (pc + 1 ∈ succ(pc) ∧ pc + 1 ∉ jmpTgt^P_m) then AS_in[m,pc + 1] := AS_out[m,pc]  end
19 end
```

Fig. 7. BC2BIR – BC method transformation. $length(\mathtt{m})$ is the size of the code of method m, $succ(\mathtt{pc})$ the set of successors of pc in m, $stackSize(\mathtt{pc})$ the stack size at point pc and $jmpTgt^{\mathtt{P}}_{\mathtt{m}}$ the set of jump targets in m.

expression is $UR^{\mathtt{C}}_{\mathtt{pc'}}$ (and a super constructor call otherwise). $UR^{\mathtt{C}}_{\mathtt{pc}}$ are used to keep track of alias information between uninitialized references, when substituting them for the local variable receiving the new object. This mechanism is similar to what is used by the BCV to check for object initialization.

Transforming the whole code of a BC method is done by BC2BIR which (i) computes the entry abstract stack used by BC2BIR_{instr} to transform the instruction, (ii) performs the BIR generation and (iii) passes on the output abstract stack to the successor points. BC2BIR is given in Figure 7. It computes three arrays: IR[m] is the BIR version of the method m, $\mathtt{AS_{in}[m]}$ and $\mathtt{AS_{out}[m]}$ respectively contain the input and output symbolic stacks used by BC2BIR_{instr}.

Most of the time, the control flow is linear (from pc to only pc + 1). In this case, we only perform the BC2BIR_{instr} generation (Lines 11 and 12) and the abstract stack resulting from BC2BIR_{instr} is transmitted as it is (Line 18). The case of control flow joins must be handled more carefully. In a program passing the BCV, we know that at every join point, the size of the stack is the same regardless of the predecessor point. Still, the content of the abstract stack might change (when e.g. the two branches of a conditional compute two different expressions). But stack elements are expressions used in the generated instructions and hence must not depend on the control flow path. We illustrate this point with the example of Figure 8. This function returns 1 or -1, depending on whether the argument x is zero or not. We focus on program point 5, whose predecessors are points 3 and 4. The abstract stack after executing the instruction goto 5 is -1 (point 3 in Figure 8(c)), while it becomes 1 after program point 4. At point 5, depending on the control flow path, the abstract stack is thus not unique.

The idea is here to store, before reaching a join point, every stack element in a temporary variable and to use, at the join point, a *normalized* stack made of all these variables. A naming convention ensures that (i) identifiers are independent of the control flow and (ii) each variable denote the same stack element: we use the identifier $\mathtt{T}^{\mathtt{i}}_{\mathtt{pc}}$ to store the ith

```
int f(int x) {return (x == 0) ? 1 : -1;}
```
(a) source function

(b) BC function	(c) Symbolic stack	(d) BIR function
`int f(x);`		`int f(x);`
`0 : load x`	$0 : []$	`0 : nop;`
`1 : if 4`	$1 : [x]$	`1 : if x 4;`
`2 : push -1`	$2 : []$	`2 : nop;`
`3 : goto 5`	$3 : [-1]$	$3 : T^1_5$:= -1; goto 5;
`4 : push 1`	$4 : []$	4 : nop; T^1_5 := 1;
`5 : vreturn`	$5 : [T^1_5]$	5 : vreturn T^1_5;

Fig. 8. Example of bytecode transformation – jumps on non-empty stacks

element of the stack for a join point at pc. All T^i_{pc} are initialized when transforming a BC instruction preceeding a join point. In Figure 8(d), at points 3 and 4, we respectively store -1 and 1 in T^1_5, the top element of the entry stack at point 5.

In the algorithm, this is done at Line 12: we prepend to the code generated by BC2BIR$_{instr}$ the assignments of all abstract stack elements to the T^i_{jp}, for all join points jp successor of pc. These assignments are generated by $TAssign(S, as)$, where S is a set of program points. The restriction Line 15 ensures these assignments are conflict-free by making the transformation fail on non-empty stack backjumps. The function *newStackJmp*(jp, *as*) (Line 7) computes the normalized stack at join point jp. It returns a stack of T^i_{jp} except that UR^C_{pc} are preserved. We need here the following constraint $C_{UR}(\mathtt{jp})$ on $\mathtt{AS_{out}}$, that we check before computing the entry abstract stack (Line 6): $\forall i.\ (\exists pc' \in pred_m(\mathtt{jp}).\ \mathtt{AS_{out}}[m, pc']_i = UR^C_{pc_0}) \Rightarrow (\forall pc' \in pred_m(\mathtt{jp}).\ \mathtt{AS_{out}}[m, pc']_i = UR^C_{pc_0})$. It means that before a join point jp, if the stack contains any UR^C_{pc} at position i, then it is the case for all predecessors of $\mathtt{jp} \in jmpTgt^P_m$.

Relative BCV-Completeness. Every case undescribed in Figures 6 and 7 yields *Fail*. Most of them are ruled out by the BCV (e.g. stack height mismatch, or uninitialised reference field assignment) but few cases remain. First, this version of the algorithm fails on non-empty stack backjumps, but they are addressed in [5]. Finally, the present transformation puts restrictions on the manipulation of uninitialised locations in the operand stack and the local variables. Transforming `store x` requires that the top expression e is not UR^C_{pc} because no valid BIR instruction would match, as constructors are folded. For the same reason, we fail to transform bytecode that does not satisfy C_{UR}: this constraint allows us not to store UR^C_{pc} stack elements. Unfortunately these patterns are not ruled out by the JVM specification and we may reject programs that pass the BCV. However this is not a limitation in practice because such patterns are not used by standard compilers. Our transformation tool has been tested on the 609209 methods of the Eclipse distribution without encountering such cases [5].

4 Correctness

The BC2BIR algorithm satisfies a precise semantics preservation property that we formalize in this section: the BIR program BC2BIR(P) simulates the initial BC program

P and both have similar execution traces. This similarity cannot be a simple equality, because some variables have been introduced by the transformation and the object allocation order is modified by BC2BIR— both heaps do not keep equal along both program executions. We define in Section 4.1 what semantic relations make us able to precisely relate BC and BIR executions. Section 4.2 formally states the semantic preservation of BC2BIR. For space reason, we only provide a proof sketch. The complete proof is given in the accompanying report [5]. We lighten the notations from now and until the end of this section by writing a BC program P, its BIR version $P' = \text{BC2BIR}(P)$.

4.1 Semantic Relations

Heap Isomorphism. The transformation does not preserve the object allocation order. However, the two heaps stay isomorphic: there exists a partial bijection between them. For example, in P (Figure 1(c)), the `B` object is allocated before the `A` object is passed as an argument to the `B` constructor. In P' (Figure 1(d)), constructors are folded and object creation is not an expression, the `A` object must thus be created (and initialized) before passing $\mathtt{t}_1$ (containing its reference) as an argument to the `B` constructor.

Heaps are not equal along the execution of the two programs: after program point `5` in P, the heap contains two objects that are not yet in the heap of P'. However, after program points `7`, each use in P' of the `A` object is synchronized with a use in P of the reference pointing to the `A` object (both objects are initialized, so both references can be used). The same reasoning can be applied just after points `8` about the `B` objects. A bijection thus exists between references of both heaps. It relates references to allocated objects as soon as their initialization has begun. Along the executions of BC and BIR programs, it is extended accordingly on each constructor call starting the initialization of a new object. In Figure 1, given an initial partial bijection on the heaps domains, it is first extended at points `7` and then again at points `8`.

Semantic Relations. This heap isomorphism has to be taken into account when relating semantic domains and program executions. Thus, the semantic relations over values, heaps, environments, configurations and observable events (see Table 1) are parametrized by a bijection β defined on the heap domains.

When relating values, the interesting case is for references. Only references related by β are in the relation. The semantic relation on heaps is as follows. First, objects related by β are exactly those existing in both heaps and on which a constructor has been called. Secondly, the related objects must have the same initialization status (hence the same class) and their fields must have related values. Here we write $tag_h(r)$ for the tag t such that $h(r) = o_t$. A BIR environment is related to a BC environment if and only if both local variables have related values. Temporary variables are, as expected, not taken into account. Execution states are related through their heaps and environments, the stack is not considered here. Program points are not related to a simple one-to-one relation: the whole block generated from a given BC instruction must be executed before falling back into the relation. Hence, a BC state is matched at the beginning of the BIR block of the same program point: the function $instrAt_{P'}(m, pc)$ gives the BIR program point $(\mathtt{pc}, \ell)$ with ℓ the complete instruction list at $\mathtt{pc}$. We only relate error states of the same kind of error. Finally, two observable events are related if they are

Table 1. Semantic relations

Relation	Definition
$v_1 \overset{\text{V}}{\sim}_\beta v_2$ $v_1, v_2 \in Value$	$\dfrac{}{Null \overset{\text{V}}{\sim}_\beta Null}$ $\quad \dfrac{n \in \mathbb{Z}}{(Num\ n) \overset{\text{V}}{\sim}_\beta (Num\ n)}$ $\quad \dfrac{\beta(r_1) = r_2}{(Ref\ r_1) \overset{\text{V}}{\sim}_\beta (Ref\ r_2)}$
$h_1 \overset{\text{H}}{\sim}_\beta h_2$ $h_1, h_2 \in Heap$	– $dom(\beta) = \{r \in dom(h_1) \mid \forall \mathtt{C}, \mathtt{pc},\ tag_{h_1}(r) \neq \widetilde{\mathtt{C}_{\mathtt{pc}}}\}$ – $rng(\beta) = dom(h_2)$ – $\forall r \in dom(h_1)$, let $o_t = h_1(r)$ and $o'_{t'} = h_2(\beta(r))$ then $(i)\ t = t' \quad (ii)\ \forall f,\ o_t(f) \overset{\text{V}}{\sim}_\beta o'_t(f)$
$l_1 \overset{\text{E}}{\sim}_\beta l_2$ $(l_1, l_2) \in Env_{\mathrm{BC}} \times Env_{\mathrm{BIR}}$	$dom(l_1) = var_{\mathrm{BC}} \cap dom(l_2)$ and $\forall x \in dom(l_1),\ l_1(x) \overset{\text{V}}{\sim}_\beta l_2(x)$
$c_1 \overset{\text{C}}{\sim}_\beta c_2$ $(c_1, c_2) \in State_{\mathrm{BC}} \times State_{\mathrm{BIR}}$	$\dfrac{h \overset{\text{H}}{\sim}_\beta ht \quad l \overset{\text{E}}{\sim}_\beta lt}{\langle h, m, \mathtt{pc}, l, s\rangle \overset{\text{C}}{\sim}_\beta \langle ht, m, (\mathtt{pc}, instrAt_{P'}(m, pc)), lt\rangle}$ $\dfrac{h \overset{\text{H}}{\sim}_\beta ht \quad rv \overset{\text{V}}{\sim}_\beta rv'}{\langle h, rv\rangle \overset{\text{C}}{\sim}_\beta \langle ht, rv'\rangle}$ $\quad \dfrac{h \overset{\text{H}}{\sim}_\beta ht \quad l \overset{\text{E}}{\sim}_\beta lt}{\langle \Omega^k, m, pc, h, l\rangle \overset{\text{C}}{\sim}_\beta \langle \Omega^k, m, pc, ht, lt\rangle}$
$\lambda_1 \overset{!}{\sim}_\beta \lambda_2$ with $\lambda_1, \lambda_2 \in Evt$	$\dfrac{}{\tau \overset{!}{\sim}_\beta \tau}$ $\quad \dfrac{}{mayinit(\mathtt{C}) \overset{!}{\sim}_\beta mayinit(\mathtt{C})}$ $\dfrac{\beta(r_1) = r_2 \quad v_1 \overset{\text{V}}{\sim}_\beta v_2}{r_1.f \leftarrow v_1 \overset{!}{\sim}_\beta r_2.f \leftarrow v_2}$ $\quad \dfrac{x \in var_{\mathrm{BC}} \quad v_1 \overset{\text{V}}{\sim}_\beta v_2}{x \leftarrow v_1 \overset{!}{\sim}_\beta x \leftarrow v_2}$ $\dfrac{\beta(r_1) = r_2 \quad \forall i = 1 \ldots n, v_i \overset{\text{V}}{\sim}_\beta v'_i}{r_1 \leftarrow C.init(v_1, \ldots, v_n) \overset{!}{\sim}_\beta r_2 \leftarrow C.init(v'_1, \ldots, v'_n)}$ $\dfrac{\beta(r_1) = r_2 \quad \forall i = 1 \ldots n, v_i \overset{\text{V}}{\sim}_\beta v'_i}{r_1.C.init(v_1, \ldots, v_n) \overset{!}{\sim}_\beta r_2.C.init(v'_1, \ldots, v'_n)}$

of the same kind, and the values they involve are related. To relate execution traces, we pointwise extend $\overset{!}{\sim}_\beta$. We now assume that $\mathtt{IR}$, $\mathtt{AS_{in}}$ and $\mathtt{AS_{out}}$ are the code and abstract stack arrays computed by BC2BIR, and so until the end of the section.

4.2 Soundness Result

The previously defined observational semantics and semantic relations allows achieving a very fine-grained correctness criterion for the transformation BC2BIR. It says that P' simulates the initial program P: starting from two related initial configurations, if the execution of P terminates in a given (normal or error) state, then P' terminates in a related state, and both execution traces are related, when forgetting temporary variables assignments in the BIR trace (we write Λ_{proj} for such a projection of Λ). More formally:

Theorem 1 (Semantic preservation)
Let $m \in \mathbb{M}$ be a method of P (and P') and $n \in \mathbb{N}$. Let $c = \langle h, m, 0, l, \varepsilon\rangle \in State_{\mathrm{BC}}$ and $ct = \langle h, m, (0, instrAt_{P'}(m, 0)), l\rangle \in State_{\mathrm{BIR}}$. Then two properties hold:

Normal return. *If $c \overset{\Lambda}{\Rightarrow}_n \langle h', v\rangle$ then there exist unique ht', v', Λ' and β such that $ct \overset{\Lambda'}{\Rightarrow}_n \langle ht', v'\rangle$ with $\langle h', v\rangle \overset{\text{C}}{\sim}_\beta \langle ht', v'\rangle$ and $\Lambda \overset{!}{\sim}_\beta \Lambda'_{proj}$.*

Error. *If* $c \stackrel{\Lambda}{\Rightarrow}_n \langle \Omega^k, m, pc', l', h' \rangle$ *then there exist unique* ht', lt', Λ' *and* β *s.t* $ct \stackrel{\Lambda'}{\Rightarrow}_n \langle \Omega^k, m, pc', lt', ht' \rangle$ *with* $\langle \Omega^k, m, pc', l', h' \rangle \stackrel{\mathrm{C}}{\sim}_\beta \langle \Omega^k, m, pc', lt', ht' \rangle$ *and* $\Lambda \stackrel{!}{\sim}_\beta \Lambda'_{proj}$.

Executions that get stuck do not need to be considered, since corresponding programs would not pass the BCV. Theorem 1 only partially deals with infinite computations: we e.g. do not show the preservation of executions when they diverge inside a method call. All reachable states (intra and inter-procedurally) could be matched giving small-step operational semantics to both languages. This would require parametrizing events by the method from which they arise, and extending the relation on configurations to all frames in the call stack.

We now provide a proof sketch of the theorem, giving an insight on the technical arguments used in the complete proof, which is given in [5]. We prove this theorem using a strong induction on the call depth n. The inductive reasoning is made possible by considering not only computations from initial states to (normal and error) return states, but also intermediate computation states. The crucial point is that BC intermediate states require dealing with the stack, to which BIR expressions must be related. Semantically, this is captured by a correctness criterion on the abstract stack used by the transformation. It intuitively means that expressions are correctly decompiled:

Definition 1 (Stack correctness: $\approx_{h,ht,lt,\beta}$**).** *Given* $h, ht \in Heap$ *such that* $h \stackrel{\mathrm{H}}{\sim}_\beta ht$ *and* $lt \in Env_{\mathrm{BIR}}$, *an abstract stack* $as \in AbstrStack$ *is said to be correct with regards to a run-time stack* $s \in Stack$ *if and only if* $s \approx_{h,ht,lt,\beta} as$:

$$\frac{}{\varepsilon \approx_{h,ht,lt,\beta} \varepsilon} \qquad \frac{ht, lt \models e \Downarrow v' \quad v \stackrel{\mathrm{V}}{\sim}_\beta v' \quad s \approx_{h,ht,lt,\beta} as}{v{::}s \approx_{h,ht,lt,\beta} e{::}as} \qquad \frac{tag_h(r) = \widetilde{\mathrm{C}}_{\mathrm{pc}} \quad s \approx_{h,ht,lt,\beta} as \quad \forall (Ref\ r') \in s,\ tag_h(r') = \widetilde{\mathrm{C}}_{\mathrm{pc}} \Rightarrow r = r'}{(Ref\ r){::}s \approx_{h,ht,lt,\beta} UR^{\mathrm{C}}_{\mathrm{pc}}{::}as}$$

where $ht, lt \models e \Downarrow v'$ *means that expression* e *evaluates to* v' *in* ht *and* lt.

The last definition rule says that the symbol $UR^{\mathrm{C}}_{\mathrm{pc}}$ correctly approximates a reference r of tag $\widetilde{\mathrm{C}}_{\mathrm{pc}}$. The alias information tracked by $UR^{\mathrm{C}}_{\mathrm{pc}}$ is made consistent if we additionally demand that all references appearing in the stack with the same status tag are equal to r (second condition of this last rule). This strong property is enforced by the restrictions imposed by the BCV on uninitialized references in the operand stack.

We are now able to state the general proposition on intermediate execution states. In order to clarify the induction hypothesis, we parametrize the proposition by the call depth and the name of the executed method:

Proposition 1 ($\mathcal{P}(n,m)$ **– BC2BIR n call-depth preservation)**
Let $m \in \mathbb{M}$ *be a method of* P *(and* P'*) and* $n \in \mathbb{N}$. *Let* β *be a partial bijection on* Ref. *Let* $c = \langle h, m, pc, l, s \rangle \in State_{\mathrm{BC}}$ *and* $ct = \langle ht, m, (pc, instrAt_{P'}(m, pc)), lt \rangle \in State_{\mathrm{BIR}}$ *such that* $c \stackrel{\mathrm{C}}{\sim}_\beta ct$ *and* $s \approx_{h,ht,lt,\beta} \mathtt{AS_{in}[m,pc]}$. *Then, for all* $c' \in State_{\mathrm{BC}}$, *whenever* $c \stackrel{\Lambda}{\Rightarrow}_n c'$, *there exist unique* ct' *and* Λ' *and a unique* β' *extending* β *such that* $ct \stackrel{\Lambda'}{\Rightarrow}_n ct'$ *with* $c' \stackrel{\mathrm{C}}{\sim}_{\beta'} ct'$ *and* $\Lambda \stackrel{!}{\sim}_{\beta'} \Lambda'_{proj}$.

In the base case $\mathcal{P}(0,m)$, we reason by induction on the number of BC steps. A step $\langle h, m, pc, l, s \rangle \stackrel{\Lambda}{\rightarrow}_0 \langle h', m, pc', l', s' \rangle$ is matched by: $\langle ht, m, (pc, IR[m, pc]), lt \rangle \stackrel{\Lambda_1}{\Rightarrow}_0$

$\langle ht, m, (pc, \texttt{code}), lt_0\rangle \overset{\Lambda_2}{\Rightarrow}_0 \langle ht', m, (pc', instrAt_{P'}(m, pc')), lt'\rangle$ where the intermediate state $\langle ht, m, (pc, \texttt{code}), lt_0\rangle$ is obtained by executing the potential additional assignments prepended to the instructions code generated by BC2BIR$_{instr}$. We obtain the second part of the matching computation thanks to a correctness lemma about BC2BIR$_{instr}$ (proved in [5]):

Lemma 1 (BC2BIR$_{instr}$ **0 call-depth one-step preservation)**
Suppose $\langle h, m, pc, l, s\rangle \overset{\Lambda}{\rightarrow}_0 \langle h', m, pc', l', s'\rangle$. *Let* ht, lt, as, β *be such that* $h \overset{\mathtt{H}}{\sim}_\beta ht$, $l \overset{\mathtt{E}}{\sim}_\beta lt$, $s \approx_{h,ht,lt,\beta} as$ *and* BC2BIR$_{instr}(pc, instrAt_P(m, pc), as) = (\texttt{code}, as')$. *There exist unique* ht', lt' *and* Λ' *such that* $\langle ht, m, (pc, \texttt{code}), lt\rangle \overset{\Lambda'}{\Rightarrow}_0 \langle ht', m, (pc', instrsAt_{P'}(m, pc')), lt'\rangle$ *with* $h' \overset{\mathtt{H}}{\sim}_\beta ht'$, $l' \overset{\mathtt{E}}{\sim}_\beta lt'$, $\Lambda \overset{!}{\sim}_\beta \Lambda'_{proj}$ *and* $s' \approx_{h',ht',lt',\beta} as'$.

It is similar to $\mathcal{P}(n, m)$, but only deals with one-step BC transitions and does not require extending the bijection (instructions at a zero call depth do not initialize any object). Moreover, considering an *arbitrary* correct entry abstract stack allows us applying the lemma with more modularity.

Lemma 1 cannot be directly applied for proving the $\overset{\Lambda_2}{\Rightarrow}_0$ step, because the entry abstract stack $\texttt{AS}_{\texttt{in}}[\texttt{m}, \texttt{pc}]$ is sometimes normalized and because of the additional assignments prepended to code. For the hypotheses of Lemma 1 to be satisfied, we thus have to show that $s \approx_{h,ht,lt_0,\beta} \texttt{AS}_{\texttt{in}}[\texttt{m}, \texttt{pc}]$. Two cases are distinguished. If $\texttt{pc} \notin jmpTgt^{\mathtt{P}}_{\mathtt{m}}$, the stack is not normalized, but additional assignments could break the stack correctness. However, as we forbid backwards jumps on non-empty stacks, all $\mathtt{T}^{\mathtt{j}}_{\mathtt{pcj}}$ (where $\texttt{pcj} \in succ(\texttt{pc})$) assigned by $\mathtt{T}Assign$ cannot be used in the stack. Now, if $\texttt{pc} \in jmpTgt^{\mathtt{P}}_{\mathtt{m}}$, then the stack is normalized. Assignments generated by $\mathtt{T}Assign$ do not alterate the stack correctness: if pcj is a join point successing pc, $\mathtt{T}^{\mathtt{k}}_{\mathtt{pcj}}$ is assigned, but all the $\mathtt{T}^{\mathtt{k'}}_{\mathtt{pc}}$ that appear in the normalized stack are distinct from $\mathtt{T}^{\mathtt{k}}_{\mathtt{pcj}}$ (pc<pcj if the stack at pcj is non-empty). Hence $s \approx_{h,ht,lt_0,\beta} \texttt{AS}_{\texttt{in}}[\texttt{m}, \texttt{pc}]$.

Applying Lemma 1 gives us that $h' \overset{\mathtt{H}}{\sim}_\beta ht'$, $l' \overset{\mathtt{E}}{\sim}_\beta lt'$ and $\Lambda \overset{!}{\sim}_\beta \Lambda_{2proj}$. Furthermore, Λ_1 is only made of temporary variable assignment events, hence Λ_{1proj} is empty, and $\Lambda \overset{!}{\sim}_\beta (\Lambda_1.\Lambda_2)_{proj}$. Because of prepended assignments, we have to show that the transmitted abstract stack $\texttt{AS}_{\texttt{in}}[\texttt{m}, \texttt{pc}']$ satisfies $s' \approx_{h',ht',lt',\beta} \texttt{AS}_{\texttt{in}}[\texttt{m}, \texttt{pc}']$. There are two cases. If pc′ is not a join point, then the transmitted abstract stack is simply $\texttt{AS}_{\texttt{out}}[\texttt{m}, \texttt{pc}]$, resulting from BC2BIR$_{instr}$. We therefore use the conclusion of Lemma 1. Now, if $\texttt{pc}' \in jmpTgt^{\mathtt{P}}_{\mathtt{m}}$, the output abstract stack is $newStackJmp(\texttt{pc}', \texttt{AS}_{\texttt{in}}[\texttt{m}, \texttt{pc}'])$. All of the $\mathtt{T}^{\mathtt{j}}_{\mathtt{pc}'}$ have been assigned, but we must show that they have not been modified by executing the BIR instructions code. As defined in Figure 6, the only assigned temporary variables are of the form $\mathtt{t}^{\mathtt{k}}_{\mathtt{pc}'}$. Our naming convention ensures $\forall \mathtt{k}. \mathtt{T}^{\mathtt{j}}_{\mathtt{pc}'} \neq \mathtt{t}^{\mathtt{k}}_{\mathtt{pc}'}$. Thus, $s' \approx_{h',ht',lt',\beta} \texttt{AS}_{\texttt{in}}[\texttt{m}, \texttt{pc}']$, which concludes the proof of $\mathcal{P}(0, m)$.

Concerning the induction case $\mathcal{P}(n + 1, m)$, the idea is to isolate one of the method calls, and to split the computation into three parts. Indeed, we know that there exist n_1, n_2 and n_3 such that a transition $c \Rightarrow_{n+1} c'$ can be decomposed into $c \Rightarrow_{n_1} c_1 \rightarrow_{n_2} c_2 \Rightarrow_{n_3} c'$, with $n_2 \neq 0$ and $n + 1 = n_1 + n_2 + n_3$. The first and third parts are easily treated applying the induction hypothesis. The method call $c_1 \rightarrow_{n_2} c_2$ is handled in a way similar to the base case. We prove an instruction-wise correctness intermediate lemma, under the induction hypothesis $\forall m' \mathcal{P}(n, m')$. The induction hypothesis is also applied on the execution of the callee, whose call depth is strictly lower.

5 Related Work

Many Java bytecode optimization and analysis tools work on an IR of bytecode that make its analysis much simpler. Soot [14] is a Java bytecode optimization framework providing three IR: Baf, Jimple and Grimp. Optimizing Java bytecode consists in successively translating bytecode into Baf, Jimple, and Grimp, and then back to bytecode, while performing diverse optimizations on each IR. Baf is a fully typed, stack-based language. Jimple is a typed stackless 3-address code. Grimp is a stackless code with tree expressions, obtained by collapsing 3-address Jimple instructions. The stack elimination is performed in two steps, when generating Jimple code from Baf code (see [15] for details). First, naive 3-address code is produced (one variable is associated to each element position of the stack). Then, numerous redundancies of variables are eliminated using a simple aggregation of single def-use pairs. Variables representing stack locations lead to type conflicts when their type is infered, so that they must be desambiguated using additional variables. Our transformation, relying on a symbolic execution, avoids this problem by only merging variables of distinct scopes. Auxiliary analyses (e.g. copy propagation) could further reduce the number of variables, but BC2BIR generates very few superfluous variables in practice [5].

The transformation technique used in BC2BIR is similar to what Whaley [16] uses for the high level IR of the Jalapeño Optimizing Compiler [3] (now part of the Jikes virtual machine [10]). The language provides explicit check operators for common runtime exceptions (`null_check`, `bound_check`...), so that they can be easily moved or eliminated by optimizations. We use a similar technique to enforce the preservation of the exception throwing order. We additionally use the `mayinit` instruction to ensure the preservation of the class initialization order, that could otherwise be broken because of folded constructors and side-effect free expressions. Our work pushes the technique further, generating tree expressions in conditional branchings and folding constructors. Unlike all works cited above, our transformation does not require iterating on the method code. Still, the number of generated variables keeps small in practice (see [5]). All these previous works have been mainly concerned with the construction of effective and powerful tools but, as far as we know, no attention has been paid to the formal semantic properties that are ensured by these transformations.

The use of a symbolic evaluation of the operand stack to recover some tree expressions in a bytecode program has been employed in several contexts of Java Bytecode analysis. The technique was already used in one of the first Sun Just-In-Time compilers [4] for direct translation of bytecode to machine instructions. Xi and Xia propose a dependent type system for array bound check elimination [18]. They use symbolic expressions to type operand stacks with *singleton* types in order to recover relations between lengths of arrays and index expressions. Besson *et al.* [2], and independently Wildmoser *et al.* [17], propose an extended interval analysis using symbolic decompilation that verifies that programs are free of out-of-bound array accesses. Besson *et al.* give an example that shows how the precision of the standard interval analysis is enhanced by including syntactic expressions in the abstract domain. Barthe *et al.* [1] also use a symbolic manipulation for the relational analysis of a simple bytecode language and prove it is as precise as a similar analysis at source level.

Among the numerous works on program transformation correctness proofs, the closest are those dealing with formal verification of the Java compiler algorithms (from Java source to Java bytecode) [12,13,7]. The present work studies a different transformation from bytecode to a higher intermediate level and handle difficulties (symbolic operand stack, non preservation of allocation order) that were not present in these previous works.

6 Conclusions and Future Work

This paper provides a semantically sound, provably correct transformation of bytecode into an IR that (i) removes the use of the operand stack and rebuilds tree expressions, (ii) makes more explicit the throwing of exception and takes care of preserving their order, (iii) rebuilds the initialization chain of an object with a dedicated instruction `x := new C(arg1, arg2, ...)`. In the accompanying technical report [5] we demonstrate on several examples of safety properties how some BIR static analysis verdicts can be translated back to the initial BC program. It would be interesting to study whether the translation of analysis results could be simplified by expressing BC2BIR in the form of annotations, as proposed by Matsuno and Ohori in [9] for the Static Single Assignment form. By the nature of the transformation, and because of the differences between BC and BIR, expressing BC2BIR in this setting would require several adaptations. The transformation is designed to work in one pass in order to make it useful in a scenario of "lightweight bytecode analysis" applied to analyses other than type checking. It has been implemented in a tool accepting full Java bytecode. Our benchmarks show the expected efficiency is obtained in practice.

Several other extensions are possible. First we would like to extend this work into a multi-threading context. This is a challenging task, especially for the formalization part that must deal with the complex Java Memory Model. Second, it would be interesting to study if the transformation scheme would fit a more multi-language support such as CIL, the output format of several compilers (`VB.NET`, `C#`...). On one hand, this would require to adapt the formalization to the low-level memory operations available in this language. On the other hand, we could lift the constraints on the use of uninitialized objects by MSIL input programs, since constructor calls are folded in CIL. Finally, we believe the current transformation would be a valuable layer on top of Bicolano, a formal JVM semantics formalized in Coq and developed during the European MOBIUS project. The Coq extraction mechanism would allow extracting certified and efficient Caml code from the Coq formalization of the algorithm.

Acknowledgments. We thank the anonymous reviewers for their thorough comments.

References

1. Barthe, G., Kunz, C., Pichardie, D., Samborski-Forlese, J.: Preservation of proof obligations for hybrid verification methods. In: Proc. of SEFM 2008, pp. 127–136. IEEE Computer Society, Los Alamitos (2008)

2. Besson, F., Jensen, T., Pichardie, D.: Proof-carrying code from certified abstract interpretation and fixpoint compression. Theor. Comput. Sci. 364(3), 273–291 (2006)
3. Burke, M.G., Choi, J., Fink, S., Grove, D., Hind, M., Sarkar, V., Serrano, M.J., Sreedhar, V.C., Srinivasan, H., Whaley, J.: The Jalapeño dynamic optimizing compiler for Java. In: Proc. of JAVA 1999, pp. 129–141. ACM, New York (1999)
4. Cramer, T., Friedman, R., Miller, T., Seberger, D., Wilson, R., Wolczko, M.: Compiling Java just in time. IEEE Micro 17(3), 36–43 (1997)
5. Demange, D., Jensen, T., Pichardie, D.: A provably correct stackless intermediate representation for Java bytecode. Research Report 7021, INRIA (2009), `http://www.irisa.fr/celtique/ext/bir/rr7021.pdf`
6. Freund, S.N., Mitchell, J.C.: The type system for object initialization in the Java bytecode language. ACM TOPLAS 21(6), 1196–1250 (1999)
7. Klein, G., Nipkow, T.: A machine-checked model for a Java-like language, virtual machine and compiler. ACM TOPLAS 28(4), 619–695 (2006)
8. Logozzo, F., Fähndrich, M.: On the relative completeness of bytecode analysis versus source code analysis. In: Hendren, L. (ed.) CC 2008. LNCS, vol. 4959, pp. 197–212. Springer, Heidelberg (2008)
9. Matsuno, Y., Ohori, A.: A type system equivalent to static single assignment. In: PPDP 2006: Proceedings of the 8th ACM SIGPLAN International Conference on Principles and Practice of Declarative Programming, pp. 249–260. ACM, New York (2006)
10. The Jikes RVM Project. Jikes rvm - home page, `http://jikesrvm.org`
11. Rose, E.: Lightweight bytecode verification. J. Autom. Reason. 31(3-4), 303–334 (2003)
12. Stark, R.F., Borger, E., Schmid, J.: Java and the Java Virtual Machine: Definition, Verification, Validation with Cdrom. Springer, New York (2001)
13. Strecker, M.: Formal verification of a Java compiler in Isabelle. In: Voronkov, A. (ed.) CADE 2002. LNCS (LNAI), vol. 2392, pp. 63–77. Springer, Heidelberg (2002)
14. Vallée-Rai, R., Co, P., Gagnon, E., Hendren, L., Lam, P., Sundaresan, V.: Soot - a Java bytecode optimization framework. In: Proc. of CASCON 1999. IBM Press (1999)
15. Vallee-Rai, R., Hendren, L.J.: Jimple: Simplifying Java bytecode for analyses and transformations (1998)
16. Whaley, J.: Dynamic optimization through the use of automatic runtime specialization. Master's thesis, Massachusetts Institute of Technology (May 1999)
17. Wildmoser, M., Chaieb, A., Nipkow, T.: Bytecode analysis for proof carrying code. In: Proc. of BYTECODE 2005, Electronic Notes in Computer Science (2005)
18. Xi, H., Xia, S.: Towards array bound check elimination in Java tm virtual machine language. In: Proc. of CASCON 1999, p. 14. IBM Press (1999)

JNI Light: An Operational Model for the Core JNI

Gang Tan

Computer Science and Engineering, Lehigh University

Abstract. Through foreign function interfaces (FFIs), software components in different programming languages interact with each other in the same address space. Recent years have witnessed a number of systems that analyze FFIs for safety and reliability. However, lack of formal specifications of FFIs hampers progress in this endeavor. We present a formal operational model, JNI Light (JNIL), for a subset of a widely used FFI—the Java Native Interface (JNI). JNIL focuses on the core issues when a high-level garbage-collected language interacts with a low-level language. It proposes abstractions for handling a shared heap, cross-language method calls, cross-language exception handling, and garbage collection. JNIL can directly serve as a formal basis for JNI tools and systems. The abstractions in JNIL are also useful when modeling other FFIs, such as the Python/C interface and the OCaml/C interface.

1 Motivation

Most modern programming languages support foreign function interfaces (FFIs) for interoperating with program modules developed in other programming languages. Recent years have witnessed a string of systems that analyze and improve FFIs for safety and reliability [1, 2, 3, 4, 5, 6, 7, 8]. However, lack of formal semantics of FFIs hampers progress in this domain. The available specifications of FFIs are in prose. Relying on prose specifications has at least two unpleasant consequences. First, prose specifications are often ambiguous and sometimes incomplete. The situation is especially acute for an FFI, whose two sides involve different programming models and language features. For instance, Lee *et al.* reported that Sun's HotSpot and IBM's J9 behave differently for four out of ten JNI test cases [8, Table 1]. In such situations, the best an FFI user can do is to perform experiments on particular implementations and make an educated guess. This may cause inconsistencies and unsoundness. Second, without formal semantics, tools and analyzers cannot provide rigorous claims about their strength. As a result, previous systems that target FFIs have to argue their hypotheses and claims informally. This leaves their strength in doubt.

While there have been many efforts in formalizing the semantics of programming languages, almost all have ignored the FFI aspect. The work by Matthews and Findler [9] formalizes the interoperation between two high-level functional languages, one typed and the other untyped. While this formalism represents significant progress in modeling language interoperation, it does not apply to FFIs.

K. Ueda (Ed.): APLAS 2010, LNCS 6461, pp. 114–130, 2010.

Most FFIs are about the interaction in the shared memory between a high-level language and a low-level language (assembly languages, C, and C++).

This paper presents the first formal operational model, named JNI Light (JNIL), for a subset of a shared-memory foreign function interface—the JNI interface. The major challenge for the modeling effort is to have the right abstractions to accommodate differences between the programming models of Java and native code, without unduly complicating the model. This is challenging because Java is a high-level OO language with a managed runtime and provides automatic garbage collection and exception handling. Native code, on the other hand, operates at a much lower level. It manually manages the heap and has no built-in exception-handling mechanism. JNIL proposes a set of abstractions to handle these differences. The abstractions make the JNIL model concise and largely straightforward.

We proceed as follows. We highlight key issues and abstractions in JNIL in Sec. 2. The formal semantics of JNIL is presented in Sec. 3. We discuss possible applications of the JNIL model in Sec. 4. Two extensions and future work are discussed in Sec. 5. We present related work in Sec. 6 and conclude in Sec. 7. Due to space limitations, we will concentrate on language-interoperation issues and leave out some technical details; we refer readers to a technical report [10].

2 Informal Discussion of JNIL

In this section, we informally discuss major challenges of modeling the JNI and highlight JNIL's solutions; formal treatment is left to Sec. 3. We also present examples that help understand the key aspects.

Background. The JNI [11] is Java's mechanism for interfacing with native code. A native method is declared in a Java class by adding the `native` modifier. For example, the following `Item` class contains a native `twice` method. Once declared, native methods are invoked in Java exactly the same as how Java methods are invoked. In the example, the `fourTimes` Java method invokes the `twice` method.

```
class Item {
   private int quantity = 17;
   private native void twice();
   public void fourTimes () {twice(); twice();}
   static {System.loadLibrary(''Item'');}
}
```

A native method is implemented in a low-level language such as C, C++, or an assembly language. Native code can use all the features provided by the native language. In addition, native code can interact with Java through a set of JNI interface functions (called JNI functions hereafter). For instance, the implementation of `twice` can invoke `GetField` to get the value of the `quantity` field, and `SetField` to set the field to double the old value. Through JNI functions, native methods can inspect, modify, and create Java objects, invoke Java methods, catch and throw Java exceptions, and so on.

Two sides of JNIL. A model of the JNI needs both a Java-side language and a native-side language. The Java-side language of JNIL is a subset of the Java Virtual Machine Language (bytecode [12]). The native-side language is a RISC-style assembly language augmented with a set of JNI functions (such as `GetField/SetField`). We choose to model an assembly language because native methods in C or C++ are compiled before loaded and linked into the JVM. Furthermore, there is less modeling overhead for an assembly language, allowing JNIL to concentrate on the interaction between Java and native code.

Many bytecode and JNI functions in JNIL work with *field IDs* and *method IDs*. For example, "GetField *fd*" gets the value of the field represented by *fd*. A field ID identifies a field by specifying three elements: a class name that the field belongs to, a field name, and its type. For example, the ID for the `quantity` field is ⟨"Item", "quantity", Int⟩. A method ID has similar information as a field ID. A method ID may identify either a Java method (implemented in bytecode) or a native method (implemented in native code).

Heap model. In the JNI, Java and native code reside in the same address space to avoid costly context switches. Consequently, JNIL needs to model a shared heap. However, modeling the shared heap poses some challenge because Java and native code's views of the heap are at different levels.

Being a high-level language, Java takes a high-level view: a heap is mathematically a map from labels to objects. The use of abstract labels hides many complexities of memory management. If a heap is rearranged and labels are renamed, the new heap is considered to be equivalent to the old one as long as the "graph" of the heap is preserved. Furthermore, in the high-level view, objects are storable values. There is no need to consider how objects are represented in memory. Previous Java models [13, 14, 15, 16] adopt the high-level view. By contrast, native code takes a low level view: a heap is mathematically a map from addresses to primitive values. An object is represented in memory as a sequence of primitive values according to an object-layout strategy. Native code can perform address arithmetic, for example, to access elements of a Java array.

JNIL adopts an unusual *block model*: (1) a heap is a map from labels to blocks; (2) a block is a map from addresses (natural numbers) to primitive values. A block may hold the representation of a Java object, or may be a memory region allocated and owned by native code.

$$\begin{aligned} \mathit{Heap} &::= \mathit{Label} \rightharpoonup \big\langle \mathsf{blk} : \mathit{Block},\ \mathsf{own} : \mathit{Owner} \big\rangle \\ \mathit{Block} &::= \mathbb{N} \rightharpoonup \mathit{Value} \end{aligned}$$

A reference value, written as $\ell[i]$, identifies a location in block ℓ with offset i.

There are two major benefits of the block heap model. First, using abstract labels instead of addresses in the heap preserves the major benefit of the high-level heap model. It simplifies the specification of GC. In particular, there is no need to worry about whether GC moves objects because the resulting heap after moving is equivalent to the previous heap.[1] The second benefit of the block

[1] We can think that there is a flatten function that maps a heap in the block model to a flat heap. A flat heap is just a map from addresses to values. Then a moving GC will only change the flatten function.

model is that it also accommodates the low-level view of native code. Values stored in blocks are primitive values. Address arithmetic is allowed within one block. Suppose a block with label ℓ holds the representation of a Java integer array, then Java may pass to native code a reference $\ell[i]$ that identifies where array elements are stored. Adding an offset n to $\ell[i]$ results in a new reference $\ell[i+n]$, which native code can use to access the nth element of the array.

Object representation and ownership. Since JNIL's heap holds only primitive values, it is necessary to represent Java objects in the heap. JNIL is parametrized by a representation function, Rep : *Object* $\rightarrow$ *Block*, for the desire of not committing to any particular object-representation strategy. The representation function maps a Java object to a block. For instance, one representation can represent Java class instances and arrays in the following way:

$$\mathrm{Rep}(\langle\!\langle fd_1 = v_1, \ldots, fd_n = v_n \rangle\!\rangle_\phi) = \{0 \mapsto \mathrm{TypeRep}(\phi), 1 \mapsto v_1, \ldots, n \mapsto v_n\}$$
$$\mathrm{Rep}([\![v_0, \ldots, v_{n-1}]\!]_{\tau[n]}) = \{0 \mapsto \mathrm{TypeRep}(\tau), 1 \mapsto n, 2 \mapsto v_0, \ldots, n+1 \mapsto v_{n-1}\}$$

In the above, $\langle\!\langle fd_1 = v_1, \ldots, fd_n = v_n \rangle\!\rangle_\phi$ is a Java instance of class ϕ with fields fd_1 to fd_n; $[\![v_0, \ldots, v_{n-1}]\!]_{\tau[n]}$ is a Java array of size n with element type τ; TypeRep($-$) is a function for representing types as primitive values.

Each block in the heap has an owner: $\omega \in \{\mathrm{J}, \mathrm{N}\}$. A heap H is conceptually divided into a subheap owned by Java (J), written as $H|_\mathrm{J}$, and a subheap owned by native code (N), written as $H|_\mathrm{N}$. The reason for adding ownership is twofold. First, it helps specify Java's GC, which recollects locations only in the Java heap. Second, ownership information could be used to define a safety policy. For instance, if the policy is that native code should not access the Java heap, then the semantics of native load/store instructions could have the ownership checking built-in.

Cross-language method calls. Java and native code may engage in so-called "ping-pong" behavior. For instance, a Java method with ID md_1 may invoke a native method with ID md_2, which in turn calls back another Java method with ID md_3. It is possible that md_3 invokes a second native method and therefore the control bounces back and forth between the Java and native sides.

To model cross-language method calls, we introduce in JNIL a *multi-language method-call stack* whose frames are either Java frames or native frames:

$$F \in \mathit{Frame} ::= \langle md, pc, s, a \rangle_\mathrm{J} \mid \langle md, pc, s, v_x, L \rangle_\mathrm{N}$$

A Java frame holds information for a Java-method execution, and a native frame for a native-method execution. Both kinds of frames include a method ID (md), a program counter (pc), and an operand stack (s). The operand stack is used for storing intermediate results and maybe also for passing arguments and results of function calls. A Java frame also includes a local variable map (a), which holds values of local variables. A native frame also includes an exception reference (v_x) and a root set (L); we will discuss their uses shortly.

For the example we discussed beforehand, the shape of the method-call stack when the control is in md_3 is presented as follows (only method IDs are shown).

$$\langle md_3, \ldots \rangle_\mathrm{J} \cdot \langle md_2, \ldots \rangle_\mathrm{N} \cdot \langle md_1, \ldots \rangle_\mathrm{J} \cdot \epsilon \quad (1)$$

The top of the stack is on the left. We treat a stack as a list of frames and use "$F \cdot S$" for the concatenation of frame F and stack S and ϵ for the empty stack.

Cross-language exception handling. The JVM has a built-in mechanism for exception handling. We define *Java exceptions* to be those that are pending in a Java method. For a Java exception, the JVM checks if there is an enclosing try/catch statement that matches the exception type in the method. If not, it pops the method off the method-call stack and checks the next method.

An exception may also be pending on the native side; we call such exceptions *JNI exceptions.* For example, if the Java method md_3 in stack configuration (1) throws an exception that is not handled by md_3, then it is a JNI exception pending in native method md_2. Native code itself may also throw exceptions by calling JNI functions such as throw. Furthermore, many JNI functions throw exceptions to indicate failures.

In contrast to how an exception is handled in a Java method, a JNI exception does not immediately disrupt the native method execution. The exception is recorded in the JVM, but the native method will keep executing. After the native method finishes execution and returns to a Java method, the exception becomes pending in the Java method and then the JVM mechanism for exceptions starts to take over.

Given this difference, the question is how to model the operational semantics when an exception becomes pending in a method-call stack that contains mixed Java and native frames. JNIL handles this issue by having different modes for indicating the presence of Java and JNI exceptions. A Java exception is indicated by a special *exception frame* $\langle \ell \rangle_{\mathrm{X}}$ at the top of the method-call stack, where ℓ is a reference to a `Throwable` object. A JNI exception is recorded in a native frame $\langle md, pc, s, v_x, L \rangle_{\mathrm{N}}$: the value v_x is null when no exception is pending and is ℓ with a pending JNI exception with label ℓ. JNIL's abstract machine proceeds differently for the two modes. Briefly, JNIL unwinds the stack for a Java exception and continues the execution of a native method for a JNI exception; we will discuss the details in the next section.

Registration of references. Java's GC is aware of only those references on the Java side. When native code retains references to Java objects, it has to register those references so that the GC will not collect the underlying objects. JNIL records the set of Java references available to a native method in a root set L. A root set is associated with a native frame so that its references are automatically "freed" when the native method finishes its execution. This semantics effectively models the so-called local references in the JNI.[2]

[2] The JNI also provides global and weak-global references. Global references are valid across multiple invocations of native methods and multiple threads. Weak global references are similar to global references except that the underlying objects can be garbage collected. These references are straightforward to model. Global references can be modeled as a global set of labels. Weak-global references have no impact on GC, although a JNI function for testing the validity of references needs to be exposed to native code. We omit their modeling in JNIL for brevity.

3 Formal Semantics of JNIL

We next present the core calculus of JNIL. A few simplifications are made to the model. First, arrays are not included. Second, it assumes a calling convention where arguments and results are passed on the operand stack when Java invokes native methods. Our technical report discusses how to generalize the model to add arrays and to parametrize over calling conventions. The bytecode language is also simplified. Following Featherweight Java [17], we avoid the object initialization problem by having a single instruction for creating and initializing an object. There is also no modeling of interfaces, subroutine calls and returns, and various other Java features. They are orthogonal to the multilingual issues we are concerned with in FFIs. A notable missing feature in JNIL is concurrency. Based on a model of concurrent bytecode (e.g., [18]), it should be straightforward to formulate an interleaving semantics for multithreaded, mixed bytecode and native code.

Notation conventions. We write $\overline{e}$ for a list (or sequence) of elements e. The empty list is ϵ, and $e \cdot s$ is the concatenation of e with list s. Appending two lists is written as $s_1 \bullet s_2$. We write $[e_1, \ldots, e_n]$ for a finite list.

Given a function f, we write $f[x \mapsto v]$ for an updated function that agrees with f except that x is mapped to v. We write $f[\overline{x} \mapsto \overline{v}]$ for a function after a sequence of updates from $\overline{x}$ to $\overline{v}$. We write "*X Option*" for an option domain of X (think of ML's option types). We write None for the none value, and $\lfloor x \rfloor$ for some x. We use $\top$ for an arbitrary value.

3.1 JNIL Programs

A JNIL program is modeled as an environment that records information for classes and methods (Fig. 1). A program P includes maps from class names and method IDs to their respective definitions. In particular, $P(\phi)$.super is the superclass of class ϕ, or None; $P(\phi)$.fields is the list of fields declared in ϕ. We write Fields(P, ϕ) for the list of all fields of ϕ, including the ones of its superclasses. Java method and native method information are separated into two maps: P_{JM} for Java methods and P_{NM} for native methods. We write JavaMD(P)

$$P = P_{\mathrm{JC}} \cup P_{\mathrm{JM}} \cup P_{\mathrm{NM}}$$
$$P_{\mathrm{JC}} : \mathit{ClassName} \rightharpoonup \langle \mathsf{super} : \mathit{ClassName\ Option},\ \mathsf{fields} : \mathit{FID\ List} \rangle$$
$$P_{\mathrm{JM}} : \mathit{MID} \rightharpoonup \left\langle \begin{array}{l} \mathsf{code} : \mathit{JInstr\ List},\ \mathsf{handlers} : \mathit{Handler\ List}, \\ \mathsf{stype} : \mathit{CodeAddr} \rightharpoonup \mathit{Type\ List},\ \mathsf{vtype} : \mathit{CodeAddr} \rightharpoonup \mathit{JVarID} \rightarrow \mathit{Type} \end{array} \right\rangle$$
$$P_{\mathrm{NM}} : \mathit{MID} \rightharpoonup \langle \mathsf{code} : \mathit{NInstr\ List} \rangle$$

$$\mathit{fd} \in \mathit{FID} ::= \langle \phi, \alpha, \tau \rangle \qquad \mathit{md} \in \mathit{MID} ::= \langle \phi, \alpha, [\tau_1, \ldots, \tau_n] \rightarrow \tau_r \rangle$$
$$\tau \in \mathit{Type} ::= \mathsf{Int} \mid \mathsf{Cls}\ \phi \mid \mathsf{Top} \qquad \eta \in \mathit{Handler} ::= \langle n_b, n_e, n_t, \phi \rangle$$

$$\phi \in \mathit{ClassName} = \mathit{String} \qquad \alpha \in \mathit{String} \qquad n \in \mathit{CodeAddr} = \mathbb{N} \qquad d \in \mathit{JVarID} = \mathbb{N}$$

Fig. 1. JNIL programs

$$
\begin{array}{rcl}
I \in \mathit{JInstr} & ::= & \mathit{arith} \mid \mathit{cond}\ n \mid \mathsf{push}\ v \mid \mathsf{pop} \mid \mathsf{localload}\ d \mid \mathsf{localstore}\ d \mid \mathsf{goto}\ n \\
 & & \mid \mathsf{getfield}\ \mathit{fd} \mid \mathsf{putfield}\ \mathit{fd} \mid \mathsf{new}\ \phi \mid \mathsf{invokevirtual}\ \mathit{md} \mid \mathsf{returnval} \mid \mathsf{throw} \\
\mathit{arith} \in \mathit{JArith} & ::= & \mathsf{add} \mid \mathsf{sub} \mid \mathsf{mul} \mid \ldots \qquad \mathit{cond} \in \mathit{JCond} ::= \mathsf{ifeq} \mid \mathsf{ifne} \mid \mathsf{ifgt} \mid \ldots
\end{array}
$$

$$
\begin{array}{rcl}
\iota \in \mathit{NInstr} & ::= & \mathit{jfun} \mid \mathit{aop}\ r_d, r_s, \mathit{op} \mid \mathit{bop}\ r_s, r_t, \mathit{op} \mid \mathsf{Mov}\ r_d, \mathit{op} \mid \mathsf{Jmp}\ \mathit{op} \\
 & & \mid \mathsf{Ld}\ r_d, r_s[r_t] \mid \mathsf{St}\ r_d[r_t], r_s \mid \mathsf{Alloc}\ r_d, n \mid \mathsf{Free}\ r_s[n] \\
 & & \mid \mathsf{SLd}\ r_d, \mathsf{sp}[n] \mid \mathsf{SSt}\ \mathsf{sp}[n], r_s \mid \mathsf{SAlloc}\ n \mid \mathsf{SFree}\ n \mid \mathsf{Ret} \\
\mathit{jfun} \in \mathit{JNIFun} & ::= & \mathsf{GetField}\ \mathit{fd} \mid \mathsf{SetField}\ \mathit{fd} \mid \mathsf{NewObject}\ \phi \mid \mathsf{CallMethod}\ \mathit{md} \\
 & & \mid \mathsf{IsInstanceOf}\ \tau \mid \mathsf{JNIThrow} \mid \mathsf{ExnClear} \mid \mathsf{ExnOccurred} \\
\mathit{aop} \in \mathit{NArith} & ::= & \mathsf{Add} \mid \mathsf{Sub} \mid \mathsf{Mul} \mid \ldots \qquad \mathit{bop} \in \mathit{NCond} ::= \mathsf{Beq} \mid \mathsf{Bneq} \mid \mathsf{Bgt} \mid \ldots \\
\mathit{op} \in \mathit{Operand} & ::= & r \mid n \qquad r \in \mathit{Register} ::= \mathsf{r1} \mid \mathsf{r2} \mid \ldots \mid \mathsf{r32}
\end{array}
$$

Fig. 2. Bytecode and native instruction sets

for the set of Java method IDs in P, and NativeMD(P) for the set of native method IDs. $P_{\mathrm{JM}}(md)$ contains a list of Java instructions (the code field), a list of exception handlers, and also type information (stype and vtype). The type information is used when type checking Java methods and is irrelevant for operational semantics. $P_{\mathrm{NM}}(md)$ simply contains a list of native instructions. We abbreviate $P(md).\mathsf{code}[pc]$ to $P(md)@pc$, the instruction at pc in md.

Java types include Int type, class type (Cls ϕ), and Top type. The predicate IsRefType(τ) holds when τ is a class type (or an array type when we consider arrays). Two special class names, `object` and `throwable`, are assumed. We write Object and Throwable for "Cls `object`" and "Cls `throwable`", respectively. An exception handler, $\langle n_b, n_e, n_t, \phi \rangle$, catches exceptions of class ϕ by transferring the control to address n_t, if the program counter is in the range $[n_b, n_e - 1]$.

Fig. 2 presents the syntax of the bytecode and native instruction sets. The bytecode instruction set is modeled after the instruction set in the JVM specification [12]; we refer readers to the specification for a detailed discussion. The native instruction set includes instructions for manipulating the heap (load, store, allocation, and deallocation), a set of instructions for manipulating the operand stack (those instructions whose operators begin with S), a Ret instruction for returning, and a set of JNI functions. We use r for a register and op for an operand, which is either a register or a constant. Finally, we note that instructions for pushing to and popping from the operand stack can be synthesized: "Push op" is "$\mathsf{SAlloc}\ 1; \mathsf{SSt}\ \mathsf{sp}[0], op$" and "Pop r" is "$\mathsf{SLd}\ r, \mathsf{sp}[0]; \mathsf{SFree}\ 1$".

Fig. 2 also includes a set of common JNI functions. Note that `GetField`, `SetField`, and `CallMethod` take field and method IDs as arguments. The JNI interface actually uses a two-step process to access a field (or call a method): first convert a string that represents the field (or method) to a field (or method) ID; the resulting ID is then used in operations such as `GetField`. JNIL omits the first step to avoid the need to axiomatize the conversion from strings to IDs.

Both the bytecode and the native instruction sets include arithmetic and binary comparison instructions. Their semantics is straightforward.

3.2 Runtime States

A runtime state is a triple $(S; H; R)$, where S is a method-call stack, H a shared heap, and R a register file. Its format is shown in Fig. 3. We have discussed the format of the method-call stack and the heap in the previous section. Recall that the heap holds only primitive values; objects are mapped to primitive values and stored in blocks. A value is either an integer n, a null value, or a reference value $\ell[i]$. We abbreviate $\ell[0]$ to ℓ.

JNIL's operational semantics is modeled as a transition relation: $P \vdash (S; H; R) \longmapsto (S'; H'; R')$. Fig. 3 also presents evaluation rules at the top level. A state steps forward because of a Java step, a native step, or a GC step.

$$\begin{array}{rcl} S \in \mathit{Stack} & ::= & \overline{F} \mid \langle \ell \rangle_{\mathrm{X}} \cdot \overline{F} \\ F \in \mathit{Frame} & ::= & \langle md, pc, s, a \rangle_{\mathrm{J}} \\ & \mid & \langle md, pc, s, v_x, L \rangle_{\mathrm{N}} \\ s \in \mathit{OpStack} & ::= & \overline{v} \\ a \in \mathit{JVarMap} & ::= & \{0 \mapsto v_0, 1 \mapsto v_1, \ldots\} \\ L \in \mathit{RootSet} & ::= & \{\ell_1, \ldots, \ell_n\} \end{array}
\qquad
\begin{array}{rcl} H \in \mathit{Heap} & ::= & \mathit{Label} \rightharpoonup \left\langle \begin{array}{l} \mathsf{blk} : \mathit{Block}, \\ \mathsf{own} : \mathit{Owner} \end{array} \right\rangle \\ b \in \mathit{Block} & ::= & \mathbb{N} \rightharpoonup \mathit{Value} \\ v \in \mathit{Value} & ::= & n \mid \mathsf{null} \mid \ell[i] \\ \omega \in \mathit{Owner} & ::= & \mathrm{J} \mid \mathrm{N} \\ o \in \mathit{Object} & ::= & \langle\!\langle fd_1 = v_1, \ldots, fd_n = v_n \rangle\!\rangle_{\phi} \end{array}$$

$$R \in \mathit{RegFile} ::= \{\mathsf{r1} \mapsto v_1, \ldots, \mathsf{r32} \mapsto v_{32}\}$$

$$\frac{P \vdash (S; H; R) \overset{\mathrm{J}}{\longmapsto} (S'; H'; R')}{P \vdash (S; H; R) \longmapsto (S'; H'; R')} \qquad \frac{P \vdash (S; H; R) \overset{\mathrm{N}}{\longmapsto} (S'; H'; R')}{P \vdash (S; H; R) \longmapsto (S'; H'; R')}$$

$$\frac{(S; H) \overset{\mathrm{GC}}{\longmapsto} (S'; H')}{P \vdash (S; H; R) \longmapsto (S'; H'; R)}$$

Fig. 3. JNIL runtime states $(S; H; R)$ and top evaluation rules

3.3 Operational Semantics of Bytecode and Native Instructions

Due to space limitation, we will present rules only for typical instructions; the full set of rules are in the technical report. Fig. 4 presents the rules for "getfield fd",

$P \vdash (\langle md, pc, s, a \rangle_{\mathrm{J}} \cdot S; H; R) \overset{\mathrm{J}}{\longmapsto} (S'; H'; R)$, where

if $P(md)@pc =$	and conditions hold,	then $S'; H' =$
getfield fd	$fd = \langle \phi, \alpha, \tau \rangle$ $\quad s = \ell \cdot s_1$ $P, H \vdash \ell : \mathsf{Cls}\ \phi$ $\mathrm{ReadFd}(H, \ell, fd) = v$	$\langle md, pc + 1, v \cdot s_1, a \rangle_{\mathrm{J}} \cdot S; H$

$P \vdash (\langle md, pc, s, v_x, L \rangle_{\mathrm{N}} \cdot S; H; R) \overset{\mathrm{N}}{\longmapsto} (S'; H'; R)$, where

if $P(md)@pc =$	and conditions hold,	then $S'; H' =$
GetField fd	$fd = \langle \phi, \alpha, \tau \rangle$ $\quad s = \ell \cdot s_1$ $P, H \vdash \ell : \mathsf{Cls}\ \phi$ $\mathrm{ReadFd}(H, \ell, fd) = v \quad v_x = \mathsf{null}$	$\langle md, pc + 1, v \cdot s_1, \mathsf{null}, L' \rangle_{\mathrm{N}} \cdot S; H$, where $L' = L \cup \mathrm{Roots}(v)$

Fig. 4. Semantics of bytecode and native instructions

$$\text{ReadFd}(H, \ell, fd) = \begin{cases} o(fd) & \text{if } H(\ell) = \langle \text{Rep}(o), \text{J} \rangle, \\ & \text{and } o = \langle\!\langle \ldots \rangle\!\rangle_\phi, \text{ and } fd \in \text{dom}(o) \\ \text{undefined otherwise} & \end{cases}$$

$$\text{Tag}(H, \ell) = \begin{cases} \phi & \text{if } H(\ell) = \langle \text{Rep}(\langle\!\langle \ldots \rangle\!\rangle_\phi), \text{J} \rangle \\ \text{undefined otherwise} & \end{cases}$$

$$\boxed{P \vdash \tau_1 <: \tau_2}$$

$$\frac{}{P \vdash \tau <: \mathsf{Top}} \qquad \frac{}{P \vdash \mathsf{Int} <: \mathsf{Int}} \qquad \frac{}{P \vdash \mathsf{Cls}\ \phi <: \mathsf{Cls}\ \phi} \qquad \frac{P \vdash \mathsf{Cls}\ \phi_1 <: \mathsf{Cls}\ \phi_2 \quad P(\phi_2).\mathsf{super} = \lfloor \phi_3 \rfloor}{P \vdash \mathsf{Cls}\ \phi_1 <: \mathsf{Cls}\ \phi_3}$$

$$\boxed{P, H \vdash v : \tau}$$

$$\frac{P, H \vdash v : \tau \quad P \vdash \tau <: \tau'}{P, H \vdash v : \tau'} \qquad \frac{}{P, H \vdash v : \mathsf{Top}}$$

$$\frac{}{P, H \vdash n : \mathsf{Int}} \qquad \frac{\text{Tag}(H, \ell) = \phi}{P, H \vdash \ell : \mathsf{Cls}\ \phi} \qquad \frac{}{P, H \vdash \mathsf{null} : \mathsf{Cls}\ \phi}$$

Fig. 5. Auxiliary definitions

a bytecode instruction, and its counterpart JNI function "GetField *fd*" (which is used in native code). The rules use a few auxiliary definitions defined in Fig. 5. $\text{ReadFd}(H, \ell, fd)$ reads the value of field *fd* from block ℓ in heap H. $\text{Tag}(H, \ell)$ returns the runtime tag of a Java object at ℓ in H. Judgment $P \vdash \tau_1 <: \tau_2$ expresses that τ_1 is a subtype of τ_2. Judgment $P, H \vdash v : \tau$ performs runtime type checking and checks that v has type τ in program P and heap H. Note a reference ℓ is of type "Cls ϕ" if the tag at ℓ is ϕ (or ϕ' and ϕ' is a subclass of ϕ). The rule itself does not mandate that the values of fields obey the fields' types. This requirement is put into a separate judgment for checking well-typed heaps, as customary in type systems for mutable references.

The semantics of "getfield *fd*" is deliberately partial. If the object reference on the operand stack does not have the class type specified in *fd*, then JNIL's abstract machine does not have a next state (that is, "getting stuck"). Similarly, the machine gets stuck if block ℓ in H is not owned by Java, does not hold an object representation, or field *fd* is not in the domain of the representation. The static type system for bytecode ensures that such cases will not happen for well-typed bytecode programs.

The semantics of "GetField *fd*" is similar to "getfield *fd*", except for a couple of differences. First, no JNI exceptions should be pending. Recall that in a native stack frame $\langle md, pc, s, v_x, L \rangle_{\text{N}}$ the value v_x records a pending JNI exception. The JNI manual specifies that "calling most JNI functions with a pending exception may lead to unexpected results". Consequently, the semantics of most JNI functions requires v_x be null. Second, some JNI functions may give native code extra references to Java objects. Since these references need to be registered with Java's GC, they are recorded in the root set of a native frame. As an example, the semantics of "GetField *fd*" adds the value of the field into the root set L, if that value is a reference value.

Cross-language method calls. The "invokevirtual md" instruction may invoke a Java or a native method, depending on what kind of method md represents. If it invokes a native method, the execution context switches to the native side. returnval may return to a Java, or a native method. JNI functions "CallMethod md" and Ret are analogous, except they are called in native code.

Semantics of method-call and return instructions are presented in Fig. 6. If "invokevirtual md" invokes a Java method, a new Java frame is constructed and parameters are copied to the local variable map of the new frame (following the JVML specification). If it invokes a native method, a native frame is constructed and arguments are put in its operand stack (recall the calling convention). The auxiliary function NewFrame constructs either a Java frame or a native frame:

$$\text{NewFrame}(P, md, [v_1, \ldots, v_n]) = \begin{cases} \langle md, 1, \epsilon, a_\top[0 \mapsto v_1, \ldots, n-1 \mapsto v_n]\rangle_{\mathrm{J}}, \\ \quad \text{if } md \in \text{JavaMD}(P), \\ \langle md, 1, v_n \cdot \ldots \cdot v_1 \cdot \epsilon, \mathsf{null}, \text{Roots}([v_1, \ldots, v_n])\rangle_{\mathrm{N}}, \\ \quad \text{if } md \in \text{NativeMD}(P) \end{cases}$$

The semantics of returnval has two cases: returning to a Java method call or a native method call. Similar to "invokevirtual md", "CallMethod md" may invoke either a Java or a native method. The JNI manual does not make it clear

$P \vdash (\langle md, pc, s, a\rangle_{\mathrm{J}} \cdot S; H; R) \overset{\mathrm{J}}{\longmapsto} (S'; H; R)$, if

$P(md)@pc =$	and cond. hold,	then $S' =$
invokevirtual md_1	$md_1 = \langle \phi, \alpha, [\tau_1, \ldots, \tau_n] \to \tau_r\rangle$ $s = v_n \cdot \ldots \cdot v_1 \cdot \ell \cdot s_1$ $\text{Tag}(H, \ell) = \phi' \quad P \vdash \mathsf{Cls}\ \phi' <: \mathsf{Cls}\ \phi$ $md' = \langle \phi', \alpha, [\tau_1, \ldots, \tau_n] \to \tau_r\rangle$	$\text{NewFrame}(P, md', [\ell, v_1, \ldots, v_n]) \cdot$ $\langle md, pc, s, a\rangle_{\mathrm{J}} \cdot S$
returnval	$md = \langle \phi, \alpha, [\tau_1, \ldots, \tau_n] \to \tau_r\rangle$ $S = \langle md', pc', \overline{v_p} \cdot \ell \cdot s', a'\rangle_{\mathrm{J}} \cdot S_1$ $\lvert\overline{v_p}\rvert = n \qquad s = v_r \cdot s_1$	$\langle md', pc' + 1, v_r \cdot s', a'\rangle_{\mathrm{J}} \cdot S_1$
returnval	$md = \langle \phi, \alpha, [\tau_1, \ldots, \tau_n] \to \tau_r\rangle$ $S = \langle md', pc', \overline{v_p} \cdot v \cdot s', v_x, L\rangle_{\mathrm{N}} \cdot S_1$ $\lvert\overline{v_p}\rvert = n \qquad s = v_r \cdot s_1$	$\langle md', pc' + 1, v_r \cdot s', v_x, L'\rangle_{\mathrm{N}} \cdot S_1$, where $L' = L \cup \text{Roots}(v_r)$

$P \vdash (\langle md, pc, s, v_x, L\rangle_{\mathrm{N}} \cdot S; H; R) \overset{\mathrm{N}}{\longmapsto} (S'; H; R)$, if

$P(md)@pc =$	and conditions hold,	then $S' =$
CallMethod md_1	$md_1 = \langle \phi, \alpha, [\tau_1, \ldots, \tau_n] \to \tau_r\rangle$ $s = v_n \cdot \ldots v_1 \cdot \ell \cdot s_1$ $\text{Tag}(H, \ell) = \phi' \quad P \vdash \mathsf{Cls}\ \phi' <: \mathsf{Cls}\ \phi$ $md' = \langle \phi', \alpha, [\tau_1, \ldots, \tau_n] \to \tau_r\rangle$ $v_x = \mathsf{null}$	$\text{NewFrame}(P, md', [\ell, v_1, \ldots, v_n]) \cdot$ $\langle md, pc, s, v_x, L\rangle_{\mathrm{N}} \cdot S$
Ret	$md = \langle \phi, \alpha, [\tau_1, \ldots, \tau_n] \to \tau_r\rangle$ $S = \langle md', pc', \overline{v_p} \cdot v \cdot s', a'\rangle_{\mathrm{J}} \cdot S_1$ $\lvert\overline{v_p}\rvert = n \qquad s = v_r \cdot s_1 \qquad v_x = \mathsf{null}$	$\langle md', pc' + 1, v_r \cdot s', a'\rangle_{\mathrm{J}} \cdot S_1$;
Ret	$md = \langle \phi, \alpha, [\tau_1, \ldots, \tau_n] \to \tau_r\rangle$ $S = \langle md', pc', \overline{v_p} \cdot v \cdot s', v'_x, L\rangle_{\mathrm{N}} \cdot S_1$ $\lvert\overline{v_p}\rvert = n \qquad s = v_r \cdot s_1 \qquad v_x = \mathsf{null}$	$\langle md', pc' + 1, v_r \cdot s', v'_x, L\rangle_{\mathrm{N}} \cdot S_1$, where $L' = L \cup \text{Roots}(v_r)$

Fig. 6. Semantics of method calls and returns

whether a native method is allowed to invoke another native method through "CallMethod *md*". Our experiments confirmed that JVM implementations allow this behavior. Both rules for Ret are for the case of no pending exceptions; a different rule for Ret with a pending exception will be presented.

Exception handling. Fig. 7 shows rules that are related to exceptions. The throw instruction pushes an exception frame onto the method-call stack. Other bytecode instructions may also generate a Java exception. For instance, "getfield *fd*" generates an exception when the object reference on the operand stack is null. When such cases happen, a `Throwable` object is allocated and an exception frame is placed onto the stack. We list these cases in the technical report.

When a Java exception is pending, JNIL unwinds the stack as shown in the second table of Fig. 7. There are three cases. If the next frame is a Java frame and there is no matched handler for the exception, the Java frame is removed. If the Java frame has a matched handler, then the control transfers to the handler. If the next frame is a native frame, the Java exception is recorded in the native frame (i.e., conceptually converted into a JNI exception) and the execution continues as normal from the next instruction in native code.

The last table in Fig. 7 shows how JNI exceptions are generated and handled. A JNI exception thrown by JNIThrow is recorded in the current native

$P \vdash (\langle md, pc, s, a\rangle_{\mathrm{J}} \cdot S; H; R) \xrightarrow{\mathrm{J}} (S'; H'; R)$, where

if $P(md)@pc =$	and conditions hold,	then $S'; H' =$
throw	$s = \ell \cdot s_1$ $\quad P, H \vdash \ell : \mathsf{Throwable}$	$\langle \ell \rangle_{\mathrm{X}} \cdot \langle md, pc, s, a\rangle_{\mathrm{J}} \cdot S; H$

$P \vdash S; H; R \xrightarrow{\mathrm{J}} S'; H; R$, if one of the following cases holds

if $S =$	and conditions hold,	then $S' =$
$\langle \ell \rangle_{\mathrm{X}} \cdot \langle md, pc, s, a\rangle_{\mathrm{J}} \cdot S_1$	$\mathrm{Tag}(H, \ell) = \phi \quad P(md).\mathsf{handlers} = \overline{\eta}$ $\mathit{CorrectHandler}(\overline{\eta}, P, pc, \phi) = \mathsf{None}$	$\langle \ell \rangle_{\mathrm{X}} \cdot S_1$
$\langle \ell \rangle_{\mathrm{X}} \cdot \langle md, pc, s, a\rangle_{\mathrm{J}} \cdot S_1$	$\mathrm{Tag}(H, \ell) = \phi \quad P(md).\mathsf{handlers} = \overline{\eta}$ $\mathit{CorrectHandler}(\overline{\eta}, P, pc, \phi) = \lfloor n_t \rfloor$	$\langle md, n_t, \ell \cdot \epsilon, a\rangle_{\mathrm{J}} \cdot S_1$
$\langle \ell \rangle_{\mathrm{X}} \cdot \langle md, pc, s, v_x, L\rangle_{\mathrm{N}} \cdot S_1$		$\langle md, pc+1, s, \ell, L\rangle_{\mathrm{N}} \cdot S_1$

$$\mathit{CorrectHandler}(\epsilon, P, pc, \phi) = \mathsf{None}$$

$$\mathit{CorrectHandler}(\langle n_b, n_e, n_t, \phi' \rangle \cdot \overline{\eta}, P, pc, \phi) = \begin{cases} \lfloor n_t \rfloor & \text{if } n_b \leq pc < n_e \text{ and } P \vdash \mathsf{Cls}\ \phi <: \mathsf{Cls}\ \phi' \\ \mathit{CorrectHandler}(\overline{\eta}, P, pc, \phi) & \text{otherwise} \end{cases}$$

$P \vdash (\langle md, pc, s, v_x, L\rangle_{\mathrm{N}} \cdot S; H; R) \xrightarrow{\mathrm{N}} (S'; H; R)$, where

if $P(md)@pc =$	and conditions hold,	then $S' =$
JNIThrow	$s = \ell \cdot s_1 \quad P, H \vdash \ell : \mathsf{Throwable}$ $v_x = \mathsf{null}$	$\langle md, pc+1, s_1, \ell, L\rangle_{\mathrm{N}} \cdot S$
ExnClear		$\langle md, pc+1, s, \mathsf{null}, L\rangle_{\mathrm{N}} \cdot S$
ExnOccurred	$v = 0$ if $v_x = \mathsf{null}$, or 1 if $v_x = \ell$	$\langle md, pc+1, v \cdot s, v_x, L\rangle_{\mathrm{N}} \cdot S$
Ret	$v_x = \ell \quad P, H \vdash \ell : \mathsf{Throwable}$	$\langle \ell \rangle_{\mathrm{X}} \cdot S$

Fig. 7. Exception handling in JNIL

frame. Native code can either clear the exception by ExnClear or return with the exception pending, in which case an exception frame is pushed onto the stack.

We present an example below showing how the method-call stack unwinds assuming 1) Java method md_1 calls native method md_2, which calls Java method md_3; 2) md_3 throws an exception; 3) md_3 and md_2 do not handle the exception, but md_1 handles the exception. Notice how md_3 and md_2 treat the exception differently.

$$
\begin{array}{ll}
\langle \ell \rangle_{\mathrm{X}} \cdot \langle md_3, \ldots \rangle_{\mathrm{J}} \cdot \langle md_2, \ldots, \mathsf{null}, \ldots \rangle_{\mathrm{N}} \cdot \langle md_1, \ldots \rangle_{\mathrm{J}} \cdot \epsilon & // md_3 \textit{ throws an exception} \\
\to \langle \ell \rangle_{\mathrm{X}} \cdot \langle md_2, \ldots, \mathsf{null}, \ldots \rangle_{\mathrm{N}} \cdot \langle md_1, \ldots \rangle_{\mathrm{J}} \cdot \epsilon & // md_3 \textit{ does not handle the exception} \\
\to \langle md_2, \ldots, \ell, \ldots \rangle_{\mathrm{N}} \cdot \langle md_1, \ldots \rangle_{\mathrm{J}} \cdot \epsilon & // md_2 \textit{ records } \ell \textit{ and continues execution} \\
\to \langle \ell \rangle_{\mathrm{X}} \cdot \langle md_1, \ldots \rangle_{\mathrm{J}} \cdot \epsilon & // md_2 \textit{ returns with a pending exception} \\
\to \langle md_1, \ldots \rangle_{\mathrm{J}} \cdot \epsilon & // md_1 \textit{ handles the exception}
\end{array}
$$

3.4 GC Step

The GC rule is presented below. A set of blocks can be removed from the heap if they are part of the Java heap, their labels are disjoint from the roots of the stack, and they are unreachable from the rest of the Java heap.

$$
\frac{L \subseteq \mathrm{dom}(H|_{\mathrm{J}}) \qquad L \cap \mathrm{Roots}(S) = \emptyset \qquad L \cap \mathrm{Reachable}((H|_{\mathrm{J}}) \setminus L) = \emptyset}{(S; H) \overset{\mathrm{GC}}{\longmapsto} (S; H \setminus L)}
$$

Roots(S) is the set of labels contained in method-call stack S and Reachable(H) is the set of labels in H. Their definitions are in the technical report.

Note that the rule is nondeterministic and L can be as small as the empty set. It is also abstract and hides the implementation details of GCs. In fact, it accommodates all garbage collectors that are based on tracing, reference counting, or combinations of both; any such garbage collector computes a set of unreachable locations [19]. Finally, recall that JNIL's heap model allows the rule to ignore the moving aspect of garbage collection.

3.5 Type Safety of Bytecode and GC Safety

The JVM always performs bytecode verification before running a bytecode program. Therefore, type checking of bytecode can be considered an essential part of the JNI. The JNIL model also performs type checking of bytecode, which largely follows a previous JVML model [15]. We highlight its top-level judgments and the main safety theorems, but leave details and proofs to the technical report [10].

Judgment "$\vdash P$ prog" checks that a program P is well typed. It ensures that all classes and all methods in its domain are well typed. When checking a Java method, each bytecode instruction in the method body is type checked with respect to pre- and post-conditions expressed in types. Note the system does not perform type inference to infer those conditions, but merely takes types as input and checks type consistency. Recall a Java method is associated with type information for the operand stack and local variables (see the fields `stype` and `vtype` in Fig. 1); the type information is input to type checking.

Judgment "$P \vdash (S;H;R)$ state" type checks runtime state $(S;H;R)$. It is well typed if 1) $H|_{\mathrm{J}}$ is a well-typed Java heap, and 2) S is a well-typed stack under P and the Java heap. Checking well-typed Java heaps requires each heap object be well typed according to its runtime tag, as customary in such kind of type systems. Checking well-typed stacks not only requires every frame be well typed, but also requires the chain of frames be a well-typed call chain—each frame is the result of a call instruction in the caller method.

Definition 1. *$(S;H;R)$ is a terminal state if 1) either $S = \langle md, pc, v_r \cdot s, a\rangle_{\mathrm{J}} \cdot \epsilon$ and $P(md)@pc$ = returnval, 2) or $S = \langle md, pc, v_r \cdot s, \textit{null}, L\rangle_{\mathrm{N}} \cdot \epsilon$ and $P(md)@pc$ = Ret, 3) or $S = \langle \ell \rangle_{\mathrm{X}} \cdot \epsilon$.*

Theorem 2 (Java Progress). *If $\vdash P$ prog, and $P \vdash (S_1;H_1;R_1)$ state, then either $(S_1;H_1;R_1)$ is a terminal state, or $\exists S_2, H_2, R_2.\ P \vdash S_1;H_1;R_1 \overset{\mathrm{J}}{\longmapsto} S_2;H_2;R_2$, or $S_1 = \langle \ldots \rangle_{\mathrm{N}} \cdot S_1'$.*

Theorem 3 (Java Preservation). *If $\vdash P$ prog, and $P \vdash (S_1;H_1;R_1)$ state, and $P \vdash S_1;H_1;R_1 \overset{\mathrm{J}}{\longmapsto} S_2;H_2;R_2$, then $P \vdash (S_2;H_2;R_2)$ state.*

Type soundness of bytecode is expressed in the standard form of progress and preservation theorems. By the progress theorem, a well-typed state will be either a terminal state, a state that can take a Java step, or a state where native code is in control. It will never get stuck when bytecode is in control. By the preservation theorem, a well-typed state steps to another well-typed state when taking Java steps. It makes no guarantee when a state takes a native step.

A GC step does not affect the type safety of bytecode, as the following theorem asserts:

Theorem 4 (GC Safety). *If $\vdash P$ prog, $P \vdash (S;H;R)$ state, and $(S;H) \overset{\mathrm{GC}}{\longmapsto} (S';H')$, then $P \vdash (S';H';R)$ state.*

4 Applications of the JNIL Model

The JNI specification does not mandate any checking of native methods. Native methods are notoriously unsafe and a rich source of software errors. Recent studies have reported hundreds of interface bugs in JNI programs [1, 5, 6].

A number of systems have been designed and implemented to improve and find misuses of the JNI interface. They have overall improved the JNI's safety and security. We classify them into three broad categories:

- *New interface languages.* Jeannie [3] is a language design that allows programmers to mix Java with C code using quasi-quoting. A Jeannie program is then compiled into JNI code by the Jeannie compiler. Jeannie helps programmers reduce errors. For instance, programmers can raise Java exceptions directly in Jeannie, avoiding the error-prone process of exception handling in native code.

- *Static checking.* Several recent systems employ static analysis to identify specific classes of errors in JNI code [1, 4, 6, 7]. These bug finders have found hundreds of errors in real JNI programs.
- *Dynamic checking.* SafeJNI [2] combines Java with CCured [20] and inserts dynamic tests that check for safety violations. Going one step further, Jinn [8] automatically generates dynamic checks based on safety specifications in terms of finite-state machines.

We argue that it would be valuable to formalize the claims of these systems in JNIL and thus provide a rigorous foundation for their strength. We envision JNIL would be useful in the following ways:

- *Formal semantics of Jeannie.* We discussed Jeannie, a language that mixes Java with C code and is translated to JNI code. Jeannie does not come with formal semantics. An interesting way of defining Jeannie's semantics would be to map Jeannie programs to JNIL programs.
- *Soundness of JNI static checking.* JNIL can serve as a basis for proving that a JNI bug finder does not miss any errors of a certain kind. One way to show the soundness is to structure the system into two components: inference and verification. The first part infers annotations (e.g., in the form of types) and the second part performs verification with annotations as hints. Then the soundness theorem is to show that programs (with annotations) that pass the verification do not incur the kind of errors in question.
- *Soundness of JNI dynamic checking.* JNIL can also serve as a basis for showing the soundness of systems that insert dynamic checks for safety (e.g., SafeJNI [2]). One way to proceed is to have an "instrumented" semantics of JNIL in which dynamic checks are embedded into its transition rules. If a dynamic check fails, the system transits to an error state. The soundness theorem expresses that a state is either a terminal state, an error state, or a state that can progress. A more ambitious attempt to formalize dynamic checking is to treat the insertion of dynamic checks as a source-to-source rewriting system. The safety theorem would then show the resulting program is safe according to the vanilla semantics of JNIL.

In the above examples, JNIL alone would not be sufficient; we would also need formal models of other parts (e.g., a model of static checking). But JNIL provides a common foundation for such formal development to proceed. With additional constraints on the native code, JNIL makes it possible to prove properties of a multilingual system.

5 Extensions and Future Work

The technical report presents two extensions of JNIL. The first extends JNIL to add support for Java arrays. Most of the new rules for arrays are straightforward. One complication is that the JNI treats primitive arrays (i.e., arrays with primitive types such as Int) differently from object arrays. The GetIntArrayElements function returns a pointer to the first element of the array and native code can then perform address arithmetic with the pointer to access array elements. Since JNIL's heap model allows address arithmetic within blocks, direct pointers to Java arrays are nicely accommodated.

For clarity, JNIL in Sec. 3 passes arguments and results through the operand stack when Java interfaces with native code. However, in reality the calling convention varies greatly, depending on compilers and architectures. Therefore, the second extension of JNIL is about how to parametrize the model over a calling convention.

One immediate next step is to develop methodology to evaluate our model. We plan to develop machine-checked semantics of JNIL in Coq. We will make the model executable so that it is possible to run benchmark programs in the model. We will also investigate whether a substantial subset of C can be translated to the native language in JNIL—a way to evaluate its practicality.

6 Related Work

The block heap model in JNIL takes inspiration from Leroy and Blazy's block memory model in the CompCert project [21]. They use the block memory model to specify the semantics of C-like languages and verify correctness of program transformations. We use the block model to reconcile differences between a high-level, garbage-collected OO language and a low-level language. The bytecode language in JNIL bears many similarities to Freund and Mitchell's JVML_f model [15]; the native language is similar to Morrisett *et al.*'s stack-based typed assembly language [22]. JNIL's emphasis is on proposing abstractions for modeling language-interoperation issues in FFIs.

Previous work proposed preliminary formalisms that capture certain aspects of the JNI. Furr and Foster justified JSaffire's soundness on a formalization of a subset of the JNI [23]. It models only the native side, and treats Java objects opaquely. Jinn [8] describes safety constraints of the JNI using finite-state machines. JNIL models both sides of the interface and proposes abstractions that address issues including a shared heap, cross-language method calls, exception handling, and the impact of garbage collection; these issues have not been addressed by previous efforts.

7 Conclusions

Most real software systems are multilingual. A safe software system depends on its building blocks and their interoperation. Even if each building block is safe in some language model with respect to some safety policy, without safe interoperation between languages there would be no safety guarantee on the whole system. Therefore, modeling and reasoning about language interoperation is critical to the safety and security of software systems. JNIL is a formal model that covers the core JNI. Its abstractions elegantly reconcile the differences between a high-level OO language and a low-level language. It can directly be used to provide a formal foundation for systems that analyze the JNI. We believe its concepts can be generalized to model other FFIs.

References

[1] Furr, M., Foster, J.S.: Polymorphic type inference for the JNI. In: Sestoft, P. (ed.) ESOP 2006. LNCS, vol. 3924, pp. 309–324. Springer, Heidelberg (2006)

[2] Tan, G., Appel, A.W., Chakradhar, S., Raghunathan, A., Ravi, S., Wang, D.: Safe Java Native Interface. In: Proceedings of IEEE International Symposium on Secure Software Engineering, pp. 97–106 (2006)

[3] Hirzel, M., Grimm, R.: Jeannie: Granting Java Native Interface developers their wishes. In: OOPSLA, pp. 19–38 (2007)

[4] Tan, G., Morrisett, G.: ILEA: Inter-language analysis across Java and C. In: OOPSLA, pp. 39–56 (2007)

[5] Tan, G., Croft, J.: An empirical security study of the native code in the JDK. In: 17th Usenix Security Symposium, pp. 365–377 (2008)

[6] Kondoh, G., Onodera, T.: Finding bugs in Java Native Interface programs. In: ISSTA 2008: Proceedings of the 2008 International Symposium on Software Testing and Analysis, pp. 109–118. ACM, New York (2008)

[7] Li, S., Tan, G.: Finding bugs in exceptional situations of JNI programs. In: Proceedings of the 16th ACM conference on Computer and communications security (CCS), pp. 442–452 (2009)

[8] Lee, B., Hirzel, M., Grimm, R., Wiedermann, B., McKinley, K.S.: Jinn: Synthesizing a dynamic bug detector for foreign language interfaces. In: ACM Conference on Programming Language Design and Implementation (PLDI), pp. 36–49 (2010)

[9] Matthews, J., Findler, R.B.: Operational semantics for multi-language programs. In: 34th ACM Symposium on Principles of Programming Languages (POPL), pp. 3–10 (2007)

[10] Tan, G.: JNI Light: An operational model for the core JNI. Technical report, Lehigh University (March 2010), `http://www.cse.lehigh.edu/~gtan/paper/jnimodel_tr.pdf`

[11] Liang, S.: Java Native Interface: Programmer's Guide and Reference. Addison-Wesley Longman Publishing Co., Inc., Amsterdam (1999)

[12] Lindholm, T., Yellin, F.: The Java Virtual Machine Specification, 2nd edn. Addison-Wesley, Reading (1999)

[13] Drossopoulou, S., Eisenbach, S.: Describing the semantics of Java and proving type soundness. In: Alves-Foss, J. (ed.) Formal Syntax and Semantics of Java. LNCS, vol. 1523, pp. 41–82. Springer, Heidelberg (1999)

[14] Flatt, M., Krishnamurthi, S., Felleisen, M.: A programmer's reduction semantics for classes and mixins. In: Alves-Foss, J. (ed.) Formal Syntax and Semantics of Java. LNCS, vol. 1523, pp. 241–269. Springer, Heidelberg (1999)

[15] Freund, S.N., Mitchell, J.C.: A type system for the Java bytecode language and verifier. Journal of Automated Reasoning 30(3-4), 271–321 (2003)

[16] Klein, G., Nipkow, T.: A machine-checked model for a Java-like language, virtual machine, and compiler. ACM Transactions on Programming Languages and Systems 28(4), 619–695 (2006)

[17] Igarashi, A., Pierce, B.C., Wadler, P.: Featherweight Java: A minimal core calculus for Java and GJ. ACM Transactions on Programming Languages and Systems 23(3), 396–450 (2001)

[18] Petri, G., Huisman, M.: BicolanoMT: a formalization of multi-threaded Java at bytecode level. In: Bytecode 2008 (2008)

[19] Bacon, D.F., Cheng, P., Rajan, V.T.: A unified theory of garbage collection. In: OOPSLA, pp. 50–68. ACM Press, New York (2004)
[20] Necula, G.C., McPeak, S., Weimer, W.: CCured: type-safe retrofitting of legacy code. In: 29th ACM Symposium on Principles of Programming Languages (POPL), pp. 128–139 (2002)
[21] Leroy, X., Blazy, S.: Formal verification of a C-like memory model and its uses for verifying program transformations. Journal of Autom. Reasoning 41(1), 1–31 (2008)
[22] Morrisett, G., Crary, K., Glew, N., Walker, D.: Stack-based typed assembly language. Journal of Functional Programming 12(1), 43–88 (2002)
[23] Furr, M., Foster, J.S.: Checking type safety of foreign function calls. ACM Transactions on Programming Languages and Systems 30(4), 1–63 (2008)

An Interactive Tool for Analyzing Embedded SQL Queries*

Aivar Annamaa[1], Andrey Breslav[2], Jevgeni Kabanov[1], and Varmo Vene[1]

[1] University of Tartu, Estonia
[2] State University ITMO, St. Petersburg, Russia

Abstract. It is conventional for Java developers to access database engines through standard JDBC API which requires passing SQL queries in plain Java strings. This is referred to as *embedding* of SQL queries into Java. The strings are not checked at compile time, and errors in the queries (e.g. syntax errors or misspelled names) are usually detected only by testing. In this paper we describe a tool which statically analyzes SQL queries embedded into Java programs. It combines a sound syntactic analyzer with a testing facility which generates small tests to detect errors in individual queries and runs them on an actual database engine. The tool is implemented as a plug-in for Eclipse IDE and allows for interactive use in real-life projects.

1 Introduction

Domain-specific languages (DSLs) are languages tailored for a concrete application domain. They offer substantial gains in expressiveness and ease of use compared with general-purpose languages in their specific domain of application. However, in production environments, complex systems are assembled from diverse software components possibly having different DSLs which should correctly integrate with a general-purpose host language. Therefore, the efficiency and robustness of interoperability between the host-language and DSLs is of great importance.

Probably the most common way of embedding external DSLs (like SQL, HTML or JavaScript) inside the general purpose host language (e.g. Java, PHP, Python) is representing DSL constructions as host language strings (we will refer to such embeddings as string-embedded DSLs). The strings are often assembled dynamically using string concatenation and other string manipulation methods. While very flexible, such an embedding can be quite error-prone, as standard development tools provide no support for string-embedded DSLs.

* This work was partially supported by the Estonian Science Foundation grant #8421, as well as the Software Technology and Applications Competence Center (STACC), and the European Regional Development Fund through the Estonian Center of Excellence in Computer Science, EXCS.

K. Ueda (Ed.): APLAS 2010, LNCS 6461, pp. 131–138, 2010.

As an example of string-embedded DSLs and problems associated with them, consider the following example Java code fragment with an embedded SQL statement:

```
public Statement ageFilter(int minimalAge) throws SQLException {
  Connection conn = getConnection();
  String sql = "SELECT name FROM people WHERE nmae IS NOT NULL";
  if (minimalAge > 0)
      sql += "AND (age >= " + minimalAge + ")";
  return conn.prepareStatement(sql);
}
```

The `ageFilter` method receives an argument `minimalAge` and produces a query which filters entries of table `people` by their age. If the method argument, `minimalAge`, is greater than zero, a condition is appended to the query to select people of this age or older. The argument `sql` passed to the JDBC API method `prepareStatement` is where we start the analysis from.

Although Java code in this method compiles without any errors, it actually does have two errors in the SQL statement. These errors are underlined in the listing above. First, if `minimalAge` happens to be greater than zero, there will be no space between keywords `NULL` and `AND`, which is a syntax error. Second, there is a typo in the `WHERE` clause: "nmae" is written instead of "name", which is a semantic error. It would be useful if these errors could be discovered without running the program.

This paper presents a tool that detects both kinds of errors mentioned above at compile-time by statically analyzing SQL statements embedded in Java programs. It can perform sound SQL syntax analysis on strings constructed by different programming constructions like conditional concatenation and method calls. Syntax analyzer is complemented by testing facility that uses actual database engine for semantic validation of embedded SQL queries. Both services can be run in parallel with program editing. No special code annotations are required for using any of the functionality mentioned. Test version of the tool can be downloaded from `http://barclay.stacc.ee/edsl`.

First we give an overview of the general architecture of the tool and then describe main components dealing respectively with SQL extraction, syntax checking, semantic validation and user experience. We then report our results on using the tool with some open source projects. Finally we compare our solution to similar tools presented before and outline possible paths for future work.

2 Architecture

The tool is implemented as a set of plug-ins for the Eclipse IDE [4]. It re-uses the capabilities of Eclipse's Java Development Tools (JDT) to acquire abstract syntax trees from Java code. Further stages of the analysis are shown in Fig. 1. The *Abstract string collector* starts with identifying Java expressions which represent SQL statements; we refer to such expressions as *hotspots*. For each hotspot the

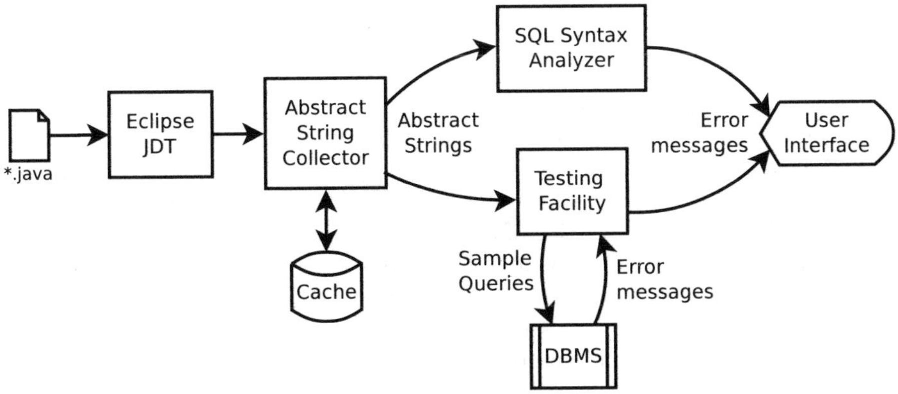

Fig. 1. Tool architecture

collector builds an *abstract string* representation, which is a regular expression representing a set of all strings the hotspot may be possibly evaluated to.

Error detection is done by the *SQL syntax analyzer* that parses abstract strings and detects syntax errors and the *testing facility* that generates sample queries from abstract strings and checks them by sending to a database engine. If the engine does not accept the query (e.g. because of a misspelled field name), the test fails and an error is reported. Error messages from both syntax analysis and tests are displayed in the Eclipse Java Editor similar to Java compiler errors.

2.1 Abstract String Collector

Abstract string collector locates hotspots and approximates sets of their possible values with abstract strings, which are regular expressions conforming to the following grammar:

$$s ::= \text{“}string\text{”} \mid [chars] \mid s^{+} \mid s\,s \mid s\,|\,s \mid (s)$$

For the SQL statement in the example above the following abstract string is constructed:

$$\text{“SELECT <...> nmae IS NOT NULL”}\left(\text{“AND (age >= ”}\;[0\text{-}9]^{+}\;\text{“)”} \mid \text{“”}\right)$$

Hotspot expressions are identified by searching the code for certain API method calls known to accept SQL statements. The exact methods can be specified by the user in a project configuration file. Text search (provided by Eclipse) is used to obtain preliminary list of hotspot locations. Corresponding compilation units are then parsed (using Eclipse JDT API) and a list of AST nodes corresponding to hotspot expressions is created.

For each hotspot expression the program slice is computed and then interprocedural path-insensitive constant propagation analysis is used for constructing the corresponding abstract string. This process includes tracking values of both immutable (`String`) and mutable (`StringBuffer` and `StringBuilder`) string objects.

Conditional appending to a string variable is represented in corresponding abstract string by choice $(a \mid b)$ between abstract strings a and b computed in either of the *if* statement branches. *While* and *for* loops are assumed to execute 0 or more times, therefore appending value x to a string variable in a loop is represented as $(\text{``''} \mid x^+)$ – choice of empty string and repetition of x.

When a method parameter is used in a hotspot expression, the corresponding abstract string is constructed as a choice of all actual arguments provided for this parameter at call sites. If a hotspot depends on a result of a (virtual) method, all implementations of this method are considered and a choice of their results is constructed. A special case when a modifiable string object[1] is passed as an argument to a method which appends to it, is also supported. The depth of interprocedural analysis is limited to a fixed number of calls in order to guarantee termination on recursive programs.

If certain unsupported Java features (e.g. global mutable state) are used in the program slice, then corresponding hotspot is marked as unsupported. For all supported hotspots, string collection algorithm is sound i.e. resulting abstract string represents a set containing all the strings this hotspot expression may possibly evaluate to. Since the analyzer uses approximation, this set may also contain strings which cannot actually appear at run time.

2.2 SQL Syntax Checker

Each abstract string is transformed into a nondeterministic finite automaton over Unicode alphabet. SQL syntax checker performs lexical analysis by transforming an automaton with a finite-state transducer (FST), which yields another automaton — over the alphabet of SQL tokens. The transducer is automatically derived from a lexical analyzer generated by JFlex [8]. This process does not introduce any loss of precision, as regular languages are closed under transformations by FSTs.

For the example given above, lexical analyzer constructs an automaton that at the end of the first string literal generates either a keyword `NULL` or an identifier `NULLAND`.

Syntactic analysis is performed using a technique called *abstract parsing* [7], which is based on simulating an LR-parser generated by Bison [3] over the automaton representing the regular expression. We have extended this technique to GLR parsing [11] to be able to use grammars with LALR(1) conflicts and even ambiguities common in grammars described in standards and manuals. For abstract strings with no repetitions (s^+) this process gives precise results. If the string set designated by an abstract string is infinite then syntax checking is equivalent to checking inclusion of a regular language into a context-free one. As this is undecidable we use an approximation based on bounding the depth

[1] For example, a `StringBuilder` object.

of stacks used by LR-parser as described in [9]. This corresponds to approximating the context-free syntax of SQL by a regular language. The analysis is sound, meaning that if no errors are reported then all possible values of the abstract string are guaranteed to comply to SQL syntax requirements. In our example, this process detects a syntax error because the `IS NOT` operator cannot be followed by an identifier `NULLAND`.

2.3 Testing Facility

Testing facility is provided for semantic validation of abstracts strings against the target database schema. Each collected abstract string is expanded to a corresponding set of concrete strings. In the expansion process, each repetition s^+ is narrowed to a finite choice $s \mid (ss)$. Concrete strings are sent to a database engine for parsing and semantic checking using standard API call (`java.sql.Connection.prepareStatement`). If database reports error for any of the concrete strings then respective abstract string is reported as erroneous.

For finite abstract strings, if all tests pass, no `prepareStatement` call will report an error during program execution, and if some test fails, there is a path in the program that leads to an error. In other words, the testing procedure is *sound* and *complete* for this case. For abstract strings containing repetition it is complete. With repetition schemes found in our benchmarks (e.g. generating a number of question marks in `IN` clause) it is also sound.

2.4 User Interface

The presented tool is integrated into Eclipse IDE. From the user perspective it adds one more checking pass to the building process of an Eclipse project. To enable checking of the string-embedded SQL in a Java project the user turns on a corresponding *project nature*, which adds a tool-specific *builder* to the project. The analysis results are reported to the user in the same manner as Java compiler errors are displayed. In addition, each hotspot is marked with an abstract string *info marker* that allows the user to see the abstract string represented as a regular expression in a tool-tip window.

The builder runs in a background thread, so the editor is not blocked during the checking process. During the first-time check the Builder collects information about hotspots and abstract strings and stores it in the *persistent cache database*, so that consequent checks run faster since only the information about updated files and dependencies has to be recomputed. These incremental checks are performed when a Java file is saved after a modification. In addition to automatic checks, user can manually invoke the checker on one or more files, packages and projects.

3 Evaluation

The tool was tested using several open source and commercial projects as benchmarks. Results for open source benchmarks are given in Fig. 2. Tests were performed using Eclipse 3.5 with Sun JRE 1.6 running on 2.8GHz Intel Core 2

		# Hotspots				Time (sec)				Mem	Cached	
Benchmark	LOC	total	bugs	FA	unsupp.	total	string	syntax	test	MB	size	time
Plazma	48520	94	4	1	3	6.0	3.8	0.5	1	65	1	0.4
Compiere	319570	1343	12	7	129	138	120	10.4	4.4	445	8	0.5

Fig. 2. Benchmark results

Quadro CPU with 4GB of RAM. Eclipse was run with 512MB limit on heap space.

In Fig. 2, *LOC* refers to lines of Java code (excluding blank lines and comments) in the specific projects analyzed. The total number of hotspots is broken down to number of actual bugs found, number of false alarms (*FA*) and number of unsupported hotspots (cases where SQL strings were constructed using certain Java features not supported by our string collector). Remaining hotspots contained no SQL errors.

Time measurements under *Time* and memory usage (*Mem*) refer to project analysis started with empty cache. Time was measured separately for string collection, syntactic analysis and testing on actual database. "Memory usage" corresponds to the peak amount of heap space used during the analysis minus the memory occupied by Eclipse at start-up.

Cached/size shows size of full cache file in MB-s. *Cached/time* refers to average time (in seconds) spent on re-analysing single file and it's dependent files using full cache, in cases when the file has at most 2 dependent files. Reanalyzing a file with more dependent files takes proportionally more time.

Plazma is a medium-size open source ERP and CRM software. We analyzed its business logic module (project *standart*) together with a required project (*framework*)[2]. All bugs were found by the testing facility and were caused by missing table definitions in schema creation scripts provided with the distribution. False alarm was caused by lack of path-sensitivity in string collection. Unsupported cases were *StringBuffer* modifications using *trim* and a method with no call sites and thus no abstract values for its parameters.

Our main open-source benchmark was *Compiere* – one of the best known ERP and CRM business solutions. Again, we analysed the business logic module (project *base*) together with its required projects. This benchmark was challenging because of the big size of the codebase and complicated constructs used for generating SQL queries.

The bugs found in Compiere include 10 errors in SQL syntax (e.g. missing space between SQL tokens), detected by syntactic analyzer and testing facility and 2 misspelled identifiers detected by testing facility. Unsupported cases include usage of global mutable state or dynamic memory. We also included among unsupported hotspots the cases where the string collector detected definite need for path-sensitive analysis. Most false alarms were caused by lack of path-sensitivity in string collection.

[2] The workspace for *Plazma* benchmark, prepared for the analysis, is available at our tool's homepage.

4 Conclusions and Related Work

In this paper we presented a tool for analyzing SQL statements embedded into Java strings. It uses abstract lexical analysis and parsing to check for syntactical errors in SQL statements and a testing facility to generate sample statements and perform semantic checks on a running database engine. These two techniques complement each other: while the former is a sound analysis, which is guaranteed to report an error if it is present, the latter is validating against a real environment and is capable of checking semantical properties and sometimes eliminating false alarms produced by syntactic analyzer. To our knowledge, no other tool presents a combination of these two techniques.

Existing tools integrated with development environments, such as IntelliJ IDEA [5], IBM pureQuery [2] and SeamlessSQL [1] perform very limited control flow analysis, supporting only basic Java constructs (mainly, string concatenation), whereas our tool performs inter-procedural analysis taking conditionals and loops into account. Additionally, these tools require explicit annotations for hotspot expressions, whereas out tool is capable of detecting hotspots from API calls.

Paper [6] reports on Java String Analyzer (JSA), a tool which performs static analysis to check syntax in embedded SQL statements as our SQL syntax checker. Our work differs from this project in several ways. First, JSA is intended for off-line analysis, whereas our tool is interactive. This is partly enabled by using a more light-weight algorithm implemented in the abstract string collector, where JSA uses a multi-step approximation based based on Mohri-Nederhof's algorithm to obtain a regular representation. Second, for syntax analysis JSA uses a manually approximated grammar where recursion depth is bound by modifying the rules. Contrary to ours, this approach is not precise even on finite sets, and does not allow for reuse of existing grammar. Additionally, JSA does not perform lexical analysis which makes grammar development harder: one has to take whitespace into account while writing productions, and prevents reuse of existing grammars.

JDBChecker tool described in [12] uses JSA for syntax analysis and performs type checking inside SQL expressions. It does not require a database connection, but is capable of detecting only some types of semantic errors and does not consider differences between semantical rules of various database engines. In contrast, our testing facility performs complete checks against the engine on which the queries will be actually executed. JDBChecker performs lexical analysis by manually implemented depth-first search based algorithm, which is less convenient for extension and does not allow to reuse existing lexical specifications, as our tool does.

Our SQL syntax checker is inspired by abstract parsing techniques proposed in [7]. The stack-depth bounding abstraction we use is proposed in [9]. The key differences of our implementation are the following: (a) syntactic analysis is separated from string collection, which makes it usable in different contexts, (b) unlike [7] and [9] we use lexical analysis which facilitates grammar development and error reporting, (c) we use a GLR-based algorithm which tolerates ambiguities in grammars, whereas the mentioned papers are based on conventional LALR(1) parsing, which complicates grammar development and adoption of specifications given in standards.

Thiemann [10] describes a different approach to analyzing syntax in embedded strings: it presents a type system for a variation of λ-calculus, where types are based on grammar nonterminals and type checking utilizes the Earley parsing algorithm. Compared to ours, this approach is rather far from practical use, for example, it is unclear if it can be adopted for the full Java language.

As possible direction for the future work we consider making abstract string collection path-sensitive which should eliminate most of the false alarms the tool currently produces. We also plan to analyze usage of result sets retrieved from executed queries to detect misspelled column names and typing errors. Additionally, we intend to develop a content-assist capability to propose table and field names inside embedded SQL queries and, probably, get-methods on result sets. As a matter of improving the overall user experience, we are going to improve the current caching mechanism to be more fine-grained and thus yield shorter delays for rechecking, we also plan to improve configuration capabilities of the tool, especially in the part of configuring it for use with multiple data sources for the same project.

References

1. SeamlessSQL (2008), `http://www.bugfreesql.com/`
2. Optim pureQuery Runtime (2009), `http://www-01.ibm.com/software/data/optim/purequery-runtime/`
3. Bison parser generator (2010), `http://www.gnu.org/software/bison/`
4. Eclipse IDE (2010), `http://www.eclipse.org`
5. IntelliJ IDEA (2010), `http://www.jetbrains.com/idea/`
6. Christensen, A.S., Møller, A., Schwartzbach, M.I.: Precise analysis of string expressions. In: Cousot, R. (ed.) SAS 2003. LNCS, vol. 2694, pp. 1–18. Springer, Heidelberg (2003)
7. Doh, K.G., Kim, H., Schmidt, D.A.: Abstract parsing: Static analysis of dynamically generated string output using LR-parsing technology. In: Palsberg, J., Su, Z. (eds.) Static Analysis. LNCS, vol. 5673, pp. 256–272. Springer, Heidelberg (2009)
8. Klein, G.: JFlex Scanner Generator (2009), `http://www.jflex.org`
9. Kong, S., Choi, W., Yi, K.: Abstract parsing for two-staged languages with concatenation. In: Proceedings of the Eighth International Conference on Generative Programming and Component Engineering, GPCE 2009, pp. 109–116. ACM, New York (2009)
10. Thiemann, P.: Grammar-based analysis of string expressions. In: Proceedings of the 2005 ACM SIGPLAN International Workshop on Types in languages Design and Implementation, TLDI 2005, pp. 59–70. ACM, New York (2005)
11. Tomita, M.: Generalized L.R. Parsing. Kluwer Academic Publishers, Norwell (1991)
12. Wassermann, G., Gould, C., Su, Z., Devanbu, P.: Static checking of dynamically generated queries in database applications. ACM Trans. Softw. Eng. Methodol. 16(4), 14 (2007)

Simple and Precise Widenings for H-Polyhedra

Axel Simon* and Liqian Chen**

[1] Informatik 2, Technische Universität München, 85748 Garching, Germany
[2] National Laboratory for Parallel and Distributed Processing, Changsha, China

Abstract. While the definition of the revised widening for polyhedra is defined in terms of inequalities, most implementations use the double description method as a means to an efficient implementation. We show how standard widening can be implemented in a simple and efficient way using a normalized H-representation (constraint-only) which has become popular in recent approximations to polyhedral analysis. We then detail a novel heuristic for this representation that is tuned to capture linear transformations of the state space while ensuring quick convergence for non-linear transformations for which no precise linear invariants exist.

1 Introduction

The lattice of convex polyhedra is a popular abstract domain [7] for inferring linear relations between variables. Implementations of the full domain [1] and its many approximations [14,17,21] were used to infer program properties (such as list sizes [16] and variable ranges) or to analyze models (such as hybrid automata [12]). The infinite ascending chains in the lattice of polyhedra require that the inferred states are widened to ensure that the fixpoint computation terminates. To this end, a widening operator extrapolates the changes between two (or more) iterates of a fixpoint computation to a state that likely includes all future iterates. Standard widening for polyhedra [10] is defined in terms of the so-called H-representation of polyhedra (a set of linear constraints), and its straightforward implementation requires a quadratic number of entailment checks [5]. In this paper, we introduce *normal widening* that implements standard widening using only simple syntactic checks, based on a normalized H-representation. It avoids the creation of redundant inequalities which, as we show, is inherent in the original definition [10]. These redundancies are avoided in classic polyhedra libraries that store a double description of a polyhedron consisting of constraints (equalities and inequalities) and generators (vertices, rays, and lines). Thus, our algorithm benefits novel implementations that only use constraints [5,18,19].

Since standard widening is often too imprecise, various heuristics have been proposed to improve the prediction of the state space growth. Most of these heuristics rely on the double description of polyhedra which makes them ill-suited to implementations using H-polyhedra. We therefore seek new heuristics that only require the H-representation and take advantage of the normal form.

* The work was supported by the DFG Emmy Noether Programme SI 1579/1.
** NSFC 60725206 and INRIA project "Abstraction" common to CNRS and ENS.

K. Ueda (Ed.): APLAS 2010, LNCS 6461, pp. 139–155, 2010.

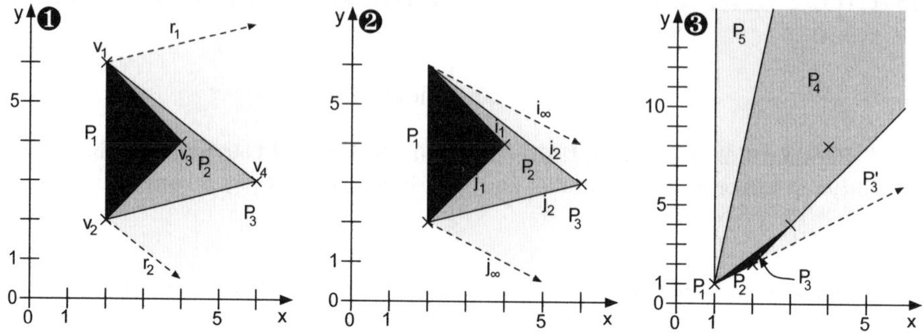

Fig. 1. Comparing the evolving-points heuristic with our method

To this end, consider the first diagram of Fig. 1 which shows how the "evolving point" heuristic [1] widens the polyhedron P_1 with respect to the next iterate P_2: The vertices v_1, v_2, v_3 in P_1 are subtracted from vertices that are new in P_2 (here only v_4) and the resulting extreme rays $r_1 = v_4 - v_2$ and $r_2 = v_4 - v_1$ are added to P_2 thereby defining the resulting polyhedron P_3. The second diagram illustrates our heuristic that rotates inequalities i_1 in P_1 and i_2 in P_2 to i_∞ which has the same distant to the evolving vertices v_3 and v_4. Performing the analog rotation for j_1, j_2 to j_∞ yields the state P_3. This result is indeed an invariant for loops that contain the statement `if (y==5) {x=x+2;y=y-1;}`. Extrapolating with the assumption that transformations are linear means that our heuristic can widen rapidly when a non-linear transformation is observed. This is illustrated in the third diagram where the polyhedra P_n show the evaluation of the loop body `x=x+1;y=2*y;` with $P_1 = \{\langle 1, 1\rangle\}$. The exact values $\langle x, y\rangle$ are indicated by crosses. The Parma Polyhedra Library [1] delays widening[1] until both polyhedra have the same dimension. Then P_3 is widened with some heuristic to give P_4 which has to be widened to P_5 which is observed to be a fixpoint in the 6th iteration. In contrast, our heuristic is able to widen P_2, yielding $P_3' = \{x \leq y, x \geq 1\}$ which is confirmed as a fixpoint in the 4th iteration. Thus, in case of non-linear transformations, polyhedra are unable to express a precise invariant (e.g. $2^x = y$) so that performing two additional iterations is likely to be a waste of time. In summary, this paper makes the following contributions:

- It presents an implementation of standard widening for H-polyhedra that requires only syntactic operations rather than expensive entailment checks.
- We present a heuristic that requires only the H-representation and which tries to guess linear transformations based on the observed changes.
- We show that our heuristic often terminates faster than classic heuristics.

The remainder of the paper is organized as follows. The next section introduces required notation. Section 3 presents the well-known standard widening and our

[1] When given one token; without any tokens, the PPL library discards all inequalities.

implementation for normalized polyhedra. Section 4 details our novel heuristic which Sect. 5 evaluates. Section 6 presents related work and concludes.

2 Preliminaries

Let $\boldsymbol{x} = \langle x_1, \ldots x_n\rangle$ denote an ordered set of variables, let $Ineq_n$ denote the set of linear inequalities $\boldsymbol{a} \cdot \boldsymbol{x} \leq c$ where $\boldsymbol{a} \in \mathbb{R}^n$ and $c \in \mathbb{R}$. Moreover, let e.g. $6x_3 \geq x_1 - 5$ abbreviate $\langle 1, 0, -6, 0, \ldots 0\rangle \cdot \boldsymbol{x} \leq 5$. Define Eq_n to denote the set of equalities of the form $\boldsymbol{a} \cdot \boldsymbol{x} = c \in Eq_n$. Given an equality set $E \subseteq Eq_n$, we use $E^{\leq} := \{\boldsymbol{a} \cdot \boldsymbol{x} \leq c, \boldsymbol{a} \cdot \boldsymbol{x} \geq c \mid \boldsymbol{a} \cdot \boldsymbol{x} = c \in E\}$ to denote the corresponding set of inequalities. Each inequality $\boldsymbol{a} \cdot \boldsymbol{x} \leq c \in Ineq_n$ induces a half-space $[\![\boldsymbol{a} \cdot \boldsymbol{x} \leq c]\!] = \{\boldsymbol{x} \in \mathbb{R}^n \mid \boldsymbol{a} \cdot \boldsymbol{x} \leq c\}$. Each finite set of inequalities $I = \{\iota_1, \ldots \iota_m\} \subseteq Ineq_n$ induces a closed, convex polyhedron $[\![I]\!] = \bigcap_{i=1}^{m} [\![\iota_i]\!]$. Let $Poly_n = \{[\![I]\!] \mid I \subseteq Ineq_n, |I| \in \mathbb{N}\}$ denote the set of all (finitely generated) polyhedra. The tuple $\langle Poly_n, \subseteq, \cap, \curlyvee\rangle$ is a lattice with $P_1 \curlyvee P_2 = cl(hull(P_1 \cup P_2))$ where cl denotes topological closure and $hull$ is the convex hull operation on sets of points. This lattice can serve as abstract domain in a program analysis where a bifurcation with condition $c \in Ineq_n$ in the control flow graph is modeled using the *meet* operation $P \cap [\![c]\!]$ and a merge of control flow edges is modeled by the *join* $P_1 \curlyvee P_2$ [7]. However, the lattice contains infinite chains $P_1 \subset P_2 \subset P_3 \ldots$ so that standard Kleene iteration may not converge onto a fixpoint in finite time. To guarantee convergence, a widening operator $\nabla : Poly_n \times Poly_n \to Poly_n$ is required, satisfying the following:

1. $\forall x, y \in Poly_n \,.\, x \subseteq x \nabla y$
2. $\forall x, y \in Poly_n \,.\, y \subseteq x \nabla y$
3. for all increasing chains $x_0 \subseteq x_1 \subseteq \ldots$, the increasing chain defined by $y_0 = x_0$ and $y_{i+1} = y_i \nabla x_{i+1}$ is ultimately stable.

All operations can be implemented by storing a set of constraints (equalities and inequalities) for each polyhedron: Suppose that $P_i = [\![I_i]\!]$, $i = 1, 2$, then $P_1 \cap P_2 = [\![I_1 \cup I_2]\!]$ and $P_1 \subseteq P_2$ iff for all $\boldsymbol{a} \cdot \boldsymbol{x} \leq c \in I_2$ it holds that $c \geq max(\boldsymbol{a} \cdot \boldsymbol{x}, I_1)$ where $max : Lin_n \times \mathcal{P}(Ineq_n) \to (\mathbb{Q} \cup \{\infty\})$ infers the maximum that $\boldsymbol{a} \cdot \boldsymbol{x}$ can take on in $[\![I_1]\!]$. Note that $max(\boldsymbol{a} \cdot \boldsymbol{x}, I)$ can be inferred using the Simplex algorithm for linear programming. Internally, this algorithm searches for a positive linear combination $\boldsymbol{\lambda} \in \mathbb{Q}^k$ of $k \leq n$ inequalities $\{\boldsymbol{a}_1 \cdot \boldsymbol{x} \leq c_1, \ldots \boldsymbol{a}_k \cdot \boldsymbol{x} \leq c_k\} \subseteq I$ such that $\boldsymbol{\lambda} \cdot (\boldsymbol{a}_1 \ldots \boldsymbol{a}_k) = \boldsymbol{a}$ and $c = \boldsymbol{\lambda} \cdot (c_1 \ldots c_k)$ maximizes $\boldsymbol{a} \cdot \boldsymbol{x}$ in $[\![I]\!]$. We use $\langle \boldsymbol{\lambda}, c\rangle = maxExt(\boldsymbol{a} \cdot \boldsymbol{x}, I)$ to calculate $\boldsymbol{\lambda}$. Linear programming has also been used to approximate the calculation of $P_1 \curlyvee P_2$ [18,19]. In this context, it is mainly used to remove redundant inequalities. An inequality $\iota \in I$ is redundant in I if $[\![I \setminus \iota]\!] \subseteq [\![I]\!]$. Throughout this paper, we assume that the representation I of a polyhedron $P = [\![I]\!]$ contains no redundant inequalities ("I is non-redundant").

The advent of approximate join operators that are solely based on constraints [18,19] raises the question how other operations, e.g., the widening, can be implemented in a constraint-only representation. The following section presents a simple constraint-only based implementation of the standard widening operator

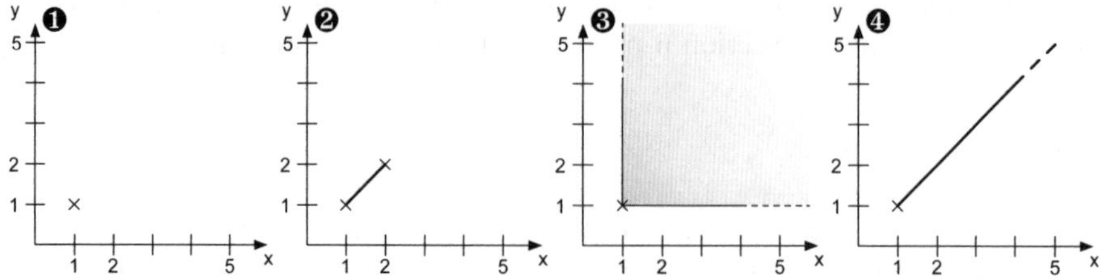

Fig. 2. Illustrating standard widening

before Sect. 4 addresses the question of additional heuristics that, so far, have only been implemented using the double description method which is a representation that uses both, constraints (equalities and inequalities) and generators (vertices, rays, and lines).

3 Widening for Polyhedra

The presence of infinite ascending chains requires a widening to accelerate and guarantee convergence of the fixpoint computation. The original widening operator on polyhedra proposed in [7] was intuitive in that all inequalities that were new are abandoned. Its improvement, presented in [10], refines this idea by making this process resilient to different representations of the same state space. The latter algorithm has specialized implementations based on the double description method and has become known as the *standard widening*. We restate the standard widening based on the constraint-only representation and present an efficient and simple implementation that does not need generators.

Definition 1 (Standard widening). *Given two polyhedra* $P_1 = [\![J_1]\!]$ *and* $P_2 = [\![J_2]\!]$ *satisfying* $P_1 \subseteq P_2$ *where* $J_1, J_2 \subseteq Ineq_n$ *are non-redundant, we define*

$$P_1 \nabla P_2 \stackrel{\text{def}}{=} [\![C_1 \cup C_2]\!]$$

where

$$C_1 = \{\, \iota_1 \in J_1 \mid [\![J_2]\!] \subseteq [\![\iota_1]\!] \,\},$$
$$C_2 = \{\, \iota_2 \in J_2 \setminus J_1 \mid \exists \iota_1 \in J_1, [\![(J_1 \setminus \iota_1) \cup \iota_2]\!] = [\![J_1]\!] \,\}.$$

The first set C_1 contains all inequalities of P_1 that are not violated by the larger P_2 and corresponds to the original widening. Standard widening adds C_2, consisting of inequalities of J_2 that can be exchanged with an inequality of J_1 without changing the represented state. This set ensures that the result is independent of the representation of P_1 and P_2. In order to illustrate this, consider Fig. 2. The first two diagrams depict the two inputs to the widening operator. Suppose that the first polyhedron P_1 is represented by $I_1 = \{1 \leq x, x \leq 1, 1 \leq y, y \leq 1\}$ whereas P_2 is represented by $I_2 = \{1 \leq x, y \leq x, x \leq y, x \leq 2\}$. Only $C_1 = \{1 \leq x, 1 \leq y\}$ is satisfied by P_2, thus the original widening returns the state depicted in the third diagram. Standard widening adds $C_2 = \{y \leq x, x \leq y\}$ since these can be exchanged with $x \leq 1, y \leq 1 \in J_1$ without changing $[\![J_1]\!]$. However, each of the $|J_1||J_2|$ entailment checks [5] requires a Simplex query. Thus, we propose to store a polyhedron in a normal form and show how this can refine the problem of making widening resilient to the representation of polyhedra.

Listing 1. Inlining equalities into an inequality

procedure $\mathit{inline}(E, \boldsymbol{a} \cdot \boldsymbol{x} \leq c)$ where $E \subseteq \mathit{Eq}_n, \boldsymbol{a} \cdot \boldsymbol{x} \leq c \in \mathit{Ineq}_n, \boldsymbol{a} \equiv \langle a_1, \ldots a_n \rangle$

for $\boldsymbol{a}^= \cdot \boldsymbol{x} = c^= \in E$ where $\boldsymbol{a}^= \equiv \langle a_1^=, \ldots a_n^= \rangle$ **do**

  $i \leftarrow \min\{i \mid a_i^= \neq 0\}$ /* *find the index of the first non-zero coefficient* */

  if $a_i = 0$ **then continue;** /* *skip loop if inequality does not contain* x_i */

  $\boldsymbol{a} \cdot \boldsymbol{x} \leq c \leftarrow (a_i^= \boldsymbol{a} - a_i \boldsymbol{a}^=) \cdot \boldsymbol{x} \leq (a_i^= c - a_i c^=)$

end for

return $\langle \boldsymbol{a} \cdot \boldsymbol{x} \leq c \rangle$

3.1 Normalizing the Constraint Representation

Given $J \subseteq \mathit{Ineq}_n$, we construct a canonical representation for $P = [\![J]\!]$ as follows:

1. We compute the affine space that P lies in by calculating $c' = -\mathit{max}(-\boldsymbol{a} \cdot \boldsymbol{x}, J)$ for each $\boldsymbol{a} \cdot \boldsymbol{x} \leq c \in J$. If $c' = c$ then $\boldsymbol{a} \cdot \boldsymbol{x} = c$ holds in P. By performing Gaussian elimination on these equalities, we obtain an equality system in reduced row echelon form, which we denote as E.
2. For each $\iota \in J$, we apply a function $\mathit{inline}(E, \iota)$, presented as Listing 1, that eliminates those variables in ι that are leading variables in E.
3. Finally, we normalize each inequality such that the leading coefficient is either 1 or -1 and remove constraints that are redundant. We get a new set of inequalities, which we denote as I.

The above steps calculate a canonical representation $\langle E, I \rangle$ of any $P \in \mathit{Poly}_n$, see e.g. [15]. For the remainder of the paper, we assume that polyhedra are represented as normalized sets of equalities and inequalities.

3.2 Standard Widening on Normalized Constraints

Given that the input constraints $[\![E_i, I_i]\!] = P_i$, $i = 1, 2$ of the widening operator are normalized, the pre-condition $P_1 \subseteq P_2$ implies that $[\![E_1]\!] \subseteq [\![E_2]\!]$. Since the affine space common to E_1 and E_2 is by definition stable, it suffices to widen the two systems $E^{\leq} \cup I_1$ and I_2 where $E \subseteq \mathit{Eq}_n$ describes the affine space of P_1 without that of P_2. For example, if $E_1 = \{x = 0, y = 0\}$ and $E_2 = \{x = y\}$ then $E_C = \{x = y\}$ is the common affine space and $E = \{y = 0\}$. In general, after normalization and omission of E_C, the constraint sets E_1, I_1, and I_2 can be written as follows:

$$\begin{array}{ll} E_1: & \mathbb{I}\boldsymbol{v} + A_E \boldsymbol{w} = \boldsymbol{c}_E \\ I_1: & A_1 \boldsymbol{w} \leq \boldsymbol{c}_1 \\ I_2: & A_2^v \boldsymbol{v} + A_2^w \boldsymbol{w} \leq \boldsymbol{c}_2 \end{array}$$

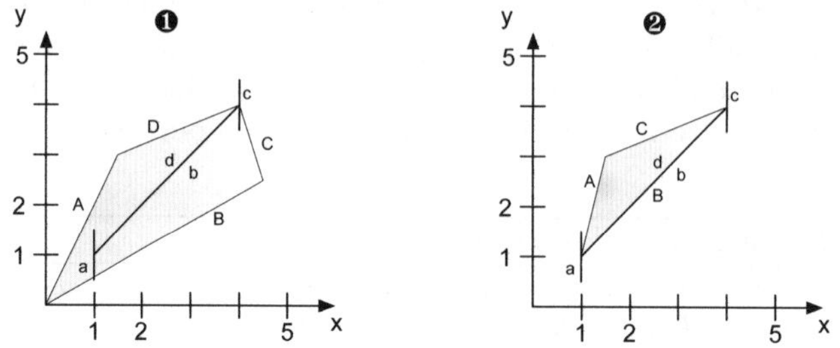

Fig. 3. Non-trivial applications of standard widening. Each letter is written on the infeasible side of the facet it denotes (i.e. the outside of the polyhedron). Lower case letters denote the constraints of the first polyhedron, capital letters those of the second.

Here, $\mathbb{I}$ denotes the identity matrix and $\langle \boldsymbol{v}, \boldsymbol{w} \rangle$ span the variable set $\boldsymbol{x}$. Restricting the input constraints to the systems above not only improves efficiency of the widening operator but also allows its implementation to be much simpler than in the definition of standard widening presented in Sect. 3. Before we show this, we observe that an inequality can be modified by inlining equalities without changing the polyhedron. The following refers to the *inline* function in Listing 1.

Lemma 1. *Let* $\iota' = \mathit{inline}(E, \iota)$ *then* $[\![I \cup \{\iota\} \cup E^{\leq}]\!] = [\![I \cup \{\iota'\} \cup E^{\leq}]\!]$.

Proof. In Listing 1, at line 4, we have $a_i^= x_i + \Sigma_{k>i} a_k^= x_k = c^=$, which is equivalent to $x_i = (c^= - \Sigma_{k>i} a_k^= x_k)/a_i^=$. Thus $\boldsymbol{a} \cdot \boldsymbol{x} \leq c$, that is, $a_i x_i + \Sigma_{k \neq i} a_k x_k \leq c$, is equivalent to $a_i(c^= - \Sigma_{k>i} a_k^= x_k)/a_i^= + \Sigma_{k \neq i} a_k x_k \leq c$. Hence, $\boldsymbol{a} \cdot \boldsymbol{x} \leq c$ is equivalent to $(a_i^= \boldsymbol{a} - a_i \boldsymbol{a}^=) \cdot \boldsymbol{x} \leq (a_i^= c - a_i c^=)$ w.r.t. the affine space E. □

We now show how standard widening can be implemented using the normal representation. To this end, suppose that the two inputs to the widening are $J_1 = E_1^{\leq} \cup I_1$ and $J_2 = I_2$ with I_1, E_1, I_2 in normal form as described above.

First, we calculate C_2 (defined in Definition 1) syntactically and call this set I_C^S. The principle is depicted on the left of Fig. 3. Here the second polyhedron $I_2 = \{A, B, C, D\}$ is widened with respect to $I_1 = \{a, c\}, E_1^{\leq} = \{b, d\}$. The resulting set according to Definition 1 is $C_1 = \emptyset$ and $C_2 = \{C, D\}$ since $[\![I_1 \setminus \{c\} \cup \{C\}]\!] = [\![I_1]\!]$ and $[\![I_1 \setminus \{c\} \cup \{D\}]\!] = [\![I_1]\!]$. The set $I_C^S \subseteq I_2$ is defined to be all $\iota \in I_2$ such that $\mathit{inline}(E, \iota)$ is in I_1 or a tautology:

Lemma 2. *Given* $J_1 = E_1^{\leq} \cup I_1$ *and* $J_2 = I_2$ *with* E_1 *in reduced row echelon form,* $I_1 = \{\mathit{inline}(E_1, \iota) \mid \iota \in I_1\}$ *and* I_1, I_2 *normalized, then* $C_2 = I_C^S$ *where*

$$I_C^S = \{\iota_2 \in J_2 \setminus J_1 \mid \mathit{inline}(E_1, \iota_2) \in I_1 \vee \mathit{inline}(E_1, \iota_2) \equiv \boldsymbol{0} \cdot \boldsymbol{x} \leq 0\}.$$

Proof. For any $\iota_2 \in J_2 \setminus J_1$ we show that $\exists\, \iota_1 \in J_1, [\![(J_1 \setminus \iota_1) \cup \{\iota_2\}]\!] = [\![J_1]\!]$ if and only if $\mathit{inline}(E_1, \iota_2) \in I_1 \vee \mathit{inline}(E_1, \iota_2) \equiv \boldsymbol{0} \cdot \boldsymbol{x} \leq 0$. We specialize this property into two separate cases depending on whether $\iota_1 \in E_{\overline{1}}^{\leq}$ or $\iota_1 \in I_1$:

$\iota_1 \in E_{\overline{1}}^{\leq}$: Show that $[\![I_1 \cup (E_{\overline{1}}^{\leq} \setminus \iota_1) \cup \{\iota_2\}]\!] = [\![J_1]\!]$ iff $\mathit{inline}(E_1, \iota_2) = \mathbf{0} \cdot \boldsymbol{x} \leq 0$: Since $\iota_1 \in E_{\overline{1}}^{\leq}$, we have $[\![I_1 \cup (E_{\overline{1}}^{\leq} \setminus \iota_1) \cup \{\iota_2\}]\!] = [\![J_1]\!]$ iff $[\![(E_{\overline{1}}^{\leq} \setminus \iota_1) \cup \{\iota_2\}]\!] = [\![E_{\overline{1}}^{\leq}]\!]$. We will show next that $[\![(E_{\overline{1}}^{\leq} \setminus \iota_1) \cup \{\iota_2\}]\!] = [\![E_{\overline{1}}^{\leq}]\!]$ iff $\mathit{inline}(E_1, \iota_2) \equiv \mathbf{0} \cdot \boldsymbol{x} \leq 0$. Given any ι_2 with $\mathit{inline}(E_1, \iota_2) \equiv \mathbf{0} \cdot \boldsymbol{x} \leq 0$ then $\iota_2 + \lambda_1 e_1 + \ldots \lambda_k e_k \equiv \mathbf{0} \cdot \boldsymbol{x} \leq 0$ for some $\lambda_1, \ldots \lambda_k > 0$ where $\{e_1, \ldots e_k\} \in E_{\overline{1}}^{\leq}$ but $\bar{e}_i \notin \{e_1, \ldots e_k\}$ for all $i \in [1, k]$ where $\bar{e}_i$ denotes the inequality in $E_{\overline{1}}^{\leq}$ that opposes e_i. In other words, $\iota_2 = \lambda_1 \bar{e}_1 + \ldots \lambda_k \bar{e}_k$. On the other hand, choose $i \in [1, k]$ such that $\iota_1 = \bar{e}_i$. Then $[\![\iota_1]\!] = [\![\lambda_i \bar{e}_i]\!] = [\![\iota_2 + \lambda_1 e_1 + \ldots \lambda_{i-1} e_{i-1} + \lambda_{i+1} e_{i+1} + \ldots \lambda_k e_k]\!]$. It follows that $[\![(E_{\overline{1}}^{\leq} \setminus \iota_1) \cup \{\iota_2\}]\!] = [\![E_1]\!]$.

$\iota_1 \in I_1$: Show that $[\![(I_1 \setminus \iota_1) \cup E_{\overline{1}}^{\leq} \cup \{\iota_2\}]\!] = [\![J_1]\!]$ iff $\mathit{inline}(E_1, \iota_2) = \iota_1$: Again, we partition $\boldsymbol{x}$ into $\boldsymbol{v}, \boldsymbol{w}$ as described previously. Then let $\iota_2 \equiv \boldsymbol{a}^v \boldsymbol{v} + \boldsymbol{a}^w \boldsymbol{w} \leq c$. Suppose that $\boldsymbol{a}^v = 0$ and thus $\mathit{inline}(E_1, \iota_2) = \iota_2$. Due to normalization $[\![\iota_2]\!] = [\![\iota_1]\!]$ iff $\iota_2 = \iota_1$ and thus $[\![(I_1 \setminus \iota_1) \cup E_{\overline{1}}^{\leq} \cup \{\iota\}]\!] = [\![J_1]\!]$ holds iff $\iota \equiv \iota_1$. Now suppose that $\boldsymbol{a}^v \neq 0$ and that $\mathit{inline}(E_1, \iota) = \iota'$ where $\iota' \equiv \boldsymbol{a}'^v \boldsymbol{v} + \boldsymbol{a}'^w \boldsymbol{w} \leq c'$. Then $\boldsymbol{a}'^v = 0$. Using Lemma 1, we obtain the equivalent $[\![(I_1 \setminus \iota_1) \cup E_{\overline{1}}^{\leq} \cup \{\iota'\}]\!] = [\![J_1]\!]$ and, since $\boldsymbol{a}'^v = 0$ this is equivalent to $[\![(I_1 \setminus \iota_1) \cup \{\iota'\}]\!] = [\![I_1]\!]$ which, due to normalization, holds iff $\iota' \equiv \iota_1$. □

As far as we know, it is not widely known that the definition of standard widening generates redundant constraints although it has been shown that these have to be removed for the correctness of future widening applications [1]. The second diagram of Fig. 3 presents an example where redundancies are produced. Here, the set $I_2 = \{A, B, C\}$ is widened with respect to $I_1 = \{a, c\}, E_{\overline{1}}^{\leq} = \{b, d\}$. Since $\mathcal{C}_1 = \{a, b, c\}$ and $\mathcal{C}_2 = \{A, C\}$, the inequalities a and c are redundant in $\mathcal{C}_1 \cup \mathcal{C}_2$. We will now show that the common constraints $I_C = (I_1 \cup E_{\overline{1}}^{\leq}) \cap I_2$ corresponds to $\mathcal{C}_1$ without such redundant inequalities, in other words, we show that $[\![I_C \cup I_C^S]\!] = [\![\mathcal{C}_1 \cup \mathcal{C}_2]\!]$. We first characterize every inequality $\iota \in \mathcal{C}_1 \setminus I_C$ with respect to I_C^S:

Lemma 3. *For any $\iota \in \mathcal{C}_1 \setminus I_C$, $[\![I_C \cup I_C^S]\!] \subseteq [\![\iota]\!]$.*

Proof. By definition of $\mathcal{C}_1$ and the fact that $[\![J_1]\!] \subseteq [\![J_2]\!]$, there exist $\lambda_j > 0$ with $\iota = \lambda_1 \iota_1 + \ldots \lambda_n \iota_n$ where $\iota_j \in I_2$, $j = 1, \ldots n$. Note that $I_C^S \subseteq J_2 \setminus J_1 = I_2 \setminus (I_1 \cup E_{\overline{1}}^{\leq})$ and hence $I_C^S \cap I_C = \emptyset$. Hence, without loss of generality, let $\iota_1, \ldots \iota_k \in I_2 \setminus I_C$ and $\iota_{k+1}, \ldots \iota_n \in I_C$. We show that $\iota_i \in I_C^S$ for all $i \leq k$. Let $\iota \equiv \boldsymbol{a} \cdot \boldsymbol{x} \leq c$. Consider $\iota_i' = \mathit{inline}(E_1, \iota_i)$. Note that ι_i is not only entailed by J_1 but also touches J_1 and so does ι_i'. Hence, if $\iota_i' \equiv \mathbf{0} \cdot \boldsymbol{x} \leq c'$ for some $c' \in \mathbb{R}$ then $c' = 0$ and $\iota_i' \in I_C^S$. Now assume $\iota_i' \equiv \boldsymbol{a}' \cdot \boldsymbol{x} \leq c'$ with $\boldsymbol{a}' \neq \mathbf{0}$ but $\boldsymbol{a}' \neq \boldsymbol{a}$. Observe that $\mathit{inline}(E_1, \iota) = \iota$ can be defined as a positive linear combination of some $\mathit{inline}(E_1, \iota_j)$, $j = 1, \ldots n$. This positive linear combination involves ι_i' and therefore cannot define ι, since J_1 entails ι_i' which would mean that

$\iota \in J_1$ is redundant. Hence $\boldsymbol{a}' = \boldsymbol{a}$. Since ι_i touches J_1, $c' = c$ and thus $\iota_i \in I_C^S$. Hence, for all $i \leq k$, $\iota_i \in I_C^S$ and thus ι is redundant in $[\![I_C \cup I_C^S]\!]$. □

Based on Lemma 2 and 3, standard widening can be implemented as follows:

Theorem 1. *Let I_1, E_1 and I_2 be in normal form. Then* $[\![\mathcal{C}_1 \cup \mathcal{C}_2]\!] = [\![I_C \cup I_C^S]\!]$.

Proof. By Lemma 2, $[\![\mathcal{C}_1 \cup \mathcal{C}_2]\!] = [\![\mathcal{C}_1 \cup I_C^S]\!]$. By Lemma 3, any $\iota \in \mathcal{C}_1 \setminus I_C$ is redundant with some inequalities in $I_C \cup I_C^S$. Thus, with $\mathcal{C}_1 = I_C \cup (\mathcal{C}_1 \setminus I_C)$, it follows that $[\![\mathcal{C}_1 \cup I_C^S]\!] = [\![I_C \cup (\mathcal{C}_1 \setminus I_C) \cup I_C^S]\!] = [\![I_C \cup I_C^S]\!]$. □

The above exercise of expressing standard widening on a normalized H-representation, which we call "normal widening", is beneficial not only to simplify an actual implementation: Standard widening still leads to certain imprecisions that are illustrated in the next section. The normalized H-representation forms the basis for heuristics that improve upon standard widening without requiring the generators of a polyhedron.

4 Improving Precision through Additional Heuristics

The standard widening algorithm is very precise when the state changes in a way that adds new inequalities. In certain situations, however, the number of inequalities does not change, but their slopes change in that they rotate via some vertex of the polyhedron. In these cases standard widening removes the inequality, which may often cause loss of bounds on the variables in that direction. One technique is to check which upper and lower bounds of variables are the same between two iterations and to add these stable bounds back in if widening makes the polyhedron unbounded. In this section we are concerned with more sophisticated techniques that anticipate the way inequalities rotate. As far as we know, our proposal is the first heuristic that does not require the double description of a polyhedron. Furthermore, in contrast to previous heuristics [1], we are interested in extrapolating to a space that can possibly be a precise linear invariant. If this likely invariant turns out to an incorrect guess, we aim to widen quickly while retaining stable upper and lower bounds on variables.

In order to illustrate a possible precision loss of standard widening, consider Fig. 4 which shows the polyhedra $P_i = [\![\{x \geq 1, y \geq 1, j_i\}]\!]$ that present consecutive iterations of a fixpoint computation. Standard widening identifies the inequalities j_i as unstable and thus return $P' = [\![\{x \geq 1, y \geq 1\}$ as fixpoint. This example is *reasonable* since the states are the result of $P_i = \bigcup_i F^i(P_0)$ where $P_0 = [\![\{x = 1, 1 \leq y \leq 3\}]\!]$ and the transfer function $F(P) = (P \sqcap \{y = 1\})[x/x-1]$ where F implements the program fragment `if (y==1) x:=x+1`. Given that the crucial statement does not change any values in the area where $y = 3$, the loss of the upper bound $y \leq 3$ is unexpected and often unacceptable. While re-adding stable bounds would fix this particular case, it cannot help when the state space development is rotated slightly which would be the case for `if (x==y) { x:=x+1; y:=y+1 }`. It is tempting to "guess" that j_i may

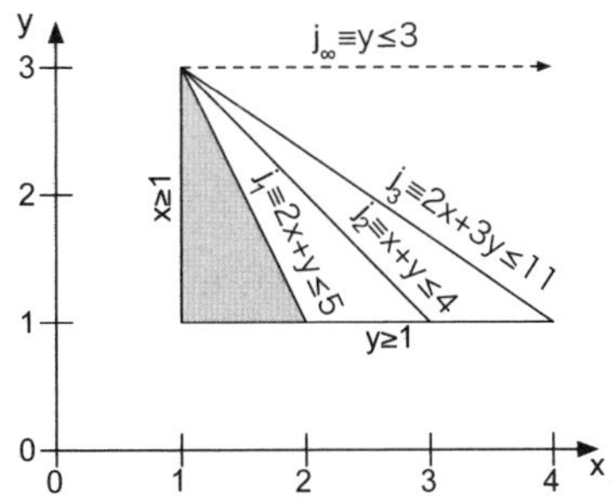

Fig. 4. Iterates with a single changing facet

evolve until it is anti-parallel to $y \geq 1$, however, as the next section will demonstrate, a reasonable opposing inequality does not always exist nor is it evident that a loop in a program should lead to opposing inequalities. The next section therefore considers the more general case of two evolving inequalities.

4.1 Widening in the Presence of Several Changing Inequalities

Defining a heuristic based on rotating inequalities is a tempting approach since these inequalities rotate because they connect a stable part of the state space with the evolving part. However, it is difficult to know how to capture rotation and how far to rotate. A rotation is defined as a multiplication with a matrix whose determinant is one which is impossible to implement with exact rational arithmetic. Instead, the difference between coefficients could be tracked which is demonstrated in Fig. 5. Here, the initial state $P_0 = [\![\{y \geq -2, y \leq 4, x = 0\}]\!]$ is repeatedly transformed by $F(P) = P \curlyvee ((P \cap [\![\{x+2y = 6\}]\!])[x/(x+4), y/(y+2)])$ which implements the program fragment `if (x+2y==6) { x:=x-4; y:=y-2; }`.

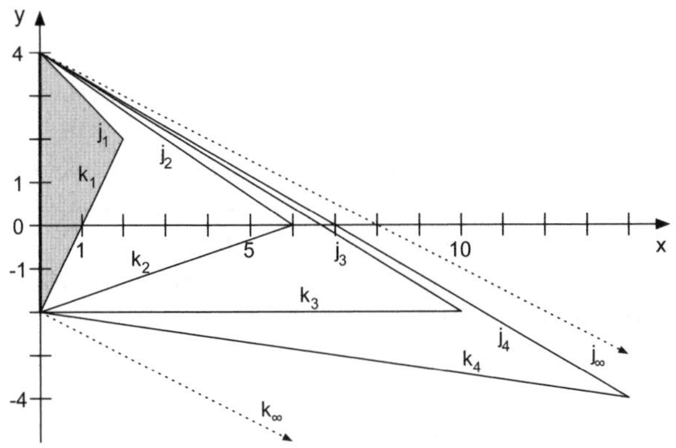

Fig. 5. An evolving sequence of polyhedra in which several facets change

Listing 2. Separating inequalities according to stability

procedure $split(E_1, I_1, I_2)$ where $E_1 \subseteq Eq_n, I_1 \subseteq Ineq_n, I_2 \subseteq Ineq_n$
  $I_C \leftarrow (I_1 \cup E_1^{\leq}) \cap I_2$
  $I_1^{\Delta} \leftarrow (I_1 \cup E_1^{\leq}) \setminus I_C$
  $I_2^{\Delta} \leftarrow I_2 \setminus I_C$
  $I_{2,t}^{\Delta} \leftarrow \{\iota_2 \in I_2 \setminus (I_1 \cup E_1^{\leq}) \mid inline(E_1, \iota_2) \in I_1 \vee inline(E_1, \iota_2) \equiv \mathbf{0} \cdot \boldsymbol{x} \leq 0\}$
  for $\boldsymbol{a} \cdot \boldsymbol{x} \leq c \in I_2^{\Delta}$ **do**
    $c' \leftarrow max(\boldsymbol{a} \cdot \boldsymbol{x}, E_1 \cup I_1)$
    if $c' = c$ **then**
      $I_{2,t}^{\Delta} \leftarrow I_{2,t}^{\Delta} \cup \{\boldsymbol{a} \cdot \boldsymbol{x} \leq c\}$
    end if
  end for
  return $\langle I_C, I_1^{\Delta}, I_2^{\Delta}, I_{2,t}^{\Delta} \rangle$

The polyhedra $P_1, \ldots P_3$ can be described by the inequality sets $\{y \geq -2, y \leq 4, x \geq 0, j_i, k_i\}$. The inequalities j_i and k_i are as follows:

$$j_0 \equiv k_0 \equiv x \leq 0$$

$$\begin{array}{ll} j_1 \equiv x + y \leq 4 & k_1 \equiv x - \frac{1}{2}y \leq 1 \\ j_2 \equiv x + \frac{3}{2}y \leq 6 & k_2 \equiv x - 3y \leq 6 \\ j_3 \equiv x + \frac{5}{3}y \leq \frac{20}{3} & k_3 \equiv -y \leq 2 \\ j_4 \equiv x + \frac{7}{4}y \leq 7 & k_4 \equiv -x - 7y \leq 14 \\ j_\infty \equiv x + 2y \leq 8 & k_\infty \equiv -x - 2y \leq 4 \end{array}$$

While certain sequences of inequalities have a constant difference between their fractions of corresponding variables (e.g., the fractions of x and y in j_1, j_2, j_3, j_4), this difference is occasionally disrupted due to normalization (c.f. k_3). Furthermore, it is not clear how to infer j_∞ and k_∞. Thus, rather than anticipating how inequalities change that connect the evolving to the stable parts of the polyhedron, we try to identify the trajectory of the evolving parts and calculate new inequalities that do not obstruct this trajectory. To this end, we first partition the inequalities of the two polyhedra using *split* in Listing 2 that, unlike the standard widening, partitions the inequality sets into *stable* inequalities I_C and *unstable* inequalities I_i^{Δ} of P_i for $i = 1, 2$. The set I_2^{Δ} is furthermore reduced to those inequalities $I_{2,t}^{\Delta} \subseteq I_2^{\Delta}$ that have changed but which still touch the polyhedron P_1. The idea is that inequalities in $I_{2,t}^{\Delta}$ connect the stable with the evolving part of the polyhedron whereas $I_2^{\Delta} \setminus I_{2,t}^{\Delta}$ only touch the evolving part and can thus not be used to reason about how the P_i will change.

Given these sets, the idea of our heuristic is illustrated in Fig. 6 which shows a modified version of the previous example. Here, $I_C = \{x \geq 0\}$ is the only common inequality and $I_i^{\Delta} = \{j_i, k_i, l_i\}$. In particular, $I_{2,t}^{\Delta} = \{j_2, k_2\}$ contains the set of inequalities that we can use to reason about the change in state. We commence by maximizing j_2 in P_1. Although we know that j_2 touches P_1 (that is, we know that the maximum is the right-hand side of j_2), the Simplex solver returns a set of inequalities whose combination is j_2. From the first diagram in Fig. 6 it can be seen that j_2 is a linear combination of $x \geq 0 \in I_C$ and $j_1 \in I_1^{\Delta}$.

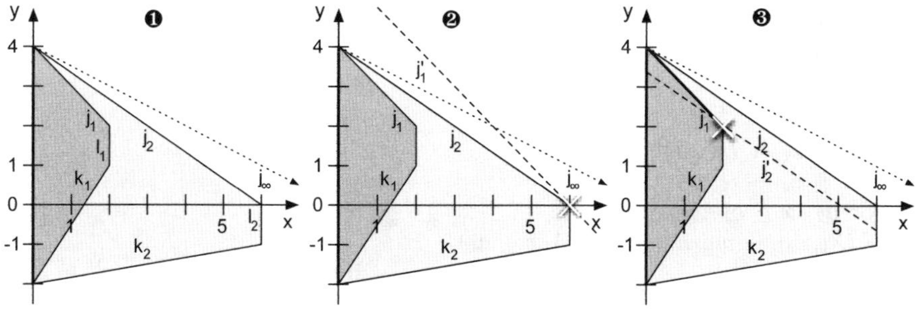

Fig. 6. Extrapolating the evolving area of the polyhedron using linear programming

Hence, we know (or assume) that j_2 has evolved from j_1 as both are unstable and touch the stable part of the state space at (at least) one vertex.

The second diagram shows how we now infer an evolving vertex that lies in j_2. Specifically, we maximize the inequality $j_1 \equiv \boldsymbol{a}_1 \cdot \boldsymbol{x} \leq c_1$ in P_2 which yields a new constant c_1' at which the displaced inequality j_1' touches the evolving vertex. This vertex is shown as white cross in the second diagram. We store this displacement as $\delta_1 = c_1' - c_1$. Diagram three now shows how we find a vertex in P_1 from which this vertex originated. In particular, we reduce P_1 to the boundary of j_1 by adding $\boldsymbol{a}_1 \cdot \boldsymbol{x} = c_1$ to its inequality set. The resulting space $P_1 \cap [\![\boldsymbol{a}_1 \cdot \boldsymbol{x} = c_1]\!]$ is indicated as thick line in the third diagram. We then minimize $j_2 \equiv \boldsymbol{a}_2 \cdot \boldsymbol{x} \leq c_2$ in this space, yielding the white vertex in the third diagram. From the inferred minimum c_2', we calculate the displacement $\delta_2 = c_2 - c_2'$. The inequality $(\delta_2 \boldsymbol{a}_1 - \delta_1 \boldsymbol{a}_2) \cdot \boldsymbol{x} \leq \delta_2 c_1 - \delta_1 c_2$ is now the sought after inequality j_∞ that is rotated around the intersection of j_1 and j_2 and has a slope that could connect the two white crosses. A similar calculation can be performed to find k_∞. Based on this general idea, the next section details the general algorithm that also works for possibly unbounded polyhedra in higher dimensions.

4.2 Implementation

Algorithm 3 implements our heuristic which we call "directed widening". The shown function takes the constraint sets describing P_1 and P_2 after they have been partitioned by Alg. 2. In terms of general structure, it calculates a set of rays R and a set of output constraints I_D. By default, line 23 will add the rays R to $[\![I_D]\!]$, and this process is detailed in Listing 5 for self-containedness.

The algorithm itself converts the constraint system representing P_1 into matrix format (line 3) which is necessary to extract a facet of P_1 that an inequality $\boldsymbol{a}_2 \cdot \boldsymbol{x} \leq c_2 \in I_{2,t}^{\Delta}$ has evolved from. In particular, the facet of P_1 that $\boldsymbol{a}_2 \cdot \boldsymbol{x} \leq c_2$ has evolved from might be a linear combination of the unstable inequalities in I_1^{Δ} rather than a single inequality. In order to find this linear combination, line 6 runs an extended linear program. The maximum c_2 in the result is ignored and only the vector of multipliers $\boldsymbol{\lambda}_1$ is kept which obeys $\boldsymbol{\lambda}_1 A_1 = \boldsymbol{a}_2$. However, $\boldsymbol{\lambda}_1$

Listing 3. Directed widening

procedure $\mathit{widen}(I_C, I_1^\Delta, I_2^\Delta, I_{2,t}^\Delta)$ where $I_C, I_1^\Delta, I_2^\Delta \subseteq \mathit{Ineq}_n, I_{2,t}^\Delta \subseteq I_2^\Delta$

1: $R \leftarrow \emptyset$
2: $I_D \leftarrow I_C$
3: $A_1\boldsymbol{x} \leq \boldsymbol{c}_1 \leftarrow I_C \cup I_1^\Delta$
4: $A_2\boldsymbol{x} \leq \boldsymbol{c}_2 \leftarrow I_C \cup I_2^\Delta$
5: **for** $\boldsymbol{a}_2 \cdot \boldsymbol{x} \leq c_2 \in I_{2,t}^\Delta$ **do**
6:     $\langle \boldsymbol{\lambda}_1, c_2 \rangle \leftarrow \mathit{maxExt}(\boldsymbol{a}_2 \cdot \boldsymbol{x}, A_1\boldsymbol{x} \leq \boldsymbol{c}_1)$
7:     $\boldsymbol{\lambda}_1^\Delta \leftarrow \langle f_1, \ldots f_m \rangle$ where $f_i = \begin{cases} \kappa_i \cdot \boldsymbol{\lambda}_1 & \text{if } (\kappa_i A) \cdot \boldsymbol{x} \leq (\kappa_i \boldsymbol{c}) \in I_1^\Delta \\ 0 & \text{otherwise} \end{cases}$
8:     $\boldsymbol{a}_1 \cdot \boldsymbol{x} \leq c_1 \leftarrow (\boldsymbol{\lambda}_1^\Delta A_1) \cdot \boldsymbol{x} \leq (\boldsymbol{\lambda}_1^\Delta \cdot \boldsymbol{c}_1)$
9:     $c_2' \leftarrow -\mathit{max}(-\boldsymbol{a}_2 \cdot \boldsymbol{x}, I_C \cup I_1^\Delta \cup \{\boldsymbol{a}_1 \cdot \boldsymbol{x} = c_1\})$
10:     $c_1' \leftarrow \mathit{max}(\boldsymbol{a}_1 \cdot \boldsymbol{x}, I_C \cup I_2^\Delta \cup \{\boldsymbol{a}_2 \cdot \boldsymbol{x} = c_2\})$
11:     **if** $c_1' < \infty \wedge c_2' > -\infty \wedge c_1' > c_1 \wedge c_2 > c_2'$ **then**
12:         $\delta_1 \leftarrow c_1' - c_1$
13:         $\delta_2 \leftarrow c_2 - c_2'$
14:         $\boldsymbol{a}_3 \leftarrow \delta_2 \boldsymbol{a}_1 - \delta_1 \boldsymbol{a}_2$
15:         $c_3 \leftarrow \mathit{max}(\boldsymbol{a}_3 \cdot \boldsymbol{x}, I_C \cup I_2^\Delta)$
16:         $I_D \leftarrow I_D \cup \{\boldsymbol{a}_3 \cdot \boldsymbol{x} \leq c_3\}$
17:     **else**
18:         $\boldsymbol{r}_1 \leftarrow \mathit{calcRay}(\boldsymbol{a}_1, \boldsymbol{a}_2)$ /* *Calculate ray with* $\boldsymbol{a}_1 \cdot \boldsymbol{r} = 0$ *and* $\boldsymbol{a}_2 \cdot \boldsymbol{r} \leq 0$. */
19:         $\boldsymbol{r}_2 \leftarrow \mathit{calcRay}(-\boldsymbol{a}_2, -\boldsymbol{a}_1)$
20:         $R \leftarrow R \cup \{\mathit{evolveRay}(\boldsymbol{r}_1, \boldsymbol{r}_2)\}$
21:     **end if**
22: **end for**
23: **for** $\boldsymbol{r} \in R$ **do**
24:     $I_D \leftarrow \mathit{addRay}(I_D, \boldsymbol{r})$
25: **end for**
26: **return** I_D

combines inequalities from I_1^Δ and I_C whereas we are only interested in a linear combination of the unstable inequalities I_1^Δ. To this end, line 7 sets all coefficients of $\boldsymbol{\lambda}_1^\Delta$ to zero that correspond to a stable inequality in I_C. Here, κ_i denotes a vector that contains a one in the ith position and is zero otherwise.

Note that $\boldsymbol{\lambda}_1^\Delta$ is non-zero since otherwise $\boldsymbol{\lambda}_1$ would only combine inequalities in I_C and thus $[\![I_C]\!] \subseteq [\![\boldsymbol{a}_2 \cdot \boldsymbol{x} \leq c_2]\!]$. In this case, since the inequalities I_C also describe P_2, the constraint $\boldsymbol{a}_2 \cdot \boldsymbol{x} \leq c_2 \in I_2^\Delta$ would be redundant in $I_C \cup I_2^\Delta$ which contradicts our assumption of a non-redundant representation.

The resulting $\boldsymbol{\lambda}_1^\Delta$ is now used in line 8 to calculate a *virtual* inequality $\boldsymbol{a}_1 \cdot \boldsymbol{x} \leq c_1$ from I_1^Δ which may be linear combination of several inequalities of I_1^Δ. As explained, we assume that $\iota_2 \equiv \boldsymbol{a}_2 \cdot \boldsymbol{x} \leq c_2$ has evolved from $\iota_1 \equiv \boldsymbol{a}_1 \cdot \boldsymbol{x} \leq c_1$. We now measure the distance that ι_2 can be moved inwards on the boundary of ι_1 in line 9. Analogously, we measure how much ι_1 can be moved outwards on the boundary of ι_2 in line 10. Note that, in order to ensure that we find a maximum on ι_2 and not on a different facet, also restrict the polyhedron P_2 to the boundary of ι_2. As an example for why this is necessary, consider adding an

Listing 4. Calculating a ray that is normal to $\boldsymbol{v}_1$

procedure *calcRay*$(\boldsymbol{v}_1, \boldsymbol{v}_2)$ where $\boldsymbol{v}_1, \boldsymbol{v}_2 \in \mathbb{Q}^n$

return $(\boldsymbol{v}_2 \cdot \boldsymbol{v}_1)\boldsymbol{v}_1 - (\boldsymbol{v}_1 \cdot \boldsymbol{v}_1)\boldsymbol{v}_2$

Listing 5. Adding a ray $\boldsymbol{r}$ to an H-polyhedron.

procedure *addRay*$(I, \boldsymbol{r})$ where $I \subseteq \mathit{Ineq}_n$, $\boldsymbol{r} \in \mathbb{Q}^n$

$I' \leftarrow \{\kappa_{n+1} \cdot \boldsymbol{x}' \leq 0\}$ /* *Let* $\boldsymbol{x}'$ *be an* $n+1$*-dimensional vector of variables.* */
for $\boldsymbol{a} \cdot \boldsymbol{x} \leq c \in I$ **do**
 $\boldsymbol{a}' \leftarrow \langle a_1, \ldots a_n, \boldsymbol{a} \cdot \boldsymbol{r}\rangle$ where $\langle a_1, \ldots a_n\rangle = \boldsymbol{a}$
 $I' \leftarrow I' \cup \{\boldsymbol{a}' \cdot \boldsymbol{x}' \leq c\}$
end for
return $\exists_{x_{n+1}}(I')$ /* $\exists_x(\cdot)$ *is a function that projects out* x */

inequality m_2 to the system in Fig 6 whose slope is between j_2 and l_2. Simply maximizing j_1 in P_2 may find the maximum at the intersection of l_2 and m_2.

If both, ι_1 and ι_2 can be translated a finite amount within the other inequality, the two distances δ_1 and δ_2 are used to calculate the slope of the new inequality $\iota_\infty \equiv \boldsymbol{a}_3 \cdot \boldsymbol{x} \leq c_3$. However, rather than calculating c_3, line 15 infers the constant c_3 using a linear program. This is necessary, since ι_∞ has a slope that may cut off some state of the current state space. By maximizing constant of ι_∞ in $I_2 = I_C \cup I_2^\Delta$ we ensure that it entails the current state.

In case ι_1 can be relaxed without ever touching a vertex in P_2, then P_2 contains a ray. The task, therefore, is to calculate a ray towards a different direction. Line 18 calculates a ray that is orthogonal to the normal vector $\boldsymbol{a}_1$ of inequality ι_1 and which lies on the feasible side of inequality ι_2. Analogously, line 19 infers a ray that is orthogonal to ι_2 but which lies on the infeasible side of inequality ι_1. Thus, $\boldsymbol{r}_1$ is contained in P_1 whereas P_2 contains both, $\boldsymbol{r}_1$ and $\boldsymbol{r}_2$. A new ray is needed that anticipates the evolution of these two rays. This task is delegated to a heuristic *evolveRay* which checks in which elements the ray is changing (modulus scaling) and sets these indices to zero. For each index i that is set to zero, the corresponding variable x_i receives a lower or upper bound. Since this heuristic has already been presented in [1] we omit it here. The resulting ray is then added to the constraint set using projection as implemented by *addRay* in Fig 5. Projection on constraints can be implemented using Fourier-Motzkin variable elimination. We now proceed to evaluate our heuristic.

5 Evaluation

Implementing standard widening by our normal widening algorithm of Sect. 3.2 refines the quadratic number of entailment checks of [5] to a few syntactic checks. Each entailment check requires a different linear program to be run and is thus rather expensive. Replacing the costly entailment checks with normal widening reduces the total analysis time from 0.210s to 0.149s in one of our larger tests.

Table 1. Counting the widening applications and comparing the precision of fixpoints

t	timed1_cl					timed2_cl					timed2					initializedRect				
	DW		PPL		FP	DW		PPL		FP	DW		PPL		FP	DW		PPL		FP
0	14	0.03	27	0.09	=	19	0.05	27	0.09	$\neq$	14	0.02	20	0.05	$\sqsupseteq$	26	0.07	33	0.11	$\sqsubseteq$
1	14	0.03	43	0.15	=	19	0.05	43	0.16	$\neq$	14	0.02	26	0.06	$\sqsupseteq$	26	0.07	42	0.15	=
	=		=			$\neq$		=			$\neq$		=			=		=		
2	26	0.06	63	0.23	=	25	0.06	59	0.23	$\neq$	19	0.03	29	0.08	=	34	0.10	51	0.19	=
	=		=			=		=			=		=			=		=		
3	42	0.11	80	0.29	=	41	0.11	73	0.32	$\neq$	25	0.04	29	0.08	=	43	0.12	60	0.23	=
	=		=			=		=			=		=			=		=		
4	62	0.17	95	0.35	=	55	0.17	85	0.37	$\neq$	28	0.05	29	0.08	=	52	0.15	69	0.27	=

t	multirate_cl					multirate					initializedSingular_cl					rectangular				
	DW		PPL		FP	DW		PPL		FP	DW		PPL		FP	DW		PPL		FP
0	19	0.04	27	0.08	$\sqsupseteq$	14	0.02	20	0.04	$\sqsupseteq$	26	0.16	51	0.34	$\sqsupseteq$	14	0.07	14	0.07	$\sqsubseteq$
1	19	0.04	43	0.12	$\sqsupseteq$	14	0.02	26	0.06	$\sqsupseteq$	26	0.16	83	0.55	$\sqsupseteq$	14	0.07	26	1.33	$\sqsupseteq$
	$\neq$		$\neq$			$\neq$		$\neq$			$\neq$		$\neq$			$\neq$		$\neq$		
2	25	0.05	63	0.19	=	19	0.03	32	0.07	=	50	0.28	123	0.81	=	26	1.30	42	5.50	=
	=		=			=		=			=		=			=		=		
3	41	0.08	87	0.26	=	25	0.03	38	0.07	=	82	0.45	171	1.15	=	42	5.45	58	10.75	=
	=		=			=		=			=		=			=		=		
4	61	0.12	115	0.34	=	31	0.04	44	0.09	=	122	0.65	227	1.50	=	58	10.67	73	15.81	=

Since the speed-up is only 40%, we conclude that the analysis time is dominated by the evaluation of the instructions in the loop body rather than by the widening algorithm itself. Thus, in order to assess the merit of a widening, it is more informative to count the number of iterations that are required to find a fixpoint.

To this end, we compared directed widening of Sect. 4 against the BHRZ03 widening [1] of the Parma Polyhedra Library which is implemented based on the double description method and combines several heuristics. A direct comparison is hampered by the use of tokens. The idea is that the user assigns a number of tokens to a widening point which can be used up to perform heuristics that may not terminate. Once all tokens are used, only heuristics may be applied that eventually terminate, e.g. standard widening. Choosing the right number of tokens is often considered "black magic". Since our directed widening tries to find linear translations in the loop body, it needs to observe the effect of two translations, say between P_0, P_1 and P_1, P_2, in order to extrapolate the change between them. Thus, the right number of tokens for our algorithm is always two. Note that tokens do not directly relate to the number of iterations required to reach a fixpoint: tokens do not have to be used when applying a heuristic that eventually terminates. For instance, the number of equalities that hold in a polyhedron can only decrease, thus, one could perform any non-terminating extrapolation while the number of equalities decreases without using up tokens.

In order to assess how quickly the widenings enforce termination and how precise the obtained fixpoint is, we picked eight example systems from the timed/hybrid automata literature [11,13], each containing several nested loops. Table 1 shows the number of tokens (column "t") that the widening was allowed to use at each loop. For each number of tokens, the double columns directed widening

"DW" and BHRZ03 widening "PPL" show the number of calls to the widening operator required to reach a fixpoint and the total analysis time (measured in seconds). The running time of the analyses is roughly proportional to the number of calls to the widening operator which, in turn, corresponds to the number of times a loop body is evaluated. We thus address after how many iterations our directed widening obtains a fixpoint that is as precise as that of the PPL.

To this end, we decorated the table with $=, \neq, \sqsubseteq, \sqsupseteq$ to compare the precision of the obtained fixpoints. Specifically, the column "FP" contains $\sqsubseteq$ if the fixpoint was better in the directed widening, and $\sqsupseteq$ if it was better in the PPL. Fixpoints can also be equal $=$ or incomparable $\neq$. For comparisons between the fixpoints of the same algorithm running with different tokens, we use $\neq$ to indicate that the fixpoint changed. As predicted, our directed widening obtains its best fixpoint with two tokens, which is sufficient to identify linear translations. Interestingly, both heuristics obtain similar precision given enough tokens. However, the number of iterations needed to obtain this precision is always lower for our directed widening, thereby leading to a faster analysis. For instance, in the seventh table "initializedSingular", both algorithms obtain their best fixpoint with two tokens. However, the PPL requires 123 evaluations of loop bodies whereas our directed widening only requires 50, yielding a considerable speed-up in the overall analysis time. Thus, even if our heuristic cannot infer more precise invariants than the combined heuristics gathered in the BHRZ03 widening of the Parma Polyhedra Library, our directed widening performs better by finding the fixpoints faster.

6 Conclusion and Related Work

We have presented a simple implementation of standard widening [10] and a precise heuristic that finds fixpoints quickly. Moreover, our heuristic operates on H-polyhedra which, to our knowledge, make it the first heuristic that does not rely on the double description. This makes our directed widening particularly interesting to implementations of polyhedra that only use constraints [18,19].

The first widening operator for the polyhedra domain was proposed in [7] and corresponds to the set $\mathcal{C}_1$ as defined in Sect. 3. Halbwachs proposed the revised widening or standard widening [10] and already provided an efficient implementation based on the double description of polyhedra. Benoy [2] showed that the above two widenings coincide when the affine spaces of the two argument polyhedra are stable. Chen et al. [5] showed that standard widening can be implemented on constraints only by using linear programming.

A wider field is the area of defining heuristics to improve standard widening. Besson et al. [3] propose a heuristic based on the generator representation that terminates since it guarantees a decreasing number of vertices and an increasing number of extreme rays. In the context of the analysis of timed automata, several heuristics have been proposed [8,12,13]. Bagnara et al. [1] compile several heuristics, such as combining constraints, evolving points, evolving rays, etc. Their heuristics require the generator representation as well as constraints.

Mostly orthogonal to improving the widening operator directly are attempts to limit the state space after widening. Besides classic narrowing [7], an established technique is *widening with thresholds* [4] which uses a finite set of user-specified values (thresholds) on individual variables up to which the state space is extrapolated. Similar to the thresholds strategy, Halbwachs et al. [11,13] propose *widening up-to* technique to improve the widening by adding additional constraints from a fixed and finite set of constraints. Chen et al. [6] lift the thresholds strategy to relational domains in order to guess the slope (i.e. the variable coefficients) to obtain possibly stable constraints. Simon et al. [20] propose *widening with landmarks* which refines widening with thresholds by collecting unsatisfiable inequalities (called landmarks) and extrapolating polyhedra to the closest landmark during widening. Gopan et al. [9] propose *lookahead widening*, which improve the precision by a tuple of polyhedra in which the first determines which branches of a program are enabled while the second polyhedron is widened and narrowed. The net effect of both methods is that no new branches are enabled as the result of widening.

References

1. Bagnara, R., Hill, P.M., Ricci, E., Zaffanella, E.: Precise Widening Operators for Convex Polyhedra. Science of Computer Programming 58(1-2), 28–56 (2005)
2. Benoy, F.: Polyhedral Domains for Abstract Interpretation in Logic Programming. PhD thesis, Computing Lab., University of Kent, Canterbury, UK (January 2002)
3. Besson, F., Jensen, T.P., Talpin, J.-P.: Polyhedral Analysis for Synchronous Languages. In: Cortesi, A., Filé, G. (eds.) SAS 1999. LNCS, vol. 1694, pp. 51–68. Springer, Heidelberg (1999)
4. Blanchet, B., Cousot, P., Cousot, R., Feret, J., Mauborgne, L., Miné, A., Monniaux, D., Rival, X.: A Static Analyzer for Large Safety-Critical Software. In: Programming Language Design and Implementation, San Diego, Calif., USA. ACM, New York (June 2003)
5. Chen, L., Miné, A., Cousot, P.: A sound floating-point polyhedra abstract domain. In: Ramalingam, G. (ed.) APLAS 2008. LNCS, vol. 5356, pp. 3–18. Springer, Heidelberg (2008)
6. Chen, L., Miné, A., Wang, J., Cousot, P.: An abstract domain to discover interval linear equalities. In: Barthe, G., Hermenegildo, M. (eds.) VMCAI 2010. LNCS, vol. 5944, pp. 112–128. Springer, Heidelberg (2010)
7. Cousot, P., Halbwachs, N.: Automatic Discovery of Linear Constraints among Variables of a Program. In: Principles of Programming Languages, Tucson, Arizona, USA, pp. 84–97. ACM, New York (January 1978)
8. Gonnord, L., Halbwachs, N.: Combining Widening and Acceleration in Linear Relation Analysis. In: Yi, K. (ed.) SAS 2006. LNCS, vol. 4134, pp. 144–160. Springer, Heidelberg (2006)
9. Gopan, D., Reps, T.: Lookahead Widening. In: Ball, T., Jones, R.B. (eds.) CAV 2006. LNCS, vol. 4144, pp. 452–466. Springer, Heidelberg (2006)
10. Halbwachs, N.: Détermination Automatique de Relations Linéaires Vérifiées par les Variables d'un Programme. Thèse de 3ème cicle d'informatique, Université scientifique et médicale de Grenoble, Grenoble, France (March 1979)
11. Halbwachs, N.: Delay analysis in synchronous programs. In: Courcoubetis, C. (ed.) CAV 1993. LNCS, vol. 697, pp. 333–346. Springer, Heidelberg (1993)

12. Halbwachs, N., Proy, Y.-E., Raymond, P.: Verification of Linear Hybrid Systems by Means of Convex Approximations. In: Le Charlier, B. (ed.) SAS 1994. LNCS, vol. 864. Springer, Heidelberg (September 1994)
13. Halbwachs, N., Proy, Y.-E., Roumanoff, P.: Verification of Real-Time Systems using Linear Relation Analysis. Formal Methods in System Design 11(2), 157–185 (1997)
14. Howe, J.M., King, A.: Logahedra: a New Weakly Relational Domain. In: Lu, Z., Ravn, A.P. (eds.) ATVA 2009. LNCS, vol. 5799, pp. 306–320. Springer, Heidelberg (2009)
15. Imbert, J.L., Van Hentenryck, P.: Redundancy Elimination with a Lexicographic Solved Form. Technical Report CS-95-02, Brown University, Providence, Rhode Island, USA (1995)
16. Mesnard, F., Bagnara, R.: cTI: a Constraint-Based Termination Inference Tool for ISO-Prolog. Theory and Practice of Logic Programming 5(1-2), 243–257 (2005)
17. Miné, A.: The Octagon Abstract Domain. In: Conference on Reverse Engineering, Stuttgart, Germany, pp. 310–319. IEEE Computer Society, Los Alamitos (October 2001)
18. Sankaranarayanan, S., Colón, M., Sipma, H.B., Manna, Z.: Efficient Strongly Relational Polyhedral Analysis. In: Emerson, E.A., Namjoshi, K.S. (eds.) VMCAI 2006. LNCS, vol. 3855, pp. 111–125. Springer, Heidelberg (2005)
19. Simon, A., King, A.: Exploiting Sparsity in Polyhedral Analysis. In: Hankin, C., Siveroni, I. (eds.) SAS 2005. LNCS, vol. 3672, pp. 336–351. Springer, Heidelberg (2005)
20. Simon, A., King, A.: Widening Polyhedra with Landmarks. In: Kobayashi, N. (ed.) APLAS 2006. LNCS, vol. 4279, pp. 166–182. Springer, Heidelberg (2006)
21. Simon, A., King, A., Howe, J.M.: Two Variables per Linear Inequality as an Abstract Domain. In: Leuschel, M. (ed.) LOPSTR 2002. LNCS, vol. 2664. Springer, Heidelberg (2003)

Metric Spaces and Termination Analyses

Aziem Chawdhary[1,2] and Hongseok Yang[2]

[1] Durham University
[2] Queen Mary University of London

Abstract. We present a framework for defining abstract interpreters for liveness properties, in particular program termination. The framework makes use of the theory of metric spaces to define a concrete semantics, relates this semantics with the usual order-theoretic semantics of abstract interpretation, and identifies a set of conditions for determining when an abstract interpreter is sound for analysing liveness properties. Our soundness proof of the framework is based on a novel relationship between unique fixpoints in metric semantics and post-fixpoints computed by abstract interpreters. We illustrate the power of the framework by providing an instance that can automatically prove the termination of programs with general (not necessarily tail) recursion.

1 Introduction

Recently, there has been great interest in the automatic verification of program termination. Quite a few techniques for automatically verifying termination or general liveness properties of imperative programs have been proposed [18,2,7,1, 6,4,8,16,5,17], some of which have led to successful tools, such as TERMINATOR [7].

In this paper, we step back from all these technological advances, and re-examine a theoretical foundation of automatic techniques for verifying termination or liveness properties of programs. Most of the proposed techniques are based on abstracting programs (in addition to clever results on well-founded relations such as [19, 3]), but these abstraction methods are justified by rather ad-hoc arguments [4]. This is in contrast with the soundness of abstraction for safety properties, which follows a standard framework of abstract interpretation [10, 11]. Our aim is to develop a theory that provides a similar systematic answer for when an abstraction is sound for proving liveness properties. By doing so, we want to relieve the burden of inventing a new way of proving soundness from designers of liveness analysis.

Our main result is a new framework for developing sound precise abstract interpreters for liveness properties of programs with general recursion. Technically, the key feature of our framework is to use a concrete semantics based on metric space [13, 20, 14] and to spell out a condition under which this concrete metric-space semantics can be related to a usual order-theoretic semantics of abstract interpretation. We illustrate the power of the framework by providing an instance that can automatically prove the termination of recursive procedures.

K. Ueda (Ed.): APLAS 2010, LNCS 6461, pp. 156–171, 2010.

Our framework uses a metric-space semantics, because such a semantics justifies a novel strategy for computing approximate fixpoints during abstract interpretation for *liveness*. Imagine that we want to develop a sound termination analysis. Our analysis needs to overapproximate the set of all computation traces of a given program and to check whether the overapproximation does not include an infinite trace. In the standard order-theoretic setting, the set of computation traces of a program is defined in terms of the greatest fixpoint of some function F [9], but overapproximating the greatest fixpoint of F precisely wrt. termination is difficult. For instance, a post-fixpoint x of F (i.e., $F(x) \sqsubseteq x$), which is normally computed by an abstract interpreter for safety, does not overapproximate the greatest fixpoint in general. Hence, fixpoint-computation strategies from safety analyses cannot be used for termination analysis without changes. Alternatively, one might consider the following sequence converging to the greatest fixpoint of F (under the assumption of the continuity of F):

$$\top \sqsupseteq F(\top) \sqsupseteq F^2(\top) \sqsupseteq F^3(\top) \sqsupseteq \ldots$$

and want to compute an overapproximating sequence $\{x_n\}$ such that $F^n(\top) \sqsubseteq x_n$ for all n, and $x_m = x_{m+1}$ for some m. In this case, a fixpoint-computation strategy finds this x_m, and returns it as a result. The problem here is that the strategy is very imprecise; it cannot prove termination of most nontrivial programs (especially those whose time complexity is not constant).

The metric-space semantics of our framework resolves this overapproximation issue. It defines the set of computation traces of a program in terms of a *unique fixpoint* of a function G, and then it guarantees that this unique fixpoint can be overapproximated by a post-fixpoint of G, as long as the post-fixpoint lives in a restricted semantic universe, such as the one with the *closed* sets of traces.[1] Thus, when developing a sound termination analysis in our framework, one can re-use fixpoint-computation strategies from existing safety analyses (which compute post-fixpoints), after adjusting the strategies so that computed post-fixpoints live in the restricted universe.

Using a metric-space semantics has another benefit that our framework can hide call stacks, which appear in a small-step operational semantics of recursive procedures. Hence, a user of the framework does not need to worry about abstracting call stacks [15], and can focus on the problem of proving a desired liveness property.

Related Work. Among the automatic techniques for proving program termination cited already, we discuss two techniques further [4, 8]. The first is our previous work [4], where we proved the soundness of a termination analysis, by directly relating greatest fixpoints in the concrete trace semantics with post-fixpoints computed by the termination analysis. Our proof relied on the fact that the language contained only tail recursions so that greatest fixpoints could be rephrased in terms of least fixpoints and infinite iterations. This rewriting is not

[1] A trace set is closed iff all Cauchy sequences in the set have limits in the set. We will explain it further in the main part of the paper.

$$e ::= x \mid r \mid e{+}e \mid r{\times}e \qquad b ::= e{=}e \mid e{\neq}e \mid e{\leq}e \mid e{<}e \mid b{\wedge}b \mid b{\vee}b \mid \neg b$$
$$c ::= x{:=}e \mid c;c \mid \mathtt{if}\, b\, c\, c \mid f() \mid \mathtt{fix}\, f.\, c$$

Fig. 1. Programming Language with General Recursion

applicable if a programming language includes non-tail recursions. In contrast, the framework of this paper can handle programs with general recursion.

The second technique is a termination analysis for recursive procedures in [8]. This technique works by replacing each recursive function call by a non-deterministic choice between entering a procedure body (in the case that the procedure does not terminate) or the application of a summary of the procedure (in the case that the procedure does terminate). The instance of our framework in this paper can be seen as a modified version of this technique where program transformations are done on the fly and termination proofs and procedure summarizations are done at the same time.

Recently Cousot et al. [12] defined bi-inductive domains to account for both infinite and finite program properties. They combine a domain for finite behaviours with another for infinite behaviours, and produce a new domain whose order is defined using the orders from the two underlying domains. A least fixpoint on this new domain can overapproximate the union of the least fixpoint in the finite domain and the greatest fixpoint in the infinite domain. However, the semantic functions may not be monotone with respect to the order of the new domain, and so cannot be computed by the usual fixpoint iteration. This limitation means that we once again have to reason about least and greatest fixpoints, a situation that we avoid in this paper by using metric spaces.

2 Programming Language

Let PName be the set of procedures names, ranged over by f, g, and let Var be a finite set of program variables x, y that contain rational numbers in $\mathbb{Q}$. We consider a simple imperative language with parameterless procedures f, g and rational variables x, y. The grammar of the language is given in Fig. 1, where we use r to denote a rational constant.

Most commands in our language are standard. The only unusual case is the definition of recursive procedure $\mathtt{fix}\, f.\, c$. It defines a recursive procedure f whose body is c, and then it immediately calls the defined procedure. Note that while loops can be expressed in this language using recursion. We write $\Gamma \vdash c$ for a finite subset Γ of PName, where Γ includes all the free function names in c.

3 Framework

In this section we describe our framework for developing a sound abstract interpreter for liveness properties. Throughout the paper, we will use $\mathbb{N}$ for the set of *positive* integers.

3.1 Review on Metric Spaces

We start with a brief review on metric spaces. For further information on metric semantics, we refer the reader to the standard book and survey on this topic [13,20].

A **metric space** is a non-empty set X with a function $d_X : X \times X \to [0, \infty)$, called metric, that satisfies the three conditions below:

1. Identity of indiscernible: $\forall x, y \in X.\ d_X(x, y) = 0 \iff x = y$.
2. Symmetry: $\forall x, y \in X.\ d_X(x, y) = d_X(y, x)$.
3. Triangular inequality: $\forall x, y, z \in X.\ d_X(x, z) \le d_X(x, y) + d_X(y, z)$.

Consider a sequence $\{x_n\}_{n \in \mathbb{N}}$ in a metric space (X, d_X). The sequence $\{x_n\}_{n \in \mathbb{N}}$ is **Cauchy** iff for all real numbers $\epsilon > 0$, there exists some $N \in \mathbb{N}$ such that $\forall m, n \ge N.\ d_X(x_m, x_n) \le \epsilon$. The sequence $\{x_n\}_{n \in \mathbb{N}}$ **converges to** x **in** X iff for all real numbers $\epsilon > 0$, there exists an $N \in \mathbb{N}$ such that $\forall m \ge N.\ d_X(x_m, x) \le \epsilon$.

A metric space X is **complete** iff every Cauchy sequence converges to some element in X. In this paper, we will consider only complete metric spaces.

Let (X, d_X) and (Y, d_Y) be metric spaces and let α be a positive real number. A function $F : X \to Y$ is **non-expansive** iff for all $x, x' \in X$, we have that $d_Y(F(x), F(x')) \le d_X(x, x')$. It is **$\alpha$-contractive** iff $d_Y(F(x), F(x')) \le \alpha \times d_X(x, x')$ holds for all $x, x' \in X$. Intuitively, the non-expansiveness means that F does not increase the distance between elements, and the contractiveness says that F actually decreases the distance.

In this paper, we use the well-known Banach's unique fixpoint theorem:

Theorem 1 (Banach's Unique Fixpoint Theorem). *Let (X, d_X) be a metric space. If X is complete and a function $F : X \to X$ is α-contractive for some $0 \le \alpha < 1$, the function F has the unique fixpoint. Furthermore, this unique fixpoint can be obtained as follows: first pick an arbitrary x_1 in X, then construct the sequence $\{x_n\}_{n \in \mathbb{N}}$ with $x_{n+1} = F(x_n)$ and finally take the limit of this sequence.*[2]

We will denote the unique fixpoint of F by $\mathsf{ufix}(F)$.

3.2 Concrete Metric-Space Semantics

Our framework consists of two parts. The first part is a concrete semantics based on metric spaces. It is parameterized by the data below, which should be provided by a user of the framework:

1. A pre-ordered complete metric space $(\mathcal{D}, d, \sqsubseteq, \top)$ with the biggest element $\top$. We require that for all Cauchy sequences $\{x_n\}_{n \in \mathbb{N}}$ in $\mathcal{D}$ and all $x \in \mathcal{D}$,

$$(\forall n \in \mathbb{N}.\ x_n \sqsubseteq x) \implies \lim_{n \to \infty} x_n \sqsubseteq x. \tag{1}$$

   Elements of $\mathcal{D}$ can be understood as semantic counterparts of syntactic commands; our concrete semantics interprets a command c as an element in $\mathcal{D}$.

[2] This limit always exists, because the constructed sequence is Cauchy.

2. Monotone non-expansive functions seq, $\mathsf{asgn}_{x,e}$ and if_b for all assignments $x{:=}e$ and all boolean conditions b:

$$\mathsf{seq} : \mathcal{D} \times \mathcal{D} \to \mathcal{D}, \qquad \mathsf{asgn}_{x,e} : \mathcal{D}, \qquad \mathsf{if}_b : \mathcal{D} \times \mathcal{D} \to \mathcal{D}.$$

   These functions define the meaning of the sequencing, assignment and conditional statements in our language.
3. A function $\mathsf{proc} : \mathsf{PName} \to \mathcal{D} \to \mathcal{D}$ for modelling the execution of procedures. We write proc_f instead of $\mathsf{proc}(f)$, and require that $\mathsf{proc}_f(-)$ be a monotone $\frac{1}{2}$-contractive function for all $f \in \mathsf{PName}$. Intuitively, an input x to $\mathsf{proc}_f(-)$ denotes all the possible computations by the body of the procedure f, and $\mathsf{proc}_f(x)$ extends each of these computations with steps taken immediately before or after running the procedure body during the call of f.
4. A subset LivProperty of $\mathcal{D}$ that is downward closed with respect to $\sqsubseteq$:

$$x \sqsubseteq y \wedge y \in \textsc{LivProperty} \implies x \in \textsc{LivProperty}.$$

   This subset consists of elements in $\mathcal{D}$ (which are semantic counterparts of commands) satisfying a desired liveness property, such as termination.

Note that the semantic domain $\mathcal{D}$ here has both pre-order and metric-space structures and that the semantic operators respect both structures by being monotone and non-expansive. These two structures are related by the requirement (1) on $\sqsubseteq$ and Cauchy sequences. One important consequence of the relationship is the lemma below, and it will play a crucial role for the soundness of our framework:

Lemma 1. *For all $\frac{1}{2}$-contractive monotone functions $F : \mathcal{D} \to \mathcal{D}$, a post-fixpoint of F overapproximates the unique fixpoint of F. That is, if x satisfies $F(x) \sqsubseteq x$, we have that $\mathsf{ufix}\, F \sqsubseteq x$, where $\mathsf{ufix}\, F$ is the unique fixpoint of F.*

Proof. Let x be a post-fixpoint of F. By the Banach fixpoint theorem, we know that the unique fixpoint $\mathsf{ufix}\, F$ of F exists and is also the limit of the following Cauchy sequence:

$$x,\ F(x),\ F^2(x),\ F^3(x),\ \ldots$$

Since x is a post-fixpoint of F (i.e., $F(x) \sqsubseteq x$) and F is monotone,

$$x \ \sqsupseteq\ F(x) \ \sqsupseteq\ F^2(x) \ \sqsupseteq\ F^3(x) \ \sqsupseteq\ F^4(x) \ \ldots$$

That is, $F^n(x) \sqsubseteq x$ for all n. Thus, the limit $\mathsf{ufix}\, F$ of $\{F^n(x)\}_{n \in \mathbb{N}}$ also satisfies $\mathsf{ufix}\ F \sqsubseteq x$ by the requirement (1) of our framework. We have just proved the lemma. □

The domain $\mathcal{D}$ and the operators above give rise to a metric-space semantics of programs. Let $[\![\Gamma]\!]$ be the domain for procedure environments (i.e., $\Pi_{f \in \Gamma} \mathcal{D}$), pre-ordered pointwise and given the product metric, where the distance between

$$[\![\Gamma \vdash c]\!] \; : \; [\![\Gamma]\!] \to \mathcal{D}$$

$$[\![\Gamma \vdash f()]\!]\eta = \eta(f) \qquad [\![\Gamma \vdash c_1; c_2]\!]\eta = \mathsf{seq}([\![\Gamma \vdash c_1]\!]\eta, [\![\Gamma \vdash c_2]\!]\eta)$$
$$[\![\Gamma \vdash x{:=}e]\!]\eta = \mathsf{asgn}_{x,e} \qquad [\![\Gamma \vdash \mathtt{if}\, b\, c_1\, c_2]\!]\eta = \mathsf{if}_b([\![\Gamma \vdash c_1]\!]\eta, [\![\Gamma \vdash c_2]\!]\eta)$$
$$[\![\Gamma \vdash \mathtt{fix}\, f.c]\!]\eta = \mathsf{ufix}\, F \qquad (\text{where } F(x) = \mathsf{proc}_f([\![\Gamma, f \vdash c]\!]\eta[f \mapsto x]))$$

Fig. 2. Concrete Semantics defined by the Framework

η and η' in $\Pi_{f\in\Gamma}\mathcal{D}$ is given by $\max_{f\in\Gamma} d(\eta(f), \eta'(f))$. The semantics interprets $\Gamma \vdash c$ as a non-expansive map from $[\![\Gamma]\!]$ to $\mathcal{D}$, and it is given in Fig. 2.

Note that the semantics defines $\mathtt{fix}\, f.c$ as the unique fixpoint of a function F modelling the meaning of the procedure body c. To ensure the existence of the fixpoint here, the semantics maintains that all commands denote only non-expansive functions. Then, it defines the function F in terms of non-expansive $[\![\Gamma, f \vdash c]\!]$ and 1/2-contractive proc_f, and ensures that F is 1/2-contractive. Hence, by the Banach fixpoint theorem, F has the unique fixpoint.

Lemma 2. *For all commands $\Gamma \vdash c$, $[\![\Gamma \vdash c]\!]$ is a well-defined non-expansive function from $[\![\Gamma]\!]$ to $\mathcal{D}$. Furthermore, $[\![\Gamma \vdash c]\!]$ is monotone.*

The use of metric spaces means that in order to design an instance of our generic framework one now needs to prove certain properties of the concrete semantics. Firstly, one has to prove that the semantic domain $\mathcal{D}$ for the meaning of commands is a complete metric space, in addition to having a pre-order structure. Secondly, one needs to show that all the semantic operators are non-expansive.

These new proof obligations often make it impossible to re-use an existing concrete semantics. For instance, a naive trace semantics, such as the one in [4], uses the powerset of traces as a semantic universe for commands, but this powerset cannot be used in our framework. This is because it does not form a complete metric space, when it is given a natural notion of distance function. In order to use the framework in this paper, one has to modify the powerset of traces, so that it has a good metric-theoretic structure, as will be done in Sec. 4.

However, these obligations come with a reward—the soundness of an order-theoretic abstract semantics, which is to be presented next.

3.3 Abstract Semantics

The second part of our framework is the abstract semantics. For a function $f : X^n \to X$ and a subset X_0 of X, we say that f can be restricted to X_0 if for all $\boldsymbol{x} \in X_0^n$, we have that $f(\boldsymbol{x}) \in X_0$. Using this terminology, we describe the parameters of our abstract semantics:

1. A set $\mathcal{A}$ with a partition $\mathcal{A}_p \uplus \mathcal{A}_t = \mathcal{A}$. The elements of $\mathcal{A}$ provide abstract meanings of commands. We call elements in $\mathcal{A}_t$ *total* and those in $\mathcal{A}_p$ *partial*. The set $\mathcal{A}$ should come with the additional data below.

(a) Distinguished elements $\bot$ and $\top$ in $\mathcal{A}$ such that $\top \in \mathcal{A}_t$.
(b) An algorithm checktot that answers the membership to $\mathcal{A}_t$ soundly but not necessarily in a complete way. That is, $\mathsf{checktot}(A) = \mathsf{true}$ means that $A \in \mathcal{A}_t$, but $\mathsf{checktot}(A) \neq \mathsf{true}$ does not mean that $A \notin \mathcal{A}_t$.
(c) A concretization function $\gamma : \mathcal{A}_t \to \mathcal{D}$, such that $\gamma(\top) = \top$. Note that the domain of γ is $\mathcal{A}_t$, not $\mathcal{A}$.

2. Functions $\mathsf{seq}^\sharp$, $\mathsf{asgn}^\sharp_{x,e}$ and $\mathsf{if}^\sharp_b$ for all assignments $x{:=}e$ and booleans b:

$$\mathsf{seq}^\sharp : \mathcal{A} \times \mathcal{A} \to \mathcal{A}, \qquad \mathsf{asgn}^\sharp_{x,e} : \mathcal{A}, \qquad \mathsf{if}^\sharp_b : \mathcal{A} \times \mathcal{A} \to \mathcal{A}.$$

These functions give the abstract meaning of the sequencing, assignment and conditional statements in our language. We require that these functions can be restricted to $\mathcal{A}_t$, and that they overapproximate their concrete counterparts:

$$\begin{aligned}\forall A_0, A_1 \in \mathcal{A}_t.\ \mathsf{seq}(\gamma(A_0), \gamma(A_1)) &\sqsubseteq \gamma(\mathsf{seq}^\sharp(A_0, A_1))\\ \wedge \quad \mathsf{asgn}_{x,e} &\sqsubseteq \gamma(\mathsf{asgn}^\sharp_{x,e})\\ \wedge \quad \mathsf{if}_b(\gamma(A_0), \gamma(A_1)) &\sqsubseteq \gamma(\mathsf{if}^\sharp_b(A_0, A_1)).\end{aligned}$$

Note that this soundness condition is only relevant for total elements in $\mathcal{A}_t$.

3. A function $\mathsf{proc}^\sharp : \mathsf{PName} \to \mathcal{A} \to \mathcal{A}$ for modelling the execution of procedures. For all $f \in \mathsf{PName}$, we require that $\mathsf{proc}^\sharp{}_f$ can be restricted to $\mathcal{A}_t$, and that it should overapproximate proc_f:

$$\forall f \in \mathsf{PName}.\ \ \forall A \in \mathcal{A}_t.\ \ \mathsf{proc}_f(\gamma(A)) \sqsubseteq \gamma(\mathsf{proc}^\sharp{}_f(A)).$$

4. A predicate $\textsc{satisfyLiv}^\sharp$ on $\mathcal{A}_t$ such that

$$\forall A \in \mathcal{A}_t.\quad \textsc{satisfyLiv}^\sharp(A) = \mathsf{true} \implies \gamma(A) \in \textsc{LivProperty}.$$

Intuitively, $\textsc{satisfyLiv}^\sharp$ identifies abstract elements denoting commands with a desired liveness property.

5. A widening operator $\triangledown : \mathcal{A} \times \mathcal{A} \to \mathcal{A}$ [10]. This operator needs to satisfy three conditions. Firstly, it can be restricted to a map from $\mathcal{A}_t$. Secondly, it overapproximates an upper bound of its right argument: $\gamma(A_2) \sqsubseteq \gamma(A_1 \triangledown A_2)$ for all $A_1, A_2 \in \mathcal{A}_t$. Finally, it turns any sequences in $\mathcal{A}$ into one with a stable element. That is, for all $\{A_n\}_{n\in\mathbb{N}}$ in $\mathcal{A}$, the widened sequence $\{A'_n\}_{n\in\mathbb{N}}$ with $A'_1 = A_1$ and $A'_{n+1} = A_n \triangledown A_{n+1}$ contains an index m with $A'_m = A'_{m+1}$.

Note that among the abstract elements in $\mathcal{A}$, only total ones in $\mathcal{A}_t$ have meanings in the concrete domain $\mathcal{D}$ via γ. That is, elements in $\mathcal{A}_p$ need not be concretizable in $\mathcal{D}$. The absence of the concretization relationship between $\mathcal{A}_p$ and $\mathcal{D}$ is intended, because it allows an analysis designer to use a flexible fixpoint strategy during abstract interpretation. Concretely, even though an abstract interpreter aims to compute a value in $\mathcal{D}$ (more precisely, $\{\gamma(A) \mid A \in \mathcal{A}_t\}$) at the end of a fixpoint computation, it can temporarily step outside of $\mathcal{D}$ and use elements in $\mathcal{A}_p$ during the computation, as long as its final result is an element in $\mathcal{D}$. We found this flexibility very useful for achieving high precision in our framework; in order to have a complete metric-space structure, a concrete domain $\mathcal{D}$ often

$$[\![\Gamma \vdash c]\!]^\sharp \;:\; [\![\Gamma]\!]^\sharp \to \mathcal{A}$$

$$[\![\Gamma \vdash f()]\!]^\sharp \eta^\sharp = \eta^\sharp(f) \qquad [\![\Gamma \vdash c_1; c_2]\!]^\sharp \eta^\sharp = \mathsf{seq}^\sharp([\![\Gamma \vdash c_1]\!]^\sharp \eta^\sharp,\ [\![\Gamma \vdash c_2]\!]^\sharp \eta^\sharp)$$

$$[\![\Gamma \vdash x{:=}e]\!]^\sharp \eta^\sharp = \mathsf{asgn}^\sharp_{x,e} \qquad [\![\Gamma \vdash \mathtt{if}\, b\, c_1\, c_2]\!]^\sharp \eta^\sharp = \mathsf{if}^\sharp_b([\![\Gamma \vdash c_2]\!]^\sharp \eta^\sharp,\ [\![\Gamma \vdash c_2]\!]^\sharp \eta^\sharp)$$

$$[\![\Gamma \vdash \mathtt{fix}\, f.c]\!]^\sharp \eta^\sharp = \lceil \mathsf{widenfix}\ F \rceil \quad (\text{where } F(A) = \mathsf{proc}^\sharp_f([\![\Gamma, f \vdash c]\!]^\sharp \eta^\sharp[f \mapsto A]))$$

Fig. 3. Abstract Semantics defined by the Framework

does not include certain semantic elements, such as the empty set, that could serve as the meaning of intermediate results of a precise fixpoint-computation strategy of an abstract interpreter.

The parameters given above are enough to induce an abstract semantics of programs, but to do so, we need to define two operators using the parameters. The first operator is the ceiling $\lceil - \rceil$, which replaces partial elements by $\top$:

$$\lceil A \rceil \;=\; \textbf{if } (\mathsf{checktot}(A) = \mathsf{true}) \textbf{ then } A \textbf{ else } \top.$$

The second is the widened fixpoint operator $\mathsf{widenfix}$. Given a function $F : \mathcal{A} \to \mathcal{A}$, the operator constructs the sequence $\{A_n\}_{n \in \mathbb{N}}$ with $A_1 = \bot$ and $A_{n+1} = A_n \nabla F(A_n)$. Then, it returns the first A_m with $A_m = A_{m+1}$. The condition on ∇ ensures that such A_m exists.

Let $[\![\Gamma]\!]^\sharp$ be the abstract domain for procedure environments (i.e., $[\![\Gamma]\!]^\sharp = \Pi_{f \in \Gamma} \mathcal{A}$). The abstract semantics interprets programs $\Gamma \vdash c$ as functions from $[\![\Gamma]\!]^\sharp$ to $\mathcal{A}$. The defining clauses in the semantics are given in Fig. 3.

The semantics in Fig. 3 are mostly standard, but the abstract semantics of $\mathsf{fix}\, f.c$ deserves attention. After computing a widened fixpoint, $[\![\Gamma \vdash \mathsf{fix}\, f.c]\!]^\sharp$ checks whether the fixpoint is a total element. If not, $[\![\Gamma \vdash \mathsf{fix}\, f.c]\!]^\sharp$ approximates the fixpoint by $\top$, which should be total by the requirement of the framework. This additional step and the requirements of our framework ensure one important property of the semantics:

Lemma 3. *For all $\Gamma \vdash c$ and $\eta^\sharp \in [\![\Gamma]\!]^\sharp$, if $\eta^\sharp(f) \in \mathcal{A}_t$ for every $f \in \Gamma$, we have that $[\![\Gamma \vdash c]\!]^\sharp \eta^\sharp \in \mathcal{A}_t$.*

Intuitively, the lemma says that $[\![\Gamma \vdash c]\!]^\sharp$ can be restricted to total elements. Using this lemma, we express the soundness of the abstract semantics:

$$\forall \eta^\sharp \in [\![\Gamma]\!]^\sharp.\ \ (\forall f \in \Gamma.\ \ \eta^\sharp(f) \in \mathcal{A}_t) \implies [\![\Gamma \vdash c]\!]\gamma(\eta^\sharp) \sqsubseteq \gamma([\![\Gamma \vdash c]\!]^\sharp \eta^\sharp). \tag{2}$$

In $\gamma(\eta^\sharp)$ above, we use the componentwise extension of γ to procedure environments. Note that although γ is not defined on partial elements, the soundness claim above is well-formed, because Lemma 3 ensures that $[\![\Gamma \vdash c]\!]^\sharp \eta^\sharp$ is total. We prove the soundness in the next theorem:

Theorem 2. *The abstract semantics is sound. That is,* (2) *holds for all $\Gamma \vdash c$.*

Proof (Sketch). Our proof is by induction on the structure of c. Here we focus on the most interesting case that $c \equiv \mathtt{fix}\, f.c_1$, where we can see the interaction between the metric structure and the pre-order structure of $\mathcal{D}$. Let $F\colon \mathcal{D} \to \mathcal{D}$ and $G\colon \mathcal{A} \to \mathcal{A}$ be functions defined by

$$F(x) = \mathsf{proc}_f([\![\Gamma, f \vdash c_1]\!]\gamma(\eta^\sharp)[f \mapsto x]), \;\; G(A) = \mathsf{proc}^\sharp_f([\![\Gamma, f \vdash c_1]\!]^\sharp\eta^\sharp[f \mapsto A]).$$

We need to prove that

$$(\mathsf{ufix}\ F) \sqsubseteq \gamma(\lceil \mathsf{widenfix}\ G \rceil). \tag{3}$$

If $\mathsf{checktot}(\mathsf{widenfix}\ G) \neq \mathsf{true}$, then $\gamma(\lceil \mathsf{widenfix}\ G \rceil) = \gamma(\top) = \top$. Thus, (3) holds. Suppose that $\mathsf{checktot}(\mathsf{widenfix}\ G) = \mathsf{true}$, which implies that $\mathsf{widenfix}\ G \in \mathcal{A}_t$. In this case, it is sufficient to prove that $\gamma(\mathsf{widenfix}\ G)$ is a post-fixpoint of F. Because then, the inequality (3) follows from Lemma 1. By the definition of $\mathsf{widenfix}$, $(\mathsf{widenfix}\ G) = (\mathsf{widenfix}\ G) \triangledown G(\mathsf{widenfix}\ G)$. Because of the condition on $\triangledown$, this implies that

$$\gamma(G(\mathsf{widenfix}\ G)) \sqsubseteq \gamma(\mathsf{widenfix}\ G). \tag{4}$$

The LHS of (4) is greater than or equal to $F(\gamma(\mathsf{widenfix}\ G))$ as shown below:

$$\begin{aligned} \gamma(G(\mathsf{widenfix}\ G)) &= \gamma\big(\mathsf{proc}^\sharp_f\ [\![\Gamma, f \vdash c_1]\!]^\sharp\eta^\sharp[f \mapsto (\mathsf{widenfix}\ G)]\big) \\ &\sqsupseteq \mathsf{proc}_f\big(\gamma([\![\Gamma, f \vdash c_1]\!]^\sharp\eta^\sharp[f \mapsto (\mathsf{widenfix}\ G)])\big) \\ &\sqsupseteq \mathsf{proc}_f\big([\![\Gamma, f \vdash c_1]\!]\gamma(\eta^\sharp)[f \mapsto \gamma(\mathsf{widenfix}\ G)]\big) \\ &= F(\gamma(\mathsf{widenfix}\ G)). \end{aligned} \tag{5}$$

The first inequality holds because $\mathsf{proc}^\sharp$ overapproximates proc. The second follows from the induction hypothesis and the monotonicity of proc_f. The inequalities in (4) and (5) imply the desired $F(\gamma(\mathsf{widenfix}\ G)) \sqsubseteq \gamma(\mathsf{widenfix}\ G)$. □

3.4 Generic Analysis

Let $\eta^\sharp_*$ be the unique abstract environment for the empty context $\Gamma = \emptyset$. Our generic analysis takes a command c with no free procedures, and computes the function: $\textsc{LivAnalysis}(c) = \textsc{satisfyLiv}^\sharp([\![c]\!]^\sharp\eta^\sharp_*)$. The result is a boolean value, indicating whether c satisfies a liveness property specified by $\textsc{LivProperty}$.

Theorem 3. *Let η_* be the unique concrete environment for the empty context $\Gamma = \emptyset$. Then, for all commands c with no free procedures, if* $\textsc{LivAnalysis}(c) = \mathsf{true}$, *we have that* $[\![c]\!]\eta_* \in \textsc{LivProperty}$.

4 Instance of the Framework

In this section, we instantiate the framework and define a sound abstract interpreter for proving the termination of programs with general recursion.

4.1 Concrete Semantics

Our instance of concrete semantics of the framework interprets commands as sets of traces satisfying certain healthiness conditions. The notion of traces here is slightly unusual, because the traces are sequences of *tagged states* and they need to meet our well-formedness conditions. In this section, we will explain the meanings of tagged states and traces, and provide parameters necessary for instantiating a concrete semantics from the framework.

Tagged States, Pre-traces and Traces. We start with the definition of traces. A **state** is a map from program variables to rational numbers, and a **tagged state** is a pair of state and tag:

$$\mathsf{Tag} = \{none\} \cup \mathsf{PName} \times \{call, ret\}, \quad \mathsf{State} = \mathsf{Var} \to \mathbb{Q}, \quad \mathsf{tState} = \mathsf{State} \times \mathsf{Tag}.$$

The tag of a tagged state indicates whether the state is the initial or the final state of a procedure call, or just a normal one not related to a call. The $(f, call)$ and (f, ret) tags mean that the state is, respectively, the initial and the final state of the call $f()$, and the *none* tag indicates that the state is a normal state, i.e., it is neither the initial nor the final state of a procedure call. We use symbol σ to denote elements in tState, and use s to denote elements in State.

A **pre-trace** τ is a nonempty finite or infinite sequence of tagged states, such that τ starts with a *none*-tagged state and if it is finite, it ends with a *none*-tagged state.

$$\mathsf{nState} = \mathsf{State} \times \{none\}, \quad \mathsf{preTrace} = \mathsf{nState}(\mathsf{tState}^*)\mathsf{nState} \cup \mathsf{nState}(\mathsf{tState}^\infty),$$

where tState^∞ means the set of (countably) infinite sequences of tagged states.

A trace τ is a pre-trace that satisfies well-formedness conditions. To define these conditions, we consider the sets $\mathcal{W}, \mathcal{O}$ of sequences of tagged states that are the least fixpoints of the below equations:

$$\begin{aligned} \mathcal{W} &= \mathsf{nState}^* \cup \mathcal{W}\mathcal{W} \cup \Big(\bigcup_{f \in \mathsf{PName}, s, s_1 \in \mathsf{State}} \{(s, (f, call))\}\, \mathcal{W}\, \{(s_1, (f, ret))\}\Big), \\ \mathcal{O} &= \mathcal{W} \cup \mathcal{O}\mathcal{O} \cup \Big(\bigcup_{f \in \mathsf{PName}, s \in \mathsf{State}} \{(s, (f, call))\}\mathcal{O}\Big). \end{aligned}$$

Intuitively, $\mathcal{W}$ describes sequences where every procedure call has a matching return and calls and returns are well-bracketed. The other set $\mathcal{O}$ defines a bigger set; in each trace in $\mathcal{O}$, some procedure calls might not have matching returns, but calls and returns should be well-bracketed.

Definition 1. *A pre-trace τ is a* **trace** *iff τ is finite and belongs to $\mathcal{W}$, or τ is infinite and all of its finite prefixes are in $\mathcal{O}$. We write* Trace *for the set of traces.*

For $\tau \in \mathsf{Trace}$ and $n \in \mathbb{N} \cup \{\infty\}$, the projection $\tau[n]$ is the n-prefix of τ; in case that $|\tau| < n$, $\tau[n] = \tau$.[3] Using this projection, we define the distance function on traces as follows:

$$d(\tau, \tau') = 2^{-\max\{n \mid \tau[n] = \tau'[n]\}} \qquad \text{(where we regard } 2^{-\infty} = 0\text{)}.$$

[3] $\tau[n]$ does not necessarily belong to Trace or even to $\mathsf{preTrace}$, but this will not cause problems for our results.

$$\begin{aligned}
\mathsf{seq}(T,T') &= \{\tau\sigma\tau' \mid (\tau\sigma \in T \cap \mathsf{tState}^+) \wedge (\sigma\tau' \in T')\} \cup (T \cap \mathsf{tState}^\infty)\\
\mathsf{asgn}_{x,e} &= \{\sigma\sigma' \mid \sigma,\sigma' \in \mathsf{nState} \wedge \mathsf{first}(\sigma') = \mathsf{first}(\sigma)[x \mapsto [\![e]\!]\mathsf{first}(\sigma)]\}\\
\mathsf{if}_b(T_0,T_1) &= \{\sigma\tau \mid (\sigma\tau \in T_0 \wedge [\![b]\!](\mathsf{first}(\sigma)) = \mathsf{true}) \vee (\sigma\tau \in T_1 \wedge [\![b]\!](\mathsf{first}(\sigma)) = \mathsf{false})\}\\
\mathsf{proc}_f(T) &= \{\sigma\sigma^{(f,call)}\tau \mid \sigma\tau \in (T \cap \mathsf{tState}^\infty)\} \cup \{\sigma\sigma^{(f,call)}\sigma^{(f,ret)}\sigma \mid \sigma \in T\}\\
&\quad \cup \{\sigma\sigma^{(f,call)}\tau\sigma_1^{(f,ret)}\sigma_1 \mid \sigma\tau\sigma_1 \in (T \cap \mathsf{tState}^+)\}
\end{aligned}$$

Here $\mathsf{first}(\sigma)$ is the first component of the tagged state σ, and $\sigma^{(f,call)}$ and $\sigma^{(f,ret)}$ are, respectively, $(\mathsf{first}(\sigma), (f, call))$ and $(\mathsf{first}(\sigma), (f, ret))$. And $[\![b]\!]$ and $[\![e]\!]$ are the standard interpretation of booleans and expressions as functions from (untagged) states to $\{\mathsf{true}, \mathsf{false}\}$ and $\mathbb{Q}$.

Fig. 4. Semantic Operators for the Instance Concrete Semantics

Lemma 4. (Trace, d) *is a complete metric space.*

Full Closed Sets of Well-formed Traces. A subset $T_0 \subseteq \mathsf{Trace}$ of traces is **closed** if for all Cauchy sequences of traces in T_0, their limits belong to T_0 as well. A trace set $T_0 \subseteq \mathsf{Trace}$ is **full** if for every *none*-tagged state $\sigma \in \mathsf{nState}$, there is a trace $\tau \in T_0$ starting with σ.

The semantic domain $(\mathcal{D}, d)$ for interpreting commands in our concrete semantics is the set $\mathcal{P}_{fcl}(\mathsf{Trace})$ of *full closed* sets of traces:

$$\mathcal{D} = \mathcal{P}_{fcl}(\mathsf{Trace}), \qquad d^\dagger(T,T') = 2^{-\max\{n \mid T[n]=T'[n]\}}.$$

Here $T[n]$ is the result of taking the prefix of every trace in T (i.e., $T = \{\tau[n] \mid \tau \in T\}$). The closedness ensures that the $d^\dagger$ just defined satisfies the axioms for being a complete metric space. Also, the condition about being full allows us to meet the non-expansiveness requirement for seq in our framework.

Our domain $\mathcal{D}$ is ordered by the subset relation $\subseteq$. With respect to this $\subseteq$ order, $\mathcal{D}$ has the top element, which is the set Trace of all traces.

Lemma 5. $(\mathcal{D}, d^\dagger)$ *is a complete metric space. Furthermore, the requirement* (1) *of our framework in Sec. 3 holds for* $\subseteq$ *and this metric space.*

Semantic Operators. So far we have defined the semantic domain for commands, the first required parameter of the framework. The next four parameters are operators working on this domain, and we describe them in Fig. 4. In the figure, the sequencing operator seq concatenates traces from T and T', while treating infinite traces from T specially. And the operator proc_f duplicates initial and final states, and tags the duplicated states with information about procedure call and return.

Lemma 6. *All the operators are well-defined, and satisfy the monotonicity and non-expansiveness or* $\frac{1}{2}$*-contractiveness requirements of our framework.*

Liveness Property. The only remaining parameter is LivProperty, which describes a desired liveness property on trace sets. Here we use a property such that if we restrict our attention to $T = [\![c]\!]\eta$ of some command c with no free procedure names, the membership of T to this property implies that T consists of finite traces only.

We say that a trace τ includes an infinite subsequence of open calls iff there exists $\{\tau_n\sigma_n\}_{n\in\mathbb{N}}$ such that

1. $\tau = \tau_1\sigma_1\tau_2\sigma_2\tau_3\sigma_3\ldots\tau_n\sigma_n\ldots$,
2. for all $i \in \mathbb{N}$, there exists some $f \in \mathsf{PName}$ such that $\mathsf{second}(\sigma_i) = (f, \mathit{call})$,
3. for all $i \in \mathbb{N}$, the corresponding return for σ_i does not appear in τ after σ_i, i.e., the return does not occur in the sequence $\tau_{i+1}\sigma_{i+1}\tau_{i+2}\sigma_{i+2}\ldots$.

We specify a desired liveness property of (semantic) commands, using the following subset LivProperty of $\mathcal{D}$: T is in LivProperty iff no traces in T include an infinite subsequence of open calls.

4.2 Abstract Semantics with Linear Ranking Relations

Our abstract semantics uses formulas φ for linear constraints. The syntax of these formulas is given in Fig. 5. Note that a formula φ can use three kinds of variables: normal program variables x; pre-primed ones ${}^{\backprime}x$ for denoting the value of x before running a program; primed ones x' that can be existentially quantified. We assume that the set Var of normal variables and the set ${}^{\backprime}\mathsf{Var}$ of pre-primed variables are finite and that there is an one-to-one correspondence between Var and ${}^{\backprime}\mathsf{Var}$, which maps x to ${}^{\backprime}x$.

Let Form be the set of formulas φ that do not contain free primed variables. Each $\varphi \in \mathsf{Form}$ defines a relation from (untagged) states ${}^{\backprime}s$ with pre-primed variables (i.e., ${}^{\backprime}s \in {}^{\backprime}\mathsf{Var} \to \mathbb{Q}$) to (untagged) states s with normal variables:

$$({}^{\backprime}s, s) \models \varphi,$$

where $\models$ is the standard satisfaction relation from the first-order logic. Let TForm be a subset of Form consisting of *total* formulas in the sense below:

$$\mathsf{TForm} \;=\; \{\varphi \in \mathsf{Form} \mid \forall {}^{\backprime}s \in ({}^{\backprime}\mathsf{Var} \to \mathbb{Q}).\ \exists s \in (\mathsf{Var} \to \mathbb{Q}).\ ({}^{\backprime}s, s) \models \varphi\}.$$

The abstract semantics in this section assumes a sound but possibly incomplete theorem prover that can answer queries of the two kinds: $\varphi \vdash \psi$ and $\vdash \forall {}^{\backprime}X.\exists X.\varphi$. Here ${}^{\backprime}X$ and X are the sets of free pre-primed variables and

$$E \;::=\; r \mid x \mid {}^{\backprime}x \mid x' \mid E+E \mid r\times E \qquad P \;::=\; E=E \mid E\neq E \mid E<E \mid E\leq E$$
$$\varphi \;::=\; P \mid \mathsf{true} \mid \varphi\wedge\varphi \mid \mathsf{false} \mid \varphi\vee\varphi \mid \exists x'.\,\varphi$$

Fig. 5. Syntax for Linear Constraints

normal variables in φ. Note that by asking the query of the second kind, we can use a prover to check, soundly, whether a formula φ belongs to TForm.

Using what we have defined or assumed so far, we define an abstract domain $\mathcal{A}$ and its subset $\mathcal{A}_t$ of total abstract elements as follows:

$$\mathcal{A} = \mathsf{Form} \times \mathsf{Form} \times \mathsf{Form}, \quad \mathcal{A}_t = \mathsf{TForm} \times \mathsf{Form} \times \mathsf{Form}, \quad \mathcal{A}_p = \mathcal{A} - \mathcal{A}_t.$$

The element $(\mathsf{false}, \mathsf{false}, \mathsf{false})$ in $\mathcal{A}$ serves the role of $\bot$, and $(\mathsf{true}, \mathsf{true}, \mathsf{true})$ the role of $\top$. The algorithm for soundly checking the totality of abstract elements is defined using the assumed prover:

$$\mathsf{checktot}(A) \;=\; \mathbf{if}\ \ (\vdash \forall\text{`}X.\exists X.\, A_1)\ \mathbf{then}\ \mathsf{true}\ \mathbf{else}\ \mathsf{unknown}$$

where A_i is the i-th component of A and $\text{`}X$ and X are the sets of free pre-primed and free normal variables in A_1.

Next, we define the concretization map γ, which will provide the intuitive meaning of abstract elements in $\mathcal{A}$. To do this, we need to introduce some additional notations. Firstly, for a (untagged) state s, we write $\text{`}s$ for the state obtained from s by renaming normal variables by corresponding pre-primed ones. Secondly, we write $\sigma \in \tau$ to mean that σ is a tagged state appearing in τ, and $\mathsf{iscall}(\sigma)$ to mean that the tag for σ is a procedure call:

$$\mathsf{iscall}(\sigma) \iff \exists f \in \mathsf{PName}.\ (\mathsf{second}(\sigma) = (f, \mathit{call})).$$

Finally, for all tagged states $\sigma_1, \sigma_2 \in \tau$, we say that σ_1 is an open call with respect to σ_2 in τ, denoted $\mathsf{open}(\sigma_1, \sigma_2, \tau)$, if both σ_1 and σ_2 are tagged with procedure calls, σ_1 appears strictly before σ_2 in τ, but the corresponding return for σ_1 does not appear before σ_2. The concretization is defined as follows:

$$\begin{aligned}\gamma(A) = \{\tau \in \mathsf{Trace} \mid\ & (\tau \in \mathsf{tState}^+ \implies (\text{`}\mathsf{first}(\mathsf{first}(\tau)), \mathsf{first}(\mathsf{last}(\tau))) \models A_1) \land \\ & (\forall \sigma \in \tau.\, \mathsf{iscall}(\sigma) \implies (\text{`}\mathsf{first}(\mathsf{first}(\tau)), \mathsf{first}(\sigma)) \models A_2) \land \\ & (\forall \sigma_1, \sigma_2.\, \mathsf{open}(\sigma_1, \sigma_2, \tau) \implies (\text{`}\mathsf{first}(\sigma_1), \mathsf{first}(\sigma_2)) \models A_3)\}.\end{aligned}$$

Here A_i is the i-th component of A. According to this concretization, A_1 relates the initial and final states of a trace τ, and A_2 and A_3 describe the relationship between certain intermediate states in τ; A_2 relates the initial state and a call state in τ, and A_3 relates states at two open calls in τ. Tracking the relationship between intermediate states is crucial for the precision of our analysis. If the abstract domain included only the first component (as in our previous work [4]), the concretizations of its elements would contain traces violating LIVPROPERTY, or they would not belong to $\mathcal{D}$.

Lemma 7. *For every $A \in \mathcal{A}_t$, the set $\gamma(A)$ is in $\mathcal{D}$, i.e., it is full and closed.*

Abstract Operators. For $\varphi, \psi \in \mathsf{Form}$, let $\varphi; \psi$ be their relational composition defined by

$$\varphi; \psi \;\equiv\; \exists Y'.(\varphi[Y'/X] \land \psi[Y'/\text{`}X]).$$

$$\begin{aligned}
\mathsf{seq}^\sharp(A, A') &= (\ A_1; A'_1,\ \ A_2 \vee (A_1; A'_2),\ \ A_3 \vee A'_3\ )\\
\mathsf{asgn}^\sharp_{x,e} &= (\ eq_{\mathsf{Var}-\{x\}} \wedge (e[`x/x] = x),\ \mathsf{false},\ \mathsf{false}\ )\\
\mathsf{if}^\sharp_b(A, A') &= \textbf{let } b_1 = \mathsf{preprime}(b) \text{ and } b_2 = \mathsf{preprime}(\mathsf{neg}(b))\\
&\quad\ \textbf{in } (\ (b_1 \wedge A_1) \vee (b_2 \wedge A'_1),\ \ (b_1 \wedge A_2) \vee (b_2 \wedge A'_2),\ \ A_3 \vee A'_3\ )\\
\mathsf{proc}^\sharp_f(A) &= (\ A_1,\ eq_{\mathsf{Var}} \vee A_2,\ A_2 \vee A_3\ )
\end{aligned}$$

Here $\mathsf{preprime}(b)$ renames all the variables with the corresponding pre-primed variables, and $\mathsf{neg}(b)$ is the negation of b where $\neg$ is removed by being pushed all the way down to atomic predicates using logical equivalences. For instance, $\mathsf{neg}(x{=}y \vee z{<}3)$ is $x{\neq}y \wedge 3{\leq}z$.

Fig. 6. Semantic Operators for the Instance Abstract Semantics

Here X and $`X$ respectively contain normal variables in φ and pre-primed variables in ψ, Y' is the set of fresh primed variables, and the cardinalities of these three sets are the same so that the substitution in $\varphi; \psi$ is well-defined. Also, for a set X of normal variables, define the formula eq_X to be the equality on the variables in X and the corresponding pre-primed ones: $eq_X \equiv \bigwedge_{x \in X}(`x = x)$.

Using these notations, we present abstract operators in Fig. 6. Note that the abstract sequencing $\mathsf{seq}^\sharp(A, A')$ is not simply the relational composition of formulas; it also describes relationships between intermediate states of a trace. For instance, the second component $A_2 \vee (A_1; A'_2)$ relates the initial state of a trace with states at procedure call in the trace. The first disjunct A_2 considers the case that a call state is from the first argument A of the sequencing, and the second $A_1; A'_2$ is for the other case that a call is from the second argument A'.

Lemma 8. *The operators in Fig. 6 meet all the requirements of our framework.*

Widening Operator. Our widening operator is parameterized by three elements. The first is a positive integer k, which bounds the number of outermost disjuncts in formulas appearing in the results of widening. We will write ∇_k to make this parameterization explicit. The second is a function lower that overapproximates a formula φ in Form by the conjunction of lower bounds on some pre-primed variables (i.e., the conjunction of formulas of the form $r \leq `x$ for some *pre-primed* variable $`x$ and rational number r):

$$\mathsf{lower}(\varphi) \quad = \quad (r_1 \leq `x_1 \ \wedge\ r_2 \leq `x_2\ \wedge\ \ldots r_n \leq `x_n)$$

such that φ entails $\mathsf{lower}(\varphi)$ semantically. The third is the dual of the second function. It is a function upper that overapproximates a formula φ in Form by the conjunction of formulas of the form $`x \leq r$.

The widening operator uses three subroutines. The first is toDNF that transforms a formula $\varphi \in \mathsf{Form}$ to a disjunctive normal form, where all existential quantifications are placed right before each conjunct. The second is the function $\mathsf{bound}_k : \mathsf{Form} \to \mathsf{Form}$ for bounding the number of outermost disjuncts to k:

$$\mathsf{bound}_k(\varphi) \ = \ \textbf{if } (\text{at most } k \text{ outermost disjuncts are in } \varphi) \textbf{ then } \varphi \textbf{ else } \mathsf{true}$$

The third is an algorithm RFS that synthesizes a linear ranking function from φ. such as RankFinder in [18]. Semantically, unless RFS returns fail, it computes an overapproximation of a disjunction-free formula $\varphi \in \mathsf{Form}$, and the overapproximation expresses a linear ranking relation, such as $10 < `x \wedge x \leq `x-1$ for the ranking function x.

Using these parameters and subroutines, we can now define the widening operator:

$$\begin{array}{rl} A \mathbin{\nabla_k} A' = \textbf{let } (\bigvee_{j\in J_i} \kappa^i_j) & = \mathsf{toDNF}(A'_i) \qquad (i = 1,2,3 \text{ here and below}) \\ \chi^i_j & = \bigwedge\{`x = x \mid x \in \mathsf{Var} \text{ and } \kappa^i_j \vdash `x = x\} \\ \xi^i_j & = \textbf{if } (\ \mathsf{RFS}(\kappa^i_j) = \zeta^i_j \text{ for some formula } \zeta^i_j\ ) \\ & \quad \textbf{then } (\ \zeta^i_j \wedge \mathsf{lower}(\kappa^i_j) \wedge \mathsf{upper}(\kappa^i_j) \wedge \chi^i_j\ ) \\ & \quad \textbf{else } (\ \mathsf{lower}(\kappa^i_j) \wedge \mathsf{upper}(\kappa^i_j) \wedge \chi^i_j\ ) \\ \delta_i & = \mathsf{bound}_k(A_i \vee \bigvee_{j\in J_i}\{\xi^i_j \mid \kappa^i_j \not\vdash A_i\}) \\ \textbf{in } (\delta_1, \delta_2, \delta_3). & \end{array}$$

Lemma 9. *The operator* $\nabla_k : \mathcal{A} \times \mathcal{A} \to \mathcal{A}$ *is a widening operator.*

Abstract Liveness Predicate. The abstract semantics uses the following predicate $\text{SATISFYLIV}^\sharp$ on $\mathcal{A}_t$ and checks whether an analysis result implies the desired liveness property:

$$\text{SATISFYLIV}^\sharp(A) \;=\; \begin{array}{l}\textbf{let } (\bigvee_{i\in I} \delta_i) = \mathsf{toDNF}(A_3) \\ \textbf{in } \big(\textbf{if } (\mathsf{RFS}(\delta_i) \neq \mathsf{fail} \text{ for all } i \in I) \textbf{ then } \mathsf{true} \textbf{ else } \mathsf{false}\big).\end{array}$$

The predicate $\text{SATISFYLIV}^\sharp$ first transforms A_3 to a disjunctive normal form. Then, it checks whether each disjunct δ_i is well-founded using the function RFS. Hence, if the predicate returns true, it means that A_3 is disjunctively well-founded. The below lemma is an easy consequence of the disjunctively well-foundedness of A_3, the result of Podelski and Rybalchenko [19] and the definition of γ.

Lemma 10. *For all* $A \in \mathcal{A}_t$*, if* $\text{SATISFYLIV}^\sharp(A) = \mathsf{true}$*, we have that* $\gamma(A) \in$ LIVPROPERTY.

5 Conclusion

In this paper, we have presented a framework for designing a sound abstract interpreter for liveness properties. The framework incorporates the theory of metric spaces in the concrete semantics. By doing so, it justifies a new strategy for approximating fixpoints for an abstract interpreter for liveness, and relieves the burden of abstracting low-level details from an analysis designer. We hope that our results help the program analysis community to exploit metric space semantics and other unexplored areas of the semantics research for developing effective program analysis algorithms.

Acknowledgments. We would like to thank Martin Escardo, Xavier Rival and Andrey Rybalchenko for helpful suggestions, comments and discussion. Peter O'Hearn has always been supportive and provided helpful suggestions. Chawdhary was supported by a Microsoft Research PhD Scholarship and ESPRC grant EP/G042322/1, and Yang was supported by EPSRC grant EP/E053041/1.

References

1. Balaban, I., Pnueli, A., Zuck, L.: Ranking abstraction as companion to predicate abstraction. In: Wang, F. (ed.) FORTE 2005. LNCS, vol. 3731, pp. 1–12. Springer, Heidelberg (2005)
2. Bradley, A., Manna, Z., Sipma, H.: Termination of polynomial programs. In: Cousot, R. (ed.) VMCAI 2005. LNCS, vol. 3385, pp. 113–129. Springer, Heidelberg (2005)
3. Bradley, A.R., Manna, Z., Sipma, H.B.: The polyranking principle. In: Caires, L., Italiano, G.F., Monteiro, L., Palamidessi, C., Yung, M. (eds.) ICALP 2005. LNCS, vol. 3580, pp. 1349–1361. Springer, Heidelberg (2005)
4. Chawdhary, A., Cook, B., Gulwani, S., Sagiv, M., Yang, H.: Ranking abstractions. In: Drossopoulou, S. (ed.) ESOP 2008. LNCS, vol. 4960, pp. 148–162. Springer, Heidelberg (2008)
5. Codish, M., Taboch, C.: A semantic basis for the termination analysis of logic programs. JLP 41(1), 103–123 (1999)
6. Cook, B., Gotsman, A., Podelski, A., Rybalchenko, A., Vardi, M.Y.: Proving that programs eventually do something good. In: POPL 2007 (2007)
7. Cook, B., Podelski, A., Rybalchenko, A.: Termination proofs for systems code. In: PLDI 2006 (2006)
8. Cook, B., Podelski, A., Rybalchenko, A.: Summarization for termination: no return! Formal Methods in System Design 35(3), 369–387 (2009)
9. Cousot, P.: Constructive design of a hierarchy of semantics of a transition system by abstract interpretation. Theor. Comput. Sci. 277(1-2), 47–103 (2002)
10. Cousot, P., Cousot, R.: Abstract interpretation: A unified lattice model for static analysis of programs by construction or approximation of fixpoints. In: Proceedings of the 4th ACM Symposium on Principles of Programming Languages, pp. 238–252 (January 1977)
11. Cousot, P., Cousot, R.: Abstract interpretation frameworks. Journal of Logic and Computation 2(4), 511–547 (1992)
12. Cousot, P., Cousot, R.: Bi-inductive structural semantics. Information and Computation 207(2), 258–283 (2009)
13. de Bakker, J., de Vink, E.: Control flow semantics. MIT Press, Cambridge (1996)
14. Escardó, M.: A metric model of PCF. unpublished research note (1998)
15. Jeannet, B., Serwe, W.: Abstracting call-stacks for interprocedural verification of imperative programs. In: Rattray, C., Maharaj, S., Shankland, C. (eds.) AMAST 2004. LNCS, vol. 3116, pp. 258–273. Springer, Heidelberg (2004)
16. Kroening, D., Sharygina, N., Tsitovich, A., Wintersteiger, C.: Termination analysis with compositional transition invariants. In: Touili, T., Cook, B., Jackson, P. (eds.) Computer Aided Verification. LNCS, vol. 6174, pp. 89–103. Springer, Heidelberg (to appear, 2010)
17. Lee, C.S., Jones, N.D., Ben-Amram, A.M.: The size-change principle for program termination. SIGPLAN Not. 36(3), 81–92 (2001)
18. Podelski, A., Rybalchenko, A.: A complete method for the synthesis of linear ranking functions. In: Steffen, B., Levi, G. (eds.) VMCAI 2004. LNCS, vol. 2937, pp. 239–251. Springer, Heidelberg (2004)
19. Podelski, A., Rybalchenko, A.: Transition invariants. In: LICS 2004 (2004)
20. van Breugel, F.: An introduction to metric semantics: operational and denotational models for programming and specification languages. Theoretical Computer Science 258(1-2), 1–98 (2001)

Amortized Resource Analysis with Polymorphic Recursion and Partial Big-Step Operational Semantics

Jan Hoffmann* and Martin Hofmann

Ludwig-Maximilians-Universität München

Abstract. This paper studies the problem of statically determining upper bounds on the resource consumption of first-order functional programs. A previous work approached the problem with an automatic type-based amortized analysis for polynomial resource bounds. The analysis is parametric in the resource and can be instantiated to heap space, stack space, or clock cycles. Experiments with a prototype implementation have shown that programs are analyzed efficiently and that the computed bounds exactly match the measured worst-case resource behavior for many functions. This paper describes the inference algorithm that is used in the implementation of the system. It can deal with resource-polymorphic recursion which is required in the type derivation of many functions. The computation of the bounds is fully automatic if a maximal degree of the polynomials is given. The soundness of the inference is proved with respect to a novel operational semantics for partial evaluations to show that the inferred bounds hold for terminating as well as non-terminating computations. A corollary is that run-time bounds also establish the termination of programs.

1 Introduction

The quantitative analysis of algorithms is a classic problem in computer science. For many applications in software development it is necessary to obtain not only asymptotic bounds but rather specific upper bounds for concrete implementations. This is especially the case for the development of embedded and safety-critical systems.

Even for basic programs, manual analysis of the specific (non-asympt.) costs is tedious and error-prone. The problem gets increasingly complex for high-level programming languages, since one needs to be aware of the translation performed by the compiler. As a result, automatic methods for analyzing the resource behavior of programs have been the subject of extensive research (see §7).

Our approach to the problem follows a line of research that was initiated by Hofmann and Jost [1]. It is based on the potential method of amortized analysis that has been invented by Sleator and Tarjan [2] to simplify the manual reasoning about the costs of a sequence of operations that manipulate a data structure. [1] showed that a fully automatic amortized resource analysis can efficiently compute bounds on the heap-space consumption of many (first-order) functional programs that admit *linear* resource bounds. The limitation to linear bounds and accordingly linear constraints was essential for the efficiency of the analysis. Subsequent research considerably extended the range

* Supported by the DFG Graduiertenkolleg 1480 (PUMA).

K. Ueda (Ed.): APLAS 2010, LNCS 6461, pp. 172–187, 2010.

of type-based amortized analysis, but the restriction to linear bounds remained. Examples are the extensions of type-based amortized analysis to object-oriented programs [3,4], to generic resource metrics [5,6], to polymorphic and higher-order programs [7], and to Java-like bytecode by means of separation logic [8].

Somewhat unexpectedly, we recently discovered a technique [9] that yields an automatic amortized analysis for polynomial bounds while still relying on linear constraint solving only. The resulting system efficiently computes resource bounds for first-order functional programs that admit bounds that are sums $\sum p_i(n_i)$ of univariate polynomials p_i. This includes bounds on the heap-space usage and the number of evaluation steps for a number of interesting functions such as quick sort, merge sort, insertion sort, longest common subsequence via dynamic programming, breadth-first traversal of a tree using a functional queue, and sieve of Eratosthenes.

The system has been implemented for *Resource Aware ML (RAML)* which is a first-order fragment of OCAML. It is available online[1] and can be run in a web browser to analyze example programs and user-generated code. Our experiments show that the computed bounds exactly match the measured worst-case behavior in many cases. For example we obtain tight evaluation-step bounds for quick sort and insertion sort.

The basic idea of the analysis is to fix a maximal degree k and then to collect linear constraints on the coefficients of polynomials of this degree. One can iteratively increase the degree so as to avoid costly computations earlier on. A fine point arises from the fact that polynomials must be nonnegative and monotone and that in order for allowing local constraint generation for pattern matches the class of allowed polynomials must be closed under the operation $p(n) \mapsto p(n+1) - p(n)$. This naturally leads to nonnegative linear combinations of binomial coefficients.

A further challenge for the inference of polynomial bounds is the need to deal with *resource-polymorphic recursion* (see §2), which is required to type most of the above example programs. However, it seems to be a hard problem to infer general resource polymorphic recursion even for the original linear system.

In this paper we present a pragmatic approach to resource-polymorphic recursion that works well and efficiently in practice. Despite being not complete with respect to the type rules, it infers types for most functions that admit a type-derivation, including the above examples. A somewhat artificial function that admits a resource-polymorphic typing that cannot be inferred by our algorithm is given in the extended version.

The main theorem of the paper (see §5) shows that the resource bounds are sound with respect to a big-step operational semantics. A dissatisfying feature of classical big-step semantics is that it does not provide evaluation judgments for non-terminating evaluations. As a result, the soundness theorems for amortized resource analyses have in the past been formulated for terminating evaluations only [1,5,7].

A secondary contribution of this paper is the introduction of a novel big-step operational semantics for partial evaluations which agrees with the usual big-step semantics on terminating computations. In this way, we retain the advantages of big-step semantics (shorter, less syntactic proofs; better agreement (arguably) with actual behaviour of computers) while capturing the resource behaviour of non-terminating programs. This enables the proof of an improved soundness result: if the type analysis has established a

[1] See `http://raml.tcs.ifi.lmu.de`

resource bound then the resource consumption of the (possibly non-terminating) evaluation does not exceed the bound. It follows that run-time bounds also ensure termination.

This paper complements a previous paper [9]. The main contributions are as follows. We introduce a novel operational semantics for partial evaluations that allows a simplified and improved soundness theorem (in §4). We present algorithmic typing rules used by the inference algorithm (in §5). An extended soundness proof shows that the inferred bounds hold for both terminating and non-terminating computations (Thm. 4). We describe an inference algorithm that efficiently computes resource-polymorphic types for most functions for which such a type exists (in §6).

An extended version of this paper is available on the first author's website. It contains proofs, a case study on sorting algorithms in RAML, and a summary of our experiments with the inference algorithm.

2 Informal Presentation

Linear Potential. The general idea of type-based amortized analysis for functional programs has been introduced in [1] as follows. First, inductive data structures are statically annotated with a positive rational number q to define a non-negative potential $\Phi(n) = q \cdot n$ as a function of the size n of the data. Second, the potential is shown to be sufficient to pay for all operations that are performed on this data structure during any possible evaluation of the program. The initial potential (summed over all input data) then describes an upper bound on the resource costs. We illustrate the idea by analyzing the heap-space consumption of the function *attach* below.

attach (x,l) = **match** l **with** | nil → nil | (y :: ys) → (x,y)::(attach (x,ys))

It takes an integer and a list of integers and returns a list of pairs of integers in which the first argument is paired with each element of the list. If we assume that a list element for a pair of integers has size 3 (two cells for the integers, one for the pointer to the next element) then the heap-space cost of an evaluation of *attach(x,l)* is $3|l|$ memory cells.

In order to infer an upper bound on the heap-space usage of the function we annotate the type of *attach* with a priori unknown resource-annotations s, s', q and p that range over non-negative rational numbers. The intuitive meaning of the resulting type *attach:* $(\mathit{int}, L^q(\mathit{int})) \xrightarrow{s/s'} L^p(\mathit{int}, \mathit{int})$ is as follows: to evaluate *attach(x,l)* one needs q memory cells per element in the list *l* and s additional memory cells. After the evaluation there are s' memory cells and p cells per element of the returned list left. We say that the list *l* has potential $\Phi(l, q) = q \cdot |l|$ and that *l'* = *attach(x,l)* has potential $\Phi(l', p) = p \cdot |l'|$.

The problem of computing a resource bound then amounts to finding valid instantiations of the resource variables, i.e., a potential that suffices to cover the costs of any possible evaluation. The validity of an instantiation can be verified statically in a sound albeit not complete type-based analysis of the program text. A valid resource annotation for *attach* can be obtained by setting $q = 3$ and $s = s' = p = 0$. The computed upper bound on the heap-space costs is then $3n$ where n is length of the input list. Another possible instantiation would be $q = 6$, $p = 3$, and $s = s' = 0$. The resulting typing of *attach* could be used for the inner occurrence of *attach* to type an expression like *attach(x,attach(z,ys))*. The associated upper bound on the heap-space costs for the evaluation of the expression is then $6|ys|$.

The use of linear potential functions relieves one of the burden of having to manipulate symbolic expressions during the analysis by a priori fixing their format. This gives rise to a particularly efficient inference algorithm for the type annotations. It works like a standard constraint-based type inference in which simple linear constraints are collected as each type rule is applied. The constraints are then solved by linear programming. To see the basic idea, consider the function *attach* in which expressions of type list are annotated with variables $q, p, r, \ldots$ that range over $\mathbb{Q}^+$. The intended meaning of l^q is that l is of type $L^q(A)$ for some type A.

attach (x, l^{q}) = **match** l$^{q'}$ **with** | nil $\rightarrow$ nil^{p} | (y :: ys^{r}) $\rightarrow$ ((x,y)::(attach (x, ys^{q}))^{p})^{p}

The syntax-directed inference then computes inequalities like $q' + s \geq 3 + p + s$. It expresses the fact that the potential q' of the first list element and the initial potential s need to cover the costs for the cons operation (3 memory cells), the potential p of a list element of the result, and the input potential s of the recursive call. To pay the cost during the recursion we require the annotation of the function arguments and the result of the recursive call to match their specification (q and p in the case of *attach*). The function is then used *resource-monomorphically*.

Polynomial Potential. Our previous work [9] showed that an automatic amortized analysis can also be used to derive *polynomial* resource bounds by extracting *linear* inequalities from a program. The main innovation is the use of potential-functions of the form $\sum_{i=1,\ldots,k} q_i \binom{n}{i}$ with $q_i \geq 0$. They are attached to inductive data structures via type annotations of the form $\vec{q} = (q_1, \ldots, q_k)$ with $q_i \in \mathbb{Q}^+$. For instance, the typing $l{:}L^{(3,2,1)}(\mathit{int})$, defines the potential $\Phi(l, (3,2,1)) = 3|l| + 2\binom{|l|}{2} + 1\binom{|l|}{3}$.

The use of binomial coefficients rather than powers of variables has many advantages as discussed in [9]. In particular, the identity $q_1 + \sum_{i=1,\ldots,k-1} q_{i+1}\binom{n}{i} + \sum_{i=1,\ldots,k} q_i\binom{n}{i} = \sum_{i=1,\ldots,k} q_i\binom{n+1}{i}$ gives rise to a local typing rule for *cons match* which naturally allows the typing of both recursive calls and other calls to subordinate functions in branches of a pattern match. This identity forms the mathematical basis of the *additive shift* $\lhd$ of a type annotation which is defined by $\lhd(q_1, \ldots, q_k) = (q_1 + q_2, \ldots, q_{k-1} + q_k, q_k)$. It appears, e.g., in the typing *tail*:$L^{\vec{q}}(\mathit{int}) \xrightarrow{0/q_1} L^{\lhd(\vec{q})}(\mathit{int})$ of the function *tail* that removes the first element from a list. The idea underlying the additive shift is that the potential resulting from the contraction xs:$L^{\lhd(\vec{q})}(\mathit{int})$ of a list *(x::xs)*:$L^{\vec{q}}(\mathit{int})$ (usually in a pattern match) is used for three purposes: (i) to pay the constant cost after and before the recursive calls (q_1), (ii) to fund calls to auxiliary functions ($(q_2, \ldots, q_n)$), and (iii) to pay for the recursive calls ($(q_1, \ldots, q_n)$).

To see how the polynomial potential annotations are used to compute polynomial resource bounds, consider the function *pairs* that computes the two-element subsets of a given set (representing sets as tuples or lists).

pairs l = **match** l **with** | nil $\rightarrow$ nil | (x :: xs) $\rightarrow$ append(attach(x,xs), pairs xs)

The function *append* consumes 3 memory cells for every element in the first argument. Similar to *attach* we can compute a tight resource bound for *append* by inferring the type *append:* $(L^{(3)}(\mathit{int}, \mathit{int}), L^{(0)}(\mathit{int}, \mathit{int})) \xrightarrow{0/0} L^{(0)}(\mathit{int}, \mathit{int})$.

The evaluation of the expression *pairs(l)* consumes 6 memory cells per element of every sub-list (suffix) of l. The inferred type for *pairs* is $L^{(0,6)}(\mathit{int}) \xrightarrow{0/0} L^{(0)}(\mathit{int}, \mathit{int})$.

It states that a list l in an expression *pairs(l)* has the potential $\Phi(l,(0,6)) = 0 \cdot |l| + 6 \cdot \binom{|l|}{2}$ and thus furnishes a tight upper bound on the heap-space usage. To type the function's body, the additive shift assigns the type $xs{:}L^{(0+6,6)}(int)$ to the variable xs in the pattern match. The potential is shared between the two occurrences of xs in the following expression by using $xs{:}L^{(6,0)}(int)$ to pay for *append* and *attach* (ii) and using $xs{:}L^{(0,6)}(int)$ to pay for the recursive call of *pairs* (iii); the constant costs (i) are zero.

To compute the bound, we start with an annotation with resource variables as before.

$$\begin{aligned} \text{pairs l} = \textbf{match } \text{l}^{(q_1,q_2)} \textbf{ with} \mid \text{nil} \to \text{nil} \\ \mid (\text{x} :: \text{xs}^{(p_1,p_2)}) \to \text{append(attach(x,xs}^{(r_1,r_2)}\text{),pairs xs}^{(s_1,s_2)}) \end{aligned}$$

The constraints that our type system computes include $q_2 \geq p_2$ and $q_1 + q_2 \geq p_1$ (additive shift); $p_1 = r_1 + s_1$ and $p_2 = r_2 + s_2$ (sharing between two variables); $r_1 \geq 6$ (pay for non-recursive function calls); $q_1 = s_1$, $q_2 = s_2$ (pay for the recursive call). This system is solvable by $q_2 = s_2 = p_1 = p_2 = r_1 = 6$ and $q_1 = s_1 = r_2 = 0$.

Polymorphic Recursion. As in the linear case, we require in the constraint system that the type of the recursive call of *pairs* matches its specification ($q_i = s_i$). But other than in the linear case, such a resource-monomorphic approach results in an unsolvable linear program for many non-tail-recursive functions with a super linear resource behavior. We illustrate this with the function *pairs'* that is a modification of *pairs* in which we permute the arguments of *append* and hence replace the expression in the cons-branch of the pattern match with *append(pairs' xs,attach(x,xs))*. The heap-space usage of *pairs'* is $3\binom{n}{2} + 3\binom{n}{3}$ since *append* is called with the intermediate results of *pairs'* in the first argument and thus consumes $\sum_{2 \leq i < n} \binom{i}{2} = \binom{n}{3}$ memory cells.

The resource-polymorphic system determines an exact heap-space bound for the function *pairs'* by computing the typing $L^{(0,3,3)}(int) \xrightarrow{0/0} L^{(0)}(int, int)$. Similar to the case of *pairs* the additive shift assigns the type $L^{(3,6,3)}(int)$ to xs in the cons-branch. The linear potential $xs{:}L^{(3,0,0)}(int)$ is passed on to the occurrence of xs in *attach*. But in order to pay the costs of *append* we have to assign a linear potential to the result of the recursive call and thus use the alternate typing *pairs'*: $L^{(0,6,3)}(int) \xrightarrow{0/0} L^{(3)}(int, int)$. The need of passing on potential of degree at most $k-1$ to the output of a function with a resource consumption of degree k is quite common in typical functions. It is present in the derivation of time bounds for most non-tail-recursive functions that we considered, e.g., quick sort and insertion sort. The classic (resource-monomorphic) inference approach of requiring the type of the recursive call to match its specification fails for these functions and it was a non-trivial problem to address it with an efficient solution.

Cost-Free Resource Metric. Our pragmatic approach is to introduce a special *cost-free* resource metric that assigns zero costs to every evaluation step. A cost-free function type $f{:}\ A \xrightarrow{a/a'} B$ then describes how to pass potential from x to $f(x)$ without paying for resource usage. Any concrete typing for a given resource metric can be superposed with a *cost-free* typing to obtain another typing for the given resource metric (cf. solutions of inhomogeneous systems by superposition with homogeneous solutions in lin. algebra).

We illustrate the idea using *pairs'*. For $A = (int, int)$, we derive the cost-free types *attach*: $(int, L^{(3)}(int)) \xrightarrow{0/0} L^{(3)}(A)$ and *append*: $(L^{(3)}(A), L^{(3)}(A)) \xrightarrow{0/0} L^{(3)}(A)$. The type inference for, e.g., *attach* works as outlined above with the inequality $q' + s \geq 3 + p + s$ replaced with $q' + s \geq p + s$. Similar, we can assign *pairs*' the cost-free type $L^{(0,3)}(\mathit{int}) \xrightarrow{0/0} L^{(3)}(\mathit{int}, \mathit{int})$. The typing $xs{:}L^{(3,3)}(\mathit{int})$ that results from the additive shift is used as $xs{:}L^{(3,0)}(\mathit{int})$ in *attach* and as $xs{:}L^{(0,3)}(\mathit{int})$ in the recursive call.

If we now want to infer the type of a function with respect to some cost metric then we deal with recursive calls by requiring them to match the functions type specification and to optionally pass potential to the result via a cost-free type. The cost-free type is then inferred resource-monomorphically. In the case of the heap-space consumption of *pairs*' we would first infer that the recursive call has to be of the form $L^{(0+q_1,3+q_2,3)}(\mathit{int}) \rightarrow L^{(0+p_1)}(\mathit{int}, \mathit{int})$ such that $L^{(q_1,q_2)}(\mathit{int}) \rightarrow L^{(p_1)}(\mathit{int}, \mathit{int})$ is a cost-free type. We then infer like in the linear case that $q_1 = 0$ and $q_2 = p_1 = 3$.

This method cannot infer every resource-polymorphic typing with respect to declarative type derivations with polymorphic recursion. This would mean to start with a (possibly infinite) set of annotated types for each function and to justify each function type with a type derivation that uses types from the initial set. With respect to this declarative view, the inference algorithm in this paper can compute every set of types for a function f that has the form $\Sigma(f) = \{T + q \cdot T_i \mid q \in \mathbb{Q}^+, 1 \leq i \leq m\}$ for a resource-annotated function type T, cost-free function types T_i, and m recursive calls of f in its function body. Since many resource-polymorphic type derivations feature a set of function types of this format, our approach leads to an effective inference method. In the algorithmic type rules (Fig. 3) we directly integrated the above format of $\Sigma(f)$ in the rule T:FUNAPP for function applications to enable an efficient inference.

3 Resource Aware ML

RAML (Resource Aware ML) is a first-order functional language with ML-style syntax, booleans, integers, pairs, lists, recursion and pattern match.

To simplify typing rules in this paper, we define the following *expressions of RAML* to be in *let normal form*. In the implementation we allow unrestricted expressions. One can use every binary operation *binop* whose worst-case cost is bounded by a constant.

$$\begin{aligned} e ::= {} & () \mid \mathit{True} \mid \mathit{False} \mid n \mid x \mid x_1\ \mathit{binop}\ x_2 \mid f(x_1,\ldots,x_n) \mid \mathit{let}\ x = e_1\ \mathit{in}\ e_2 \\ & \mid \mathit{if}\ x\ \mathit{then}\ e_t\ \mathit{else}\ e_f \mid (x_1,x_2) \mid \mathit{match}\ x\ \mathit{with}\ (x_1,x_2) \rightarrow e \\ & \mid \mathit{nil} \mid \mathit{cons}(x_h,x_t) \mid \mathit{match}\ x\ \mathit{with}\ \mid \mathit{nil} \rightarrow e_1 \mid \mathit{cons}(x_h,x_t) \rightarrow e_2 \end{aligned}$$

In the implementation of RAML we included a destructive pattern match and the extended version of [9] describes how polynomial potential can be applied to tree-like data types. The inference algorithm can easily be adopted to handle these extensions.

We define the well-typed expressions of RAML by assigning a *simple type*, a usual ML type without resource annotations, to well-typed expressions. Simple types are data types and first-order types as given by the grammars below.

$$A ::= \mathit{unit} \mid \mathit{bool} \mid \mathit{int} \mid L(A) \mid (A,A) \qquad\qquad F ::= A \rightarrow A$$

A *typing context* Γ is a partial, finite mapping from variable identifiers to data types. A *signature* Σ is a finite, partial mapping of function identifiers to first-order types. The typing judgment $\Gamma \vdash_{\Sigma} e : A$ states that the expression e has type A under the signature Σ in the context Γ. The typing rules that define the typing judgment are standard and identical with the resource-annotated typing rules from §5 if the resource annotations are omitted. A *RAML program* consists of a signature Σ and a family $(e_f, y_f)_{f \in \text{dom}(\Sigma)}$ of expressions with a variable identifier such that $y_f{:}A \vdash_{\Sigma} e_f{:}B$ if $\Sigma(f) = A \to B$.

4 Operational Semantics

We define a big-step operational semantics that measures the quantitative resource consumption of programs. It is parametric in the resource of interest and can measure every quantity whose usage in a single evaluation step can be bounded by a constant. The actual constants for a step on a specific system architecture can be derived by analyzing the translation of the step in the compiler implementation for that architecture [5].

The semantics is formulated with respect to a stack and a heap: A value $v \in \text{Val}$ is either a location $l \in \text{Loc}$, a boolean constant b, an integer n, a null value NULL or a pair of values (v_1, v_2). A *heap* is a finite partial mapping $\mathcal{H} : \text{Loc} \to \text{Val}$ from locations to values. A *stack* is a finite partial mapping $\mathcal{V} : \text{VID} \to \text{Val}$ from variable identifiers to values. Since we also consider resources like memory that can become available during an evaluation, we have to track the *watermark* of the resource usage, i.e., the maximal number of resources units that are simultaneously used during an evaluation. In order to derive a watermark of a sequence of evaluations from the watermarks of the sub evaluations one has also to take into account the number of resource units that are available after each sub evaluation.

The operational evaluation rules in Fig. 1 thus define an evaluation judgment of the form $\mathcal{V}, \mathcal{H} \vdash e \rightsquigarrow v, \mathcal{H}' \mid (q, q')$ expressing the following. If the stack $\mathcal{V}$ and the initial heap $\mathcal{H}$ are given then the expression e evaluates to the value v and the new heap $\mathcal{H}'$. In order to evaluate e one needs at least $q \in \mathbb{Q}^+$ resource units and after the evaluation there are at least $q' \in \mathbb{Q}^+$ resource units available. The actual resource consumption is then $\delta = q - q'$. The quantity δ is negative if resources become available.

In contrast to similar versions in earlier works there is at most one pair (q, q') such that $\mathcal{V}, \mathcal{H} \vdash e \rightsquigarrow v, \mathcal{H}' \mid (q, q')$ for an expression e and fixed $\mathcal{H}$ and $\mathcal{V}$. The non-negative number q is the watermark of simultaneous resources usage during the evaluation.

It is handy to view the pairs (q, q') in the evaluation judgments as elements of a monoid[2] $\mathcal{R} = (\mathbb{Q}^+ \times \mathbb{Q}^+, \cdot)$. The neutral element is $(0, 0)$ which means that resources are neither used nor restituted. The operation $(q, q') \cdot (p, p')$ defines how to account for an evaluation consisting of evaluations whose resource consumptions are defined by (q, q') and (p, p'), respectively. We define

$$(q, q') \cdot (p, p') = \begin{cases} (q + p - q',\ p') & \text{if } q' \leq p \\ (q,\ p' + q' - p) & \text{if } q' > p \end{cases}$$

The intuition is that we need q resource units to perform the first evaluation after which q' restituted units remain. The second operation needs then p units. If $q' \leq p$ then we additionally need $p - q'$ resources to pay for both evaluations and have p' resources left

[2] It is possible to define the evaluation more abstractly with respect to an arbitrary monoid M.

$$\frac{}{\mathcal{V},\mathcal{H} \vdash () \rightsquigarrow \text{NULL},\mathcal{H} \mid K^{\text{unit}}}\text{E:ConstU} \qquad \frac{x_1,x_2 \in \text{dom}(\mathcal{V}) \qquad v = op(\mathcal{V}(x_1),\mathcal{V}(x_2))}{\mathcal{V},\mathcal{H} \vdash x_1\; op\; x_2 \rightsquigarrow v,\mathcal{H} \mid K^{\text{op}}}\text{E:BinOp}$$

$$\frac{n \in \mathbb{Z}}{\mathcal{V},\mathcal{H} \vdash n \rightsquigarrow n,\mathcal{H} \mid K^{\text{int}}}\text{E:ConstI} \qquad \frac{\mathcal{V}(x){=}v \qquad [y_f \mapsto v],\mathcal{H} \vdash e_f \rightsquigarrow v',\mathcal{H}' \mid (q,q')}{\mathcal{V},\mathcal{H} \vdash f(x) \rightsquigarrow v',\mathcal{H}' \mid K_1^{\text{app}}\cdot(q,q')\cdot K_2^{\text{app}}}\text{E:FunApp}$$

$$\frac{b \in \{\mathit{True},\mathit{False}\}}{\mathcal{V},\mathcal{H} \vdash b \rightsquigarrow b,\mathcal{H} \mid K^{\text{bool}}}\text{E:ConstB} \qquad \frac{\mathcal{V}(x) = \mathit{True} \qquad \mathcal{V},\mathcal{H} \vdash e_t \rightsquigarrow v,\mathcal{H}' \mid (q,q')}{\mathcal{V},\mathcal{H} \vdash \mathit{if}\; x\; \mathit{then}\; e_t\; \mathit{else}\; e_f \rightsquigarrow v,\mathcal{H}' \mid K_1^{\text{conT}}\cdot(q,q')\cdot K_2^{\text{conT}}}\text{E:CondT}$$

$$\frac{\mathcal{V}(x) = \mathit{False} \qquad \mathcal{V},\mathcal{H} \vdash e_f \rightsquigarrow v,\mathcal{H}' \mid (q,q')}{\mathcal{V},\mathcal{H} \vdash \mathit{if}\; x\; \mathit{then}\; e_t\; \mathit{else}\; e_f \rightsquigarrow v,\mathcal{H}' \mid K_1^{\text{conF}}\cdot(q,q')\cdot K_2^{\text{conF}}}\text{E:CondF}$$

$$\frac{\mathcal{V},\mathcal{H} \vdash e_1 \rightsquigarrow v_1,\mathcal{H}_1 \mid (q,q') \qquad \mathcal{V}[x \mapsto v_1],\mathcal{H}_1 \vdash e_2 \rightsquigarrow v_2,\mathcal{H}_2 \mid (p,p')}{\mathcal{V},\mathcal{H} \vdash \mathit{let}\; x = e_1\; \mathit{in}\; e_2 \rightsquigarrow v_2,\mathcal{H}_2 \mid K_1^{\text{let}}\cdot(q,q')\cdot K_2^{\text{let}}\cdot(p,p')\cdot K_3^{\text{let}}}\text{E:Let}$$

$$\frac{x_1,x_2 \in \text{dom}(\mathcal{V}) \qquad v = (\mathcal{V}(x_1),\mathcal{V}(x_2))}{\mathcal{V},\mathcal{H} \vdash (x_1,x_2) \rightsquigarrow v,\mathcal{H} \mid K^{\text{pair}}}\text{E:Pair} \qquad \frac{}{\mathcal{V},\mathcal{H} \vdash \mathit{nil} \rightsquigarrow \text{NULL},\mathcal{H} \mid K^{\text{nil}}}\text{E:Nil}$$

$$\frac{x \in \text{dom}(\mathcal{V})}{\mathcal{V},\mathcal{H} \vdash x \rightsquigarrow \mathcal{V}(x),\mathcal{H} \mid K^{\text{var}}}\text{E:Var} \qquad \frac{x_h,x_t \in \text{dom}(\mathcal{V}) \quad v{=}(\mathcal{V}(x_h),\mathcal{V}(x_t)) \quad l \notin \text{dom}(\mathcal{H})}{\mathcal{V},\mathcal{H} \vdash \mathit{cons}(x_h,x_t) \rightsquigarrow l,\mathcal{H}[l \mapsto v] \mid K^{\text{cons}}}\text{E:Cons}$$

$$\frac{\mathcal{V}(x) = (v_1,v_2) \qquad \mathcal{V}[x_1 \mapsto v_1, x_2 \mapsto v_2],\mathcal{H} \vdash e \rightsquigarrow v,\mathcal{H}' \mid (q,q')}{\mathcal{V},\mathcal{H} \vdash \mathit{match}\; x\; \mathit{with}\; (x_1,x_2) \to e \rightsquigarrow v,\mathcal{H}' \mid K_1^{\text{matP}}\cdot(q,q')\cdot K_2^{\text{matP}}}\text{E:MatP}$$

$$\frac{\mathcal{V}(x) = \text{NULL} \qquad \mathcal{V},\mathcal{H} \vdash e_1 \rightsquigarrow v,\mathcal{H}' \mid (q,q')}{\mathcal{V},\mathcal{H} \vdash \mathit{match}\; x\; \mathit{with}\; \mid \mathit{nil} \to e_1 \mid \mathit{cons}(x_h,x_t) \to e_2 \rightsquigarrow v,\mathcal{H}' \mid K_1^{\text{matN}}\cdot(q,q')\cdot K_2^{\text{matN}}}\text{E:MatN}$$

$$\frac{\mathcal{V}(x){=}l \qquad \mathcal{H}(l){=}(v_h,v_t) \qquad \mathcal{V}[x_h{\mapsto}v_h, x_t{\mapsto}v_t],\mathcal{H} \vdash e_2 \rightsquigarrow v,\mathcal{H}' \mid (q,q')}{\mathcal{V},\mathcal{H} \vdash \mathit{match}\; x\; \mathit{with}\; \mid \mathit{nil} \to e_1 \mid \mathit{cons}(x_h,x_t) \to e_2 \rightsquigarrow v,\mathcal{H}' \mid K_1^{\text{matC}}\cdot(q,q')\cdot K_2^{\text{matC}}}\text{E:MatC}$$

Fig. 1. Big-step operational semantics

in the end. If $q' > p$ then q units suffices to perform both evaluations. Additionally, the $q' - p$ units that are not needed for the second evaluation are added to the resources becoming finally available. If resources are never restituted (as with time) then we can restrict to elements of the form $(q,0)$ and $(q,0)\cdot(p,0)$ is just $(q+p,0)$.

We identify (positive and negative) rational numbers with elements of $\mathcal{R}$ as follows: $q \geq 0$ denotes $(q,0)$ and $q < 0$ denotes $(0,-q)$. This notation avoids case distinctions in the evaluation rules since the constants K that appear in the rules might be negative.

Partial Evaluations. A shortcoming of classic big-step operational semantics is that it does not provide judgments for evaluations that diverge. This is problematic if one intends to prove statements for divergent and convergent computations.

A straightforward remedy is to use a small-step semantics. But in the context of resource analysis, the use of big-step rules seems to be more favorable. First, big-step rules can more directly axiomatize the resource behavior of compiled code on specific machines. Secondly, it allows for shorter and less syntactic proofs.

$$\frac{}{\mathcal{V},\mathcal{H}\vdash e \rightsquigarrow\mid 0}\text{ P:ZERO} \qquad \frac{b\in\{\mathit{True},\mathit{False}\}}{\mathcal{V},\mathcal{H}\vdash b \rightsquigarrow\mid K^{\text{bool}}}\text{ P:CONSTB} \qquad \frac{}{\mathcal{V},\mathcal{H}\vdash () \rightsquigarrow\mid K^{\text{unit}}}\text{ P:CONSTU}$$

$$\frac{n\in\mathbb{Z}}{\mathcal{V},\mathcal{H}\vdash n \rightsquigarrow\mid K^{\text{int}}}\text{ P:CONSTI} \qquad \frac{x\in\text{dom}(\mathcal{V})}{\mathcal{V},\mathcal{H}\vdash x \rightsquigarrow\mid K^{\text{var}}}\text{ P:VAR} \qquad \frac{x_1,x_2\in\text{dom}(\mathcal{V})}{\mathcal{V},\mathcal{H}\vdash (x_1,x_2) \rightsquigarrow\mid K^{\text{pair}}}\text{ P:PAIR}$$

$$\frac{\mathcal{V}(x)=v \qquad [y_f\mapsto v],\mathcal{H}\vdash e_f \rightsquigarrow\mid q}{\mathcal{V},\mathcal{H}\vdash f(x) \rightsquigarrow\mid K_1^{\text{app}}+q}\text{ P:FUNAPP} \qquad \frac{\mathcal{V},\mathcal{H}\vdash e_1 \rightsquigarrow\mid q}{\mathcal{V},\mathcal{H}\vdash \mathit{let}\, x=e_1\, \mathit{in}\, e_2 \rightsquigarrow\mid K_1^{\text{let}}+q}\text{ P:LET1}$$

$$\frac{\mathcal{V},\mathcal{H}\vdash e_1 \rightsquigarrow v_1,\mathcal{H}_1\mid (q,q') \qquad \mathcal{V}[x\mapsto v_1],\mathcal{H}_1\vdash e_2 \rightsquigarrow\mid p \qquad K_1^{\text{let}}\cdot(q,q')\cdot K_2^{\text{let}}\cdot(p,0)=(r,r')}{\mathcal{V},\mathcal{H}\vdash \mathit{let}\, x=e_1\, \mathit{in}\, e_2 \rightsquigarrow\mid r}\text{ P:LET2}$$

$$\frac{\mathcal{V}(x)=\mathit{True} \qquad \mathcal{V},\mathcal{H}\vdash e_t \rightsquigarrow\mid q}{\mathcal{V},\mathcal{H}\vdash \mathit{if}\, x\, \mathit{then}\, e_t\, \mathit{else}\, e_f \rightsquigarrow\mid K_1^{\text{conT}}+q}\text{ P:CONDT} \qquad \frac{x_1,x_2\in\text{dom}(\mathcal{V})}{\mathcal{V},\mathcal{H}\vdash x_1\, \mathit{op}\, x_2 \rightsquigarrow\mid K^{\text{op}}}\text{ P:BINOP}$$

$$\frac{\mathcal{V}(x)=\mathit{False} \qquad \mathcal{V},\mathcal{H}\vdash e_f \rightsquigarrow\mid q}{\mathcal{V},\mathcal{H}\vdash \mathit{if}\, x\, \mathit{then}\, e_t\, \mathit{else}\, e_f \rightsquigarrow\mid K_1^{\text{conF}}+q}\text{ P:CONDF} \qquad \frac{x_h,x_t\in\text{dom}(\mathcal{V})}{\mathcal{V},\mathcal{H}\vdash \mathit{cons}(x_h,x_t) \rightsquigarrow\mid K^{\text{cons}}}\text{ P:CONS}$$

$$\frac{\mathcal{V}(x)=(v_1,v_2) \qquad \mathcal{V}[x_1\mapsto v_1,x_2\mapsto v_2],\mathcal{H}\vdash e \rightsquigarrow\mid q}{\mathcal{V},\mathcal{H}\vdash \mathit{match}\, x\, \mathit{with}\, (x_1,x_2)\to e \rightsquigarrow\mid K_1^{\text{matP}}+q}\text{ P:MATP} \qquad \frac{}{\mathcal{V},\mathcal{H}\vdash \mathit{nil} \rightsquigarrow\mid K^{\text{nil}}}\text{ P:NIL}$$

$$\frac{\mathcal{V}(x)=\text{NULL} \qquad \mathcal{V},\mathcal{H}\vdash e_1 \rightsquigarrow\mid q}{\mathcal{V},\mathcal{H}\vdash \mathit{match}\, x\, \mathit{with}\, \mid \mathit{nil}\to e_1 \mid \mathit{cons}(x_h,x_t)\to e_2 \rightsquigarrow\mid K_1^{\text{matN}}+q}\text{ P:MATN}$$

$$\frac{\mathcal{V}(x)=l \qquad \mathcal{H}(l)=(v_h,v_t) \qquad \mathcal{V}[x_h\mapsto v_h,x_t\mapsto v_t],\mathcal{H}\vdash e_2 \rightsquigarrow\mid q}{\mathcal{V},\mathcal{H}\vdash \mathit{match}\, x\, \mathit{with}\, \mid \mathit{nil}\to e_1 \mid \mathit{cons}(x_h,x_t)\to e_2 \rightsquigarrow\mid K_1^{\text{matC}}+q}\text{ P:MATC}$$

Fig. 2. Partial big-step operational semantics

An alternative approach is to use coinductively defined big-step semantics [10,11]. However, coinductive semantics lends itself less well to formulating and proving semantic soundness theorems of the form "if the program is well-typed and the operational semantics says X then Y holds" (like Thm. 4). For example, in Leroy's Lemmas 17-22 [11] the coinductive definition appears in the conclusion rather than as a premise.

That is why we use a novel approach to the problem here by defining a *big-step semantics for partial evaluations* that directly corresponds to the rules of the big-step semantics in Fig. 1. It defines a statement of the form $\mathcal{V},\mathcal{H}\vdash e \rightsquigarrow\mid q$ for a stack $\mathcal{V}$, a heap $\mathcal{H}$, $q\in\mathbb{Q}^+$ and an expression e. The meaning is that there is a partial evaluation of e with the stack $\mathcal{V}$ and the heap $\mathcal{H}$ that consumes q resources. Here, q is the watermark of the resource usage. We do not have to keep track of the restituted resources.

Note that the rule P:ZERO is essential for the partiality of the semantics. It can be applied at any point to stop the evaluation and thus yields to a non-deterministic evaluation judgment.

Since there might be negative constants K, the partial evaluation rules in Fig. 2 have conclusions of the form $\mathcal{V},\mathcal{H}\vdash e \rightsquigarrow\mid \max(q,0)$ to ensure non-negative values. We simply write $\mathcal{V},\mathcal{H}\vdash e \rightsquigarrow\mid q$ instead of $\mathcal{V},\mathcal{H}\vdash e \rightsquigarrow\mid \max(q,0)$ in each conclusion.

We prove that if an expression converges in a given environment then the resource-usage watermark of the evaluation is an upper bound for the resource usage of every partial evaluation of the expression in that environment.

Theorem 1. *If* $\mathcal{V},\mathcal{H} \vdash e \rightsquigarrow v,\mathcal{H}' \mid (q,q')$ *and* $\mathcal{V},\mathcal{H} \vdash e \rightsquigarrow \mid p$ *then* $p \leq q$.

A stack $\mathcal{V}$ and a heap $\mathcal{H}$ are *well-formed* with respect to a context Γ if, for every $x \in \text{dom}(\Gamma)$, $\mathcal{V}(x)$ is a value matching the type $\Gamma(x)$ or a location in $\mathcal{H}$ that contains a value matching $\Gamma(x)$. We then write $\mathcal{H} \vDash \mathcal{V}{:}\Gamma$. Similarly, we write $\mathcal{H} \vDash v{:}A$ if v is a value matching type A in $\mathcal{H}$. A formal definition is given in [7].

Thm. 2 states that, in a well-formed environment, every well-typed expression either diverges or evaluates to a value of the stated type. To this end we instantiate the resource constants in the rules to count the number of evaluation steps.

Theorem 2. *Let the resource constants be instantiated by* $K^x = 1$, $K^x_1 = 1$ *and* $K^x_m = 0$ *for all* x *and all* $m > 1$. *If* $\Gamma \vdash_\Sigma e{:}A$ *and* $\mathcal{H} \vDash \mathcal{V}{:}\Gamma$ *then* $\mathcal{V},\mathcal{H} \vdash e \rightsquigarrow v,\mathcal{H}' \mid (n,0)$ *for an* $n \in \mathbb{N}$ *or* $\mathcal{V},\mathcal{H} \vdash e \rightsquigarrow \mid m$ *for every* $m \in \mathbb{N}$.

Cost-Free Metric. The type inference algorithm makes use of the *cost-free* resource metric. This is the metric in which all constants K that appear in the rules are instantiated to zero. We will use it in §5 to define a resource-polymorphic recursion where we use cost-free function types to pass potential from the argument to the result.

With the cost-free resource metric the resource usage of evaluations is always zero: If $\mathcal{V},\mathcal{H} \vdash e \rightsquigarrow v,\mathcal{H}' \mid (q,q')$ then $q = q' = 0$ and if $\mathcal{V},\mathcal{H} \vdash e \rightsquigarrow \mid q$ then $q = 0$.

5 Resource Annotated Types

Resource-annotated types are simple types where lists are annotated with non-negative vectors $\vec{p} \in \mathbb{Q}^n$. Here we only give a short definition of the potential functions defined by annotated types. More explanations can be found in [9].

Let $\vec{p} = (p_1,\ldots,p_k)$ be an annotation.The *additive shift* of $\vec{p}$ is $\lhd(\vec{p}) = (p_1{+}p_2, p_2{+}p_3,\ldots,p_{k-1}+p_k,p_k)$. Let $\mathcal{H}$ be a heap, A be a resource-annotated type and let v be a value matching type A in $\mathcal{H}$. The *potential* $\Phi_\mathcal{H}(v{:}A)$ is then defined as follows.

$$\Phi_\mathcal{H}(v{:}A) = 0 \text{ if } v = \text{NULL} \text{ or } A \in \{\mathit{unit}, \mathit{int}, \mathit{bool}\}$$
$$\Phi_\mathcal{H}((v_1,v_2){:}(A_1,A_2)) = \Phi_\mathcal{H}(v_1{:}A_1) + \Phi_\mathcal{H}(v_2{:}A_2)$$
$$\Phi_\mathcal{H}(l{:}L^{\vec{p}}(A')) = p_1 + \Phi_\mathcal{H}(v'{:}A') + \Phi_\mathcal{H}(l'{:}\,L^{\lhd(\vec{p})}(A')) \text{ if } \mathcal{H}(l){=}(v',l')$$

If l_1 is a location that points to a list then we write $\mathcal{H}(l_1) = [v_1,\ldots,v_n]$ if $\mathcal{H}(l_i) = (v_i,l_{i+1})$ for $i = 1,\ldots,n$ and $l_{n+1} = \text{NULL}$. If $l_1 = \text{NULL}$ then $\mathcal{H}(l_1) = []$. Thm. 3 shows how to express the potential $\Phi_\mathcal{H}(v{:}A)$ of a value v with respect the heap $\mathcal{H}$ and a matching annotated type A in terms of polynomials in the lengths of the lists that are reachable from v. A proof can be found in the extended version of [9].

Theorem 3. *Let* $\mathcal{H}$ *be a heap and let* $\mathcal{H}(l) = [v_1\ldots,v_n]$ *be a list of length* n. *Then* $\Phi_\mathcal{H}(l{:}L^{\vec{p}}(A)) = \sum_{i=1}^k p_i\binom{n}{i} + \sum_{i=1}^n \Phi_\mathcal{H}(v_i{:}A)$.

As in the case of simple types, a *typing context* is a finite partial mapping from variable identifiers to annotated data types. The potential of a context Γ with respect to a heap $\mathcal{H}$ and a stack $\mathcal{V}$ is $\Phi_{\mathcal{V},\mathcal{H}}(\Gamma) = \sum_{x\in\text{dom}(\Gamma)} \Phi_\mathcal{H}(\mathcal{V}(x){:}\Gamma(x))$.

Resource-annotated first-order types have the form $A \xrightarrow{q/q'} B$ for $q, q' \in \mathbb{Q}^+$ and annotated data types A, B. A *resource-annotated signature* Σ is a finite, partial mapping from function identifiers to resource-annotated first-order types.

A *resource-annotated typing judgment* has the form $\Sigma; \Gamma \;{}^{k}\!\vdash^{q}_{q'}\; e{:}A$ where e is a RAML expression, $k \in \mathbb{N}^+$ is the length of the list annotations, $q, q' \in \mathbb{Q}^+$ are non-negative rational numbers, Σ is a resource-annotated signature, Γ is a resource-annotated context and A is a resource-annotated data type. The intended meaning of this judgment is that if there are more than $q + \Phi(\Gamma)$ resource units available then this is sufficient to evaluate e and there are more than $q' + \Phi(v{:}A)$ resource units if e evaluates to the value v.

A RAML program with resource-annotated types of degree k consists of a resource-annotated signature Σ and a family $(e_f, y_f)_{f \in \mathrm{dom}(\Sigma)}$ of expressions with variables identifiers such that for each e_f we have $\Sigma; y_f{:}A \;{}^{k}\!\vdash^{q}_{q'}\; e_f{:}B$ if $\Sigma(f) {=} A \xrightarrow{q/q'} B$.

We write $\Sigma; \Gamma \;{}^{cf(k)}\!\vdash^{q}_{q'}\; e{:}A$ to refer to cost-free type judgments where all constants K in the rules are zero. It is used to define a resource-polymorphic recursion where we use cost-free function types to pass potential from the argument to the result (see §2).

In the typing rules in Fig. 3 we write $e[z/x]$ to denote the expression e with all free occurrences of the variable x replaced with the variable z. We assume that a fixed but arbitrary global resource-annotated signature Σ is given. Furthermore, there is the implicit constraint $q \geq 0$ for every resource annotation q.

The rules are mostly algorithmic versions of the typing rules in [9]. The most important difference is the rule T:FUNAPP which enables resource-polymorphic recursion. It states that one can add any cost-free typing of the function body to the function type that is given by the signature Σ. The signature Σ_{cf} is a fresh signature such that $(e_f, y_f)_{f \in \Sigma_{cf}}$ is a valid RAML program with cost-free types of degree $k - 1$. It can differ in every application of the rule. The idea is as follows. To pay for the resource costs of a function call $f(x)$, the available potential ($\Phi(x{:}B) + q$) must meet the requirements of the functions' signature ($\Phi(x{:}B') + p$). Additionally available potential ($\Phi(x{:}B_{cf}) + p_{cf}$) can be passed to a cost-free typing of the function body. The potential after the function call ($\Phi(f(x){:}A) + q'$) is then the sum of the potentials that are assigned by the cost-free typing ($\Phi(f(x){:}A_{cf}) + p_{cf}$) and by the function signature ($\Phi(f(x){:}A') + p$). As a result, $f(x)$ can be used resource-polymorphically with a specific typing for each recursive call while the resource monomorphic function signature enables an efficient type inference.

The *sharing relation* $\curlyvee$ defines how potential can be shared between multiple occurrences of a variable. Intuitively, if $\curlyvee(A \mid A_1, A_2)$ holds then $x{:}A$ can be used twice, once with type A_1 and once with type A_2. We define $\curlyvee(A \mid A, A)$ if $A \in \{$*unit, bool, int*$\}$; $\curlyvee(L^{\vec{p}}(A) \mid L^{\vec{q}}(A_1), L^{\vec{r}}(A_2))$ if $\curlyvee(A \mid A_1, A_2)$ and $\vec{p} = \vec{q} + \vec{r}$; and $\curlyvee((A, B) \mid (A_1{,}B_1), (A_2, B_2))$ if $\curlyvee(X \mid X_1, X_2)$ for $X{=}A, B$. The sharing relation is analogously extended to contexts $\Gamma, \Gamma_1, \Gamma_2$ with $\mathrm{dom}(\Gamma) = \mathrm{dom}(\Gamma_1) = \mathrm{dom}(\Gamma_2)$ in a per element way.

A data type A is a *subtype* of a data type B, $A <: B$, only if A and B are structurally identical, and if $\Phi(v{:}A) \geq \Phi(v{:}B)$ holds for every value v. We define $C <: C$ if $C \in \{$*unit, bool, int*$\}$; $(A_1, A_2) <: (B_1, B_2)$ if $A_1 <: B_1$ and $A_2 <: B_2$; and $L^{\vec{p}}(A) <: L^{\vec{q}}(B)$ if $A <: B$ and $\vec{p} \geq \vec{q}$.

$$\frac{q \geq q' + K^{\text{var}}}{\Gamma, x{:}A \;{}^{k}\vdash^{q}_{q'}\; x : A}\;\textsc{(T:Var)} \qquad \frac{q \geq q' + K^{\text{unit}}}{\Gamma \;{}^{k}\vdash^{q}_{q'}\; ()\!:\!\mathit{unit}}\;\textsc{(T:ConstU)} \qquad \frac{n \in \mathbb{Z} \quad q \geq q' + K^{\text{int}}}{\Gamma \;{}^{k}\vdash^{q}_{q'}\; n : \mathit{int}}\;\textsc{(T:ConstI)}$$

$$\frac{b \in \{\mathit{True}, \mathit{False}\} \quad q \geq q' + K^{\text{bool}}}{\Gamma \;{}^{k}\vdash^{q}_{q'}\; b{:}\mathit{bool}}\;\textsc{(T:ConstB)} \qquad \frac{op \in \{\mathit{or}, \mathit{and}\} \quad q \geq q' + K^{\text{op}}}{\Gamma, x_1{:}\mathit{bool}, x_2{:}\mathit{bool} \;{}^{k}\vdash^{q}_{q'}\; x_1 \; op \; x_2 : \mathit{bool}}\;\textsc{(T:BinOpB)}$$

$$\frac{q \geq q' + K^{\text{pair}}}{\Gamma, x_1{:}A_1, x_2{:}A_2 \;{}^{k}\vdash^{q}_{q'}\; (x_1, x_2){:}(A_1, A_2)}\;\textsc{(T:Pair)} \qquad \frac{op \in \{+, -, *, \ldots\} \quad q \geq q' + K^{\text{op}}}{\Gamma, x_1{:}\mathit{int}, x_2{:}\mathit{int} \;{}^{k}\vdash^{q}_{q'}\; x_1 \; op \; x_2 : \mathit{int}}\;\textsc{(T:BinOpI)}$$

$$\frac{k = 1 \quad \Sigma(f) = B \xrightarrow{p/p'} A \quad q = p + c + K^{\text{app}}_1 \quad q' = p' + c - K^{\text{app}}_2}{\Gamma, x{:}B \;{}^{k}\vdash^{q}_{q'}\; f(x) : A}\;\textsc{(T:FunApp1)}$$

$$\frac{\begin{array}{c}\Sigma(f) = B' \xrightarrow{p/p'} A' \quad \curlyvee(A \,|\, A', A_{cf}) \quad \curlyvee(B \,|\, B', B_{cf}) \quad \Sigma_{cf}(f) = B_{cf} \xrightarrow{p_{cf}/p'_{cf}} A_{cf} \\ q = p + p_{cf} + c + K^{\text{app}}_1 \quad q' = p' + p'_{cf} + c - K^{\text{app}}_2 \quad \Sigma_{cf}; y_f{:}B_{cf} \;{}^{cf(k-1)}\vdash^{p_{cf}}_{p'_{cf}}\; e_f{:}A_{cf}\end{array}}{\Gamma, x{:}B \;{}^{k}\vdash^{q}_{q'}\; f(x) : A}\;\textsc{(T:FunApp)}$$

$$\frac{\begin{array}{c}q \geq p_1 + K^{\text{let}}_1 \quad p'_1 \geq p_2 + K^{\text{let}}_2 \quad p'_2 \geq q' + K^{\text{let}}_3 \quad \curlyvee(\Delta \mid \Delta_1, \Delta_2) \\ \mathrm{Var}(\Gamma_1) \cap \mathrm{Var}(\Gamma_2) = \emptyset \quad \Gamma_1, \Delta_1 \;{}^{k}\vdash^{p_1}_{p'_1}\; e_1{:}B \quad \Gamma_2, \Delta_2, x{:}B \;{}^{k}\vdash^{p_2}_{p'_2}\; e_2{:}A\end{array}}{\Gamma_1, \Gamma_2, \Delta \;{}^{k}\vdash^{q}_{q'}\; \mathit{let}\; x = e_1 \;\mathit{in}\; e_2 : A}\;\textsc{(T:Let)}$$

$$\frac{\begin{array}{c}q \geq p_t + K^{\text{conT}}_1 \quad q \geq p_f + K^{\text{conF}}_1 \quad p'_t \geq q' + K^{\text{conT}}_2 \\ p'_f \geq q' + K^{\text{conF}}_2 \quad A_i <: A \text{ for } i = 1, 2 \quad \Gamma \;{}^{k}\vdash^{p_t}_{p'_t}\; e_t : A_1 \quad \Gamma \;{}^{k}\vdash^{p_f}_{p'_f}\; e_f : A_2\end{array}}{\Gamma, x{:}\mathit{bool} \;{}^{k}\vdash^{q}_{q'}\; \mathit{if}\; x \;\mathit{then}\; e_t \;\mathit{else}\; e_f : A}\;\textsc{(T:Cond)}$$

$$\frac{q \geq p + K^{\text{matP}}_1 \quad p' \geq q' + K^{\text{matP}}_2 \quad \Gamma, x_1{:}B_1, x_2{:}B_2 \;{}^{k}\vdash^{p}_{p'}\; e{:}A}{\Gamma, x{:}(B_1, B_2) \;{}^{k}\vdash^{q}_{q'}\; \mathit{match}\; x \;\mathit{with}\; (x_1, x_2) \to e : A}\;\textsc{(T:MatP)} \qquad \frac{q \geq q' + K^{\text{nil}}}{\Gamma \;{}^{k}\vdash^{q}_{q'}\; \mathit{nil}{:}L(A)}\;\textsc{(T:Nil)}$$

$$\frac{\vec{p} = (p_1, \ldots, p_k) \quad \vec{r} \geq \lhd(\vec{p}) \quad q \geq q' + p_1 + K^{\text{cons}} \quad A_i <: A \text{ for } i = 1, 2}{\Gamma, x_h{:}A_1, x_t{:}L^{\vec{r}}(A_2) \;{}^{k}\vdash^{q}_{q'}\; \mathit{cons}(x_h, x_t){:}L^{\vec{p}}(A)}\;\textsc{(T:Cons)}$$

$$\frac{\begin{array}{c}q + p_1 \geq s_c + K^{\text{matC}}_1 \quad q \geq s_n + K^{\text{matN}}_1 \quad s'_c \geq q' + K^{\text{matC}}_2 \quad s'_n \geq q' + K^{\text{matN}}_2 \quad \Gamma \;{}^{k}\vdash^{s_n}_{s'_n}\; e_1{:}A_1 \\ \vec{p} = (p_1, \ldots, p_k) \quad A_i <: A \text{ for } i = 1, 2 \quad \Gamma, x_h{:}B, x_t{:}L^{\lhd(\vec{p})}(B) \;{}^{k}\vdash^{s_c}_{s'_c}\; e_2{:}A_2\end{array}}{\Gamma, x{:}L^{\vec{p}}(B) \;{}^{k}\vdash^{q}_{q'}\; \mathit{match}\; x \;\mathit{with}\; \mid \mathit{nil} \to e_1 \mid \mathit{cons}(x_h, x_t) \to e_2 : A}\;\textsc{(T:MatL)}$$

Fig. 3. Algorithmic type rules

The introduction of the partial evaluation rules enables us to formulate a stronger soundness theorem than, e.g., in [9]. It states that the bounds derived from an annotated type statement also hold for non-terminating evaluations. Additionally, the new notation that we use in the operational semantics allows for a more concise statement.

Theorem 4 (Soundness). *Let* $\mathcal{H} \vDash \mathcal{V}{:}\Gamma$ *and* $\Gamma \;{}^{k}\vdash^{q}_{q'}\; e{:}A$. *(1) If* $\mathcal{V}, \mathcal{H} \vdash e \rightsquigarrow v, \mathcal{H}' \mid (p, p')$ *then* $p \leq \Phi_{\mathcal{V},\mathcal{H}}(\Gamma) + q$ *and* $p - p' \leq \Phi_{\mathcal{V},\mathcal{H}}(\Gamma) + q - (\Phi_{\mathcal{H}'}(v{:}A) + q')$.
(2) If $\mathcal{V}, \mathcal{H} \vdash e \rightsquigarrow \mid p$ *then* $p \leq \Phi_{\mathcal{V},\mathcal{H}}(\Gamma) + q$.

It follows from Thm. 4 and Thm. 2 that run-time bounds also prove termination.

Corollary 1. *Let the resource constants be instantiated by* $K^x = 1$, $K_1^x = 1$ *and* $K_m^x = 0$ *for all* x *and all* $m > 1$. *If* $\mathcal{H} \models \mathcal{V}{:}\Gamma$ *and* $\Gamma \;{}_k\vdash^{q}_{q'}\; e{:}A$ *then there is an* $n \in \mathbb{N}, n \leq \Phi_{\mathcal{V},\mathcal{H}}(\Gamma) + q$ *such that* $\mathcal{V}, \mathcal{H} \vdash e \rightsquigarrow v, \mathcal{H}' \mid (n, 0)$.

Thm. 4 is proved by induction on the derivation of the evaluation statements $\mathcal{V}, \mathcal{H} \vdash e \rightsquigarrow v, \mathcal{H}' \mid (p, p')$ and $\mathcal{V}, \mathcal{H} \vdash e \rightsquigarrow\mid p$, respectively. There is one proof for all possible instantiations of the resource constants. It is technically involved but conceptually unsurprising. Compared to earlier works [7,9], further complexity arises from the matching of the constraints in the type rules with the monoid elements in the semantics. The proof can be found in the extended version of this paper.

6 The Inference Algorithm

The inference algorithm is mainly defined by the type rules in the previous section. It works like a standard type inference in which each type is annotated with resource variables and the corresponding linear constraints are collected as each type rule is applied. The main innovation in comparison to the classic algorithm [1] is the resource-polymorphic recursion enabled by the rule T:FUNAPP.

The number of computed constraints grows linearly in the maximal degree k that has to be provided by the user. There is a trade-off between the quality of the analysis and the size of the constraint system. The reason is that one sometimes has to analyze function applications context-sensitively with respect to the call stack. Recall, e.g., the expression *attach(x,attach(y,xs))* from §1 where we used two different types for *attach*.

In our implementation we collapse the cycles in the call graph and analyze each function once for every path in the resulting graph. In a nutshell, the algorithm computes inequalities for annotations of degree k for a strongly connected component (SCC) F of the call graph as follows.

1. Annotate the signature of each function $f \in F$ with fresh resource variables.
2. Use the type rules from §5 to type the corresponding expressions e_f. Introduce fresh resource variables for each type annotation in the derivation and collect the corresponding inequalities.
   (a) For a function application $g \in F$: if $k = 1$ or in the cost-free case use the function resource-monomorphically with the signature from (1). Otherwise, go to (1) and derive a cost-free typing of e_g with a fresh signature. Store the arising inequalities and use the resource variables from the obtained typing together with the signature from (1) in T:FUNAPP.
   (b) For a function application $g \notin F$: repeat the algorithm for the SSC of g. Store the arising inequalities and use the obtained annotated type of g.

The context sensitivity can lead to an exponential blow up of the constraint system if there is a sequence of function $f_1, \ldots, f_n$ such that f_i calls f_{i+1} several times. But such sequences are short in most programs. It would not be a substantial limitation in practice to restrict oneself to programs that feature a collapsed call graph with a fixed maximal path length to obtain a constraint system that is linear in the program size.

In general, the computed constraint systems are simple and can be quickly solved by standard LP-solvers. The objective function states that annotations of arguments in function signatures have to be minimized and that annotations of high degree are more expensive then annotations of low degree.

In the extended version one finds a comparison of the computed evaluation-step bounds with the actual worst-case time behavior for several example programs together with the run times of the analyses. The inference algorithm works efficiently and infers resource-polymorphic types for all programs that we manually typed in our system. However, it is not complete with respect to full resource-polymorphism. This would mean to start with a (possibly infinite) set of annotated function types for each function and to justify each type with a derivation that uses first-order types from the initial set.

The extended version of the paper contains a somewhat artificial example that admits a resource-polymorphic type derivation that cannot be inferred by our algorithm. It seems to be unlikely that there is a method to infer a typing for such functions with a method that uses only linear constraints. One could move to quadratic constraints to address the problem but the efficiency of such an approach is unclear. We plan to also experiment with SMT solvers to deal which such constraints.

7 Related Work

Most closely related is the previous work on automatic amortized analysis [9,1,3,4,5,7] (see §1). This paper focuses on polymorphic recursion and is the first that investigates relations of the inferred bounds to non-terminating computations.

Other resource analyses that can in principle obtain polynomial bounds are approaches based on recurrences pioneered by Grobauer [12] and Flajolet [13]. In those systems, an a priori unknown resource bounding function is introduced for each function in the code; by a straightforward intraprocedural analysis a set of recurrence equations or inequations for these functions is then derived. A type-based extraction of such recurrences has been given in [14]. Even for relatively simple programs the resulting recurrences are quite complicated and difficult to solve with standard methods. In the COSTA project [15,16] progress has been made with the solution of those recurrences. In an automatic complexity analysis for higher-order Nuprl terms Benzinger uses Mathematica to solve the generated recurrence equations [17]. Still, we find that amortization yields better results in cases where resource usage of intermediate functions depends on factors other than input size, e.g., sizes of partitions in quick sort. Also compositions of functions seem to be better dealt with by amortization.

A successful method to estimate time bounds for C++ procedures with loops and recursion was recently developed by Gulwani et al. [18,19] in the SPEED project. They annotate programs with counters and use automatic invariant discovery between their values using off-the-shelf program analysis tools which are based on abstract interpretation. A recent innovation for non-recursive programs is the combination of disjunctive invariant generation via abstract interpretation with proof rules that employ SMT-solvers [20]. In contrast to our method, these techniques can not fully automatically analyze iterations over data structures. Instead, the user needs to define numerical "quantitative functions". A methodological difference is that we infer (using linear programming) an abstract potential function which indirectly yields a resource-bounding function. The potential-based approach may be favorable in the presence of compositions and data scattered over different locations (partitions in quick sort). Moreover, our method infers tight bounds for functions like insertion sort that admit a worst-case time usage of the form $\sum_{1\leq i\leq n} i$. In contrast, [18] indicates that a nested loop on $1 \leq i \leq n$ and $1 \leq j \leq i$ is over-approximated with the bound n^2.

The examples from loc. cit. suggest that the two approaches are complementary in the sense that the method of Gulwani et al. works well for programs with little or no recursion but integrate interaction of linear arithmetic with loops. Our method, on the other hand, does not model the interaction of integer arithmetic with resource usage, but is particularly good for analyzing recursive programs involving inductive data types. Moreover, type derivations can be seen as certificates and can be automatically translated into formalized proofs in program logic [21].

Another related approach is the use of sized types [22,23,24] which provide a general framework to represent the size of the data in its type. Sized types are a very important concept and we also employ them indirectly. Our method adds a certain amount of data dependency and dispenses with the explicit manipulation of symbolic expressions in favour of numerical potential annotations.

Polynomial resource bounds have also been studied in [25] that addresses the derivation of polynomial size bounds for functions whose exact growth rate is polynomial.

8 Conclusion and Future Research

We have continued our work on automatic type-base amortized analysis for polynomial resource bounds. To deal with the challenge of resource-polymorphic recursion we have introduced a new inference algorithm. It uses a special cost-free resource metric to compute alternate function types for recursive calls. The algorithm has been implemented and it has been shown by experiments that it efficiently computes types for interesting examples such as sorting algorithms. To prove the non-trivial soundness of the algorithm for terminating and non-terminating evaluations we introduced a novel partial big-step operational semantics. It models non-termination with non-deterministic inductive rules.

Even though there are examples that the inference algorithm cannot handle we find it to be a good compromise between efficiency and performance. Therefore, our future research will focus mainly on conceptual extensions of the type system that will employ the same inference method. Most notably we plan an extension to mixed potential capable of inferring bounds like $n \cdot m$, an extension to recursion on non-inductive data like integers, and the integration of higher-order and polymorphism.

References

1. Hofmann, M., Jost, S.: Static Prediction of Heap Space Usage for First-Order Functional Programs. In: 30th ACM Symp. on Principles of Prog. Langs. (POPL 2003), pp. 185–197 (2003)
2. Tarjan, R.E.: Amortized Computational Complexity. SIAM J. Algebraic Discrete Methods 6(2), 306–318 (1985)
3. Hofmann, M., Jost, S.: Type-Based Amortised Heap-Space Analysis. In: Sestoft, P. (ed.) ESOP 2006. LNCS, vol. 3924, pp. 22–37. Springer, Heidelberg (2006)
4. Hofmann, M., Rodriguez, D.: Efficient Type-Checking for Amortised Heap-Space Analysis. In: Grädel, E., Kahle, R. (eds.) CSL 2009. LNCS, vol. 5771, pp. 317–331. Springer, Heidelberg (2009)

5. Jost, S., Loidl, H.W., Hammond, K., Scaife, N., Hofmann, M.: Carbon Credits for Resource-Bounded Computations using Amortised Analysis. In: Cavalcanti, A., Dams, D.R. (eds.) FM 2009. LNCS, vol. 5850, pp. 354–369. Springer, Heidelberg (2009)
6. Campbell, B.: Amortised Memory Analysis using the Depth of Data Structures. In: Castagna, G. (ed.) ESOP 2009. LNCS, vol. 5502, pp. 190–204. Springer, Heidelberg (2009)
7. Jost, S., Hammond, K., Loidl, H.W., Hofmann, M.: Static Determination of Quantitative Resource Usage for Higher-Order Programs. In: 37th ACM Symp. on Principles of Prog. Langs. (POPL 2010), pp. 223–236 (2010)
8. Atkey, R.: Amortised Resource Analysis with Separation Logic. In: Gordon, A.D. (ed.) Programming Languages and Systems. LNCS, vol. 6012, pp. 85–103. Springer, Heidelberg (2010)
9. Hoffmann, J., Hofmann, M.: Amortized Resource Analysis with Polynomial Potential. In: Gordon, A.D. (ed.) Programming Languages and Systems. LNCS, vol. 6012, pp. 287–306. Springer, Heidelberg (2010)
10. Cousot, P., Cousot, R.: Inductive Definitions, Semantics and Abstract Interpretations. In: 19th ACM Symp. on Principles of Prog. Langs. (POPL 1992), pp. 83–94 (1992)
11. Leroy, X.: Coinductive Big-Step Operational Semantics. In: Sestoft, P. (ed.) ESOP 2006. LNCS, vol. 3924, pp. 54–68. Springer, Heidelberg (2006)
12. Grobauer, B.: Cost Recurrences for DML Programs. In: 6th Intl. Conf. on Funct. Prog. (ICFP 2001), pp. 253–264 (2001)
13. Flajolet, P., Salvy, B., Zimmermann, P.: Automatic Average-case Analysis of Algorithms. Theoret. Comput. Sci. 79(1), 37–109 (1991)
14. Crary, K., Weirich, S.: Resource Bound Certification. In: 27th ACM Symp. on Principles of Prog. Langs. (POPL 2000), pp. 184–198 (2000)
15. Albert, E., Arenas, P., Genaim, S., Puebla, G., Zanardini, D.: Cost Analysis of Java Bytecode. In: De Nicola, R. (ed.) ESOP 2007. LNCS, vol. 4421, pp. 157–172. Springer, Heidelberg (2007)
16. Albert, E., Arenas, P., Genaim, S., Puebla, G.: Automatic Inference of Upper Bounds for Recurrence Relations in Cost Analysis. In: Alpuente, M., Vidal, G. (eds.) SAS 2008. LNCS, vol. 5079, pp. 221–237. Springer, Heidelberg (2008)
17. Benzinger, R.: Automated Higher-Order Complexity Analysis. Theor. Comput. Sci. 318(1-2), 79–103 (2004)
18. Gulwani, S., Mehra, K.K., Chilimbi, T.M.: SPEED: Precise and Efficient Static Estimation of Program Computational Complexity. In: 36th ACM Symp. on Principles of Prog. Langs. (POPL 2009), pp. 127–139 (2009)
19. Gulavani, B.S., Gulwani, S.: A Numerical Abstract Domain Based on Expression Abstraction and Max Operator with Application in Timing Analysis. In: Gupta, A., Malik, S. (eds.) CAV 2008. LNCS, vol. 5123, pp. 370–384. Springer, Heidelberg (2008)
20. Gulwani, S., Zuleger, F.: The Reachability-Bound Problem. In: Conf. on Prog. Lang. Design and Impl. (PLDI 2010), pp. 292–304 (2010)
21. Beringer, L., Hofmann, M., Momigliano, A., Shkaravska, O.: Automatic Certification of Heap Consumption. In: Baader, F., Voronkov, A. (eds.) LPAR 2004. LNCS (LNAI), vol. 3452, pp. 347–362. Springer, Heidelberg (2005)
22. Hughes, J., Pareto, L., Sabry, A.: Proving the Correctness of Reactive Systems Using Sized Types. In: Symp. Princ. of Prog. Langs. (POPL 1996), pp. 410–423 (1996)
23. Hughes, J., Pareto, L.: Recursion and Dynamic Data-structures in Bounded Space: Towards Embedded ML Programming. In: 4th Intl. Conf. on Funct. Prog. (ICFP 1999), pp. 70–81 (1999)
24. Chin, W.N., Khoo, S.C.: Calculating Sized Types. High.-Ord. and Symb. Comp. High.-Ord. and Symb. Comp. 14(2-3), 261–300 (2001)
25. Shkaravska, O., van Kesteren, R., van Eekelen, M.C.: Polynomial Size Analysis of First-Order Functions. In: Della Rocca, S.R. (ed.) TLCA 2007. LNCS, vol. 4583, pp. 351–365. Springer, Heidelberg (2007)

Interprocedural Control Flow Reconstruction

Andrea Flexeder, Bogdan Mihaila, Michael Petter, and Helmut Seidl

Technische Universität München, Boltzmannstrasse 3, 85748 Garching, Germany
{flexeder,mihaila,petter,seidl}@cs.tum.edu

Abstract. In this paper we provide an interprocedural algorithm for reconstructing the control flow of assembly code in presence of indirect jumps, call instructions and returns. In case that the underlying assembly code is the output of a compiler, indirect jumps primarily originate from high-level switch statements. For these, our methods succeed in resolving indirect jumps with high accuracy. We show that by explicitly handling procedure calls, additional precision is gained at calls to procedures exiting the program as well as through the analysis of side-effects of procedures onto the local state of the caller. Our prototypical implementation applied to real-world examples shows that this approach yields reliable and meaningful results with decent efficiency.

Keywords: static analysis, binary analysis, control flow reconstruction, reverse engineering.

1 Introduction

In contrast to high-level languages as e.g. C at the assembler level the semantics of a program can be fully specified, i.e. the effect of every assembler instruction is formally given by the instruction manual of the processor vendor. Consequently, an analysis of executables can provide more reliable results than a source-code analysis [5]. Full information about the behaviour of an assembly program is required e.g. for *reverse engineering* [8], i.e. to obtain an understanding of the structure of an executable, or when *analysing safety-critical real-time applications*. For instance, determining tight bounds for the worst-case execution time of an application [12] or checking safety properties of micro-controllers [7] for flawless functionality, demand for analysing the compiler output. Sometimes only the executable is available or the compiler may even contain bugs, s.t. the executable provides the basis for a static analysis. However, in order to perform analyses on assembly code, the control flow has to be reconstructed first. Resolving the jump targets for *indirect calls* and *indirect jumps* requires an analysis of the values of registers as well as of memory locations. Many architectures have specific instructions for both local jumps and procedure calls. However, not all occurrences of call instructions semantically denote procedure calls in the sense of temporary transfer of control to a subroutine. For instance consider the call to procedure exit in figure 1, which never returns control back to the caller. An analysis that assumes that every function returns can be misled by a call to such a non-returning function, since the immediately following program point should not be influenced by such a call. Thus, it is essential to deal with procedure calls for reconstructing meaningful control flow graphs.

K. Ueda (Ed.): APLAS 2010, LNCS 6461, pp. 188–203, 2010.

Moreover, switch-statements at the assembler level are often translated to indirect jumps [9], as e.g. demonstrated by example 1. These jumps are controlled by a *jump table* containing relative jump targets for each case statement. In our setting this table is located in the read-only data segment of the executable and thus its entries are never changed. The target address of such an indirect jump is computed via the following instruction sequence: First via a comparison instruction (cf. instruction `0x08`) the value range of the index register is restricted. For example 1 register $r0$ is restricted to $0 \leq r0 \leq 5$. Note that the unsigned comparison instruction cmplwi treats its operands as unsigned integers (cf. [23]), i.e. all the negative numbers are rejected because their two's complement representation is larger than that of any positive number. If the value of register $r0$ is not inside these bounds, then the default case is executed, which results in a call to the exit function (cf. instruction `0x14`). Otherwise the instructions starting at `0x18` will be considered. Here, register $r0$ serves as an index into the jump table. Before the indirect jump is performed (cf. instruction `0x30`) the address offset read from the jump table is added to the table base address (cf. instruction `0x2C`).

In this paper we present our example programs and our implementation for the *PowerPC* architecture (PPC) [23] which is still broadly used in embedded systems, as e.g. automotive industry, aeronautics or robotics. However, our approach can be applied to arbitrary architectures as well.

```
int i = read();
switch(i)
{
  case 1: i += 11;   break;
  case 2: i += 22;   break;
  case 3: f(i);      break;
  case 4: i += 44;   break;
  case 5: i += 55;   break;
 default: exit(1);   break;
}
```

The jump table is given by:

```
.ro_data
51c60:ff fa e3 d4 //51c60-34
51c64:ff fa e3 dc //51c60-3c
51c68:ff fa e3 e4 //51c60-44
51c6C:ff fa e3 ec //51c60-4c
51c70:ff fa e3 f4 //51c60-54
```

```
//i = read();
00: call    0x70
04: mr      r0,r3
//switch(i) {
08: cmplwi  cr7,r0,5
0C: jle     cr7,0x18
10: li      r3,1
14: call    0x80<exit>
18: mulli   r2,r0,4
1C: lis     r9,5
20: addi    r10,r9,7264
24: add     r9,r2,r10
28: lwz     r11,0(r9)
2C: add     r11,r11,r10
30: jump    r11
//case 1: i += 11; break;
34: addi    r0,r0,11
38: jump    0x64<postswitch>
//case 2: i += 22; break;
3C: addi    r0,r0,22
40: jump    0x64<postswitch>
...
//<exit>:
80: li      r10,99
84: halt
```

Fig. 1. Switch statement in PPC assembler

Before elaborating our framework in detail we present related approaches in the area of control flow reconstruction.

Related Work. Several tools tackle the problem of reconstructing the control flow from executables. Using a simple linear-sweep disassembler, as e.g. gcc's *objdump*, is not sufficient for identifying the code sections of an executable [21]. Therefore modern control flow reconstruction additionally relies on extra information either through code patterns used by compilers or static program analysis.

The first category of tools using *compiler patterns* for control flow reconstruction are e.g. *exec2crl* by AbsInt [25,24], *dcc* by Cifuentes et al. [1,10] and IDAPro [2]. exec2crl is a tool which extracts the control flow from well-formed compiler-generated assembly code of time-critical embedded systems. There, special coding conventions must be adhered to which prevent the use of function pointers and dynamic data structures. Additionally precise knowledge about the compiler and the target architecture is given. Under these restrictions a complete and sound control flow reconstruction is possible. The drawback of such a compiler-pattern driven approach is that for every compiler and change in the code generation schemes the set of patterns has to be adjusted.

Cifuentes et al. [10] propose slicing and substitution of expressions for obtaining normal forms for indirect jumps and calls. This normal form is matched against their repository of compiler patterns to recover high-level data flow information from executables. They only use heuristics if local memory is used to compute the address expression for an indirect jump or call. These heuristics make their tool unsound.

Our experiments with IDAPro [2] lead us to assume that the latest version 5.5 also uses compiler patterns to resolve those indirect jumps that represent switch statements.

The second category relies on *static analyses*. These approaches are used by tools such as e.g. *CodeSurfer* by Reps et al. [20,5], *Jakstab* by Kinder and Veith [14,15] and the work of Myreen [18]. In [15] Kinder and Veith present an analysis framework based on partial control flow graphs to resolve indirect jumps. They present a generic worklist algorithm to dynamically extend the control flow of a program. In [15] they claim that their approach yields *"the most precise overapproximation of the control flow graph w.r.t. the precision of the provided abstract domain."* However, they rely on an intra-procedural framework only, inlining newly detected procedures. Recursive procedures may lead to assembly code which is not manageable by their framework.

CodeSurfer works upon the control flow reconstruction of IDAPro. Reps et al. are aware of the fact that IDAPro yields an unsafe as well as incomplete control flow graph in presence of indirect jumps and calls. Thus, they attempt to augment and correct the information provided by IDAPro [5]. Their practical tool CodeSurfer, however, is not available to us.

In the context of program proving, Myreen [18] has presented a semantics-based control flow reconstruction via a translation into tail-recursive functions.

In this paper we present an analysis that safely reconstructs an overapproximation of the control flow for compiler-generated assembler programs by carefully examining call and jump instructions. Here, we follow the approach of Kinder and Veith [15] for dealing with indirect jumps and extend it with a treatment of procedure calls. One particular problem we deal with are abort and exit functions, which do *not return* to the corresponding call site, but terminate the whole program whenever they are called.

The structure of the paper is as follows: In Section 2 we present the concrete semantics our control flow reconstruction analysis builds on. Then, in Section 3 we describe a general interprocedural framework to overapproximate the control flow and call graph of an executable. Additionally we present a concrete instantiation of this framework in order to resolve common indirect jump instructions. We present experimental results and discuss several practical issues when analysing real-world code in Section 4. And finally we conclude.

2 The Concrete Semantics

Here, we present an instrumented concrete semantics w.r.t. which the control flow graph is defined. Let $\mathbf{X} = \{\mathbf{x}_1, \ldots, \mathbf{x}_k\}$ denote the set of registers of the processor. The instructions of the program are stored at the set of addresses $\mathbf{N} \subseteq \mathbb{N}$. For every executable we assume that we are given a unique start address $\mathsf{start} \in \mathbf{N}$ where program execution starts. The mapping $I : \mathbf{N} \to \mathbf{Instr}$ provides the processor instruction for a given program address from $\mathbf{N}$. Depending on the architecture, the width of an instruction may vary. For the PPC architecture, however, all instructions have equal width 4. In this paper, we consider the set **Instr** of processor instructions consisting of:

- stm: assignment statements $\mathbf{x}_i := e$, i.e. the value of expression e is assigned to register $\mathbf{x}_i \in \mathbf{X}$, memory read instructions $\mathbf{x}_i := M[e]$, where the content of the memory location specified by e is assigned to register $\mathbf{x}_i$ and memory write instructions $M[e_1] := e_2$, where the value of e_2 is assigned to the memory location specified by e_1;
- call $\mathbf{x}_i$: procedure calls, where the value of register $\mathbf{x}_i$ denotes the start address of a procedure;
- jump e $\mathbf{x}_i$: jump instructions, which transfer control to the address specified by $\mathbf{x}_i$ iff e evaluates to 0;
- return: the return-instruction transfers control back to the caller and
- halt: the program exit instruction which terminates execution of the whole program and transfers control back to the operating system.

Here, e, e_1, e_2 denote expressions as provided by the syntax of assembler instructions.

A procedure call call $\mathbf{x}_i$ transfers control to the callee whose address is given by the value of $\mathbf{x}_i$. We consider every address which is jumped to by a call instruction as the start address of a procedure. The address of the instruction directly following the procedure call is saved in a dedicated register, the *link* register of the processor. For instance, instruction `0x00` from figure 1 sets the link register to address `0x04`. The instruction return is nothing but an indirect jump to the address currently stored in the link register. For our control flow reconstruction, we only consider programs where return-statements transfer control back to the caller. This means that it is up to the callee to save the content of the link register (if necessary) and to restore it before executing the return. We leave it for supplementary analyses to verify that the link register is handled correctly.

For the sake of our analysis, we combine the comparison instruction and the succeeding branch instruction to the guarded jump instruction jump e $\mathbf{x}_i$. In concrete machine architectures, these instructions need not follow each other directly (see Section 4).

In the concrete semantics, we consider states σ assigning values to registers $\mathbf{X}$ and to memory locations from some address space $\mathbf{N}'$ which is disjoint from $\mathbf{N}$. Let V denote the set of all possible values. The set of all such states then is given by $\Sigma = (\mathbf{X} \cup \mathbf{N}') \to V$. Additionally, the instrumented operational semantics maintains a pair (c, f) where c is the address of the last call and f is the start address of the current procedure, with $c, f \in \mathbf{N}$. Processor instructions from $\mathbf{Instr}$ modify the current state $\sigma \in \Sigma$. The semantics of a single processor instruction s on a given program state σ is defined via the semantic function $[\![s]\!] : \Sigma \to \Sigma$. Besides modifying the state, it transfers control to another instruction (if it is an assignment or a jump), to another procedure (if it is a call) or to the environment (if it is a halt instruction). The transfer of control is provided by the partial function $\mathsf{next}_I : (\mathbf{N} \times \Sigma) \to \mathbf{N}$ which computes for every program point u with state σ, the next program point according to the semantics of the processor instruction $I(u)$:

$$\mathsf{next}_I(u, \sigma) = \begin{cases} \sigma(\mathbf{x}_i) \text{ with } [\![e]\!]\sigma = 0 & \text{if } I(u) = \mathsf{jump}\ e\ \mathbf{x}_i \\ u + 4 \text{ with } [\![e]\!]\sigma \neq 0 & \text{if } I(u) = \mathsf{jump}\ e\ \mathbf{x}_i \\ u + 4 & \text{otherwise} \end{cases}$$

Here, the function $[\![e]\!]\sigma$ evaluates an expression e and returns a value which is interpreted as an integer. In case of a jump-instruction the successor node is either the immediately following program point, if condition e does not evaluate to 0, or the value of the jump target register $\mathbf{x}_i$, otherwise. For procedure calls, the successor node is the immediately following program point (given that the called procedure returns).

Due to the presence of procedures, the small-step operational semantics is based on the two transition relations $\vdash_S$ and $\vdash_R$ denoting one step of intra-procedural and inter-procedural execution, respectively. These relations are defined by:

$$\begin{array}{ll} (u, \sigma, (c, f)) \vdash_S (\mathsf{next}_I(u, \sigma), \sigma', (c, f)) & \text{if } I(u) = \mathsf{call}\ \mathbf{x}_i \wedge f' = \sigma(\mathbf{x}_i) \wedge \\ & (f', \sigma, (u, f')) \vdash_S^* (r, \sigma', (u, f')), \\ & I(r) = \mathsf{return} \\ (u, \sigma, (c, f)) \vdash_S (\mathsf{next}_I(u, \sigma), [\![I(u)]\!]\sigma, (c, f)) & \text{if } I(u) \text{ not a call} \\ (u, \sigma, (c, f)) \vdash_R (f', \sigma, (u, f')) & \text{if } I(u) = \mathsf{call}\ \mathbf{x}_i \wedge f' = \sigma(\mathbf{x}_i) \\ (u, \sigma, (c, f)) \vdash_R (u', \sigma', (c, f)) & \text{if } (u, \sigma, (c, f)) \vdash_S (u', \sigma', (c, f)) \end{array}$$

An initial program state is given by $(\mathsf{start}, \sigma, (\mathsf{start}, \mathsf{start}))$ for suitable $\sigma \in \Sigma$.

Given this operational semantics, an approximation of the control flow of the program is a pair $(N, \mathsf{next}_I^{\sharp\sharp})$ where $N \subseteq \mathbf{N}$ and $\mathsf{next}_I^{\sharp\sharp} : \mathbf{N} \to 2^{\mathbf{N}}$ is a mapping such that for every initial configuration $\mathsf{conf} = (\mathsf{start}, \sigma_0, (\mathsf{start}, \mathsf{start}))$ the following holds:

- If $\mathsf{conf} \vdash_R^* (u, \sigma, (c, f))$ then $u \in N$;
- If $\mathsf{conf} \vdash_R^* (u, \sigma, (c, f)) \vdash_S (u', \sigma', (c, f))$ then $u' \in \mathsf{next}_I^{\sharp\sharp}(u)$.

Let $\mathsf{calls} \subseteq \mathbf{N}$ denote the subset of program points u where $I(u)$ is a call instruction. Then an approximation of the call graph of the program is a pair $(F, \mathsf{fun}_I^{\sharp\sharp})$ where $F \subseteq \mathbf{N}$ and $\mathsf{fun}_I^{\sharp\sharp} : \mathsf{calls} \to 2^F$ is a mapping such that for every initial configuration $\mathsf{conf} = (\mathsf{start}, \sigma_0, (\mathsf{start}, \mathsf{start}))$, $\mathsf{conf} \vdash_R^* (u, \sigma, (c, f))$ for some $I(u) = \mathsf{call}\, \mathbf{x}_i$, implies that $\sigma(\mathbf{x}_i) \subseteq \mathsf{fun}_I^{\sharp\sharp}(u)$.

3 Interprocedural Control Flow Reconstruction

Our goal is to construct sufficiently small pairs $(N, \mathsf{next}_I^{\sharp\sharp})$ and $(F, \mathsf{fun}_I^{\sharp\sharp})$. For that, we must determine tight approximations to the values of registers $\mathbf{x}_i$ occurring in indirect jump instructions $\mathsf{jump}\ e\ \mathbf{x}_i$ and indirect call instructions $\mathsf{call}\ \mathbf{x}_i$. In the following, we abstract from the concrete contents of the main memory and concentrate on the values of registers only. In order to be as precise as possible with the values of registers, we directly use the powerset domain 2^V ordered by subset inclusion as our abstract domain. Thus, an abstract state is described by a mapping $\sigma^\sharp$ from registers to the abstract domain $\mathbf{X} \to 2^V$. Only when sets of values grow, we may insert a widening to an enclosing interval [19]. However, the interval domain also requires a widening operation [11] to ensure termination of the fixpoint iteration. Typically, loops and recursive functions may lead to infinitely ascending chains. In our analysis framework, we therefore insert widening operators at back-edges and at procedure entries.

The general framework relies on an arbitrary complete lattice $\Sigma^\sharp$ of abstract states together with a concretisation $\gamma : \Sigma^\sharp \to 2^\Sigma$ where $\gamma(\sigma^\sharp)$ returns the set of concrete states described by $\sigma^\sharp$. Additionally, we require for every instruction s the corresponding abstract transformer $[\![s]\!]^\sharp : \Sigma^\sharp \to \Sigma^\sharp$ which safely approximates the concrete semantics of s, i.e., which satisfies:

$$[\![s]\!]\sigma \in \gamma([\![s]\!]^\sharp\sigma^\sharp) \text{ whenever } \sigma \in \gamma(\sigma^\sharp)$$

Given the abstract lattice $\Sigma^\sharp$ and the concretisation γ, we define the abstract next function $\mathsf{next}_I^\sharp : \mathbf{N} \times \Sigma^\sharp \to 2^\mathbf{N}$ by:

$$\mathsf{next}_I^\sharp(u, \sigma^\sharp) = \begin{cases} \gamma(\sigma^\sharp(\mathbf{x}_i)) \cap \mathbf{N} \text{ with } ([\![e]\!]^\sharp\sigma^\sharp) = \{0\} & \text{if } I(u) = \mathsf{jump}\ e\ \mathbf{x}_i \\ \{u+4\} \text{ with } ([\![e]\!]^\sharp\sigma) \not\ni 0 & \text{if } I(u) = \mathsf{jump}\ e\ \mathbf{x}_i \\ \{u+4\} \cup \gamma(\sigma^\sharp(\mathbf{x}_i)) \cap \mathbf{N} \text{ otherwise} & \text{if } I(u) = \mathsf{jump}\ e\ \mathbf{x}_i \\ \{u+4\} & \text{otherwise} \end{cases}$$

Here, the abstract evaluation function $[\![e]\!]^\sharp$ takes an expression and returns a set of possible values of e.

For guarded jump instructions the set of successor program points is specified by the value of register $\mathbf{x}_i$ in the current register valuation if condition e is fulfilled, by the immediately following program point if e is not fulfilled or both sets otherwise. For all other processor instructions $\mathsf{next}_I^\sharp$ yields the immediately following program point.

Our analysis determines for each possible procedure entry node f a pair $\mu(f) = (\sigma^\sharp, C)$ where $\sigma^\sharp \in \Sigma^\sharp$ describes all possible concrete states at return points reachable from f on the same level (i.e., through $\vdash_S$), and $C \subseteq \mathbf{N}$ is the superset of all possible call sites for f. Additionally, the analysis determines for every program point u a pair $\eta(u) = (\sigma^\sharp, R)$ where $\sigma^\sharp$ describes the set of all states attained at u when reaching u from an initial state, and $R \subseteq \mathbf{N} \times \mathbf{N}$ is a set of pairs (c, f) of call sites c for procedure entry points f such that the current program point is reachable from f on the same level (i.e., w.r.t. $\vdash_S$).

Assume that $\eta(u) = (\sigma^\sharp, R)$. Then we refer to the i-th component of the pair $\eta(u)$ via $\eta_i(u)$. The components of the pair $\mu(f)$ will be accessed analogously.

The values $\mu(f)$ and $\eta(u)$ can be characterised as a solution of the following constraint system:

$$
\begin{array}{llll}
(1)\ \mu(f) & \sqsupseteq ((c,f) \in \eta_2(u)); (\eta_1(u), \{c\}) & & \text{if } I(u) = \mathsf{return} \\
(2)\ \eta(\mathsf{start}) & \sqsupseteq (\top, \{(\mathsf{start}, \mathsf{start})\}) & & \\
(3)\ \eta(v) & \sqsupseteq (f \in \gamma(\eta_1(u)(\mathbf{x}_i)) \wedge (u \in \mu_2(f))); & & \text{if } I(u) = \mathsf{call}\ \mathbf{x}_i \wedge \\
 & \quad (H^\sharp(\eta_1(u), \mu_1(f)), \eta_2(u)) & & \quad v = u + 4 \\
(4)\ \eta(f) & \sqsupseteq (f \in \gamma(\eta_1(u)(\mathbf{x}_i))); (E^\sharp(\eta_1(u)), \{(u,f)\}) & & \text{if } I(u) = \mathsf{call}\ \mathbf{x}_i \\
(5)\ \eta(v) & \sqsupseteq (v \in \mathsf{next}_I^\sharp(u, \eta_1(u))); ([\![s]\!]^\sharp(\eta_1(u)), \eta_2(u)) & & \text{if } I(u) = s \in \mathsf{stm}
\end{array}
$$

Here, the operator ";" is defined by:

$$
(x \in A); B = \begin{cases} B & \text{if } x \in A \\ \bot & \text{otherwise} \end{cases}
$$

Constraint (1) describes the effect of a possibly called procedure f which may reach a return point. For constraint system η, initially at the start point start no information about possible variable valuations is known. Additionally we mark the start point as reachable by managing the relation (start, start), as constraint (2) specifies. Constraint (3) treats the case of a procedure call call $\mathbf{x}_i$. There, on the one hand the set of successor nodes is specified by the set of possible values of register $\mathbf{x}_i$, i.e., the set of entry points of the callees, and on the other hand, by the immediately following program point — given that any of the possibly called procedures returns. The value after the procedure call $u + 4$ consists of the set of call site - callee - relations valid before the call to procedure f together with the combination of the data flow value before the procedure call with the procedure summary $\mu_1(f)$. This combination is computed by the function $H^\sharp$. The function $E^\sharp$ computes the contribution of the abstract state of the current call site to the start point f of the callee. Additionally we relate the current call site u to the entry point of procedure f. This is defined by constraint (4). Constraint (5) treats all other forms of statements, which have no influence on the call site - callee relations. The successor node is computed by the abstract next function.

Note that for a procedure f which does not return, $\mu(f)$ yields $\bot$. Thus, in case of a call instruction at program point u the directly following program point $u + 4$ will not be reached.

A safe approximation of $E^\sharp$ and $H^\sharp$ independent of the abstraction $\Sigma^\sharp$ is:

$$
\begin{array}{ll}
E^\sharp(\sigma^\sharp) & = \sigma^\sharp \\
H^\sharp(\sigma_c^\sharp, \sigma^\sharp) & = \sigma^\sharp
\end{array}
$$

Assume we are given a (not necessarily least) solution (μ, η) of the constraint system. Then we can extract both an approximate control flow $(N, \mathsf{next}_I^{\sharp\sharp})$ and an approximate call graph $(F, \mathsf{fun}_I^{\sharp\sharp})$ by:

$$
\begin{array}{lll}
N & = \{u \mid \eta(u) \neq (\bot, \emptyset)\} & \\
\mathsf{next}_I^{\sharp\sharp}(u) & = \mathsf{next}_I^\sharp(u, \eta_1(u)) & \\
F & = \bigcup\{f \mid \eta_2(u) = \{\_, f\}\} & \\
\mathsf{fun}_I^{\sharp\sharp}(u) & = \gamma(\eta_1(u))(\mathbf{x}_i) \cap \mathbf{N} & \quad \text{if } I(u) = \mathsf{call}\ \mathbf{x}_i
\end{array}
$$

F captures all possible procedure entry points of both functions that may return to the caller and functions that do definitely not return.

The following theorem relates the least solution of our constraint system with the (instrumented) operational semantics of the program as specified through the relations $\vdash_S$ and $\vdash_R$.

Theorem 1. (Correctness) *Let (μ, η) denote the least solution of the constraint system. Then the following holds:*

1. *Assume that* $\eta(u) = (\sigma^\sharp, R)$ *and* $(\mathsf{start}, \sigma_0, (\mathsf{start}, \mathsf{start})) \vdash_R^* (u, \sigma, (c, f))$. *Then* $(c, f) \in R$ *and* $\sigma \in \gamma(\sigma^\sharp)$.
2. *Assume that* $\mu(f) = (\sigma^\sharp, C)$ *and* $(\mathsf{start}, \sigma_0, (\mathsf{start}, \mathsf{start})) \vdash_R^* (f, \sigma, (c, f)) \vdash_S^* (u, \sigma_u, (c, f))$ *where* $I(u) = \mathsf{return}$. *Then* $c \in C$ *and* $\sigma_u \in \gamma(\sigma^\sharp)$.

The proof of theorem 1 is by induction on the length of the respective execution steps $\vdash_S$ and $\vdash_R$, respectively. As an immediate corollary, we obtain:

Corollary 1. *The pairs* $(N, \mathsf{next}_I^{\sharp\sharp})$ *and* $(F, \mathsf{fun}_I^{\sharp\sharp})$ *are approximations of the control flow and call graph of the input program.* □

Instead of abstracting the state at a program point u only, we may also abstract the transformer along the path to program point u. The abstract domain $\Sigma^\sharp$ can be enhanced by additionally accumulating an abstraction of the state transformer from $\mathbb{T}$ corresponding to the current procedure. Thus, we consider the abstract domain $\Sigma^\natural = \Sigma^\sharp \times \mathbb{T}$. Accordingly we have to adjust the abstract semantic function $[\![s]\!]^\natural : \Sigma^\natural \to \Sigma^\natural$ to elements from $\Sigma^\natural$:

$$[\![s]\!]^\natural(\sigma^\sharp, \tau) = ([\![s]\!]^\sharp \sigma^\sharp, [\![s]\!]^\natural_{\mathbb{T}} \circ^\natural \tau)$$

where $\circ^\natural$ denotes the composition of transformers τ from $\mathbb{T}$ and $[\![s]\!]^\natural_{\mathbb{T}} : \mathbb{T}$ denotes the abstract semantic function on a processor instruction s, i.e. is a state transformer from $\mathbb{T}$.

This enhancement by abstracting the state transformers enables a more precise definition of the function $H^\sharp$ w.r.t. the domain $\Sigma^\natural$.

$$H^\sharp((\sigma_1^\sharp, \tau_1), (\sigma_2^\sharp, \tau_2)) = (\iota(\tau_2, \iota(\tau_1, \sigma_1^\sharp)), \tau_2 \circ^\natural \tau_1)$$

with $\iota : \mathbb{T} \to \Sigma^\sharp \to \Sigma^\sharp$. $\iota(\tau, \sigma^\sharp)$ transforms an abstract state $\sigma^\sharp$ by means of the state transformer $\tau \in \mathbb{T}$ which is interpreted in the context of the abstract domain $\Sigma^\sharp$. Additionally the function $E^\sharp$ is given by:

$$E^\sharp((\sigma^\sharp, \_)) = (\sigma^\sharp, \mathsf{Id}^\sharp)$$

with $\mathsf{Id}^\sharp$ the identity mapping.

One specific instance of this abstraction $\mathbb{T}$ records e.g. the set of registers which have definitely not been modified since procedure entry. For that, we choose $\Sigma^\natural = (\mathbf{X} \to 2^V) \times 2^{\mathbf{X}}$. Then $H^\sharp$ can be refined to:

$$\begin{aligned} H^\sharp((\sigma_c^\sharp, X), (\sigma^\sharp, X')) &= (\tilde{\sigma}^\sharp, X' \cap X) \qquad \text{where} \\ \tilde{\sigma}^\sharp(\mathbf{x}) &= \begin{cases} \sigma_c^\sharp(\mathbf{x}) & \text{if } \mathbf{x} \in X' \\ \sigma^\sharp(\mathbf{x}) & \text{otherwise} \end{cases} \end{aligned}$$

where for the instantiation of $H^\sharp$, $\circ^\natural$ is the intersection of both register sets. Combining the effect of a called procedure with the state of the call site results in a register valuation $\tilde{\sigma}^\sharp$ which takes its values from the register valuation before the call for all registers which are not modified by the called procedure and the values at procedure return for the remaining ones. Additionally, the set of definitely not modified registers for the caller after the call is given by the intersection of the respective sets of the caller before the call and the callee.

The value for the start point of a procedure is given by the register valuation $\sigma^\sharp$ at the call site for the procedure together with the set of all registers:

$$E^\sharp(\sigma^\sharp, X) = (\sigma^\sharp, \mathbf{X})$$

In this instance of domain $\mathbb{T}$, $\mathsf{Id}^\sharp$ is given by the set of all registers.

The constraint system as specified above, is not really tractable. In particular, the set of program locations is not known beforehand. In order to overcome this obstacle, we extend the approach of [15] and explore the reachable program locations as they are encountered during fixpoint computation. Besides indirect jumps, our extension also handles calls and returns.

In case of a return instruction at program point r, we rely on the fixpoint algorithm for updating the summaries $\mu(f)$ of procedure entries f from which r is (intra-procedurally) reachable, and let it re-consider the call sites of f if the summary $\mu(f)$ has changed. This results in the worklist-based fixpoint algorithm 1.

Fixpoint Algorithm 1

$W \leftarrow \{(\mathsf{start}, (\top, \{(\mathsf{start}, \mathsf{start})\}))\}$;
while $(W \neq \emptyset)$ **do**
  $(u, s) = \mathsf{extract}(W)$;
  if $(s \not\sqsubseteq \eta(u))$ **then**
    $\eta(u) \leftarrow \eta(u) \sqcup s$;
    $(\sigma^\sharp, R) = \eta(u)$;
    if $(I(u) = \mathsf{jump}\ e\ \mathbf{x}_i \wedge \sigma^\sharp(\mathbf{x}_i) = \top)$ **then**
      $\mathsf{abort}()$;
    else if $(I(u) = \mathsf{call}\ \mathbf{x}_i \wedge \sigma^\sharp(\mathbf{x}_i) = \top)$ **then**
      $W \leftarrow W \cup \{(u+4, (\top, R))\}$;
    else if $(I(u) = \mathsf{call}\ \mathbf{x}_i \wedge \sigma^\sharp(\mathbf{x}_i) \neq \top)$ **then**
      $W \leftarrow W \cup \{(f, (E^\sharp(\sigma^\sharp), \{(u, f)\})) \mid f \in \gamma(\sigma^\sharp(\mathbf{x}_i))\}$;
    else if $(I(u) = \mathsf{return})$ **then**
      for all $((\_, f) \in R)$ **do**
        if $((\sigma^\sharp, \{c \mid (c, f) \in R\}) \not\sqsubseteq \mu(f))$ **then**
          $\mu(f) \leftarrow \mu(f) \sqcup (\sigma^\sharp, \{c \mid (c, f) \in R\})$;
          $(\sigma^\sharp_f, R_f) = \mu(f)$;
          $W \leftarrow W \cup \{(c+4, (H^\sharp(\eta_1(c), \sigma^\sharp_f), \eta_2(c))) \mid (c, \_) \in R_f\}$;
    else
      $W \leftarrow W \cup \{(v, (\llbracket I(u) \rrbracket^\sharp \sigma^\sharp, R)) \mid v \in \mathsf{next}^\sharp_I(u, \sigma^\sharp)\}$;

Initially, we assume that $\eta(u)$ is (implicitly) initialised with the least possible value $(\bot, \emptyset)$ for all possible values of u. Likewise, we assume that μ assigns $(\bot, \emptyset)$ to all possible entry points of procedures.

Algorithm 1 maintains a worklist W consisting of all pairs (u, s) of program points together with a potential update s for the value $\eta(u)$. The algorithm terminates when all these updates have been processed. For processing one pair (u, s), the algorithm first checks whether s is already subsumed by the current value of $\eta(u)$. If this is not the case, s is added to $\eta(u)$, and this change is propagated to all consumers of the value $\eta(u)$. Here, a case distinction on the instruction at program point u is performed.

In case the target addresses of a call-instruction are not known (cf. line 9), we at least assume that the called function returns and overapproximate the return state with $\top$. Otherwise, we extend the worklist by pairs, consisting of all the targets f that may be called and their corresponding states (cf. line 12). In case of a return-instruction in procedure f we propagate the effect of f to all its call sites (cf. line 18). For all other kinds of program instructions the worklist is extended by pairs, consisting of all the successor nodes (computed via the abstract next function) and the corresponding state update (computed via the abstract semantic evaluation function).

With our current instantiation of $\Sigma^\sharp$ which only keeps track of the values of registers, we are only able to resolve *static* procedure calls. A more sophisticated instantiation, however, which additionally analyses the memory in greater detail, would also allow to compute a safe approximation of the control flow of a larger class of programs.

An assembly program can be either *stripped*, i.e. symbol table and debugging information is missing, or *unstripped*. The symbol table contains all the start addresses of the procedures F provided by the executable. In case we have a symbol table we start our analysis from all procedure start points. Furthermore, we can make the assumption that only those procedures may be called, which are listed in the symbol table in case of a call-instruction whose target addresses are unknown. In case of analysing a stripped executable, procedure start addresses are uncovered on the fly. Every executable is provided with a unique start address, specified in the header of the executable. Typically, the entry point of an executable is the start address of the .text section. If the target address of a call instruction call $\mathbf{x}_i$ is unknown, we must assume that an unknown procedure is called, which may call any other procedure in any state. Thus, a safe approximation of $E^\sharp$ and $H^\sharp$ is only given by:

$$\begin{aligned} E^\sharp(\sigma^\sharp) &= \top \\ H^\sharp(\sigma_c^\sharp, \sigma^\sharp) &= \top \end{aligned}$$

The function abort (cf. line 8 of algorithm 1) indicates that the reconstruction of the control flow graph has failed. For unknown target addresses of jump-instructions (cf. line 7 of algorithm 1) we abort control flow reconstruction. Section 4 shows that an instantiation of our framework which tracks both the values of registers and memory locations is able to resolve all indirect jumps (resolvable by a static analysis) on all our benchmark programs. We fail in resolving some of the indirect calls since we do not track code addresses stored in the heap.

On regular termination, let (μ, η) be the variable valuations computed by algorithm 1, and let $F = \bigcup\{f \mid \eta_2(u) = \{(\_, f)\}\}$ and $N = \{u \in \mathbf{N} \mid \eta(u) \neq (\bot, \emptyset)\}$. Then the pair $(\mu|_F, \eta|_N)$ is a solution of our constraint system when restricted to procedure entries from F and program points from N. In particular, this means that the control flow graph $(N, \mathsf{next}_I^{\sharp\sharp})$ and the call graph $(F, \mathsf{fun}_I^{\sharp\sharp})$ constructed from (η, μ) are indeed approximations of the control flow and the call graph of the program.

Our experiments show that in case of switch-statements which are realised by jump table look-ups, we have to take memory into account. The jump table can either contain absolute addresses or address offsets, as e.g. is the case in our example in figure 1. Jump tables $T : \mathbf{N}'' \to V$ are located in the read-only memory $\mathbf{N}'' \subset \mathbf{N}'$ of an executable. Thus, in our instantiation of the framework we handle all those memory read accesses $\mathbf{x}_i := M[\mathbf{x}_j]$ to the read-only data section only. Then the abstract semantic function on memory access expressions is defined by:

$$[\![M[\mathbf{x}_j]]\!]^\sharp \sigma^\sharp = \begin{cases} \{T[c] \mid c \in \sigma^\sharp(\mathbf{x}_i)\} & \text{if } \sigma^\sharp(\mathbf{x}_i) \setminus \mathbf{N}'' = \emptyset \\ V & \text{otherwise} \end{cases}$$

In compiler-generated switch statements, typically no procedure calls are involved in the address computation for the jump target. Nevertheless, our experiments with real-world applications reveal that procedure calls may occur in-between this address computation, as figure 1 illustrates. The compiler omits a jump to the end of the switch statements, if an exit-procedure is called within the default branch of the switch-statement. Only a sufficiently precise treatment of procedure calls can avoid the loss of essential information for resolving the jump instruction at address `0x30` in figure 1.

4 Practical Issues and Experiments

Based on our theoretical approach, we implemented a prototypical control flow reconstruction tool to explore the quality of the resulting control flow graph and identify the next challenges by means of real-world programs. Our current implementation tracks the values of registers and memory locations but completely neglects the heap.

We conducted our experiments on a $2,2$ GHz quad-core machine equipped with physical memory of 16GB. All our benchmark programs have been compiled with GCC version $4.4.3$ using optimisation levels 0 and 2 *without* debug information for the *PowerPC* architecture. For the moment we only inspect fully statically linked and stripped executable programs. Hence our benchmark programs contain the whole *GNU C library* code. Our prototypical implementation (VoTUM [4]) consists in the following steps: First GCC's *objdump* is applied to the binaries to extract the assembler instructions. Then, we parse these assembler instructions and use them as the basis for our control flow reconstruction. The following two tables present the performance of our analyser on the benchmark programs.

Within these tables we specify: the binary file size **`Size`**; the number of procedure entries **`Procs`** (which is provided by the symbol table of the corresponding unstripped version of the binary) and in parentheses the number of procedures identified by our analyser; the number of assembler instructions **`Instr`**; the number of indirect jumps

bctr and indirect calls **bctrl**; the number of *unresolved* indirect jumps **ures** and in parentheses the number of statically not resolvable indirect jumps due to runtime linkage; the number of *resolved* indirect calls **res**; **ureac** denotes the number of *unreachable* indirect jump and call instructions which the analyser did not reach when starting from the entry point of the stripped binary; the number of static call instructions **bl**; the memory consumption **M** in GB and the time consumption **T(s)** in seconds of our analyser.

For our benchmark suite on the one hand we concentrate on applications from embedded systems, as e.g. communication protocols **openSSL**, lightweight HTTP servers **thttpd** and a SCADE generated vehicle control program **control** from [3]. On the other hand we took a home-made example program **switches** with several characteristics of switches: nested switches, switches in loops, etc. **coreutils** consists of five selected programs (**ls, basename, vdir, chmod, chgrp**) taken from the *GNU Coreutils* package of Unix in order to demonstrate the applicability of our approach to ordinary desktop software and **gzip** to be comparable to other tools which refer to *SPECint*.

Some of our benchmark programs use lazy binding of procedure addresses via indirect jumps within the trampoline code to the so-called Procedure Linkage Table (**PLT**) [16]. The absolute address of such a dynamically loaded procedure is loaded from a constant memory location in the **PLT** section and then branched to via a **bctr**-instruction. If this location is not yet initialised, the trampoline branches to the runtime linker, which provides the dynamic address of the corresponding procedure. However, the address of this runtime linker is not present in the binary – it is only provided after loading the binary. Thus, *no static value* for the target of such a **bctr** instruction can be determined. Consequently, we list this kind of unresolvable **bctr** instructions in parentheses within our benchmark tables.

Table 1. Benchmark suite for programs with optimisation level 0

Program	Size	Procs	Instr	bctr	ures	ureac	bctrl	res	ureac	bl	M	T(s)
openSSL	3.8MB	6708(375)	769511	163	0(4)	129	1352	20	1219	35709	4	203
thttpd	884kB	1197(464)	196493	77	0(5)	42	321	21	189	6092	1.2	67
switches	636kB	825(364)	138178	82	0(4)	42	302	20	184	3680	0.8	45
control	633kB	817(354)	139917	83	0(4)	49	302	16	184	3670	0.8	42
coreutils	3.9MB	5671(2371)	852322	431	0(26)	219	1648	101	1004	24159	1.3	527
gzip	0.7MB	1076(472)	166213	79	0(4)	44	310	20	188	4634	1.1	132

Table 2. Benchmark suite for programs with optimisation level 2

Program	Size	Procs	Instr	bctr	ures	ureac	bctrl	res	ureac	bl	M	T(s)
openSSL	2.9MB	6232(380)	613882	150	0(4)	116	1355	20	1217	34405	3	156
thttpd	852kB	1147(469)	189034	77	0(5)	42	320	17	190	5890	1	60
switches	625kB	826(358)	137833	77	0(4)	41	302	17	184	3673	0.8	44
control	629kB	817(354)	138589	81	0(4)	47	302	20	184	3670	0.8	40
coreutils	3.8MB	5372(2534)	830407	424	0(28)	202	1634	104	959	23504	1.3	459
gzip	0.7MB	1026(384)	162380	83	0(5)	44	309	20	190	4587	1	117

Summarising, our instantiation of the framework is able to provide tight bounds for all of the statically resolvable indirect jumps within the benchmark programs. We fail in resolving some of the indirect call instructions due to the fact that we have not modelled bit operations in our semantics yet and do not take the heap into account.

Position-Independent Code. Within position-independent code (PIC) we also examined switch-constructs. PIC is common in shared libraries [16]. Such code accesses all constant addresses through the global offset table (GOT), located in the read/write data section of the program. Consider the following example:

```
04: call    0x08
08: mflr    r30
0C: lwz     r0,-24(r30)
10: add     r30,r0,r30
....
2C: lwz     r0, 24(r1)
30: cmplwi  cr7,r0,5
34: bgt     cr7,0x70<default>
38: mulli   r9,r0,4
3C: lwz     r0,-32764(r30)
40: add     r9,r9,r0
44: lwz     r9,0(r9)
48: add     r9,r9,r0
4C: jump    r9
```

After instruction `0x10` register $r30$ contains the address of the GOT (cf. instructions `0x04`–`0x10`). Typically, in order to obtain the address of the GOT, *instruction pointer relative addressing* is used. This is realised via a call instruction to the immediately following location. The effect of this local jump is that the continuation address is saved in the link register. This continuation address serves as a fixed point in the code section and via a constant difference the GOT can be addressed, although its absolute address is not known until runtime.

After instruction `0x38` register $r9$ holds the value of the switch index variable. The base address of the switch table is computed via a look-up in the GOT, as instruction `0x3C` illustrates. Finally, an access into the jump table (in the read-only data section) is performed at instruction `0x44`. Under the assumption that the location with offset 32764 to the GOT (cf. instruction `0x3c`) is definitely not overwritten, we can safely infer the base address of the jump table.

Control Flow Splitting. For our semantics we assumed that the `compare`- and `branch`-instructions are either directly following each other (cf. instructions `0x08, 0x0C` in example 1) or the processor instructions in between the `compare` and the `branch`-instructions do not modify the register the compare is based on. This assumption, however, need not always be satisfied. In order to deal with this case we propose the technique of control flow splitting, as described in [22].

Function Pointers. At the assembler level, function pointers are realised via indirect calls.

Consider the following example code motivated by a Linux kernel driver, as for instance `linux-2.6.33/drivers/md/md.c`, where a bunch of initialisation functions is managed in a global array. Procedure `global_init` sequentially calls all the initialisation functions.

```
const fptr inits[] =
    {init1,init2,init3};
void global_init() {
  int j = sizeof(inits);
  int i;
  for (i=0; i<j; i++)
    inits[i]();
}
```

```
//for (i=0; i<j; i++)
00: li      r0,0
04: stw     r0,8(r1)
08: jump    0x30
//inits[i]();
0C: lis     r9,10
10: addi    r9,r9,6908
14: mulli   r0,r0,4
18: add     r9,r0,r9
1C: lwz     r0,0(r9)
20: call    r0
24: lwz     r9,8(r1)
28: addi    r0,r9,1
2C: stw     r0,8(r1)
30: cmpwi   cr7,r0,12
34: blt     cr7,0x0C
```

Assuming that the global array `inits` is located in the read-only memory, our control flow reconstruction analysis allows to infer the targets for the call-instruction `0x20`. There are common compilers arranging all constant global data in the read-only memory. However, if this is not the case we either have to enhance our (theoretical) analysis framework with a memory analysis or rely on a may-analysis of modified memory locations. Let B denote such a set of possibly modified memory locations. Then, in our analysis framework we only have to adjust the abstract effect function for memory read accesses:

$$[\![M[\mathbf{x}_j]]\!]^\sharp\sigma^\sharp = \begin{cases} \{M[c] \mid c \in \sigma^\sharp(\mathbf{x}_i)\} & \text{if } (\sigma^\sharp(\mathbf{x}_i) \setminus \mathbf{N}') \cap B = \emptyset \\ V & \text{otherwise} \end{cases}$$

Our benchmark examples show that the number of indirect call-instructions (column **`bctrl`** in table 1) is significantly smaller than the number of static call-instructions (column **`bl`** in table 2). Our current implementation of the framework neither supports a precise handling of bit operations nor of the heap memory and thus fails in resolving some of the indirect calls.

Optimisation Levels. Our instantiation of the framework speaks about register valuations, only. Thus, the control flow reconstruction yields precise results as long as values are kept in registers only. This is the case for assembly code generated by compilers with a higher optimisation level. However, in case of unoptimised code or register pressure compilers store values on the stack. In order to analyse unoptimised assembly code, we extended our implementation of the framework by a stack analysis. Via the approach of inferring linear relations as presented in [17], we detect local and global memory locations. Since in such code the values of stack locations are temporarily cached in registers [13], also an analysis of relations between registers and memory locations is mandatory to precisely track the values of both registers and memory locations.

5 Conclusion

We have presented a framework for static analysis to jointly approximate the control flow and the call graph in presence of indirect jumps and calls. Such an approach is less restrictive than approaches relying on compiler patterns only. Furthermore, we discussed the challenges and possible solutions for code generated via different optimisation levels. In order to precisely reconstruct the control flow in presence of indirect calls, abstract domains are required which capture side-effects of procedures, and possibly also track code addresses which are stored in the heap [6].

For our prototypical implementation, we have assumed that the code to be analysed adheres to the coding conventions for calls to and returns from procedures. It remains for future work to extend these techniques to deal with code which deliberately violates these conventions. On the one hand, it remains to show that the executable to analyse adheres to our assumptions, such as e.g. a correct management of the return address. On the other hand, there are several areas for which code that does not adhere to the calling conventions offers interesting challenges, as e.g. self-modifying code, self-extracting executables or hand-made assembly code, as e.g. malicious code or optimised library code.

References

1. DCC decompiler, `http://www.itee.uq.edu.au/~cristina/dcc.html`
2. IDAPro disassembler, `http://www.hex-rays.com/idapro/`
3. Sicherheitsgarantien Unter REALzeitanforderungen, `http://www.sureal-projekt.org/`
4. VoTUM, `http://www2.in.tum.de/votum`
5. Balakrishnan, G.: WYSINWYX: What You See Is Not What You eXecute. PhD thesis, University of Wisconsin, Madison, WI, USA (August 2007)
6. Balakrishnan, G., Reps, T.W.: Recency-abstraction for heap-allocated storage. In: Yi, K. (ed.) SAS 2006. LNCS, vol. 4134, pp. 221–239. Springer, Heidelberg (2006)
7. Brauer, J., King, A.: Automatic abstraction for intervals using boolean formulae. In: Static Analysis Symposium (SAS 2010), Perpignan, France. LNCS. Springer, Heidelberg (2010)
8. Cifuentes, C.: Reverse Compilation Techniques. Ph.D. thesis, Queensland University of Technology (July 1994)
9. Cifuentes, C., Emmerik, M.V.: Recovery of jump table case statements from binary code. Science of Computer Programming 40, 171–188 (2001)
10. Cifuentes, C., Simon, D., Fraboulet, A.: Assembly to high-level language translation. In: ICSM, pp. 228–237 (1998)
11. Cousot, P., Cousot, R.: Comparing the Galois connection and widening/narrowing approaches to abstract interpretation. In: Bruynooghe, M., Wirsing, M. (eds.) PLILP 1992. LNCS, vol. 631, pp. 269–295. Springer, Heidelberg (1992)
12. Ferdinand, C., Heckmann, R., Langenbach, M., Martin, F., Schmidt, M., Theiling, H., Thesing, S., Wilhelm, R.: Reliable and precise WCET determination for a real-life processor. In: Henzinger, T.A., Kirsch, C.M. (eds.) EMSOFT 2001. LNCS, vol. 2211, pp. 469–485. Springer, Heidelberg (2001)
13. Flexeder, A., Petter, M., Seidl, H.: Analysis of Executables for WCET Concerns. Technical Report TUM-I0838, Technische Universität München (2008)

14. Kinder, J., Veith, H.: Jakstab: A static analysis platform for binaries. In: Gupta, A., Malik, S. (eds.) CAV 2008. LNCS, vol. 5123, pp. 423–427. Springer, Heidelberg (2008)
15. Kinder, J., Veith, H., Zuleger, F.: An abstract interpretation-based framework for control flow reconstruction from binaries. In: Jones, N.D., Müller-Olm, M. (eds.) VMCAI 2009. LNCS, vol. 5403, pp. 214–228. Springer, Heidelberg (2009)
16. Levine, J.R.: Linkers and Loaders. Morgan Kaufmann Publishers Inc., San Francisco (1999)
17. Müller-Olm, M., Seidl, H.: Precise interprocedural analysis through linear algebra. In: 31st ACM Symp. on Principles of Programming Languages (POPL), pp. 330–341 (2004)
18. Myreen, M.O.: Formal verification of machine-code programs. PhD thesis, University of Cambridge (2008)
19. Ramon, F.B., Moore, E.: Methods and Applications of Interval Analysis (SIAM Studies in Applied and Numerical Mathematics) (Siam Studies in Applied Mathematics, 2). Soc. for Industrial & Applied Math. (1979)
20. Reps, T., Balakrishnan, G., Lim, J.: Intermediate-representation recovery from low-level code. In: PEPM 2006: Proceedings of the 2006 ACM SIGPLAN symposium on Partial evaluation and semantics-based program manipulation, pp. 100–111 (2006)
21. Schwarz, B., Debray, S., Andrews, G.: Disassembly of executable code revisited. In: WCRE 2002: Proceedings of the Ninth Working Conference on Reverse Engineering (WCRE 2002), Washington, DC, USA, p. 45. IEEE Computer Society, Los Alamitos (2002)
22. Simon, A.: Splitting the control flow with boolean flags. In: Alpuente, M., Vidal, G. (eds.) SAS 2008. LNCS, vol. 5079, pp. 315–331. Springer, Heidelberg (2008)
23. Sobek, S., Burke, K.: PowerPC Embedded Application Binary Interface (EABI): 32-Bit Implementation. Freescale Semiconductor (2004), `http://www.freescale.com/files/32bit/doc/app_note/PPCEABI.pdf`
24. Theiling, H.: Extracting safe and precise control flow from binaries. In: RTCSA 2000: Proceedings of the Seventh International Conference on Real-Time Systems and Applications, Washington, DC, USA, p. 23. IEEE Computer Society, Los Alamitos (2000)
25. Theiling, H.: Control Flow Graphs for Real-Time System Analysis. PhD thesis, Universität des Saarlandes (2003)

Data Structure Fusion

Peter Hawkins, Alex Aiken, Kathleen Fisher, Martin Rinard, and Mooly Sagiv

Stanford University, AT&T Labs Research, MIT, Tel Aviv University

Abstract. We consider the problem of specifying data structures with complex sharing in a manner that is both declarative and results in provably correct code. In our approach, abstract data types are specified using relational algebra and functional dependencies; a novel *fuse* operation on relational indexes specifies where the underlying physical data structure representation has sharing. We permit the user to specify different concrete shared representations for relations, and show that the semantics of the relational specification are preserved.

1 Introduction

Consider the data structure used in an operating system kernel to represent the set of available file systems. There are two kinds of objects: *file systems* and *files*. Each file system has a list of its files, and each file may be in one of two states, either currently *in use* or currently *unused*. Figure 1 sketches the data structure typically used:[1] each file system is the head of a linked list of its files, and two other linked lists maintain the set of files in use and files not in use. Thus, every file participates in two lists: the list of files in its file system, and one of the in-use or not-in-use lists. A characteristic feature of this example is the sharing: the files participate in multiple data structures. Sharing usually implies that there are non-trivial high-level invariants to be maintained when the structure is updated. For example, in Figure 1, if a file is removed from a file system, it should be removed from the in-use or not-in-use list as well. A second characteristic is that the structure is highly optimized for a particular expected usage pattern. In Figure 1, it is easy to enumerate all of the files in a file system, but without adding a parent pointer to the file objects we have only a very slow way to discover which file system owns a particular file.

We are interested in the problem of how to support high-level, declarative specification of complex data structures with sharing while also achieving efficient and safe low-level implementations. Existing languages provide at most one or the other. Modern functional languages provide excellent support for inductive data structures, which are all essentially trees of some flavor. When multiple such data structures overlap (i.e., when there is more than one inductive structure and they are not separate), functional languages do not provide any support beyond what is available in conventional object-oriented and procedural languages. All of these languages require the programmer to build and

[1] This example is a simplified version of the file system representation in Linux, where file systems are called *superblocks* and files are *inodes*.

K. Ueda (Ed.): APLAS 2010, LNCS 6461, pp. 204–221, 2010.

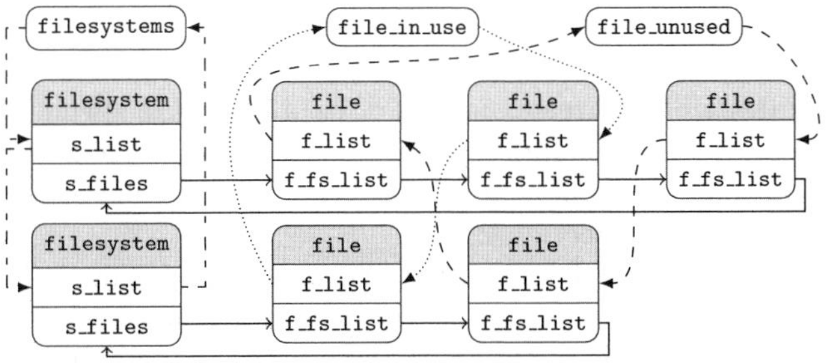

Fig. 1. File objects simultaneously participate in multiple circular lists. Different line types denote different lists.

maintain mutable structures with sharing by using explicit pointers or reference cells. While the programmer can get exactly the desired representation, there is no support for maintaining or even describing invariants of the data structure.

Languages built on relations, such as SQL and logic programming languages, provide much higher-level support. We could encode the example above using the relation:

$$\text{file}(\textit{filesystem} : \mathsf{int}, \textit{fileid} : \mathsf{int}, \textit{inuse} : \mathsf{bool})$$

Here integers suffice as unique identifiers for file systems and files, and a boolean records whether or not the file is in use. Using standard query facilities we can conveniently find for a file system *fs* all of its files file(*fs*, _, _) as well as all of the files not in use file(_, _, false). Even better, using *functional dependencies* we can specify important high-level invariants, such as that every file is part of exactly one file system, and every file is either in use or not; i.e., the *fileid* functionally determines the *filesystem* and *inuse* fields. Thus, there is only one tuple in the relation per *fileid*, and when the tuple with a *fileid* is deleted all trace of that file is provably removed from the relation. Finally, relations are general; since pointers are just relationships between objects, any pointer data structure can be described by a set of relations. Adding relations to general-purpose programming languages is a well-accepted idea. Missing from existing proposals is the ability to provide highly specialized implementations of relations, and in particular to take advantage of the potential for mutable data structures with sharing.

Our vision is a programming language where low-level pointer data structures are specified using high-level relations. Furthermore, because of the high-level specification, the language system can produce code that is correct by construction; even in cases where the implementation has complex sharing and destructive update, the implementation is guaranteed to be a faithful representation of the relational specification. In this paper, we take only the first step in realizing this plan, focusing on the core problem of what it means to represent a given high-level relation by a low-level representation (possibly with sharing) that is provably correct. We do not address in this paper the design of a surface syntax for integrating relational operations into a full programming language (there are many existing proposals).

This paper is organized into several parts, each of which highlights a separate contribution of our work:

- We begin by describing three examples of data structure specification. Our approach separates the semantic content of a data structure from details of its implementation, while allowing the programmer to control the low-level physical representation (Section 2).
- A key contribution is the design of a language for specifying *indices*, which are a mapping between a relational specification and concrete data structures (Section 3). This language allows us to define *cross-linking* and *fusion* constructs which, although common in practice, express sharing that is difficult or impossible to express using standard data abstraction techniques.
- We describe adequacy conditions that ensure that the low-level representation of a relation is capable of implementing its higher-level specification.
- We describe the implementations of the core relation primitives, and we prove that the low-level implementations are sound with respect to the higher-level specifications (Section 4 and Section 5).

Due to space limitations we have not included all supporting lemmas or any proofs in this paper. All lemmas and proofs are in the on-line tech report [10].

2 Relation Representations and Indices

In this section we motivate and describe three different representations for relations, at different levels of abstraction, using three examples: directed graphs, a process scheduler, and a Minesweeper game. The highest level is the *logical representation* of a relation, which is the usual mathematical description of a finite relation as a set of tuples. The lowest level is the *physical representation* of a relation, which represents a relation in a program's heap using pointer-based data structures. Bridging the gap we have an intermediate *tree decomposition* of a relation, which decomposes the relation into a tree form corresponding to an index without yet committing to a specific physical representation.

First, we need to fix notation.

Values, Tuples, Relations. For our formal development we assume a universe of untyped values $\mathbb{V}$, which includes the integers, that is, $\mathbb{Z} \subseteq \mathbb{V}$. We write v to denote one value, $\mathbf{v}$ for a sequence of values, and V to denote a set of values.

A *tuple* $t = \langle c_1 \mapsto v_1, c_2 \mapsto v_2, \dots \rangle$ is a mapping from a set of *columns* $\{c_1, c_2, \dots\}$ to values drawn from $\mathbb{V}$. We write $t(c)$ to denote the value of column c in tuple t, and we write $t(\mathbf{c})$ to denote the sequence of values corresponding to a sequence of columns. We write $s \subseteq t$ if the tuple t is an extension of tuple s, that is we have $t(c) = s(c)$ for all c in the domain of s. In an abuse of notation we sometimes use a sequence of columns $\mathbf{c}$ as a set. A *relation* r is a set of tuples $\{x, y, z, \dots\}$ over the same set of column names C.

Relational Algebra. We use the standard notation of relational algebra [6]: union ($\cup$), intersection ($\cap$), set difference ($\setminus$), selection $\sigma_f\, r$, projection $\pi_C\, r$, projection onto the complement of a set of columns C: $\pi_{\overline{C}}\, r$, and natural join $r_1 \bowtie r_2$; we also allow tuples in place of relations as arguments to relation operators.

2.1 Logical Representation of Relations

We begin with the problem of representing the edges of a weighted directed graph (V, E) where $E \subseteq V \times \mathbb{Z} \times V$. We return to this example throughout the paper. One popular way to represent sparse graphs is as an adjacency list, which records the list of successors and predecessors of each vertex $v \in V$. In ML, we might represent a graph via adjacency lists as the type

$$\mathsf{type}\ g = (v, (v * \mathsf{int})\ \mathsf{list})\ \mathsf{btree} * (v, (v * \mathsf{int})\ \mathsf{list})\ \mathsf{btree},$$

assuming v is the type of vertices, and (α, β) btree is a binary tree mapping keys of type α to values of type β. Here the graph is represented as two collaborating data structures, namely a binary tree mapping each vertex to a list of its successors, together with the corresponding edge weights, and a binary tree mapping each vertex to a list of its predecessors, and the corresponding edge weights.

One problem with our proposed ML representation is that the successor and predecessor data structures represent the same set of edges; however it is the programmer's responsibility to ensure that the two data structure representations remain consistent. Another problem is that with only tree-like data structures there is no natural place to put the edge weight—we can place it in either the successor data structure or the predecessor data structure, increasing the time complexity of certain queries, or we can duplicate the weight, as we have here, which increases the space cost and introduces the possibility of inconsistencies.

Instead, we can use a relation. We represent the edges of our directed graph as a relation g with three columns $(src, dst, weight)$, in which each tuple represents the source, destination, and weight of an edge. The graph shown in Figure 5(a) can be represented as the relation $\{\langle 1, 2, 17\rangle, \langle 1, 3, 42\rangle\}$. We call the usual mathematical view of a relation as a set of tuples the *logical representation.*

We extend ML with a new type constructor $(\alpha_1, \ldots, \alpha_k)$ relation which represents relations of arity k, together with a set of primitive operations to manipulate relations. Relations are mutable data structures conceptually similar to $(\alpha_1 * \cdots * \alpha_k)$ list ref, with a very different representation. The primitives with which the client programmer manipulates relations, shown in Figure 2, are creating an empty relation, operations to insert and remove tuples from a relation, and query, which returns the list of tuples matching a *tuple pattern*, a tuple in

$$\begin{aligned}
\mathsf{empty}_d &: \mathsf{unit} \to (\alpha_1, \ldots, \alpha_k)\ \mathsf{relation}_d \\
\mathsf{insert}_d &: \alpha_1 * \cdots * \alpha_k \to (\alpha_1, \ldots, \alpha_k)\ \mathsf{relation}_d \to \mathsf{unit} \\
\mathsf{remove}_d &: \alpha_1 * \cdots * \alpha_k \to (\alpha_1, \ldots, \alpha_k)\ \mathsf{relation}_d \to \mathsf{unit} \\
\mathsf{query}_d &: (\alpha_1, \ldots, \alpha_k)\ \mathsf{relation}_d \to \alpha_1\ \mathsf{option} * \cdots * \alpha_k\ \mathsf{option} \to (\alpha_1 * \cdots \alpha_k)\ \mathsf{list}
\end{aligned}$$

Fig. 2. Primitive operations on logical relations

which some fields are missing. We describe a minimal interface to make proofs easier; a practical implementation should provide a richer set of primitives, such as an interface along the lines of LINQ [15].

2.2 Indices and Tree Decompositions

The data structure designer describes how to represent a logical relation using an *index*, which specifies how to decompose the relation into a collection of nested map and join operations over unit relations containing individual tuples. Different decompositions lead to different operations being particularly efficient. We do not maintain an underlying list of tuples; the only representation of a relation is that described by an index. Beyond the index definition programmers can remain oblivious of details of how relations are represented.

Every relation r has an associated *index* d describing how to decompose the relation into a tree and how to lay that tree out in memory; Figure 3 shows the syntax of indices. Given an index d and a relation r we can form a *tree decomposition* ρ whose structure is governed by d; Figure 4 defines the syntax of tree decompositions. There are three kinds of index that we can use to decompose a relation, each of which has a corresponding kind of tree-decomposition node:

- *Joins* allow the data-structure designer to specify how to divide the relation into pieces. These pieces can have different structures, each supporting different access patterns efficiently. We require that the natural join of the pieces be equal to the original relation. Formally, a $\mathsf{join}(d_1, d_2, L)$ index represents a relation as the natural join of two different sub-relations (ρ_1, ρ_2), where d_1 is an index that describes how to represent ρ_1 and d_2 is an index that describes how to represent ρ_2. The set L consists of *cross-linking* and *fusion* declarations, which we will describe shortly.
- *Maps* allow the data-structure designer to specify that certain columns of the relation can be used to lookup other columns. The map operator allows the programmer to specify the data structure ψ that should be used for this mapping, with options including singly- and doubly-linked lists and binary trees. Formally, a $\mathsf{map}(\psi, \mathbf{c}, d')$ index represents a relation as a mapping $\{\mathbf{v}_i \mapsto \rho_i\}_{i \in I}$ from a sequence of *key* columns $\mathbf{c}$ to a set of *residual relations* ρ_i, one for each valuation $\mathbf{v}_i$ of the key columns. We further decompose each residual relation ρ_i using an index d'.

$$
\begin{array}{rll}
d ::= & \mathsf{unit}(\mathbf{c}) \mid \mathsf{map}(\psi, \mathbf{c}, d') \mid \mathsf{join}(d_1, d_2, L) & \text{indices} \\
\psi ::= & \mathsf{option} \mid \mathsf{slist} \mid \mathsf{dlist} \mid \mathsf{btree} & \text{data struct.} \\
l \in L ::= & (\mathsf{fuse}, \mathbf{z}_1, \mathbf{z}_2) \mid (\mathsf{link}, \mathbf{z}_1, \mathbf{z}_2) & \text{cross-links} \\
\mathbf{z} \in \mathit{contour} ::= & \{\mathtt{m}, \mathtt{l}, \mathtt{r}\}^* & \text{stat. contours} \\
\mathbf{y} \in \mathit{dcontour} ::= & \{\mathtt{m}_{\mathbf{v}}, \mathtt{l}, \mathtt{r}\}^* & \text{dyn. contours}
\end{array}
$$

Fig. 3. Syntax of indices

$$\rho ::= \{\} \mid \{\mathbf{v}\} \mid \{\mathbf{v}_i \mapsto \rho_i\}_{i \in I} \mid (\rho_1, \rho_2)$$

Fig. 4. Tree decompositions

- *Unit* indices are the base case, and represent individual tuples. Formally, a $\mathsf{unit}(\mathbf{c})$ index represents a relation over a sequence of columns $\mathbf{c}$ with cardinality either 0 or 1; such a relation can either be the empty set $\{\}$, or contain a single sequence of values $\{\mathbf{v}\}$.

We assume we are given correct implementations of a set of primitive data structures such as singly- and doubly-linked lists and trees. Our focus is on assembling such building blocks into nested and overlapping data structures.

Static Contours. We annotate each term in the index with a unique name called a *static contour.* Formally, a static contour $\mathbf{z}$ is a path in an index d which identifies a specific sub-index d'. A static contour $\mathbf{z}$ is drawn from the set $\{\mathtt{m}, \mathtt{l}, \mathtt{r}\}^*$, where $\mathtt{m}$ means "move to the child index of a map index", $\mathtt{l}$ means "move to the left sub-index of a join index", and $\mathtt{r}$ means "move to the right sub-index of a join index". We write $d.\mathbf{z}$ to denote the sub-index of d identified by a contour $\mathbf{z}$.

In our directed graph we want to find the set of successors and find the set of predecessors of a vertex efficiently. One index that satisfies this constraint is

$$\begin{aligned} d_g = \mathsf{join}^{\cdot}(&\mathsf{map}^{\mathtt{l}}(\mathsf{btree}, [\mathit{src}], \mathsf{map}^{\mathtt{lm}}(\mathsf{slist}, [\mathit{dst}], \mathsf{unit}^{\mathtt{lmm}}([\mathit{weight}]))), \\ &\mathsf{map}^{\mathtt{r}}(\mathsf{btree}, [\mathit{dst}], \mathsf{map}^{\mathtt{rm}}(\mathsf{slist}, [\mathit{src}], \mathsf{unit}^{\mathtt{rmm}}([]))), \{(\mathsf{fuse}, \mathtt{rmm}, \mathtt{lmm})\}) \end{aligned}$$

The index d_g states that we should represent the relation as the natural join of two sub-indices. The left sub-index is a binary tree mapping each value of the *src* column to a distinct singly-linked list, which in turn maps each *dst* column value (for the given *src*) to its corresponding *weight*. The right sub-index is a binary tree mapping each value of the *dst* column to a linked list of *src* values.

Tree Decompositions. An index determines a useful intermediate representation of the associated relation, decomposing it into a tree according to the operations in the index. We call this representation the *tree decomposition* of a relation. As an example, Figure 5(b) depicts the tree decomposition ρ of the graph relation g given index d_g. We write ρ mathematically as

$$\left({}^{\cdot}\begin{cases} {}^{\mathtt{l}}\left\{ 1 \mapsto \left\{^{\mathtt{lm_1}} 2 \mapsto \{^{\mathtt{lm_1m_2}} \langle 17 \rangle\}, 3 \mapsto \{^{\mathtt{lm_1m_3}} \langle 42 \rangle\}\right\}\right\}, \\ {}^{\mathtt{r}}\left\{ 2 \mapsto \left\{^{\mathtt{rm_2}} 1 \mapsto \{^{\mathtt{rm_2m_1}} \langle\rangle\}\right\}, 3 \mapsto \left\{^{\mathtt{rm_3}} 1 \mapsto \{^{\mathtt{rm_3m_1}} \langle\rangle\}\right\}\right\} \end{cases} \right), \tag{1}$$

Dynamic Contours. We assign each term of a tree decomposition a unique label, called a *dynamic contour.* A *dynamic contour* $\mathbf{y}$ is a path in a tree decomposition ρ under index d that identifies a specific subtree of ρ. Each dynamic contour in a tree decomposition corresponds to an instance of a static contour in an index. In a dynamic contour we annotate the $\mathtt{m}$ operator with a sequence of key values $\mathbf{v}$; a tree decomposition via a map index has one subtree for each sequence of key values, and hence when navigating to a subtree we must specify which subtree we mean. We do not need any extra dynamic information for a join index, so we leave the `l` and `r` operators unannotated. For example, the part of the tree labeled `r` corresponds with the sub-index of d_g labeled `r`, and maps *dst* values of the relation to a list of tree decompositions corresponding to index `rm`.

2.3 Physical Representations, Cross-Linking, and Fusion

In Section 2.2 we showed how to represent logical relations as tree decompositions. Given a relation and an accompanying index, our implementation generates a *physical representation* with the structure given by the index. This representation is the concrete realization of the tree-decomposed relation in memory. Each term in the tree-decomposition becomes an object in memory, and we use the data structures specified in the index to lay out and link those objects together.

Sharing declarations allow the programmer to specify connections between objects in different parts of the index. Such sharing declarations come in two flavors: *fusion* and *cross-linking.* Fuse declarations indicate that the objects should be merged, with each structure containing a pointer to the shared object, while link operations indicate that one structure should contain a pointer to an object in another structure. Effectively these constructs collapse the tree decomposition into a directed acyclic graph.

In the graph example, we would like to share the weight of each edge between the two representations. Observe that given a (src, dst) pair, the weight is the same whether we traverse the links in the left or the right tree. That is, there is a functional dependency: any (src, dst) pair determines a unique weight, and it does not matter whether we visit the *src* or the *dst* first. Hence instead of replicating the weight, we can share it between the two trees, specified here by the *fuse* declaration. The declaration says that the data structure we get after looking up a *src* and then a *dst* in the left tree should be fused with the data structure we get by looking up a *dst* and then a *src* in the right tree.

Each join index takes an argument L which is a set of cross-linking declarations $(\mathsf{link}, \mathbf{z}_1, \mathbf{z}_2)$ and fusion declarations $(\mathsf{fuse}, \mathbf{z}_1, \mathbf{z}_2)$. A cross-linking declaration $(\mathsf{link}, \mathbf{z}_1, \mathbf{z}_2)$ states that a pointer should be maintained from each object with static contour $\mathbf{z}_1$ to the corresponding object with static contour $\mathbf{z}_2$. Similarly, a fusion declaration $(\mathsf{fuse}, \mathbf{z}_1, \mathbf{z}_2)$ states that objects with static contour $\mathbf{z}_1$ should be placed adjacent to the corresponding object with static contour $\mathbf{z}_2$. By "corresponding" object we mean the object with static contour $\mathbf{z}_2$, whose column values are drawn from the set bound by following static contour $\mathbf{z}_1$.

In the graph example, the contour `rmm` names the data structure we get by looking in the right component of the join (`r`) and then navigating down two map indices (`mm`), *i.e.*, looking in the right tree and then following first the *dst* and then the *src* links. The contour `lmm` names the corresponding location in the left tree. The fuse declaration indicates these two nodes should be merged, with the *weight* data structure from the left tree being fused with the empty data structure from the right tree. Figure 5(b) depicts the index structure after

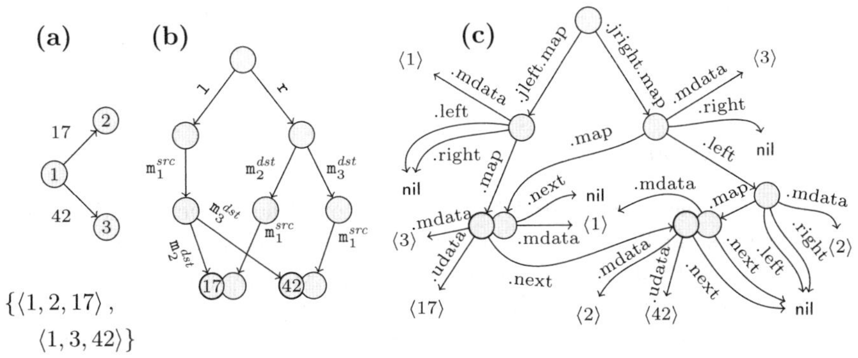

Fig. 5. Representations of a weighted directed graph: **(a)** An example graph, and its representation as a relation, **(b)** A tree decomposition of the relation in (a), with fused data structures shown as conjoined nodes, and **(c)** a diagram of the memory state that represents (b)

fusion. Figure 5(c) graphically depicts the resulting physical memory state that represents the graph of Figure 5(b). The conjoined nodes in the figure are placed at a constant field offset from one another on the heap.

2.4 Process Scheduler

As another example, suppose we want to represent the data for a simple operating system process scheduler (as in [13]). The scheduler maintains a list of live processes. A live process can be in any one of a number of states, e.g. running or sleeping. The scheduler also maintains a list of possible process states; for each state we maintain a tree of processes with that state. We represent the scheduler's data by a relation live(*pid*, *state*, *uid*, *walltime*, *cputime*), and the index

$$\mathsf{join}^{\cdot}\big(\mathsf{map}^{\mathtt{l}}\big(\mathsf{btree}, [pid], \mathsf{unit}^{\mathtt{lm}}([uid, walltime, cputime])\big),\\ \mathsf{map}^{\mathtt{r}}\big(\mathsf{dlist}, [state], \mathsf{map}^{\mathtt{rm}}(\mathsf{btree}, [pid], \mathsf{unit}^{\mathtt{rmm}}([]))\big), \{(\mathsf{fuse}, \mathtt{rmm}, \mathtt{lm})\}\big)$$

The index allows us both to efficiently find the information associated with the *pid* of a particular process, and to manipulate the set of processes with any given

$$(\textsc{TWfEmp})\ \{\} \models_T \mathsf{unit}(\mathbf{c}) \qquad (\textsc{TWfUnit})\ \frac{|\mathbf{v}| = |\mathbf{c}|}{\{\mathbf{v}\} \models_T \mathsf{unit}(\mathbf{c})}$$

$$(\textsc{TWfMap})\ \frac{\forall i \in I.\, |\mathbf{v}_i| = |\mathbf{c}| \qquad \forall i \in I.\, \rho_i \models_T d \qquad \forall i \in I.\, \alpha_t(\rho_i, d) \neq \emptyset}{\{\mathbf{v}_i \mapsto \rho_i\}_{i \in I} \models_T \mathsf{map}(\psi, \mathbf{c}, d)}$$

$$(\textsc{TWfJoin})\ \frac{\begin{array}{ll}\rho_1 \models_T d_1 & \alpha_t(\rho_1, d_1) \models \operatorname{dom} d_1 \cap \operatorname{dom} d_2 \to \operatorname{dom} d_1 \setminus \operatorname{dom} d_2 \\ \rho_2 \models_T d_2 & \pi_{\operatorname{dom} d_1 \cap \operatorname{dom} d_2}\, \alpha_t(\rho_1, d_1) = \pi_{\operatorname{dom} d_1 \cap \operatorname{dom} d_2}\, \alpha_t(\rho_2, d_2)\end{array}}{(\rho_1, \rho_2) \models_T \mathsf{join}(d_1, d_2, L)}$$

Fig. 6. Well-formed tree decompositions: $\rho \models_T d$

state and their associated data. In this case the fuse construct allows us to jump directly between the *pid* entry in a per-state binary tree and the data such as *walltime* and *cputime* associated with the process.

2.5 Minesweeper

Another example is motivated by the game of Minesweeper. A Minesweeper board consists of a 2-dimensional matrix of cells. Each cell may or may not have a mine; each cell may also be concealed or exposed. Every cell starts off in the unexposed state; the goal of the game is to expose all of the cells that do not have mines without exposing a cell containing a mine. Some implementations of Minesweeper also implement a "peek" cheat code that iterates over the set of unexposed cells, temporarily displaying them as exposed. We represent a board by the relation board$(x, y, \mathit{ismined}, \mathit{isexposed})$, with the index:

$$\begin{aligned}&\mathsf{join}^{\cdot}\big(\mathsf{map}^{\mathtt{l}}\big(\mathsf{btree}, [x], \mathsf{map}^{\mathtt{lm}}(\mathsf{btree}, [y], \mathsf{unit}^{\mathtt{lmm}}([\mathit{ismined}, \mathit{isexposed}]))\big),\\ &\quad \mathsf{map}^{\mathtt{r}}\big(\mathsf{slist}, [\mathit{isexposed}], \mathsf{map}^{\mathtt{rm}}(\mathsf{btree}, [x, y], \mathsf{unit}^{\mathtt{rmm}}([]))\big), \{(\mathsf{link}, \mathtt{rmm}, \mathtt{lmm})\}\big)\end{aligned}$$

In this example, the index specifies a *cross-link* rather than a fusion. Cross-linking adds a pointer from one object in a tree decomposition to another object, providing a "short-cut" from one data structure to another.

3 Abstraction, Well-Formedness, and Adequacy

In this and subsequent sections we give the details of how we can specify data structures with sharing at a high-level using relations and then faithfully translate those specifications into efficient low-level representations. There are two main complications. First, not every index can represent every relation; we introduce a notion of *adequacy* to characterize which relations an index can represent. Second, our proof strategy requires two steps: first showing that the intermediate *tree decomposition* of a relation is correct with respect to the logical relation, and second showing that the *physical representation* is correct with respect to the tree decomposition (Sections 4 and 5).

3.1 Tree Decompositions

Abstraction Function. Finally, we can relate the pieces we have defined so far. The abstraction function $\alpha_t(\rho, d)$ maps a tree decomposition ρ according to some index d to the corresponding high-level logical relation, showing what relation the tree decomposition represents:

$$\begin{aligned}\alpha_t(V, \mathsf{unit}(\mathbf{c})) &= \{\langle \mathbf{c} \mapsto \mathbf{v}\rangle \mid \mathbf{v} \in V\}\\ \alpha_t(\{\mathbf{v}_i \mapsto \rho_i\}_{i\in I}, \mathsf{map}(\psi, \mathbf{c}, d)) &= \bigcup\nolimits_{i\in I}(\langle \mathbf{c} \mapsto \mathbf{v}_i\rangle \times \alpha(\rho_i, d))\\ \alpha_t((\rho_1, \rho_2), \mathsf{join}(d_1, d_2, L)) &= \alpha_t(\rho_1, d_1) \bowtie \alpha_t(\rho_2, d_2)\end{aligned}$$

Functional Dependencies. A relation r has a *functional dependency* (FD) $B \to C$, if any pair of tuples in r that are equal on the set of columns B are also equal on columns C. We write Δ to denote a set of functional dependencies; we write $r \models \Delta$ if a relation r has the set of FDs Δ. If a FD $A \to B$ is a consequence of set of FDs Δ we write $\Delta \vdash_{\mathrm{fd}} A \to B$; sound and complete inference rules for functional dependencies are standard [1].

Well-Formed Decompositions. We define a class of well-formed tree decompositions ρ for an index d with a judgment $\rho \models_T d$ shown in Figure 6. The (TWfEmp) and (TWfUnit) check that a unit node is either the empty set or a sequence of values of the right length. The (TWfMap) rule checks that each sequence of key values has the right length, and that there are no key values that map to empty subtrees. The (TWfJoin) rule ensures the relation actually has the functional dependency promised by the adequacy judgment, and that we do not have "dangling" tuples on one side of a join without a matching tuple on the other side. Note that rule (TWfJoin) does not place any restrictions on the fusion declaration L; valid fusions are the subject of the physical adequacy rules of Figure 9. We write $\operatorname{dom} d$ for the set of columns that appear in an index.

3.2 Logical Adequacy

Digressing briefly, we observe that we cannot decompose every relation with every index. In general an index can only represent a class of relations satisfying particular functional dependencies.

For our running graph example the index d_g is not capable of representing every possible relation of three columns. For example, the relation $r' = \{\langle 1,2,3\rangle, \langle 1,2,4\rangle\}$ cannot be represented, because d_g can only represent a single *weight* for each pair of *src* and *dst* vertices. However r' does not correspond to a well-formed graph; all well-formed graphs satisfy a functional dependency *src*, *dst* $\to$ *weight*, which allows at most one weight for any pair of vertices.

We say that an index d is *adequate* for a class of relations R if for every relation $r \in R$ there is some tree decomposition ρ such that $\alpha_t(\rho, d) = r$. Figure 7 lists inference rules for a judgment $C; \Delta \vdash_l d$ that is a sufficient condition for an index to be adequate for the class of relations with columns C that satisfy a set of FDs Δ. The inference rules enforce two properties. Firstly, the (LAUnit) and (LAMap) rules ensure that every column of a relation must be represented by

$$(\text{LAUnit})\ \frac{\Delta \vdash_{\mathrm{fd}} \emptyset \to \mathbf{c}}{\mathbf{c}; \Delta \vdash_l \mathsf{unit}(\mathbf{c})} \qquad (\text{LAMap})\ \frac{C_2; \Delta/\mathbf{c}_1 \vdash_l d}{\mathbf{c}_1 \uplus C_2; \Delta \vdash_l \mathsf{map}(\psi, \mathbf{c}_1, d)}$$

$$(\text{LAJoin})\ \frac{\Delta \vdash_{\mathrm{fd}} C_1 \to C_2 \qquad C_1 \cup C_2; \Delta \vdash_l d_1 \qquad C_1 \cup C_3; \Delta \vdash_l d_2}{C_1 \uplus C_2 \uplus C_3; \Delta \vdash_l \mathsf{join}(d_1, d_2, L)}$$

$$\text{where } \Delta/C = \big\{(A \setminus C) \to (B \setminus C) \mid (A \to B) \in \Delta\big\}$$

Fig. 7. Rules for logical adequacy $C; \Delta \vdash_l d$

$f \in \{\text{link}_{(\mathbf{z}_1,\mathbf{z}_2)}, \text{fuse}_{(\mathbf{z}_1,\mathbf{z}_2)}, \ldots\}$	field names	$\mathbb{A} = \mathbb{Z} \times f^*$	addresses
$\mu : \mathbb{A} \to \mathbb{A} \cup \mathbb{V}$	memory	$\Lambda : dcontour \to \mathbb{A}$	layout

Fig. 8. Heaps

the index; every column must appear in a unit or map index. Secondly, in order to split a relation into two parts using a join index, the (LAJoin) rule requires a functional dependency to prevent anomalies such as spurious tuples.

We have the following lemma:

Lemma 1 (Soundness of Adequacy Judgement). *If $C; \Delta \vdash_l d$ then for each relation r with columns C such that $r \models \Delta$ there is some ρ such that $\rho \models_T d$ and $\alpha_t(\rho, d) = r$.*

3.3 Physical Representation

Heaps. Figure 8 defines the syntax for our model of memory. We represent the heap as function μ from a set of heap locations to a set of heap values. Our model of a heap location is based on C structs, except that we abstract away the layout of fields within each heap object. Heap locations are drawn from an infinite set $\mathbb{A}$, and consist of a pair $(n, \mathbf{f})$ of an integer address identifying a heap object, together with a string of field offsets. Each integer location notionally has a infinite number of field slots, although we only ever use a small and bounded number, which can then be laid out in consecutive memory locations. The contents of each heap cell can either be a value drawn from $\mathbb{V}$ or an address drawn from $\mathbb{A}$; we assume that the two sets are disjoint.

The set of columns that are bound by following a static contour $\mathbf{z}$ is given by the function $\mathsf{bound}(\mathbf{z}, d)$, defined as

$$\mathsf{bound}(\cdot, d) = \emptyset \qquad \mathsf{bound}(\mathtt{m}\mathbf{z}, \mathsf{map}(\psi, \mathbf{c}, d)) = \mathbf{c} \cup \mathsf{bound}(\mathbf{z}, d)$$
$$\mathsf{bound}(\mathtt{l}\mathbf{z}, \mathsf{join}(d_1, d_2, L)) = \mathsf{bound}(\mathbf{z}, d_1) \quad \mathsf{bound}(\mathtt{r}\mathbf{z}, \mathsf{join}(d_1, d_2, L)) = \mathsf{bound}(\mathbf{z}, d_2)$$

Layouts. We use dynamic contours to name positions in a tree. A *layout* function Λ is a mapping from the dynamic contours of a tree to addresses from $\mathbb{A}$. Layout functions allow us to translate from semantic names for memory locations to a more machine-level description of the heap; the extra layer of indirection allows us to ignore details of memory managers and layout policies, and to describe fusion and cross-linking succinctly. All layouts must be injective; that is, different tree locations must map to different physical locations. We define operators that strip and add prefixes to the domain of a layout

$$\Lambda / x = \{\mathbf{y} \mapsto a \mid (x\mathbf{y} \mapsto a) \in \Lambda\}, \text{ and } \Lambda \times x = \{x\mathbf{y} \mapsto a \mid (\mathbf{y} \mapsto a) \in \Lambda\}.$$

Data Structures. In our present implementation, a map index can be represented by an option type (option), a singly-linked list (slist), a doubly-linked list (dlist), or a binary tree (btree). It is straightforward to extend the set of data structures

$$\text{(PAUnit)}\quad \Delta;\Phi \vdash_p \mathsf{unit}(\mathbf{c}) \qquad \text{(PAMap)}\ \frac{\Delta/\mathbf{c}_1; \{\mathbf{x} \mid \mathtt{m}\mathbf{x} \in \Phi\} \vdash_p d}{\Delta;\Phi \vdash_p \mathsf{map}(\psi, \mathbf{c}_1, d)}$$

$$\text{(PAJoin)}\ \frac{\forall l \in L.\, \Delta;\Phi \vdash_p d; l \qquad \Phi' = \Phi \cup \{\mathbf{z} \mid (\mathsf{fuse}, \mathbf{z}, \mathbf{z}') \in L\} \qquad \Delta; \{\mathbf{x} \mid \mathtt{l}\mathbf{x} \in \Phi'\} \vdash_p d_1 \qquad \Delta; \{\mathbf{x} \mid \mathtt{r}\mathbf{x} \in \Phi'\} \vdash_p d_1}{\Delta;\Phi \vdash_p \mathsf{join}(d_1, d_2, L)}$$

$$\text{(PALink)}\ \frac{\mathsf{bound}(\mathtt{r}\mathbf{z}_1\mathtt{m}, d) \supseteq \mathsf{bound}(\mathtt{l}\mathbf{z}_2, d)}{\Delta;\Phi \vdash_p d; (\mathsf{link}, \mathtt{r}\mathbf{z}_1\mathtt{m}, \mathtt{l}\mathbf{z}_2)} \qquad \text{(PAFuse)}\ \frac{\mathtt{r}\mathbf{z}_1\mathtt{m} \notin \Phi \qquad \mathsf{bound}(\mathtt{r}\mathbf{z}_1\mathtt{m}, d) = \mathsf{bound}(\mathtt{l}\mathbf{z}_2, d)}{\Delta;\Phi \vdash_p d; (\mathsf{fuse}, \mathtt{r}\mathbf{z}_1\mathtt{m}, \mathtt{l}\mathbf{z}_2)}$$

Fig. 9. Rules for physical adequacy $\Delta;\Phi \vdash_p d\ [;\ l]$

by implementing a common data structure interface—we present this particular selection merely for concreteness. The common interface views each data structure as a set of key-value pairs, which is a good fit to many, but not all possible data structures. Each data structure must provide low-level functions: $\mathsf{pempty}_\psi\ a$ which creates a new structure with its root pointer located at address a, $\mathsf{pisempty}_\psi\ a$ which tests emptiness of the structure rooted at a, $\mathsf{plookup}_\psi\ a\ \mathbf{v}$ which returns the address a' of the entry with value $\mathbf{v}$, if any, $\mathsf{pscan}_\psi\ a$ which returns the set of all $(a', \mathbf{v})$ pairs of a value $\mathbf{v}$ and its address a', $\mathsf{pinsert}_\psi\ a\ \mathbf{v}\ a'$ which inserts a new value $\mathbf{v}$ into the data structure rooted at address a', and $\mathsf{premove}_\psi\ a\ \mathbf{v}\ a'$ which removes a value $\mathbf{v}$ at address a' from a data structure. Typical implementations can be found in the tech report [10].

For cross-linking and fusion to be well-defined in an index d, we need d to be physically adequate. This condition ensures that for cross-linking and fusion operations between static contours $\mathbf{z}_1$ and $\mathbf{z}_2$, the mapping from $\mathbf{z}_1$ to $\mathbf{z}_2$ is a function for each cross-link declaration and an injective function for each fusion declaration. Further, as fusions constrain the location of an object in memory, we require any object is fused at most once for feasibility. We use the judgment form $\Delta;\Phi \vdash_p d$ and the associated rules in Figure 9 to indicate that index d is physically adequate for functional dependencies Δ where Φ denotes the set of static contours that have already been fused. The (PALink) and (PAFuse) rules ensure a suitable mapping by requiring the set of fields bound by the target contour of a link be a subset of the set of fields bound by the source contour; in the case of a fusion we require equality. The rule (PAFuse) ensures that no contour is fused twice. We assume that all indices are physically adequate.

Abstraction Function. We define a second abstraction function $\alpha_m(\mu, a, d) = \rho$, which given a memory state μ, root address a, and an index d constructs the corresponding tree decomposition ρ:

$$\alpha_m(\mu, a, \mathsf{unit}(\mathbf{c})) = \mathsf{if}\ !a.\text{ulen} = 0\ \mathsf{then}\ \{\}\ \mathsf{else}\ \{!a.\text{udata}\}$$
$$\alpha_m(\mu, a, \mathsf{map}(\psi, \mathbf{c}, d)) = \{\mathbf{v} \mapsto \alpha_m(\mu, a', d) \mid (\mathbf{v}, a') \in \mathsf{pscan}_\psi\ a.\text{map}\}$$
$$\alpha_m(\mu, a, \mathsf{join}(d_1, d_2, L)) = (\alpha_m(\mu, a.\text{jleft}, d_1),\ \alpha_m(\mu, a.\text{jright}, d_2))$$

4 Queries

Up to this point we have focused on defining how relations are represented as data structures; now we turn to describing how high-level queries on relations correspond to low-level sequences of operations traversing those data structures. Recall that we define a query operation that extracts the set of tuples in a relation whose fields match a tuple pattern, i.e., $\mathsf{query}\ r\ t = r \bowtie t$, where $\operatorname{dom} t \subseteq \operatorname{dom} r$. We define *query plans* on the data structure representation, and establish sufficient conditions for a query plan to be *valid*, meaning that the query plan correctly implements a particular query on both the tree decomposition and physical representations.

One problem we do not address is selecting an efficient query plan from all possible valid query plans, but we can make a few observations. First, there is always a trivial valid query plan that uses the entire index; more efficient plans avoid traversing parts of data structures unneeded for a particular query. Second, all possible query plans can be enumerated and checked for validity; there are only so many ways to traverse an index. Finally, we expect that profile-directed database methods for selecting good query plans can be adapted to our setting; we leave that as future work.

4.1 Query Plans

A query plan is a tree of query plan operators, which take as input a *query state*, a pair $(t, \mathbf{y})$ of a tuple pattern t and a dynamic contour $\mathbf{y}$, and produce as output a set of tuples. The input tuple t maps previously bound variables to their values, whereas the dynamic contour represents the position in the index tree to which the query operator applies. Query plans are defined inductively:

None. The qnone operator determines whether an index is empty or non-empty, and returns either the empty set $\{\}$ or the singleton set $\{\langle\rangle\}$ respectively.

Unit. The qunit operator returns the tuple represented by a unit index, if any.

Scan. The $\mathsf{qscan}(q')$ operator retrieves the list of key values that match t in a map index and invokes query operator q' for each sub-tree. Since the qscan operator iterates over the contents of a map data structure, it typically takes time linear in the number of entries in the map.

Lookup. The $\mathsf{qlookup}(q')$ operator looks up a particular sequence of key values in a $\mathsf{map}(\psi, \mathbf{c}, d)$ index; each of the key columns must be bound in the input tuple t. Query operator q' is invoked on the relevant subtree, if any. The complexity of the qlookup depends on the particular choice of data structure ψ; in general we expect qlookup to have better time complexity than qscan.

Left/Right Join. The $\mathsf{qljoin}(q_1, q_2)$ operator first executes query q_1 in the left subtree of a join index, then executes query q_2 in the right subtree, and returns the natural join of the two results. The $\mathsf{qrjoin}(q_1, q_2)$ operator is similar, but executes the two queries in the opposite order. Both joins produce identical results, however the computational complexity may differ.

Fuse Join. The $\mathsf{qfusejoin}(\mathbf{z}_0, l, q_1, q_2)$ operator switches the current index data structure by following a fuse or cross-link l and executes query q_2; it then switches back to the original location and executes q_1. The result is the natural join of the two sub-queries. Parameter $\mathbf{z}_0$ identifies the join index that contains l; position $\mathbf{y}$ must be an instantiation of the source of l.

For example, suppose in the directed graph example of Section 2.1 we want to find the set of successors of graph vertex 1, together with their edge weights. Figure 10 depicts one possible, albeit inefficient, query plan q consisting of the operations

$$q = \mathsf{qrjoin}(\mathsf{qnone}, \mathsf{qscan}(\mathsf{qlookup}(\mathsf{qfusejoin}(\cdot, (\mathsf{fuse}, \mathtt{rmm}, \mathtt{lmm}), \mathsf{qunit}, \mathsf{qunit})))).$$

Intuitively, to execute this plan we use the right-hand side of the join to iterate over every possible value for the *dst* field. For each *dst* value we check to see whether there is a *src* value that matches the query input, and if so we use a fuse join to jump over to the left-hand side of the join and retrieve the corresponding weight. (A better query plan would look up the *src* on the left-hand side of the join first, and then iterate over the set of corresponding *dst* nodes and their weights, but our goal here is to demonstrate the role of the qfusejoin operator.)

To find successors using query plan q, we start with the state $(\langle src \mapsto 1\rangle, \cdot)$. Since the left branch of the join is qnone, the join reduces to a recursive execution of the query $\mathsf{qscan}(\cdots)$ with input $(\langle src \mapsto 1\rangle, \mathtt{r})$. The qscan recursively invokes qlookup on each of the states $(\langle src \mapsto 1, dst \mapsto 2\rangle, \mathtt{rm}_2)$ and $(\langle src \mapsto 1, dst \mapsto 3\rangle, \mathtt{rm}_3)$. The qlookup operator in turn recursively invokes the qfusejoin operator on $(\langle src \mapsto 1, dst \mapsto 2\rangle, \mathtt{rm}_2\mathtt{m}_1)$ and the state $(\langle src \mapsto 1, dst \mapsto 3\rangle, \mathtt{rm}_3\mathtt{m}_1)$. To execute its second query argument the fuse join maps each instantiation of contour $\mathtt{rmm}$ to the corresponding instantiation of contour $\mathtt{lmm}$; we are guaranteed that exactly one such contour instantiation exists by index adequacy. The fuse join produces the states $(\langle src \mapsto 1, dst \mapsto 2\rangle, \mathtt{lm}_1\mathtt{m}_2)$ and $(\langle src \mapsto 1, dst \mapsto 3\rangle, \mathtt{lm}_1\mathtt{m}_3)$. Finally the invocations of qunit on each state produces the tuples

$$\{\langle src \mapsto 1, dst \mapsto 2, weight \mapsto 17\rangle, \\ \langle src \mapsto 1, dst \mapsto 3, weight \mapsto 17\rangle\}.$$

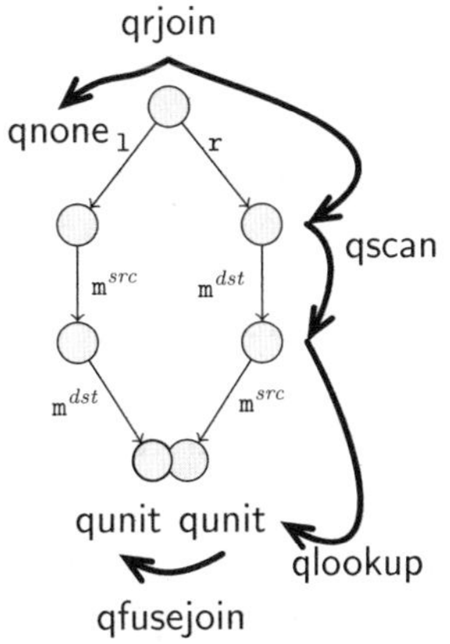

Fig. 10. A possible query plan for the graph example of Section 2.1

We need a criteria for determining whether a particular query plan does in fact return all of the tuples that match a pattern. We say a query plan is *valid*, written $d, \mathbf{z}, X \vdash_q q, Y$ if q correctly answers queries in index d at dynamic instantiations of contour $\mathbf{z}$, where X is the set of columns bound in the input tuple pattern t and Y is the set of columns bound in the output tuples (see the technical report [10]).

5 Relational Operations

In this section we describe implementations for the primitive relation operators for the tree-decomposition and physical representations of a relation, and we prove our main result: that these primitive operators are sound with respect to their higher-level specification. Complete code is given in the tech report [10].

5.1 Operators on the Tree Decomposition

We implement queries over tree decompositions by a function tquery $d\ t\ \rho$, which finds tuples matching pattern t over tree decompositions ρ under index d. The core routine is a function tqexec $\rho\ d\ q\ t\ \mathbf{y}$ which, given a tree decomposition ρ, index d, and a tuple t, executes plan q at the position of the dynamic contour $\mathbf{y}$.

Creation/update are handled by tempty d, which constructs a new empty relation with index d, tinsert $d\ t\ \rho$, which inserts a tuple t into a tree-decomposed relation ρ with index d, and tremove $d\ t\ \rho$ which removes a tuple t from a tree-decomposed relation ρ with index d. It is the client's responsibility to ensure that functional dependencies are not violated; the implementation contains dynamic checks that abort if the client fails to comply. These checks can be removed if there is an external guarantee that the client will never violate the dependencies.

To show that the primitive operations on tree decompositions faithfully implement the corresponding primitive operations on logical relations, we first show executing valid queries over tree decompositions soundly implements logical tuple pattern queries. We then prove a soundness result by induction.

Lemma 2 (Tree Decomposition Query Soundness). *For all ρ, r, d such that $\rho \models_T d$ and $\alpha_t(\rho, d) = r$, if $d, \cdot, \mathrm{dom}\, t \vdash_q q, \mathrm{dom}\, d$ for a tuple pattern t and query plan q we have* tqexec $\rho\ d\ q\ t\ \cdot =$ query $r\ t$.

Theorem 1 (Tree Decomposition Soundness). *Suppose a sequence of* insert *and* remove *operators starting from the empty relation produce a relation r. The corresponding sequence of* tinsert *and* tremove *operators given* tempty d *as input either produce ρ such that $\rho \models_T d$ and $\alpha_t(\rho, d) = r$, or abort with an error.*

5.2 Physical Representation Operators

In this section we describe implementations of each of the primitive relation operations that operate over the physical representation of a relation. We prove soundness of the physical implementation with respect to the tree decomposition. For space reasons we omit the code for physical operators but we give a brief synopsis of each function; for a complete definition see the full paper [10].

We execute physical queries via a query execution function pqexec $d\ q\ y\ a\ \mathbf{y}$. Function pqexec is structurally very similar to the query execution function tqexec over tree decompositions. Instead of a tree decomposition ρ the physical function accesses the heap, and in place of a dynamic contour $\mathbf{y}$ the physical function represents a position in the data structure by a pair $(\mathbf{z}, a)$ of a static contour $\mathbf{z}$ and an address a. The main difference in implementation is that the qfusejoin case follows a fusion or cross-link simply by performing pointer arithmetic or a pointer dereference, respectively, rather than traversing the index.

Creation/update are handled by pempty $d\ a$ (creates an empty relation with index d rooted at address a), pinsert $d\ t\ a$ (inserts tuple t into a relation with index d rooted at a), and premove $d\ t\ a$ (removes tuple t). The main difference with corresponding operations on the tree decomposition is in pinsert, which needs to create fusions and cross-links. To fuse two nodes we simply place the data of a node being fused in a subfield of the node into which it is fused. To create a cross-link, we first construct the tree structure and then add pointers between each pair of linked nodes.

Analogous to the soundness proof for tree decompositions, we prove soundness by proving a set of commutative diagrams relating physical representations of relations with their tree decomposition counterparts. We need a well-formedness invariant for physical states. A memory state μ is *well-formed* for index d with layout Λ if there exists an injective function Λ such that the judgment $\mu; \Lambda \models_p d$ holds, defined by the inference rules in [10].

We show that valid queries over physical memory states are sound with respect to the tree decomposition. We then show soundness by induction.

Lemma 3 (Physical Query Soundness). *Suppose we have* $\mu; \Lambda \models_p d$ *and* $\alpha_m(\mu, \Lambda(\cdot), d) = \rho$ *for some* μ, Λ, d. *Then for all queries* q *and tuples* t *such that* $d, \cdot, \mathrm{dom}\, t \vdash_q q, \mathrm{dom}\, d$ *we have* pqexec $d\ q\ t\ a\ \cdot =$ tqexec $\rho\ d\ q\ t\ \cdot$, *where* pqexec *is executed in memory state* μ.

Theorem 2 (Physical Soundness). *Let* d *be an index, and suppose a sequence of* tinsert *and* tremove *operators starting from the* $\rho =$ tempty d *produce a relation* ρ'. *Let* μ *be the heap produced by* pempty $d\ a$ *where* a *is a location initially present in the heap. Then the corresponding sequence of* pinsert *and* premove *operators given* μ *as input either produce a memory state* μ' *such that* $\mu'; \Lambda \models_p d$ *for some* Λ *and* $\alpha_m(\mu, a, d) = \rho'$, *or abort with an error.*

6 Related Work

Relations. Many authors propose adding relations to both general- and special-purpose programming languages (e.g., [3; 15; 19; 16]). We focus on the orthogonal problem of specifying and implementing shared representations for data. Our approach can benefit from much of this past work; in particular, database techniques for query planning are likely to prove useful.

Automatic Data Structure Selection. Automatic data structure selection was studied in SETL [20; 4; 17] and has also been pursued for Java collection implementations [21]. Our index language describes a mapping between abstract data and its concrete implementations with a similar goal to [7]. We focus on composing and expressing sharing between data structures which is important in many practical situations. Our work can be combined with static and dynamic techniques to infer suitable data structures.

Specifying Shared Representations. Graph types [11] extend tree-structured types with extra pointers functionally determined by the structure of the tree backbone. One way to view our cross-linking and fusion constructs is adding extra pointers determined by the semantics of data and not by its structure. Separation Logic allows elegant specifications of disjoint data structures [18]. Various extensions of separation logic enable proofs about some types of sharing [2; 8].

Inferring Shared Representations. Some static analysis algorithms infer some sharing between data structures in low level code [13; 12]. In contrast we allow the programmer to specify sharing in a concise way and guarantee consistency only assuming that functional dependencies are maintained. Functional dependencies or their equivalent are an essential invariant for any shared data structure.

Verification Approaches. The Hob system uses abstract sets of objects to specify and verify properties that characterize how multiple data structures share objects [14]. Monotonic typestates enable aliased objects to monotonically change their typestates in the presence of sharing without violating type safety [9]. Researchers have developed systems to mechanically verify data structures (e.g., hash tables) that implement binary relational interfaces [22; 5]. The relation implementation presented here is more general, allowing relations of arbitrary arity and substantially more sophisticated data structures than previous research.

7 Conclusion

We have presented a system for specifying and operating on data structures at a high level as relations while implementing those relations as the composition of low-level pointer data structures. Most unusually we can express, and prove correct, the use of complex sharing in the low-level representation, allowing us to express many practical examples beyond the capabilities of previous techniques.

References

[1] Beeri, C., Fagin, R., Howard, J.H.: A complete axiomatization for functional and multivalued dependencies in database relations. In: SIGMOD, pp. 47–61. ACM, New York (1977)
[2] Berdine, J., Calcagno, C., Cook, B., Distefano, D., O'Hearn, P., Wies, T., Yang, H.: Shape analysis for composite data structures. In: Damm, W., Hermanns, H. (eds.) CAV 2007. LNCS, vol. 4590, pp. 178–192. Springer, Heidelberg (2007)
[3] Bierman, G., Wren, A.: First-class relationships in an object-oriented language. In: Black, A.P. (ed.) ECOOP 2005. LNCS, vol. 3586, pp. 262–286. Springer, Heidelberg (2005)
[4] Cai, J., Paige, R.: Look ma, no hashing, and no arrays neither. In: POPL, pp. 143–154 (1991)
[5] Chlipala, A.J., Malecha, J.G., Morrisett, G., Shinnar, A., Wisnesky, R.: Effective interactive proofs for higher-order imperative programs. In: ICFP, pp. 79–90 (2009)
[6] Codd, E.F.: A relational model of data for large shared data banks. Commun. ACM 13(6), 377–387 (1970)

[7] Dewar, R.B.K., Grand, A., Liu, S.-C., Schwartz, J.T., Schonberg, E.: Programming by refinement, as exemplified by the SETL representation sublanguage. ACM Trans. Program. Lang. Syst. 1(1), 27–49 (1979)

[8] Distefano, D., Parkinson, M.J.: jStar: towards practical verification for Java. In: OOPSLA, pp. 213–226 (2008)

[9] Fahndrich, M., Leino, R.: Heap monotonic typestates. In: Int. Work. on Alias Confinement and Ownership (July 2003)

[10] Hawkins, P., Aiken, A., Fisher, K., Rinard, M., Sagiv, M.: Data structure fusion, full (2010), `http://theory.stanford.edu/~hawkinsp/papers/rel-full.pdf`

[11] Klarlund, N., Schwartzbach, M.I.: Graph types. In: POPL, Charleston, South Carolina, pp. 196–205. ACM, New York (1993)

[12] Kreiker, J., Seidl, H., Vojdani, V.: Shape analysis of low-level C with overlapping structures. In: Barthe, G., Hermenegildo, M. (eds.) VMCAI 2010. LNCS, vol. 5944, pp. 214–230. Springer, Heidelberg (2010)

[13] Kuncak, V., Lam, P., Rinard, M.: Role analysis. In: POPL, pp. 17–32 (2002)

[14] Lam, P., Kuncak, V., Rinard, M.C.: Generalized typestate checking for data structure consistency. In: Cousot, R. (ed.) VMCAI 2005. LNCS, vol. 3385, pp. 430–447. Springer, Heidelberg (2005)

[15] Meijer, E., Beckman, B., Bierman, G.: LINQ: Reconciling objects, relations and XML in the .NET framework. In: SIGMOD, p. 706. ACM, New York (2006)

[16] Olston, C., et al.: Pig Latin: A not-so-foreign language for data processing. In: SIGMOD (June 2008)

[17] Paige, R., Henglein, F.: Mechanical translation of set theoretic problem specifications into efficient RAM code. J. Sym. Com. 4(2), 207–232 (1987)

[18] J. C. Reynolds. Separation logic: A logic for shared mutable data structures. In LICS (2002) (invited paper)

[19] Rothamel, T., Liu, Y.A.: Efficient implementation of tuple pattern based retrieval. In: PEPM, pp. 81–90. ACM, New York (2007)

[20] Schonberg, E., Schwartz, J.T., Sharir, M.: Automatic data structure selection in SETL. In: POPL, pp. 197–210 (1979)

[21] Shacham, O., Vechev, M., Yahav, E.: Chameleon: adaptive selection of collections. In: PLDI, pp. 408–418 (2009)

[22] Zee, K., Kuncak, V., Rinard, M.C.: Full functional verification of linked data structures. In: PLDI, pp. 349–361 (2008)

Categorical Descriptional Composition

Shin-ya Katsumata

Research Institute for Mathematical Sciences
Kyoto University, Kyoto, 606-8502, Japan
sinya@kurims.kyoto-u.ac.jp

Abstract. Descriptional composition is a method to fuse two term transformation algorithms described by attribute couplings (AC, attribute grammars over terms) into one. In this article, we provide a general categorical framework for the descriptional composition based on traced symmetric monoidal categories and the **Int** construction by Joyal et al. We demonstrate that this framework can handle the descriptional composition of SSUR-ACs, nondeterministic SSUR-ACs, quasi-SSUR ACs and quasi-SSUR stack ACs.

1 Introduction

Descriptional composition [6,7,8] is a method to fuse two term transformation algorithms described by attribute couplings (ACs; attribute grammars over terms) into one. The AC yielded by the descriptional composition computes the composition of two ACs without constructing the intermediate data structure passed between two ACs; hence it saves time and space in many cases. The descriptional composition was first introduced as an optimisation method for compilers described by ACs [7]. Around the same time Bartha introduced a similar composition method for linear attributed tree transformations [1]. Later, it was realised that ACs can be used to represent functional programs with accumulating parameters [10], and the descriptional composition inspired various fusion transformations of such functional programs [19,22].

The descriptional composition was first given for the ACs consisting only of term constructors [7]. Later, extensions of the ACs have been studied in [18,20,3]. In [3], Boyland considered an extension of ACs with conditional expressions. In [18], Nakano introduces stacks to ACs so that complex parsing functions can be expressed. In each work, the descriptional composition was also considered to these extended ACs. In general, the descriptional composition is sensitive on the language describing ACs, and formulating the descriptional composition verifying its correctness tend to be involved when expressive power of the language increases.

The question we address here is to find a mathematical framework that can uniformly treat these extensions of ACs and the descriptional composition of them. In this paper, we propose such a general categorical framework based on the theory of *traced symmetric monoidal categories* (TSMCs) and the **Int** *construction* by Joyal et al. The key observation in the categorical treatment of ACs and the descriptional composition is that every attribute grammar determines a traced symmetric strict monoidal functor $F : \mathcal{L}(\Sigma) \to \mathbf{Int}(\mathbb{C})$ where $\mathcal{L}(\Sigma)$ is a free TSMC over a signature Σ, and especially every AC satisfying *syntactic single use condition (SSUR)*, which is the essential condition for

K. Ueda (Ed.): APLAS 2010, LNCS 6461, pp. 222–238, 2010.

the descriptional composition to work, determines a traced symmetric monoidal functor $G : \mathcal{L}(\Sigma) \to \mathbf{Int}(\mathcal{L}(\Delta))$. With this functorial presentation, the descriptional composition becomes the composition of functors, and its associativity can be easily verified. This story scales up to the TSMCs with extra structures, provided that the **Int** construction is also extended to such TSMCs; examples include nondeterministic ACs, quasi-SSUR ACs (an affine version of SSUR AC), and ACs with stacks [18].

In this paper we do not exclude circular terms and recursive computation as meaningless things. Hence every AG assigns some meaning to a given term.

Conventions and Notations. Signatures are all many-typed and first-order. We reserve Δ, Σ, Ξ for ranging over signatures. By $\rho \in \Sigma$ and $o \in \Sigma^{\rho_1 \cdots \rho_n \to \rho}$ we mean that ρ is a type of Σ and o is an operator of type $\rho_1 \cdots \rho_n \to \rho$, respectively. We declare the signature for binary trees, cons-lists and natural numbers by

$$\Sigma_{\text{tree}} = (\{*\}, \mathsf{L}^*, \mathsf{N}^{** \to *}), \quad \Sigma_{\text{list}} = (\{*\}, []^*, a :: (-)^{* \to *}), \quad \Sigma_{\text{nat}} = (\{*\}, \mathsf{Z}^*, \mathsf{S}^{* \to *}).$$

For a type $\sigma \in \Sigma$ and sequence of Σ-types $\rho_1 \cdots \rho_n$, by $T^{\sigma}_{\Sigma}(\rho_1 \cdots \rho_n)$ we mean the set of open Σ-terms that may contain some variables x_i of type ρ_i ($1 \le i \le n$). We then extend this notation by $T^{\sigma_1 \cdots \sigma_m}_{\Sigma}(\rho_1 \cdots \rho_n) = T^{\sigma_1}_{\Sigma}(\rho_1 \cdots \rho_n) \times \cdots \times T^{\sigma_m}_{\Sigma}(\rho_1 \cdots \rho_n)$. By Σ^+ we mean that Σ contains a special type #; such signature is called *rooted*. We assume that the readers are familiar with the concept of symmetric monoidal categories [17]. We also employ the 2-category theory and the theory of pseudo-monads and pseudo-distributive laws; see e.g. [21].

2 Classical Attribute Couplings and Descriptional Composition

A classical attribute grammar (AG) for a signature Δ is a triple $\mathcal{A} = (I, S, a)$ where for each type $\rho \in \Delta$, $I\rho$ and $S\rho$ are resp. sets of inherited and synthesised attribute values, and for each operator $o \in \Delta^{\rho_1, \cdots, \rho_n \to \rho}$, a_o is a function called the *attribute calculation rule*[1]:

$$a_o : S\rho_1 \times \cdots \times S\rho_n \times I\rho \to S\rho \times I\rho_1 \times \cdots \times I\rho_n. \tag{1}$$

This function captures the input-output relation of a computation unit that processes bidirectional information flow (Figure 1, left). Given a Δ-term M, we connect the assigned computation units according to the shape of M (Figure 1, right). The function corresponding to the entire circuit is the meaning $\mathcal{A}[\![M]\!]$ assigned to M by the AG $\mathcal{A}$. Depending on the configuration of the attribute calculation rules, such function may not exist in general, but if any combination of attribute calculation rules does not yield cyclic information dependency (such AGs are called *non-circular*), the function $\mathcal{A}[\![M]\!]$ uniquely exists for any M. See [14,15] for the detail.

An *attribute coupling* (AC) from Δ to Σ is a special AG such that the set assigned to $I\rho$ (resp. $S\rho$) is a set $T^{\sigma_1, \cdots, \sigma_n}_{\Sigma}$ of tuples of Σ-terms for some $\sigma_1, \cdots, \sigma_n \in \Sigma$, and each attribute calculation rule comprises only of Σ-operators rather than arbitrary functions. Briefly speaking, ACs are AGs constructing Σ-terms. We can extract the essential information from such AGs and redefine ACs from Δ to Σ as the tuple $\mathcal{A} = (I, S, a)$,

[1] This form of attribute calculation rule is called *Bochmann normal form*.

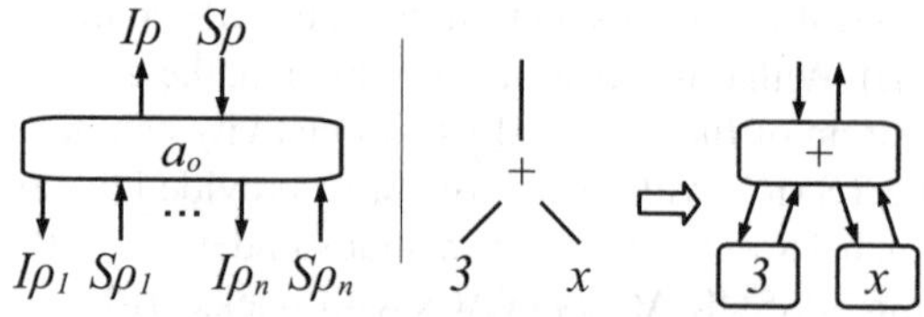

Fig. 1. Attribute Grammars

where for each type $\rho \in \Delta$, $I\rho$ and $S\rho$ are sequences of Σ-types, and for each operator $o \in \Delta^{\rho_1,\cdots,\rho_n \to \rho}$, a_o is a tuple of (open) Σ-terms:

$$a_o \in T_{\Sigma}^{S\rho, I\rho_1, \cdots, I\rho_n}(S\rho_1, \cdots, S\rho_n, I\rho).$$

We write $\mathbf{AC}(\Delta, \Sigma)$ for the set of ACs from Δ to Σ. We assume that ACs (I, S, a) between the signatures containing the special type # satisfy $I\# = \epsilon$ and $S\# = \#$. With this convention we can view every non-circular AC $\mathcal{A}$ from Δ^+ to Σ^+ as a term transformation function $T\mathcal{A} : T^{\#}_{\Delta^+} \to T^{\#}_{\Sigma^+}$, defined by $T\mathcal{A}(M) = \mathcal{A}[\![M]\!]$.

Let $\mathcal{A} \in \mathbf{AC}(\Delta^+, \Sigma^+)$ and $\mathcal{B} \in \mathbf{AC}(\Sigma^+, \Xi^+)$ be non-circular ACs. We seek for an AC $\mathcal{B} \copyright \mathcal{A}$ such that $T(\mathcal{B} \copyright \mathcal{A}) = T\mathcal{B} \circ T\mathcal{A}$. In general such AC may not exist, but when $\mathcal{A}$ satisfies a condition called *syntactic single-use restriction (SSUR)*, we can build $\mathcal{B} \copyright \mathcal{A}$ by the *descriptional composition*, which we illustrate below.

Suppose that the attribute calculation rules of $\mathcal{A}$ and $\mathcal{B}$ look like the left of Figure 2. There, $\mathcal{A}$ assigns to a Δ^+-operator f a computation unit that constructs Σ^+-terms, which is drawn as a circuit. Similarly, $\mathcal{B}$ assigns to a Σ^+-operator a a computation unit b, which is just drawn as a round box. We now replace each wire in the right hand side of the attribute calculation rule of $\mathcal{A}$ with bidirectional wire, and replace each Σ^+-term constructor with the computation unit assigned by $\mathcal{B}$. The result of this replacement is drawn on the right of Figure 2, which is a new attribute coupling from Δ^+ to Ξ^+. This is the descriptional composition $\mathcal{B} \copyright \mathcal{A}$.

The hidden point in the above process is that the computation unit (circuit) assigned by $\mathcal{A}$ should not contain any branching wires nor terminals. This is because we do not know how to make branches and terminals bidirectional (Figure 3). This suggests that each attribute calculation rule assigned by $\mathcal{A}$ should use each variable exactly once, and an AC satisfying this linearity condition is called *syntactic single use restriction* (*SSUR*) AC. We will see its precise definition in Section 2.2, and reformulate it as an AG in a linear recursive language, which we introduce below.

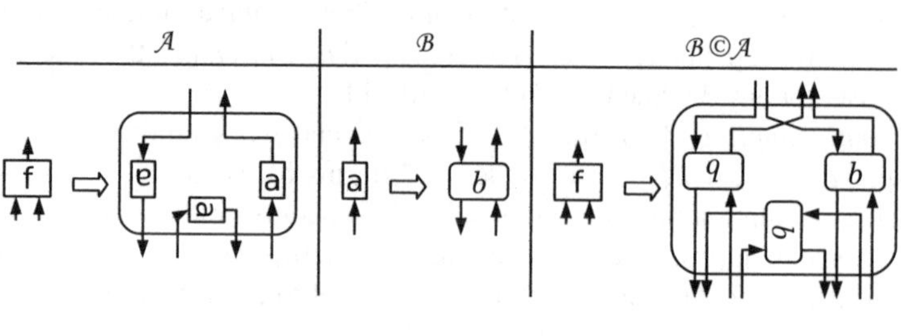

Fig. 2. The descriptional composition

Fig. 3. How to Make Branches and Terminals Bidirectional?

2.1 The Linear Recursive Language $\mathcal{L}(\Sigma)$

We introduce a simply-typed first-order linear language with recursive declarations called $\mathcal{L}(\Sigma)$. It has only one form of raw-expressions:

$$\lambda x_1, \cdots, x_n \,.\, \mathsf{let}\; y_1 = M_1, \cdots, y_l = M_l \;\mathsf{in}\; z_1, \cdots, z_m,$$

and they are given a type $\sigma_1, \cdots, \sigma_n \to \tau_1, \cdots, \tau_m$ by the type system in Figure 4, where U and D are typing contexts defined by

$$\mathrm{U} = \Gamma_1 \cup \cdots \cup \Gamma_n \cup \{z_1 : \tau_1, \cdots, z_m : \tau_m\}$$
$$\mathrm{D} = \{x_1 : \sigma_1, \cdots, x_n : \sigma_n, y_1 : \rho_1, \cdots, y_l : \rho_l\},$$

such that x_i, y_j, z_k and variables in $\Gamma_1, \cdots, \Gamma_n$ are different from each other. The leading λ of expressions is a formal binder for $x_1, \cdots, x_n$, rather than the lambda abstraction in the lambda calculus. Expressions are treated modulo α-equivalence.

Expressions of $\mathcal{L}(\Sigma)$ are identified by the rules in Figure 4, where the sequence of variable declarations after let is abbreviated as D. The first axiom allows us to permute D without affecting the meaning of expressions. In the second axiom, $D[w/v]$ denotes the sequence of variable declarations obtained by replacing v in D with w. This axiom allows us to forward v to w when $v = w$ is contained in D.

Here are some examples of $\mathcal{L}(\Sigma_{\mathrm{tree}})$-expressions:

$$\vdash_M \lambda x \,.\, \mathsf{let}\; y = \mathsf{N}(l, x), l = \mathsf{L} \;\mathsf{in}\; y : * \to *$$
$$\vdash_M \lambda x, y, z \,.\, \mathsf{let}\; w = \mathsf{N}(x, w), l = \mathsf{L}, v = \mathsf{N}(l, z) \;\mathsf{in}\; y, v : *** \to **. \qquad (2)$$

Note that in (2) the variable w can not be used for output due to the linearity constraint. This means that when the underlying signature has a binary operator then there is a way to discard inputs.

$$\frac{\rho \in \Sigma}{x : \rho \vdash_E x : \rho} \qquad \frac{o \in \Sigma^{\rho_1 \cdots \rho_n \to \rho}}{x_1 : \rho_1, \cdots, x_n : \rho_n \vdash_E o(x_1, \cdots, x_n) : \rho}$$

$$\frac{\Gamma_1 \vdash_E M_1 : \rho_1 \quad \cdots \quad \Gamma_l \vdash_E M_l : \rho_l \quad \mathrm{U} = \mathrm{D}}{\vdash_M \lambda \boldsymbol{x} \,.\, \mathsf{let}\; y_1 = M_1, \cdots, y_l = M_l \;\mathsf{in}\; \boldsymbol{z} : \sigma_1, \cdots, \sigma_n \to \tau_1, \cdots, \tau_m}$$

$$(\lambda \boldsymbol{x} \,.\, \mathsf{let}\; D \;\mathsf{in}\; \boldsymbol{z}) = (\lambda \boldsymbol{x} \,.\, \mathsf{let}\; \pi(D) \;\mathsf{in}\; \boldsymbol{z})$$
$$(\lambda \boldsymbol{x} \,.\, \mathsf{let}\; v = w, D \;\mathsf{in}\; \boldsymbol{z}) = (\lambda \boldsymbol{x} \,.\, \mathsf{let}\; D[w/v] \;\mathsf{in}\; \boldsymbol{z}[w/v]) \quad (v \neq w)$$

Fig. 4. Type System and Axiom for $\mathcal{L}(\Sigma)$

2.2 SSUR-ACs as Attribute Grammars in $\mathcal{L}(\Sigma)$

An AC $(I, S, a) \in \mathbf{AC}(\Delta, \Sigma)$ satisfies the *syntactic single use restriction* (*SSUR*) [6] if each attribute calculation rule satisfies the following linearity condition. We let l be the length of the concatenation $S\rho, I\rho_1, \cdots, I\rho_n$, and write τ_i $(1 \leq i \leq l)$ for the i-th component of this sequence. We prepare sequences Γ_i $(1 \leq i \leq l)$ of Σ-types such that $S\rho_1, \cdots, S\rho_n, I\rho$ is a permutation of the concatenation $\Gamma_1, \cdots, \Gamma_l$. We then ask the attribute calculation rule to be in the following set:

$$a_o \in T_\Sigma^{\tau_1}(\Gamma_1) \times \cdots \times T_\Sigma^{\tau_l}(\Gamma_l), \tag{3}$$

and, moreover, in the i-th component of a_o, each variable occurs exactly once.

We observe that there is a one-to-one correspondence between such a tuple and a $\mathcal{L}(\Sigma)$-expression of type $S\rho_1, \cdots, S\rho_n, I\rho \to S\rho, I\rho_1, \cdots, I\rho_n$. We exploit this correspondence to redefine the concept of SSUR-AC.

Definition 1. *An SSUR-AC from Δ to Σ is a triple (I, S, a) where for each type $\rho \in \Delta$, $I\rho$ and $S\rho$ are sequences of Σ-types, and for each $o \in \Delta^{\rho_1, \cdots, \rho_n \to \rho}$, a_o is an $\mathcal{L}(\Sigma)$-expression of type $a_o : S\rho_1, \cdots, S\rho_n, I\rho \to S\rho, I\rho_1, \cdots, I\rho_n$. We write* **SSUR-AC**$(\Delta, \Sigma)$ *for the set of SSUR-ACs from Δ to Σ. When Δ, Σ contains the special type #, we assume that every SSUR-AC (I, S, a) from Δ to Σ satisfies $I\# = \epsilon$ and $S\# = \#$.*

We note that this correspondence is not surjective, as $\mathcal{L}(\Sigma)$ permits recursively defined variables that can not be expressed by SSUR-ACs.

3 Categorical Aspect of Attribute Couplings

3.1 $\mathcal{L}(\Sigma)$ as a Traced Symmetric Monoidal Category

We next view $\mathcal{L}(\Sigma)$ as a category. We regard a sequence $\boldsymbol{\rho} = \rho_1 \cdots \rho_n$ of types in Σ as an object, and an equivalence class of expressions of type $\boldsymbol{\rho} \to \boldsymbol{\sigma}$ as a morphism from $\boldsymbol{\rho}$ to $\boldsymbol{\sigma}$. The composition is defined by

$$(\lambda \boldsymbol{x} \,.\, \mathsf{let}\ D\ \mathsf{in}\ \boldsymbol{y}) \circ (\lambda \boldsymbol{z} \,.\, \mathsf{let}\ D'\ \mathsf{in}\ \boldsymbol{w}) = \lambda \boldsymbol{z} \,.\, \mathsf{let}\ D[\boldsymbol{w}/\boldsymbol{x}], D'\ \mathsf{in}\ \boldsymbol{y}[\boldsymbol{w}/\boldsymbol{x}];$$

here we assume that every bound variable in the above expression is distinct from each other. The category $\mathcal{L}(\Sigma)$ has an evident symmetric strict monoidal structure. The unit object is the empty sequence and the tensor product of two objects is the concatenation of them. The tensor product of two morphisms is defined by merging two expressions:

$$(\lambda \boldsymbol{x} \,.\, \mathsf{let}\ D\ \mathsf{in}\ \boldsymbol{y}) \otimes (\lambda \boldsymbol{z} \,.\, \mathsf{let}\ D'\ \mathsf{in}\ \boldsymbol{w}) = \lambda \boldsymbol{x}, \boldsymbol{z} \,.\, \mathsf{let}\ D, D'\ \mathsf{in}\ \boldsymbol{y}, \boldsymbol{w}.$$

The symmetry morphism is given by $\lambda \boldsymbol{x}, \boldsymbol{y} \,.\, \mathsf{let}\ \epsilon\ \mathsf{in}\ \boldsymbol{y}, \boldsymbol{x}$.

In addition to this, the following *trace operator* constructs recursive declarations in expressions. Let $\boldsymbol{x}, \boldsymbol{y}, \boldsymbol{z}, \boldsymbol{w}$ be sequences of different variables, and $\boldsymbol{\rho}, \boldsymbol{\sigma}, \boldsymbol{\tau}$ be sequences of types such that $|\boldsymbol{x}| = |\boldsymbol{\rho}|, |\boldsymbol{z}| = |\boldsymbol{\sigma}|, |\boldsymbol{y}| = |\boldsymbol{w}| = |\boldsymbol{\tau}|$. We define the *trace operator* $\mathrm{tr}^{\boldsymbol{\tau}}_{\boldsymbol{\rho},\boldsymbol{\sigma}}$ as follows:

$$\mathrm{tr}^{\boldsymbol{\tau}}_{\boldsymbol{\rho},\boldsymbol{\sigma}}(\lambda \boldsymbol{x}, \boldsymbol{y} \,.\, \mathsf{let}\ D\ \mathsf{in}\ \boldsymbol{z}, \boldsymbol{w}) = \lambda \boldsymbol{x} \,.\, \mathsf{let}\ \boldsymbol{y} = \boldsymbol{w}, D\ \mathsf{in}\ \boldsymbol{z}.$$

A pair of a symmetric monoidal category and a trace operator is called *traced symmetric monoidal category* (see Appendix B). In this article we only consider the traced symmetric *strict* monoidal categories, and call them TSMC. [2] The above discussion is summarised as follows:

Proposition 1. *The above data make $\mathcal{L}(\Sigma)$ a TSMC.*

We call a symmetric strong monoidal functor between TSMCs *traced* if it preserves the trace operator in an evident way (see Appendix B). We write **TSMC** for the 2-category of TSMCs, traced symmetric strong monoidal functors and monoidal natural isomorphisms. Its 2-subcategory consisting of traced symmetric strict monoidal functors will be denoted by $\mathbf{TSMC}_s$.

From a traced strong monoidal functor $(F, \phi^F_\epsilon, \phi^F_{\rho,\sigma}) \in \mathbf{TSMC}(\mathcal{L}(\Sigma), \mathbb{C})$, we can construct a traced strict monoidal functor $\mathbf{Str}(F) \in \mathbf{TSMC}_s(\mathcal{L}(\Sigma), \mathbb{C})$ which is naturally isomorphic to F. The strict functor is constructed as follows:

$$\mathbf{Str}(F)(\rho_1 \cdots \rho_n) = F\rho_1 \otimes \cdots \otimes F\rho_n \qquad \mathbf{Str}(F)(f : \rho \to \sigma) = (\phi^F_\sigma)^{-1} \circ Ff \circ \phi^F_\rho.$$

The assignment $F \mapsto \mathbf{Str}(F)$, which we will call *strictification operator*, extends to an equivalence of categories $\mathbf{Str} : \mathbf{TSMC}(\mathcal{L}(\Sigma), \mathbb{C}) \to \mathbf{TSMC}_s(\mathcal{L}(\Sigma), \mathbb{C})$. It satisfies the following property: for any $F \in \mathbf{TSMC}_s(\mathcal{L}(\Sigma), \mathbb{D}), G \in \mathbf{TSMC}(\mathbb{D}, \mathbb{E}), H \in \mathbf{TSMC}(\mathbb{E}, \mathbb{F})$, we have $\mathbf{Str}(F) = F$ and $\mathbf{Str}(H \circ G \circ F) = \mathbf{Str}(H \circ \mathbf{Str}(G \circ F))$.

3.2 Monoidal Attribute Grammar

We generalise the underlying semantic domain of AGs to arbitrary $\mathbb{C} \in \mathbf{TSMC}$. This generalisation is done by replacing sets with objects and attribute calculation rules with $\mathbb{C}$-morphisms.

Definition 2 ([12]). *Let $\mathbb{C} \in$ **TSMC**. A* monoidal attribute grammar *(MAG) for Δ in $\mathbb{C}$ is a triple (I, S, a) where for each type $\rho \in \Sigma$, $I\rho$ and $S\rho$ are $\mathbb{C}$-objects (of domains of inherited and synthesised attributes), and for each operator $o \in \Delta^{\rho_1 \cdots \rho_n \to \rho}$, a_o is a $\mathbb{C}$-morphism of type $a_o : S\rho_1 \otimes \cdots \otimes S\rho_n \otimes I\rho \to S\rho \otimes I\rho_1 \otimes \cdots \otimes I\rho_n$. We write $\mathbf{MAG}(\Delta, \mathbb{C})$ for the collection of MAGs for Δ in $\mathbb{C}$.*

Some instances of MAGs are studied in [12]; in the category ω**CPPO** of pointed CPOs and ω-continuous functions, monoidal attribute grammars are equivalent to Chirica and Martin's K-systems [4]. The category **Rel** of sets and relations has traced biproducts [11], and MAGs in this traced symmetric monoidal category are *local dependency graphs*, which are the standard tool to represent dependencies between the attributes in attribute calculation rules. MAGs over the compact closed structure on **Rel** are *relational attribute grammars* [5]. In addition to this, by comparing Definition 1 and 2, we conclude that SSUR-ACs are exactly MAGs in $\mathcal{L}(\Sigma)$.

Proposition 2. $\mathbf{SSUR\text{-}AC}(\Delta, \Sigma) = \mathbf{MAG}(\Delta, \mathcal{L}(\Sigma))$.

[2] Every traced symmetric monoidal category is equivalent to a traced symmetric strict monoidal category (coherence theorem).

3.3 MAGs as Algebras in $\mathbf{Int}(\mathbb{C})$

Below we give two concepts that are equivalent to MAG: one is algebras in the categories obtained by Joyal, Street and Verity's **Int** construction [11], and the other is traced symmetric strict monoidal functors of type $\mathcal{L}(\Sigma) \to \mathbf{Int}(\mathbb{C})$.

Let $\mathbb{C} \in \mathbf{TSMC}$. The category $\mathbf{Int}(\mathbb{C})$ is defined by the following data: an object is a pair (A^+, A^-) of $\mathbb{C}$-objects, and homsets are defined by

$$\mathbf{Int}(\mathbb{C})((A^+, A^-), (B^+, B^-)) = \mathbb{C}(A^+ \otimes B^-, B^+ \otimes A^-).$$

In category $\mathbf{Int}(\mathbb{C})$ we can naturally model computation over bidirectional information flow. An object (A^+, A^-) denotes the type of upward and downward information; in the context of attribute grammar, they correspond to the type of synthesised and inherited attributes, respectively. A morphism $f : (A^+, A^-) \to (B^+, B^-)$ then represents a computation that processes bidirectional information flow.

We give a symmetric strict monoidal structure to $\mathbf{Int}(\mathbb{C})$ by

$$\mathbf{I}^{\mathbf{Int}(\mathbb{C})} = (\mathbf{I}^{\mathbb{C}}, \mathbf{I}^{\mathbb{C}}), \qquad (A^+, A^-) \otimes^{\mathbf{Int}(\mathbb{C})} (B^+, B^-) = (A^+ \otimes^{\mathbb{C}} B^+, A^- \otimes^{\mathbb{C}} B^-).$$

The category $\mathbf{Int}(\mathbb{C})$ has a *compact closed structure* [11], which yields the *canonical trace operator* with respect to the above symmetric monoidal structure. The mapping $\mathbb{C} \mapsto \mathbf{Int}(\mathbb{C})$ extends to a 2-endofunctor over **TSMC**, and moreover, to a pseudo-monad $(\mathbf{Int}, (N, n), (M, m), \tau, \lambda, \rho)$ over **TSMC**; see Appendix B for the detail.

We extend the concept of Σ-algebra from the set-theoretic one to the categorical one. A Σ-algebra in a monoidal category $\mathbb{C}$ is a pair (A, a) where A is a family of $\mathbb{C}$-objects indexed by Σ-types and a is a family of $\mathbb{C}$-morphisms indexed by Σ-operators, such that the type of a_o is $A\rho_1 \otimes \cdots \otimes A\rho_n \to A\rho$ for each operator $o \in \Sigma^{\rho_1 \cdots \rho_n \to \rho}$. We write $\mathbf{Alg}_\Sigma(\mathbb{C})$ for the collection of Σ-algebras in $\mathbb{C}$. The concept of Σ-algebras has another presentation: there is a natural bijection between Σ-algebras in $\mathbb{C}$ and traced symmetric strict monoidal functors from $\mathcal{L}(\Sigma)$ to $\mathbb{C}$:

$$\mathbf{Alg}_\Sigma(\mathbb{C}) \simeq \mathbf{TSMC}_s(\mathcal{L}(\Sigma), \mathbb{C}) \tag{4}$$

Let (I, S, a) be a MAG for Δ in $\mathbb{C} \in \mathbf{TSMC}$. We define $A\rho$ to be the pair $(S\rho, I\rho)$ of $\mathbb{C}$-objects (note that it is an object in $\mathbf{Int}(\mathbb{C})$). Then for each operator $o \in \Sigma^{\rho_1 \cdots \rho_n \to \rho}$, the $\mathbb{C}$-morphism a_o can be seen as an $\mathbf{Int}(\mathbb{C})$-morphism:

$$a_o \in \mathbb{C}(S\rho_1 \otimes \cdots \otimes S\rho_n \otimes I\rho, S\rho \otimes I\rho_1 \otimes \cdots \otimes I\rho_n) = \mathbf{Int}(\mathbb{C})(A\rho_1 \otimes \cdots \otimes A\rho_n, A\rho).$$

This means that every MAG determines a Δ-algebra (A, a) in $\mathbf{Int}(\mathbb{C})$, and the other way around. We summarise these concepts by the following bijective correspondences:

$$\mathbf{MAG}(\Delta, \mathbb{C}) \simeq \mathbf{Alg}_\Delta(\mathbf{Int}(\mathbb{C})) \simeq \mathbf{TSMC}_s(\mathcal{L}(\Delta), \mathbf{Int}(\mathbb{C})) \tag{5}$$

$$\mathbf{SSUR\text{-}AC}(\Delta, \Sigma) \simeq \mathbf{TSMC}_s(\mathcal{L}(\Delta), \mathbf{Int}(\mathcal{L}(\Sigma))). \tag{6}$$

These three equivalent forms have different advantages. The first form is the actual data we give when defining AGs. The second form is used to explain the initial algebra semantics of AGs [12]. The third form is suitable for discussing the descriptional composition. We mainly adopt the functorial representation of AGs and ACs below.

4 Descriptional Composition

We begin with a categorical formulation of the descriptional composition of SSUR-ACs. Let $\mathcal{A} \in$ **SSUR-AC**(Δ, Σ) and $\mathcal{B} \in$ **MAG**$(\Sigma, \mathbb{C})$, regarded as functors. We define their (categorical) descriptional composition $\mathcal{B} \circledcirc \mathcal{A}$ by

$$\mathcal{B} \circledcirc \mathcal{A} = \mathbf{Str}(\mathcal{B}^{\#} \circ \mathcal{A}),$$

where $\mathcal{B}^{\#} = M_{\mathbb{C}} \circ \mathbf{Int}(\mathcal{B})$ is the Kleisli lifting of $\mathcal{B}$ by the pseudo-monad **Int**. We insert the strictification operator **Str** (Section 3.1) as $\mathcal{B}^{\#}$ is not strict monoidal.[3] The SSUR-AC $\mathcal{A}$ constructs bidirectional networks of Σ-operators, while $\mathcal{B}$ can only accept single-directional networks of them. The Kleisli lifting extends the domain of $\mathcal{B}$ to the bidirectional network of Σ-operators (see Figure of 5) so that this mismatch is resolved.

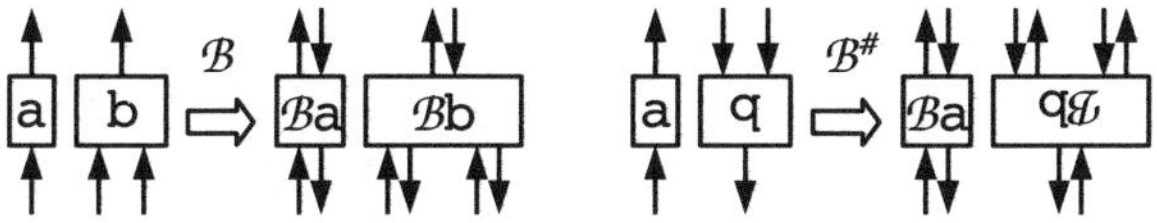

Fig. 5. Kleisli Lifting of $\mathcal{B}$

Theorem 1. *1. SSUR-ACs are closed under the descriptional composition.*
*2. The descriptional composition is associative up to a natural isomorphisms; for any $\mathcal{A} \in$ **SSUR-AC**$(\Delta, \Sigma), \mathcal{B} \in$ **SSUR-AC**(Σ, Ξ) and $C \in$ **MAG**$(\Xi, \mathbb{C})$, there is a natural isomorphism between $(C \circledcirc \mathcal{B}) \circledcirc \mathcal{A}$ and $C \circledcirc (\mathcal{B} \circledcirc \mathcal{A})$.*

We do not prove this theorem as it is subsumed by Theorem 2. We note that the associativity of the descriptional composition holds only up to a natural isomorphism. This isomorphism has no computational meaning; it just permutes the order of arguments. This permutation is invisible in the syntactic study of the descriptional composition because arguments are passed by records rather than tuples.

We extend this formulation of the descriptional composition to a more general setting where TSMCs are equipped with some extra structures, such as nondeterminism, undefined values, stacks, etc. To capture such extensions, we introduce the concept of *extension of TSMC*.

Definition 3. *We call the following situation an* extension of TSMC.

1. *There is a 2-category* **TSMC**$'$ *and its 2-subcategory* **TSMC**$'_s$.
2. *There is a 2-functor U :* **TSMC**$'$ $\to$ **TSMC** *that can be restricted to a 2-functor U_s :* **TSMC**$'_s$ $\to$ **TSMC**$_s$*. Furthermore, U_s, as an ordinary functor, has a left adjoint F. We write $\overline{(-)}$: $|\mathbf{TSMC}(F\mathbb{C}, \mathbb{D})| \to |\mathbf{TSMC}(\mathbb{C}, U_s\mathbb{D})|$ for the bijection between homsets, and $\underline{(-)}$ for its inverse.*
3. *There is a pseudo-monad $(\mathbf{Int}', (N', n'), (M', m'), \tau', \lambda', \rho')$ over* **TSMC**$'$ *such that* **Int**$'$ *is a 2-functor, and is a strict lifting of the pseudo-monad* **Int** *along U, that is, $U \circ \mathbf{Int}' = \mathbf{Int} \circ U$, $U(N'_F) = N_{UF}$, $U\tau'_{\mathbb{C}} = \tau_{U\mathbb{C}}$, etc. We note that the Kleisli lifting $(-)^{\flat}$ of* **Int**$'$ *also commutes with U, that is, $U((\mathcal{A})^{\flat}) = (U\mathcal{A})^{\#}$.*

[3] This is because the multiplication $M_{\mathbb{C}} : \mathbf{Int}^2(\mathbb{C}) \to \mathbf{Int}(\mathbb{C})$ is not strict monoidal.

4. *There is an equivalence* $\overline{\mathbf{Str}'} : \mathbf{TSMC}'(F\mathcal{L}(\Sigma), \mathbb{C}) \to \mathbf{TSMC}'_s(F\mathcal{L}(\Sigma), \mathbb{C})$ *such that* $\overline{\mathbf{Str}'(F)} = \mathbf{Str}(\overline{F})$, *and for any functor* $F \in \mathbf{TSMC}'_s$ *and* $G, H \in \mathbf{TSMC}'$ *of appropriate type,* $\mathbf{Str}'(F) = F$ *and* $\mathbf{Str}'(H \circ G \circ F) = \mathbf{Str}'(H \circ \mathbf{Str}'(G \circ F))$.

We express such a situation by a tuple $\mathcal{E} = (F, U, \mathbf{Int}')$.

Definition 4. *Let* $\mathcal{E} = (F, U, \mathbf{Int}')$ *be an extension of TSMC. We define the collection of* $\mathcal{E}$*-MAG for* Δ *in* $\mathbb{C} \in \mathbf{TSMC}'$ *and* $\mathcal{E}$*-AC from* Δ *to* Σ *by*

$$\mathcal{E}\text{-}\mathbf{MAG}(\Delta, \mathbb{C}) = \mathbf{TSMC}_s(\mathcal{L}(\Delta), \mathbf{Int}(U\mathbb{C})) \simeq \mathbf{MAG}(\Delta, U\mathbb{C})$$
$$\mathcal{E}\text{-}\mathbf{AC}(\Delta, \Sigma) = \mathbf{TSMC}_s(\mathcal{L}(\Delta), \mathbf{Int}(UF\mathcal{L}(\Sigma))) \simeq \mathbf{MAG}(\Delta, UF\mathcal{L}(\Sigma)).$$

Let $\mathcal{A} \in \mathcal{E}\text{-}\mathbf{AC}(\Delta, \Sigma)$ and $\mathcal{B} \in \mathcal{E}\text{-}\mathbf{MAG}(\Sigma, \mathbb{C})$. We define their descriptional composition $\mathcal{B} \copyright \mathcal{A}$ by

$$\mathcal{B} \copyright \mathcal{A} = \mathbf{Str}(U((\underline{\mathcal{B}})^{\flat}) \circ \mathcal{A}).$$

We write $H_{\mathbb{C}} : \mathbb{C} \to FU_s\mathbb{C}$ for the unit of the adjunction $F \dashv U_s$. We assume that any $\mathcal{E}$-AC $\mathcal{A}$ between rooted signatures satisfies $\mathcal{A}(\#) = (\mathbf{I}, H(\#))$. We define the translation $T\mathcal{A} : UF\mathcal{L}(\Delta^+)(\mathbf{I}, H\#) \to UF\mathcal{L}(\Sigma^+)(\mathbf{I}, H\#)$ induced by $\mathcal{A} \in \mathcal{E}\text{-}\mathbf{AC}(\Delta^+, \Sigma^+)$ as follows:

$$T\mathcal{A}(f) = \text{unique } g \text{ such that } U\underline{\mathcal{A}}(f) = N_{UF\mathcal{L}(\Sigma)}(g).$$

This is well-defined as N is full and faithful [11]. When we do not consider the extension ($F = U = \mathrm{Id}$), the translation $T\mathcal{A}$ is just a mapping of $f \in \mathcal{L}(\Delta^+)(\epsilon, \#)$ to a morphism in $\mathcal{L}(\Sigma^+)(\epsilon, \#)$. Under the identification of terms and morphisms in a free TSMC, $T\mathcal{A}$ represents the term translation induced by the attribute coupling $\mathcal{A}$.

Theorem 2. *Let* $\mathcal{E}$ *be an extension of TSMC.*

1. $\mathcal{E}$*-ACs are closed under descriptional composition.*
2. *For any* $\mathcal{A} \in \mathcal{E}\text{-}\mathbf{AC}(\Delta, \Sigma), \mathcal{B} \in \mathcal{E}\text{-}\mathbf{AC}(\Sigma, \Xi)$ *and* $C \in \mathcal{E}\text{-}\mathbf{MAG}(\Xi, \mathbb{C})$, *there is a natural isomorphism between* $(C \copyright \mathcal{B}) \copyright \mathcal{A}$ *and* $C \copyright (\mathcal{B} \copyright \mathcal{A})$.
3. *For any* $\mathcal{A} \in \mathcal{E}\text{-}\mathbf{AC}(\Delta^+, \Sigma^+), \mathcal{B} \in \mathcal{E}\text{-}\mathbf{AC}(\Sigma^+, \Xi^+)$ *and* $f \in \mathcal{L}(\Delta^+)(\epsilon, \#)$, *we have* $T(\mathcal{B} \copyright \mathcal{A}) \circ H_{\mathcal{L}(\Delta^+)}(f) = T\mathcal{B} \circ T\mathcal{A} \circ H_{\mathcal{L}(\Delta^+)}(f)$.

The proof is in Appendix A.

Corollary 1. *For any composable SSUR-ACs* $\mathcal{A}, \mathcal{B}$, *we have* $T(\mathcal{B} \copyright \mathcal{A}) = T\mathcal{B} \circ T\mathcal{A}$.

In the subsequent sections, we show that some useful extensions of (SSUR)-ACs can be captured as attribute couplings in extensions of TSMC. From the above general theorem, the associativity of the descriptional composition and the closure property of extended ACs under the descriptional composition.

4.1 Descriptional Composition for Nondeterministic ACs

We look at an example of an extension of TSMC arising from a symmetric monoidal monad $(T, \eta, \mu, \phi_{\mathbf{I}}, \phi_{A,B})$ over **Set**. [4] Given such a monad, for a category $\mathbb{C}$, we define a

[4] This is equivalent to a commutative monad [16].

new category $T_*(\mathbb{C})$ by the following data: $|T_*(\mathbb{C})| = |\mathbb{C}|$ and $T_*(\mathbb{C})(A,B) = T(\mathbb{C}(A,B))$. The identity and composition of $T_*(\mathbb{C})$ defined as follows:

$$1 \xrightarrow{\phi_I} T1 \xrightarrow{T(\mathrm{id}^{\mathbb{C}}_A)} T_*(\mathbb{C})(A,A)$$

$$T_*(\mathbb{C})(B,C) \times T_*(\mathbb{C})(A,B) \xrightarrow{\phi_{\mathbb{C}(B,C),\mathbb{C}(A,B)}} T(\mathbb{C}(B,C) \times \mathbb{C}(A,B)) \xrightarrow{T(comp^{\mathbb{C}})} T_*(\mathbb{C})(A,C).$$

This construction is well-known as *change-of-base* in enriched category theory. The mapping $\mathbb{C} \mapsto T_*\mathbb{C}$ extends to a 2-monad (T_*, μ_*, η_*) over **TSMC** and $\mathbf{TSMC}_s$. We write $\mathbf{TSMC}^{T_*}$ for the 2-category of strict T_*-algebras (which are exactly T-algebra enriched TSMCs), strict T_*-algebra morphisms and T_*-algebra transformations; see [2] for the detail. We also write $\mathbf{TSMC}_s^{T_*}$ for its 2-subcategory such that T_*-algebra morphisms belong to $\mathbf{TSMC}_s$. The Eilenberg-Moore 2-adjunction $F \dashv U : \mathbf{TSMC}^{T_*} \to \mathbf{TSMC}$ can be restricted to $F_s \dashv U_s : \mathbf{TSMC}_s^{T_*} \to \mathbf{TSMC}_s$. One can easily extend the strictification operator **Str** to the one satisfying the condition 4 of Definition 3.

To lift the pseudo-monad **Int** to the 2-category $\mathbf{TSMC}^{T_*}$, we (necessarily) give a pseudo-distributive law [21] of T_* over **Int**. In fact, it consists only of identities, as the components of **Int** and T_* commutes with each other, such as $\mathbf{Int}(T_*(\mathbb{C})) = T_*(\mathbf{Int}(\mathbb{C}))$, $T_*(N_{\mathbb{C}}) = N_{T_*\mathbb{C}}$, $\mathbf{Int}((\mu_*)_{\mathbb{C}}) = (\mu_*)_{\mathbf{Int}(\mathbb{C})}$, etc. Thus the above data determine an extension of TSMC.

Example 1. We write $\mathcal{P} : \mathbf{Set} \to \mathbf{Set}$ for the covariant powerset monad. Let $\mathbb{C} \in \mathbf{TSMC}$. A monoidal attribute grammar (I, S, a) for Σ in $\mathcal{P}_*(\mathbb{C})$ assigns $\mathbb{C}$-objects $I\rho, S\rho$ to each type $\rho \in \Sigma$, and a $\mathcal{P}_*(\mathbb{C})$-morphism

$$a_o \in \mathcal{P}_*(\mathbb{C})(S\rho_1 \otimes \cdots \otimes S\rho_n \otimes I\rho, S\rho \otimes I\rho_1 \otimes \cdots \otimes I\rho_n)$$

to each operator $o \in \Sigma^{\rho_1 \cdots \rho_n \to \rho}$; this means that a $\mathcal{P}_*$-MAG assigns an attribute calculation rule *nondeterministically* to each operator in Σ. For instance, we consider the following $\mathcal{P}_*$-AC from Σ_{nat} to Σ_{list}:

$$I(*) = \epsilon, \qquad S(*) = *,$$

$$a_{\mathsf{Z}} = \{[]\}, \qquad a_{\mathsf{S}} = \{(\lambda x\,.\,\mathsf{let}\ y = 0 :: x\ \mathsf{in}\ y), (\lambda x\,.\,\mathsf{let}\ y = 1 :: x\ \mathsf{in}\ y)\}.$$

This AC maps each natural number $\mathsf{S}^{(n)}(\mathsf{Z})$ to the set of all binary digit with length n, represented as morphisms of type $\epsilon \to *$ in $\mathcal{P}_*(\mathcal{L}(\Sigma_{\mathrm{list}}))$.

4.2 Descriptional Composition for Quasi-SSUR ACs

In [20], Nishimura and Nakano introduced a relaxation of SSUR called *quasi-SSUR*. It relaxes the linear use (exactly once) of variables to affine use (at most once), and introduces a constant denoting the undefined value to the language for attribute calculation rules. We formulate their quasi-SSUR ACs and the descriptional composition of them in our categorical framework.

First, we introduce the language $\mathcal{A}(\Sigma)$ that modifies the typing rules of $\mathcal{L}(\Sigma)$ so that variables can be discarded, and that has an extra constant $\bot_\rho$ for each type $\rho \in \Sigma$. These features directly correspond to Nishimura and Nakano's modification of SSUR. The detail of $\mathcal{A}(\Sigma)$ is the following:

1. We replace the typing rule of $\mathcal{L}(\Sigma)$ in Figure 4 as follows:

$$\frac{\Gamma_1 \vdash_E M_1 : \rho_1 \quad \cdots \quad \Gamma_l \vdash_E M_l : \rho_l \quad \mathrm{U} \subseteq \mathrm{D}}{\vdash_M \lambda x \,.\, \mathsf{let}\, y_1 = M_1, \cdots, y_l = M_l \,\mathsf{in}\, z : \sigma_1, \cdots, \sigma_n \to \tau_1, \cdots, \tau_m}$$

   What is new to $\mathcal{L}(\Sigma)$ is that some defined variables may be unused ($\mathrm{U} \subseteq \mathrm{D}$). For instance, the following is now a valid derivation in $\mathcal{A}(\Sigma)$:

$$\frac{}{\vdash_M \lambda x_1 \cdots x_n \,.\, \mathsf{let}\, \epsilon \,\mathsf{in}\, \epsilon : \rho_1 \cdots \rho_n \to \epsilon}$$

   We write this expression $\top_{\rho_1 \cdots \rho_n}$.
2. We add to $\mathcal{L}(\Sigma)$ a constant $\bot_\rho : \rho$ for each type $\rho \in \Sigma$, corresponding to undef in [20]. We then extend this to any sequence of Σ-types by

$$\bot_{\rho_1 \cdots \rho_n} = (\lambda \epsilon \,.\, \mathsf{let}\, x_1 = \bot_{\rho_1}, \cdots, x_n = \bot_{\rho_n} \,\mathsf{in}\, x_1, \cdots, x_n).$$

Definition 5. *A quasi-SSUR AC from Δ to Σ is a triple (I, S, a) where for each type $\rho \in \Delta$, $I\rho$ and $S\rho$ are sequences of Σ-types, and for each $o \in \Delta^{\rho_1, \cdots, \rho_n \to \rho}$, a_o is an $\mathcal{A}(\Sigma)$-expression of type $a_o : S\rho_1, \cdots, S\rho_n, I\rho \to S\rho, I\rho_1, \cdots, I\rho_n$.*

We next introduce the concept of *bipointed TSMC*. It is a triple $(\mathbb{C}, \top, \bot)$ where $\mathbb{C} \in$ **TSMC** and $\top, \bot$ are $\mathbb{C}$-object indexed families of morphisms $\top_A : A \to \mathbf{I}$ and $\bot_A : \mathbf{I} \to A$ such that

$$\top_{\mathbf{I}} = \mathrm{id}_{\mathbf{I}}, \qquad \top_{A \otimes B} = \top_A \otimes \top_B, \qquad \bot_{\mathbf{I}} = \mathrm{id}_{\mathbf{I}}, \qquad \bot_{A \otimes B} = \top_A \otimes \top_B. \tag{7}$$

Discarding variables is modelled by the morphism $\top$. We say that a traced symmetric strong monoidal functor $(F, \phi_{\mathbf{I}}, \phi_{A,B})$ *preserves bipoints* if it satisfies $F(\bot_A) \circ \phi_{\mathbf{I}} = \bot_{FA}$ and $\phi_{\mathbf{I}} \circ \top_{FA} = F(\top_A)$. We write $\mathbf{TSMC}^\bullet$ for the 2-category of bipointed TSMCs, traced symmetric strong monoidal functors preserving bipoints and monoidal natural isomorphisms. We write $\mathbf{TSMC}^\bullet_s$ for its 2-subcategory consisting of traced symmetric strict monoidal functors. There is an evident forgetful functor $U^\bullet : \mathbf{TSMC}^\bullet \to \mathbf{TSMC}$ that can be restricted to $U^\bullet_s : \mathbf{TSMC}^\bullet_s \to \mathbf{TSMC}_s$, and it has an ordinary left adjoint $F^\bullet : \mathbf{TSMC}_s \to \mathbf{TSMC}^\bullet_s$ that freely adds morphisms $\bot_A : \mathbf{I} \to A$ and $\top_A : A \to \mathbf{I}$, subject to the equations in (7).

The **Int** construction can be lifted over $\mathbf{TSMC}^\bullet$. For a bipointed TSMC $(\mathbb{C}, \bot, \top)$, we define $\mathbf{Int}(\mathbb{C})$-morphisms $\bot^{\mathbf{Int}(\mathbb{C})}_A$ and $\top^{\mathbf{Int}(\mathbb{C})}_A$ by

$$\bot^{\mathbf{Int}(\mathbb{C})}_A = \bot_{A^+} \otimes \top_{A^-}, \qquad \top^{\mathbf{Int}(\mathbb{C})}_A = \top_{A^+} \otimes \bot_{A^-}.$$

Then we define $\mathbf{Int}^\bullet(\mathbb{C}, \bot, \top)$ to be the tuple $(\mathbf{Int}(\mathbb{C}), \bot^{\mathbf{Int}(\mathbb{C})}, \top^{\mathbf{Int}(\mathbb{C})})$. One can easily check that this is a bipointed TSMC. The mapping $(\mathbb{C}, \bot, \top) \mapsto \mathbf{Int}^\bullet(\mathbb{C}, \bot, \top)$ extends to a 2-functor over $\mathbf{TSMC}^\bullet$, and the pseudo-monad structure of **Int** also makes $\mathbf{Int}^\bullet$ a pseudo-monad. Furthermore, it is a strict lifting of **Int** along U.

Proposition 3. *The triple $\mathcal{E}^\bullet = (F^\bullet, U^\bullet, \mathbf{Int}^\bullet)$ forms an extension of TSMCs.*

Proposition 4. *The tuple $(\mathcal{A}(\Sigma), \bot, \top)$ is a bipointed TSMC, and it is equivalent to $F(\mathcal{L}(\Sigma))$. Therefore, quasi-SSUR ACs are $\mathcal{E}^\bullet$-ACs.*

4.3 Descriptional Composition for Stack AGs

In [18], Nakano introduced an extension of AC called *stack AC*, where we can use stacks in attribute calculation rules. He then showed that the stack ACs satisfying certain linearity condition are closed under the descriptional composition. Inspired by his extension, below we express his theory of stack ACs in our categorical framework by setting-up an appropriate extension of TSMC. Our approach differs from Nakano's work as follows: 1) the concept of stack ACs given below allow stacks to be stack elements, and 2) we represent the empty stack by undefined stack $\bot$, and combine stack deconstructors (head, tail) into single operator dec.

We introduce a language $\mathcal{S}(\Sigma)$ and capture the stack ACs satisfying a linearity condition as AGs in $\mathcal{S}(\Sigma)$. In this language we can use a stack of type ρ, whose type is denoted by ρ^∞. Stacks are then manipulated by two operators: constructor $\mathsf{cons} : \rho, \rho^\infty \to \rho^\infty$ and deconstructor $\mathsf{dec} : \rho^\infty \to \rho, \rho^\infty$. The operator cons pushes a given value on a given stack, while dec separates the top value of a given stack from the rest of it.

We move on to the formal definition of $\mathcal{S}(\Sigma)$. First, we define $\mathcal{S}(\Sigma)_0$ to be the set of pairs of the form (n, ρ) where n is a natural number and ρ is a Σ-type. We identify a type $\rho \in \Sigma$ and the pair $(0, \rho) \in \mathcal{S}(\Sigma)_0$. We denote a pair (n, ρ) by $\rho^{\infty\cdots\infty}$, where n is the length of ∞'s on the shoulder. Next, we define $|\mathcal{S}(\Sigma)|$ to be the set of finite sequences of $\mathcal{S}(\Sigma)_0$. Below we use metavariables B and C to denote elements in $\mathcal{S}(\Sigma)_0$ and $|\mathcal{S}(\Sigma)|$, respectively. The set of raw terms of $\mathcal{S}(\Sigma)$ is defined by

$$M ::= \lambda \boldsymbol{x}.\, \mathrm{let}\ \boldsymbol{D}\ \mathrm{in}\ \boldsymbol{x}$$
$$D ::= x = x \mid x = o(\boldsymbol{x}) \mid x = \bot_B \mid x = \mathsf{cons}_B(x, x) \mid x, x = \mathsf{dec}_B(x).$$

The typing rules of $\mathcal{S}(\Sigma)$ extends the one for $\mathcal{A}(\Sigma)$ with cons and dec:

$$\frac{}{x : B \vdash_E x : B} \qquad \frac{}{\vdash_E \bot_B : B} \qquad \frac{o \in \Sigma^{\rho_1 \cdots \rho_n \to \rho}}{x_1 : \rho_1, \cdots, x_n : \rho_n \vdash_E o(x_1, \cdots, x_n) : \rho}$$

$$\frac{}{x : B, y : B^\infty \vdash_E \mathsf{cons}_B(x, y) : B^\infty} \qquad \frac{}{x : B^\infty \vdash_E \mathsf{dec}_B(x) : B, B^\infty}$$

$$\frac{\Gamma_1 \vdash_E M_1 : C_1 \quad \cdots \quad \Gamma_l \vdash_E M_l : C_l \quad \mathrm{U} \subseteq \mathrm{D}}{\vdash_M \lambda \boldsymbol{x}\,.\ \mathsf{let}\ \boldsymbol{y}_1 = M_1, \cdots, \boldsymbol{y}_l = M_l\ \mathsf{in}\ \boldsymbol{z} : C' \to C''}$$

where $\mathrm{U} = \Gamma_1 \cup \cdots \cup \Gamma_l \cup \{\boldsymbol{z} : C''\}$ and $\mathrm{D} = \{\boldsymbol{x} : C', \boldsymbol{y}_1 : C_1, \cdots, \boldsymbol{y}_l : C_l\}$, and each variable in $\Gamma_1, \cdots, \Gamma_n, \boldsymbol{x}, \boldsymbol{y}, \boldsymbol{z}$ is different from the other. The set of axioms for $\mathcal{S}(\Sigma)$-expressions extends the one for $\mathcal{A}(\Sigma)$ with the following rules (leading λ is omitted):

$$(\mathsf{let}\ x, y = \mathsf{dec}_B(z), z = \mathsf{cons}_B(x', y'), D\ \mathsf{in}\ \boldsymbol{v}) = (\mathsf{let}\ x = x', y = y', D\ \mathsf{in}\ \boldsymbol{v})$$
$$(\mathsf{let}\ x, y = \mathsf{dec}_B(z), z = \bot_{B^\infty}, D\ \mathsf{in}\ \boldsymbol{v}) = (\mathsf{let}\ x = \bot_B, y = \bot_{B^\infty}, D\ \mathsf{in}\ \boldsymbol{v})$$
$$(\mathsf{let}\ z = \mathsf{cons}_B(x, y), D\ \mathsf{in}\ \boldsymbol{v}) = (\mathsf{let}\ D\ \mathsf{in}\ \boldsymbol{v} \quad (z \notin FV(D) \cup \boldsymbol{v} \cup \{y\})).$$

Definition 6. *A quasi-SSUR stack AC from Δ to Σ is a triple (I, S, a) where for each type $\rho \in \Delta$, $I\rho, S\rho \in |\mathcal{S}(\Sigma)|$, and for each operator $o \in \Delta^{\rho_1, \cdots, \rho_n \to \rho}$, a_o is an $\mathcal{S}(\Sigma)$-expression of type $a_o : S\rho_1, \cdots, S\rho_n, I\rho \to S\rho, I\rho_1, \cdots, I\rho_n$.*

Example 2. This example is from [18]. We consider a stack AC that converts reverse-polish notations to ordinary expressions. Let Σ_p and Σ_e be signatures defined as follows:

$$\Sigma_p = (\{*\}, \{\mathsf{p}_n^{*\to*}, \mathsf{a}^{*\to*}, \mathsf{m}^{*\to*}, \mathsf{r}^{\to*}\}) \quad (n \in \mathbf{N}),$$
$$\Sigma_e = (\{*\}, \{\mathsf{num}_n^{\to*}, \mathsf{add}^{*,*\to*}, \mathsf{mul}^{*,*\to*}\}) \quad (n \in \mathbf{N}).$$

The signature Σ_p is for the reverse-polish notation of expressions. For instance, a Σ_p-expression $\mathsf{p}_3(\mathsf{p}_2(\mathsf{p}_5(\mathsf{a}(\mathsf{m}(\mathsf{r})))))$ denotes $(5+2)*3$. The stack AC (I, S, a) that constructs Σ_e-terms from reverse-polish expressions is the following (type annotations are omitted):

$$I* = (*)^\infty, O* = *$$
$$a_{\mathsf{p}_n} = \lambda s_1, i\,.\, \mathsf{let}\ i_1 = \mathsf{cons}(\mathsf{num}_n, i)\ \mathsf{in}\ s_1, i_1$$
$$a_{\mathsf{a}} = \lambda s_1, i\,.\, \mathsf{let}\ h_1, t_1 = \mathsf{dec}(i), h_2, t_2 = \mathsf{dec}(t_1), i_1 = \mathsf{cons}(\mathsf{add}(h_1, h_2), t_2)\ \mathsf{in}\ s_1, i_1$$
$$a_{\mathsf{m}} = \lambda s_1, i\,.\, \mathsf{let}\ h_1, t_1 = \mathsf{dec}(i), h_2, t_2 = \mathsf{dec}(t_1), i_1 = \mathsf{cons}(\mathsf{mul}(h_1, h_2), i_2)\ \mathsf{in}\ s_1, i_1$$
$$a_{\mathsf{r}} = \lambda i\,.\, \mathsf{let}\ h, t = \mathsf{dec}(i)\ \mathsf{in}\ h.$$

Definition 7. *A* TSMC with stack *is a tuple* $(\mathbb{C}, \bot, \top, (-)^\infty, \mathsf{cons}, \mathsf{dec})$ *where*

- $(\mathbb{C}, \bot, \top)$ *is a bipointed TSMC,*
- $(-)^\infty : |\mathbb{C}| \to |\mathbb{C}|$ *is a mapping such that* $\mathbf{I}^\infty = \mathbf{I}$ *and* $(A \otimes B)^\infty = A^\infty \otimes B^\infty$,
- $\mathsf{cons}_A : A \otimes A^\infty \to A^\infty$ *and* $\mathsf{dec}_A : A^\infty \to A \otimes A^\infty$ *are* $\mathbb{C}$*-object indexed families of morphisms such that*

$$\mathsf{dec}_A \circ \mathsf{cons}_A = \mathrm{id}_{A\otimes A^\infty}, \qquad \mathsf{dec}_{\mathbf{I}} = \mathsf{cons}_{\mathbf{I}} = \mathrm{id}_{\mathbf{I}},$$
$$\mathsf{dec}_A \circ \bot_A = \bot_A \otimes \bot_{A^\infty}, \qquad \top_A \circ \mathsf{cons}_A = \top_A \otimes \top_{A^\infty},$$
$$\mathsf{cons}_{A\otimes B} = (\mathsf{cons}_A \otimes \mathsf{cons}_B) \circ (A \otimes \sigma_{B\otimes A^\infty} \otimes B^\infty),$$
$$\mathsf{dec}_{A\otimes B} = (A \otimes \sigma_{A^\infty\otimes B} \otimes B^\infty) \circ (\mathsf{dec}_A \otimes \mathsf{dec}_B).$$

A stack-preserving functor *between TSMCs with stack is a traced symmetric strong monoidal functor* $(F, \phi_{\mathbf{I}}, \phi_{A,B})$ *such that it preserves bipoints,* $F(A^\infty) = (FA)^\infty$ *and*

$$F(\mathsf{cons}_A) \circ \phi_{A,A^\infty} = \mathsf{cons}_{FA} \qquad \phi_{A,A^\infty} \circ \mathsf{dec}_{FA} = F(\mathsf{dec}_A).$$

We define $\mathbf{TSMC}^S$ *to be the 2-category of TSMCs with stack, stack-preserving functors and monoidal natural isomorphisms. Its 2-subcategory consisting of traced symmetric strict monoidal functors is denoted by* $\mathbf{TSMC}^S_s$*. We write* $U^S : \mathbf{TSMC}^S \to \mathbf{TSMC}$ *for the canonical forgetful functor.*

Next, U^S can be restricted to a 2-functor $U^S_s : \mathbf{TSMC}^S_s \to \mathbf{TSMC}_s$, and when viewed as an ordinary functor, it has a left adjoint $F^S : \mathbf{TSMC}_s \to \mathbf{TSMC}^S_s$. This left adjoint constructs a syntactic TSMC with stacks from a given category. We omit its detail, but an object of the category $F^S\mathbb{C}$ is an element of the countably infinite coproduct of the monoid $(|\mathbb{C}|, \mathbf{I}, \otimes)$, that is, a sequence $(k_1, C_1)\cdots(k_n, C_n)$ such that $k_i \in \mathbf{N}$, $C_i \in |\mathbb{C}|$ $(1 \le i \le n)$ and $k_i \ne k_j$ if $i \ne j$. The unit $H_{\mathbb{C}}$ and counit $E_{\mathbb{C}}$ of the adjunction is defined by (on objects) $H_{\mathbb{C}}(C) = (0, C)$ and $H_{\mathbb{C}}(k_1, C_1)\cdots(k_n, C_n) = \bigotimes_{i=1}^n C_i^{\infty(k_i)}$. The category $F^S\mathcal{L}(\mathbb{C})$ admits the strictification operator $\mathbf{Str}^S$ satisfying the condition 4 of Definition 3; on objects it is defined by $\mathbf{Str}^S(F)((k_1, \rho_1)\cdots(k_n, \rho_n)) = \bigotimes_{1\le i\le n, 1\le j\le|\rho_i|}(F\rho_{ij})^{\infty(k_i)}$.

Let $(\mathbb{C}, \bot, \top, (-)^\infty, \mathsf{cons}, \mathsf{dec}) \in \mathbf{TSMC}^S$, which we just write $\mathbb{C}$. We define the tuple $\mathbf{Int}^S(\mathbb{C}) = (\mathbf{Int}(\mathbb{C}), \bot^{\mathbf{Int}(\mathbb{C})}, \top^{\mathbf{Int}(\mathbb{C})}, (-)^{\infty^{\mathbf{Int}(\mathbb{C})}}, \mathsf{cons}^{\mathbf{Int}(\mathbb{C})}, \mathsf{dec}^{\mathbf{Int}(\mathbb{C})})$ by

$$\bot_A^{\mathbf{Int}(\mathbb{C})} = \bot_{A^+} \otimes \top_{A^-}, \quad \top_A^{\mathbf{Int}(\mathbb{C})} = \top_{A^+} \otimes \bot_{A^-}, \quad A^{\infty^{\mathbf{Int}(\mathbb{C})}} = ((A^-)^\infty, (A^+)^\infty),$$
$$\mathsf{cons}_A^{\mathbf{Int}(\mathbb{C})} = \mathsf{cons}_{A^+} \otimes \mathsf{dec}_{A^-}, \quad \mathsf{dec}_A^{\mathbf{Int}(\mathbb{C})} = \mathsf{dec}_{A^+} \otimes \mathsf{cons}_{A^-}.$$

We define $\mathbf{Int}^S$ of 1-cells and 2-cells in $\mathbf{TSMC}^S$ to be **Int** of them. In this way $\mathbf{Int}^S$ becomes a 2-functor. One can check that we can adopt the structure of the pseudo-monad **Int** to make $\mathbf{Int}^S$ a pseudo-monad over $\mathbf{TSMC}^S$. Thus we obtain a pseudo-monad $\mathbf{Int}^S : \mathbf{TSMC}^S \to \mathbf{TSMC}^S$ which is a strict lifting of the pseudo-monad **Int** along U^S.

Proposition 5. *The triple $\mathcal{E}^S = (F^S, U^S, \mathbf{Int}^S)$ forms an extension of TSMC.*

Proposition 6. *The tuple $(\mathcal{S}(\Sigma), \bot, \top, (-)^\infty, \mathsf{cons}, \mathsf{dec})$ is a TSMC with stack, and is equivalent to $F^S(\mathcal{L}(\Sigma))$. Therefore, quasi-SSUR stack ACs are $\mathcal{E}^S$-ACs.*

5 Conclusion and Discussion

We presented a categorical framework for capturing various extensions of ACs and their descriptional composition. By setting up appropriate extensions of TSMCs, the descriptional composition of non-deterministic ACs, quasi-SSUR ACs and quasi-SSUR stack ACs are covered by our framework. The framework uniformly guarantees the associativity of the descriptional composition and the closure property of extended ACs under the descriptional composition.

We strongly believe that our framework will contribute to extending the fusion transformation of functions with accumulating parameters. In attribute grammar framework, the fusion problem is reformulated as the descriptional composition of attribute couplings that represent functions with accumulating parameters. Extending this approach with extra language features is a delicate task (see e.g. [18]), and our categorical framework indicates the direction of the extension of ACs so that the descriptional composition works. For instance, one may consider introducing the map operator to stack ACs. In our framework, this is done by promoting the operator $(-)^\infty$ in Section 4.3 to a functor, then form a suitable extension of TSMCs.

We also expect that our framework can provide an alternative account for the existing fusion methods that use circular let bindings to express fusion results as first-order functional programs [22,19,13]. An interesting connection between these transformations and the category theory is that, these fusion results, when viewed as morphisms, often have the same pattern as the composition of morphisms in $\mathbf{Int}(\mathbb{C})$; this is also observed in [13]. Through this similarity, our categorical view of the descriptional composition will be helpful to understand these fusion methods, and hopefully provide an equational proof of their correctness.

One possible future work is to implement the descriptional composition based on our categorical framework. The major task will be to define the data structure representing TSMCs and implement the **Int** construction on them. The implementation task breaks down the descriptional composition into fundamental operations on categories and functors, each of which will be easily verifiable.

Acknowledgement. The author is grateful to Susumu Nishimura and Craig Pastro for discussions, and Masahito Hasegawa for his encouragement and helpful feedback.

References

1. Bartha, M.: Linear deterministic attributed transformations. Acta Cybern. 6, 125–147 (1983)
2. Blackwell, R., Kelly, G.M., Power, A.J.: Two-dimentional monad theory. Journal of pure and applied algebra 59, 1–41 (1989)
3. Boyland, J.: Conditional attribute grammars. ACM Trans. Program. Lang. Syst. 18(1), 73–108 (1996)
4. Chirica, L.M., Martin, D.F.: An order-algebraic definition of Knuthian semantics. Mathematical Systems Theory 13, 1–27 (1979)
5. Courcelle, B., Deransart, P.: Proofs of partial correctness for attribute grammars with applications to recursive procedures and logic programming. Inf. Comput. 78(1), 1–55 (1988)
6. Ganzinger, H.: Increasing modularity and language-independency in automatically generated compilers. Sci. Comput. Program. 3(3), 223–278 (1983)
7. Ganzinger, H., Giegerich, R.: Attribute coupled grammars. In: SIGPLAN Symposium on Compiler Construction 1984, pp. 157–170. ACM, New York (1984)
8. Giegerich, R.: Composition and evaluation of attribute coupled grammars. Acta Inf. 25(4), 355–423 (1988)
9. Hasegawa, M.: Models of Sharing Graphs: A Categorical Semantics of let and letrec. Springer, Heidelberg (1999)
10. Johnsson, T.: Attribute grammars as a functional programming paradigm. In: Kahn, G. (ed.) FPCA 1987. LNCS, vol. 274, pp. 154–173. Springer, Heidelberg (1987)
11. Joyal, A., Street, R., Verity, D.: Traced monoidal categories. Mathematical Proceedings of the Cambridge Philosophical Society 119(3), 447–468 (1996)
12. Katsumata, S.: Attribute grammars and categorical semantics. In: Aceto, L., Damgrd, I., Goldberg, L.A., Halldórsson, M.M., Ingólfsdóttir, A., Walukiewicz, I. (eds.) ICALP 2008, Part II. LNCS, vol. 5126, pp. 271–282. Springer, Heidelberg (2008)
13. Katsumata, S., Nishimura, S.: Algebraic fusion of functions with an accumulating parameter and its improvement. In: Reppy, J.H., Lawall, J.L. (eds.) ICFP, pp. 227–238. ACM, New York (2006)
14. Knuth, D.E.: Semantics of context-free languages. Mathematical Systems Theory 2(2), 127–145 (1968)
15. Knuth, D.E.: Correction: Semantics of context-free languages. Mathematical Systems Theory 5(1), 95–96 (1971)
16. Kock, A.: Strong functors and monoidal monads. Archiv. der Math. 23(1), 113–120 (1972)
17. MacLane, S.: Categories for the Working Mathematician, 2nd edn. Graduate Texts in Mathematics, vol. 5. Springer, Heidelberg (1998)
18. Nakano, K.: Composing stack-attributed tree transducers. Theory Comput. Syst. 44(1), 1–38 (2009)
19. Nishimura, S.: Deforesting in accumulating parameters via type-directed transformations. In: APLAS 2002, pp. 145–159 (2002)
20. Nishimura, S., Nakano, K.: XML stream transformer generation through program composition and dependency analysis. Sci. Comput. Program. 54(2-3), 257–290 (2005)
21. Tanaka, M., Power, J.: Pseudo-distributive laws and axiomatics for variable binding. Higher-Order and Symbolic Computation 19(2-3), 305–337 (2006)
22. Voigtländer, J.: Using circular programs to deforest in accumulating parameters. Higher-Order and Symbolic Computation 17(1-2), 129–163 (2004)

A Proof of Theorem 2

1) Obvious. 2) First, we introduce an auxiliary binary operator ©′. For functors $\mathcal{A} \in \mathbf{TSMC}'_s(F\mathcal{L}(\Delta), \mathbf{Int}'F\mathcal{L}(\Sigma))$ and $\mathcal{B} \in \mathbf{TSMC}'_s(F\mathcal{L}(\Sigma), \mathbf{Int}'(\mathbb{C}))$, we define $\mathcal{B} \copyright' \mathcal{A}$ to be $\mathbf{Str}'((\mathcal{B})^\flat \circ \mathcal{A})$. It is associative up to an isomorphism:

$$\mathcal{C} \copyright' (\mathcal{B} \copyright' \mathcal{A}) = \mathbf{Str}'((\mathcal{C})^\flat \circ (\mathcal{B})^\flat \circ \mathcal{A}) \cong \mathbf{Str}'(((\mathcal{C})^\flat \circ \mathcal{B})^\flat \circ \mathcal{A}) \cong (\mathcal{C} \copyright' \mathcal{B}) \copyright' \mathcal{A}.$$

Let $\mathcal{A} \in \mathbf{TSMC}_s(\mathcal{L}(\Delta), \mathbf{Int}UF\mathcal{L}(\Sigma))$ and $\mathcal{B} \in \mathbf{TSMC}_s(\mathcal{L}(\Sigma), \mathbf{Int}U\mathbb{C})$. Then we have

$$\mathcal{B} \copyright \mathcal{A} = \mathbf{Str}(U((\underline{\mathcal{B}})^\flat) \circ \mathcal{A}) = \mathbf{Str}(\overline{(\underline{\mathcal{B}})^\flat \circ \underline{\mathcal{A}}}) = \overline{\mathbf{Str}'((\underline{\mathcal{B}})^\flat \circ \underline{\mathcal{A}})} = \overline{(\underline{\mathcal{B}} \copyright' \underline{\mathcal{A}})}.$$

The bijection $\overline{(-)} : |\mathbf{TSMC}'_s(F\mathbb{C}, \mathbb{D})| \to |\mathbf{TSMC}_s(\mathbb{C}, U\mathbb{D})|$ extends to an ordinary functor $\mathbf{TSMC}'_s(F\mathbb{C}, \mathbb{D}) \to \mathbf{TSMC}_s(\mathbb{C}, U\mathbb{D})$, because it is defined as $\overline{F} = UF \circ H_{\mathbb{C}}$. Therefore if F and G are naturally isomorphic, so are $\overline{F}$ and $\overline{G}$. Then we have

$$\mathcal{C} \copyright (\mathcal{B} \copyright \mathcal{A}) = \overline{\underline{\mathcal{C}} \copyright' (\underline{\mathcal{B}} \copyright' \underline{\mathcal{A}})} \cong \overline{(\underline{\mathcal{C}} \copyright' \underline{\mathcal{B}}) \copyright' \underline{\mathcal{A}}} = \mathcal{C} \copyright (\mathcal{B} \copyright \mathcal{A}).$$

3) Note that $N(T\mathcal{A}(H(f))) = \mathcal{A}(f)$. Since N is faithful, it is sufficient to show $N \circ T(\mathcal{B} \copyright \mathcal{A}) \circ H(f) = N \circ T\mathcal{B} \circ T\mathcal{A} \circ H(f)$.

$$\begin{aligned} N(T(\mathcal{B} \copyright \mathcal{A})(H(f))) &= \mathbf{Str}((U\underline{\mathcal{B}})^\# \circ \mathcal{A})(f) = (U\underline{\mathcal{B}})^\#(N(T\mathcal{A}(H(f)))) \\ &= (U\underline{\mathcal{B}})(T\mathcal{A}(H(f))) = N(T\mathcal{B}(T\mathcal{A}(H(f)))). \end{aligned}$$

B Traced Symmetric Monoidal Categories and the Int Construction

Traced Symmetric Monoidal Category We recall the concept of trace operator [11]. A *trace operator* on a symmetric strict monoidal category $(\mathbb{C}, \mathbf{I}, \otimes, \sigma)$ is a mapping $\mathrm{tr}^A_{B,C} : \mathbb{C}(B \otimes A, C \otimes A) \to \mathbb{C}(B, C)$ satisfying the following equations.

(Naturality)	$h \circ \mathrm{tr}^A_{B,C}(f) \circ g = \mathrm{tr}^A_{B',C'}((h \otimes A) \circ f \circ (g \otimes A))$
(Dinaturality)	$\mathrm{tr}^A_{B,C}((C \otimes g) \circ f) = \mathrm{tr}^{A'}_{B,C}(f \circ (B \otimes g))$
(Vanishing I)	$\mathrm{tr}^{\mathbf{I}}_{A,B}(f) = f$
(Vanishing II)	$\mathrm{tr}^{A \otimes B}_{C,D}(g) = \mathrm{tr}^A_{C,D}(\mathrm{tr}^B_{C \otimes A, D \otimes A}(g))$
(Superposing)	$\mathrm{tr}^A_{B \otimes C, B \otimes D}(B \otimes f) = B \otimes \mathrm{tr}^A_{C,D} f$
(Yanking)	$\mathrm{tr}^A_{A,A}(\sigma_{A,A}) = \mathrm{id}.$

We simplify the superposing axiom in [11] using naturality and dinaturality [9]. A *traced symmetric strict monoidal category* (TSMC) is a pair of a symmetric strict monoidal category and a trace operator on it. We say that a symmetric strong monoidal functor $(F, \phi_{\mathbf{I}}, \phi_{A,B}) : \mathbb{C} \to \mathbb{D}$ between TSMCs $\mathbb{C}, \mathbb{D}$ is *traced* if it satisfies $F(\mathrm{tr}^C_{A,B}(f)) = \mathrm{tr}^{FC}_{FA,FB}(\phi^{-1}_{B,C} \circ Ff \circ \phi_{A,C})$.

The **Int** *Construction* Joyal, Street and Verity showed that the forgetful functor from the 2-category of tortile monoidal categories to that of traced (braided) monoidal categories has a left biadjoint, which they called **Int** [11]. This biadjunction can be restricted to the one between **TSMC** and the 2-category of strict compact closed categories, strong monoidal functors and monoidal natural isomorphisms. Like the usual construction of monads from adjunctions, we obtain a pseudo-monad over **TSMC**, which we also write **Int**. Below we give an explicit definition of this pseudo-monad **Int**.

Let $\mathbb{C} \in \mathbf{TSMC}$. We define the TSMC $\mathbf{Int}(\mathbb{C})$ by the following data. An object is a pair (A^+, A^-) of $\mathbb{C}$-objects. Below, when A is declared as an $\mathbf{Int}(\mathbb{C})$-object, by A^+ and A^- we mean its first and second component. A morphism from A to B is a $\mathbb{C}$-morphism $f : A^+ \otimes B^- \to B^+ \otimes A^-$. The identity is defined by $\mathrm{id}_A^{\mathbf{Int}(\mathbb{C})} = \mathrm{id}_{A^+ \otimes A^-}$, and the composition of $f : A \to B$ and $g : B \to C$ is defined by $g \circ^{\mathbf{Int}(\mathbb{C})} f = \mathrm{tr}^{B^-}_{A^+ \otimes C^-, C^+ \otimes A^-}(h)$ where $h = (C^+ \otimes \sigma_{B^-,A^-}) \circ (g \otimes A^-) \circ (B^+ \otimes \sigma_{A^-,C^-}) \circ (f \otimes C^-) \circ (A^+ \otimes \sigma_{C^-,B^-})$. The (strict) tensor product in $\mathbf{Int}(\mathbb{C})$ is given by $A \otimes^{\mathbf{Int}(\mathbb{C})} B = (A^+ \otimes B^+, A^- \otimes B^-)$ and $f \otimes^{\mathbf{Int}(\mathbb{C})} g = (B^+ \otimes \sigma_{A^-,D^+} \otimes C^-) \circ (f \otimes g) \circ (A^+ \otimes \sigma_{C^+,B^-} \otimes D^-)$. The unit object of this tensor product is given by $(\mathbf{I}, \mathbf{I})$. The symmetry morphism is $\sigma^{\mathbf{Int}(\mathbb{C})}_{A,B} = \sigma_{A^+,B^+} \otimes \sigma_{A^-,B^-}$. We give the trace operator with respect to the above symmetric monoidal structure by $(\mathrm{tr}^{\mathbf{Int}(\mathbb{C})})^C_{A,B}(f) = \mathrm{tr}^{C^+ \otimes C^-}_{A^+ \otimes B^-, B^+ \otimes A^-}((B^+ \otimes \sigma_{C^+,A^-} \otimes C^-) \circ f \circ (A^+ \otimes \sigma_{B^-,C^+} \otimes C^-))$.

We next give a functor $\mathbf{Int}_{\mathbb{C},\mathbb{D}} : \mathbf{TSMC}(\mathbb{C}, \mathbb{D}) \to \mathbf{TSMC}(\mathbf{Int}(\mathbb{C}), \mathbf{Int}(\mathbb{D}))$, which we simply write by **Int**. We define **Int** of a traced symmetric strong monoidal functor $(F, \phi_{\mathbf{I}}, \phi_{A,B}) : \mathbb{C} \to \mathbb{D}$ to be the tuple $(\mathbf{Int}(F), \phi^{\mathbf{Int}(F)}_{\mathbf{I}}, \phi^{\mathbf{Int}(F)}_{A,B}) : \mathbf{Int}(\mathbb{C}) \to \mathbf{Int}(\mathbb{D})$ defined by $\mathbf{Int}(F)(A) = (FA^+, FA^-)$, $\mathbf{Int}(F)(f) = \phi^{-1}_{B^+,B^-} \otimes Ff \otimes \phi_{A^+,A^-}$, $\phi^{\mathbf{Int}(F)}_{\mathbf{I}} = \phi_{\mathbf{I}} \otimes \phi^{-1}_{\mathbf{I}}$ and $\phi^{\mathbf{Int}(F)}_{A,B} = \phi_{A^+,B^+} \otimes \phi^{-1}_{A^-,B^-}$. For a monoidal natural isomorphism $\alpha : F \to G$, we define $\mathbf{Int}(\alpha) : \mathbf{Int}(F) \to \mathbf{Int}(G)$ by $\mathbf{Int}(\alpha)_A = \alpha_{A^+} \otimes \alpha^{-1}_{A^-}$. These data determine a 2-endofunctor $\mathbf{Int} : \mathbf{TSMC} \to \mathbf{TSMC}$.

Let $\mathbb{C} \in \mathbf{TSMC}$. A calculation shows that the homset $\mathbf{Int}^2(\mathbb{C})(A, B)$ is identical to $\mathbb{C}(A^{++} \otimes B^{-+} \otimes B^{+-} \otimes A^{--}, B^{++} \otimes A^{-+} \otimes A^{+-} \otimes B^{--})$; thus we manipulate morphisms in $\mathbf{Int}^2(\mathbb{C})$ as $\mathbb{C}$-morphisms. The unit of the pseudo-monad **Int** is the traced symmetric strict monoidal functor $N_{\mathbb{C}} : \mathbb{C} \to \mathbf{Int}(\mathbb{C})$ defined by $N_{\mathbb{C}}(A) = (\mathbf{I}, A)$ and $N_{\mathbb{C}}(f) = f$, while the multiplication of **Int** is the traced symmetric strong monoidal functor $M_{\mathbb{C}} : \mathbf{Int}^2(\mathbb{C}) \to \mathbf{Int}(\mathbb{C})$ defined by $M_{\mathbb{C}}(A) = (A^{--} \otimes A^{++}, A^{-+} \otimes A^{+-})$ and $M_{\mathbb{C}}(f) = r^{-1}_{B,A} \circ f \circ r_{A,B}$, where $r_{A,B}$ is the symmetry morphism $\sigma_{A^{--},A^{++} \otimes B^{-+} \otimes B^{+-}}$ in $\mathbb{C}$. We also define monoidal natural isomorphisms $n_F : \mathbf{Int}(F) \circ N_{\mathbb{C}} \to N_{\mathbb{D}} \circ F$ and $m_F : \mathbf{Int}^2(F) \circ M_{\mathbb{C}} \to M_{\mathbb{D}} \circ \mathbf{Int}(F)$ for $(F, \phi_{\mathbf{I}}, \phi_{A,B}) \in \mathbf{TSMC}(\mathbb{C}, \mathbb{D})$ by $(n_F)_A = \mathrm{id}_{FA} \otimes \phi_{\mathbf{I}}$ and $(m_F)_A = \phi^{-1}_{A^{--},A^{++}} \otimes \phi_{A^{-+},A^{+-}}$. These data determine pseudo-natural transformations $(N, n) : \mathrm{Id} \to \mathbf{Int}$ and $(M, m) : \mathbf{Int}^2 \to \mathbf{Int}$.

Finally, we define modifications $\lambda_{\mathbb{C}} : M_{\mathbb{C}} \circ \mathbf{Int}(N_{\mathbb{C}}) \to \mathrm{Id}_{\mathbf{Int}(\mathbb{C})}$ and $\rho_{\mathbb{C}} : M_{\mathbb{C}} \circ N_{\mathbf{Int}(\mathbb{C})} \to \mathrm{Id}_{\mathbf{Int}(\mathbb{C})}$ to be identities, and $\tau_{\mathbb{C}} : M_{\mathbb{C}} \circ \mathbf{Int}(M_{\mathbb{C}}) \to M_{\mathbb{C}} \circ M_{\mathbf{Int}(\mathbb{C})}$ by $(\tau_{\mathbb{C}})_A = (\sigma_{A^{--+},A^{-+-} \otimes A^{+--}} \otimes A^{+++}) \otimes (\sigma^{-1}_{A^{---},A^{-++} \otimes A^{+-+}} \otimes A^{++-})$.

Theorem 3. *The tuple* $(\mathbf{Int}, (N, n), (M, m), \tau, \lambda, \rho)$ *forms a pseudo-monad on* **TSMC**.

Bisimulation Proof Methods in a Path-Based Specification Language for Polynomial Coalgebras*

Xiao-cong Zhou, Yong-ji Li, Wen-jun Li, Hai-yan Qiao, and Zhong-mei Shu

Sun Yat-sen University, Guangzhou, 510275, P.R. China

Abstract. Bisimulation is one of the fundamental concepts of the theory of coalgebras. However, it is difficult to verify whether a relation is a bisimulation. Although some categorical bisimulation proof methods for coalgebras have been proposed, they are not based on specification languages of coalgebras so that they are difficult to be used in practice. In this paper, a specification language based on paths of polynomial functors is proposed to specify polynomial coalgebras. Since bisimulation can be defined by paths, it is easy to transform Sangiorgi's bisimulation proof methods for labeled transition systems to reasoning rules in such a path-based specification language for polynomial coalgebras. The paper defines the notions of progressions and sound functions based on paths, then introduces the notion of faithful contexts for the language and presents a bisimulation-up-to context proof technique for polynomial coalgebras. Several examples are given to illustrate how to make use of the bisimulation proof methods in the language.

1 Introduction

The theory of coalgebras provides a uniform mathematical foundation for modeling state-based dynamical systems, such as streams, automata, objects and processes [1]. The state space of such a system is usually considered as a black-box, and then the properties of the system are specified via its observational behaviors. As a result, two states of the system are said to be *bisimilar* rather than be equal.

The most popular method to verify two states s and t are bisimilar is to find a bisimulation relation containing the pair (s,t) [2]. However, in many cases, it is not easy to find such a bisimulation relation. Sangiorgi proposed effective bisimulation proof methods for labeled transition systems [3]. We use $P \xrightarrow{a} Q$ to denote a state transition of a labeled transition system, where P, Q are processes, and label a is drawn from some alphabet of actions. Two basic notions in Sangiorgi's work are *progression* and *sound function*. A binary relation R on processes *progresses* to a relation S, abbreviated $R \rightarrowtail S$, if $(P,Q) \in R$ implies:

(i) whenever $P \xrightarrow{a} P'$, there is Q' such that $Q \xrightarrow{a} Q'$ and $(P',Q') \in S$;
(ii) whenever $Q \xrightarrow{a} Q'$, there is P' such that $P \xrightarrow{a} P'$ and $(P',Q') \in S$.

* Supported by the National Natural Science Foundation of China under Grant No. 60673050.

K. Ueda (Ed.): APLAS 2010, LNCS 6461, pp. 239–254, 2010.

A function ϕ on relations is called a *sound function* if $R \rightarrowtail \phi(R)$ implies $R \subseteq \sim$ for all relations R, where $\sim$ is the largest bisimulation (i.e. the bisimilarity) on processes. By using a sound function ϕ, a bisimulation-up-to ϕ proof technique can be used to demonstrate two processes P and Q are bisimilar, that is, to find a relation R such that $(P, Q) \in R$ and $R \rightarrowtail \phi(R)$. With the help of ϕ, the relation R can contain less state pairs, and then it is easier to find such a relation than to find a bisimulation directly.

The most powerful class of sound functions provided by Sangiorgi is the class of *contextual functions* which give the closure of a relation under contexts. For example, a simple context of a process language is an expression C with a hole $[-]$. Actually, the hole can be regarded as a special variable for building the expression, and $C[P]$ is the process obtained by filling the hole $[-]$ with P. A contextual function $\phi_{\mathcal{C}}$ is of the form $\phi_{\mathcal{C}}(R) = \bigcup_{C \in \mathcal{C}}\{(C[P], C[Q]) \mid (P, Q) \in R\}$, where $\mathcal{C}$ is a set of contexts. When $\mathcal{C}$ satisfies certain conditions, for example, when it is a *faithful* context set, $\phi_{\mathcal{C}}$ becomes a sound function, and hence yields a bisimulation-up-to context proof technique which is proved to be a powerful proof method in practice for process algebras like CCS and pi-calculus [4].

It is natural to consider applying Sangiorgi's ideas to build bisimulation proof methods for the theory of coalgebras. In order to apply the bisimulation-up-to sound function proof techniques to general coalgebras, a notion of progressions based on the notions in the theory of coalgebras has to be defined. Particularly, an appropriate specification language for coalgebras is necessary for the powerful bisimulation-up-to context proof technique, since the definition of contexts heavily relies on a certain language. In addition, such a language should be able to express and reason about bisimulations directly.

However, it seems not easy to give a notion of progressions based on categorical definitions of coalgebra and bisimulations. Moreover, the current specification languages of coalgebras, such as CCSL [5], languages used in [6,7,8,9], and recent regular expressions for polynomial coalgebras [10,11] do not provide a way to reasoning about bisimulations, i.e. getting new bisimulations from existing bisimulations logically. In this paper, a notion of progressions based on paths [8,12] of polynomial functors is presented, and hence the bisimulation-up-to sound function proof techniques are built for polynomial coalgebras. Furthermore, a specification language for polynomial coalgebras based on paths is proposed to express and reason about bisimulations directly. In particular, a notion of faithful contexts in this language is introduced, and hence the bisimulation-up-to context proof technique can be transformed to a reasoning rule in the inference system of the language.

The remainder of this paper is organized as follows. Section 2 gives some basic notions of coalgebras. Section 3 defines the syntax and semantics of a path-based specification language for polynomial coalgebras. Section 4 investigates the bisimulation-up-to proof techniques, especially the notion of faithful contexts and the bisimulation-up-to context proof method, and illustrates them with examples. Section 5 discusses related work. Finally, Section 6 concludes the paper and discusses future work briefly.

2 Preliminaries

A functor $\boldsymbol{T} : \mathcal{S}et \rightarrow \mathcal{S}et$ on the category of sets is called a *polynomial functor*, if it is constructed from the identity functor, constant functors by finitely many applications of products, coproducts and constant exponents [13]:

$$\boldsymbol{T} ::= \mathbf{Id} \mid \boldsymbol{K}_D \mid \boldsymbol{T} \times \boldsymbol{T} \mid \boldsymbol{T} + \boldsymbol{T} \mid \boldsymbol{T}^D$$

Let $\boldsymbol{T} : \mathcal{S}et \rightarrow \mathcal{S}et$ be a functor. A $\boldsymbol{T}$-*coalgebra* is a pair (A, α), where A is a set, and $\alpha : A \rightarrow \boldsymbol{T}A$ is a function. A $\boldsymbol{T}$-coalgebra is called a *polynomial coalgebra* when $\boldsymbol{T}$ is a polynomial functor. A coalgebra *homomorphism* from one coalgebra (A, α) to another coalgebra (B, β) is a function $f : A \rightarrow B$ such that $\beta \circ f = \boldsymbol{T}f \circ \alpha$.

If (A, α) and (B, β) are $\boldsymbol{T}$-coalgebras, then a relation $R \subseteq A \times B$ is a *bisimulation (relation)* from (A, α) to (B, β) if there exists a transition structure $\rho : R \rightarrow \boldsymbol{T}R$ on R such that the relation projections $\pi_1 : R \rightarrow A, \pi_2 : R \rightarrow B$ are coalgebra homomorphisms from (R, ρ) to (A, α) and (B, β) respectively.

In this paper, we focus on polynomial coalgebras, because they are simple but enough to capture many of the interesting examples in computer science. For example, both automata and classes in object-oriented programming languages are polynomial coalgebras. In addition, polynomial functors allow us to define the notion of paths, which is the cornerstone of this paper. The notion of paths of polynomial functors is first studied by Rößiger in [14,8], and explored by Jacobs in details [15,12].

A *path* from one polynomial functor $\boldsymbol{T}$ to another polynomial functor $\boldsymbol{S}$, denoted as $p : \boldsymbol{T} \rightsquigarrow \boldsymbol{S}$, is a finite list of symbols $\pi_1, \pi_2, \kappa_1, \kappa_2, ev(d)$, for elements $d \in D$ of sets D occurring as exponent in T. Let $\boldsymbol{T}$ and $\boldsymbol{S}$ be polynomial functors. The set of paths from $\boldsymbol{T}$ to $\boldsymbol{S}$ is the least set generated by the following clauses:

(1) $\langle\rangle : \boldsymbol{T} \rightsquigarrow \boldsymbol{T}$, where $\langle\rangle$ is the empty list.
(2) $\pi_i \cdot p : \boldsymbol{T}_1 \times \boldsymbol{T}_2 \rightsquigarrow \boldsymbol{S}$ for $p : \boldsymbol{T}_i \rightsquigarrow \boldsymbol{S}$, where $i = 1, 2$.
(3) $\kappa_i \cdot p : \boldsymbol{T}_1 + \boldsymbol{T}_2 \rightsquigarrow \boldsymbol{S}$ for $p : \boldsymbol{T}_i \rightsquigarrow \boldsymbol{S}$, where $i = 1, 2$.
(4) $ev(d) \cdot p : \boldsymbol{T}_1^D \rightsquigarrow \boldsymbol{S}$ for all $d \in D$ and $p : \boldsymbol{T}_1 \rightsquigarrow \boldsymbol{S}$.

A path $p : \boldsymbol{T} \rightsquigarrow \boldsymbol{S}$ is a *state path* if $\boldsymbol{S} = \mathbf{Id}$, and an *observation path* if $\boldsymbol{S} = \boldsymbol{K}_D$ for some set D. The set of all state paths from $\boldsymbol{T}$ is denoted as $\mathtt{SPATH}(\boldsymbol{T})$, the set of all observation paths from $\boldsymbol{T}$ is denoted as $\mathtt{OPATH}(\boldsymbol{T})$, and their union is denoted as $\mathtt{OSPATH}(\boldsymbol{T})$.

A path $p : \boldsymbol{T} \rightsquigarrow \boldsymbol{S}$ induces a partial function $\widehat{p}_A : \boldsymbol{T}A \rightharpoonup \boldsymbol{S}A$ for each set A, defined by induction on the length of p as follows.

(1) $\widehat{\langle\rangle}_A : \boldsymbol{T}A \rightharpoonup \boldsymbol{T}A$ is the identity function $id_{\boldsymbol{T}A}$, so it is totally defined.

(2) $\widehat{(\pi_j \cdot p)}_A = \widehat{p}_A \circ \pi_j (j = 1, 2)$, where π_j is the product projection.

(3) $\widehat{(\kappa_j \cdot p)}_A = \widehat{p}_A \circ \varepsilon_j (j = 1, 2)$, where ε_j is the coproduct extraction [13], $y \in \mathrm{Dom}(\varepsilon_j)$ iff $y = \kappa_j\ x$ for some $x \in A_j$, and then $\varepsilon_j(y) = x$.

(4) $\widehat{(ev(d) \cdot p)}_A = \widehat{p}_A \circ ev_d$, where $ev_d(f) = f(d)$ for each $f \in (\boldsymbol{T}A)^D$.

Because partial functions is frequently involved in our discussions, we use some conventions to simplify the discussions. Let E be an expression probably containing partial functions, "$E \Downarrow$" means that the value of E is well-defined. Let

E_1 and E_2 be two expressions, R be a binary relation, "$E_1 \ R \ E_2$" means that $E_1 \Downarrow$ **iff** $E_2 \Downarrow$ **and** $(E_1, \ E_2) \in R$ **when they are both well-defined**.

The following proposition given by Goldblatt (c.f. Theorem 5.5 in [13]) shows that a bisimulation can be characterised as a relation that is "preserved" by the partial functions induced by state and observation paths.

Proposition 1. *Let* (X, α) *and* (Y, β) *be two* $\boldsymbol{T}$*-coalgebras. Then a relation* $R \subseteq X \times Y$ *is a bisimulation if, and only if, for any* $x \in X$ *and* $y \in Y$, $x \ R \ y$ *implies (1) for all* $p \in \mathtt{OPATH}(\boldsymbol{T})$, $\widehat{p}_X(\alpha(x)) = \widehat{p}_Y(\beta(y))$*; and (2) for all* $p \in \mathtt{SPATH}(\boldsymbol{T})$, $\widehat{p}_X(\alpha(x)) \ R \ \widehat{p}_Y(\beta(y))$. □

3 A Path-Based Language for Polynomial Coalgebras

In this section, we present a specification language for specifying polynomial coalgebras. Like algebraic specification languages, a signature over a polynomial functor is used to construct terms of the language, and then the terms are used to form formulas according to an equational approach. A distinctive feature of the language is that paths are used as function symbols to construct terms.

For a polynomial functor $\boldsymbol{T}$, we use $\mathbb{O}_{\boldsymbol{T}}$ to denote the set of the constant sets occurring in the observation paths of $\boldsymbol{T}$, that is, $\mathbb{O}_{\boldsymbol{T}} = \{D \mid \exists p : \boldsymbol{T} \rightsquigarrow \mathbf{K}_D\}$.

Definition 1. *Let* $\boldsymbol{T}$ *be a polynomial functor. A* ***signature*** *over* $\boldsymbol{T}$ *is a pair* $\mathsf{Sg}_{\boldsymbol{T}} = (\mathsf{Sort}_{\boldsymbol{T}}, \mathsf{Op}_{\boldsymbol{T}})$, *where (1)* $\mathsf{Sort}_{\boldsymbol{T}}$, *called* ***types*** *of the signature, satisfies that (i)* $\mathsf{State} \in \mathsf{Sort}_{\boldsymbol{T}}$, *i.e. there exists a type* State*; (ii) for each* $D \in \mathbb{O}_{\boldsymbol{T}}$, *there exists a type* $s_D \in \mathsf{Sort}_{\boldsymbol{T}}$. *(2)* $\mathsf{Op}_{\boldsymbol{T}}$ *is a set of* ***function symbols****, each with a* ***signature*** $f : s_1, s_2, \cdots, s_n \rightarrow s$, *where* $s_i (i = 1, \cdots n), s \in \mathsf{Sort}_{\boldsymbol{T}}$. *The subscript* $\boldsymbol{T}$ *is often omitted for convenience. The type* State *is called the* ***state type****, and all other types are called* ***observation types****.*

To define terms of the language, we use a family of variables $\mathbf{Var} = \{V_s \mid s \in \mathsf{Sort}\}$. We assume that if $s_1 \neq s_2$ then $V_{s_1} \cap V_{s_2} = \varnothing$.

Definition 2. *Let* $\mathsf{Sg}_{\boldsymbol{T}} = (\mathsf{Sort}_{\boldsymbol{T}}, \mathsf{Op}_{\boldsymbol{T}})$ *be a signature, and* $\mathbf{Var}$ *be a family of variables. The* ***term*** *and its type are inductively defined by the following clauses.*

(1) For each variable $x \in V_s$, x *is a term with type* s.

(2) If M *is a term with type* State, $p : \boldsymbol{T} \rightsquigarrow \mathbf{K}_D$ *is an observation path, then* $p^\sharp(M)$ *is a term with type* s_D.

(3) If M *is a term with type* State, $p : \boldsymbol{T} \rightsquigarrow \mathbf{Id}$ *is a state path, then* $p^\sharp(M)$ *is a term with type* State.

(4) If $f : s_1, s_2, \cdots, s_n \rightarrow s$ *is a function symbol in* $\mathsf{Op}_{\boldsymbol{T}}$, $M_1, M_2, \cdots, M_n$ *are terms with type* $s_1, s_2, \cdots, s_n$ *respectively, then* $f(M_1, M_2, \cdots, M_n)$ *is a term with type* s.

The set of all terms over Sg and $\mathbf{Var}$ is denoted as $\mathbf{Term}(\mathsf{Sg}, \mathbf{Var})$. A term M with the type State is called *state term*; all other terms are called *observation terms*. Given a term M, its type is denoted as $type(M)$, and the set of variables occurring in M is denoted as $fv(M)$. $M[N_1/x_1, \cdots, N_n/x_n]$ denotes the simultaneous substitution of $N_1, \cdots, N_n$ for variables $x_1, \cdots, x_n$ in M, where $type(N_i) = type(x_i)$ for $i = 1, \cdots, n$.

Definition 3. *A* ***(semantic) model*** *of* ***Term***$(Sg, \mathbf{Var})$ *is a pair* $\mathcal{M} = (\mathcal{X}, I)$, *where (1)* $\mathcal{X} = (X, \alpha : X \to \mathbf{T}X)$ *is a* $\mathbf{T}$*-coalgebra; (2)* I *is an interpretation of the signature* Sg*, i.e. for each type* $s \in Sort$*, there exists a set* $[\![s]\!]_{\mathcal{M}}$ *as its interpretation, and for each function symbol* $f : s_1, \cdots, s_n \to s$*, there exists a function* $[\![f]\!]_{\mathcal{M}} : [\![s_1]\!]_{\mathcal{M}} \times \cdots \times [\![s_n]\!]_{\mathcal{M}} \to [\![s]\!]_{\mathcal{M}}$ *as its interpretation. Moreover,* I *satisfies that* $[\![State]\!]_{\mathcal{M}} = X$ *and* $[\![s_D]\!]_{\mathcal{M}} = D$.

Definition 4. *Given a model* $\mathcal{M} = (\mathcal{X}, I)$ *of* ***Term***$(Sg, \mathbf{Var})$*, an* ***assignment*** $\sigma = \{\sigma_s \mid s \in Sort\}$ *is a family of partial functions* $\sigma_s : V_s \rightharpoonup [\![s]\!]$.

It is worth noting that partial functions are used in assignments. Consequently, the value of a variable x, i.e. $[\![x]\!]^\sigma$, is probably not well-defined under an assignment σ. This will not lead to problems in our language, since the value of a term is probably not well-defined in general. Instead, as we shall explain later, using partial functions simplifies the semantics of substitutions.

For a model $\mathcal{M} = (\mathcal{X}, I)$ and an assignment σ, the value of a term M under $\mathcal{M}$ and σ is written as $[\![M]\!]^\sigma_{\mathcal{M}}$ ($[\![M]\!]$ or $[\![M]\!]^\sigma$ for short). Since paths are used as function symbols to construct terms and they only induce partial functions, $[\![M]\!]$ is not always well-defined. The following definition gives when $[\![M]\!]$ is well-defined and how to compute $[\![M]\!]$ (when it is well-defined) inductively.

Definition 5. *Let* $\mathcal{M} = (\mathcal{X}, I)$ *be a model and* σ *be an assignment. The value of a term* M *under* $\mathcal{M}$ *and* σ *is defined inductively by the following clauses.*

(1) If M *is a variable* $x \in V_s$*, then* $[\![x]\!] \Downarrow$ *iff* $x \in \mathrm{Dom}(\sigma_s)$*, and* $[\![x]\!] = \sigma_s(x)$.

(2) If M *has the form of* $p^\sharp(M_1)$*, then* $[\![M]\!] \Downarrow$ *iff* $[\![M_1]\!] \Downarrow$ *and* $\widehat{p}_X(\alpha([\![M_1]\!])) \Downarrow$*, and* $[\![M]\!] = \widehat{p}_X(\alpha([\![M_1]\!]))$.

(3) If M *has the form of* $f(M_1, \cdots, M_n)$*, then* $[\![M]\!] \Downarrow$ *iff* $[\![M_1]\!] \Downarrow, \cdots, [\![M_n]\!] \Downarrow$*, and* $[\![M]\!] = [\![f]\!]([\![M_1]\!], \cdots, [\![M_n]\!])$.

To give the semantics of substitutions, we consider the value of a term under different assignments. Let $x_1, \cdots, x_n$ be variables with type $s_1, \cdots, s_n$ respectively, and $E_1, \cdots, E_n$ be expressions such that the value of E_i is in $[\![s_i]\!]$ when $E_i \Downarrow$ for $i = 1, \cdots, n$. Given an assignment σ, a new assignment $\sigma[E_1/x_1, \cdots, E_n/x_n] = \{\sigma'_s \mid s \in \mathsf{Sort}\}$ can be defined: for each $s \in \mathsf{Sort}$, if there exists i such that $x = x_i$, then $\sigma'_s(x) = E_i$, otherwise $\sigma'_s(x) = \sigma_s(x)$.

Lemma 1. *Let* σ *be an assignment,* M *be a term,* $x_1, \cdots, x_n$ *be variables, and* $N_1, \cdots, N_n$ *be terms with* $type(N_i) = type(x_i)$ *for* $i = 1, \cdots, n$*. Then* $[\![M[N_1/x_1, \cdots, N_n/x_n]]\!]^\sigma = [\![M]\!]^{\sigma'}$*, where* $\sigma' = \sigma[[\![N_1]\!]^\sigma/x_1, \cdots, [\![N_n]\!]^\sigma/x_n]$. □

We can use $\sigma[[\![N_1]\!]^\sigma/x_1, \cdots, [\![N_n]\!]^\sigma/x_n]$ even if $[\![N_i]\!]^\sigma$ is not well-defined for some i, since partial functions are allowed in an assignment. Moreover, we always have $[\![M[N_1/x_1, \cdots, N_n/x_n]]\!]^\sigma \Downarrow$ iff $[\![M]\!]^{\sigma'} \Downarrow$. However, if we define an assignment as a family of (total) functions, then the condition that $[\![N_i]\!] \Downarrow$ for all $i = 1, \cdots, n$ is necessary for using $\sigma[[\![N_1]\!]^\sigma/x_1, \cdots, [\![N_n]\!]^\sigma/x_n]$ and obtaining that $[\![M[N_1/x_1, \cdots, N_n/x_n]]\!]^\sigma \Downarrow$ iff $[\![M]\!]^{\sigma'} \Downarrow$.

Like algebraic specification languages, we use an equational approach to construct formulas for our coalgebraic specification language. However, a major difference between our language and algebraic languages is that we specify that two state terms are bisimilar rather than equal. In addition, because a term probably has no value under a semantic model, a formula of the form $M \Downarrow$ is used to specify whether the value of M is well-defined.

Therefore, the language has three kinds of basic formulas: (1) $M \Downarrow$, called *term definition formula*; (2) $M_1 \approx M_2$, called *observation equation*, where M_1 and M_2 are two observation terms; (3) $M_1 \simeq M_2$, called *state bisimulation formula*, where M_1 and M_2 are two state terms. Then, the formulas of the language are constructed from basic formulas by using Boolean operators:

$$\varphi, \psi \ ::= \ M \Downarrow | \ M_1 \approx M_2 \mid M_1 \simeq M_2 \mid \neg\varphi \mid \varphi \wedge \psi \mid \varphi \vee \psi \mid \phi \rightarrow \psi \mid \phi \leftrightarrow \psi$$

We use $fv(\varphi)$ to denote the set of variables occurring in φ, and $\varphi[N_1/x_1, \cdots, N_n/x_n]$ to denote the simultaneous substitution of $N_1, \cdots, N_n$ for variables $x_1, \cdots, x_n$ in φ, where $type(N_i) = type(x_i)$ for $i = 1, \cdots, n$.

Definition 6. *Let $\mathcal{M} = (\mathcal{X}, I)$ be a model and σ be an assignment. The truth value of a formula, written $[\![\varphi]\!]^\sigma_\mathcal{M}$ ($[\![\varphi]\!]$ or $[\![\varphi]\!]^\sigma$ for short), is defined inductively by the following clauses.*

(1) If φ has the form of $M \Downarrow$, then $[\![\varphi]\!] = \mathsf{true}$ iff $[\![M]\!] \Downarrow$.

(2) If φ has the form of $M_1 \approx M_2$, then $[\![\varphi]\!] = \mathsf{true}$ iff $[\![M_1]\!] = [\![M_2]\!]$.

(3) If φ has the form of $M_1 \simeq M_2$, then $[\![\varphi]\!] = \mathsf{true}$ iff $[\![M_1]\!] \sim [\![M_2]\!]$, where $\sim$ is the largest bisimulation relation on the coalgebra $\mathcal{X}$.

(4) If φ is constructed by Boolean operators, its truth value is calculated in the standard way.

We write $\mathcal{M}, \sigma \vDash \varphi$ when $[\![\varphi]\!]^\sigma_\mathcal{M} = \mathsf{true}$, and write $\mathcal{M} \vDash \varphi$ when $\mathcal{M}, \sigma \vDash \varphi$ for all σ. By Lemma 1, it is not hard to prove the following lemma.

Lemma 2. *Let σ be an assignment, φ be a formula, $x_1, \cdots, x_n$ be variables, and $N_1, \cdots, N_n$ be terms with $type(N_i) = type(x_i)$ for $i = 1, \cdots, n$. Then $[\![\varphi[N_1/x_1, \cdots, N_n/x_n]]\!]^\sigma = [\![\varphi]\!]^{\sigma'}$, where $\sigma' = \sigma[[\![N_1]\!]^\sigma/x_1, \cdots, [\![N_n]\!]^\sigma/x_n]$.* □

We give some examples to illustrate the usage of the language. These examples will be continued later to show how to validate state bisimulation formulas logically by using bisimulation proof methods in the language. Such a process of validation is thought of as a process of reasoning about bisimulations.

Example 1. We consider the signature functor of streams on real numbers, i.e. $\boldsymbol{T}X = \mathbb{R} \times X$, which has an observation path $\pi_1 : \boldsymbol{T} \rightsquigarrow \boldsymbol{K}_\mathbb{R}$ and a state path π_2.

We give a signature $\mathsf{Sg} = (\mathsf{Sort}, \mathsf{Op})$ over $\boldsymbol{T}$, defined as $\mathsf{Sort} = \{\mathsf{State}, s_\mathbb{R}\}$ and $\mathsf{Op} = \{+ : s_\mathbb{R}, s_\mathbb{R} \rightarrow s_\mathbb{R},\ \cdot : s_\mathbb{R}, s_\mathbb{R} \rightarrow s_\mathbb{R},\ [\,] : s_\mathbb{R} \rightarrow \mathsf{State}, \oplus : \mathsf{State}, \mathsf{State} \rightarrow \mathsf{State},\ \times : \mathsf{State}, \mathsf{State} \rightarrow \mathsf{State}\}$. The intended meanings of these operators can refer to the stream calculus presented by Rutten [16]. For any state term M, we use more meaningful notation $head(M)$ for $\pi_1^\sharp(M)$, and $tail(M)$ for $\pi_2^\sharp(M)$.

Let x, y be two variables with the type State, and r be a variable with type $s_\mathbb{R}$, the following formulas give the specification of stream operators $\oplus$(sum) and

$\times$(convolution product) defined in the stream calculus in [16] (for convenience, we use the function symbols as infix operators) :

$$head(x \oplus y) \approx head(x) + head(y) \quad tail(x \oplus y) \simeq tail(x) \oplus tail(y)$$
$$head(x \times y) \approx head(x) \cdot head(y) \quad tail(x \times y) \simeq ([head(x)] \times tail(y)) \oplus (tail(x) \times y)$$

Example 2. We consider the functor $\boldsymbol{T}X = A \times (1 + X \times X)$, which is the signature functor of binary tree given in [17]. The functor has two observation paths $p_1 = \pi_1 : \boldsymbol{T} \rightsquigarrow \mathbf{K}_A$ and $p_2 = \pi_2 \cdot \kappa_1 : \boldsymbol{T} \rightsquigarrow \mathbf{K}_1$, and two state paths $p_3 = \pi_2 \cdot \kappa_2 \cdot \pi_1$ and $p_4 = \pi_2 \cdot \kappa_2 \cdot \pi_2$.

We give a signature Sg over $\boldsymbol{T}$, which has types State, s_A, s_1, and a function symbol $mirror : \mathsf{State} \to \mathsf{State}$. In [17], Jacobs gives some semantic models for this signature. For any state term M, we use more meaningful notation $label(M)$ for $p_1^\sharp(M)$, $nochild(M)$ for $p_2^\sharp(M)$, $lchild(M)$ for $p_3^\sharp(M)$, and $rchild(M)$ for $p_4^\sharp(M)$.

Let x be a variable with the type State, the following formulas specify the properties of $mirror$:

$$label(mirror(x)) \approx label(x) \qquad nochild(mirror(x)) \Downarrow \leftrightarrow nochild(x) \Downarrow$$
$$rchild(mirror(x)) \Downarrow \leftrightarrow lchild(x) \Downarrow \quad rchild(mirror(x)) \simeq mirror(lchild(x))$$
$$lchild(mirror(x)) \Downarrow \leftrightarrow rchild(x) \Downarrow \quad lchild(mirror(x)) \simeq mirror(rchild(x))$$

Let Γ be a set of formulas, a formula φ is called a *semantic consequence* of Γ, written $\Gamma \models \varphi$, if, for any model $\mathcal{M}$, $\mathcal{M} \models \Gamma$ implies $\mathcal{M} \models \varphi$, where $\mathcal{M} \models \Gamma$ means $\mathcal{M} \models \psi$ for every $\psi \in \Gamma$. Obviously, the semantic consequence relation here has the properties as in propositional logic. In addition, certain properties of the semantic consequence relation can be induced by the fact that equalities and bisimilarities are equivalent relations. Due to the limit space, here we only give some properties of the semantic consequence relation induced by the properties of terms and formulas defined in our specification language.

Lemma 3. *Let Γ be a formula set. (1) For any function symbol f and terms $M_1, \cdots, M_n$, $\Gamma \models f(M_1, \cdots, M_n) \Downarrow$ iff $\Gamma \models M_1 \Downarrow \wedge \cdots \wedge M_n \Downarrow$. (2) For any path p and term M, $\Gamma \models p^\sharp(M) \Downarrow$ implies $\Gamma \models M \Downarrow$.* □

Let $\sigma' = \sigma[[\![N_1]\!]^\sigma/x_1, \cdots, [\![N_n]\!]^\sigma/x_n]$, by Lemma 2, we can obtain that $[\![\varphi[N_1/x_1, \cdots, N_n/x_n]]\!]^\sigma_\mathcal{M} = [\![\varphi]\!]^{\sigma'}_\mathcal{M}$ for any model $\mathcal{M}$ and any assignment σ. And thus we have the following important result.

Theorem 1. *Let Γ be a formula set, φ be a formula, $x_1, \cdots, x_n$ be variables, and $N_1, \cdots, N_n$ be terms. Then $\Gamma \models \varphi$ implies $\Gamma \models \varphi[N_1/x_1, \cdots, N_n/x_n]$.* □

From the above theorem, we obtain that substitutions preserve term definition formulas, i.e. $\Gamma \models M \Downarrow$ implies $\Gamma \models M[N_1/x_1, \cdots, N_n/x_n] \Downarrow$. Note that this holds even when $\Gamma \models N_i \Downarrow$ does not hold for some $i (1 \leq i \leq n)$. Moreover, by this theorem, if M_1, M_2 are observation terms then $\Gamma \models M_1 \approx M_2$ implies $\Gamma \models M_1[N_1/x_1, \cdots, N_n/x_n] \approx M_2[N_1/x_1, \cdots, N_n/x_n]$; and if M_1, M_2 are state terms then $\Gamma \models M_1 \simeq M_2$ implies $\Gamma \models M_1[N_1/x_1, \cdots, N_n/x_n] \simeq M_2[N_1/x_1, \cdots, N_n/x_n]$. In short, substitutions also preserve observation equations and state bisimulation formulas.

4 Bisimulation Proofs in the Language

In this section, we present some bisimulation proof methods for polynomial coalgebras. First, we define a notion of progression based on the relationship between bisimulations and paths, as well as a notion of sound function based on this progression. Then, we discuss how to use these notions to form reasoning rules on bisimulation proofs from a semantic prospective for the specification language presented in Section 3. Finally, we define a notion of faithful context and give a sound function based on faithful contexts to form a bisimulation-up-to context proof method for the langauge.

Definition 7. *Let (X, α) and (Y, β) be two $\mathbf{T}$-coalgebras. A relation $R \subseteq X \times Y$ is called a* ***quasi-bisimulation****, if, for all $x \in X$ and $y \in Y$, $(x, y) \in R$ implies (1) for all $p \in$ OSPATH($\mathbf{T}$), $\widehat{p}_X(\alpha(x)) \Downarrow$ iff $\widehat{p}_Y(\beta(y)) \Downarrow$; and (2) for all $p \in$ OPATH($\mathbf{T}$), $\widehat{p}_X(\alpha(x)) = \widehat{p}_Y(\beta(y))$.*

Definition 8. *Let R be a quasi-bisimulation between two $\mathbf{T}$-coalgebras (X, α) and (Y, β), and $S \subseteq X \times Y$ is an ordinary relation. We say R* ***progresses to*** *S, written $R \overset{\alpha,\beta}{\Longrightarrow} S$ ($R \Longrightarrow S$ for short), if, for all $(x, y) \in R$ and all state paths $p \in$ SPATH($\mathbf{T}$), $\widehat{p}_X(\alpha(x)) \Downarrow$ and $\widehat{p}_Y(\beta(y)) \Downarrow$ imply $(\widehat{p}_X(\alpha(x)), \widehat{p}_X(\beta(y))) \in S$.*

By Proposition 1, a quasi-bisimulation R is a bisimulation iff $R \Longrightarrow R$. Intuitively, for a quasi-bisimulation R, $(s, t) \in R$ implies that s and t have the same observational outputs and the same possible state transitions. In addition to the notion of quasi-bisimulations, the notion of progressions describes which relation a state pair in a quasi-bisimulation reaches after one possible state transition.

Definition 9. *Let (X, α) and (Y, β) be two $\mathbf{T}$-coalgebras. A function ϕ : $\mathcal{P}(X \times Y) \rightarrow \mathcal{P}(X \times Y)$ is called a* ***sound function****, if (1) ϕ preserves quasi-bisimulations, that is, if R is a quasi-bisimulation, so is $\phi(R)$; and (2) ϕ preserves progressions, that is, for any quasi-bisimulation R and any ordinary relation S, if $R \subseteq S$ and $R \Longrightarrow S$, then $\phi(R) \subseteq \phi(S)$ and $\phi(R) \Longrightarrow \phi(S)$.*

Theorem 2. *Let (X, α) and (Y, β) be two $\mathbf{T}$-coalgebras, ϕ be a sound function, and $R \subseteq X \times Y$ be a quasi-bisimulation. Then, $R \Longrightarrow \phi(R)$ implies $R \subseteq \sim$, where $\sim$ is the largest bisimulation between (X, α) and (Y, β).*

Proof. (c.f. Theorem 2.11 in [3]) We inductively define a sequence of relations $(R_i)_{i \in \mathbb{N}}$: $R_0 = R$, $R_{i+1} = R_i \cup \phi(R_i)$ for all $i \geq 1$. Since ϕ preserves quasi-bisimulation, R_i is a quasi-bisimulation for all $i \in \mathbb{N}$. Then, it is easy to show that $\bigcup_{i \in \mathbb{N}} R_i$ is a bisimulation. □

Actually, the condition (2) in the above definition of sound functions is the same as the property of respectful functions in [3]. Here we require a sound function satisfies one more condition, i.e. preserving quasi-bisimulations, which is critical for showing that R_n is a quasi-bisimulation in the above proof.

As in [3], the identity function and the constant-to-$\sim$, mapping every relation to $\sim$, are two primitive sound functions, and sound functions are closure under constructors including composition, union and chaining. Using these primitive sound functions and constructors, the function $\phi_B(R) = \sim \circ R \circ \sim$ is a sound function. As a corollary, we obtain the following bisimulation proof method, which is called bisimulation-up-to bisimilarity in process algebras:

Corollary 1. *Let (X, α) be a $\mathbf{T}$-coalgebra. A relation R on X is contained in the bisimilarity $\sim$ on X, if it satisfies that, for all $x, y \in X$, $(x, y) \in R$ implies (1) for all path $p \in$ OSPATH($\mathbf{T}$), $\widehat{p}_X(\alpha(x)) \Downarrow$ iff $\widehat{p}_X(\alpha(y)) \Downarrow$; (2) for all observation path $p \in$ OPATH($\mathbf{T}$), $\widehat{p}_X(\alpha(x)) = \widehat{p}_X(\beta(x))$; and (3) for all state path $p \in$ SPATH($\mathbf{T}$), if $\widehat{p}_X(\alpha(x)) \Downarrow$ and $\widehat{p}_X(\alpha(y)) \Downarrow$, then there exist $x', y' \in X$ such that $x' \sim \widehat{p}_X(\alpha(x)), y' \sim \widehat{p}_X(\alpha(y))$ and $(x', y') \in R$.* □

Since paths are used to construct terms in the specification language defined by us in Section 3, the above proof method can be transformed to a reasoning rule for bisimulation proofs in the language as follows.

Theorem 3. *Let M_1 and M_2 be two state terms, $x_1, \cdots x_n$ be variables, and Γ be a formula set. Then $\Gamma \models M_1 \simeq M_2$ if (1) $\Gamma \models M_1 \Downarrow \leftrightarrow M_2 \Downarrow$; (2) for all $p \in$ OPATH($\mathbf{T}$), $\Gamma \models p^\sharp(M_1) \approx p^\sharp(M_2)$; and (3) for all $p \in$ SPATH($\mathbf{T}$), there exist terms $N_1, N_2, \cdots, N_n$ such that*

$$\Gamma \models (p^\sharp(M_1) \simeq M_1[N_1/x_1, \cdots N_n/x_n])$$
$$\Gamma \models (p^\sharp(M_2) \simeq M_2[N_1/x_1, \cdots N_n/x_n])$$

Proof. (Sketch) Let $\mathcal{M}$ be a model, (X, α) be the coalgebra of $\mathcal{M}$. Assume that $\mathcal{M} \models \Gamma$, we define a relation $R \subseteq X \times X$:

$$R = \{([\![M_1]\!]^\sigma,\ [\![M_2]\!]^\sigma) \mid \sigma \text{ is an assignment such that } [\![M_1]\!]^\sigma \Downarrow \text{ and } [\![M_2]\!]^\sigma \Downarrow\}$$

Then $\mathcal{M} \models M_1 \simeq M_2$ follows from $R \subseteq \sim$, which can be shown by Corollary 1. □

Although the above theorem just gives how to validate a state bisimulation formula from the perspective of semantic consequence relations, it is not difficult to form a corresponding rule in the inference system of the language for reasoning about bisimulations. The details of the formal rules and the inference system of the language will be considered when we implement the language in the future. For the sake of simplicity, in this paper, we give the bisimulation proof methods in the form of semantic consequence relations, and use some examples to illustrate how to make use of these methods in our language.

Example 3. Considering the signature Sg given in Example 1, let x, y be state variables, $r, r_1, r_2, r_1', r_2', r_3$ be variables with type $s_{\mathbb{R}}$, and

$$\begin{aligned}\Gamma = \{&x \Downarrow,\ r_1 \approx r_1' \wedge r_2 \approx r_2' \rightarrow r_1 + r_2 \approx r_1' + r_2',\ r_1 + r_2 \approx r_2 + r_1,\\ &r_1 \approx r_1' \wedge r_2 \approx r_2' \rightarrow r_1 \cdot r_2 \approx r_1' \cdot r_2',\ r_1 \cdot (r_2 + r_3) \approx (r_1 \cdot r_2) + (r_1 \cdot r_3),\\ &head(x \oplus y) \approx head(x) + head(y),\ tail(x \oplus y) \simeq tail(x) \oplus tail(y),\\ &head(x \times y) \approx head(x) \cdot head(y),\\ &tail(x \times y) \simeq ([head(x)] \times tail(y)) \oplus (tail(x) \times y)\}\end{aligned}$$

Let $M_1 = x \oplus y$ and $M_2 = y \oplus x$. It is easy to obtain that $\Gamma \models M_1 \Downarrow \leftrightarrow M_2 \Downarrow$ from $\Gamma \models x \Downarrow$, and $\Gamma \models head(M_1) \approx head(M_2)$ from $\Gamma \models r_1 + r_2 \approx r_2 + r_1$. Then, by Theorem 3, $\Gamma \models M_1 \simeq M_2$ follows from that

$$\Gamma \models tail(M_1) \simeq M_1[tail(x)/x, tail(y)/y]$$
$$\Gamma \models tail(M_2) \simeq M_2[tail(x)/x, tail(y)/y]$$

However, we cannot show that $\Gamma \models x \times (y \oplus z) \simeq (x \times y) \oplus (x \times z)$ by using Theorem 3. Hence, we need more powerful bisimulation proof methods.

We consider sound functions based on contexts of the language. A term M is called a ***(state) context***, if it is a state term and all variables occurring in it are state variables. Let M and M' be two state contexts, a ***variable mapping*** from M' to M is a function of the form $\rho : fv(M') \rightarrow fv(M) \times (1 + \mathtt{SPATH}(\boldsymbol{T}))$.

Now, we give our core definition, i.e. the definition of faithful contexts.

Definition 10. *Let Γ be a set of formulas, $\mathcal{C}$ be a set of state contexts. $\mathcal{C}$ is called a* ***faithful context set with respect to*** *Γ, if every state context M in $\mathcal{C}$ satisfies the following three conditions (assume that $fv(M) = \{x_1, \cdots, x_n\}$):*

(1) it is ***well-defined****, that is, $\Gamma \models \varphi_{wd} \rightarrow \psi_{wd}$ for all paths $p \in \mathtt{OSPATH}(\boldsymbol{T})$ and all state terms $N_1, \cdots, N_n$, where φ_{wd} and ψ_{wd} are defined as follows:*

$$\varphi_{wd} \stackrel{\text{def}}{=} M[N_1/x_1, \cdots, N_n/x_n] \Downarrow$$
$$\psi_{wd} \stackrel{\text{def}}{=} p^\sharp(M[N_1/x_1, \cdots, N_n/x_n]) \Downarrow \;\leftrightarrow\; (p^\sharp(N_1) \Downarrow \wedge \cdots \wedge p^\sharp(N_n) \Downarrow)$$

(2) it ***preserves observations****, that is, $\Gamma \models \varphi_{po} \rightarrow \psi_{po}$ for all observation paths $p \in \mathtt{OPATH}(\boldsymbol{T})$ and all state terms $N_1, \cdots, N_n, L_1, \cdots, L_n$, where φ_{po} and ψ_{po} are defined as follows:*

$$\varphi_{po} \stackrel{\text{def}}{=} p^\sharp(N_1) \approx p^\sharp(L_1) \wedge \cdots \wedge p^\sharp(N_n) \approx p^\sharp(L_n)$$
$$\psi_{po} \stackrel{\text{def}}{=} p^\sharp(M[N_1/x_1, \cdots, N_n/x_n]) \approx p^\sharp(M[L_1/x_1, \cdots, N_n/x_n])$$

(3) it has ***faithful progressions****, that is, for all state paths $p \in \mathtt{SPATH}(\boldsymbol{T})$, there exist a state context M_p in $\mathcal{C}$ and a variable mapping $\rho_p : fv(M_p) \rightarrow fv(M) \times (1 + \mathtt{SPATH}(\boldsymbol{T}))$ such that (assume that $fv(M_p) = \{y_1, \cdots, y_m\}$)*

$$\Gamma \models p^\sharp(M[N_1/x_1, \cdots, N_n/x_n]) \simeq M_p[L_1/y_1, L_2/y_2, \cdots, L_m/y_m]$$

for all state terms $N_1, \cdots, N_n$, where $L_j (j = 1, \cdots, m)$ is defined as follows: if $\rho_p(y_j) = (x_i, \kappa *)$, then $L_j \stackrel{\text{def}}{=} N_i$, and if $\rho_p(y_j) = (x_i, \kappa p')$, then $L_j \stackrel{\text{def}}{=} p'^\sharp(N_i)$. A state context M is called a ***faithful context with respect to*** *Γ, if there exists a faithful context set $\mathcal{C}$ with respect to Γ such that $M \in \mathcal{C}$.*

The above definition looks complicated, however, the names of the three conditions indicate the key ideas of the definition. We use some simple examples to illustrate the intended meaning of the definition.

Example 4. Continue to Example 3. It is easy to show that $x \oplus y$ is a faithful context with respect to Γ. However, $x \times y$ is not a faithful context with respect to Γ, since $[head(x)]$ is not an observation or state transition induced by path.

Example 5. Considering the signature Sg given in Example 2, let x, y be state variables, and

$$\begin{aligned}\Gamma = \{ & nochild(x) \Downarrow \leftrightarrow \neg(lchild(x) \Downarrow),\ lchild(x) \Downarrow \leftrightarrow rchild(x) \Downarrow, \\ & label(x) \Downarrow \leftrightarrow x \Downarrow,\ label(mirror(x)) \approx label(x), \\ & nochild(x) \approx nochild(y),\ nochild(mirror(x)) \Downarrow \leftrightarrow nochild(x) \Downarrow, \\ & rchild(mirror(x)) \Downarrow \leftrightarrow lchild(x) \Downarrow,\ lchild(mirror(x)) \Downarrow \leftrightarrow rchild(x) \Downarrow, \\ & rchild(mirror(x)) \simeq mirror(lchild(x)), \\ & lchild(mirror(x)) \simeq mirror(rchild(x)) \ \}\end{aligned}$$

We show that $M = mirror(x)$ is a faithful context with respect to Γ.

First, from that substitutions preserve term definition formulas, it is easy to show that $\Gamma \models label(M) \Downarrow \leftrightarrow M \Downarrow$, $\Gamma \models nochild(M) \Downarrow \leftrightarrow nochild(x) \Downarrow$, $\Gamma \models lchild(M) \Downarrow \leftrightarrow lchild(x) \Downarrow$ and $\Gamma \models rchild(M) \Downarrow \leftrightarrow rchild(x) \Downarrow$. Therefore, $mirror(x)$ is well-defined.

Second, from that substitutions preserve observation equations, it is not hard to show that $\Gamma \models (label(x) \approx label(y)) \rightarrow (label(mirror(x)) \approx label(mirror(y)))$ and $\Gamma \models nochild(mirror(x)) \approx nochild(mirror(y))$. Therefore, $mirror(x)$ also preserves observations.

Finally, the following imply that $mirror(x)$ has faithful progressions.

$$\Gamma \models lchild(M) \simeq M[rchild(x)/x] \qquad \Gamma \models rchild(M) \simeq M[lchild(x)/x]$$

Theorem 4. *Faithful contexts preserve bisimulations.* *Let Γ be a formula set, M be a faithful context with respect to Γ with $fv(M) = \{x_1, \cdots, x_n\}$. For all state terms $N_1, \cdots, N_n, L_1, \cdots, L_n$, if $\Gamma \models N_i \simeq L_i$ for all $i = 1, \cdots, n$, and $\Gamma \models M[N_1/x_1, \cdots, N_n/x_n] \Downarrow \leftrightarrow M[L_1/x_1, \cdots, L_n/x_n] \Downarrow$, then*

$$\Gamma \models M[N_1/x_1, \cdots, N_n/x_n] \simeq M[L_1/x_1, \cdots, L_n/x_n]$$

Proof. *(Sketch) Let $\mathcal{C}$ be the set of all faithful contexts with respect to Γ. For any model $\mathcal{M}$, let (X, α) be the coalgebra of $\mathcal{M}$. If $\mathcal{M} \models \Gamma$, we define a relation $R \subseteq X \times X$ as follows.*

$$\begin{aligned} R \ = \ \bigcup_{T \in \mathcal{C}} \{ \ & ([\![T[P_1/y_1, \cdots, P_n/y_n]]\!]^\sigma,\ [\![T[Q_1/y_1, \cdots, Q_n/y_n]]\!]^\sigma) \ \mid \\ & \sigma \ \text{ is an assignment, } fv(T) = \{y_1, y_2, \cdots, y_n\}, \\ & P_i, Q_i \text{ are state terms and } [\![P_i]\!]^\sigma \sim [\![Q_i]\!]^\sigma \text{ for all } i = 1, \cdots, n, \\ & [\![T[P_1/y_1, \cdots, P_n/y_n]]\!]^\sigma \Downarrow, \text{ and } [\![T[Q_1/y_1, \cdots, Q_n/y_n]]\!]^\sigma \Downarrow \ \} \end{aligned}$$

Using Corollary 1, we can prove that $R \subseteq \sim$. Then, it is not hard to show that $\Gamma \models M[N_1/x_1, \cdots, N_n/x_n] \simeq M[L_1/x_1, \cdots, L_n/x_n]$. □

Example 6. Continue to Example 5, we show $\Gamma \models mirror(mirror(x)) \simeq x$. By $\Gamma \models lchild(mirror(x)) \simeq mirror(rchild(x))$, we get $\Gamma \models lchild(mirror(mirror(x))) \simeq mirror(rchild(mirror(x)))$. Since $mirror(x)$ is a faithful context respect to Γ and $\Gamma \models rchild(mirror(x)) \simeq mirror(lchild(x))$, by Theorem 4, we obtain

$$\Gamma \models mirror(rchild(mirror(x))) \simeq mirror(mirror(lchild(x)))$$

And hence, let $M_1 = mirror(mirror(x))$ and $M_2 = x$, we obtain

$$\Gamma \models lchild(M_1) \simeq M_1[lchild(x)/x] \qquad \Gamma \models lchild(M_2) \simeq M_2[lchild(x)/x]$$

Similarly, we obtain that $\Gamma \models rchild(M_1) \simeq M_1[rchild(x)/x]$ and $\Gamma \models rchild(M_2) \simeq M_2[rchild(x)/x]$. Thus, by Theorem 3, $\Gamma \models M_1 \simeq M_2$, since it is not hard to show that $\Gamma \models M_1 \Downarrow \leftrightarrow M_2 \Downarrow$, $\Gamma \models label(M_1) \approx label(M_2)$, and $\Gamma \models nochild(M_1) \approx nochild(M_2)$.

Now, we present the following theorem as the main result of the paper, which gives how to define sound functions based on faithful contexts.

Theorem 5. *Let Γ be a formula set, $\mathcal{C}$ be a faithful context set with respect to Γ, $\mathcal{M}$ be a model with $\mathcal{M} \models \Gamma$, and (X, α) be the coalgebra in $\mathcal{M}$. A function $\phi_{\mathcal{C}} : \mathcal{P}(X \times X) \to \mathcal{P}(X \times X)$ is defined as follows. For $R \subseteq X \times X$,*

$$\begin{aligned}\phi_{\mathcal{C}}(R) = \{(t, s) \mid\ & t, s \in X, \exists M \in \mathcal{C} \text{ with } fv(M) = \{x_1, x_2, \cdots, x_n\}, \text{an} \\ & \text{assignment } \sigma, \text{ and state terms } P_1, \cdots, P_n, Q_1, \cdots, Q_n, \text{such that} \\ & t \sim [\![M[P_1/x_1, \cdots, P_n/x_n]]\!]^\sigma,\ s \sim [\![M[Q_1/x_1, \cdots, Q_n/x_n]]\!]^\sigma, \\ & \text{where } [\![M[P_1/x_1, \cdots, P_n/x_n]]\!]^\sigma \Downarrow,\ [\![M[Q_1/x_1, \cdots, Q_n/x_n]]\!]^\sigma \Downarrow, \\ & \text{and, for all } i = 1, \cdots, n,\ P_i = Q_i \text{ or } ([\![P_i]\!]^\sigma, [\![Q_i]\!]^\sigma) \in R \ \}\end{aligned}$$

Then $\phi_{\mathcal{C}}$ is a sound function.

Proof. (Sketch) (1) Let R be a quasi-bisimulation on X. For any state pair $(s, t) \in \phi_{\mathcal{C}}(R)$, there exist a faithful context $M \in \mathcal{C}$ with $fv(M) = \{x_1, \cdots, x_n\}$, an assignment σ, and state terms $P_1, \cdots, P_n, Q_1, \cdots, Q_n$, such that

(i) $[\![M[P_1/x_1, \cdots, P_n/x_n]]\!]^\sigma \Downarrow$ and $[\![M[Q_1/x_1, \cdots, Q_n/x_n]]\!]^\sigma \Downarrow$, in addition, these imply $[\![P_i]\!]^\sigma \Downarrow$ and $[\![Q_i]\!]^\sigma \Downarrow$ for all $i = 1, \cdots, n$;

(ii) either $P_i = Q_i$ or $([\![P_i]\!]^\sigma, [\![Q_i]\!]^\sigma) \in R$ for all $i = 1, \cdots, n$;

(iii) $t \sim [\![M[P_1/x_1, \cdots, P_n/x_n]]\!]^\sigma$ and $s \sim [\![M[Q_1/x_1, \cdots, Q_n/x_n]]\!]^\sigma$.

For showing that $\phi_{\mathcal{C}}(R)$ is a quasi-bisimulation, we note that

$$\begin{aligned}\widehat{p}_X(\alpha(t)) \Downarrow &\iff \widehat{p}_X(\alpha([\![M[P_1/x_1, \cdots, P_n/x_n]]\!]^\sigma)) \Downarrow && \text{(iii) and Proposition 1} \\ &\iff [\![p^\sharp(M[P_1/x_1, \cdots, P_n/x_n])]\!]^\sigma \Downarrow && \text{(i) and Definition 5} \\ &\iff [\![p^\sharp(P_i)]\!]^\sigma \Downarrow \text{ for all } i = 1, \cdots, n && M \text{ is well-defined}\end{aligned}$$

and $\widehat{p}_X(\alpha(t)) = [\![p^\sharp(M[P_1/x_1, \cdots, P_n/x_n])]\!]^\sigma$ when $p \in$ OPATH($\mathbf{T}$). Similarly, $\widehat{p}_X(\alpha(s)) \Downarrow$ iff $[\![p^\sharp(Q_i)]\!]^\sigma \Downarrow$, and $\widehat{p}_X(\alpha(s)) = [\![p^\sharp(M[Q_1/x_1, \cdots, Q_n/x_n])]\!]^\sigma$ when $p \in$ OPATH($\mathbf{T}$). Then, $\widehat{p}_X(\alpha(t)) \Downarrow$ iff $\widehat{p}_X(\alpha(s)) \Downarrow$, and when p is an observation *path,* $\widehat{p}_X(\alpha(t)) = \widehat{p}_X(\alpha(s))$*, since* $P_i = Q_i$ *or* $([\![P_i]\!]^\sigma, [\![Q_i]\!]^\sigma) \in R$*,* R *is a quasi-bisimulation and* M *preserves observations.*

(2) Let S *be a relation with* $R \subseteq S$ *and* $R \Longrightarrow S$*. Obviously,* $\phi_{\mathcal{C}}(R) \subseteq \phi_{\mathcal{C}}(S)$*. From the above condition (iii),* $\widehat{p}_X(\alpha(t)) \sim [\![p^\sharp(M[P_1/x_1, \cdots, P_n/x_n])]\!]^\sigma$ *and* $\widehat{p}_X(\alpha(s)) \sim [\![p^\sharp(M[Q_1/x_1, \cdots, Q_n/x_n])]\!]^\sigma$ *when* $\widehat{p}_X(\alpha(t)) \Downarrow$ *and* $\widehat{p}_X(\alpha(s)) \Downarrow$*. On the other hand, because* M *is a faithful context with respect to* Γ*, there exist* $M_p \in \mathcal{C}$ *with* $fv(M_p) = \{y_1, \cdots, y_m\}$ *and a variable mapping* ρ*, such that*

$$\Gamma \models p^\sharp(M[P_1/x_1, \cdots, P_n/x_n]) \simeq M_p[N_1/y_1, N_2/y_2, \cdots, N_m/y_m]$$
$$\Gamma \models p^\sharp(M[Q_1/x_1, \cdots, Q_n/x_n]) \simeq M_p[L_1/y_1, L_2/y_2, \cdots, L_m/y_m]$$

where, for $j = 1, \cdots, m$*, if* $\rho_p(y_j) = (x_i, \kappa *)$*, then* $N_j \stackrel{\text{def}}{=} P_i$ *and* $L_j \stackrel{\text{def}}{=} Q_i$*, and if* $\rho_p(y_j) = (x_i, \kappa p')$*, then* $N_j \stackrel{\text{def}}{=} p'^\sharp(P_i)$ *and* $L_j \stackrel{\text{def}}{=} p'^\sharp(Q_i)$*. In all cases of the definition of* ρ*, it is not hard to show that either* $N_j = L_j$ *or* $([\![N_j]\!]^\sigma, [\![L_j]\!]^\sigma) \in S$ *since either* $P_i = Q_i$ *or* $([\![P_i]\!]^\sigma, [\![Q_i]\!]^\sigma) \in R$ *and* $R \Longrightarrow S$*. Thus,* $(\widehat{p}_X(\alpha(t)), \widehat{p}_X(\alpha(s))) \in \phi_{\mathcal{C}}(S)$*. These show that* $\phi_{\mathcal{C}}(R) \Longrightarrow \phi_{\mathcal{C}}(S)$*.* □

By Theorem 5, we obtain the following theorem, which can be regarded as the bisimulation-up-to context proof method for polynomial coalgebras.

Theorem 6. *Let* M_1 *and* M_2 *be two state terms,* $x_1, \cdots x_n$ *be variables in* $fv(M_1) \cap fv(M_2)$*, and* Γ *be a formula set. Then* $\Gamma \models M_1 \simeq M_2$ *if*

(1) $\Gamma \models M_1 \Downarrow \leftrightarrow M_2 \Downarrow$*;*

(2) for all $p \in \mathit{OPATH}(\mathbf{T})$*,* $\Gamma \models p^\sharp(M_1) \approx p^\sharp(M_2)$ *; and*

(3) for all $p \in \mathit{SPATH}(\mathbf{T})$*, there exist a faithful context* M_p *with respect to* Γ *with* $fv(M_p) = \{y_1, \cdots, y_m\}$*, and state terms* $N_1, \cdots, N_m, L_1, \cdots, L_m$ *such that* $\Gamma \models M_p[N_1/y_1, \cdots, N_m/y_m] \Downarrow \leftrightarrow M_p[L_1/y_1, \cdots, L_m/y_m] \Downarrow$ *and*

$$\Gamma \models p^\sharp(M_1) \simeq M_p[N_1/y_1, \cdots, N_m/y_m]$$
$$\Gamma \models p^\sharp(M_2) \simeq M_p[L_1/y_1, \cdots, L_m/y_m]$$

where, for $j = 1, \cdots, m$*, either* $N_j = L_j$*, or there exist terms* $Q_{j_1}, \cdots, Q_{j_n}$ *such that* $N_j = M_1[Q_{j_1}/x_1, \cdots, Q_{j_n}/x_n]$ *and* $L_j = M_2[Q_{j_1}/x_1, \cdots, Q_{j_n}/x_n]$*.*

Proof. (Sketch) Let $\mathcal{M}$ *be a model,* (X, α) *be the coalgebra of* $\mathcal{M}$*. Assume that* $\mathcal{M} \models \Gamma$*, we define a relation* $R \subseteq X \times X$*:*

$$R = \{ \ ([\![M_1]\!]^\sigma, [\![M_2]\!]^\sigma) \mid \sigma \text{ is an assignment}, [\![M_1]\!]^\sigma \Downarrow, \text{ and } [\![M_2]\!]^\sigma \Downarrow \ \}$$

It is not hard to show that R *is a quasi-bisimulation and* $R \Longrightarrow \phi_{\mathcal{C}}(R)$*, where* $\phi_{\mathcal{C}}$ *is defined as in Theorem 5. And then,* $\mathcal{M} \models M_1 \simeq M_2$ *follows from* $R \subseteq \sim$*.* □

Example 7. Continue to Example 4, we use Theorem 6 to show that $\Gamma \models x \oplus (y \times z) \simeq (x \times y) \oplus (x \times z)$. Let $M_1 = (x \times y) \oplus (x \times z)$ and $M_2 = x \times (y \oplus z)$. From $\Gamma \models r_1 \cdot (r_2 + r_3) \approx (r_1 \cdot r_2) + (r_1 \cdot r_3)$, we obtain $\Gamma \models \mathit{head}(M_1) \approx \mathit{head}(M_2)$. And from $\Gamma \models tail(x \times y) \simeq ([head(x)] \times tail(y)) \oplus (tail(x) \times y)$ and $\Gamma \models (x \oplus y) \simeq (y \oplus x)$, it is not hard to show that

$$\Gamma \models tail(M_1) \simeq (x \oplus y)[N_1/x, N_2/y] \qquad \Gamma \models tail(M_2) \simeq (x \oplus y)[L_1/x, L_2/y]$$

where $N_1 = M_1[[head(x)]/x, tail(y)/y, tail(z)/z]$, $N_2 = M_1[tail(x)/x, y/y, z/z]$, $L_1 = M_2[[head(x)]/x, tail(y)/y, tail(z)/z]$, $L_2 = M_2[tail(x)/x, y/y, z/z]$. Therefore, by Theorem 6, $\Gamma \models x \oplus (y \times z) \simeq (x \times y) \oplus (x \times z)$ as required.

Generally, it is not hard to prove that $x_1 \oplus x_2 \oplus \cdots \oplus x_n$ is a faithful context with respect to Γ, and then the bisimulation-up-to proof method in Rutten's stream calculus (c.f. Theorem 4.2 in [16]) is an instance of Theorem 6.

5 Related Work

The coalgebraic specification language presented in this paper can be thought of as a simple version of CCSL [5]. A major difference between our language and CCSL stands in the use of paths of polynomial functors. Names of class methods are used to construct terms in CCSL for specifying classes in object-oriented programming. From Example 1 and 2, one may note that paths can give more detailed observations and state transitions than class methods. Most importantly, the relationship between paths and bisimulations enable us to express and reason about bisimulations through using state bisimulation formulas in our language. There exist other equational approaches (e.g. [6,9]), as well as modal logic approaches (e.g. [18,7,8,19,20]), to specify coalgebras. However, none of them provide a way to express and reason about bisimulations directly.

Recently, Bonsangue, Rutten and Silva generalize Kleene's regular expressions to a specification language for polynomial coalgebras, and present a sound and complete (with respect to bisimulation) axiomatization for the equational system of this language [10,11]. Actually, an expression in this language indicates how to construct an element of final coalgebra, and all expressions (modulo equivalence defined in the equational system) form a subcoalgebra of final coalgebra. Compared with this language, a distinctive feature of our language is that functional operators can be used to construct terms. And then the bisimulation proof methods are used to reason about the relationship between bisimulations and those operators. It would be interesting to investigate the precise connection between our language and this language, and see whether the bisimulation proof methods could also be formulated in terms of the regular expressions.

Instead of investigating bisimulation proof methods in coalgebraic specification languages, there exist a few categorical descriptions of bisimulation proof principles for coalgebras in the literature. Lenisa presented a notion of $\boldsymbol{F}$-bisimulation "up-to $\boldsymbol{T}$" [21]; and Bartels generalized Lenisa's idea by introducing a notion of λ-bisimulations [22]. Luo Lingyun introduced a notion of consistent functions [23], which is close to the notion of sound functions in [3]. Actually, Luo defined a notion of progressions by using relation lifting $Rel(\boldsymbol{T})(-)$ [24] of functor $\boldsymbol{T}$: a relation R progresses to S iff, $(x, y) \in R$ implies $(\alpha(x), \beta(y)) \in Rel(\boldsymbol{T})(S)$, where (X, α) and (Y, β) are $\boldsymbol{T}$-coalgebras. And then, the notion of consistent functions in [23] is essentially the same as the notion of sound functions. So, Luo applied the Sangiorgi's ideas from labeled transition systems to the coalgebras of the functors whose relation lifting has certain properties (e.g. Proposition 2.2 in [23]). However, he could not give a bisimulation-up-to context proof method, since his study is not based on a specification language.

Our work can be seen as an extension of Luo's work for polynomial coalgebras. The notion of sound functions in this paper is essentially equivalent to the notion of consistent functions for polynomial coalgebras, but we can provide more powerful sound functions based on faithful contexts to further facilitate the bisimulation proofs for polynomial coalgebras since our work is based on a coalgebraic specification language. Compared with the work presented by Lenisa [21] and Bartels [22], the bisimulation proof methods based on sound functions are more practicable than λ-bisimulations, because the notion of λ-bisimulations is too abstract, and one should make an effort to verify properties of involved structures to form a distributive law.

6 Conclusions

In this paper, a term calculus based on paths of polynomial coalgebras is presented for building formulas to specify polynomial coalgebras. The fact that bisimulations can be defined by paths enables the specification language to express bisimulations explicitly and to reason about them by using certain bisimulation proof methods as reasoning rules. Sangiorgi's bisimulation proof methods for labeled transition systems are transformed to reasoning rules in the form of semantic consequence relations for the language.

The major contribution of this paper is twofold: (i) We use paths of polynomial functors to define an equational coalgebraic specification language. As to our knowledge, this is a novel approach to specify properties of polynomial coalgebras. (ii) We provide the first study on bisimulation proof methods in coalgebraic specification languages for the theory of coalgebras. We give path-based definitions of progressions and sound functions, and introduce the notion of faithful contexts for our proposed coalgebraic specification language. And then, we are able to apply Sangiorgi's bisimulation-up-to proof methods, including bisimulation-up-to context proof methods, to this language.

The work presented in this paper is a fundamental study of the path-based specification language for polynomial coalgebras. We shall study the language further in the future, for example, to investigate the connections with other languages, to explore the congruence formats for polynomial coalgebras, such as GSOS-like formats for polynomial coalgebras, and to look at under what conditions for the specification of function symbols a semantic model of the specification can form a λ-bialgebra. Of course, we shall use the language to specify more practical examples of polynomial coalgebras, especially classes in object-oriented programs. Moreover, in order to automate the bisimulation proofs, we shall implement tools for translating the rules induced by the bisimulation proof methods presented in this paper to theorem proving assistant systems (e.g. PVS).

Acknowledgements. Thanks to Prof. Jun ZHANG for helpful discussions on improving the paper. We would also like to thank the reviewers for giving us valuable feedback and suggestions.

References

1. Rutten, J.: Universal coalgebra: A theory of systems. TCS 249(1), 3–80 (2000)
2. Sangiorgi, D.: On the origins of bisimulation and coinduction. TOPLAS, Articale 15 31(4) (2009)
3. Sangiorgi, D.: On the bisimulation proof method. Mathematical Structures in Computer Science 8, 447–479 (1998)
4. Sangiorgi, D., Walker, D.: The pi-calculus: a Theory of Mobile Processes. Cambridge University Press, Cambridge (2001)
5. Rothe, J., Tews, H., Jacobs, B.: The coalgebraic class specification language CCSL. Journal of Universal Computer Science 7(2), 175–193 (2001)
6. Cîrstea, C.: Integrating Observatins and Computations in the Specification of State-based, Dynamical Systems. PhD thesis, University of Oxford (2000)
7. Kurz, A.: Specifying coalgebras with modal logic. TCS 260(1-2), 119–138 (2001)
8. Rößiger, M.: From modal logic to terminal coalgebras. TCS 260, 209–228 (2001)
9. Goldblatt, R.: Equational logic of polynomial coalgebras. In: Balbiani, P., Suzuki, N.-Y., Wolter, F., Zakharyaschev, M. (eds.) Advances in Modal Logic, vol. 4, pp. 149–184. King's College Publications (2003)
10. Bonsangue, M., Rutten, J., Silva, A.: Regular expressons for polynomial coalgebras. CWI Report SEN-E0703 (2007)
11. Bonsangue, M., Rutten, J., Silva, A.: An algebra for Kripke polynomial coalgebras. In: 24th Annual IEEE Symposium on Logic in Computer Science, pp. 49–58. IEEE Press, Los Alamitos (2009)
12. Jacobs, B.: Towards a duality result in coalgebraic modal logic. ENTCS 33 (2000)
13. Goldblatt, R.: A calculus of terms for coalgebras of polynomial functors. ENTCS 44, 161–184 (2001)
14. Rößiger, M.: Languages for coalgebras on datafunctors. ENTCS 19, 39–60 (1999)
15. Jacobs, B.: The temporal logic of coalgebras via galois algebras. Technical Report CSI-R9906, Computer Science Institution, University of Nijmegen (1999)
16. Rutten, J.: Elements of stream calculus (an extensive exercise in coinduction). ENTCS 45, 1–66 (2001)
17. Jacobs, B.: Exercises in coalgebraic specification. In: Backhouse, R., Crole, R., Gibbons, J. (eds.) Algebraic and Coalgebraic Methods in the Mathematics of Program Construction. LNCS, vol. 2297, pp. 237–280. Springer, Heidelberg (2002)
18. Moss, L.: Coalgebraic logic. APAL 96(1-3), 277–317 (1999)
19. Jacobs, B.: Many-sorted coalgeraic modal logic: a model-theoretical study. ITA 35(1), 31–59 (2001)
20. Pattinson, D.: Coalgebraic modal logic: soundness, completeness and decidability of local consequence. TCS 309(1-3), 177–193 (2003)
21. Lenisa, M.: From set-theoretic coinduction to coalgebraic coinduction: some resuults, some problems. ENTCS 19, 1–21 (1999)
22. Bartels, F.: Generalised coinduction. Mathematical Structures in Computer Science 13, 321–348 (2003)
23. Lingyun, L.: An effective coalgebraic bisimulation proof method. ENTCS 164, 105–119 (2006)
24. Jacobs, B.: Introduction to Coalgebra: Towards Mathematics of States and Observations. Book Draft (2005), `http://www.cs.ru.nl/~bart`

Context-Preserving XQuery Fusion

Hiroyuki Kato[1], Soichiro Hidaka[1], Zhenjiang Hu[1],
Keisuke Nakano[2], and Yasunori Ishihara[3]

[1] National Institute of Informatics, Japan
{kato,hidaka,hu}@nii.ac.jp
[2] The University of Electro-Communications, Japan
ksk@cs.uec.ac.jp
[3] Osaka University, Japan
ishihara@ist.osaka-u.ac.jp

Abstract. XQuery is a DBPL for querying XML databases. The semantics of XQuery is context sensitive and requires preservation of document order. In this paper, we propose, as far as we are aware, the first XQuery fusion that can deal with both the document order and the context of XQuery expressions. More specifically, we carefully design a context representation of XQuery expressions based on the Dewey order encoding, develop a context-preserving XQuery fusion for ordered trees by static emulation of the XML store, and prove that our fusion is correct. Our XQuery fusion has been implemented, and all the examples in this paper have passed the system.

1 Introduction

Fusion [22,2,5] is a well-known technique for improving efficiency by removing unnecessary intermediate data from the computation. Although it has been applied to optimize query languages such as SQL [3] and object query languages [5], it remains a challenge to implement fusion for XQuery optimization. This is because XQuery has more complicated semantics [12]; *it is context sensitive and requires preservation of document order*. One may consider, for example, the following naive fusion transformation[1] (as studied in [4]).

$$\langle e \rangle E_1, \ldots, E_n \langle /e \rangle / c \mapsto \sigma_c(E_1), \ldots, \sigma_c(E_n)\ ^2 \qquad \text{(F)}$$

This transformation works correctly only if the order of the XML document and the context can be ignored. However, order is an important issue in XML documents [6,1], and various index structure for ordered trees have been developed for XML documents [21,15,25]. When we view an XML document as an ordered tree, an existing fusion transformation like (F) by naive elimination of element constructors does not work correctly because the context, which is a navigation of newly constructed trees, is missing during the transformation.

[1] Analogous to relational algebra operators, σ_c is used as a selection, which extracts data with their element name being c.

[2] We use "narrow" angle brackets for XML tags. For example, we use $\langle e \rangle$ instead of <e>.

K. Ueda (Ed.): APLAS 2010, LNCS 6461, pp. 255–270, 2010.

```
<na>
  <lhs>
    <item><a/></item>
    <item><b/></item>
  </lhs>
  <rhs>
    <item><c/></item>
    <item><d/></item>
  </rhs>
</na>
```

```
<sa>
    (<lhs>/na/rhs/item</lhs>,
      <rhs>/na/lhs/item</rhs>)
</sa>
```

```
<sa>
  <lhs>
    <item><c/></item>
    <item><d/></item>
  </lhs>
  <rhs>
    <item><a/></item>
    <item><b/></item>
  </rhs>
</sa>
```

Fig. 1. Source XML:S (left). XQuery expression: e_m (middle) and the serialized result: T (right).

Consider the simple case illustrated in Figure 1, where the query e_m (the middle) is applied to the source S (the left), and the target T (the right) is obtained as the serialized result. Let us apply the following query e_1 to the serialized T,

$$e_1 : \textbf{let } \$v := (/\mathsf{sa}/\mathsf{rhs}, /\mathsf{sa}/\mathsf{lhs}) \textbf{ return } \$v/\mathsf{item}.$$

Since the semantics of "axis access" by using "/" in XQuery (and XPath) requires sorting without duplicates in the document order, the correct result is the following sequence of "item" elements:

$$\langle\mathsf{item}\rangle\langle\mathsf{c}/\rangle\langle/\mathsf{item}\rangle, \langle\mathsf{item}\rangle\langle\mathsf{d}/\rangle\langle/\mathsf{item}\rangle, \langle\mathsf{item}\rangle\langle\mathsf{a}/\rangle\langle/\mathsf{item}\rangle, \langle\mathsf{item}\rangle\langle\mathsf{b}/\rangle\langle/\mathsf{item}\rangle.$$

However, for the composite query $e_1 \circ e_m$, by unfolding the expression e_m, we can get

$$\begin{array}{l} \textbf{let } \$t := \langle\mathsf{sa}\rangle\{(\langle\mathsf{lhs}\rangle/\mathsf{na}/\mathsf{rhs}/\mathsf{item}\langle/\mathsf{lhs}\rangle, \langle\mathsf{rhs}\rangle/\mathsf{na}/\mathsf{lhs}/\mathsf{item}\langle/\mathsf{rhs}\rangle)\}\langle/\mathsf{sa}\rangle \\ \textbf{return let } \$v := (\$t/\mathsf{rhs}, \$t/\mathsf{lhs}) \textbf{ return } \$v/\mathsf{item}. \end{array}$$

Now if we perform the calculation according to the context-insensitive fusion rule (F):

$$\begin{array}{ll} & e_1 \circ e_m \\ \rightarrow & \{(\text{variable expansion for } \$t); (\text{F})\} \\ & \textbf{let } \$v := (\langle\mathsf{rhs}\rangle/\mathsf{na}/\mathsf{lhs}/\mathsf{item}\langle/\mathsf{rhs}\rangle, \langle\mathsf{lhs}\rangle/\mathsf{na}/\mathsf{rhs}/\mathsf{item}\langle/\mathsf{lhs}\rangle) \\ & \textbf{return } \$v/\mathsf{item} \\ \rightarrow & \{(\text{variable expansion for } \$v); (\text{F})\} \\ & (/\mathsf{na}/\mathsf{lhs}/\mathsf{item}, /\mathsf{na}/\mathsf{rhs}/\mathsf{item}) \end{array}$$

then evaluating the transformed query $(/\mathsf{na}/\mathsf{lhs}/\mathsf{item}, /\mathsf{na}/\mathsf{rhs}/\mathsf{item})$ on S gives

$$\langle\mathsf{item}\rangle\langle\mathsf{a}/\rangle\langle/\mathsf{item}\rangle, \langle\mathsf{item}\rangle\langle\mathsf{b}/\rangle\langle/\mathsf{item}\rangle, \langle\mathsf{item}\rangle\langle\mathsf{c}/\rangle\langle/\mathsf{item}\rangle, \langle\mathsf{item}\rangle\langle\mathsf{d}/\rangle\langle/\mathsf{item}\rangle$$

whose order of "item" elements is different from the expected result. Furthermore, if we consider the query e_2 on T:

$$e_2 : \textbf{let } \$v := /\mathsf{sa}/\mathsf{rhs}/\mathsf{item} \textbf{ return } \$v/..$$

then although the expected result of e_2 to T is the "rhs" element, the result of the transformed query from $e_2 \circ e_m$ via similar steps above is the "lhs" element. In both examples, the problem is caused by not having the context, which is a tree navigation over the newly constructed XML fragment using ⟨sa⟩...⟨/sa⟩ in e_m.

The problem of the existing fusion transformation lies in that the naive elimination of element constructors during the transformation does not preserve the (computation) context because element constructors construct ordered trees. This implies that eliminating element constructors in XQuery expressions and preserving the context of the expressions are conflicting requirements. The purpose of our work is to propose a new fusion mechanism to meet these two requirements. To this end, we should find a way to manage the context of the original expressions in developing a correct fusion transformation.

While we will show the concrete solution to both examples at the end of this paper, we shall give an intuitive idea of our solution to the first example here. For two step expressions /na/rhs/item and /na/lhs/item in e_m which constructs the ordered tree T, there is a fact that the items of the sequence generated by /na/rhs/item always precede ones generated by /na/lhs/item in the ordered tree T for an arbitrary XML store. By adding this information to these two step expressions, for given $e_1 \circ e_m$, we can formulate the correct XQuery expression (/na/rhs/item, /na/lhs/item) from this information. We call this information, context.

We propose a novel context-preserving XQuery fusion for when an XML document is modeled as an ordered tree. Our basic idea is *to lift dynamic operations on XML store to the static level of expression*. Our main contributions can be summarized as follows.

- To keep track of context, we carefully design the context representation of XQuery expressions to reflect the properties of element constructions. This enable us to statically emulate newly created XML fragments — created by element constructors — in the XML store.
- We develop a context-preserving fusion for XQuery by partial evaluation and prove the correctness of our fusion. Our fusion introduces an annotated XQuery, which is an XQuery expression with the context as an annotation, to preserve the context of the input expressions even when the element constructors are eliminated during our fusion transformation.

The paper proceeds as follows. Section 2 reviews the XQuery semantics and introduces value equivalent expressions to show our fusion concisely. In Section 3, we carefully design the context of XQuery expressions by extending Dewey code and its order to suite the semantics of XQuery expressions. Section 4 presents the algorithm of context-preserving fusion using the extended Dewey code and its order. We discuss related work in Section 5 and conclude the paper in Section 6.

2 XQuery Semantics

To show our XQuery fusion concisely and that it is semantics-preserving, we briefly review the semantics of the core part of XQuery that is based on [12]. Our target XQuery expressions, a subset of XQuery, are as follows.

$$\begin{aligned} e ::= &\ \$\mathrm{v} \mid (e, e, ..., e) \mid () \mid e/\alpha::\tau \mid \mathbf{for}\ \$\mathrm{v}\ \mathbf{in}\ e\ \mathbf{return}\ e \\ \mid &\ \mathbf{let}\ \$\mathrm{v} := e\ \mathbf{return}\ e \mid \langle t \rangle e \langle /t \rangle \end{aligned}$$

A query expression can be a variable $\$v$, a sequence expression $(e_1, \ldots, e_n)$ where each subexpression e_i is not a sequence expression, an empty sequence (), a location step expression $e/\alpha::\tau$ where α is an axis which can be child, self, parent (..), and τ is a name test which can be a tag name t or $*$ (an arbitrary tag), a "for"-expression, a "let"-expression, or an element construction expression $\langle t \rangle e \langle /t \rangle$. Since we focus on newly constructed trees that consist of XML nodes, to simplify the presentation, a constant c is represented by "empty-element tags" like $\langle$c /$\rangle$. Although constants themselves are not nodes, they become a (text) node when they occur in an element constructor. For example, a constant "abc" is not a node i.e., this constant does not populate any ordered trees. On the other hand, consider $\langle$a$\rangle$"abc"$\langle$/a$\rangle$; in this expression, the constant "abc" is a text node because the constant occurs in the element construction of $\langle$a$\rangle$(...)$\langle$/a$\rangle$, i.e., this constant is a child node of the element node of a. We could define the semantics of constants with such behavior, but this would make our presentation unnecessarily complex.

2.1 Sequence: Data Model in XQuery

The data model of XQuery is *sequences* [23]. A sequence is an ordered collection of zero or more items. One important characteristic of the data model is that sequences are *flat* in the sense that a sequence never contains other sequences; if sequences are combined, the result is always a flattened sequence. In addition, there is no distinction between an item and a singleton sequence containing that item, i.e., we often write $[a]$ as a or vice versa.

We denote the empty sequence as [], non-empty sequences for example as [a,b,c], and the concatenation of two sequences s_1 and s_2 as $s_1 +\!\!+ s_2$. We use $\in$ for sequence containment in addition to set containment and $[d | d \in D \wedge \phi(d)]$ for a sequence of d obtained by selecting them from D, all items that satisfy $\phi(d)$.

2.2 Dewey Order Encoding and XML Store

An XML document is modeled as an ordered tree. *Document order* in an XML document is a total order defined over the nodes in a tree, and this order is determined by a preorder traversal of the tree. This order plays an important role in the semantics of XQuery, especially in node creation and axis accesses. An XQuery expression is evaluated against an XML store which contains XML fragments with their document order. This store contains fragments that are created as intermediate results, in addition to the initial XML documents [12].

Dewey order encoding of XML nodes is a lossless representation of a position in the document order [15,21]. In Dewey order, each node is represented by a path from a root using '.' : (1) a root node is encoded by $r \in \mathcal{R}$, where $\mathcal{R}$ is a countably infinite set of special codes; (2) say that a node a is the n-th child of a node b; then the Dewey code of a, $did(a)$, is $did(b).n$. The fact that the relative order of nodes in distinct trees is implementation-dependent leads to nondeterminism in XQuery. Therefore, if two Dewey codes begin with different codes, it implies that the two nodes are in different ordered trees. By using Dewey order encoding, one can easily compute axis relations. For example, $\texttt{ancestor}(d_1, d_2)$ holds when d_1 has the form $d_2.n_1.n_2.\cdots.n_k$.

Let $\mathcal{T}$ be a set of symbols for element names, and $\mathcal{D}$ be a countably infinite set of Dewey codes on which a strict partial order $<$ and the equality $=$ is defined.

Definition 1 (Simple XML Store). *A simple XML store is a pair $St = (D, \nu)$, where (a) D is a finite subset of $\mathcal{D}$ and (b) ν is a partial function $\nu : \mathcal{D} \mapsto \mathcal{T}$ that maps a Dewey code to its element name.*

For instance, the store of the source S in Figure 1 is defined as $St_0 = (D_0, \nu_0)$, where $D_0 = \{s, s.1, s.1.1, s.1.1.1, s.1.2, s.1.2.1, s.2, s.2.1, s.2.1.1, s.2.2, s.2.2.1\}$ and $\nu_0(s) = \mathtt{na}$, $\nu_0(s.1) = \mathtt{lhs}$, $\nu_0(s.2) = \mathtt{rhs}$, $\nu_0(s.1.1) = \nu_0(s.1.2) = \nu_0(s.2.1) = \nu_0(s.2.2) = \mathtt{item}$, $\nu_0(s.1.1.1) = \mathtt{a}$, $\nu_0(s.1.2.1) = \mathtt{b}$, $\nu_0(s.2.1.1) = \mathtt{c}$, $\nu_0(s.2.2.1) = \mathtt{d}$. In what follows, we will refer to a simple XML store as an XML store. We denote the disjoint union of two stores St_1 and St_2 as $St_1 \cup St_2$ (combining D and ν independently).

Definition 2 (Value Equivalence, $\equiv_{(St_1,St_2)}$). *Given two stores St_1, St_2, and two nodes, d_1 in St_1 and d_2 in St_2, d_1 and d_2 are said to be value equal, denoted as $d_1 \equiv_{(St_1,St_2)} d_2$, if d_1 and d_2 refer to two isomorphic trees, i.e., there is a one-to-one function $h : D_1 \mapsto D_2$ with $D_1 = \{d | d \in D_{St_1} \wedge \mathtt{ancestor\text{-}or\text{-}self}(d, d_1)\}$ and $D_2 = \{d | d \in D_{St_2} \wedge \mathtt{ancestor\text{-}or\text{-}self}(d, d_2)\}$, such that for each d and $d' \in D_1$, it holds that (1) $h(d) \in D_2$, (2) $\nu(d) = \nu(h(d))$, and (3) $d < d'$ iff $h(d) < h(d')$. This definition can be extended to the value equivalence over two sequences, straightforwardly.*

2.3 Formal Semantics

The formal semantics of XQuery established by W3C is defined over XQuery Core, which is a subset of XQuery [24]. While XQuery Core does not have a location step expression, the reason why our target has is that (1) evaluating path expressions is more efficient than "for"-expressions [8,19], although theoretically, it can be translated into "for"-expressions; and (2) previous work on XQuery dealt with location steps [14,10,9].

Figure 2 shows the semantics of our target XQuery using a set of inference rules. In these rules, a judgment of the form $St; En \vdash e \Rightarrow (St', s)$ indicates that the evaluation of expression e against the store St and environment En (mapping variables to values) results in a (new) store St' and value s. The semantics of sequence expressions, "let"-expressions and variables are straightforward. The semantics of a "for"-expression (**for** $\$v$ **in** e_1 **return** e_2) is the concatenation of the results of e_2 evaluated N times for each item in the result of e_1 but with v in the environment bound to the item in question in the result of e_1, where N is the length of the sequence of the result of e_1. The semantics of the element constructor ($\langle t \rangle e \langle /t \rangle$) and location step ($e/\alpha :: \tau$) are worth futher attention because they are evaluated using the document order. The semantics of $\langle t \rangle e \langle /t \rangle$ is as follows. A new store St_2 that contains a new root node having t as its name and having contents is created. The contents are the value-equivalent sequence to the result of e. St_2 is added to the input store, and the newly created root node is returned. The semantics of $e/\alpha :: \tau$ is as follows. First, e is evaluated. Then, for each node d_i in its result, construct a sequence s_i such that for each content d'_i in s_i, d'_i is contained in St_0, and α-relation holds for d_i and d'_i, and the element name of d'_i is

$$\frac{}{St; En \vdash () \Rightarrow (St, [])} \qquad \frac{St; En \vdash e_1 \Rightarrow (St_1, s_1) \quad \cdots \quad St_{N-1}; En \vdash e_N \Rightarrow (St_N, s_N)}{St; En \vdash (e_1, \ldots, e_N) \Rightarrow (St_N, s_1 ++ \ldots ++ s_N)}$$

$$\frac{\begin{array}{c} St; En \vdash e_1 \Rightarrow (St_0, [d_1, \cdots, d_N]) \\ St_0; En + \{\$v \mapsto d_1\} \vdash e_2 \Rightarrow (St_1, s_1) \\ \cdots \\ St_{N-1}; En + \{\$v \mapsto d_N\} \vdash e_2 \Rightarrow (St_N, s_N) \end{array}}{St; En \vdash \textbf{for } \$v \textbf{ in } e_1 \textbf{ return } e_2 \Rightarrow (St_N, s_1 ++ \cdots ++ s_N)}$$

$$\frac{\begin{array}{c} St; En \vdash e_1 \Rightarrow (St_1, s_1) \\ St_1; En + \{\$v \mapsto s_1\} \vdash e_2 \Rightarrow (St_2, s_2) \end{array}}{St, En \vdash \textbf{let } \$v := e_1 \textbf{ return } e_2 \Rightarrow (St_2, s_2)} \qquad \frac{}{St; En \vdash \$v \Rightarrow (St, En(\$v))}$$

$$\frac{\begin{array}{cc} St; En \vdash e \Rightarrow (St_1, s_1) & \text{a fresh } r \in \mathcal{R} \\ d \in D_{St_2} \Rightarrow d \text{ begins with } r & \nu_{St_2}(r) = t \\ \textbf{ddo}_{St_2}[d' | d' \in D_{St_2} \wedge \textbf{child}(d', r)] = s_2 & s_1 \equiv_{(St_1, St_2)} s_2 \end{array}}{St; En \vdash \langle t \rangle e \langle /t \rangle \Rightarrow (St \cup St_2, [r])}$$

$$\frac{\begin{array}{c} St; En \vdash e \Rightarrow (St_0, [d_1, \cdots, d_N]) \\ [d'_1 | d'_1 \in D_{St_0} \wedge \alpha(d'_1, d_1) \wedge \nu_{St_0}(d'_1) = \tau] = s_1 \\ \cdots \\ [d'_N | d'_N \in D_{St_0} \wedge \alpha(d'_N, d_N) \wedge \nu_{St_0}(d'_N) = \tau] = s_m \end{array}}{St; En \vdash e/\alpha :: \tau \Rightarrow (St_0, \textbf{ddo}_{St_0}(s_1 ++ \cdots ++ s_m))}$$

Fig. 2. Semantics of XQuery using the simple XML store

τ. The results of these sequences are concatenated. Finally, this sequence is sorted in the document order and duplicates are removed from it because an axis access by "/" requires sorting and duplicate elimination in the document order. This sorting without duplicates is performed by using the function **ddo** (distinct-doc-order).

Value equivalent expressions are introduced in order to prove the correctness of our fusion later.

Definition 3 (Value Equivalent Expressions). *Given a store St, an environment En, and two XQuery expressions e_1 and e_2, e_1 and e_2 are said to be value equivalent, if the following conditions hold; $St; En \vdash e_1 \Rightarrow (St_1, s_1)$, $St; En \vdash e_2 \Rightarrow (St_2, s_2)$ and $s_1 \equiv_{(St_1, St_2)} s_2$.*

3 Emulating XML Stores with Extended Dewey Codes

The problem of the existing fusion transformation is that the naive elimination of element constructors during the transformation does not preserve the context. To give a correct fusion transformation, we should be able to emulate (keep track of) the context information (i.e., XML store) during the static transformation when an element is constructed. Our idea is to *lift dynamic operations on XML store to the static level of expression*, and it is based on the observation that Dewey order encoding of the result of the evaluation of an expression corresponds well to the structure of the expression.

3.1 XML Store Emulation on Expression

First, we show an important property for element constructors in terms of Dewey code: The Dewey order encoding of the result of an evaluation of an expression corresponds to the structure of the expression. This enables us to associate the static transformation world with the dynamic evaluation world by using Dewey code.

Given an element construction $\langle t\rangle e\langle /t\rangle$, we denote its relation with its result by $\langle t\rangle e\langle /t\rangle \sim r$ if there exist St, En, St' such that $St; En \vdash \langle t\rangle e\langle /t\rangle \Rightarrow (St', r)$.

Property 1 (Dewey code correspondence in element construction). For an element construction, $\langle t\rangle e\langle /t\rangle$, the following properties hold.

(i) $\langle t\rangle e\langle /t\rangle \sim r$, where $r \in \mathcal{R}$ and r is not in the input store.
(ii) $\langle t\rangle e\langle /t\rangle \sim r$ and $e \sim [r_1, \cdots, r_n]$ imply $r_i = r.i$.
(iii) For $\langle t\rangle(e_1, e_2)\langle /t\rangle$, $(e_1, e_2) \sim [r_1, r_2]$ and $d_1 \in r_1$ and $d_2 \in r_2$ imply $d_1 < d_2$.
(iv) $\langle t_1\rangle e_1\langle /t_1\rangle \sim r_1$ and $\langle t_2\rangle e_2\langle /t_2\rangle \sim r_2$ imply $r_1 \neq r_2$, where $r_1, r_2 \in \mathcal{R}$.

The above correspondence property hints that we should associate each expression with a Dewey code, so that these codes can be used to keep track of context information during the fusion transformation. For instance, for the element construction $\langle t\rangle(\$v/c, \$v/a)\langle /t\rangle$, we may give the following Dewey order encoding to the expression:

$$(\langle t\rangle(\$v/c)^{r.1}, (\$v/a)^{r.2}\langle /t\rangle)^r$$

where e^d denotes that d is the Dewey order encoding of the expression e (we will define this formally in Section 4.)

One difficulty, however, remains in associating Dewey codes to expressions to keep the context information: how do we deal with the "for" ("let") expressions in XQuery? We have to extend Dewey code for this purpose.

3.2 Extended Dewey Code

To be able to associate XQuery expressions with suitable context information, we propose an *extended Dewey code* (xD), defined by

$$\begin{aligned} \hat{d} &::= n\ \hat{x} \mid \underline{\epsilon} \mid \underline{[\hat{d}, \hat{d}, \ldots, \hat{d}]} \\ \hat{x} &::= \epsilon \mid \text{"."}\ \hat{d} \mid \underline{\text{"\#"}\ \hat{d}} \end{aligned}$$

where $n \in (\mathcal{R} \cup \mathcal{I})$ with $\mathcal{R}$ being a set of special codes[3] and $\mathcal{I}$ being a set of integers. It has a hierarchical structure, the same as in XQuery expressions, because xD is an annotation for an XQuery expression. Here, the underlined parts are our extension, and ϵ is used for a termination, so, every xD ends with ϵ. Intuitively, the form of xD is

[3] The special code is used to exploit *Property* 1 (i).

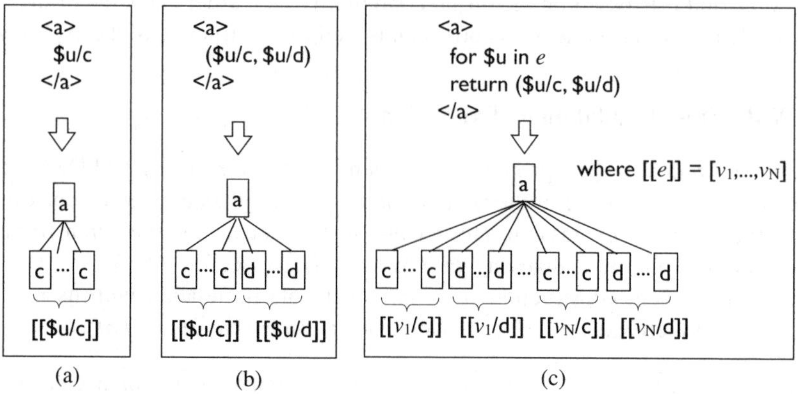

Fig. 3. A simple example for the document order in element creations

as follows. ϵ is annotated to an expression, which does not occur inside an element constructor. A sequence construction has the form of sequence[4] is used. The delimiter ".", which plays the same role as in the original Dewey codes, is used to represent parent-child relationships.

The delimiter "#", which is our extension, represents the association of a "return" clause with a "for" or "let" expression and is used to resolve sortings with duplicate elimination for multiple "for" or "let" expressions that are derived from identical "for" or "let" expressions. Figure 3 (c) shows how an element is constructed with the "for" expression (Q1).

$$\text{Q1: } \langle a\rangle\, \textbf{for}\ \$u\ \textbf{in}\ e\ \textbf{return}\ (\$u/c, \$u/d)\langle/a\rangle$$

To show the idea behind the design of our delimiter "#", let us consider the fusion transformation for the expression ((Q1)/d, (Q1)/c)/ **self** :: $*$. For the expressions (Q1)/d and (Q1)/c, we can get the *value equivalent* expressions (Q2) and (Q3), respectively, from the XQuery semantics.

$$\text{Q2: } \textbf{for}\ \$u\ \textbf{in}\ e\ \textbf{return}\ \$u/d$$

$$\text{Q3: } \textbf{for}\ \$u\ \textbf{in}\ e\ \textbf{return}\ \$u/c$$

Now consider the following expression (Q4).

$$\text{Q4: } (((\text{Q2})), ((\text{Q3})))/\ \textbf{self} :: *$$

As described in the previous section, since axis access by "/" requires sorting and duplicate elimination in document order, the correct transformation of (Q4) should result in (Q5), in which two "for" expressions (Q2) and (Q3) are merged.

[4] This sequence is the same as the data model of XQuery. So, it is flattened, and singleton and its element cannot be distinguished.

Q5: $\textbf{for}\ \$u\ \textbf{in}\ e\ \textbf{return}\ (\$u/c, \$u/d)$

Here, we can capture the order of the two expressions in the "return" expressions by using "#". Thus, by encoding (Q1) into

$$(\langle a\rangle(\textbf{for}\ \$u\ \textbf{in}\ e\ \textbf{return}\ (\$v/c, \$v/d))^{r.1\#[1,2]}\langle/a\rangle)^r$$

and encoding (Q2) and (Q3) into

$$(\textbf{for}\ \$u\ \textbf{in}\ e\ \textbf{return}\ \$v/d)^{r.1\#2}\ \text{and}\ (\textbf{for}\ \$u\ \textbf{in}\ e\ \textbf{return}\ \$v/c)^{r.1\#1}$$

we can apply the transformation to (Q5) (See Section 4), thanks to sorting on subsequences produced by the "for" expressions.

Returning to our extend Dewey codes, we can introduce the context position of sorting and duplicate elimination over $\hat{d}$ in a similar way to the original Dewey code (See [13] for details). Therefore, we can use the functions dc_sort and remove_dup for sorting and duplicate elimination, respectively. The difference from the sorting of the original Dewey code is in merging two extended codes sharing the same prefix until they reach $\#$. For instance, sorting $[r.1\#2, r.1\#1]$ results in $[r.1\#[1,2]]$.

4 XQuery Fusion

This section describes our algorithm for automatic fusion of XQuery expressions so that unnecessary element constructions can be correctly eliminated. Basically, we will focus on fusing the following subexpression,

$$e/\alpha{::}\tau$$

so that unnecessary element constructions in the query expression in e are eliminated under the context of "selection" by $\alpha{::}\tau$.

We add annotations of the extended Dewey codes to the XQuery expression (Figure 4). We sometimes omit the annotation if it is clear from the context. To simplify our presentation, we will assume that there is a global environment for storing all annotated expressions during our fusion transformation, and a function

$$getExpGlobal(r)$$

that can be used to extract the expression whose code is r from the global environment.

$$\begin{aligned} e^{\hat{d}} ::= &\ \$v^{\hat{d}} \mid (e^{\hat{d}}, e^{\hat{d}}, ..., e^{\hat{d}})^{\hat{d}} \mid (e^{\hat{d}}/\alpha{::}\tau)^{\hat{d}} \mid (\textbf{for}\ \$\text{v}\ \textbf{in}\ e^{\hat{d}}\ \textbf{return}\ e^{\hat{d}})^{\hat{d}} \\ \mid &\ (\textbf{let}\ \$\text{v} := e^{\hat{d}}\ \textbf{return}\ e^{\hat{d}})^{\hat{d}} \mid (\langle t\rangle e^{\hat{d}}\langle/t\rangle)^{\hat{d}} \end{aligned}$$

Fig. 4. Annotated XQuery

$$\begin{aligned}
\text{peval } () \ \Theta &= ()^{[]} \\
\text{peval } \$v \ \Theta &= \begin{cases} \Theta(\$v) & \text{if \$v is letvar} \\ \$v & \text{otherwise} \end{cases} && \text{(PEVR)} \\
\text{peval } (e_1, ..., e_N) \ \Theta &= \underline{\text{let}}\, e'_i = \text{peval } e_i \ \Theta && \text{(PESEQ)} \\
&\qquad d_i = \text{extract_dc}(e'_i) \\
&\quad \underline{\text{in}} \text{ flatten } ((e'_1, ..., e'_N)^{[d_1,..,d_N]}) \\
\text{peval } (e/\textbf{child} :: \tau) \ \Theta &= \mathcal{F}_c\,(\text{peval } e \ \Theta)\ \tau && \text{(PECSTP)} \\
\text{peval } (e/\textbf{self} :: \tau) \ \Theta &= \mathcal{F}_s\,(\text{peval } e \ \Theta)\ \tau && \text{(PESSTP)} \\
\text{peval } (e/\textbf{parent} :: \tau) \ \Theta &= \mathcal{F}_p\,(\text{peval } e \ \Theta)\ \tau && \text{(PEPSTP)} \\
\text{peval } (\textbf{let } \$\text{v} := e_1 \textbf{ return } e_2) \ \Theta &= \underline{\text{let}}\, e'_1 = \text{peval } e_1 \ \Theta \\
&\qquad e'_2 = \text{peval } e_2 \ (\Theta \cup \{\$\text{v} \mapsto (e'_1, \textbf{let})\}) \\
&\quad \underline{\text{in}}\, e'_2 && \text{(PELET)} \\
\text{peval } (\textbf{for } \$\text{v} \textbf{ in } e_1 \textbf{ return } e_2) \ \Theta &= \underline{\text{let}}\, e'_1 = \text{peval } e_1 \ \Theta \\
&\qquad e'_2 = \text{peval } e_2 \ (\Theta \cup \{\$\text{v} \mapsto (e'_1, \textbf{for})\}) \\
&\qquad d = \text{extract_dc } e'_2 \\
&\quad \underline{\text{in}}\, (\textbf{for } \$\text{v} \textbf{ in } e'_1 \textbf{ return } e'_2)^{\#d} && \text{(PEFOR)} \\
\text{peval } (\langle t \rangle e \langle /t \rangle) \ \Theta &= \underline{\text{let}}\, e' = \text{peval } e \ \Theta && \text{(PEEC)} \\
&\qquad \text{a fresh } r \in \mathcal{R} \\
&\quad \underline{\text{in}} \text{ dc_assign } \langle t \rangle e' \langle /t \rangle \ r
\end{aligned}$$

Fig. 5. Fusion by partial evaluation

4.1 Fusion Transformation

Figure 5 summarizes our fusion transformation on XQuery expressions. Fusion is defined by a partial evaluation function peval:

$$\text{peval} \ :: \ e \to \Theta \to e^{\hat{d}}$$

which accepts an XQuery expression and an environment Θ (mapping variables bound by "let" or "for" to expressions):

$$\Theta :: Var \to (e^{\hat{d}}, \textbf{let} \mid \textbf{for})$$

and produces a more efficient XQuery expression in which subexpressions are annotated by the extended Dewey codes. As will be seen later, the annotation is used to keep track of information of the order and the context among expressions, and it plays an important role in our fusion transformation. When the fusion transformation is finished, we can ignore all the annotations and get a normal XQuery expression as the final result.

The definition of peval in Figure 5 is straightforward. For a variable, if it is bounded by the outside "let", we retrieve its corresponding expression from the environment; otherwise, it must be a variable bound by the outside "for", and we leave it as is. For a sequence expression, we partially evaluate each element expression and group them into a new sequence annotated with Dewey codes from the results of each element expression. Note that we use flatten to remove nested sequences (e.g.,

$$\begin{aligned}
\mathsf{dc_assign}\ ()^{-}\ r &= ()^{[]} \\
\mathsf{dc_assign}\ \$v^{-}\ r &= \$v^{r} \\
\mathsf{dc_assign}\ (e/c)^{-}\ r &= (e/c)^{r} && \text{(DCSTP)} \\
\mathsf{dc_assign}\ (e_1,\ldots,e_n)^{-}\ r &= \underline{\text{let}}\ r_0 = r && \text{(DCPSEQ)} \\
&\qquad e'_i = \mathsf{dc_assign}\ e_i\ r_{i-1} \\
&\qquad r_i = \mathsf{succ}(\mathsf{extract_dc}\ e'_i) \\
&\quad \underline{\text{in}}\ (e_1,\ldots,e_n)^{[r_1,\ldots,r_n]} \\
\mathsf{dc_assign}\ (\texttt{<}t\texttt{>}e\texttt{</}t\texttt{>})^{-}\ r &= \underline{\text{let}}\ e' = \mathsf{dc_assign}\ e_i\ r.1 && \text{(DCPEC)} \\
&\quad \underline{\text{in}}\ \texttt{<}t\texttt{>}e'\texttt{</}t\texttt{>}^{r} \\
\mathsf{dc_assign}\ (\textbf{for}\ \$v\ \textbf{in}\ e_0\ \textbf{return}\ e)^{-}\ r &= \underline{\text{let}}\ e' = \mathsf{dc_assign}\ e\ 1 && \text{(DCPFOR)} \\
&\qquad bs = \mathsf{extract_dc}\ e' \\
&\quad \underline{\text{in}}\ (\textbf{for}\ \$v\ \textbf{in}\ e_0\ \textbf{return}\ e')^{r\#bs}
\end{aligned}$$

Fig. 6. Dewey code propagation

$\mathsf{flatten}((e_{11}^{r_1}, e_{12}^{r_2})^{[r_1,r_2]}, e_3^{r_3})^{[[r_1,r_2],r_3]} = (e_{11}^{r_1}, e_{12}^{r_2}, e_3^{r_3})^{[r_1,r_2,r_3]})$, and extract_dc to get annotated Dewey code from an expression (i.e., extract_dc $e^d = d$). For a location step expression $e/\alpha{::}\tau$, we perform fusion transformation to eliminate unnecessary element constructions in e after partially evaluating e. We will discuss the definitions of the three important fusion functions $\mathcal{F}_c$, $\mathcal{F}_s$, and $\mathcal{F}_p$, later. For a "let" expression, we first partially evaluate the expression e_1, and then partially evaluate e_2 with an updated environment and return it as the result. We do similarly for a "for" expression except that we finally produce a new "for" expression by gluing partially evaluated results together. For an element construction, after partially evaluating its content expression e into e', we create a new Dewey code for annotating this element and propagate this Dewey code information to all subexpressions in e' (with the function dc_assign) so that we can access (recover) this element constructor when processing the subexpressions of e'. It is this trick that helps to solve the problem of $e_2 \circ e_m$ in the Introduction.

Dewey Code Propagation. Propagating the Dewey code of an element construction to its subexpressions plays an important role in constructing our fusion rules, described later, for correct fusion transformation.

Figure 6 defines a function dc_assign $e^-\ r$:

$$\mathsf{dc\_assign} :: e^{\hat{d}} \to \hat{d} \to e^{\hat{d}}$$

which is to propagate the Dewey code r into an annotated expression e by assigning proper new Dewey codes to e and its subexpressions. In what follows, we will explain some of the important equations in this definition. Note that we write e^- to denote that the Dewey code of e is "don't care".

The equation (DCPSEQ) horizontally numbers sequence expressions. The function succ is used to enforce numberings using a strictly greater value relative to previously processed expressions (e.g., succ $r.1 = r.2$). (DCPEC) introduces a vertical structure

$$\mathcal{F}_{\mathsf{c}} :: e^{\hat{d}} \to \tau \to e^{\hat{d}}$$

$$\mathcal{F}_{\mathsf{c}}\ e^{d}\ \tau = \begin{cases} \mathsf{remove\_dup}\ (e'_1, ..., e'_N) & \text{if dc\_sort succeeds} \\ (e^{d}/\,\mathbf{child} :: \tau)^{\epsilon} & \text{otherwise} \end{cases}$$

$$\text{where } (e'_1, ..., e'_N) = \mathsf{dc\_sort}(\mathsf{filter}(\mathsf{equal\_to}\,\tau)(\mathsf{get\_children}\ e^{d})) \qquad (\text{CFUSION})$$

$$\mathcal{F}_{\mathsf{s}} :: e^{\hat{d}} \to \tau \to e^{\hat{d}}$$

$$\mathcal{F}_{\mathsf{s}}\ e^{d}\ \tau = \begin{cases} \mathsf{remove\_dup}\ (e'_1, ..., e'_N) & \text{if dc\_sort succeeds} \\ (e^{d}/\,\mathbf{self} :: \tau)^{\epsilon} & \text{otherwise} \end{cases}$$

$$\text{where } (e'_1, ..., e'_N) = \mathsf{dc\_sort}(\mathsf{filter}(\mathsf{equal\_to}\,\tau)(\mathsf{get\_self}\ e^{d})) \qquad (\text{SFUSION})$$

$$\mathcal{F}_{\mathsf{p}} :: e^{\hat{d}} \to \tau \to e^{\hat{d}}$$

$$\mathcal{F}_{\mathsf{p}}\ e^{d}\ \tau = \begin{cases} \mathsf{remove\_dup}\ (e'_1, ..., e'_N) & \text{if dc\_sort succeeds} \\ (e^{d}/\,\mathbf{parent} :: \tau)^{\epsilon} & \text{otherwise} \end{cases}$$

$$\text{where } (e'_1, ..., e'_N) = \mathsf{dc\_sort}(\mathsf{filter}(\mathsf{equal\_to}\,\tau)(\mathsf{get\_parent}\ e^{d})) \qquad (\text{PFUSION})$$

$$\mathsf{get\_children} :: e^{\hat{d}} \to e^{\hat{d}}$$

$$\mathsf{get\_children}\ \$v^{\text{-}} = (\$v/\,\mathbf{child} :: *)^{\epsilon} \quad \mathsf{get\_children}\ ()^{[]} = ()^{[]}$$

$$\mathsf{get\_children}\ (e_1, ..., e_N)^{\text{-}} = \mathsf{flatten}\ ((e'_1, ..., e'_N)^{[d_1, .., d_N]})$$

$$\text{where } e'_i = \mathsf{get\_children}\ e_i \quad d_i = \mathsf{extract\_dc}(e'_i) \qquad (\text{GCSEQ})$$

$$\mathsf{get\_children}\ (e/\,\mathbf{child} :: en)^{\text{-}} = (e/\,\mathbf{child} :: en/\,\mathbf{child} :: *)^{\epsilon}$$

$$\mathsf{get\_children}\ (\langle en\rangle e^{d} \langle /en\rangle)^{\text{-}} = e^{d} \qquad (\text{GCEC})$$

$$\mathsf{get\_children}\ (\mathbf{for}\ \$v\ \mathbf{in}\ e\ \mathbf{return}\ (e_1, ..., e_N))^{r\#[b_1, ..., b_N]}$$

$$= \left(\begin{array}{ll} \mathbf{for}\ \$v\ \mathbf{in}\ e\ \mathbf{return} & (e_{11}, e_{12}, \ldots, e_{1n_1}, \\ & \ e_{21}, e_{22}, \ldots, e_{2n_2}, \\ & \ \ldots \\ & \ e_{N1}, e_{N2}, \ldots, e_{Nn_n}) \end{array} \right)^{r'}$$

$$\begin{array}{lll} \text{where} & (e_{i1}, \ldots, e_{in_i}) = \mathsf{get\_children}\, e_i & r_{ij} = \mathsf{extract\_dc}\, e'_{ij} \\ & r' = r\#\,[b_1.r_{11}, \ldots, b_1.r_{1n_1}, & \\ & \qquad b_2.r_{21}, \ldots, b_2.r_{2n_2}, & \\ & \qquad \ldots & \\ & \qquad b_N.r_{N1}, \ldots, b_N.r_{Nn_n}] & \end{array} \qquad (\text{GCFOR})$$

$$\mathsf{get\_self}, \mathsf{get\_parent} :: e^{\hat{d}} \to e^{\hat{d}}$$

$$\mathsf{get\_self}\ e^{r} = e^{r} \quad \mathsf{get\_parent}\ e^{r.n} = \mathit{getExpGlobal}(r)$$

Fig. 7. Fusion rules for three kinds of *axis*

to the numbering by initiating dc_assign for the subexpression e by adding ".1" to its second parameter. The equations that needs additional attention are (DCSTP) and (DCPFOR). In (DCSTP), it may seem unusual for dc_assign not to recurse subexpression e. However, considering that the path expression itself does not introduce an additional parent-child relationship and that dc_assign always handles expressions already partially evaluated expressions, there is no additional chance to simplify the path expression further by using the Dewey code allocated to the subexpression. In particular, the characteristic equation (DCPFOR), which introduces # structure to the Dewey code, numbers the expression e at the return clause. Note that the second parameter of the recursive call for e is reset to 1. bs that reflects the horizontal structure produced by the return clause is combined with the # sign to produce $r\#bs$ as the top level code allocated to the "for" expression.

Lemma 1. *From the definition of* dc_assign, *given an XQuery expression* e, *the extended Dewey code assigned by* dc_assign e^{-} r *satisfies* Property *1.*

Fusion Rules. Our fusion transformation on $e/\alpha{::}\tau$ is based on the three fusion rules (functions) $\mathcal{F}_{\mathsf{c}}$, $\mathcal{F}_{\mathsf{s}}$ and $\mathcal{F}_{\mathsf{p}}$ in Figure 7 that respectively correspond to three axis types. The basic procedure is as follows:

1. Extract (get) subexpressions according to the axis α;
2. Select those that produce nodes whose name is equal to the tag name τ by using a filter;
3. Sort the remaining subexpressions according to their Dewey codes;
4. If the above sort step succeeds, remove the duplicated subexpressions and return its sequence as the result; otherwise, end fusion.

More concretely, let us consider the definition of $\mathcal{F}_{\mathsf{c}}$. We use get_children e to get a sequence of subexpressions that contribute to producing children of the XML document that can be obtained by evaluating e, and use the filter(equal_to τ) function to keep those that are equal to τ, where filter $p\ xs = [x \mid x \leftarrow xs, p\ x]$. The resulting sequence expression is sorted according to their Dewey codes by dc_sort. This sorting may fail since not all of the Dewey codes are comparable. If the sorting succeeds, we return a sequence expression by removing all duplicated element subexpressions; otherwise, we end fusion by returning the original expression $e/$ **child** $::\ \tau$.

Our fusion transformation always terminates and is correct, as summarized by the following theorem.

Theorem 1 (Correctness of Fusion). *For an XQuery expression* e, *if* peval $e\ \{\} = e'^{d'}$ *then* e *and* e' *are value equivalent expressions.*

Proof. (sketch): It is sufficient to show the correctness for location step expressions. For other expressions, it is straightforward to show the correctness by using structural induction on the expressions. For location step expressions, the correctness is implied by **Lemma** 1 and a property of the sorting without duplicates on xD (See [13] for details) together with the semantics of the location step expressions. □

Simple Example. For $e_1 \circ e_m$ described in the introduction, our fusion function peval works as follows.

$$
\begin{array}{ll}
 & \mathsf{peval}\ e_1 \circ e_m\ \{\} \\
\rightsquigarrow & \{(\text{PECSTP}); (\text{PELET}); (\text{PEEC})\} \\
 & \mathbf{let}\ \$t := \langle\mathsf{sa}\rangle\{(\ \langle\mathsf{lhs}\rangle/\mathsf{na}/\mathsf{rhs}/\mathsf{item}^{r.1.1}\langle/\mathsf{lhs}\rangle^{r.1}, \\
 & \qquad\qquad \langle\mathsf{rhs}\rangle/\mathsf{na}/\mathsf{lhs}/\mathsf{item}^{r.2.1}\langle/\mathsf{rhs}\rangle^{r.2})^{[r.1,r.2]}\}\langle/\mathsf{sa}\rangle^{r} \\
 & \mathbf{return}\ \mathbf{let}\ \$v := (\$t/\mathsf{rhs}, \$t/\mathsf{lhs})\ \mathbf{return}\ \$v/\mathsf{item} \\
\rightsquigarrow & \{(\text{PELET}); (\text{PESEQ}); (\text{PECSTP}); (\text{PECSTP})\} \\
 & \mathbf{let}\ \$v := (\ \langle\mathsf{rhs}\rangle/\mathsf{na}/\mathsf{lhs}/\mathsf{item}^{r.2.1}\langle/\mathsf{rhs}\rangle^{r.2}, \\
 & \qquad \langle\mathsf{lhs}\rangle/\mathsf{na}/\mathsf{rhs}/\mathsf{item}^{r.1.1}\langle/\mathsf{lhs}\rangle^{r.1})^{[r.2,r.1]} \\
 & \mathbf{return}\ \$v/\mathsf{item} \\
\rightsquigarrow & \{(\text{PECSTP})\} \\
 & \mathsf{remove\_dup}\ (\mathsf{dc\_sort}\ (/\mathsf{na}/\mathsf{lhs}/\mathsf{item}^{r.2.1}, /\mathsf{na}/\mathsf{rhs}/\mathsf{item}^{r.1.1})) \\
\rightarrow & \\
 & (/\mathsf{na}/\mathsf{rhs}/\mathsf{item}^{r.1.1}, /\mathsf{na}/\mathsf{lhs}/\mathsf{item}^{r.2.1})
\end{array}
$$

For $e_2 \circ e_m$, which is also from the introduction, peval performs the correct transformation.

$$
\begin{array}{ll}
 & \mathsf{peval}\ e_2 \circ e_m\ \{\} \\
\rightsquigarrow & \{(\text{PELET}); (\text{PESEQ}); (\text{PECSTP}); (\text{PECSTP})\} \\
 & \mathbf{let}\ \$t := \langle\mathsf{sa}\rangle\{(\ \langle\mathsf{lhs}\rangle/\mathsf{na}/\mathsf{rhs}/\mathsf{item}^{r.1.1}\langle/\mathsf{lhs}\rangle^{r.1}, \\
 & \qquad\qquad \langle\mathsf{rhs}\rangle/\mathsf{na}/\mathsf{lhs}/\mathsf{item}^{r.2.1}\langle/\mathsf{rhs}\rangle^{r.2})^{[r.1,r.2]}\}\langle/\mathsf{sa}\rangle^{r} \\
 & \mathbf{return}\ \mathbf{let}\ \$v := \$t/\mathsf{rhs}/\mathsf{item}\ \mathbf{return}\ \$v/.. \\
\rightsquigarrow & \{(\text{PELET}); (\text{PECSTP}); (\text{PEPSTP}); (\text{PEVR})\} \\
 & /\mathsf{na}/\mathsf{lhs}/\mathsf{item}^{r.2.1}/.. \\
\rightsquigarrow & \{(\text{PFUSION})\} \\
 & \langle\mathsf{rhs}\rangle/\mathsf{na}/\mathsf{lhs}/\mathsf{item}^{r.2.1}\langle/\mathsf{rhs}\rangle^{r.2}
\end{array}
$$

5 Related Work

There are many studies on rewriting XQueries into other XQueries [11,18,14,20]. The study most related to ours in the sense of eliminating redundant expressions is [11]. The authors of [11] proposed a rewriting optimization that replaces expressions which return empty sequences with () by using an emptiness detection based on static analysis. In contrast, our rewriting eliminates redundant element constructors as well.

Koch [14] and Page et al. [18] introduced some classes for composite XQuery and proposed XQuery-to-XQuery transformations over the classes of XQuery they defined. Their target queries don't contain newly constructed nodes. In the real world, however, practical expressions such as schema mapping always return newly constructed elements.

Tatarinov et al. proposed an efficient query reformulation in data integration systems, in which XML and XQuery are used for the data model and schema mapping, respectively [20]. In this system, the composition of the element construction is typical because the schema mapping that maps one element to an other element involves element construction. They treat the actual reformulation algorithm as a black box. Our work attempts to open the box and exploit some of its properties.

Fusion has been extensively studied in the functional programming (FP) community [22,2,7,17]. Referentially transparent FP languages allow naive fusion rules (F), as we saw in the Introduction, if the element constructor behaves like the constructors in FP. However, since the element constructor introduces a new node identity in each evaluation, thereby breaking the referential transparency, it is not directly applicable. It would be interesting to promote the identity as a first class object by using the technique described in [16], but our focus here is to perform XQuery-to-XQuery transformations, and the node identity is not a first class object in XQuery.

6 Conclusion

We proposed a new rewriting technique for XQuery fusion to eliminate unnecessary element constructions in the expressions while preserving the document order. The prominent feature of our framework is its static emulation of the XML store and assignment of extended Dewey codes to the expressions. The result is easy construction of correct fusion transformations.

We implemented a prototype system in Objective Caml. It consists of about 4600 lines of code. Currently it works stand-alone by reading XQuery expressions from standard input and produces rewritten XQueries to standard outputs. The system is available at `http://www.biglab.org/fusion`.

We believe that our approach can be generalized straightforwardly to handle the other axes including "transitive" axes like **ancestor**.

Acknowledgments. We would like to thank the anonymous reviewers for their extensive and extremely helpful comments. Part of this work was supported by Grant-in-Aid for Scientific Research No. 22300012, No. 20500043, and No. 20700035.

References

1. Amano, S., Libkin, L., Murlak, F.: XML Schema Mappings. In: PODS, pp. 33–42 (2009)
2. Chin, W.: Safe Fusion of Functional Expressions. In: Proc. Conference on Lisp and Functional Programming, San Francisco, California, pp. 11–20 (June 1992)
3. Daniels, S., Graefe, G., Keller, T., Maier, D., Schmidt, D., Vance, B.: Query optimization in revelation, an overview. Data Eng. 14(2), 58–62 (1991)
4. Deutsch, A., Papakonstantinou, Y., Xu, Y.: The NEXT Framework for Logical XQuery Opimization. In: Proc. of VLDB, pp. 168–179 (2004)
5. Fegaras, L., Maier, D.: Optimizing object queries using an effective calculus. ACM Trans. Database Syst. 25(4), 457–516 (2000)
6. Fernamdez, M., Hidders, J., Michiels, P., Simeon, J., Vercammen, R.: Optimizing sorting and duplicate elimination in XQuery path expressions. In: Andersen, K.V., Debenham, J., Wagner, R. (eds.) DEXA 2005. LNCS, vol. 3588, pp. 554–563. Springer, Heidelberg (2005)
7. Gill, A., Launchbury, J., Jones, S.L.P.: A short cut to deforestation. In: FPCA 1993: Proceedings of the conference on Functional programming languages and computer architecture, pp. 223–232. ACM Press, New York (1993)

8. Gottlob, G., Koch, C., Pichler, R.: Efficient Algorithms for Processing XPath Queries. ACM TODS (June 2005)
9. Grust, T., Mayr, M., Rittinger, J.: Let SQL drive the XQuery workhorse (XQuery join graph isolation). In: EDBT, pp. 147–158 (2010)
10. Grust, T., Sakr, S., Teubner, J.: XQuery on SQL Hosts. In: VLDB, pp. 252–263 (2004)
11. Gueni, B., Abdessalem, T., Cautis, B., Waller, E.: Pruning Nested XQuery Queries. In: CIKM 1992, pp. 541–550 (2008)
12. Hidders, J., Paredaens, J., Vercammen, R., Demeyer, S.: A Light but Formal Introduction to XQuery. In: Bellahsène, Z., Milo, T., Rys, M., Suciu, D., Unland, R. (eds.) XSym 2004. LNCS, vol. 3186, pp. 5–20. Springer, Heidelberg (2004)
13. Kato, H., Hidaka, S., Hu, Z., Nakano, K., Ishihara, Y.: Context-Preserving XQuery Fusion. Technical Report GRACE-TR-2010-07, GRACE Center, National Institute of Informatics (September 2010)
14. Koch, C.: On the role of composition in XQuery. In: Proceedings of Eighth International Workshop on the Web and Databases, WebDB 2005 (2005)
15. Lu, J., Ling, T.W., Chan, C.-Y., Chen, T.: From Region Encoding To Extended Dewey: On Efficient Processing of XML Twig pattern Matching. In: Proc. of VLDB (2005)
16. Ohori, A.: Representing object identity in a pure functional language. In: Kanellakis, P.C., Abiteboul, S. (eds.) ICDT 1990. LNCS, vol. 470, pp. 41–55. Springer, Heidelberg (1990)
17. Ohori, A., Sasano, I.: Lightweight fusion by fixed point promotion. SIGPLAN Not. 42(1), 143–154 (2007)
18. Page, W.L., Hidders, J., Michiels, P., Paredaens, J., Vercammen, R.: On the expressive power of node construction in XQuery. In: Proceedings of Eighth International Workshop on the Web and Databases, WebDB 2005 (2005)
19. Parys, P.: XPath evaluation in linear time with polynomial combined complexity. In: Paredaens, J., Su, J. (eds.) PODS, pp. 55–64. ACM, New York (2009)
20. Tatarinov, I., Halevy, A.: Efficient Query Reformulation in Peer Data Management Systems. In: Proceedings of the ACM International Conference on Management of Data, pp. 539–550 (2004)
21. Tatarinov, I., Viglas, S.D., Beyer, K., Shanmugasundaram, J., Shekita, E., Zhang, C.: Storing and Querying Ordered XML Using a Relational Database System. In: Proc. of SIGMOD (2002)
22. Wadler, P.: Deforestation: Transforming programs to eliminate trees. In: Ganzinger, H. (ed.) ESOP 1988. LNCS, vol. 300, pp. 344–358. Springer, Heidelberg (1988)
23. World Wide Web Consortium. XQuery1.0 : An XML Query Language, W3C Recommendation (January 2007)
24. World Wide Web Consortium. XQuery1.0 and XPath2.0 Formal Semantics, W3C Recommendation (January 2007)
25. Xu, L., Ling, T.W., Wu, H., Bao, Z.: DDE: From Dewey to a Fully Dynamic XML Labeling Scheme. In: SIGMOD Conference, pp. 719–730 (2009)

Index-Compact Garbage Collection

Liangliang Tong and Francis C.M. Lau

Department of Computer Science,
The University of Hong Kong,
Pokfulam Road, Hong Kong
{lltong,fcmlau}@cs.hku.hk

Abstract. Automatic garbage collection is currently adopted by many object-oriented programming systems. Among the many variants, a mark-compact garbage collector offers high space efficiency and cheap object allocation, but suffers from poor virtual memory interactions. It needs to linearly scan through the entire available heap, triggering many page faults which may lead to excessively long collection time. We propose building an object reference index while tracing the heap, which in the following stages can be used to directly locate the live objects. As the dead objects are not touched, the collection time becomes dependent only on the size of the live data set. We have implemented a prototype in Jikes RVM, which shows promising results with the SPECjvm98 benchmarks.

Keywords: Index, Virtual Memory, Compacting Garbage Collection.

1 Introduction

In order to avoid the errors of manual memory management, the idea of a garbage collector to automatically reclaim dead objects was introduced [1]. But to precisely determine which objects will no longer be used by the program is undecidable. A somewhat conservative approach was therefore adopted which identified reachable objects by tracing the heap from the program roots [1], and many improvements followed, including some that took advantage of the presence or work around the limits of virtual memory.

Theoretically there is an unlimited address space in a virtual memory system. However, as the working set of a program increases its span in the virtual space, live objects mingle with dead objects and pages gradually become sparsely occupied (by live objects). Ultimately something must be done, otherwise many of the pages will be pushed to secondary storage which leads to frequent swaps [19]. Traditionally a free-list is used to mitigate the problem, unfortunately it would create memory fragments. So garbage collectors that move live objects together in space were devised and became popular.

There are two major kinds of moving garbage collectors: semi-space (also known as copying collector) and mark-compact. The former [14] is faster, but it needs to reserve half of available space for copying live objects. The latter [2] does not need to reserve any space, but takes much more time to do a collection. There are two reasons for the longer collection time:

K. Ueda (Ed.): APLAS 2010, LNCS 6461, pp. 271–286, 2010.

- Compaction needs multiple passes over the objects, while copying takes only one pass.
- Some phases[1] of compaction will walk the entire available heap, including garbage objects, but semi-space collectors only need to touch[2] the live objects and hence their collection work is proportional only to the amount of live data [7].

Much research has been conducted to reduce the number of passes required by compaction, such as [3], but to the best of our knowledge nearly no attention has been paid to the second issue. Regarding this issue, we note that, as indicated in [17], unreachable objects tend to cluster together. In our experiments, the size of some clusters even exceeded that of a page. In the presence of virtual memory, such pages with only garbage are never or rarely visited and therefore should be evicted out of the main storage. To touch them will trigger many page faults hence prolong the operation time.

In this paper we propose an improvement to compacting collectors, called an index-compact garbage collector. It builds an address (index) table during marking. This index table contains all the references to the live objects in the available heap in address order. After all the live objects have been visited, this index is sorted by the values of the references to make it address ordered. In the following phases of garbage collection, the index is used to efficiently locate live objects for pointer adjustment and object compaction. Because the index is sorted, the corresponding movements of objects will not cause them to overlap and data will not be lost. During these phases, the garbage objects are never touched, which substantially reduces the working set of the garbage collector. We have implemented a prototype based on this idea on JikesRVM [12] and the experiment clearly showed that the collection time depends only on the size of live objects for the benchmarks tested.

The improvement does not come without a cost—we need at least extra space for the index and extra time to sort it. In the following, we expound on the overhead incurred by our algorithm and suggest several possible methods to mitigate its side effects. Considering that almost all the enterprise garbage collected systems are generational[9], we also give a separate discussion on how to build generations using our algorithm. Compared with copying, compaction saves resources but requires multiple phases to complete its work, so it will be interesting if we can somehow combine the two to achieve a balance between space and time.

Our contributions can be summarized as follows.

- We put forward the case that reducing page faults should be one of the main tasks of garbage collectors in a virtual memory based system.
- We propose the index-compact garbage collector which can avoid touching the garbage while compacting the working heap. The result is reduced page swaps, and the collection time can be made proportional only to the amount

[1] If a process needs to visit the heap from the start again, we call that a phase.

[2] An object is touched if any bytes in this object is visited.

of live objects. This mechanism can be even more effective if the collector is generational because of the higher infant mortality of young spaces.
- We have implemented a preliminary version of our collector in JikesRVM. The experiment behaved as expected and showed a collection time that is correlated with the size of live objects.
- We also suggest several techniques, such as cluster indexing and page remapping, that can further extend the proposed idea and improve the performance of the proposed collector. A fine-grain blending of copying and compacting collectors is discussed, which can achieve a balance between time and space costs.

The remainder of this paper is organized as follows. Sec. 2 provides a comparison between copying and compacting garbage collectors and gives the motivation for constructing an index for compacting collectors. Sec. 3 presents the basic design and implementation of our collector. Sec. 4 describes the experimental environment and reports the experimental results. Sec. 5 gives a discussion of the overheads and extensions of our algorithm. Related works are overviewed in Sec. 6. We summarize our contributions and point out possible future work in Sec. 7.

2 Comparison and Motivation

Semi-space collectors reserve half of the available heap and copy every reachable object to that space. Because the reserved space contains no object at the beginning of collection, there is no need to consider whether different objects may overlap or not. The active object tree is traced on the fly and every reached object is copied to the reserved half heap. After the collection, the live objects align in the new space by breadth-first order regardless of the addresses they are originally stored at. The situation of mark-compact collectors is different: live objects must be compacted in address order, or different objects may be moved to the same place and data will be damaged. We illustrate this situation in Fig. 1.

In this figure, garbage objects are colored white, and live objects grey. Assume at the moment the root points at object C which is now marked and needs to be relocated. If this is a copying collector, this object will be immediately copied to the new space, and its header will store a forward pointer so that the following pointers to this object can be updated. But in a compacting garbage collector, no extra space is reserved, and so this object must be moved to the start of the

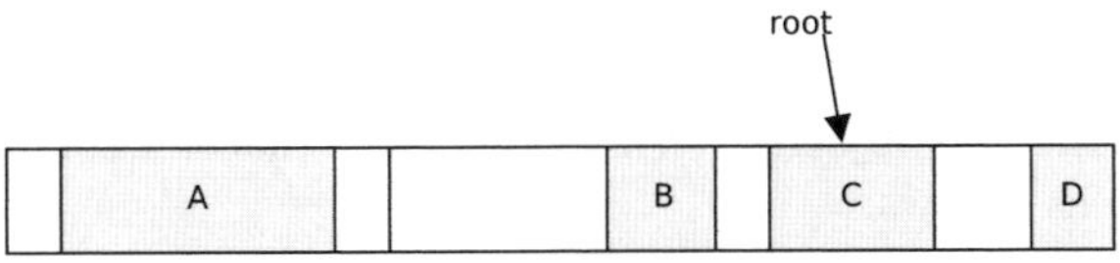

Fig. 1. The Traced Heap

heap. If we do so, however, C will land right on the live object A, damaging its content. Therefore, a compacting garbage collector must first linearly scan through the whole available heap for live objects and mark them. Then beginning from the start of the heap, the collector walks through the objects (including the dead ones), and when encountering a live one, say A, it relocates the object to the start of the heap; and similarly for the following marked objects, which are, B, C and D.

Touching garbage objects can be detrimental, since they mainly reside on secondary storage, and this might trigger a page fault. It also unnecessarily enlarges the program's working set, pollutes the cache memory with the garbage, and leads to mass misses as a result. In view of this undesirable situation, we need a mechanism to keep track of live objects in address order after tracing the entire heap. In this paper we propose such a mechanism which employs an index table to store every live object reference.

3 Index-Compact Garbage Collector

3.1 Design

Traditionally a compacting garbage collector reclaims memory in four phases:

1. Compute the root set of the running program and push them into a FIFO queue. To start the tracing, pop an object reference out of the queue and completely scan it for pointers. The objects referred to by any pointers are marked and pushed into the queue. This operation continues until the queue becomes empty, at which time all the reachable objects have been marked as alive.
2. Scan linearly through the available heap where objects are allocated and calculate the forward addresses for the marked objects by adding up their sizes to the heap's start address.
3. Trace the active program tree again and update the pointers to the forward addresses.
4. Walk sequentially through the heap and move the marked objects to their forward addresses.

It can be seen that at least phases 2 and 4 need to touch (specifically to check the mark bit of) the garbage objects because there is no auxiliary information on how to locate just the live objects. If we can create and maintain a global data structure to store this information, we can skip over the garbage objects completely.

Fig. 2 shows an address index table where each entry points at the start address of an active object. In phases 2, 3 and 4, this index can be used to directly locate the live objects. With this index in place, a compacting garbage collector works as follows:

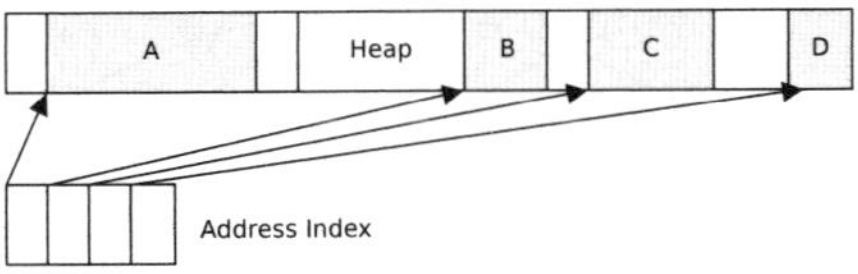

Fig. 2. The Index-Compact Garbage Collector

1. Compute the root set, and push all the object references into the *index* and iteratively trace them. Note that this time the object references are not popped out of the index. After completion, the index is sorted by the reference address values of the items.
2. Calculate the forward addresses using this index. Touching of garbage is therefore avoided.
3. Update the pointers of objects referred to by items in the index to their forward addresses.
4. Pop every item in the index and move the object pointed by it to the forward address.

The above descriptions shows that the index stores only the references to the reached objects, thus the garbage will never be touched. Consequently the number of page faults will be reduced. In this paper, we present a simple algorithm for our idea for the sake of understanding, and leave any enhancements which we will discuss in the following paragraphs to future implementations.

3.2 Implementation

Where to store the index is an issue. Since the index stores all the pointers to live objects, so it must be efficient. We cannot use the Java classes to implement a linked list for this purpose, because that will bring in extra object headers. In Java [30] this overhead comprises two words, which is too costly and will triple the overall size of the index.

We notice that every compacting garbage collector has some auxiliary data structure, such as the trace queue, which must be stored somewhere in the heap. The size of these data is largely unpredictable, and thus in real-life platforms the address space allocated for them is extremely large in order to cope with any unexpected cases. Because they are meta data there is no header to consume extra spaces. We therefore store the index in such an area.

Since this area has other usages with different data intersecting with each other, some data structure must be put in place to differentiate them. In this paper, we partition this area into 4KB blocks (whose size is identical to the page adopted by most current computer systems) and store two pointers (*next* and *pre*) at the end of each block allocated for the index. Inside each block the object references are stored in array style. Once a block is exhausted, we allocate a new block, and set up the *next* and *pre* pointers of the two blocks. This is depicted

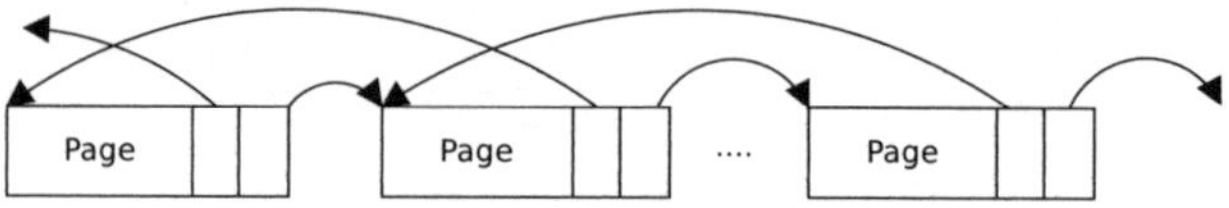

Fig. 3. The Structure of Overall Index

in Fig. 3. So for every block only two pointers are maintained, corresponding to a space overhead of less than 0.1%.

The index also eliminates the need of building a tracing queue and marking. When a garbage collection is triggered due to memory exhaustion, the root set is scanned and their object references are pushed into the index. We create an iterator to point to its first item. Then one by one, every item is checked for pointers. The reference of every object reached is added to the end of the index. After the object is entirely scanned, the iterator moves on to the next object and this process repeats until it meets the end of the index. We use an MSD radix exchange algorithm to sort this index, which is relatively quick and requires no extra space. This is also the reason why the index blocks are doubly linked, because this kind of algorithm needs to search from both top and bottom.

4 Methodology

Based on where to store the forward address, there are three types of compacting garbage collectors: Lisp-2 [6], break table [8], and threading [18]. Our algorithm can be applied to all of them, but we only select Lisp-2 to work on for illustration's sake. Similar improvements can be achieved for threading compactors by avoiding touching the garbage, and better optimizations are possible for table-based compaction as the break table can be completely removed.

4.1 Experimental Setup

The computer which runs our experiments has a 2 GHz Intel Core 2 Duo CPU and 2 GB main memory. Every core has an independent 8-way associative 32 KB L1 cache and shares a 4 MB L2 cache. We use Ubuntu 8.04 operating system [29] with kernel version 2.6.24-24.

Our collector is implemented on MMTk [11] of the Jikes RVM [12]. MMTk partitions the address heap of the RVM into the several spaces: metadata, immortal, large object and small object space. We modify the current mark-compact collector and create the index in the metadata space. The iterator is placed in the immortal space, since it will always be needed during the entire program execution. Literally the large object space stores objects that are larger than 32KB, and normal allocations and collections happen in the small object space.

All the applications in SPECjvm98 are tested in our experiments except *mpegaudio* which rarely allocates any new objects and triggers almost no collection.

We calculate the average size consumed by the index at every collection and subtract it from the working heap space. In this way, the sizes of memory used by both the mark and the index compactor are approximately the same. In the experiment we found that the index seldom exceeds 1 MB (See Fig. 1, and so the initial average size is set to this number.

The only assumption for our collector to work well is what makes a garbage collector run efficiently: the heap residency of an application, which is the ratio between the size of live objects and the heap size, must be low enough so that there is room for new allocations. We did not include other benchmarks, but it can be expected that if the heap residency is not too high then they will also present good performance. Average object size being too small may also affect the collector's efficiency, for it will result in an overly large index table. We figure that the minimum size of Java objects is 8 bytes (to store the header), and in fact, many previous experiments have suggested that the average size of Java object ranges from 20 bytes to 60 bytes, which will work fine for our algorithm.

4.2 Results

We firstly profiled MMTk to obtain the dynamic object characteristics of the SPECjvm98 benchmarks, which are summarized in Tab. 1. The table shows that the average object size is small, which is bad news for us because this means the number of objects would be large and correspondingly so would be the size of the index. For this particular situation, we offer several optimizations in Sec. 5.

Table 1. Object Characteristics for SPECjvm98 Benchmarks

Benchmark	Average Object Size (bytes)	Average Cluster Number	Average Index Size (bytes)
compress	513	252	348720
db	26	1070	377265
jack	37	912	443048
javac	31	23263	1516896
jess	34	1204	503380
mtrt	24	780	973696

Attention must be paid to the second column of the table, which represents a very common phenomenon of memory usage: objects are created en masse, and they also tend to die together. Although the third column suggests that the size of the index sometimes grows beyond 1 MB, the number of object clusters[3] remains moderate. This motivates us to propose in the discussion section the cluster-wise idea, as opposed to the simple address-wise way of building the index. Yet by employing our simple, address-wise indexing algorithm, the results are still encouraging.

[3] An object cluster is a continuous heap block with only live objects.

We implement the index compactor (*ic*) and compare its performance with that of a Lisp-2 mark compactor (*mc*), as reported in the following figures. Fig. 4[4] shows the overall benchmark execution times for both compactors. In the figure, two benchmarks, *jess* and *jack*, clearly demonstrate the superiority of *ic*, while for three other benchmarks, *db*, *javac* and *mtrt*, *ic* only wins after the heap grows beyond a certain size. This is reasonable, since the advantage of our compactor comes from not touching the garbage objects. The live object (survival) rate of the former two benchmarks is as low as 30% even for a $20MB$ heap; this rate would not come down for the latter three benchmarks until the heap grows to a certain extent. We tuned the heap size for these benchmarks, and found that the turning point is approximately at 40%. That is, for *ic* to outperform *mc* the heap residency should be less than this turning point rate. Furthermore, it is also the turning point where the execution time drops dramatically, since garbage collectors require enough space to work well.

This characteristic makes our algorithm perfect for applying to the young space of a generational collector, where this rate is well below 10%. Because of the same reason, the performance of the benchmark *compress* degrades with *ic*. After allocating about $4MB$ of normal objects in the small object space (where our algorithm is used), the program only creates large objects in the large object space. It can be seen from Tab. 1 that its average object size is very large as compared to that of the other benchmarks. To make the situation worse, the $4MB$ small objects are never disposed of until the end of the program execution, which pushes the live object rate to be close to 100% at every collection. In a nutshell, for *compress*, an index is redundant, because all the objects are alive. The degradation in performance as compared to *mc* is due to the extra computation time to build and sort the index.

Fig. 5 compares the collection times of the two compactors. It portrays a similar picture to Fig. 4, and shows a difference that increases monotonically as the heap grows. This is within our expectation that the performance of our algorithm improves as the heap residency reduces. Because of the similarity between *ic* and *mc*, there is virtually no difference in mutation time for both collectors. Combining the temporal performance of the above two figures, it can be perceived that the size of index table matters a lot. *javac* and *mtrt* generate the biggest indexes. As a result, the performance of *ic* will not outstrip *mc* until the heap approaches $40MB$. To reduce the size of index table, we propose several methods in the discussion section.

As we have stressed, *ic* does not touch the garbage objects at all, which contributes to the interesting characteristic of *ic* as presented in Fig. 6. In the figure, we can easily spot that the average collection time of *ic* is insensitive to the heap size, whereas this time increases as the heap grows for *mc*. It is worth pointing out that as the heap grows the number of collections decreases, and this is why the total collection number keeps falling while the average collection time remains roughly unchanged.

[4] The size of the heap is normalized by 20MB. That is, 1 denotes 20MB, 2 denotes 40MB, etc.

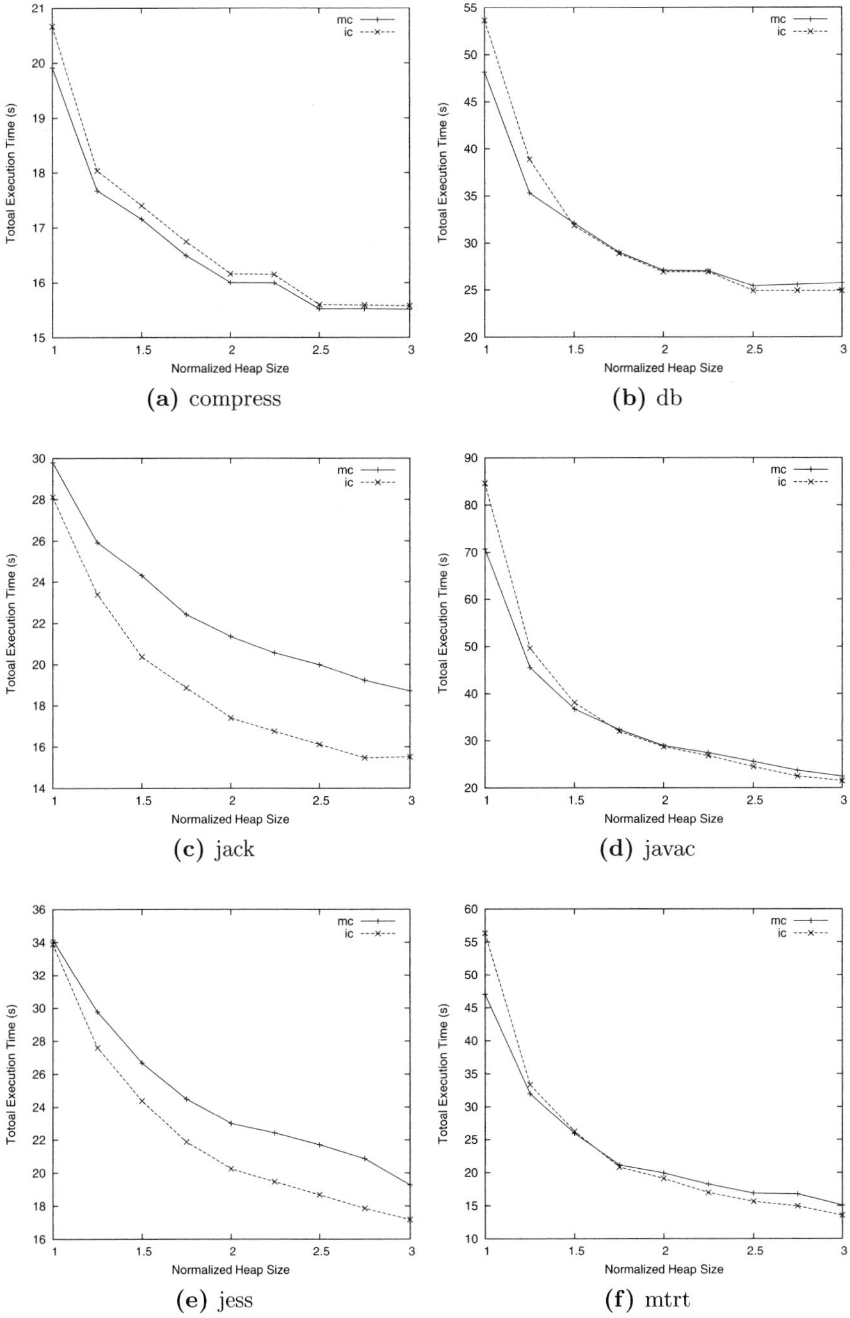

Fig. 4. Total Execution Time for Mark- and Index-Compact Collectors

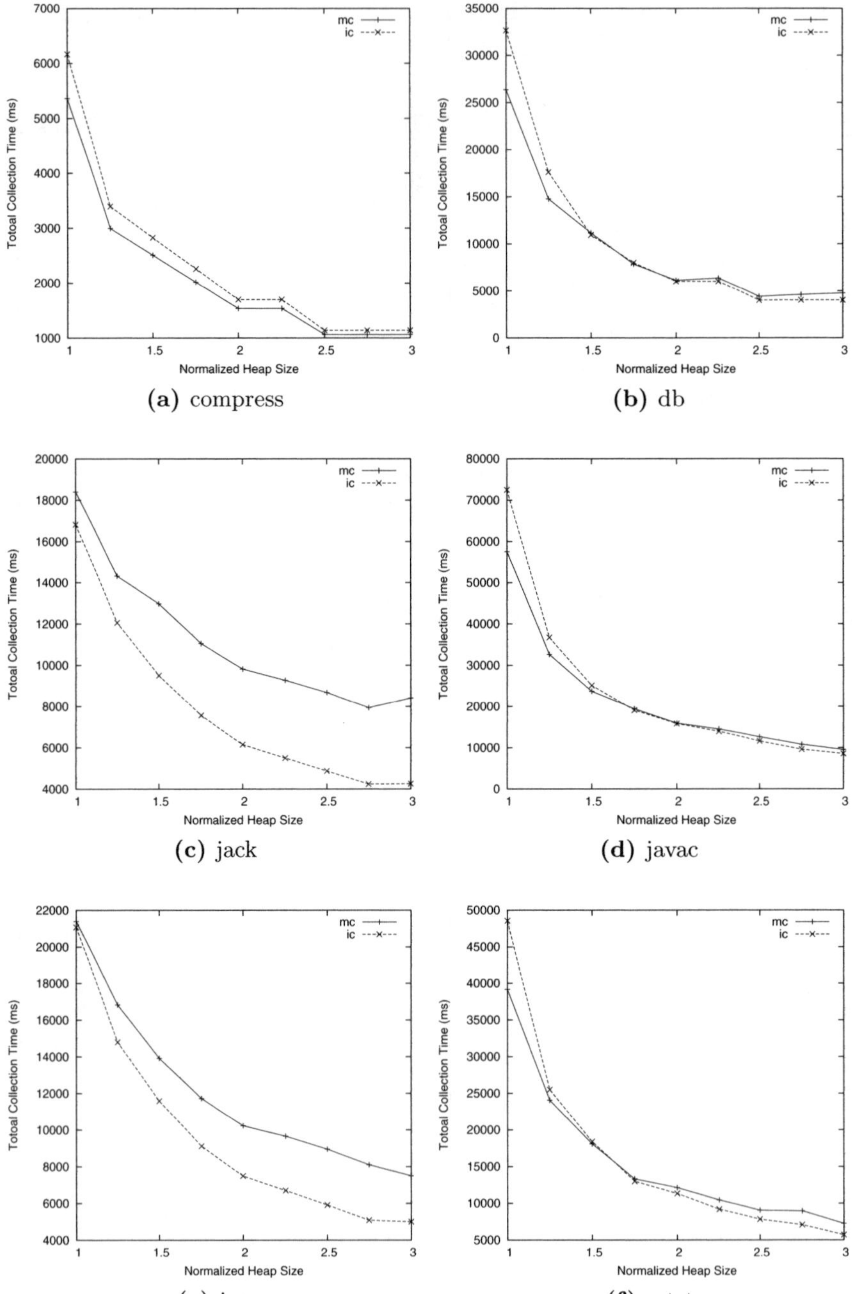

(a) compress **(b)** db

(c) jack **(d)** javac

(e) jess **(f)** mtrt

Fig. 5. Total Collection Time for Mark- and Index-Compact Collectors

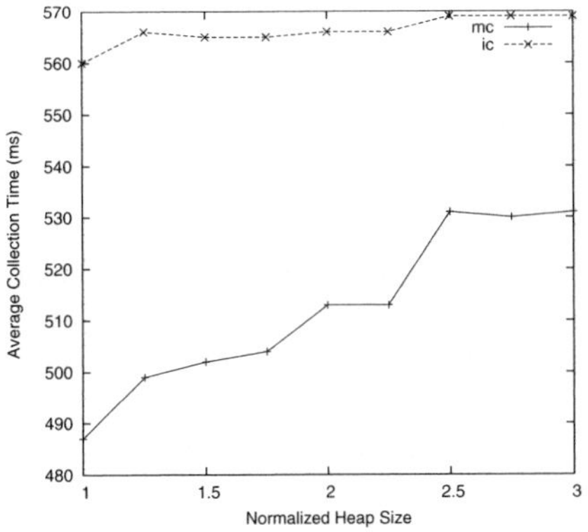

(a) compress

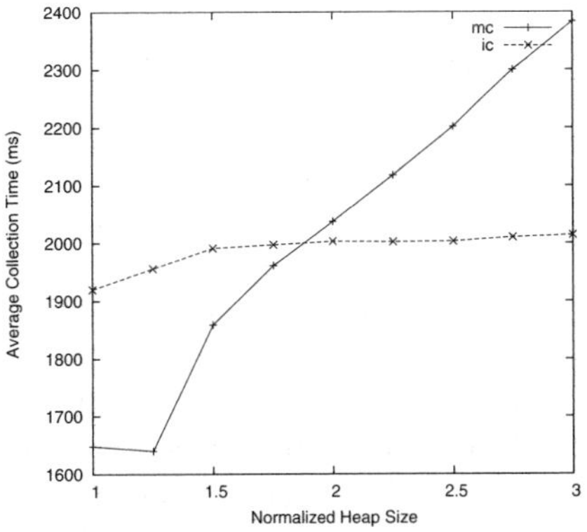

(b) db

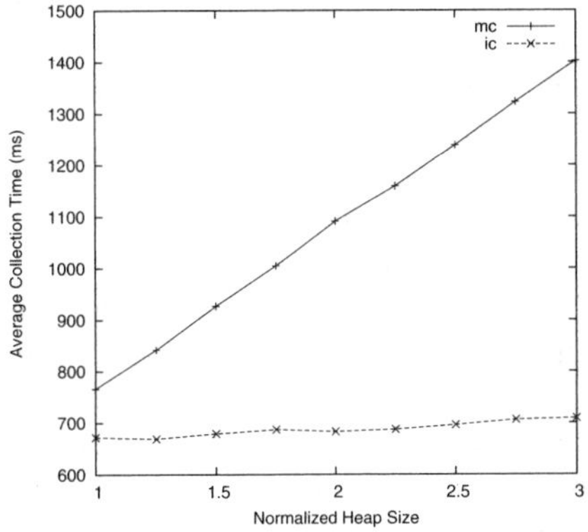

(c) jack

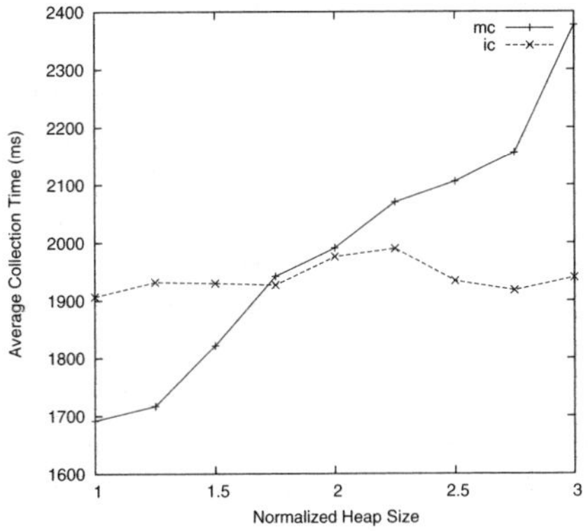

(d) javac

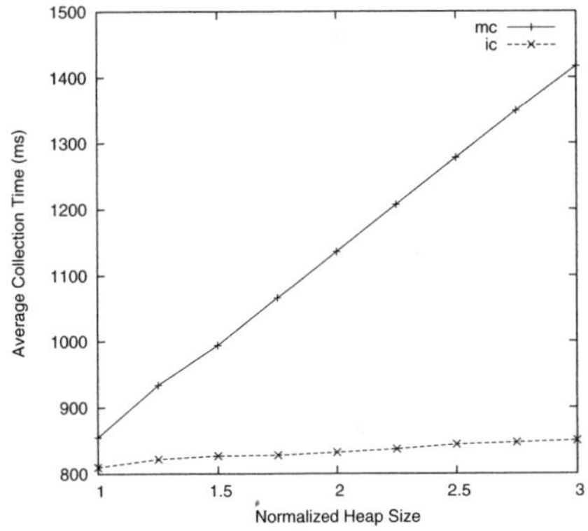

(e) jess

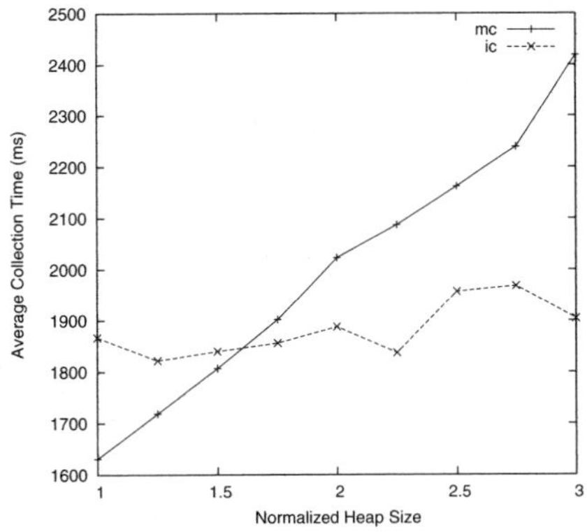

(f) mtrt

Fig. 6. Average Collection Time for Mark- and Index-Compact Collectors

5 Discussions

5.1 Improvement Techniques

The above experiments show that after introducing an index table to guide the compactors, the collection time can be made dependent only on the size of live objects, instead of the size of heap which is the case for traditional compactors. For most of the time the two compactor versions operate in a similar fashion. Our algorithm requires some extra time to sort the index. Therefore, it must be due to avoiding touching garbage that the pages faults triggered by our collectors are reduce. As a result, the overall collection time is reduced.

Compared with traditional mark-compact, our compactor needs extra space to store the index and extra time to sort the index. In [28] it is revealed that most of the objects created in typical programs tend to be very small (See Tab. 1) and the number of objects tends to be large. For the SPECjvm98 benchmarks, the average object size ranges mainly from 24 to 37 bytes, whereas an index entry takes up four bytes (in order to represent an address in a 32-bit machine). It means that the size of the index can grow to be as large as one eighth of the total size of live objects, and occasionally it can be larger than $1MB$.

As the size of the index grows, so does the space needed to store and the time spent to sort it. In Sec. 4, we mention that live objects are likely to cluster together. The number of clusters can be considerably smaller than that of live objects. Tab. 1 shows that this number falls well below 1000 for most of the benchmarks. This gives us a good opportunity to adopt another way of building the index. Fig. 7 shows a cluster-wise index, where every entry contains two pointers, pointing to the start and the end of a cluster respectively. Note that this time each index entry must be stored as a node of a linked list. We cannot construct an array for the index any more, because the tracing may not be address ordered. For instance, if the first and third cluster in Fig. 7 are traversed before the second, then an array structure is not adequate for handling this case.

Having a cluster-wise index eases the pressure on space, but it may increase the computation time. In order to make sure that every first reference address of the block index is ordered, the index must be built as a linked list and every insertion requires a search for the desired insertion point. If the objects do not cluster as much, such as the case of *javac*, this process will introduce considerable overhead. Furthermore, because the insertion happens for every live object, it

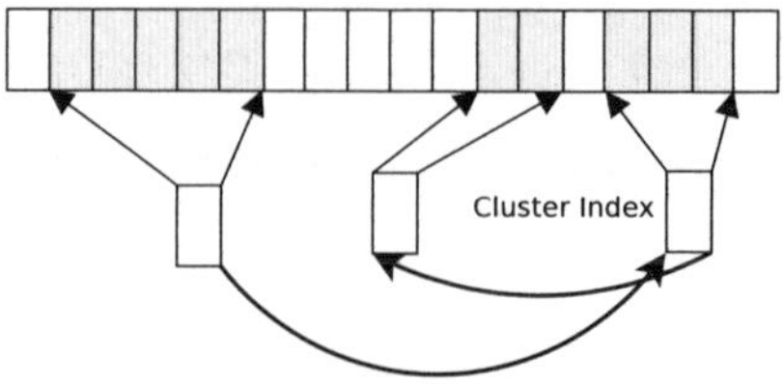

Fig. 7. The Cluster-wise Index Table

will be better to build a hash for this index to accelerate searching. Because of space limitation and that the purpose of this paper is to introduce the basic indexing idea, we skip further details on and results for the cluster-wise variant.

In the experiments we spotted that the residency of a considerable portion of the pages was nearly full. The extreme example is *compress* whose pages in the small object space are virtually all filled with live objects. For these pages, there is no need for compaction. Instead, we can remap the virtual addresses of these full pages so that they become continuous and update those pointers pointing to them. This would substantially decrease the size of the index and avoid the cost of moving full pages. For *compress*, in particular, compaction can be totally avoided in the small object space, which should help our collector to outstrip other normal compactors even when the heap becomes densely populated.

5.2 Generational Variant

Because most of the state-of-the-art collectors are generational, we suggest here how our algorithm can be applied to these collectors. As said before, the object mortality rate in the young space is much lower than that of the whole heap. It can be observed that most of the time, the survival rate is well below 10%. Since 40% is the observed turning point, it can be expected that our algorithm will perform excellently there. For older spaces, a free-list collector is probably enough, since it will not be touched as often. To fight against memory fragments, a compactor can be triggered from time to time to tidy up the room for these older spaces.

Copying-based collectors are most desirable for young space, because of their time efficiency. However, the low survival rate there makes it space inefficient, as it still needs to conserve half the available heap for copying live objects. Our collector can give a hand at this juncture to achieve a space-time balance for garbage collection, using an algorithm as described in [10]. This algorithm would manually set the portion of reserved space to be 30% of the working space, and fall back to a mark-compactor if this prediction turns out wrong during actual collection. This fallback compactor can now be replaced by our index-compact collector to avoid touching the garbage. Most of the objects in the to-be-compacted area would have already been copied to the reserved space, and what remains is a sparsely populated space for which our compactor will work better than an ordinary mark compactor. We will report our implementation of these ideas in a future paper.

6 Related Works

Since our algorithm is concerned with compaction and virtual memory, we briefly introduce several existing works that fall into these domains. For details on their implementation, please refer to [7].

6.1 Compact Collectors

Implementations of compacting garbage collectors can be classified into three classes: Lisp-2 [6], table-based [8] and threading [18][4]. In [20], a comparison between different compacting algorithms is given, and the authors argue that Lisp-2 is the most time efficient collector. Yet since all of these compactors need four phases and two heap passes to complete, none of them are good enough to be used widely in real-life systems.

Because compactors would move objects, they are frequently employed as an auxiliary method to curb memory fragmentation for non-moving collectors [22][21]. To take advantage of compactors' space efficiency over copying collectors, [16] designs a hot-swapping mechanism based on memory residency, and [10] resorts to compaction in case when its copying reserve prediction falls through. Note that in [10], the fallback compactor needs to touch the entire heap even after most of garbage have been collected by the preceding copying collector. Our algorithm should be a much better choice at this point than traditional compactors, as we have explained in the previous section. There are also research efforts on how to cut down on the phases required for compaction. For example, [3] combines marking and compaction into a two-step algorithm with one phase. But in any case, all of them need to touch the garbage objects.

6.2 VM-Aware Design

To design a VM-aware collector, some researchers have focused directly on reducing the overall consumed memory, for example, via object reuse [23]. Although there are works on how to reap the merits of virtual memory system [26][25][27], these proposed mechanisms are mostly ignored by current garbage collectors, as pointed out in [24] where the authors propose to build barriers between secondary storage and the main memory in order to avoid collection paging. We should also mention [5] which describes a concurrent, incremental and parallel algorithm designed for compactors. This collector uses two equal virtual address spaces to perform a copying-like compaction without touching the garbage. Their implementation is based on a markbit vector, whereas our algorithm uses an object reference index which is more portable and extensible to other usage scenarios, as has been explained in Sec. 5.

7 Conclusion

The slow collection time of compactors is a well known headache. They need to traverse the heap multiple times; while touching the garbage objects they trigger lots of page swaps. Many researchers have presented different techniques to reduce the number of phases in compaction, but little has been done on the problem of page swapping.

In this paper, we argue that virtual memory performance is one of the most important factors in the performance of garbage collection, and every garbage collector should endeavor to minimize page faults. We then designed an indexing algorithm that can avoid touching the garbage objects for compactors. We have implemented a preliminary basic version of the algorithm and its collector in Jikes RVM. The results confirmed our point about page swapping during garbage collection, and showed improved overall performance over traditional mark compactors. To furthermore enhance our collector's performance, we have sketched out several related advanced methods, including an application of our algorithm in a generational collector.

Further work can be done to make this compactor more suitable for real use, such as to optimize the sorting algorithm, to make the compaction parallel, to reduce the phases by storing the relocation pointers in the index, etc. In real life, our algorithm may not be suitable for certain programs, for example Lisp programs whose objects are typically even smaller than those of Java. It will be an interesting exploration to see if we can dynamically decide whether to use an index or fall back to a traditional compactor.

Acknowledgement. This work is supported in part by a Hong Kong RGC CERG grant (7141/06E). We are thankful to the anonymous reviewers and Prof. Ueda for their excellent comments and great help in the final stage of the writing.

References

1. McCarthy, J.: Recursive Functions Symbolic Expressions and Their Computation by Machine. Communication of the ACM 3(4), 184–195 (1960)
2. Saunders, R.A.: The LISP System for the Q-32 Computer. In: Berkeley and Bobrow, pp. 220–231 (1964)
3. Martin, J.J.: An efficient garbage compaction algorithm. Communications of the ACM 25(8), 571–580 (1982)
4. Morris, F.L.: A Time- and Space- Efficient Garbage Compaction Algorithm. Communications of the ACM 21(8), 662–665 (1978)
5. Kermany, H., Petrank, E.: The Compressor: Concurrent, Incremental, and Parallel Compaction. In: ACM Conference on Programming Language Design and Implementation, pp. 354–363 (2006)
6. Jones, R., Lins, R.: Garbage Collection: Algorithm for Automatic Dynamic Memory Management. John Wiley&Sons, Chichester (1997)
7. Wilson, P.R.: Uniprocessor Garbage Collection Techniques. In: Proceedings of the International Workshop on Memory Management, pp. 1–42 (1992)
8. Haddon, B.K., Waite, W.M.: A Compaction Procedure for Variable Length Storage Element. The Computer Journal 10(2), 162–165 (1967)
9. Lieberman, H., Hewitt, C.: A Real-time Garbage Collection Based on the Lifetimes of Objects. Communication of the ACM 26(6), 419–429 (1983)
10. MaGachey, P., Hosking, A.L.: Reducing Generational Copy Reserve Overhead with Fallback Compaction. In: International Symposium on Memory Management, pp. 17–28 (2006)
11. Blackburn, S.M., Cheng, P., McKinley, K.S.: Oil and Water? High Performance Garbage Collection in Java with MMTk. In: International Conference on Software Engineering, pp. 137–146 (2004)

12. Alpern, B., Augart, S., Blackburn, S.M.: The Jikes Research Virtual Machine Project: Building an Open-source Research Community. IBM Systems Journal special issue on Open Source Software 44(2), 399–417 (2005)
13. Alpern, B., Attanasio, C.R., Barton, J.J.: The Jalapeno Virtual Machine. IBM Systems Journal 39(1), 211–238 (2000)
14. Cheney, C.J.: A Nonrecursive List Compacting Algorithm. Communication of the ACM 13(11), 677–678 (1970)
15. Jonkers, H.B.M.: A Fast Garbage Compaction Algorithm. Information Processing Letters 9(9), 25–30 (1979)
16. Sansom, P.M.: Combining Single-Space and Two-Space Compacting Garbage Collectors. In: Proceedings of the Glasgow Workshop on Functional Programming (1991)
17. Wegiel, M., Krintz, C.: The mapping collector: virtual memory support for generational, parallel, and concurrent compaction. In: International Conference on Architectural Support for Programming Languages and Operating Systems, pp. 91–102 (2008)
18. Fisher, D.A.: Bounded Workspace Garbage Collection in an Address Order Preserving List Processing Environment. Information Processing Letters 3(1), 25–32 (1974)
19. Baecker, H.D.: Garbage Collection for Virtual Memory Computer Systems. Communications of the ACM 15(11), 981–986 (1972)
20. Cohen, J., Nicolau, A.: Comparison of Compacting Algorithms for Garbage Collection. ACM Transactions on Programming Languages and Systems 5(4), 532–553 (1983)
21. Ossia, Y., Yitzhak, O.B., Segal, M.: Mostly Concurrent Compaction for Mark-Sweep GC. In: International Symposium on Memory Management, pp. 25–36 (2004)
22. Printezis, T.: Hot-swapping between a mark&sweep and a mark&compact garbage collector in a generational environment. In: Symposium on JavaTM Virtual Machine Research and Technology Symposium, pp. 20–32 (2001)
23. Yu, Z.C.H., Lau, F.C.M., Wang, C.-L.: Exploiting Java Objects Behavior for Memory Management and Optimizations. In: Asian Symposium on Programming Language and Systems, pp. 437–452 (2004)
24. Hertz, M., Feng, Y., Berger, E.D.: Garbage collection without paging. In: ACM SIGPLAN Conference on Programming Language Design and Implementation, pp. 143–153 (2005)
25. Yang, T., Berger, E.D., Kaplan, S.F.: CRAMM: virtual memory support for garbage-collected applications. In: Symposium on Operating Systems Design and Implementation, pp. 103–116 (2006)
26. Wilson, P.R., Lam, M.S., Moher, T.G.: Effective "Static-graph" Reorganization to Improve Locality in Garbage-Collected Systems. ACM SIGPLAN Notices 26(6), 177–191 (1991)
27. Spoonhower, D., Blelloch, G., Harper, R.: Using Page Residency to Balance Tradeoffs in Tracing Garbage Collection. In: ACM/USENIX International Conference on Virtual Execution Environments, pp. 57–67 (2005)
28. Shuf, Y., Gupta, M., Bordawekar, R., Singh, J.R.: Exploiting Prolific Types for Memory Management and Optimizations. In: ACM Symposium on Principles of Programming Languages, pp. 295–306 (2002)
29. The Ubuntu Operating System, http://www.ubuntu.com
30. The Java Hotspot Virtual Machine, White Paper, http://java.sun.com/products/hotspot/index.html
31. The SPEC Java Virtual Machine Benchmarks, http://spec.org/jvm98

Live Heap Space Bounds for Real-Time Systems

Martin Kero, Paweł Pietrzak, and Johan Nordlander

Department of Computer Science and Electrical Engineering
Luleå University of Technology
{martin.kero,pawel.pietrzak,johan.nordlander}@ltu.se

Abstract. Live heap space analyses have so far been concerned with the standard sequential programming model. However, that model is not very well suited for embedded real-time systems, where fragments of code execute concurrently and in orders determined by periodic and sporadic events. Schedulability analysis has shown that the programming model of real-time systems is not fundamentally in conflict with static predictability, but in contrast to accumulative properties like time, live heap space usage exhibits a very state-dependent behavior that renders direct application of schedulability analysis techniques unsuitable.

In this paper we propose an analysis of live heap space upper bounds for real-time systems based on an accurate prediction of task execution orders. The key component of our analysis is the construction of a non-deterministic finite state machine capturing all task executions that are legal under given timing assumptions. By adding heap usage information inferred for each sequential task, our analysis finds an upper bound on the inter-task heap demands as the solution to an integer linear programming problem. Values so obtained are suitable inputs to other analyses depending on the size of a system's persistent state, such as running time prediction for a concurrent tracing garbage collector.

1 Introduction

Recent years have seen a respectable development in techniques for analysis of live heap space usage of programs [3,14,9,18]. The common goal of this line of research is to obtain an a priori upper bound on the size of heap memory reachable from various points in a program, expressed as a function of its input data. To this end, a standard sequential programming model has been assumed, where a program reads all its input initially, computes internally without further interaction, and eventually terminates with a deterministic result.

Unfortunately, very few embedded real-time systems – for which static predictability and failure-free operation are of particular concern – fit such a traditional programming model. Instead of terminating with a result, an embedded system typically maintains an ongoing interaction with its environment, executing fragments of code at predefined intervals or in response to sporadic events. Moreover, code fragments are often allowed to execute in parallel or under arbitrary interleaving, which introduces another source of non-determinism in such

K. Ueda (Ed.): APLAS 2010, LNCS 6461, pp. 287–303, 2010.

systems. It is clear that both these deviations from purely sequential execution adds significant complexity to the problem of predicting heap space usage.

The substantial body of results in *real-time scheduling theory* has however demonstrated that sporadic events and concurrent execution are not fundamentally at odds with static predictability. What is required is just some carefully chosen restrictions on how tasks (i.e., code fragments) may interact with each other, and what time-patterns external events may exhibit [16]. In this paper we present a technique for lifting live heap space analysis to a real-time programming model of a similar vein, sufficiently restricted to make static analysis feasible, but still expressive enough to fit a large class of real-world systems.

However, unlike schedulability analysis – which is only concerned with the number of CPU cycles a task needs to be allocated before its deadline expires – a prediction of heap space usage cannot ignore the order in which deadline-avoiding tasks actually execute at run-time. For an example, consider a task A that allocates heap memory and a task B that frees up any previous allocations. To the combined heap demand of these tasks, it makes a fundamental difference whether an A is always followed by a B or if two A can sometimes occur in a row, even if this distinction might be irrelevant for the purpose of meeting deadlines. For the same reason, heap space analysis cannot ignore the actual interleaving of tasks that are allowed to run concurrently, unless the effect each task has on live memory can be considered atomic.

The main contribution of this paper is a technique for calculating upper bounds on live heap memory of real-time systems, that is safe even in the presence of state- and order-dependent tasks driven by external sporadic events. Our strategy for doing so consists of the following key ideas:

1. We impose a modest restriction on the tasks we consider: every root of live memory must be protected by some locking mechanism, and all the locks a task requires must be held throughout its whole execution (Section 2). This is arguably a stronger restriction than necessary to guarantee atomicity, but it is appealingly simple and "obviously" correct for our purpose. We further elaborate on the realism of our task model at the end of Section 2.
2. We assume a uniform event model where each task is characterized by a minimum and (possibly infinite) maximum distance in time between the events that may trigger it. This allows us to employ techniques from *timed automata* [5] to construct a non-deterministic finite state machine (FSM) for every given task set, which adequately models all possible task execution orderings that are possible according to the given timing assumptions (Section 3).
3. We apply a standard variant of abstract interpretation to each task for inferring *size relations* [11], which capture how each individual task affects an abstract notion of size for every persistent state variable (Section 5). The input to this step is a variant of the rule-based representation (RBR) introduced in [2] for describing sequential imperative code that may involve iterative or recursive computations (Section 4).

4. We combine the results from the FSM construction and the size relation analysis in order to obtain an *integer linear programming problem*, whose solution includes a provably safe upper bound on the total live heap size observable between all possible task executions (Section 6). A set of examples illustrating how the implemented analysis algorithm behaves in practice are also given in Section 7.

Our interest in this paper is to bound the size of the heap-allocated state a system needs to preserve between its event-triggered activations, to serve as input to other analyses that crucially depend on this value, like worst-case execution time estimation for an idle time garbage collector, for example. The related problem of finding a size-bound on the total memory that must be set aside for a system's heap is not directly addressed, but we will return to the question of how our analysis fits this larger picture in Section 9.

2 Real-Time System Model

Here we define the model of execution we will work with in the rest of the paper. Our model connects fairly well to task models used in the real-time scheduling literature [16], while drawing its concrete inspiration from the execution principles underlying the real-time programming language Timber [17].

We consider a real-time system to consist of a finite set $\tau = \{t_1, \ldots, t_m\}$ of *tasks*, and a finite set $\sigma = \{s_1, \ldots, s_n\}$ of *shared state variables*. Each task is supposed to be triggered by a recurring event whose origin we know nothing about, but for which we can make timing assumptions. To this end we assume that each task $t_i \in \tau$ is characterized by a minimum and a maximum inter-arrival time between activation events ($P_i^{min}, P_i^{max} \in \mathbb{N}$). Furthermore, we assume that there is a deadline ($D_i \in \mathbb{N}$) associated with each task, and that every task is scheduled correctly (that is, every task will execute to completion within D_i time units after each triggering event). A task set is *well-formed* if the following is true:

Definition 1. *A task set τ is well-formed iff $\forall t_i \in \tau \,.\, 0 < P_i^{min} \leq P_i^{max}$ and $0 \leq D_i \leq P_i^{min}$.*

In other words, *aperiodic* tasks are excluded from our model (i.e., tasks for which $P_i^{min} = 0$), motivated by the unbounded load such tasks can place on the processor as well as on the heap. For technical reasons we also exclude tasks for which the permissible execution window of one instance is allowed to overlap with the next one (i.e., where $D_i > P_i^{min}$).

Periodic tasks are captured in this model by letting $P_i^{min} = P_i^{max}$, and fully sporadic tasks by $P_i^{max} = \infty$. Note that the model allows a continuum of behaviors between these extremes, even though the typical cases will be found at either end of the scale.

Shared State. Each shared state variable s_j is assumed to be protected by some mutual exclusion mechanism, and we furthermore require every task that either reads or writes to s_j to maintain exclusive access to s_j throughout its whole execution. This way every pair of tasks with any state variables in common will be forced to execute in some sequential order rather than in a potentially interleaved fashion. Tasks which do not share any state variables are allowed to execute under arbitrary interleaving, but the effect such tasks have on the global state is consequently independent of the interleaving pattern, and thus equivalent to their sequential execution in some arbitrary order.

Furthermore, we make our analysis independent of the actual processing power of the chosen execution platform by assuming that tasks may run arbitrarily fast[1]; that is, task execution can be associated with a point in time rather than a time interval. What we achieve under these hypotheses is that we may approximate the concurrent execution of a real-time system by a *set of sequential task orderings*, strictly governed by the underlying inter-arrival time assumptions and deadline requirements, and notably independent of any task execution times and scheduling policies. In Section 3 we will show how to concretely represent this set of task orderings in the form of a non-deterministic finite state machine.

Keeping all accessed state variables locked for the duration of full task executions is of course detrimental to the concurrent schedulability of a system, and thus not a very realistic model of concrete real-time software. However, we argue that for the purpose of the specific analysis of this paper, our simplistic model is an accurate description of a much more general class of concurrent systems that actually do occur in practice. Indeed, the Timber language that we target in our analysis implementation uses a run-time model that closely follows the principles of Baker's Stack Resource Policy [6]: state variables are partitioned into logical units called resources (or objects), each resource uses a common lock for its set of variables, and tasks (or methods) are required to lock and unlock resources in a stack-like fashion according to a total resource order (a resource may only be acquired if it is of less rank than those already held).

The only restriction this paper effectively adds to the SRP model is that we prohibit non-nested sequential resource access: new resources may not be locked once a previously held resource has been released. Under this assumption we are able to describe all relevant state update sequences of a system in terms of its possible task orderings, which is a key to the tractability of our technique and from an analysis point of view equivalent to locking all resources at once. In our experience, this additional restriction is not very burdening in practice; in the Timber language it simply corresponds to limiting the use of synchronous inter-object method calls to at most one per metod. Nevertheless, we do consider lifting the nesting requirement as an important topic for future work, and one approach we have been pondering is to automatically split tasks not conforming to the restriction into smaller parts until they do. This approach does however require that the FSM construction algorithm can be modified to take the implied sequential order of such sub-tasks into account.

Task Bodies. The sole purpose of a task is to modify the contents of the system state variables $\sigma = \{s_1, \ldots, s_n\}$. For the purpose of this paper, external ports

[1] Or arbitrarily slow, provided that all deadlines are still met.

and other observable state containers such as operating system services also count as state variables. Apart from these global state variables, we require that variables and data structures are *immutable* and thus never change their values once they are assigned. To better capture the freedom from arbitrary side-effects during task runs, we make threading of the system state through each task t_i explicit by representing it as a procedure $t_i(\overline{x}, \overline{y})$ that maps an input state vector $\overline{x}$ to an output state vector $\overline{y}$. The intention is then that the global scheduling mechanism of a system uses the output state vector to destructively update the system state, which we henceforth never need to make explicit. The exact format of each task body is further explained in Section 4.

Worked Example. Throughout the paper we will work with the following example through the steps of our analysis. Suppose we have two tasks, a and b, sharing two lists x_1 and x_2 in the following manner:

- a extends x_1 with one element, leaving x_2 as is.
- b sets $x_2 := x_1$ and $x_1 := []$ (empty list), i.e. x_2 becomes the list that x_1 was, and x_1 becomes empty.
- Initially, x_1 and x_2 are both empty.

For the purpose of the example, let a and b have the following timing characteristics:

task	P^{min}	P^{max}	D
a	10	∞	10
b	10	20	10

Our underlying analysis question is: what is the maximum sum of the sizes of x_1 and x_2 that ever may occur?

3 FSM Representation

As a core technical idea of our approach we choose to express the behaviour of a given task set as a *Timed Automaton*, itself constructed as the parallel composition of timed automata representing every individual task. The observable transitions of this automaton are the execution points of the tasks, i.e., the momentary points in time where we consider a task to perform its mutation of the system state. We then apply standard techniques for obtaining a finite *untimed* representation of the timed automaton, representing all possible task execution orders of the system in a compact form.

3.1 Real-Time Systems as Timed Automata

We follow a notation similar to Bengtsson and Yi [7] for representing the legal orders of execution for a real-time task set. A timed automaton is defined by a tuple $\mathcal{A} = \langle L, l_0, A, C, I, E \rangle$, where L is a set of locations, l_0 an initial location, A a set of labels (including the silent label ε), C a set of clock variables, I a mapping from locations to clock variable constraints, and E a set of transitions (characterized by a label, a transition guard, and a set of clock variables to reset as a side-effect).

For a well-formed task set τ, let each task $t_i \in \tau$ be represented by a timed automaton $\mathcal{A}_i = \langle L_i, l_{0i}, A_i, C_i, I_i, E_i \rangle$ defined as follows:

$$
\begin{aligned}
L_i &= \{\texttt{idle}, \texttt{released}\} \\
l_{0i} &= \texttt{idle} \\
A_i &= \{t_i, \varepsilon\} \\
C_i &= \{c_i\} \\
I_i &= \{(\texttt{idle}, c_i \le P_i^{max}), (\texttt{released}, c_i \le D_i)\} \\
E_i &= \{(\texttt{idle}, c_i \ge P_i^{min}, \varepsilon, \{c_i\}, \texttt{released}), (\texttt{released}, \mathit{true}, t_i, \emptyset, \texttt{idle})\}
\end{aligned}
$$

Fig. 1 shows the the definition above in a graphical notation.

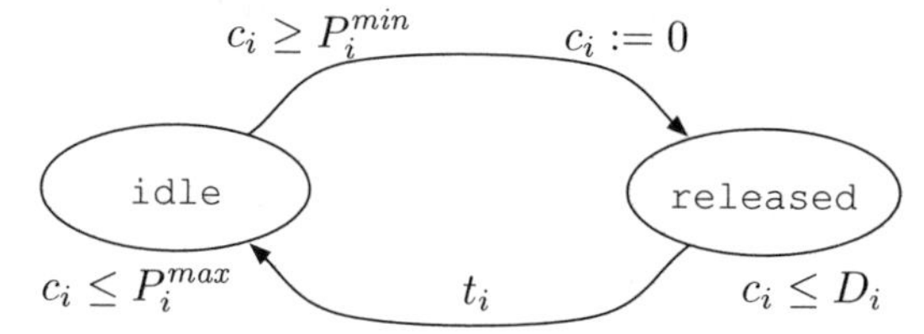

Fig. 1. Timed automaton $\mathcal{A}_i$ capturing the execution points of task t_i

The transitions of $\mathcal{A}_i$ capture the execution points of t_i: either the silent arrival of a triggering event for t_i, or the observable execution of t_i. Location `idle` denotes the state when the task is neither executing nor pending. Clock variable c_i increases in synchrony with real time and is reset whenever an event transition is taken, thus the invariant $(c_i \le P_i^{max})$ ensures that the time between two triggering events for t_i never exceeds P_i^{max}. Moreover, the guard $(c_i \ge P_i^{min})$ on the event transition forces the inter-arrival time to be at least P_i^{min}. The invariant in the `released` location guarantees that execution must take place within the deadline $(c_i \le D_i)$. Because of the well-formedness assumption we know that $D_i \le P_i^{min}$, which means that we can capture the timing constraint of the deadline with the same clock used for inter-arrival times (i.e., whenever the execution transition is taken, we know that $c_i \le D_i \le P_i^{min}$).

The timed automaton of the whole task set τ is then constructed by parallel composition $\mathcal{A}_\tau = \|_{t_i \in \tau} \mathcal{A}_i$. The resulting automaton is entirely straightforward, with locations and invariants being conjunctions of the individual automata counterparts (see [4] for further details on parallel automata composition).

3.2 Untimed Automata

Our goal is to construct a compact FSM that accurately captures all legal orders of task executions. In reachability analysis for timed automata, such faithful constructions of FSMs are usually referred to as *untimed* automata.

The operational semantics of timed automata is described as a transition system of which states are pairs $\langle l, u \rangle$ where l is a location in the original timed automaton and u is a *clock valuation* mapping clock variables to real values [5].

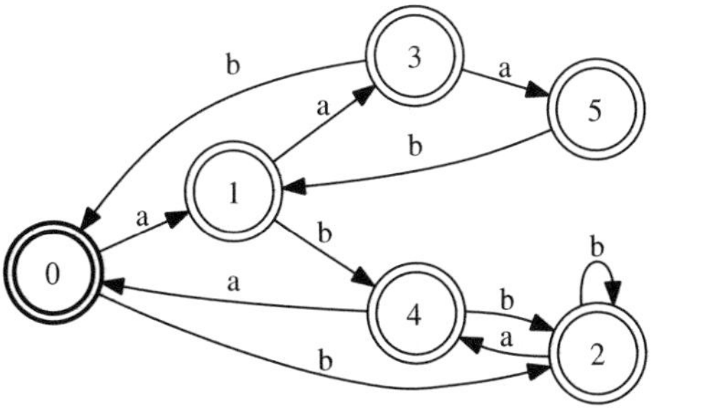

Fig. 2. Minimal FSM representation of the execution orders of the worked example

State space and transitions are defined based on the locations and transitions in the timed automaton, combined with the condition that u satisfies the implied clock constraints from invariants, guards, and resets. The state space of this transition system can efficiently (and finitely) be quotiented by configurations $\langle l, D_\varphi \rangle$, called *zones*, where D_φ is a convex set of clock valuations (called *clock zone*) defined by the clock constraint φ. The transitions of the *zone graph* is defined as follows.

$$\begin{array}{lll} \langle l, D_\varphi \rangle \longrightarrow \langle l, [{D_\varphi}^{\Uparrow} \cap D_{I(l)}] \rangle & & \\ \langle l, D_\varphi \rangle \stackrel{\alpha}{\longrightarrow} \langle l', [\delta(D_\varphi \cap D_\psi) \cap D_{I(l')}] \rangle & & \text{if } (l, \psi, \alpha, \delta, l') \in E \end{array}$$

The operations on clock zones in the definition are: *delay* (${D_\varphi}^{\Uparrow}$) which computes the strongest post condition of φ (i.e., the clock zone containing all valuations after an arbitrary delay); *reset* ($\delta(D_\varphi)$) which computes the new clock zone to capture the resets of δ; and *normalization* ($[D_\varphi]$) which widens the clock zone based on the maximum constants used in clock constraints of the timed automaton.

The zone graph accurately accepts all legal sequences of untimed labels as of the original timed automaton, while faithfully keeping track of both locations and clock valuations. However, our analysis only requires a faithful representation of the untimed language accepted by the zone graph (i.e., reachability of particular locations and clock valuations are irrelevant), we may apply standard FSM transformation techniques (such as determinization and minimization) to possibly improve the automaton. The *raw* zone graph of our worked example contains 31 zones and 59 transitions of which 34 are ε-transitions (delays and events). After determinization and minimization we get a FSM of 6 states and 11 transitions. The minimized FSM is shown in Fig. 2.

However, as we will see in Section 7, it is not necessary an improvement of performance of our analysis to make these quite costly transformations.

4 Rule-Based Representation

Following [1,2] we express the actual code a task executes in a *rule-based representation*, or RBR for short. Our RBR is essentially a slight simplification of the format used in [2]. We assume four distinct name-spaces: ordinary variables ranged over by x and y, procedure names ranged over by p and q, as well as constructor names and field names (ranged over by c and f, respectively). The syntax of our rule-based language is given in Fig. 3.

Variables can take atomic values (we limit ourselves to integers), or compound values (lists, trees, etc.), in which case the variable is a reference to a *constructed* and possibly heap-allocated object. A program consists of a set of procedures, of which some are designated as *tasks*. A procedure with a head $p(\overline{x}, \overline{y})$ has input ($\overline{x}$) and output ($\overline{y}$) parameters, and is defined by one or more *rules*. Each rule is guarded by a boolean applicability condition g, which may be either the unconditional constant *true*, a simple arithmetic comparison, or the special form $\mathsf{type}(x, c)$, which tests whether x is a reference to a constructed c object. The guard is followed by the procedure *body*, which might contain a variable assignment, an object creation instruction (with a vector of field initializations within braces), an assignment with field selection, or a (possibly recursive) procedure call. Since we do not support mutation of any other data than the system state vector, we make it an implicit condition that all variables in a procedure body are assigned only once.

$$
\begin{aligned}
P &::= R_1, \dots, R_n \\
R &::= p(\overline{x}, \overline{y}) \leftarrow g, b_1, \dots, b_n \\
g &::= \mathit{true} \mid e \; \mathit{op} \; e \mid \mathsf{type}(x, c) \\
b &::= x := e \mid x := \textbf{new } c\, \{\overline{f} := \overline{e}\} \mid x := y.f \mid q(\overline{x}, \overline{y}) \\
e &::= x \mid n \mid e - e \mid e + e \mid e * e \mid e/e \\
\mathit{op} &::= \; > \mid \; < \mid \; \geq \mid \; \leq \mid \; = \mid \; \neq
\end{aligned}
$$

Fig. 3. Syntax of rule-based representation

With the rule-based representation, the code of the tasks of our worked example looks as shown in Fig. 4 (assuming *value* is some suitable integer element). We use constructors *cons* and *nil* for building lists, where **new** *nil* {} denotes a "null pointer" (i.e., a zero-arity constructed value requiring no additional heap space).

$$
\begin{aligned}
&a(\langle x_1, x_2\rangle, \langle x_1', x_2'\rangle) \leftarrow x_1' := \textbf{new } \mathit{cons}\, \{\mathit{head} := \mathit{value}, \mathit{tail} := x_1\}, x_2' := x_2 \\
&b(\langle x_1, x_2\rangle, \langle x_1', x_2'\rangle) \leftarrow x_2' := x_1, x_1' := \textbf{new } \mathit{nil}\, \{\}
\end{aligned}
$$

Fig. 4. The worked example in the rule-based representation

In addition to rules defining tasks, we always include a predefined procedure *init* with just a single vector of output parameters carrying the initial values for a system's state variables. For the worked example we have:

$$\mathit{init}(\langle x_1, x_2\rangle) \leftarrow x_1 := \textbf{new } \mathit{nil}\, \{\}, x_2 := \textbf{new } \mathit{nil}\, \{\}$$

From [2] we also adopt an operational semantics for our rule-based programs, as depicted in Fig. 5. A value v is either an integer constant or a tagged heap reference r^c, where c is a constructor name. A heap h maps references to objects o, which in turn are mappings from field names to values. Execution steps are described as transitions $S \leadsto S'$, where S is a configuration $A : h$ containing a stack A of activation records (of the form $\langle p, bs, \rho\rangle$, where p is a procedure name, bs a sequence of instructions, and ρ an environment mapping variables to values), and a heap. We write $\rho(x)$ for the value referred to by x in ρ, and $\rho[x \mapsto v]$ for the mapping identical to ρ except that x maps to v. Both notations extend to vectors of variables and values, and also apply to mappings o and h in a similar manner.

Rule (1) deals with evaluating expressions and storing the resulting value in the environment. We assume that function $\mathsf{eval}(e, \rho)$ evaluates exp in the context of ρ. Rule (2) shows extension of the heap with a new tagged object reference r^c, mapped to an object associating each field with its evaluated value. Field access is shown in rule (3). Rules (4) and (5) illustrate calling and returning from a procedure, respectively. The notation $p[\overline{y}, \overline{y}']$ stands for a saved association between the formal and actual output parameters of p.

$$\frac{b \equiv x := e \quad v = \mathsf{eval}(e, \rho)}{\langle p, (b, bs), \rho\rangle \cdot A : h \rightsquigarrow \langle p, bs, \rho[x \mapsto v]\rangle \cdot A : h} \tag{1}$$

$$\frac{b \equiv x := \mathbf{new}\ c\{\overline{f} := \overline{e}\} \quad \overline{v} = \mathsf{eval}(\overline{e}, \rho) \quad r^c \notin dom(h)}{\langle p, (b, bs), \rho\rangle \cdot A : h \rightsquigarrow \langle p, bs, \rho[x \mapsto r^c]\rangle \cdot A : h[r^c \mapsto [\overline{f} \mapsto \overline{v}]\,]} \tag{2}$$

$$\frac{b \equiv x := y.f \quad h(\rho(x)) = o}{\langle p, (b, bs), \rho\rangle \cdot A : h \rightsquigarrow \langle p, bs, \rho[x \mapsto o(f)]\rangle \cdot A : h} \tag{3}$$

$$\frac{b \equiv q(\overline{x}, \overline{y}) \quad q(\overline{x}', \overline{y}') \leftarrow g, bs' \text{ is a rule} \quad \rho'(\overline{x}') = \rho(\overline{x}) \quad \mathsf{eval}(g, \rho') = true}{\langle p, (b, bs), \rho\rangle \cdot A : h \rightsquigarrow \langle q, bs', \rho'\rangle \cdot \langle p[\overline{y}, \overline{y}'], bs, \rho\rangle \cdot A : h} \tag{4}$$

$$\frac{}{\langle q, \epsilon, \rho\rangle \cdot \langle p[\overline{y}, \overline{y}'], bs), \rho'\rangle \cdot A : h \rightsquigarrow \langle p, bs, \rho'[\overline{y} \mapsto \rho(\overline{y}')]\rangle \cdot A : h} \tag{5}$$

Fig. 5. Operational semantics of rule-based programs

Note that since we model state variables as explicit input and output parameters, we can avoid mutation of the heap altogether in the formal semantics.

Executions can be seen as traces $S_0 \rightsquigarrow S_1 \rightsquigarrow \cdots \rightsquigarrow S_m$. Let $\overset{*}{\rightsquigarrow}$ denote a transitive closure of $\rightsquigarrow$. Complete execution of a single task t_i corresponds to the trace (called *complete trace*) $\langle \bot, t_i(\sigma, \sigma), \rho\rangle : h \overset{*}{\rightsquigarrow} \langle \bot, \epsilon, \rho'\rangle : h'$, where $\bot$ stands for the "scheduler" procedure, σ contains the names of the global state variables, and ρ and ρ' hold the state variable values before and after executing t_i, respectively.

5 Inferring Size Relations

The notion of size of a heap allocated object can vary depending on what exact purpose our analysis will serve. Let $size_{\mathcal{X}}(o)$ denote *size* of a heap-allocated object o, where the size is determined by the cost model $\mathcal{X}$ and may denote $\mathcal{M}$ (memory size occupied by o), $\mathcal{R}$ (number of reference fields in o), and $\mathcal{O}$ (number of objects in o – i.e., 1).

The above notation also extends over sequences of objects: $size_{\mathcal{X}}(\overline{o}) = [size_{\mathcal{X}}(o_1), \ldots, size_{\mathcal{X}}(o_n)]$. Inferring size relations, similarly to e.g. [8,1,2] is performed in two steps. The first one is *abstract compilation* of rules into linear constraints capturing relations between sizes of program variables. In the second step the fixpoint of the linear constraints system is computed in a bottom-up fashion. We apply the approach and implementation of [8], which originally was designed to compute size relations in logic programs. Since we represent the tasks as rules rather than logic programs, we do compile our rules to constraint logic programs (CLP), but we use a different abstract compilation scheme, as described in the following section.

Abstract Compilation of Rules. In the abstractly compiled version of a program we keep the original variable names, possibly with scripts or overlines, and use boldface to denote their sizes, with respect to a given cost model $\mathcal{X}$. For example, $\mathbf{x}$ denotes size of x. We shall extend the notation to expressions, writing $\mathbf{e}$ for a size of an expression e in which every variable x has been replaced by $\mathbf{x}$. A size of an integer number is its value [11]. Size of a compound structure $c\{...\}$ is a sum of sizes of its elements, plus a size $k_c^{\mathcal{X}}$ of a single node, suitable for a cost model $\mathcal{X}$. Abstract compilation proceeds over rules in the program as depicted in Fig. 6.

$$\begin{aligned}
\mathsf{Abs}_P[\![R_1, \ldots, R_n]\!] &= \mathsf{Abs}_R[\![R_1]\!], \ldots, \mathsf{Abs}_R[\![R_n]\!] \\
\mathsf{Abs}_R[\![p(\overline{x}, \overline{y}) \leftarrow g, b_1, \ldots, b_n]\!] &= p(\overline{\mathbf{x}}, \overline{\mathbf{y}}) \leftarrow \overline{\mathbf{x}} \geq 0, \overline{\mathbf{y}} \geq 0, \mathsf{Abs}_g[\![g]\!], \mathsf{Abs}_b[\![b_1]\!], \ldots, \mathsf{Abs}_b[\![b_n]\!]
\end{aligned}$$

$$\begin{aligned}
\mathsf{Abs}_g[\![true]\!] &= true \\
\mathsf{Abs}_g[\![e_1 \; op \; e_2]\!] &= \text{if } e_1 \text{ and } e_2 \text{ are linear then } \mathbf{e}_1 \; op \; \mathbf{e}_2 \text{ else } true \\
\mathsf{Abs}_g[\![\mathsf{type}(x, c)]\!] &= true
\end{aligned}$$

$$\begin{aligned}
\mathsf{Abs}_b[\![x := e]\!] &= \text{if } e \text{ is linear then } \mathbf{x} = \mathbf{e} \text{ else } true \\
\mathsf{Abs}_b[\![x := \textbf{new } c\{\overline{f_i} := \overline{e_i}\}]\!] &= \mathbf{x} \leq k_c^{\mathcal{X}} + \textstyle\sum_i \mathsf{norm}(c, f_i, e_i) \\
\mathsf{Abs}_b[\![x := y.f]\!] &= \mathbf{x} < \mathbf{y} \\
\mathsf{Abs}_b[\![q(\overline{x}, \overline{y})]\!] &= q(\overline{\mathbf{x}}, \overline{\mathbf{y}})
\end{aligned}$$

$$\mathsf{norm}(c, f, e) = \text{if the type of field } f \text{ of a } c \text{ is integer then } 0 \text{ else } \mathbf{e}$$

Fig. 6. Abstract compilation to CLP

Note that for compiling an object creation instruction ($x :=$ **new** $c\{...\}$) does not result in an equality, but rather in an inequality. This is the effect of possible sharing between fields of $c\{...\}$ which we do not try to detect.

Given a rule-based program P, its compiled version $\mathsf{Abs}_P[\![P]\!]$ is a CLP program over real numbers (CLP($\mathbb{R}$)). We refer, for instance, to [13] for further reading on CLP. Let us assume the *model-theoretic (or algebraic)* semantics[2]

[2] This is an arbitrary choice made for an illustrative purpose only. All kinds of semantics of CLP coincide is some well-defined sense, so choosing any other semantics would be equally valid.

of CLP($\mathbb{R}$), where semantics of programs is given by means of *models* over $\mathbb{R}$ ($\mathbb{R}$-models), and standard interpretation of arithmetic functions (see e.g. [12] for details). The following lemma shows the soundness of the abstract compilation. It is shown that relation between sizes of input and output parameters of a given procedure is correctly captured by the resulting CLP program.

Lemma 1. *Given a program P and procedure p, assume the trace $\langle q, (p(\overline{x}, \overline{y}), bs), \rho\rangle : h \overset{*}{\rightsquigarrow} \langle q, bs, \rho'\rangle : h'$. The atomic formula $p(k, l)$ where $k = size_{\mathcal{X}}(h(\rho(\overline{x})))$ and $l = size_{\mathcal{X}}(h(\rho'(\overline{y})))$ belongs to the least $\mathbb{R}$- model of* $\mathsf{Abs}_P[\![P]\!]$.

Proof: By induction over depth of recursion in P.

Assume that $k^{\mathcal{M}}_{cons} = 3$ and $k^{\mathcal{M}}_{null} = 0$. The abstractly compiled worked example is shown in Fig. 7

$$
\begin{aligned}
init(\langle \mathbf{x}_1, \mathbf{x}_2\rangle) &\leftarrow \mathbf{x}_1 \geq 0, \mathbf{x}_2 \geq 0, \mathbf{x}_1 \leq 0, \mathbf{x}_2 \leq 0 \\
a(\langle \mathbf{x}_1, \mathbf{x}_2\rangle, \langle \mathbf{x}'_1, \mathbf{x}'_2\rangle) &\leftarrow \mathbf{x}_1 \geq 0, \mathbf{x}_2 \geq 0, \mathbf{x}'_1 \geq 0, \mathbf{x}'_2 \geq 0, \mathbf{x}'_1 \leq \mathbf{x}_1 + 3, \mathbf{x}'_2 = \mathbf{x}_2 \\
b(\langle \mathbf{x}_1, \mathbf{x}_2\rangle, \langle \mathbf{x}'_1, \mathbf{x}'_2\rangle) &\leftarrow \mathbf{x}_1 \geq 0, \mathbf{x}_2 \geq 0, \mathbf{x}'_1 \geq 0, \mathbf{x}'_2 \geq 0, \mathbf{x}'_2 = \mathbf{x}_1, \mathbf{x}'_1 \leq 0
\end{aligned}
$$

Fig. 7. The worked example after abstract compilation

In general, right hand sides of abstractly compiled rules might contain recursive calls. In this case a bottom-up fixpoint algorithm is applied to infer, for each procedure p, a set linear constraints ϕ_p (or $\phi_p[\overline{\mathbf{x}}, \overline{\mathbf{y}}]$ if we want to make the involved variables explicit). See [8] for the details of the fixpoint iteration algorithm. Theorem 1 states soundness of size relation inference.

Theorem 1. *Given a trace $\langle \bot, t_i(\sigma, \sigma), \rho\rangle : h \overset{*}{\rightsquigarrow} \langle \bot, \epsilon, \rho'\rangle : h'$, the vector pair $size_{\mathcal{X}}(h(\rho(\sigma))), size_{\mathcal{X}}(h'(\rho'(\sigma)))$ satisfies ϕ_{t_i}; that is, the formula $\phi_{t_i}[size_{\mathcal{X}}(h(\rho(\sigma))), size_{\mathcal{X}}(h'(\rho'(\sigma)))]$ is true.*

Proof: By Lemma 1 and the soundness of size relation analysis of [8].

Example. Let us illustrate the behaviour of the size relation analyzer by means of the following list concatenation procedure:

$$
\begin{aligned}
app(\langle x, y\rangle, \langle z\rangle) &\leftarrow x = null(), z := y \\
app(\langle x, y\rangle, \langle z\rangle) &\leftarrow x \neq null(),\ x' := x.tail,\ app(\langle x', y\rangle, z'), \\
&\qquad z := \textbf{new}\ cons(x.head, z')
\end{aligned}
$$

Abstract compilation of the above two rules, with respect to the cost model $\mathcal{O}$, results in

$$
\begin{aligned}
app(\langle \mathbf{x}, \mathbf{y}\rangle, \langle \mathbf{z}\rangle) &\leftarrow \mathbf{x} \geq 0, \mathbf{y} \geq 0, \mathbf{z} \geq 0, \mathbf{y} = \mathbf{z} \\
app(\langle \mathbf{x}, \mathbf{y}\rangle, \langle \mathbf{z}\rangle) &\leftarrow \mathbf{x} \geq 0, \mathbf{y} \geq 0, \mathbf{z} \geq 0, \mathbf{x}' \geq 0, \mathbf{z}' \geq 0, \mathbf{x}' \leq \mathbf{x} - 1, \\
&\qquad app(\langle \mathbf{x}', \mathbf{y}\rangle, \mathbf{z}'), \mathbf{z} \leq \mathbf{z}' + 1
\end{aligned}
$$

Observe that $z := \textsf{new}\ cons(x.head, z')$ has been compiled to $\mathbf{z} \leq \mathbf{z}' + 1$ rather than $\mathbf{z} = \mathbf{z}' + 1$, due to possible sharing. Computing bottom-up fixpoint over convex polyhedra domain, as described in [8], gives the final size relations:

$$app(\langle \mathbf{x}, \mathbf{y} \rangle, \langle \mathbf{z} \rangle) \leftarrow \mathbf{x} \geq 0, \mathbf{y} \geq 0, \mathbf{z} \geq 0, \mathbf{z} \leq \mathbf{x} + \mathbf{y}$$

6 Upper Bounds

The crucial observation is that the value we are looking for is the upper bound of live memory size occupied by state variables after any possible completion of any task executed in the concurrent environment, that is in every possible schedule. The size value is not accumulated over recursive calls that might take place while executing the tasks. Therefore, for our purpose we do not need cost relations in the form of [1,2], but rather than that we work directly with the size relations introduced in the previous section. Based on the FSM representation of task execution orders and size relations for each task, we set up a system of linear constraints which is essentially an ILP (integer linear programming) problem that can be solved by any standard solver. The ILP problem, whose construction is shown below, captures the upper bounds of live memory usage.

Assume there are n state (shared) variables $s_1, \ldots, s_n$. In previous steps, for every task $m(\overline{x}, \overline{y})$ we infer size relations ϕ_m which in the matrix form can be written as

$$\mathbf{Y} \leq \mathbf{A}_m \mathbf{X} + \mathbf{C}_m, \quad \mathbf{X} \geq \mathbf{0} \tag{6}$$

where $\mathbf{X} = [\mathbf{x}_1, \ldots, \mathbf{x}_n]$, $\mathbf{Y} = [\mathbf{y}_1, \ldots, \mathbf{y}_n]$, n is a number of states variables. For an initialization method *init* (which has no input parameters) the constraints take form:

$$\mathbf{X}_0 \leq \mathbf{C}_{init}, \quad \mathbf{X}_0 \geq \mathbf{0} \tag{7}$$

Thus the vector $\mathbf{C}_{init}$ describes sizes of initial values of the state variables. The size relation matrices with respect to cost model $\mathcal{M}$ for the worked example look like the following:

$$\mathbf{A}_a = \begin{bmatrix} 1 & 0 \\ 0 & 1 \end{bmatrix} \quad \mathbf{C}_a = \begin{bmatrix} 3 \\ 0 \end{bmatrix} \quad \mathbf{A}_b = \begin{bmatrix} 0 & 0 \\ 1 & 0 \end{bmatrix} \quad \mathbf{C}_b = \begin{bmatrix} 0 \\ 0 \end{bmatrix}$$

In order to find an upper bound of $\mathbf{X}$'s, for every state i in the FSM we assign a vector of sizes of the state variables, written $\hat{\mathbf{X}}_i$. For a transition $i \stackrel{m}{\rightarrow} j$ we set up a set of constraints

$$\hat{\mathbf{X}}_j \geq \mathbf{A}_m \hat{\mathbf{X}}_i + \mathbf{C}_m \tag{8}$$

and for the initialization

$$\hat{\mathbf{X}}_0 \geq \mathbf{C}_{init} \tag{9}$$

For the ε-transitions we have $\mathbf{A}_\varepsilon = \mathbf{I}_n$ (the $n \times n$ unit matrix) and $\mathbf{C}_\varepsilon = \mathbf{0}$.

We require the size relation matrices ($\mathbf{A}$'s) to only contain non-negative coefficients. If, for some task, a size relation matrix with negative coefficients is inferred (this might occur if, for instance, the task definition is incomplete), we simply replace those coefficients by 0's. For our purpose, which is finding upper bounds, increasing coefficients in $\mathbf{A}$ is a relaxation and always a safe step to do. The reason for this requirement is that $\hat{\mathbf{X}}_i$ and $\hat{\mathbf{X}}_j$ represent upper bounds, which means that the inferred constraints for $\hat{\mathbf{X}}_j$ must be safe for any sizes between $\mathbf{0}$ and $\hat{\mathbf{X}}_i$.

Let $i_0 \overset{m_0}{\rightarrow} i_1 \overset{m_1}{\rightarrow} i_2 \overset{m_2}{\rightarrow} \cdots$ be a run of the state machine. With every step k we assign variables $\mathbf{X}_k$ denoting sizes of state variables in k, in according to (6) and (7).

Lemma 2. *Consider a run of the state machine and its k-th step. Let i_k denote the state in step k. For any solution of (8) + (9), any k we have* $\hat{\mathbf{X}}_{i_k} \geq \mathbf{X}_k$.

Proof: Inductive over k.

Base case: *Trivially holds by combining (7) and (9).*
Inductive step: *By inductive assumption we know that* $\hat{\mathbf{X}}_{i_{k-1}} \geq \mathbf{X}_{k-1}$, *and by the fact that* $\mathbf{A}_{m_{k-1}}$ *contains only non-negative values we conclude that* $\mathbf{A}_{m_{k-1}} \hat{\mathbf{X}}_{i_{k-1}} + \mathbf{C}_{m_{k-1}} \geq \mathbf{A}_{m_{k-1}} \mathbf{X}_{k-1} + \mathbf{C}_{m_{k-1}}$ *By combining the above with (6) and (8) we can observe that* $\hat{\mathbf{X}}_{i_k} \geq \mathbf{X}_k$, *which concludes the proof.*

Lemma 2 suggests the way to compute upper bounds of state variable sizes. In addition to (9) and (8) we add $\hat{X} \geq \mathbf{H} \cdot \hat{\mathbf{X}}_l$ for every state l; where $\mathbf{H} = [\mathbf{h}_1, \ldots, \mathbf{h}_n]$ and $\mathbf{h}_i = 1$ if s_i is heap allocated, $\mathbf{h}_i = 0$ otherwise. Let the cost function $c = \hat{X}$ and c^* denote its minimum value. The following theorem states soundness of the analysis.

Theorem 2. *Let T be a set of all complete traces, over all feasible (possibly infinite) schedules. The following holds:*

$$max\{\sum size_{\mathcal{X}}(h'(\rho'(y))) \mid \langle \bot, p(\overline{x}, \overline{y}), \rho\rangle : h \overset{*}{\leadsto} \langle \bot, \epsilon, \rho'\rangle : h' \in T\} \leq c^*$$

Proof: Follows directly from Theorem 1 and construction of (8) and (9), and Lemma 2.

The constraints (wrt cost model $\mathcal{M}$) for our worked example are shown below. The minimum solution to its corresponding cost function is $c^* = 30$.

$\mathbf{x1}_1 \geq \mathbf{x1}_0 + 3$	$\mathbf{x2}_1 \geq \mathbf{x2}_0$	$\mathbf{x2}_2 \geq \mathbf{x1}_0$	$\mathbf{x1}_3 \geq \mathbf{x1}_1 + 3$
$\mathbf{x2}_3 \geq \mathbf{x2}_1$	$\mathbf{x2}_4 \geq \mathbf{x1}_1$	$\mathbf{x1}_4 \geq \mathbf{x1}_2 + 3$	$\mathbf{x2}_4 \geq \mathbf{x2}_2$
$\mathbf{x2}_2 \geq \mathbf{x1}_2$	$\mathbf{x1}_5 \geq \mathbf{x1}_3 + 3$	$\mathbf{x2}_5 \geq \mathbf{x2}_3$	$\mathbf{x2}_0 \geq \mathbf{x1}_3$
$\mathbf{x1}_0 \geq \mathbf{x1}_4 + 3$	$\mathbf{x2}_0 \geq \mathbf{x2}_4$	$\mathbf{x2}_2 \geq \mathbf{x1}_4$	$\mathbf{x2}_1 \geq \mathbf{x1}_5$

$\mathbf{x1}_0 \geq 0$	$\mathbf{x1}_1 \geq 0$	$\mathbf{x1}_2 \geq 0$	$\mathbf{x1}_3 \geq 0$
$\mathbf{x1}_4 \geq 0$	$\mathbf{x1}_5 \geq 0$	$\mathbf{x2}_0 \geq 0$	$\mathbf{x2}_1 \geq 0$
$\mathbf{x2}_2 \geq 0$	$\mathbf{x2}_3 \geq 0$	$\mathbf{x2}_4 \geq 0$	$\mathbf{x2}_5 \geq 0$
$\hat{X} \geq \mathbf{x1}_0 + \mathbf{x2}_0$	$\hat{X} \geq \mathbf{x1}_1 + \mathbf{x2}_1$	$\hat{X} \geq \mathbf{x1}_2 + \mathbf{x2}_2$	
$\hat{X} \geq \mathbf{x1}_3 + \mathbf{x2}_3$	$\hat{X} \geq \mathbf{x1}_4 + \mathbf{x2}_4$	$\hat{X} \geq \mathbf{x1}_5 + \mathbf{x2}_5$	

7 Examples

Our analysis relies on constructing an integer linear programming problem, whose solution includes a provably safe upper-bound on the live heap size observable between all possible task executions. Solving such problems can be done by standard solvers. However, the complexity of solving such problems depends on both the number of unknowns and the number of constraints. In our case, the number of unknowns is determined by the number of states in the FSM. Similarly, the number of constraints is dependent on the number of transitions in the FSM. Both these multiplied by the number of shared state variables.

Task set	P^{min}	P^{max}	D	#states zone graph	#states FSM
τ_1	{17,19,23}	$\{\infty, \infty, \infty\}$	{17,19,23}	1255	1
τ_2	{10,300}	{20,350}	{10,300}	200	699
τ_3	{10,20,30,40,50}	{10,20,30,40,50}	{10,20,30,40,50}	10368	3393
τ_4	{17,23,29}	{17,23,29}	{17,23,29}	12968	6343

Fig. 8. Zone graph and minimal FSM sizes of four different example task sets

It is well-known that the number of zones is exponential to the number of clocks present in the timed automaton [10]. I.e., in our case, we have an exponential growth of zones w.r.t. number of tasks. In Figure 8, the zone graph and minimal FSM sizes for four different example task sets are shown. Observe that, for τ_2, the number of states is less in the zone graph than in the determinized and minimized FSM. However, as τ_1 shows, the minimized FSM can be as small as 1 state (the order between fully sporadic tasks is in fact completely arbitrary), even though the original zone graph contains many more states. Appendix A contains an extended example of our analysis. The required times by our prototype implementation for constructing the zone graphs of the task sets in Figure 8 and Appendix A are neglectable (< 1 s). Solving the ILP problem of the example in Appendix A took about 25 seconds, using `lp_solve version 5.5.2.0`. [3]

8 Related Work

To the best of our knowledge, there is no existing work on predicting global live heap space for real-time systems similar to those we describe in Section 2. Nonetheless, a substantial body of work has been presented for analyzing live heap space bounds for standard sequential programs. In this section we briefly describe some of the more recent contributions in this line of research.

As already mentioned, for each task we borrow from [2,3], the rule-based representation of programs along with semantics, which we could however simplify due to special treatment of state variables and lack of mutation. We also adopt from their work the step of inferring size relations. Jost et al. [14] presents a

[3] Platform: 3.06GHz Intel Core 2 Duo, 4 GB RAM, Mac OS X 10.6.4.

generic type-based resource analysis for inferring linear bounds on resource consumption for higher-order polymorphic programs. The corresponding type inference is based on a standard linear programming solver. Chin et al. [9] presents a memory resource analysis for low-level assembly programs. They infer both net usage and a high watermark bound for each computation unit based on explicit allocation and deallocation of heap space. Unnikrishnan et al. [18] presents a live heap space analysis based on program transformation and symbolic evaluation. The transformed program mimics the memory behavior and essentially keeps the same computational complexity as of the original program.

9 Conclusion and Further Work

We have proposed a technique for computing upper bounds on live heap memory of real-time systems, that is safe even in the presence of state- and order-dependent tasks driven by external sporadic events.

Our key contribution is based on the derivation of an accurate prediction of task execution orders according to timing assumptions of each task (inter-arrival times and deadlines). This is done by representing the task set as a timed automaton and apply standard techniques used in reachability analysis to construct an FSM representation of task execution orders. We infer linear input/output size relations for each task on the persistent state of the system, which is then combined with the execution order FSM to obtain an integer linear programming problem, whose solution includes a provably safe upper bound on the total live heap size observable between all possible task executions.

Heap Space Usage and Schedulability. In real-time systems where tasks share heap data (as we describe in Section 2) it is in general impossible to manage heap memory manually. If such systems are to be memory managed by a concurrent garbage collector, the key question is how it affects schedulability. In fact, the problem is twofold; (1) will all tasks meet their deadlines, and (2) how much heap memory will be needed? These two interests are obviously in conflict since running the garbage collector will reduce the memory needs while it may cause tasks to miss their deadlines. On the other hand, avoiding to run the collector might keep tasks meeting deadlines but at the same time cause the system to exhaust memory resources.

A tracing garbage collector recycles the dead (non-reachable) part of the heap and the running time of such collectors is directly dependent on the amount of live (reachable) memory. Thus, finding bounds on the global live heap space of such systems are crucial for both determining schedulability of the task set as well as predicting the total heap space usage.

In [15], Kero and Aittamaa presents a schedulability analysis, called *garbage collection demand analysis*, for a concurrent copying garbage collector in a reactive real-time system. Their garbage collector is restricted to run only during idle time, which enables them to rely on regular schedulability analysis of the task set to ensure (1). The analysis determines an upper bound on the start to finish time of the garbage collector as well as the amount of memory consumed during that time.

Further Work. One key observation is that the execution order FSM accepts traces of task executions that are *legal* according to the timing assumptions of each task. In our case, we have left those timing assumptions as open as possible, containing only inter-arrival times and deadlines. Generally, the schedulability requirement leaves the choice of order in which released tasks are executed open as long as all individual deadlines are met. In reality, schedulability is typically reached by a myopic scheduling policy (e.g., EDF, RM, etc.), which has a fully deterministic outcome. Thus, from any zone in the zone graph, if assuming a particular scheduling policy, one can reduce the number of labelled transitions to a maximum of one. Apart from tighter bounds, preliminary experimental results show significant improvements in FSM sizes (down to 25 % of the original size). Along the same line, the zone graph accepts traces where the release of a task and its execution point occurs at the very same instant. Adding a safe lower bound on execution time for each task will reduce the time windows in which task execution points may occur, ultimately reducing the number of possible execution orders. Although standard solvers of ILP problems are quite efficient nowadays, the complexity of finding the optimal solution is still exponential. However, sub-optimal solutions to our ILP problems are still safe bounds (although less precise), which opens up the possibility to use heuristics to reduce complexity.

References

1. Albert, E., Arenas, P., Genaim, S., Puebla, G., Zanardini, D.: Cost Analysis of Java Bytecode. In: 16th European Symposium on Programming (2007)
2. Albert, E., Genaim, S., Gómez-Zamalloa, M.: Live heap space analysis for languages with garbage collection. In: ISMM (2009)
3. Albert, E., Genaim, S., Gómez-Zamalloa, M.: Parametric inference of memory requirements for garbage collected languages. In: ISMM (2010)
4. Alur, R.: Timed automata. In: Halbwachs, N., Peled, D.A. (eds.) CAV 1999. LNCS, vol. 1633, pp. 8–22. Springer, Heidelberg (1999)
5. Alur, R., Dill, D.: A theory of timed automata. Journal of Theoretical Computer Science 126(2) (1994)
6. Baker, T.P.: Stack-based scheduling for realtime processes. Real-Time Syst. 3(1), 67–99 (1991)
7. Bengtsson, J., Yi, W.: Timed automata: Semantics, algorithms and tools. In: Lectures on Concurrency and Petri Nets (2003)
8. Benoy, F., King, A.: Inferring argument size relationships with CLPR. In: Workshop on Logic-based Program Synthesis and Transformation (1997)
9. Chin, W.N., Nguyen, H.H., Popeea, C., Qin, S.: Analysing memory resource bounds for low-level programs. In: ISMM (2008)
10. Courcoubetis, C., Yannakakis, M.: Minimum and maximum delay problems in real-time systems. Formal Methods in System Design 1(4) (1992)
11. Cousot, P., Halbwachs, N.: Automatic discovery of linear restraints among variables of a program. In: POPL (1978)
12. Jaffar, J., Maher, M., Marriott, K., Stuckey, P.: The semantics of constraint logic programs. Journal of Logic Programming 37 (1–3) (1998)
13. Jaffar, J., Maher, M.J.: Constraint logic programming: A survey. Journal of Logic Programming 19 & 20 (1994)

14. Jost, S., Loid, H.W., Hammond, K., Hofmann, M.: Static determination of quantitative resource usage for higher-order programs. In: POPL (2010)
15. Kero, M., Aittamaa, S.: Scheduling garbage collection in real-time systems. In: CODES (2010)
16. Krishna, C.M., Shin, K.G.: Real-Time Systems. McGraw-Hill, New York (1997)
17. Nordlander, J., Carlsson, M., Gill, A., Lindgren, P., von Sydow, B.: The Timber home page (2008), `http://timber-lang.org`
18. Unnikrishnan, L., Stoller, S.D., Liu, Y.A.: Optimized live heap bound analysis. In: Zuck, L.D., et al. (eds.) VMCAI 2003. LNCS, vol. 2575, pp. 70–85. Springer, Heidelberg (2002)

Appendix A – Extended Example

task	P^{min}	P^{max}	D
$sample_1$	10	15	5
$sample_2$	20	20	5
$lphigh$	100	100	10
$acquire$	1000	1000	1000

	#states	#arcs
zone graph:	6100	14072
minimal FSM:	3510	8428

$$sample_1(\langle gval, gbuf, buf_1, buf_2\rangle, \langle gval', gbuf', buf'_1, buf'_2\rangle) \leftarrow$$
$$gval' := gval, \quad gbuf' := gbuf, \quad buf'_2 := buf_2, \quad val_1 := buf_1.head,$$
$$buf'_1 := \textbf{new}\ cons\,\{head := (sensor_1 + 99 * val_1)/100, tail := buf_1\}.$$

$$sample_2(\langle gval, gbuf, buf_1, buf_2\rangle, \langle gval', gbuf', buf'_1, buf'_2\rangle) \leftarrow$$
$$gval' := gval, \quad gbuf' := gbuf, \quad buf'_1 := buf_1, \quad val_2 := buf_2.head,$$
$$buf'_2 := \textbf{new}\ cons\,\{head := (sensor_2 + 99 * val_2)/100, tail := buf_2\}.$$

$$lphigh(\langle gval, gbuf, buf_1, buf_2\rangle, \langle gval', gbuf', buf'_1, buf'_2\rangle) \leftarrow$$
$$gval' := gval, \quad mean(\langle buf_1\rangle, \langle m_1\rangle), \quad mean(\langle buf_2\rangle, \langle m_2\rangle), \quad buf'_1 := \textbf{new}\ nil\,\{\},$$
$$buf'_2 := \textbf{new}\ nil\,\{\}, \quad gbuf' := \textbf{new}\ cons\,\{head := (m_1 + m_2)/2, tail := gbuf\}.$$

$$acquire(\langle gval, gbuf, buf_1, buf_2\rangle, \langle gval', gbuf', buf'_1, buf'_2\rangle) \leftarrow$$
$$mean(\langle gbuf\rangle, \langle gval''\rangle), \quad gval' := (gval + gval'')/2, \quad gbuf' := \textbf{new}\ nil\,\{\},$$
$$buf'_1 := buf_1, \quad buf'_2 := buf_2.$$

$$init(\langle gval, gbuf, buf_1, buf_2\rangle) \leftarrow$$
$$gval := 0, \quad gbuf := \textbf{new}\ nil\,\{\}, \quad buf_1 := \textbf{new}\ nil\,\{\}, \quad buf_2 := \textbf{new}\ nil\,\{\}.$$

For cost model $\mathcal{M}$ ($k^{\mathcal{M}}_{cons} = 3$ and $k^{\mathcal{M}}_{null} = 0$) we get the following matrices:

$$\mathbf{A}_{sample_1} = \begin{bmatrix}1&0&0&0\\0&1&0&0\\0&0&1&0\\0&0&0&1\end{bmatrix} \quad \mathbf{A}_{sample_2} = \begin{bmatrix}1&0&0&0\\0&1&0&0\\0&0&1&0\\0&0&0&1\end{bmatrix} \quad \mathbf{A}_{lphigh} = \begin{bmatrix}1&0&0&0\\0&1&0&0\\0&0&0&0\\0&0&0&0\end{bmatrix} \quad \mathbf{A}_{acquire} = \begin{bmatrix}1&0&0&0\\0&0&0&0\\0&0&1&0\\0&0&0&1\end{bmatrix}$$

$$\mathbf{C}_{sample_1} = \begin{bmatrix}0\\0\\3\\0\end{bmatrix} \quad \mathbf{C}_{sample_2} = \begin{bmatrix}0\\0\\0\\3\end{bmatrix} \quad \mathbf{C}_{lphigh} = \begin{bmatrix}0\\3\\0\\0\end{bmatrix} \quad \mathbf{C}_{acquire} = \begin{bmatrix}0\\0\\0\\0\end{bmatrix}$$

The minimum solution to c is $c^* = 111$.

A Quick Tour of the VeriFast Program Verifier

Bart Jacobs*, Jan Smans, and Frank Piessens

Department of Computer Science, Leuven, Belgium
{bart.jacobs,jan.smans,frank.piessens}@cs.kuleuven.be

Abstract. This paper describes the main features of VeriFast, a sound and modular program verifier for C and Java. VeriFast takes as input a number of source files annotated with method contracts written in separation logic, inductive data type and fixpoint definitions, lemma functions and proof steps. The verifier checks that (1) the program does not perform illegal operations such as dividing by zero or illegal memory accesses and (2) that the assumptions described in method contracts hold in each execution.

Although VeriFast supports specifying and verifying deep data structure properties, it provides an interactive verification experience as verification times are consistently low and errors can be diagnosed using its symbolic debugger. VeriFast and a large number of example programs are available online at: `http://www.cs.kuleuven.be/~bartj/verifast`

1 Introduction

To tame the problems caused by aliasing when reasoning about imperative programs, O'Hearn, Reynolds and Yang [1,2] proposed a variant of Hoare logic [3] called separation logic. Separation logic extends Hoare logic with new assertions to describe the structure of the heap. These additional assertions allow for local reasoning through the frame rule:

$$\frac{\{P\}\ C\ \{Q\}}{\{P * R\}\ C\ \{Q * R\}}$$

Informally, the frame rule states that to reason about the behavior of a command C, it is safe to ignore memory locations not accessed by C (here R).

To automate the ideas behind separation logic, Berdine *et al.* [4] proposed an efficient verification algorithm based on symbolic execution and implemented this algorithm for a small, imperative language in Smallfoot. Variants of this algorithm were soon implemented in static analyzers (e.g. Space Invader [5]) and in automatic (e.g. jStar [6]) and interactive program verifiers (e.g. Ynot [7]).

This paper describes the main features of VeriFast, a program verifier that brings the ideas of Berdine *et al.* to (subsets of) C and Java. Contrary to Smallfoot, we focus more on fast verification, expressive power, and the ability to diagnose errors easily than on automation. In the remainder of this paper, we

* Bart Jacobs is a Postdoctoral Fellow of the Research Foundation - Flanders (FWO).

K. Ueda (Ed.): APLAS 2010, LNCS 6461, pp. 304–311, 2010.

explain the core specification concepts by showing how one can specify and verify full functional correctness of a C implementation of a stack (Section 2), and discuss our experience with our implementation (Section 3).

2 Building Blocks

In this section, we introduce the building blocks of the VeriFast approach: method contracts written in separation logic, inductive data types, fixpoint functions and lemma functions. We do so by specifying a C implementation of a stack.

```
struct node { int value; struct node * next; };

struct node * create_node(int v, struct node * nxt)
   requires emp;
   ensures result→value ↦ v * result→next ↦ nxt * malloc_block_node(result);
{
  struct node * n := malloc(sizeof(struct node));
  if(n = 0) abort();
  n→value := v; n→next := nxt;
  return n;
}
```

Fig. 1. The function *create_node* and its method contract

2.1 Method Contracts

In VeriFast, developers can specify the behavior of a C function via a method contract consisting of two assertions, a precondition and a postcondition. Both assertions must be written in a form of separation logic. As an example, consider the program of Figure 1. The function *create_node* creates a new node, initializes its fields, and returns a pointer to the caller. As *create_node* can be called at all times, its precondition (keyword **requires**) imposes no restriction on callers. Its postcondition (keyword **ensures**) guarantees that the fields *value* and *next* of the returned pointer are valid memory locations that respectively hold the values *v* and *nxt*. In addition, the conjunct *malloc_block_node*(*result*) guarantees that the return value is a pointer returned by *malloc*, that can be passed to *free*[1] to deallocate **sizeof**(**struct** *node*) bytes of memory. Note that all aforementioned conjuncts of the postcondition are separated by a separating conjunction (denoted by $*$), indicating that modification of one conjunct will not affect the others.

In Figure 1 and the remainder of this paper, annotations are marked by a gray background. In our implementation annotations must be placed inside special comments that are ignored by the C compiler, but recognized by VeriFast.

[1] In C, only pointers returned by *malloc* should be passed to *free*.

2.2 Inductive Data Types

To allow developers to specify rich properties, VeriFast supports inductive data types. For example, the first line of Figure 2 defines the well-known inductive data type *list*: a list is either empty, *nil*, or the concatenation of a head element and a tail. Note that the definition is generic in the type of the list elements (here *t*). As we will soon show, inductively defined lists can be used in specifications.

```
inductive list<t> = nil | cons(t, list<t>);

predicate lseg(struct node *f, struct node *t; list<int> vs) =
  f = t ?
    vs = nil :
    f ≠ 0 * f→value ↦?v * f→next ↦?n * malloc_block_node(f)*
      lseg(n, t, ?vs0) * vs = cons(v, vs0);

struct stack { struct node *head; };

predicate stack(struct stack *s; list<int> vs) =
  s→head ↦?h * malloc_block_stack(s) * lseg(h, 0, vs);
```

```
struct stack *create_stack()
  requires emp;
  ensures stack(result, nil);
{
  struct stack *s :=
    malloc(sizeof(struct stack));
  if(s = 0)abort();
  s→head := 0;
  return s;
}
```

```
void push(struct stack *s, int x)
  requires stack(s, ?vs);
  ensures stack(s, cons(x, vs));
{
  s→head := create_node(x, s→head);
}
```

Fig. 2. A small program illustrating inductive data types and predicates

To describe recursive data structures and to allow for information hiding, VeriFast supports separation logic predicates. A predicate is a named assertion. For example, Figure 2 defines the predicates *lseg* and *stack*. The former predicate denotes a chain of valid nodes starting at f and ending in t containing exactly the values in the mathematical list *vs*. More specifically, if f equals t, then *vs* is the empty list; otherwise, f is a node with some value v (the question mark preceding v indicates that $f \rightarrow value$ can have an arbitrary value, which is called v in the remainder of the assertion), there exists a sequence of node objects at f's next pointer with values *vs0* and *vs* is the concatenation of v and *vs0*. The latter predicate states that s is a valid stack that holds the values *vs*.

The aforementioned predicates are used in Figure 2 to specify the behavior of *create_stack* and *push* in an implementation-independent manner. More specifically, *create_stack* can be called at all times, and guarantees that the returned pointer refers to a valid, but empty stack. The precondition of *push* requires that s is a pointer to a valid stack containing an arbitrary sequence of values called vs. *push*'s postcondition ensures that s still is a valid stack with the value x added at the top.

Both *lseg* and *stack* are precise predicates. This means that their input parameters uniquely determine (1) the structure of the heap described by those predicates and (2) the values of the output parameters. In VeriFast, input parameters are separated from output parameters by a semicolon. For example, f and t are input parameters of *lseg*, while vs is an output parameter. VeriFast automatically tries to fold and unfold precise predicate instances whenever necessary. For instance, the predicate instance $stack(s, vs)$ is opened automatically inside *push* such that $s{\rightarrow}head$ can be read. As shown in Figure 5, developers can insert explicit fold (**close**) and unfold (**open**) proofs steps in the form of ghost commands for non-precise predicates or when the automatic folding and unfolding does not suffice.

2.3 Fixpoint Functions

In addition to inductive data types, VeriFast also supports fixpoint functions. Just like predicates and inductive data types, fixpoint functions can only be mentioned in specifications, not in the C code itself. Figure 3 contains 3 fixpoint functions, that respectively compute the head, tail and length of an inductively defined list. Note that the aforementioned fixpoints functions are generic in the element type of the list.

```
fixpoint t head<t>(list<t> l) {
  switch(l) {
    case nil : return default<t>;
    case cons(hd, tl) : return hd;
  }
}
```

```
fixpoint list<t> tail<t>(list<t> l) {
  switch(l) {
    case nil : return default<t>;
    case cons(hd, tl) : return tl;
  }
}
```

```
fixpoint int length<t>(list<t> l) {
  switch(l) {
    case nil : return 0; case cons(hd, tl) : return 1 + length(tl);
  }
}
```

Fig. 3. The fixpoint functions *head*, *tail* and *length*

The body of a fixpoint function must be a switch statement over one of the fixpoint's inductive arguments. To ensure soundness of the encoding of fixpoints, VeriFast checks that fixpoints terminate. In particular, VeriFast enforces that whenever a fixpoint g is called in the body of a fixpoint f that either g appears before f in the program text or that the call decreases the size of an inductive argument. For example, the call $\mathit{length}(\mathit{tl})$ in the body of *length* itself is allowed because tl is a component of l (and hence smaller than l).

As shown in Figure 4, *pop*'s function contract uses fixpoint functions: given a non-empty stack with values vs, *pop* removes the top of the stack (i.e. the head of vs) and returns this value to the caller. The function *dispose* deallocates a stack and its constituent nodes. To dispose the nodes, *dispose* walks over the list of nodes in a loop and deallocates them one by one. To reason about loops, VeriFast requires developers to provide loop invariants (keyword **invariant**). Developers may provide an optional loop variant, an integer-valued expression that decreases in each iteration but never becomes negative, to enforce termination. In the example, the length of the sequence of nodes that is not deallocated yet is the loop variant.

```
int pop(struct stack * s)
    requires stack(s, vs) * vs ≠ nil;
    ensures stack(s, tail(vs))*
        result = head(vs);
{
    int r := s→head→value;
    struct node * n := s→head;
    s→head := n→next;
    free(n);
    return r;
}
```

```
void dispose(struct stack * s)
    requires stack(s, ?vs);
    ensures emp;
{
    struct node * n := s→head;
    while(n ≠ 0)
        invariant lseg(n, 0, ?vs0);
        decreases length(vs0);
    {
        struct node * tmp := n→next;
        free(n); n := tmp;
    }
    free(s);
}
```

Fig. 4. The functions *pop* and *dispose*

2.4 Lemma Functions

Lemma functions allow developers to prove properties of their inductive data types, fixpoints and predicates, and allow them to use these properties when reasoning about programs. A lemma is a function without side-effects marked **lemma**. The contract of a lemma function corresponds to the property itself, its body to the proof and a lemma function call corresponds to an application of the property. VeriFast has two types of lemma functions, pure and spatial lemmas.

```
fixpoint list<t> append<t>(list<t> a, list<t> b) {
  switch(a) {
    case nil : return b; case cons(hd, tl) : return cons(hd, append(tl, b));
  }
}

lemma void append_assoc<t>(list<t> a, list<t> b, list<t> c)
  requires true; ensures append(append(a, b), c) = append(a, append(b, c));
{ switch(a) { case nil : ; case cons(hd, tl) : append_assoc(tl, b, c); } }

lemma void lseg_add(struct node * a)
  requires lseg(a, ?b, ?vs1) * b→next ↦?n * b → value ↦?v*
    malloc_block_node(b) * lseg(n, 0, ?vs2);
  ensures lseg(a, n, append(vs1, cons(v, nil))) * lseg(n, 0, vs2);
{
  if(a = b){ open lseg(a, b, vs1); } else { lseg_add(a→next); }
  open lseg(n, 0, vs2); close lseg(n, 0, vs2); // get info from predicate body
}

int size(struct stack * s)
  requires stack(s, ?vs); ensures stack(s, vs) * result = length(vs);
{
  int c := 0; struct node * n := s→head; struct node * head := n;
  while(n ≠ 0)
    invariant lseg(head, n, ?vs1) * lseg(n, 0, ?vs2)*
      c = length(vs1) * vs = append(vs1, vs2);
    decreases length(vs2);
  {
    c++; n := n→next;
    lseg_add(head); append_assoc(vs1, cons(head(vs2), nil), tail(vs2));
  }
  return c;
}
```

Fig. 5. The correctness of the C function *size* is established using the lemma functions *lseg_add* and *append_assoc*

A pure lemma is a function whose contract only contains pure assertions, and whose body proves that the precondition implies the postcondition. *append_assoc* shown in Figure 5 is a pure lemma that proves by induction on a's size that the fixpoint *append* is associative[2]. More specifically, the case *nil* of the switch statement corresponds to the base case, while the case *cons* corresponds to the inductive step. Note that switches over inductive data types do not require break statements.

As opposed to pure lemmas, contracts of spatial lemmas can mention spatial assertions such as predicates and points-to assertions. A spatial lemma with precondition P and postcondition Q states that the program state described by P is equivalent to the state described by Q. A spatial lemma call does not modify the underlying values in the heap, but changes the symbolic representation of the program state. *lseg_add* shown in Figure 5 is an example of a spatial lemma that shows that a list segment from a to b can be extended provided b itself is a valid node. The body of the C function *size*, which computes the number of elements in a stack s, calls *lseg_add* and *append_assoc* to prove that the loop invariant is preserved by the loop's body.

3 Implementation and Experience

The VeriFast program verifier, a large number of examples, and additional documentation is available online at: `http://www.cs.kuleuven.be/~bartj/verifast`. VeriFast has been used for teaching several courses on program verification at K.U.Leuven (Belgium) and ETH Zurich (Switzerland). The documentation includes a tutorial, which describes the supported subset of C via a number of examples and covers many features of VeriFast not discussed here such as fractional permissions, higher-order predicates, overflow checking, function pointers, predicate families and concurrency.

VeriFast has been used in a number of case studies as shown in the table below. These case studies do not consist of large code bases, but rather focus on proving correctness of challenging specification and verification patterns (e.g. composite).

program	total # lines	# annotation lines	time taken (seconds)
chat server	242	114	0.08
linked list and iterator	332	194	0.09
composite	345	263	0.09
JavaCard applet	340	95	0.51
GameServer	383	148	0.23

To make it easier for developers to diagnose verification errors, VeriFast has an IDE that supports symbolic debugging. That is, when verification fails, one can inspect the symbolic states encountered during symbolic execution on the path to the failure. A screenshot of the IDE is shown in Figure 6.

[2] Our pure prover, Z3 [8], does not perform induction and therefore cannot derive associativity of *append* solely based on its definition.

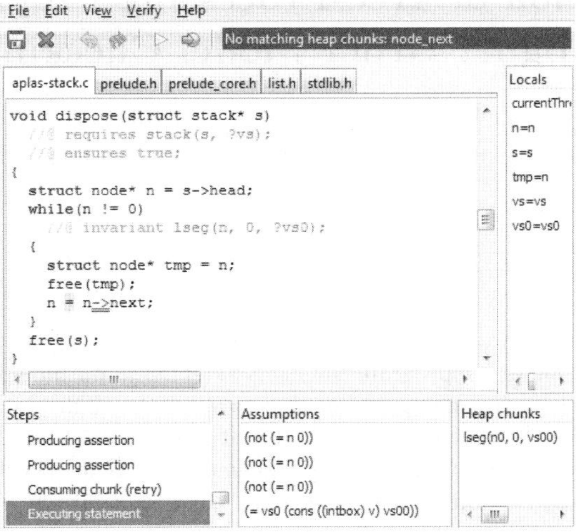

Fig. 6. A screenshot of the VeriFast IDE. Developers can use the symbolic debugger in the IDE to diagnose verification errors and inspect the symbolic state at each program point. The box on the bottom left of the screen shows the symbolic states encountered on the current path. The components of the selected state are shown in the boxes on the bottom center (path condition), bottom right (symbolic heap), and top right (symbolic store).

References

1. O'Hearn, P., Reynolds, J., Yang, H.: Local reasoning about programs that alter data structures. In: Fribourg, L. (ed.) CSL 2001 and EACSL 2001. LNCS, vol. 2142, p. 1. Springer, Heidelberg (2001)
2. Reynolds, J.C.: Separation logic: A logic for shared mutable data structures. In: Symposium on Logic in Computer Science (2002)
3. Hoare, C.A.R.: An axiomatic basis for computer programming. Communications of the ACM 12 (1969)
4. Berdine, J., Calcagno, C., O'Hearn, P.W.: Symbolic execution with separation logic. In: Yi, K. (ed.) APLAS 2005. LNCS, vol. 3780, pp. 52–68. Springer, Heidelberg (2005)
5. Calcagno, C., Distefano, D., O'Hearn, P.W., Yang, H.: Compositional shape analysis by means of bi-abduction. In: POPL (2009)
6. Distefano, D., Parkinson, M.: jStar: Towards practical verification for Java. In: OOPSLA (2008)
7. Nanevski, A., Morrisett, G., Shinnar, A., Govereau, P., Birkedal, L.: Ynot: Reasoning with the awkward squad. In: ICFP (2008)
8. de Moura, L., Bjørner, N.: Z3: An efficient SMT solver. In: Ramakrishnan, C.R., Rehof, J. (eds.) TACAS 2008. LNCS, vol. 4963, pp. 337–340. Springer, Heidelberg (2008)

Verification of Tree-Processing Programs via Higher-Order Model Checking

Hiroshi Unno, Naoshi Tabuchi, and Naoki Kobayashi

Tohoku University

Abstract. We propose a new method to verify that a higher-order, tree-processing functional program conforms to an input/output specification. Our method reduces the verification problem to multiple verification problems for higher-order multi-tree transducers, which are then transformed into higher-order recursion schemes and model-checked. Unlike previous methods, our new method can deal with arbitrary higher-order functional programs manipulating algebraic data structures, as long as certain invariants on intermediate data structures are provided by a programmer. We have proved the soundness of the method and implemented a prototype verifier.

1 Introduction

The model checking of higher-order recursion schemes [20], or higher-order model checking for short, has been extensively studied recently. Ong [20] has shown the decidability of higher-order model checking. Kobayashi [13,12] then developed a practical model checking algorithm and applied it to program verification. The present work is an extension of that line of work, trying to apply higher-order model checking to verification of a wider range of higher-order programs.

From a programming language point of view, recursion schemes are terms of the simply-typed λ-calculus with recursion and tree constructors (but not destructors). One can also encode finite data domains (such as booleans) by using Church encoding. Based on this observation, Kobayashi [13] applied model checking to resource usage verification of simply-typed functional programs with recursion, booleans, and resource primitives. The limitation of this approach was that programs manipulating infinite data domains such as lists and trees could not be handled. To relax this limitation, in our previous work [15], we have introduced higher-order multi-parameter tree transducers (HMTTs) as an extension of recursion schemes with tree destructors. HMTTs are a kind of tree transducers that take (possibly infinite) input trees, which can be destructed, and outputs a (possibly infinite) tree. However, there still remains a gap between HMTTs and ordinary functional programs that use recursive data structures since HMTTs do not support intermediate data structures: an HMTT cannot destruct trees constructed by the HMTT itself.

In this paper, we propose a verification method for an extension of HMTTs called EHMTTs. In essence, EHMTTs are higher-order, simply-typed functional

K. Ueda (Ed.): APLAS 2010, LNCS 6461, pp. 312–327, 2010.

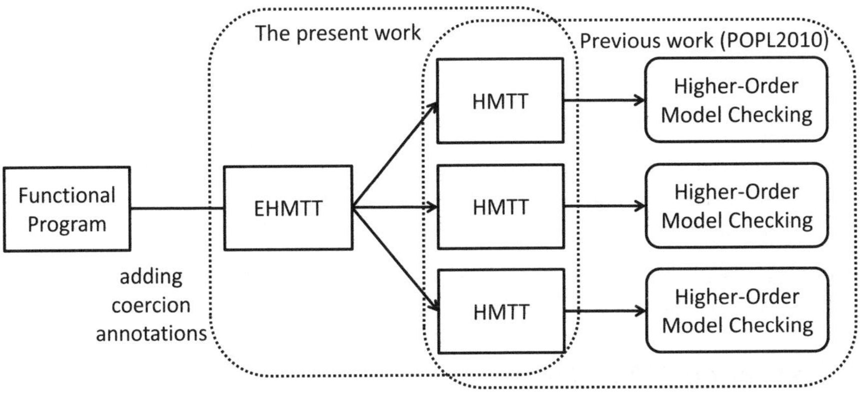

Fig. 1. Overall Structure of EHMTT Verification Method

programs with recursion and tree primitives. Unlike our previous HMTTs [15], there is no fundamental restriction on tree constructors/destructors, except that special annotations (called coercion) are required for destructing trees constructed in a program. Our method can check whether the output trees generated by a given EHMTT conform to a given output specification whenever the input trees conform to given input specifications. We can apply our method to verification of ordinary functional programs that manipulate algebraic data structures by encoding them as trees and adding annotations to the programs.

The overall structure of our method is shown in Figure 1. A given EHMTT verification problem is reduced to multiple HMTT verification problems, which are then solved by an HMTT verification method presented in our previous work [15]. The HMTT verification method further reduces the HMTT verification problems to model checking problems of recursion schemes, which are finally solved by Kobayashi's higher-order model checker TRecS [12]. In this paper, we have formalized the reduction from an EHMTT verification problem to HMTT verification problems, and proved the soundness of the reduction. Our verification method is not complete, however, since the verification problem is undecidable in general. We have implemented a prototype verifier and verified functional programs that manipulate XML and user-defined recursive data structures.

The rest of the paper is organized as follows. Section 2 presents some preliminary definitions and notations. In Section 3, we introduce EHMTTs. Section 4 formalizes our verification method for EHMTTs. Section 5 reports on the experimental results. We compare our method with related work in Section 6, and conclude the paper with some remarks on future work in Section 7.

2 Preliminaries

We write $\mathrm{dom}(f)$ for the domain of a map f, and $f\{x \mapsto v\}$ for the map f' such that $\mathrm{dom}(f') = \mathrm{dom}(f) \cup \{x\}$, $f'(x) = v$ and $f'(y) = f(y)$ for $y \in \mathrm{dom}(f) \setminus \{x\}$.

We write X^* for the set of sequences of elements of X. We write ϵ for the empty sequence, and $v_1 \cdots v_n$ for the sequence consisting of $v_1, \ldots, v_n$. We write $s_1 \cdot s_2$ for the concatenation of sequences s_1 and s_2. A sequence $v_1 \cdots v_n$ is often abbreviated to $\widetilde{v}$.

A *ranked alphabet* Σ is a map from a finite set of symbols to non-negative integers. For each symbol $a \in \mathrm{dom}(\Sigma)$, $\Sigma(a)$ denotes the arity of a. We write A_Σ to denote the largest arity of the symbols in $\mathrm{dom}(\Sigma)$. A *Σ-labeled ranked tree* T is a map from a subset of $\{1, \cdots, A_\Sigma\}^*$ to $\mathrm{dom}(\Sigma)$ such that:

- $\mathrm{dom}(T)$ is prefix-closed, i.e. if $\pi \cdot i \in \mathrm{dom}(T)$, then $\pi \in \mathrm{dom}(T)$; and
- if $T(\pi) = a$, then $\{i \mid \pi \cdot i \in \mathrm{dom}(T)\} = \{1, \ldots, \Sigma(a)\}$.

3 Extended HMTTs

In this section, we introduce extended HMTTs (EHMTTs). From a programming language point of view, an EHMTT is a simply-typed, call-by-name, higher-order functional program that takes possibly infinite trees as input and outputs a possibly infinite tree. The main differences from ordinary functional programs is that trees are classified into input and output trees. Input trees can only be destructed, and output trees can only be constructed in a program, as in other tree transducers. Special annotations ($\mathbf{coerce}^L(\cdot)$ introduced below) are however provided to convert output trees to input trees, so that, unlike ordinary tree transducers, trees constructed in a program can be destructed again in the same program. Thus, the class of EHMTTs is actually Turing complete.

We fix below a ranked alphabet Σ. We call elements of $\mathrm{dom}(\Sigma)$ *terminal symbols*, and use the meta-variable a for them.

Definition 1 (EHMTT). *An EHMTT $\mathcal{P}$ is a pair (D, S) where D is a set of function definitions of the form $\{F_1\,\widetilde{x}_1 = t_1, \ldots, F_n\,\widetilde{x}_n = t_n\}$, and S is a function name. Here, t ranges over the set of terms, given by:*

$$t ::= a \mid x \mid F \mid t_1\ t_2 \mid \mathbf{case}\ t\ \mathbf{of}\ \{a_i\ \widetilde{y}_i \Rightarrow t_i\}_{i=1}^{n} \mid \mathbf{coerce}^L(t) \mid \mathbf{gen}^L$$

Here, L denotes a set of trees. An EHMTT (D, S) is well-sorted *under $\mathcal{K}$ if $S : \mathbf{i} \to \cdots \to \mathbf{i} \to \mathbf{o} \in \mathcal{K}$ and $\vdash D : \mathcal{K}$ is derivable by using the sort assignment rules in Figure 2. An HMTT is an EHMTT that does not contain $\mathbf{coerce}^L(t)$.*

In the figure, the sorts $\mathbf{i}$ and $\mathbf{o}$ describe input and output trees respectively. The sort $\kappa_1 \to \kappa_2$ denotes functions that take a tree or tree function of sort κ_1 and return a tree or tree function of sort κ_2. $\widetilde{\kappa} \to \mathbf{o}$ and $\widetilde{x} : \widetilde{\kappa}$ are shorthand forms of $\kappa_1 \to \cdots \to \kappa_k \to \mathbf{o}$ and $x_1 : \kappa_1, \ldots, x_k : \kappa_k$ respectively. We consider only well-sorted EHMTTs below.

The term $\mathbf{case}\ t\ \mathbf{of}\ \{a_i\ \widetilde{y}_i \Rightarrow t_i\}_{i=1}^{n}$ is reduced to $[\widetilde{u}_i/\widetilde{y}_i]t_i$ if t evaluates to $a_i\ \widetilde{u}_i$. If t does not match any pattern, the term evaluates to a special terminal symbol `fail`.[1] The term $\mathbf{coerce}^L(t)$ asserts that the tree generated by t belongs

[1] Thus, verification of the absence of pattern match errors can be encoded as a problem of checking that the tree generated by EHMTT does not contain `fail`, which is an instance of EHMTT verification problems considered below.

Syntax of Sorts:

$$\kappa ::= \mathbf{i} \mid \mathbf{o} \mid \kappa_1 \rightarrow \kappa_2$$

Sort Assignment Rules:

$$\mathcal{K} \vdash F : \mathcal{K}(F) \quad \text{(T-Fun)}$$

$$\mathcal{K} \vdash a : \underbrace{\mathbf{o} \rightarrow \cdots \rightarrow \mathbf{o}}_{\Sigma(a)} \rightarrow \mathbf{o} \quad \text{(T-Con)}$$

$$\mathcal{K}, x : \kappa \vdash x : \kappa \quad \text{(T-Var)}$$

$$\frac{\mathcal{K} \vdash t_1 : \kappa_1 \rightarrow \kappa_2 \qquad \mathcal{K} \vdash t_2 : \kappa_1}{\mathcal{K} \vdash t_1\ t_2 : \kappa_2} \quad \text{(T-App)}$$

$$\frac{\mathcal{K} \vdash t : \mathbf{i} \qquad \mathcal{K}, \widetilde{y_i} : \widetilde{\mathbf{i}} \vdash t_i : \mathbf{o} \quad \text{(for all } i = 1, \ldots, N)}{\mathcal{K} \vdash \mathbf{case}\ t\ \mathbf{of}\ \{a_i\ \widetilde{y_i} \Rightarrow t_i\}_{i=1}^{n} : \mathbf{o}} \quad \text{(T-Case)}$$

$$\mathcal{K} \vdash \mathbf{gen}^L : \mathbf{i} \quad \text{(T-Gen)}$$

$$\frac{\mathcal{K} \vdash t : \mathbf{o}}{\mathcal{K} \vdash \mathbf{coerce}^L(t) : \mathbf{i}} \quad \text{(T-Coerce)}$$

$$\frac{\mathcal{K} = \{F_1 : \widetilde{\kappa_1} \rightarrow \mathbf{o}, \ldots, F_n : \widetilde{\kappa_1} \rightarrow \mathbf{o}\} \qquad \mathcal{K}, \widetilde{x_i} : \widetilde{\kappa_i} \vdash t_i : \mathbf{o} \text{ (for each } i)}{\vdash \{F_1\ \widetilde{x_1} = t_1, \ldots, F_n\ \widetilde{x_n} = t_n\} : \mathcal{K}} \quad \text{(T-Def)}$$

Operational Semantics

$$\begin{aligned} t \text{ (extended terms)} &::= \cdots \mid \underline{a} \mid \mathbf{o2i}(t) \mid \mathbf{assert}^L(t) \\ E \text{ (evaluation contexts)} &::= [\,] \mid a\ t_1 \cdots t_{j-1}\ E\ t_{j+1} \cdots t_{\Sigma(a)} \\ &\quad\mid \mathbf{case}\ E\ \mathbf{of}\ \{a_i\ \widetilde{y_i} \Rightarrow t_i\}_{i=1}^{n} \mid \mathbf{o2i}(E) \mid \mathbf{assert}^L(E) \end{aligned}$$

$$\frac{F\ \widetilde{x} = t \in D}{E[F\ \widetilde{t}] \longrightarrow_{\mathcal{P}} E[[\widetilde{t}/\widetilde{x}]t]} \quad \text{(E-App)}$$

$$E[\mathbf{case}\ \underline{a_i}\ \widetilde{t}\ \mathbf{of}\ \{a_i\ \widetilde{y_i} \Rightarrow t_i\}_{i=1}^{n}] \longrightarrow_{\mathcal{P}} E[[\widetilde{t}/\widetilde{y_i}]t_i] \quad \text{(E-Case)}$$

$$\frac{a \notin \{a_1, \ldots, a_n\}}{E[\mathbf{case}\ \underline{a}\ \widetilde{t}\ \mathbf{of}\ \{a_i\ \widetilde{y_i} \Rightarrow t_i\}_{i=1}^{n}] \longrightarrow_{\mathcal{P}} E[\mathtt{fail}]} \quad \text{(E-Case-Fail)}$$

$$\frac{a\ L_1 \cdots L_n \subseteq L}{E[\mathbf{gen}^L] \longrightarrow_{\mathcal{P}} E[\underline{a}\ \mathbf{gen}^{L_1} \ldots \mathbf{gen}^{L_n}]} \quad \text{(E-Gen)}$$

$$E[\mathbf{coerce}^L(t)] \longrightarrow_{\mathcal{P}} \mathbf{assert}^L(t) \quad \text{(E-Coerce-Assert)}$$

$$E[\mathbf{coerce}^L(t)] \longrightarrow_{\mathcal{P}} E[\mathbf{o2i}(t)] \quad \text{(E-Coerce-Input)}$$

$$E[\mathbf{o2i}(a_i\ \widetilde{t})] \longrightarrow_{\mathcal{P}} E[\underline{a_i}\ \mathbf{o2i}(\widetilde{t})] \quad \text{(E-Input)}$$

$$\frac{t^{\perp} \notin L^{\perp}}{\mathbf{assert}^L(t) \longrightarrow_{\mathcal{P}} \mathbf{Error}} \quad \text{(E-Assert-Error)}$$

Fig. 2. Sort Assignment Rules and Call-by-Name Operational Semantics

to a set L of trees, and converts the tree to an input tree. $\mathbf{gen}^L$ generates an element of L non-deterministically.

Example 1. Consider the EHMTT $\mathcal{P}_{rev} = (D, \mathit{Reverse})$, where D consists of:

$$\begin{aligned}
\mathit{Reverse}\ x = \mathbf{case}\ x\ \mathbf{of}\ & \mathtt{e} \Rightarrow \mathtt{e} \\
& \mid \mathtt{a}\ x' \Rightarrow \mathit{Append}\ (\mathbf{coerce}^{\mathtt{b}^*\mathtt{a}^*\mathtt{e}}(\mathit{Reverse}\ x'))\ (\mathtt{a}\ \mathtt{e}) \\
& \mid \mathtt{b}\ x' \Rightarrow \mathit{Append}\ (\mathbf{coerce}^{\mathtt{b}^*\mathtt{e}}(\mathit{Reverse}\ x'))\ (\mathtt{b}\ \mathtt{e}). \\
\mathit{Append}\ x\ y = \mathbf{case}\ x\ \mathbf{of}\ & \mathtt{e} \Rightarrow y \\
& \mid \mathtt{a}\ x' \Rightarrow \mathtt{a}\ (\mathit{Append}\ x'\ y) \\
& \mid \mathtt{b}\ x' \Rightarrow \mathtt{b}\ (\mathit{Append}\ x'\ y).
\end{aligned}$$

P_{rev} takes a tree of the form $\mathtt{a}^m(\mathtt{b}^n(\mathtt{e}))$ as input, and outputs a tree $\mathtt{b}^n(\mathtt{a}^m(\mathtt{e}))$. The coercions $\mathbf{coerce}^{\mathtt{b}^*\mathtt{a}^*\mathtt{e}}(\cdot)$ and $\mathbf{coerce}^{\mathtt{b}^*\mathtt{e}}(\cdot)$ assert that their arguments belong to $\{\mathtt{b}^m(\mathtt{a}^n(\mathtt{e})) \mid m, n \geq 0\}$ and $\{\mathtt{b}^m(\mathtt{e}) \mid m \geq 0\}$ respectively, and convert them to input trees. Note that *Reverse* and *Append* have sorts $\mathbf{i} \to \mathbf{o}$ and $\mathbf{i} \to \mathbf{o} \to \mathbf{o}$ respectively, so that $\mathit{Reverse}\ x'$ returns an output tree. □

Figure 2 shows the formal semantics of the language. In the semantics, the set of terms are extended as follows. An underlined symbol $\underline{a}$ denotes an input tree constructor (which, by the restriction of EHMTT, occurs only at run-time, not in source programs). $\mathbf{o2i}(t)$ and $\mathbf{assert}^L(t)$ are used to define the semantics of $\mathbf{coerce}^L(t)$: the former converts an output tree to an input tree, and the latter asserts that the tree generated by t belong to L. In the rule E-Assert-Error, $t^\perp$ is a finite $(\Sigma \cup \{\perp \mapsto 0\})$-labeled ranked tree, defined by:

$$t^\perp = \begin{cases} a\ t_1^\perp \cdots t_n^\perp & (\text{if } t = a\ t_1\ \cdots\ t_n) \\ \perp & (\text{otherwise}) \end{cases}$$

$L^\perp$ is the set $\{T \mid T \preceq T' \in L\}$, where $T \preceq T'$ means that T is obtained from T' by replacing some nodes of T' with $\perp$.

Remark 1. Note that EHMTT is call-by-name. This is because our verification method is based on the model checking of higher-oder recursion schemes, whose semantics is call-by-name. To deal with call-by-value programs, it suffices to apply CPS transformation before applying our verification method. The reasons why we allow infinite trees as inputs and outputs for EHMTTs are as follows. First, we would like to verify programs that manipulate not only finite but also infinite data structures (such as streams). Secondly, we would like to model a program that contains non-deterministic branches (which is typically obtained by abstracting branching information of a user program) as an EHMTT that generates a single tree describing all the possible outputs of the program. In that case, even if a program manipulates only finite data structures, the output of the EHMTT can be an infinite tree.

The goal of our verification is to check that a given EHMTT conforms to a given specification on input and output. As EHMTTs manipulate infinite trees, we use top-down tree automata called *trivial automata* (which are Büchi tree automata with a trivial acceptance condition) as specifications (as well as for annotations L in $\mathbf{coerce}^L(\cdot)$ and $\mathbf{gen}^L$).

Definition 2 (trivial automaton). *A* trivial automaton $\mathcal{M}$ *is a quadruple* (Σ, Q, Δ, q_0)*, where:*

- Σ *is a ranked alphabet.*
- Q *is a finite set of states.*
- Δ *is a finite subset of* $Q \times \mathrm{dom}(\Sigma) \times Q^*$ *called a* transition relation *such that if* $(q, a, \widetilde{q}) \in \Delta$*, then the length of the sequence* $\widetilde{q}$ *is* $\Sigma(a)$*.*
- q_0 *is a state called an* initial state.

A Σ*-labeled ranked tree* T *is* accepted *by* $\mathcal{M}$ *if there is a* Q*-labeled tree* R *such that:*

- $\mathrm{dom}(T) = \mathrm{dom}(R)$.
- *For any* $\pi \in \mathrm{dom}(R)$, $(R(\pi), T(\pi), R(\pi \cdot 1) \cdots R(\pi \cdot \Sigma(T(\pi)))) \in \Delta$.
- $R(\epsilon) = q_0$.

We write $\mathcal{L}(\mathcal{M})$ *for the set of* Σ*-labeled ranked trees accepted by* $\mathcal{M}$*.*

When restricted to finite trees, the class of languages recognized by trivial automata is equivalent to the class of regular tree languages.

Example 2. Recall Example 1. A trivial automaton for accepting $\mathtt{b}^*\mathtt{a}^*\mathtt{e}$ is defined by $(\Sigma, \{q_0, q_1\}, \Delta, q_0)$, where:

$$\Sigma = \{\mathtt{a} \mapsto 1, \mathtt{b} \mapsto 1, \mathtt{e} \mapsto 0\}$$
$$\Delta = \{(q_0, \mathtt{b}, q_0), (q_0, \mathtt{a}, q_1), (q_0, \mathtt{e}, \epsilon), (q_1, \mathtt{a}, q_1), (q_1, \mathtt{e}, \epsilon)\}$$ □

We now formalize our verification problem:

Definition 3. *Given an EHMTT* $\mathcal{P} = (D, S)$ *and trivial automata* $\mathcal{M}_1, \ldots, \mathcal{M}_k$, $\mathcal{M} = (\Sigma, Q, \Delta, q_0)$*, we write* $\models (\mathcal{P}, \mathcal{M}_1, \ldots, \mathcal{M}_k, \mathcal{M})$ *if for all* $T_1 \in \mathcal{L}(\mathcal{M}_1), \ldots$, $T_k \in \mathcal{L}(\mathcal{M}_k)$,

1. $S\ T_1 \cdots T_k \longrightarrow^*_{\mathcal{P}} t$ *implies* $t^\perp \in \mathcal{L}(\mathcal{M}^\perp)$*, and*
2. $S\ T_1 \cdots T_k \not\longrightarrow^*_{\mathcal{P}} \mathbf{Error}$.

Here, $\mathcal{M}^\perp$ *is the trivial automaton* $(\Sigma \cup \{\perp \mapsto 0\}, Q, \Delta \cup \{(q, \perp, \epsilon) \mid q \in Q\}, q_0)$*. An EHMTT verification problem* $(\mathcal{P}, \mathcal{M}_1, \ldots, \mathcal{M}_k, \mathcal{M})$ *is the problem to check that* $\models (\mathcal{P}, \mathcal{M}_1, \ldots, \mathcal{M}_k, \mathcal{M})$*.*

The first condition of an EHMTT verification problem says that given input trees that conform to the input specification, the EHMTT generates a valid tree.[2] The second condition means that the EHMTT in fact never causes a coercion error.

[2] Because of the presence of $\perp$, only safety properties are guaranteed; there is no guarantee that the EHMTT eventually generates a tree that belongs to $\mathcal{L}(\mathcal{M})$.

In [15], we have presented a (sound but incomplete) method for the restricted case (which we call *HMTT verification problems*) where $\mathcal{P}$ is an HMTT (i.e., for the case where $\mathcal{P}$ does not contain $\mathbf{coerce}^L(\cdot)$). In the next section, we reduce an EHMTT verification problem to HMTT verification problems.

4 Verification Method for EHMTTs

We now present a method for reducing an EHMTT verification problem to HMTT verification problems (which can then be solved by the previous method [15]). The idea is to reduce each of the two conditions in Definition 3 to HMTT verification problems.

Let $(\mathcal{P}, \mathcal{M}_1, \ldots, \mathcal{M}_k, \mathcal{M})$ be a given EHMTT verification problem, and suppose that $\mathcal{P}$ contains m occurrences of coercions: $\mathbf{coerce}^{L_1}(\cdot), \ldots, \mathbf{coerce}^{L_m}(\cdot)$. We construct HMTTs $\mathcal{P}^{\mathcal{A}}, \mathcal{P}^{\mathcal{B}_1}, \ldots, \mathcal{P}^{\mathcal{B}_m}$ such that:

- $\mathcal{P}^{\mathcal{A}}$ approximates the output of $\mathcal{P}$, by assuming that coercions never fail.
- $\mathcal{P}^{\mathcal{B}_i}$ approximates all the possible arguments of $\mathbf{coerce}^{L_i}(\cdot)$.

Then, the verification problem $(\mathcal{P}, \mathcal{M}_1, \ldots, \mathcal{M}_k, \mathcal{M})$ can be reduced to $m+1$ HMTT verification problems: $(\mathcal{P}^{\mathcal{A}}, \mathcal{M}_1, \ldots, \mathcal{M}_k, \mathcal{M})$, $(\mathcal{P}^{\mathcal{B}_1}, \mathcal{M}_1, \ldots, \mathcal{M}_k, \mathcal{B}(L_1))$, $\ldots$, $(\mathcal{P}^{\mathcal{B}_m}, \mathcal{M}_1, \ldots, \mathcal{M}_k, \mathcal{B}(L_m))$ (where $\mathcal{B}(L)$ is an automaton for accepting trees representing subsets of L; see Section 4.2 below). Sections 4.1 and 4.2 below show the constructions of $\mathcal{P}^{\mathcal{A}}$ and $\mathcal{P}^{\mathcal{B}_i}$ respectively.

4.1 Construction of $\mathcal{P}^{\mathcal{A}}$

Let $\mathcal{P}^{\mathcal{A}}$ be the HMTT obtained by just replacing every occurrence of $\mathbf{coerce}^{L_i}(\cdot)$ in $\mathcal{P}$ with $\mathbf{gen}^{L_i}$. Then, $\mathcal{P}^{\mathcal{A}}$ approximates the output of $\mathcal{P}$, assuming that no coercion error occurs.

Theorem 1. *Let $\mathcal{P} = (D, S)$ be an EHMTT such that $\models (\mathcal{P}^{\mathcal{A}}, \mathcal{M}_1, \ldots, \mathcal{M}_k, \mathcal{M})$ holds. For any $T_1 \in \mathcal{L}(\mathcal{M}_1), \ldots, T_k \in \mathcal{L}(\mathcal{M}_k)$, if $S\ T_1 \cdots T_k \not\longrightarrow^*_{\mathcal{P}}$* **Error** *and $S\ T_1 \cdots T_k \longrightarrow^*_{\mathcal{P}} t$, then $t^{\perp} \in \mathcal{L}(\mathcal{M}^{\perp})$.*

A proof is given in the full version of this paper [23].

Example 3. Recall $\mathcal{P}_{rev}$ in Example 1. $\mathcal{P}^{\mathcal{A}}_{rev}$ is $(D, \mathit{Reverse}^{\mathcal{A}})$ where D is given by:

$$
\begin{aligned}
\mathit{Reverse}^{\mathcal{A}}\ x^{\mathcal{A}} &= \mathbf{case}\ x^{\mathcal{A}}\ \mathbf{of}\ \mathsf{e} \Rightarrow \mathsf{e} \\
&\qquad \mid \mathsf{a}\ x'^{\mathcal{A}} \Rightarrow \mathit{Append}^{\mathcal{A}}\ \mathbf{gen}^{\mathsf{b^*a^*e}}\ (\mathsf{a}\ \mathsf{e}) \\
&\qquad \mid \mathsf{b}\ x'^{\mathcal{A}} \Rightarrow \mathit{Append}^{\mathcal{A}}\ \mathbf{gen}^{\mathsf{b^*e}}\ (\mathsf{b}\ \mathsf{e}) \\
\mathit{Append}^{\mathcal{A}}\ x^{\mathcal{A}}\ y^{\mathcal{A}} &= \mathbf{case}\ x^{\mathcal{A}}\ \mathbf{of}\ \mathsf{e} \Rightarrow y^{\mathcal{A}} \\
&\qquad \mid \mathsf{a}\ x'^{\mathcal{A}} \Rightarrow \mathsf{a}\ (\mathit{Append}^{\mathcal{A}}\ x'^{\mathcal{A}}\ y^{\mathcal{A}}) \\
&\qquad \mid \mathsf{b}\ x'^{\mathcal{A}} \Rightarrow \mathsf{b}\ (\mathit{Append}^{\mathcal{A}}\ x'^{\mathcal{A}}\ y^{\mathcal{A}})
\end{aligned}
$$

4.2 Construction of $\mathcal{P}^{\mathcal{B}_i}$

The construction of $\mathcal{P}^{\mathcal{B}_i}$ is more involved, for the following reasons.

1. Given an input, $\mathcal{P}$ may invoke $\mathbf{coerce}^{L_i}(\cdot)$ more than once. For example, given $\mathtt{b(b(e))}$ as input, $\mathcal{P}_{rev}$ in Example 1 invoke $\mathbf{coerce}^{\mathtt{b^*e}}(\cdot)$ twice, with different parameters $\mathtt{e}$ and $\mathtt{b(e)}$. Thus, $\mathcal{P}^{\mathcal{B}_i}$ should approximate the *set* of trees that are passed to $\mathbf{coerce}^{L_i}(\cdot)$.
2. How a function invokes $\mathbf{coerce}^{L_i}(\cdot)$ may depend on its arguments. For example, consider a higher-order function F defined by $F\ g\ x = g(x)$. Obviously, how $\mathbf{coerce}^{L_i}(\cdot)$ is invoked during evaluation of $F\ t_1\ t_2$ depends on t_1 and t_2.

To address the first issue, we represent a (possibly infinite) set of trees by a single (possibly infinite) tree. We use special terminal symbols $\mathtt{br}$ and $\mathtt{emp}$, which represent the set union and an empty set respectively. For example, the set $\{\mathtt{e}, \mathtt{b(e)}\}$ is represented by $\mathtt{br\ e\ (b(e))}$. $\mathcal{P}^{\mathcal{B}_i}$ outputs such a tree representation of (an over-approximation of) the set of trees passed to $\mathbf{coerce}^{L_i}(\cdot)$.

To address the second issue, we duplicate each parameter x of a function into $x^{\mathcal{A}}$ and $x^{\mathcal{B}}$. The parameter $x^{\mathcal{A}}$ is used to compute (an approximation of) the original value of x, while the parameter $x^{\mathcal{B}}$ computes (an approximation of) the set of trees passed to $\mathbf{coerce}^{L_i}(\cdot)$ during evaluation of x. For example, $F\ g\ x = g(x)$ is transformed to: $F^{\mathcal{B}}\ g^{\mathcal{A}}\ g^{\mathcal{B}}\ x^{\mathcal{A}}\ x^{\mathcal{B}} = g^{\mathcal{B}}\ x^{\mathcal{A}}\ x^{\mathcal{B}}$. Here, $F^{\mathcal{B}}$ computes an approximation of the set of trees passed to $\mathbf{coerce}^{L_i}(\cdot)$ by calling $g^{\mathcal{B}}$ with duplicated parameters $x^{\mathcal{A}}$ and $x^{\mathcal{B}}$.

We give below more concrete examples to explain the construction of $\mathcal{P}^{\mathcal{B}_i}$.

Example 4. Recall $\mathcal{P}_{rev}$ in Example 1. For the first coercion $\mathbf{coerce}^{L_1}(\mathit{Reverse}\ x')$ (where $L_1 = \mathtt{b^*a^*e}$), we construct the following HMTT $\mathcal{P}_{rev}^{\mathcal{B}_1}$:

$$
\begin{aligned}
&\mathit{Reverse}^{\mathcal{B}}\ x^{\mathcal{A}}\ x^{\mathcal{B}} = \\
&\quad \mathtt{br}\ x^{\mathcal{B}}\ (\mathbf{case}\ x^{\mathcal{A}}\ \mathbf{of}\ \mathtt{e} \Rightarrow \mathtt{emp} \\
&\qquad\qquad \mid \mathtt{a}\ x'^{\mathcal{A}} \Rightarrow \mathit{Append}^{\mathcal{B}}\ \mathbf{gen}^{\mathtt{b^*a^*e}}\ (\mathtt{br}\ (\mathit{Reverse}^{\mathcal{A}}\ x'^{\mathcal{A}}) \\
&\qquad\qquad\qquad\qquad\qquad\qquad (\mathit{Reverse}^{\mathcal{B}}\ x'^{\mathcal{A}}\ \mathtt{emp})) \\
&\qquad\qquad\qquad\qquad (\mathtt{a\ e})\ \mathtt{emp} \\
&\qquad\qquad \mid \mathtt{b}\ x'^{\mathcal{A}} \Rightarrow \mathit{Append}^{\mathcal{B}}\ \mathbf{gen}^{\mathtt{b^*e}}\ (\mathit{Reverse}^{\mathcal{B}}\ x'^{\mathcal{A}}\ \mathtt{emp}) \\
&\qquad\qquad\qquad\qquad (\mathtt{b\ e})\ \mathtt{emp}) \\
&\mathit{Append}^{\mathcal{B}}\ x^{\mathcal{A}}\ x^{\mathcal{B}}\ y^{\mathcal{A}}\ y^{\mathcal{B}} = \\
&\quad \mathtt{br}\ x^{\mathcal{B}}\ (\mathbf{case}\ x^{\mathcal{A}}\ \mathbf{of}\ \mathtt{e} \Rightarrow y^{\mathcal{B}} \\
&\qquad\qquad \mid \mathtt{a}\ x'^{\mathcal{A}} \Rightarrow \mathit{Append}^{\mathcal{B}}\ x'^{\mathcal{A}}\ \mathtt{emp}\ y^{\mathcal{A}}\ y^{\mathcal{B}} \\
&\qquad\qquad \mid \mathtt{b}\ x'^{\mathcal{A}} \Rightarrow \mathit{Append}^{\mathcal{B}}\ x'^{\mathcal{A}}\ \mathtt{emp}\ y^{\mathcal{A}}\ y^{\mathcal{B}})
\end{aligned}
$$

As mentioned above, the parameters of *Reverse* and *Append* have been duplicated. When $\mathit{Reverse}\ t$ is called in $\mathcal{P}_{rev}$, there are two cases where $\mathbf{coerce}^{L_1}(\cdot)$

may be called: the case where t contains $\mathbf{coerce}^{L_1}(\cdot)$ and it is called when t is evaluated by the case statement (note that our language is call-by-name); and the case where $\mathbf{coerce}^{L_1}(\cdot)$ is called in a case branch. In the body of the definition of $\mathit{Reverse}^{\mathcal{B}}$, the part $x^{\mathcal{B}}$ approximates the set of trees passed to $\mathbf{coerce}^{L_1}(\cdot)$ in the former case, and the part $\mathbf{case}\ x^{\mathcal{A}}\ \mathbf{of}\ \cdots$ approximates the set of trees for the latter case.

In the clause for $\mathtt{a}(x'^{\mathcal{A}})$, $\mathit{Append}^{\mathcal{B}}$ is used to compute an approximation of the set of trees passed to $\mathbf{coerce}^{L_1}(\cdot)$. The first and third parameters approximate the values of the original parameters of *Append*. The second parameter $(\mathtt{br}\ (\mathit{Reverse}^{\mathcal{A}}\ x'^{\mathcal{A}})\ (\mathit{Reverse}^{\mathcal{B}}\ x'^{\mathcal{A}}\ \mathtt{emp}))$ approximates the set of trees passed to $\mathbf{coerce}^{L_1}(\cdot)$ during the computation of $\mathbf{coerce}^{L_1}(\mathit{Reverse}\ x')$. Here, there are two cases where coercion can occur: (i) the value of $\mathit{Reverse}\ x'$ is computed and passed to $\mathbf{coerce}^{L_1}(\cdot)$ and (ii) $\mathbf{coerce}^{L_1}(\cdot)$ is invoked during the computation of $\mathit{Reverse}\ x'$. The parts $(\mathit{Reverse}^{\mathcal{A}}\ x'^{\mathcal{A}})$ and $(\mathit{Reverse}^{\mathcal{B}}\ x'^{\mathcal{A}}\ \mathtt{emp})$ cover the former and the latter cases respectively. In the latter, the second parameter of $(\mathit{Reverse}^{\mathcal{B}}$ is an empty set, as the trees passed to $\mathbf{coerce}^{L_1}(\cdot)$ during the computation of x' are already covered by $x^{\mathcal{B}}$. □

The reduction works similarly for EHMTTs with higher-order functions.

Example 5. Let us consider a higher-order version of the list reverse program:

$$\begin{aligned}
\mathit{Reverse}\ x &= \mathit{Reverseh}\ \mathit{Append}\ x\\
\mathit{Reverseh}\ f\ x &= \mathbf{case}\ x\ \mathbf{of}\ \mathtt{e} \Rightarrow \mathtt{e}\\
&\qquad\qquad\qquad \mid \mathtt{a}\ x' \Rightarrow f\ (\mathbf{coerce}^{\mathtt{b}^*\mathtt{a}^*\mathtt{e}}(\mathit{Reverseh}\ f\ x'))\ (\mathtt{a}\ \mathtt{e})\\
&\qquad\qquad\qquad \mid \mathtt{b}\ x' \Rightarrow f\ (\mathbf{coerce}^{\mathtt{b}^*\mathtt{e}}(\mathit{Reverseh}\ f\ x'))\ (\mathtt{b}\ \mathtt{e})
\end{aligned}$$

We get the following HMTT for the first coercion $\mathbf{coerce}^{\mathtt{b}^*\mathtt{a}^*\mathtt{e}}(\mathit{Reverseh}\ f\ x')$:

$$\begin{aligned}
&\mathit{Reverse}^{\mathcal{B}}\ x^{\mathcal{A}}\ x^{\mathcal{B}} = \mathit{Reverseh}^{\mathcal{B}}\ \mathit{Append}^{\mathcal{A}}\ \mathit{Append}^{\mathcal{B}}\ x^{\mathcal{A}}\ x^{\mathcal{B}}\\
&\mathit{Reverseh}^{\mathcal{B}}\ f^{\mathcal{A}}\ f^{\mathcal{B}}\ x^{\mathcal{A}}\ x^{\mathcal{B}} =\\
&\quad \mathtt{br}\ x^{\mathcal{B}}\ (\mathbf{case}\ x^{\mathcal{A}}\ \mathbf{of}\ \mathtt{e} \Rightarrow \mathtt{emp}\\
&\qquad\qquad \mid \mathtt{a}\ x'^{\mathcal{A}} \Rightarrow f^{\mathcal{B}}\ \mathbf{gen}^{\mathtt{b}^*\mathtt{a}^*\mathtt{e}}\ (\mathtt{br}\ (\mathit{Reverseh}^{\mathcal{A}}\ f^{\mathcal{A}}\ x'^{\mathcal{A}})\\
&\qquad\qquad\qquad\qquad (\mathit{Reverseh}^{\mathcal{B}}\ f^{\mathcal{A}}\ f^{\mathcal{B}}\ x'^{\mathcal{A}}\ \mathtt{emp}))\\
&\qquad\qquad\qquad (\mathtt{a}\ \mathtt{e})\ \mathtt{emp}\\
&\qquad\qquad \mid \mathtt{b}\ x'^{\mathcal{A}} \Rightarrow f^{\mathcal{B}}\ \mathbf{gen}^{\mathtt{b}^*\mathtt{e}}\ (\mathit{Reverseh}^{\mathcal{B}}\ f^{\mathcal{A}}\ f^{\mathcal{B}}\ x'^{\mathcal{A}}\ \mathtt{emp})\\
&\qquad\qquad\qquad (\mathtt{b}\ \mathtt{e})\ \mathtt{emp})
\end{aligned}$$

Here, $\mathit{Append}^{\mathcal{A}}$ is the one obtained in Example 3. Note that $\mathit{Reverseh}^{\mathcal{B}}$ requires an additional argument $f^{\mathcal{B}}$, which generates all the trees passed to the coercion by f. □

Formally, given an EHMTT $\mathcal{P} = (D, S)$, $\mathcal{P}^{\mathcal{B}_i}$ is $(\mathcal{B}_i(D), S)$ where:

$$\begin{aligned}\mathcal{B}_i(D) = \{&S\ x_1 \cdots x_k = S^{\mathcal{B}_i}\ x_1\ \texttt{emp} \cdots x_k\ \texttt{emp}\} \cup \\ \{&a^{\mathcal{B}_i}\ x_1^{\mathcal{A}}\ x_1^{\mathcal{B}_i} \cdots x_{\Sigma(a)}^{\mathcal{A}}\ x_{\Sigma(a)}^{\mathcal{B}_i} = \texttt{br}\ x_1^{\mathcal{B}_i} \cdots x_{\Sigma(a)}^{\mathcal{B}_i} \mid a \in \mathrm{dom}(\Sigma)\} \cup \\ \{&F^{\mathcal{A}}\ x_1^{\mathcal{A}} \cdots x_n^{\mathcal{A}} = \mathcal{A}(t) \mid F\ x_1 \cdots x_n = t \in D\} \cup \\ \{&F^{\mathcal{B}_i}\ x_1^{\mathcal{A}}\ x_1^{\mathcal{B}_i} \cdots x_n^{\mathcal{A}}\ x_n^{\mathcal{B}_i} = \mathcal{B}_i(t) \mid F\ x_1 \cdots x_n = t \in D\}\end{aligned}$$

$$\begin{aligned}&\mathcal{B}_i(a) = a^{\mathcal{B}_i} \qquad \mathcal{B}_i(x) = x^{\mathcal{B}_i} \qquad \mathcal{B}_i(F) = F^{\mathcal{B}_i} \\ &\mathcal{B}_i(t_1\ t_2) = \mathcal{B}_i(t_1)\ \mathcal{A}(t_2)\ \mathcal{B}_i(t_2) \\ &\mathcal{B}_i(\textbf{case}\ t\ \textbf{of}\ \{a_j\ \widetilde{y}_j \Rightarrow t_j\}_{j=1}^n) = \\ &\qquad \texttt{br}\ \mathcal{B}_i(t)\ (\textbf{case}\ \mathcal{A}(t)\ \textbf{of}\ \{a_j\ \widetilde{y}_j^{\mathcal{A}} \Rightarrow [\widetilde{\texttt{emp}}/\widetilde{y}_j^{\mathcal{B}_i}]\mathcal{B}_i(t_j)\}_{j=1}^n) \\ &\mathcal{B}_i(\textbf{gen}^L) = \texttt{emp} \\ &\mathcal{B}_i(\textbf{coerce}^{L_j}(t)) = \begin{cases} \texttt{br}\ \mathcal{A}(t)\ \mathcal{B}_i(t) & (\text{if } i = j) \\ \mathcal{B}_i(t) & (\text{otherwise}) \end{cases}\end{aligned}$$

Here, $\mathcal{A}(t)$ is the term obtained by replacing every coercion $\textbf{coerce}^L(\cdot)$, variable x, and function name F in t with $\textbf{gen}^L$, $x^{\mathcal{A}}$, and $F^{\mathcal{A}}$ respectively. $\texttt{br}\ t_1 \cdots t_n$ stands for $\texttt{br}\ t_1\ (\texttt{br}\ t_2\ (\texttt{br} \cdots (\texttt{br}\ t_{n-1}\ t_n)))$ if $n \geq 2$, t_1 if $n = 1$, and $\texttt{emp}$ if $n = 0$. For each terminal $a \in \mathrm{dom}(\Sigma)$, we obtain the new function $a^{\mathcal{B}_i}$ that generates all the trees passed to the i-th coercion by the actual arguments of a.

Given a trivial automaton $\mathcal{M}(L_i) = (\Sigma, Q, \Delta, q_0)$ for accepting L_i, the output specification for $\mathcal{P}^{\mathcal{B}_i}$ is the trivial automaton $\mathcal{B}(L_i) = (\Sigma', Q, \Delta', q_0)$, where:

$$\begin{aligned}\Sigma' &= \Sigma \cup \{\texttt{br} \mapsto 2, \texttt{emp} \mapsto 0\} \\ \Delta' &= \Delta \cup \{(q, \texttt{br}, q \cdot q), (q, \texttt{emp}, \epsilon) \mid q \in Q\}\end{aligned}$$

The following theorem states the correctness of the construction of $\mathcal{P}^{\mathcal{B}_i}$. See the full version of this paper for the proof [23].

Theorem 2. *Let $\mathcal{P} = (D, S)$ be an EHMTT and suppose that the coercions in $\mathcal{P}$ are* $\textbf{coerce}^{L_1}(\cdot), \ldots, \textbf{coerce}^{L_m}(\cdot)$. *If* $\models (\mathcal{P}^{\mathcal{B}_i}, \mathcal{M}_1, \ldots, \mathcal{M}_k, \mathcal{B}(L_i))$ *holds for each* $i \in \{1, \ldots, m\}$, *for any* $T_1 \in \mathcal{L}(\mathcal{M}_1), \ldots, T_k \in \mathcal{L}(\mathcal{M}_k)$, $S\ T_1 \cdots T_k \not\longrightarrow_{\mathcal{P}}^* \textbf{Error}$.

Our reduction from EHMTT to HMTT verification problems is incomplete, however, i.e. there is a case that an EHMTT satisfies a given specification, but the generated HMTTs do not satisfy the required properties. There are two main reasons for this.

- Coercion annotations may not be good enough. For example, if coercions are annotated with the empty language $\emptyset$, the derived HMTTs obviously do not satisfy the property. Actually, there may be no good way to annotate coercions. For example, consider the EHMTT $S\ x = \mathit{Zip}\ (\textbf{coerce}^L(\mathit{Unzip}\ x))$, where *Unzip* takes an input $\texttt{s}^n\ \texttt{z}$ that encodes a natural number n and returns an output tree $\texttt{pair}\ (\texttt{s}^n\ \texttt{z})\ (\texttt{s}^n\ \texttt{z})$, and *Zip* takes an input tree of the form $\texttt{pair}\ (\texttt{s}^{n_1}\ \texttt{z})\ (\texttt{s}^{n_2}\ \texttt{z})$ and outputs $\texttt{fail}$ if and only if $n_1 \neq n_2$. To verify that $S\ x$ never outputs $\texttt{fail}$ for any $x \in \{\texttt{s}^n\ \texttt{z} \mid n \geq 0\}$, we need the coercion annotation $L = \{\texttt{pair}\ (\texttt{s}^n\ \texttt{z})\ (\texttt{s}^n\ \texttt{z}) \mid n \geq 0\}$, which cannot be expressed by a trivial automaton or a regular language. As another example, consider the following variant of a reverse function:

$$\begin{aligned} &\mathit{Reverse}\ x = \textbf{case}\ x\ \textbf{of}\ \texttt{e} \Rightarrow \texttt{e} \\ &\qquad\qquad\qquad\qquad \mid \texttt{cons}\ z\ x' \Rightarrow \mathit{Append}\ (\textbf{coerce}^{L}(\mathit{Reverse}\ x'))\ (\texttt{cons}\ z\ \texttt{e}) \\ &\mathit{Append}\ x\ y = \cdots \end{aligned}$$

Here, we have used a list-like representation of sequences of a, b. In this case, the appropriate annotation depends on the value of z (L should be $\texttt{b}^*\texttt{a}^*\texttt{e}$ if z is a while $\texttt{b}^*\texttt{e}$ if z is b), which cannot be expressed in our language. One way to avoid this problem is to duplicate a part of the code so that appropriate annotations can be inserted.

- The output specification $\mathcal{B}(L_i)$ for $\mathcal{P}^{\mathcal{B}_i}$ is too restrictive. When the automaton for accepting L_i is non-deterministic, $\mathcal{B}(L_i)$ does not accept all the tree representations of subsets of L_i. This problem can easily be remedied, however, by using a more elaborate construction of $\mathcal{B}(L_i)$, hence not a fundamental limitation.

Our overall method is also incomplete because of the incompleteness of the HMTT verification method [15] (unsurprisingly, as the HMTT verification problem is undecidable in general).

5 Experiments

We have implemented the reduction method from an EHMTT verification problem to HMTT verification problems presented in Section 4. For solving the HMTT verification problems, we adopted an HMTT verification method in [15] and Kobayashi's higher-order model checker TRecS [12].

Table 1 shows the results of preliminary experiments. The column "O" shows the order of each EHMTT which is the largest order of the sorts of the functions. The order of a sort is defined by:

$$\mathit{order}(\mathbf{i}) = \mathit{order}(\mathbf{o}) = 0 \qquad \mathit{order}(\kappa_1 \rightarrow \kappa_2) = \mathit{max}(\mathit{order}(\kappa_1) + 1, \mathit{order}(\kappa_2))$$

The column "C" shows the number of coercions in each EHMTT. The columns "R" and "S" are the number of rules and the size of each EHMTT respectively. The size of an EHMTT is measured by the number of symbols occurring in the right-hand side of the rewriting rules. "$\mathrm{Sum_R}$" and "$\mathrm{Sum_S}$" respectively are the sum of the numbers of the rules and the sum of the sizes of all HMTTs derived from each EHMTT. "$\mathrm{Q_I}$" and "$\mathrm{Q_O}$" respectively show the numbers of the states of trivial automata for the input and output specifications. The column "$\mathrm{T_{Red}}$" shows the elapsed time, in milliseconds, of reduction from an EHMTT verification problem to HMTT verification problems. The column "Y/N" indicates whether each EHMTT was proved correct (Y) or rejected (N). The column "$\mathrm{T_{MC}}$" shows the total running time of the higher-order model checker TRecS to solve all the HMTT verification problems derived from each EHMTT.

Table 1. Experimental Results

Programs	O	C	R	S	Sum_R	Sum_S	Q_I	Q_O	T_Red	Y/N	T_MC
`Reverse`	1	2	3	32	23	222	4	2	1	Y	4
`Isort`	1	1	4	29	16	115	3	2	1	Y	3
`Msort`	2	4	8	131	88	1,731	3	2	2	Y	224
`HomRep-Rev`	4	1	12	90	43	362	6	2	1	Y	31
`Split`	2	1	6	126	33	572	23	9	3	Y	132
`Bib2Html`	2	1	13	493	126	2,303	59	50	52	Y	52
`XMarkQ1`	2	1	12	454	118	2,136	99	23	29	Y	168
`XMarkQ2`	1	2	9	461	207	3,797	99	4	77	Y	92
`Gapid-Html`	3	1	17	374	75	1,642	16	7	2	Y	112
`JWIG-guess`	2	1	6	465	98	2,331	64	50	588	Y	50
`JWIG-cal`	1	2	12	475	222	4,045	60	50	72	Y	73
`MinCaml-K`	2	8	19	605	563	16,117	5	3	5	Y	647
`Split'`	2	1	6	126	33	572	23	9	3	N	27
`JWIG-guess'`	2	1	6	465	98	2,331	64	50	586	N	49
`JWIG-cal'`	1	2	12	475	222	4,045	60	50	2	N	55

The program `Reverse` is the same as the one presented in the paper. `Isort` performs insertion sort on the lists encoded as linear trees over $\Sigma = \{\mathtt{a} \mapsto 1, \mathtt{b} \mapsto 1, \mathtt{e} \mapsto 0\}$. `Msort` performs merge sort instead of insertion sort on the same linear trees. `HomRep-Rev` takes a word homomorphism h over linear trees $(\mathtt{a}+\mathtt{b})^*\mathtt{e}$, a number n and a word $w \in (\mathtt{a}+\mathtt{b})^*\mathtt{e}$, and produces the reverse of the image $h^n(w)$. We let $h = \{\mathtt{a} \mapsto \mathtt{bb}, \mathtt{b} \mapsto \mathtt{a}\}$ and verified that if n is an even number and $w \in \mathtt{a}^*\mathtt{b}^*\mathtt{e}$, then the reversed image is in $\mathtt{b}^*\mathtt{a}^*\mathtt{e}$. The program `Split` presented in Figure 3 is taken from sample programs of CDuce [2], a higher-order XML-oriented functional language. `Split` takes a list of persons, and splits it into two lists of men and women. `Bib2Html` also simulates a CDuce program that transforms a list of bibliography into an XHTML. `XMarkQ1` and `XMarkQ2` taken from Q1 and Q2 of XMark benchmark suite [21] simulate simple XQuery queries. The program `Gapid-Html` is a composition of Tozawa's high-level tree transducers [22]. It takes a document of the following DTD:

```
type Doc      = doc[Preface, (Div|P|Note)*]
type Preface  = preface[Header, P*]
type Header   = header[A*]
type P        = p[A*]
type Div      = div[(Div|P|Note|A)*]
type Note     = note[(P|A)*]
type A        = a[A*]
```

and another tree as inputs. It checks whether the children of each node of the document are empty, and if so, replaces the empty children with a "hole". The program then inserts the given tree into the holes. The program finally transforms the result to an XHTML. The programs `JWIG-guess` and `JWIG-cal` are taken from sample programs of JWIG (`http://www.brics.dk/JWIG/`), a programming language for interactive Web services. A main feature of JWIG is document templates. For example, the following document template represents an HTML document with a hole named `x`:

```
<html>
  <head><title> ... </title></head>
  <body><[x]></body>
</html>
```

We can instantiate the template by substituting another document or template for `x`. In EHMTTs, the template can be encoded as the following rule for a function T with an argument x:

$$T\ x \rightarrow \texttt{html}\ (\texttt{head}\ (\texttt{title}\ (\texttt{text leaf leaf})\ \texttt{leaf})\ (\texttt{body}\ x\ \texttt{leaf}))\ \texttt{leaf}$$

The program `JWIG-guess` is a number guessing game. The program `JWIG-cal` is a web-based calendar service. `MinCaml-K` simulates the K-normalization routine of the MinCaml compiler (`http://min-caml.sourceforge.net/index-e.html`). Finally, `Split'`, `JWIG-guess'` and `JWIG-cal'` are respectively the same as `Split`, `JWIG-guess` and `JWIG-cal` except that they involve wrong coercions which lead to an **Error** to see that programs with wrong coercions are rejected. These programs (except for `Reverse`, `Isort`, `Msort` and `HomRep-Rev`) are manually translated from original source codes to EHMTTs.

All the valid programs have been proved correct by our verification method despite its incompleteness, while wrong programs are correctly rejected. The number of coercions (thus the number of annotations required by our method) is much smaller than the number of rules (functions) in all cases. Though these numbers depend on the particular encoding, this result witnesses that our verification method usually requires fewer annotations than existing verification methods [9,2,4], which require type annotations for every function definition. Further comparison with the existing methods on this point is given in Section 6.

All the programs were proved correct within 1 second. From this, we can expect that our method can verify non-trivial programs reasonably fast despite the high time complexity (n-EXPTIME complete, where n is the order) of higher-order model checking.

6 Related Work

As shown in Section 1, our verification method is based on recent advances on higher-order model checking [11,1,20,14]. Ong [20] has proven the decidability of the model checking problem for recursion schemes, and Kobayashi has developed and implemented a type-based model checking algorithm [14].

As we have shown in Section 5, our EHMTT verification method can be applied to verification of functional programs that manipulate various data structures such as strings, lists, trees, XML, and user-defined recursive data structures

```
Split x = case x of person g n c =>
  case c of children cs => case g of gender gend =>
    Let gend n (coerce qPair (MakePair cs nil nil))
Let gend n x = case gend of
  m => Make man (Copy n) x
| f => Make woman (Copy n) x
MakePair ps ms fs = case ps of nil => pair ms fs
| cons p sib => case p of person g n c => case g of gender gend =>
  case gend of
   m => MakePair sib (cons (person (gender m) (Copy n) (Copy c)) ms) fs
  |f => MakePair sib ms (cons (person (gender f) (Copy n) (Copy c)) fs)
Make tag name sdpair = case sdpair of pair s d =>
  tag name (sons (RevMap Split s nil))
           (daughters (RevMap Split d nil))
RevMap f l ac =
  case l of nil => ac | cons x xs => RevMap f xs (cons (f x) ac)
```

Fig. 3. Split

by encoding them as trees and adding coercion annotations to the programs. We compare our method with existing verification methods below.

Refinement types [7,4] can be used for verification of functional programs that manipulate user-defined recursive data structures. The original refinement type system [7] uses a naïve least fixed-point algorithm to infer the most precise refinement types of functions, and does not seem to scale for higher-order functions. Another refinement type system proposed by Davies [4] requires users to write type annotations for each function. For example, for $\mathcal{P}_{rev}$ in Example 1, *Reverse* and *Append* need to be annotated with the following intersection types:

$$\mathit{Reverse} : (\mathtt{a}^*\mathtt{b}^*\mathtt{e} \to \mathtt{b}^*\mathtt{a}^*\mathtt{e}) \wedge (\mathtt{b}^*\mathtt{e} \to \mathtt{b}^*\mathtt{e})$$
$$\mathit{Append} : (\mathtt{b}^*\mathtt{a}^*\mathtt{e} \to \mathtt{a}^*\mathtt{e} \to \mathtt{b}^*\mathtt{a}^*\mathtt{e}) \wedge (\mathtt{b}^*\mathtt{e} \to \mathtt{b}^*\mathtt{e} \to \mathtt{b}^*\mathtt{e})$$

In contrast, our method requires only the annotations $\mathbf{coerce}^{\mathtt{b}^*\mathtt{a}^*\mathtt{e}}(\mathit{Reverse}\ x')$ and $\mathbf{coerce}^{\mathtt{b}^*\mathtt{e}}(\mathit{Reverse}\ x')$ in the definition of *Reverse*. As in this case, we expect that coercion annotations required in our approach tends to be simpler than refinement type declarations. Because of the limitation of our approach discussed at the end of Section 4, however, it may be useful to combine both approaches.

Several research groups have proposed typed XML processing languages [9,2]. Their type systems can be used for verification of XML processing programs. As in the Davies's refinement type system, these type systems require type annotations for each function for type checking. Thus, our method can be used as an alternative for a verification purpose. Meanwhile their type systems support advanced programming features such as parametric polymorphism [8] and regular expression pattern matching [10]. Extensions of our method with these features are left for future work. While the type checking of the XML processing languages are incomplete, extensive work has been done on complete type checking of various tree transducers [18,17]. They are not Turing-complete, however, and thus less expressive than our EHMTTs. As shown in [16], ordinary macro and high-level tree transducers [5,6] are subsumed by linear HMTTs, for which our EHMTT verification method is sound and complete.

String analysis [3,19] can verify programs that manipulate strings by approximating a string-processing program as a regular or a context-free grammar. In contrast, our method is more precise since we can naturally model programs as EHMTTs, which are strictly more expressive than context-free grammars.

Our approach of reducing EHMTT verification to simpler verification problems based on coercion annotations is a reminiscent of program verification techniques for imperative languages based on verification condition generation from loop invariants: coercion annotations are invariants, and generated HMTT verification problems can be considered verification conditions. The main differences are that our target is a higher-order functional language and that not all recursions (or loops) need to be annotated with invariants.

7 Conclusion

We have proposed a verification method for tree-processing programs based on reduction to higher-order model checking, and shown its effectiveness through experiments. We plan to investigate techniques for inferring coercion annotations, which would enable fully automatic verification of tree-processing programs. If the derived HMTTs are ordinary macro or high-level tree transducers [5,6], annotations can indeed be inferred by the inverse inference technique. For general EHMTTs, we plan to apply techniques of machine learning. Addressing the limitations discussed at the end of Section 4 is also left for future work.

Acknowledgment

We would like to thank anonymous referees for useful comments.

References

1. Aehlig, K., de Miranda, J.G., Ong, C.H.L.: The monadic second order theory of trees given by arbitrary level-two recursion schemes is decidable. In: Urzyczyn, P. (ed.) TLCA 2005. LNCS, vol. 3461, pp. 39–54. Springer, Heidelberg (2005)
2. Benzaken, V., Castagna, G., Frisch, A.: CDuce: an XML-centric general-purpose language. In: ICFP 2003, pp. 51–63. ACM, New York (2003)
3. Christensen, A.S., Møller, A., Schwartzbach, M.I.: Precise analysis of string expressions. In: Cousot, R. (ed.) SAS 2003. LNCS, vol. 2694, pp. 1–18. Springer, Heidelberg (2003)
4. Davies, R.: Practical refinement-type checking. Ph.D. thesis, Carnegie Mellon University, chair-Pfenning, Frank (2005)
5. Engelfriet, J., Vogler, H.: Macro tree transducers. Journal of Computer and System Sciences 31(1), 71–146 (1985)
6. Engelfriet, J., Vogler, H.: High level tree transducers and iterated pushdown tree transducers. Acta Informatica 26(1/2), 131–192 (1988)

7. Freeman, T., Pfenning, F.: Refinement types for ML. In: PLDI 1991, pp. 268–277. ACM, New York (1991)
8. Hosoya, H., Frisch, A., Castagna, G.: Parametric polymorphism for XML. ACM Transactions on Programming Languages and Systems 32(1), 1–56 (2009)
9. Hosoya, H., Pierce, B.C.: XDuce: A statically typed XML processing language. ACM Transactions on Internet Technology 3(2), 117–148 (2003)
10. Hosoya, H., Vouillon, J., Pierce, B.C.: Regular expression types for XML. In: ICFP 2000, pp. 11–22. ACM, New York (2000)
11. Knapik, T., Niwinski, D., Urzyczyn, P.: Higher-order pushdown trees are easy. In: Nielsen, M., Engberg, U. (eds.) FOSSACS 2002. LNCS, vol. 2303, pp. 205–222. Springer, Heidelberg (2002)
12. Kobayashi, N.: Model-checking higher-order functions. In: PPDP 2009, pp. 25–36. ACM, New York (2009)
13. Kobayashi, N.: Types and higher-order recursion schemes for verification of higher-order programs. In: POPL 2009, pp. 416–428. ACM, New York (2009)
14. Kobayashi, N., Ong, C.-H.L.: A type system equivalent to the modal mu-calculus model checking of higher-order recursion schemes. In: LICS 2009, pp. 179–188. IEEE, Los Alamitos (2009)
15. Kobayashi, N., Tabuchi, N., Unno, H.: Higher-order multi-parameter tree transducers and recursion schemes for program verification. In: POPL 2010, pp. 495–508. ACM, New York (2010)
16. Kobayashi, N., Tabuchi, N., Unno, H.: Higher-order multi-parameter tree transducers and recursion schemes for program verification. An extended version (2010), `http://www.kb.ecei.tohoku.ac.jp/~koba/papers/hmtt.pdf`
17. Maneth, S., Berlea, A., Perst, T., Seidl, H.: XML type checking with macro tree transducers. In: PODS 2005, pp. 283–294. ACM, New York (2005)
18. Milo, T., Suciu, D., Vianu, V.: Typechecking for XML transformers. Journal of Computer and System Sciences 66(1), 66–97 (2003)
19. Minamide, Y.: Static approximation of dynamically generated web pages. In: WWW 2005, pp. 432–441. ACM, New York (2005)
20. Ong, C.-H.L.: On model-checking trees generated by higher-order recursion schemes. In: LICS 2006, pp. 81–90. IEEE, Los Alamitos (2006)
21. Schmidt, A., Waas, F., Kersten, M., Carey, M.J., Manolescu, I., Busse, R.: XMark: a benchmark for XML data management. In: VLDB 2002, pp. 974–985. VLDB Endowment (2002)
22. Tozawa, A.: XML type checking using high-level tree transducer. In: Hagiya, M., Wadler, P. (eds.) FLOPS 2006. LNCS, vol. 3945, pp. 81–96. Springer, Heidelberg (2006)
23. Unno, H., Tabuchi, N., Kobayashi, N.: Verification of tree-processing programs via higher-order model checking. An extended version (2010), `http://www.kb.ecei.tohoku.ac.jp/~uhiro/papers/aplas2010.pdf`

Automatically Inferring Quantified Loop Invariants by Algorithmic Learning from Simple Templates*

Soonho Kong[1], Yungbum Jung[1], Cristina David[2], Bow-Yaw Wang[3], and Kwangkeun Yi[1]

[1] Seoul National University
[2] National University of Singapore
[3] INRIA, Tsinghua University, and Academia Sinica

Abstract. By combining algorithmic learning, decision procedures, predicate abstraction, and simple templates, we present an automated technique for finding quantified loop invariants. Our technique can find arbitrary first-order invariants (modulo a fixed set of atomic propositions and an underlying SMT solver) in the form of the given template and exploits the flexibility in invariants by a simple randomized mechanism. The proposed technique is able to find quantified invariants for loops from the Linux source, as well as for the benchmark code used in the previous works. Our contribution is a simpler technique than the previous works yet with a reasonable derivation power.

1 Introduction

Recently, algorithmic learning has been successfully applied to invariant generation. The new approach formalizes the invariant generation problem as an instance of algorithmic learning: to generate an invariant is to learn a concept from a teacher. Using a learning algorithm as a black box, one only needs to design a mechanical teacher that guides the learning algorithm to invariants. The learning-based framework not only simplifies the invariant generation algorithms, the new approach can also automatically generate invariants for realistic C loops at a reasonable cost [15].

Figure 1 shows the new framework proposed in [15]. In the figure, the CDNF algorithm is used to drive the search of quantifier-free invariants. The CDNF algorithm is an exact learning algorithm for Boolean formulae. It computes a

* This work was supported by the Engineering Research Center of Excellence Program of Korea Ministry of Education, Science and Technology(MEST) / National Research Foundation of Korea(NRF) (Grant 2010-0001717). This work was partly supported by MoE Tier-2 grant R-252-000-411-112 and by the National Science Council of Taiwan projects No. NSC97-2221-E-001-003-MY3, NSC97-2221-E-001-006-MY3, the FORMES Project within LIAMA Consortium, and the French ANR project SIVES ANR-08-BLAN-0326-01.

K. Ueda (Ed.): APLAS 2010, LNCS 6461, pp. 328–343, 2010.

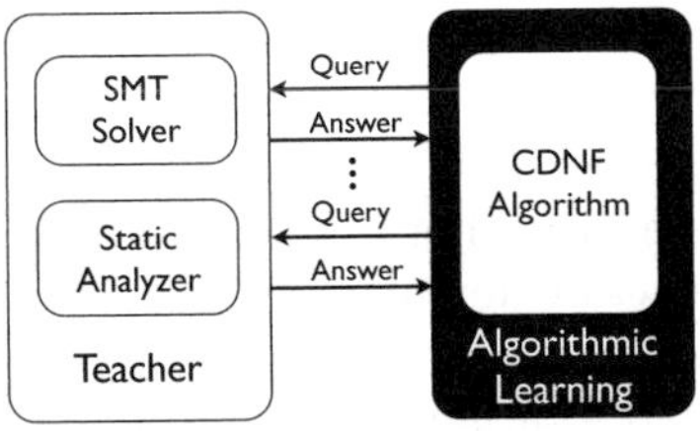

Fig. 1. The learning-based framework

representation of an unknown target formula by asking a teacher two types of queries. A membership query asks if a valuation to Boolean variables satisfies the unknown target; an equivalence query asks if a candidate formula is equivalent to the target. With predicate abstraction, the new approach formulates an unknown quantifier-free invariant as the unknown target Boolean formula. One only needs to automate the query resolution process to infer an invariant.

If an invariant was known, a mechanical teacher to resove queries can be implemented straightforwardly. In the context of invariant generation, no invariant is known. However, a simple randomized automatic teacher is proposed in [15]. With the help of SMT solvers, user-provided annotations, and coin tossing, one can resolve both types of queries by a simple reduction to the satisfiability problem of quantifier-free formulae. An ingenious feature of this design is its random walk. Due to the lack of information, some queries cannot be resolved decisively. In this case, the teacher simply gives a random answer. The learning algorithm will then look for invariants consistent with both decisive and random answers from the teacher. Since there are sufficiently many invariants for an annotated loop in practice, almost certainly the learning algorithm can find one.

The work [15] has, however, one obvious limitation; it can only generate quantifier-free invariants. Yet loops iterating over arrays often require invariants quantified over indices. It will be very useful to extend the new approach to quantified invariants. However, a naïve extension would not work. First of all, it is not clear how to associate an arbitrarily quantified formula with a quantified Boolean formula. There is no counterpart (a Boolean formula) for quantified variables in, say, $\forall i.i > 10$. Second, there is no exact learning algorithm for quantified Boolean formulae to the best of our knowledge. Even if an abstraction for quantified formulae was available, we could not adopt the same learning-based framework. Third, computability issues must be addressed because the satisfiability problem for arbitrarily quantified formulae is undecidable. Developing an effective invariant generation algorithm for quantified invariants is therefore an interesting challenge to the learning-based framework.

This article is about our findings in generating *quantified* invariants with algorithmic learning:

- We show that a simple combination of algorithmic learning, decision procedures, predicate abstraction, and templates can automatically infer quantified loop invariants. The technique is as powerful as the previous approaches [9,20] yet is much simpler.
- The technique needs a very simple template such as "$\forall k.[]$" or "$\forall k.\exists i.[]$." Our algorithm can generate any quantified invariants expressible by a fixed set of atomic propositions in the form of the given template. Moreover, the correctness of generated invariants is verified by an SMT solver.
- The technique works in realistic settings: The proposed technique can find quantified invariants for some Linux library, kernel, and device driver sources, as well as for the benchmark code used in the previous work [20].
- The technique's future improvement is free. Since our algorithm uses the two key technologies (exact learning algorithm and decision procedures) as black boxes, future advances of these technologies will straightforwardly benefit our approach.

1.1 Motivating Example

In order to illustrate how our algorithm works, we briefly describe the learning process for the `max` example from [20].

$$\{m = 0 \wedge i = 0\}$$
$$\texttt{while } i < n \texttt{ do if } a[m] < a[i] \texttt{ then } m = i \texttt{ fi}; \ i = i + 1 \texttt{ end}$$
$$\{\forall k. k < n \Rightarrow a[k] \leq a[m]\}$$

The `max` example examines $a[0]$ through $a[n-1]$ and finds the index of the maximal element in the array. This simple loop is annotated with the precondition $m = 0 \wedge i = 0$ and the postcondition $\forall k. 0 \leq k < n \Rightarrow a[k] \leq a[m]$.

Template and Atomic Propositions A template and atomic propositions are provided manually by user. We provide the template $\forall k.[]$. The postcondition is universally quantified with k and gives a hint to the form of an invariant. By extracting from the annotated loop and adding the last two atomic propositions from the user's guidance, we use the following set of atomic propositions:

$$\{i < n, \ m = 0, \ i = 0, \ a[m] < a[i], \ a[k] \leq a[m], \ k < n, \ k < i\}.$$

Query Resolution In this example, 20 membership queries and 6 equivalence queries are made by the learning algorithm on average. For simplicity, let us find an invariant that is weaker than the precondition but stronger than the postcondition. We describe how the teacher resolves some of these queries.

- Equivalence Query: The learning algorithm starts with an equivalence query $EQ(\mathtt{T})$, namely whether $\forall k.\mathtt{T}$ can be an invariant. The teacher answers *NO* since $\forall k.\mathtt{T}$ is weaker than the postcondition. Additionally, by employing an SMT solver, the teacher returns a counterexample $\{m = 0, \ k = 1, \ n = 2, \ i = 2, \ a[0] = 0, \ a[1] = 1\}$, under which $\forall k.\mathtt{T}$ evaluates to true, whereas the postcondition evaluates to false.

– Membership Query: After a few equivalence queries, a membership query asks whether $\bigwedge\{i \geq n,\ m = 0,\ i = 0,\ k \geq n,\ a[k] \leq a[m],\ a[m] \geq a[i]\}$ is a part of an invariant. The teacher replies *YES* since the query is included in the precondition and therefore should also be included in an invariant.
– Membership Query: The membership query $MEM(\bigwedge\{i < n,\ m = 0,\ i \neq 0,\ k < n,\ a[k] > a[m],\ k < i,\ a[m] \geq a[i]\})$ is not resolvable because the template is not *well-formed* (Definition 1) by the given membership query. In this case, the teacher gives a random answer (*YES* or *NO*). Interestingly, each answer leads to a different invariant for this query. If the answer is *YES*, we find an invariant $\forall k.(i < n \wedge k \geq i) \vee (a[k] \leq a[m]) \vee (k \geq n)$; if the answer is *NO*, we find another invariant $\forall k.(i < n \wedge k \geq i) \vee (a[k] \leq a[m]) \vee (k \geq n \wedge k \geq i)$. This shows how our approach exploits a multitude of invariants for the annotated loop.

1.2 Organization

We organize this paper as follows. After preliminaries in Section 2, we present problems and solutions in Section 3. Our abstraction is briefly described in Section 4. The details of our technique are described in Section 5. We report experiments in Section 6, discuss related work in Section 7, then conclude in Section 8.

2 Preliminaries

The abstract syntax of our simple imperative language is given below:

$$\begin{aligned}
\mathsf{Stmt} \triangleq\ & \mathtt{nop} \mid \mathsf{Stmt};\ \mathsf{Stmt} \mid x := \mathsf{Exp} \mid b := \mathsf{Prop} \mid a[\mathsf{Exp}] := \mathsf{Exp} \mid \\
& a[\mathsf{Exp}] := \mathtt{nondet} \mid x := \mathtt{nondet} \mid b := \mathtt{nondet} \mid \\
& \mathtt{if}\ \mathsf{Prop}\ \mathtt{then}\ \mathsf{Stmt}\ \mathtt{else}\ \mathsf{Stmt} \mid \{\ \mathsf{Pred}\ \}\ \mathtt{while}\ \mathsf{Prop}\ \mathtt{do}\ \mathsf{Stmt}\ \{\ \mathsf{Pred}\ \} \\
\mathsf{Exp} \triangleq\ & n \mid x \mid a[\mathsf{Exp}] \mid \mathsf{Exp} + \mathsf{Exp} \mid \mathsf{Exp} - \mathsf{Exp} \\
\mathsf{Prop} \triangleq\ & \mathtt{F} \mid b \mid \neg\mathsf{Prop} \mid \mathsf{Prop} \wedge \mathsf{Prop} \mid \mathsf{Exp} < \mathsf{Exp} \mid \mathsf{Exp} = \mathsf{Exp} \\
\mathsf{Pred} \triangleq\ & \mathsf{Prop} \mid \forall x.\mathsf{Pred} \mid \exists x.\mathsf{Pred} \mid \mathsf{Pred} \wedge \mathsf{Pred} \mid \neg\mathsf{Pred}
\end{aligned}$$

The language has two basic types: Booleans and natural numbers. A term in Exp is a natural number; a term in Prop is a quantifier-free formula and of Boolean type; a term in Pred is a first-order formula. The keyword `nondet` is used for unknown values from user's input or complex structures (e.g, pointer operations, function calls, etc.). In an annotated loop $\{\delta\}$ `while` κ `do` S $\{\epsilon\}$, $\kappa \in \mathsf{Prop}$ is its *guard*, and $\delta, \epsilon \in \mathsf{Pred}$ are its *precondition* and *postcondition* respectively. Quantifier-free formulae of the forms b, $\pi_0 < \pi_1$, and $\pi_0 = \pi_1$ are called *atomic propositions*. If A is a set of atomic propositions, then Prop_A and Pred_A denote the set of quantifier-free and first-order formulae generated from A, respectively.

A *template* $t[] \in \tau$ is a finite sequence of quantifiers followed by a hole to be filled with a quantifier-free formula in Prop_A.

$$\tau \triangleq [] \mid \forall I.\tau \mid \exists I.\tau.$$

Let $\theta \in \mathsf{Prop}_A$ be a quantifier-free formula. We write $t[\theta]$ to denote the first-order formula obtained by replacing the hole in $t[]$ with θ. Observe that any first-order formula can be transformed into the prenex normal form; it can be expressed in the form of a proper template.

A *precondition* $Pre(\rho, S)$ for $\rho \in \mathsf{Pred}$ with respect to a statement S is a first-order formula that guarantees ρ after the execution of the statement S. Let $\{\delta\}$ `while` κ `do` S $\{\epsilon\}$ be an annotated loop and $t[] \in \tau$ be a template. The *invariant generation problem with template* $t[]$ is to compute a first-order formula $t[\theta]$ such that (1) $\delta \Rightarrow t[\theta]$; (2) $\neg\kappa \wedge t[\theta] \Rightarrow \epsilon$; and (3) $\kappa \wedge t[\theta] \Rightarrow Pre(t[\theta], S)$. Observe that the condition (2) is equivalent to $t[\theta] \Rightarrow \epsilon \vee \kappa$. We have $\delta \Rightarrow t[\theta]$ and $t[\theta] \Rightarrow \epsilon \vee \kappa$ for any invariant $t[\theta]$. δ and $\epsilon \vee \kappa$ are subsequently called the *strongest under-approximation* and *weakest over-approximation* to invariants respectively.

A *valuation* ν is an assignment of natural numbers to integer variables and truth values to Boolean variables. If A is a set of atomic propositions and $Var(A)$ is the set of variables occurred in A, $Val_{Var(A)}$ denotes the set of valuations for $Var(A)$. A valuation ν is a *model* of a first-order formula ρ (written $\nu \models \rho$) if ρ evaluates to $\mathtt{T}$ under ν. Let B be a set of Boolean variables. We write Bool_B for the class of Boolean formulae over Boolean variables B. A *Boolean valuation* μ is an assignment of truth values to Boolean variables. The set of Boolean valuations for B is denoted by Val_B. A Boolean valuation μ is a *Boolean model* of the Boolean formula β (written $\mu \models \beta$) if β evaluates to $\mathtt{T}$ under μ.

Given a first-order formula ρ, a *satisfiability modulo theories (SMT) solver* [6,16] returns a model of ν if it exists. In general, SMT solver is incomplete over quantified formulae and may return a potential model (written $SMT(\rho) \xrightarrow{!} \nu$). It returns $UNSAT$ (written $SMT(\rho) \rightarrow UNSAT$) if the solver proves the formula unsatisfiable. Note that an SMT solver can only err when it returns a (potential) model. If $UNSAT$ is returned, the input formula is certainly unsatisfiable.

CDNF Learning Algorithm [3]. The CDNF (Conjunctive Disjunctive Normal Form) algorithm is an exact algorithm that computes a representation for any *target* $\lambda \in \mathsf{Bool}_B$ by asking a *teacher* queries. The teacher is required to resolve two types of queries:

- *Membership query* $MEM(\mu)$ where $\mu \in Val_B$. If the valuation μ is a Boolean model of the target Boolean formula λ, the teacher answers *YES*. Otherwise, the teacher answers *NO*;
- *Equivalence query* $EQ(\beta)$ where $\beta \in \mathsf{Bool}_B$. If the target Boolean formula λ is equivalent to β, the teacher answers *YES*. Otherwise, the teacher gives a counterexample. A *counterexample* is a valuation $\mu \in Val_B$ such that β and λ evaluate to different truth values under μ.

For a Boolean formula $\lambda \in \mathsf{Bool}_B$, define $|\lambda|_{CNF}$ and $|\lambda|_{DNF}$ to be the sizes of minimal Boolean formulae equivalent to λ in conjunctive and disjunctive normal forms respectively. The CDNF algorithm infers any target Boolean formula $\lambda \in \mathsf{Bool}_B$ with a polynomial number of queries in $|\lambda|_{CNF}$, $|\lambda|_{DNF}$, and $|B|$ [3].

3 Problems and Solutions

Given an annotated loop and a template, we apply algorithmic learning to find an invariant in the form of the given template. We follow the framework proposed in [15] and deploy the CDNF algorithm to drive the search of invariants. Since the learning algorithm assumes a teacher to answer queries, it remains to mechanize the query resolution process (Figure 1). Let $t[]$ be the given template and $t[\theta]$ an invariant. We will devise a teacher to guide the CDNF algorithm to infer $t[\theta]$.

To achieve this goal, we need to address two problems. First, the CDNF algorithm is a learning algorithm for Boolean formulae, not quantifier-free nor quantified formulae. Second, the CDNF algorithm assumes a teacher who knows the target $t[\theta]$ in its learning model. However, an invariant of the given annotated loop is yet to be computed and hence unknown to us. We need to devise a teacher without assuming any particular invariant $t[\theta]$.

For the first problem, we adopt predicate abstraction to associate Boolean formulae with quantified formulae. Recall that the formula θ in the invariant $t[\theta]$ is quantifier-free. Let α be an abstraction function from quantifier-free to Boolean formulae. Then $\lambda = \alpha(\theta)$ is a Boolean formula and serves as the target function to be inferred by the CDNF algorithm.

For the second problem, we need to design algorithms to resolve queries about the Boolean formula λ without knowing $t[\theta]$. This is achieved by exploiting the information derived from annotations and by making a few random guesses. Recall that any invariant must be weaker than the strongest under-approximation and stronger than the weakest over-approximation. Using an SMT solver, queries can be resolved by comparing with these invariant approximations. For queries unresolvable through approximations, we simply give random answers.

Following a similar framework to [15], we are able to infer quantified invariants of a given template for annotated loops. Our solution to the quantified invariant generation problem for annotated loops is in fact very general. It only requires users to provide a sequence of quantifiers and a fixed set of atomic propositions. With a number of coin tossing, our technique can infer arbitrary quantified invariants representable by the user inputs. This suggests that the algorithmic learning approach to invariant generation has great potential in invariant generation problems.

4 Predicate Abstraction with a Template

We begin with the association between Boolean formulae and first-order formulae in the form of a given template. Let A be a set of atomic propositions and $B(A) \triangleq \{b_p : p \in A\}$ the set of corresponding Boolean variables. Figure 2 shows the abstraction used in our algorithm. The left box represents the class Pred_A of first-order formulae generated from A. The middle box corresponds to the class Prop_A of quantifier-free formulae generated from A. Since we are looking for quantified invariants in the form of the template $t[]$, Prop_A is in fact the essence of generated quantified invariants. The right box contains the class $\mathsf{Bool}_{B(A)}$ of

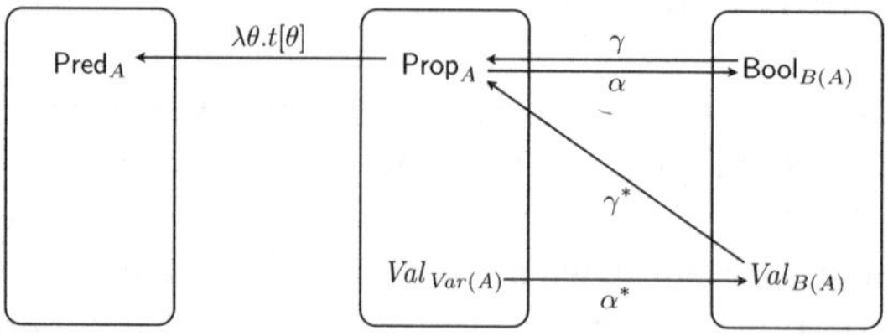

Fig. 2. The domains Pred_A, Prop_A, and $\mathsf{Bool}_{B(A)}$

Boolean formulae over the Boolean variables $B(A)$. The CDNF algorithm infers a target Boolean formula by posing queries in this domain.

The pair (γ, α) gives the correspondence between the domains $\mathsf{Bool}_{B(A)}$ and Prop_A. Let us call a Boolean formula $\beta \in \mathsf{Bool}_{B(A)}$ a *canonical monomial* if it is a conjunction of literals, where each variable appears exactly once. Define

$$\gamma : \mathsf{Bool}_{B(A)} \to \mathsf{Prop}_A \qquad\qquad \alpha : \mathsf{Prop}_A \to \mathsf{Bool}_{B(A)}$$

$$\gamma(\beta) = \beta[\overline{b}_p \mapsto \overline{p}]$$
$$\alpha(\theta) = \bigvee\{\beta \in \mathsf{Bool}_{B(A)} : \beta \text{ is a canonical monomial and } \theta \wedge \gamma(\beta) \text{ is satisfiable}\}.$$

Concretization function $\gamma(\beta) \in \mathsf{Prop}_A$ simply replaces Boolean variables in $B(A)$ by corresponding atomic propositions in A. On the other hand, $\alpha(\theta) \in \mathsf{Bool}_{B(A)}$ is the abstraction for any quantifier-free formula $\theta \in \mathsf{Prop}_A$.

A Boolean valuation $\mu \in Val_{B(A)}$ is associated with a quantifier-free formula $\gamma^*(\mu)$ and a first-order formula $t[\gamma^*(\mu)]$. A valuation $\nu \in Var(A)$ moreover induces a natural Boolean valuation $\alpha^*(\nu) \in Val_{B(A)}$.

$$\gamma^*(\mu) = \bigwedge_{p \in A} \{p : \mu(b_p) = \mathtt{T}\} \wedge \bigwedge_{p \in A} \{\neg p : \mu(b_p) = \mathtt{F}\}$$
$$\alpha^*(\nu)(b_p) = \nu \models p$$

The following lemmas characterize relations among these functions:

Lemma 1 ([15]). *Let A be a set of atomic propositions, $\theta \in \mathsf{Prop}_A$, $\beta \in \mathsf{Bool}_{B(A)}$, and ν a valuation for $Var(A)$. Then*

1. *$\nu \models \theta$ if and only if $\alpha^*(\nu) \models \alpha(\theta)$; and*
2. *$\nu \models \gamma(\beta)$ if and only if $\alpha^*(\nu) \models \beta$.*

Lemma 2 ([15]). *Let A be a set of atomic propositions, $\theta \in \mathsf{Prop}_A$, and μ a Boolean valuation for $B(A)$. Then $\gamma^*(\mu) \Rightarrow \theta$ if and only if $\mu \models \alpha(\theta)$.*

5 Learning Quantified Invariants

We present our query resolution algorithms, followed by the invariant generation algorithm. The query resolution algorithms exploit the information derived from

Algorithm 1. Resolving Equivalence Queries

```
/* ι̲ : an under-approximation; ῑ : an over-approximation        */
/* t[]: the given template                                          */
```

Input: $\beta \in \mathsf{Bool}_{B(A)}$

Output: *YES*, or a counterexample ν s.t. $\alpha^*(\nu) \models \beta \oplus \lambda$

1 $\rho := t[\gamma(\beta)]$;

2 **if** $SMT(\underline{\iota} \wedge \neg\rho) \rightarrow UNSAT$ **and** $SMT(\rho \wedge \neg\bar{\iota}) \rightarrow UNSAT$ **and**

3 $\quad SMT(\kappa \wedge \rho \wedge \neg Pre(\rho, S)) \rightarrow UNSAT$ **then return** *YES*;

4 **if** $SMT(\underline{\iota} \wedge \neg\rho) \xrightarrow{!} \nu$ **then return** $\alpha^*(\nu)$;

5 **if** $SMT(\rho \wedge \neg\bar{\iota}) \xrightarrow{!} \nu$ **then return** $\alpha^*(\nu)$;

6 **if** $SMT(\rho \wedge \neg\underline{\iota}) \xrightarrow{!} \nu_0$ **or** $SMT(\bar{\iota} \wedge \neg\rho) \xrightarrow{!} \nu_1$ **then**

7 $\quad$ **return** $\alpha^*(\nu_0)$ *or* $\alpha^*(\nu_1)$ *randomly*;

the given annotated loop $\{\delta\}$ `while` κ `do` S $\{\epsilon\}$. Let $\underline{\iota}, \bar{\iota} \in \mathsf{Pred}$. We say $\underline{\iota}$ is an *under-approximation* to invariants if $\delta \Rightarrow \underline{\iota}$ and $\underline{\iota} \Rightarrow \iota$ for some invariant ι of the annotated loop. Similarly, $\bar{\iota}$ is an *over-approximation* to invariants if $\bar{\iota} \Rightarrow \epsilon \vee \kappa$ and $\iota \Rightarrow \bar{\iota}$ for some invariant ι. The strongest under-approximation δ is an under-approximation; the weakest over-approximation $\epsilon \vee \kappa$ is an over-approximation. Better invariant approximations can be obtained by other techniques; they can be used in our query resolution algorithms.

5.1 Equivalence Queries

An equivalence query $EQ(\beta)$ with $\beta \in \mathsf{Bool}_{B(A)}$ asks if β is equivalent to the unknown target λ. Algorithm 1 gives our equivalence resolution algorithm. It first checks if $\rho = t[\gamma(\beta)]$ is indeed an invariant for the annotated loop by verifying $\underline{\iota} \Rightarrow \rho$, $\rho \Rightarrow \bar{\iota}$, and $\kappa \wedge \rho \Rightarrow Pre(\rho, S)$ with an SMT solver (line 2 and 3). If so, the CDNF algorithm has generated an invariant and our teacher acknowledges

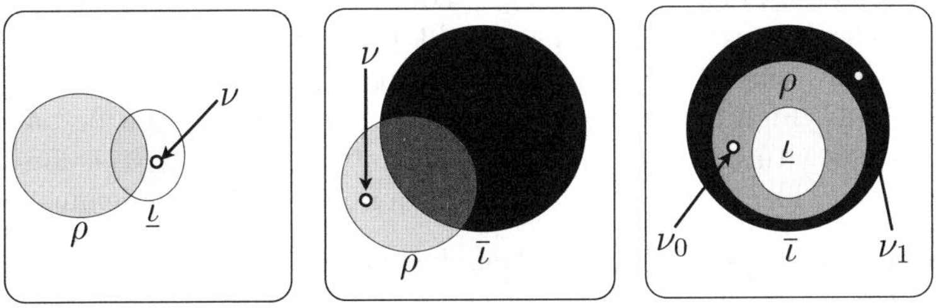

(a) (b) (c)

Fig. 3. Counterexamples in equivalence query resolution (c.f. Algorithm 1): (a) a counterexample inside the under-approximation $\underline{\iota}$ but outside the candidate ρ (line 4); (b) a counterexample inside the candidate ρ but outside the over-approximation $\bar{\iota}$ (line 5); (c) a random counterexample ν_0 (or ν_1) inside the candidate ρ (or over-approximation $\bar{\iota}$) but out of the under-approximation $\underline{\iota}$ (or candidate ρ), respectively (line 6 and 7).

Algorithm 2. Resolving Membership Queries

/* $\underline{\iota}$: an under-approximation; $\overline{\iota}$: an over-approximation */
/* $t[]$: the given template */
Input: a valuation μ for $B(A)$
Output: *YES* or *NO*
1 **if** $SMT(\gamma^*(\mu)) \rightarrow UNSAT$ **then return** *NO*;
2 $\rho := t[\gamma^*(\mu)]$;
3 **if** $SMT(\rho \wedge \neg\overline{\iota}) \stackrel{!}{\rightarrow} \nu$ **then return** *NO*;
4 **if** $SMT(\rho \wedge \neg\underline{\iota}) \rightarrow UNSAT$ **and** $isWellFormed(t[], \gamma^*(\mu))$ **then return** *YES*;
5 **return** *YES or NO randomly*

that the target has been found. If the candidate ρ is not an invariant, we need to provide a counterexample. Figure 3 describes the process of counterexample discovery. The algorithm first tries to generate a counterexample inside of under-approximation (a), or outside of over-approximation (b). If it fails to find such counterexamples, the algorithm tries to return a valuation distinguishing ρ from invariant approximations as a random answer (c).

Recall that SMT solvers may err when a potential model is returned (line 4 – 6). If it returns an incorrect model, our equivalence resolution algorithm will give an incorrect answer to the learning algorithm. Incorrect answers effectively guide the CDNF algorithm to different quantified invariants. Note also that random answers do not yield incorrect results because the equivalence query resolution algorithm uses an SMT solver to *verify* that the found first-order formula is indeed an invariant.

5.2 Membership Queries

In a membership query $MEM(\mu)$, our membership query resolution algorithm (Algorithm 2) should answer whether $\mu \models \lambda$. Note that any relation between atomic propositions A is lost in the abstract domain $\mathsf{Bool}_{B(A)}$. A valuation may not correspond to a consistent quantifier-free formula (for example, $b_{x=0} = b_{x>0} = \mathtt{T}$). If the valuation $\mu \in Val_{B(A)}$ corresponds to an inconsistent quantifier-free formula (that is, $\gamma^*(\mu)$ is unsatisfiable), we simply answer *NO* to the membership query (line 1). Otherwise, we compare $\rho = t[\gamma^*(\mu)]$ with invariant approximations. Figure 4 shows the scenarios when queries can be answered by comparing ρ with invariant approximations. In case 4(a), $\rho \Rightarrow \overline{\iota}$ does not hold and we would like to show $\mu \not\models \lambda$. This requires the following lemma:

Lemma 3. *Let* $t[] \in \tau$ *be a template. For any* $\theta_1, \theta_2 \in \mathsf{Prop}_A$, $\theta_1 \Rightarrow \theta_2$ *implies* $t[\theta_1] \Rightarrow t[\theta_2]$.[1]

By Lemma 3 and $t[\gamma^*(\mu)] \not\Rightarrow \overline{\iota}$ (line 3), we have $\gamma^*(\mu) \not\Rightarrow \gamma(\lambda)$. Hence $\mu \not\models \lambda$ (Lemma 2).

For case 4(b), we have $\rho \Rightarrow \underline{\iota}$ and would like to show $\mu \models \lambda$. However, the implication $t[\theta_1] \Rightarrow t[\theta_2]$ carries little information about the relation between θ_1

[1] Complete proofs are in [5].

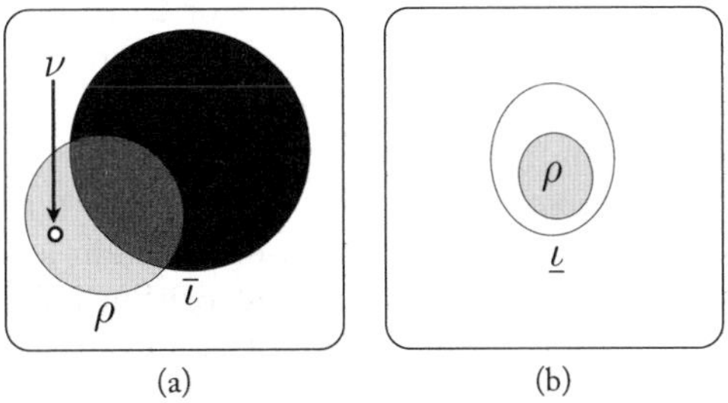

Fig. 4. Resolving a membership query with invariant approximations (c.f. Algorithm 2): (a) the guess ρ is not included in the over-approximation $\bar{\iota}$ (line 3); (b) the guess ρ is included in the under-approximation $\underline{\iota}$ (line 4)

and θ_2. Consider $t[] \equiv \forall i.[]$, $\theta_1 \equiv i < 10$, and $\theta_2 \equiv i < 1$. We have $\forall i.i < 10 \Rightarrow \forall i.i < 1$ but $i < 10 \not\Rightarrow i < 1$. In order to infer more information from $\rho \Rightarrow \underline{\iota}$, we introduce a subclass of templates.

Definition 1. *Let $\theta \in \mathsf{Prop}_A$ be a quantifier-free formula over A. A* well-formed *template $t[]$ with respect to θ is defined as follows.*

- *$[]$ is well-formed with respect to θ;*
- *$\forall I.t'[]$ is well-formed with respect to θ if $t'[]$ is well-formed with respect to θ and $t'[\theta] \Rightarrow \forall I.t'[\theta]$;*
- *$\exists I.t'[]$ is well-formed with respect to θ if $t'[]$ is well-formed with respect to θ and $\neg t'[\theta]$.*

Using an SMT solver, it is straightforward to check if a template $t[]$ is well-formed with respect to a quantifier-free formula θ by a simple recursion. For instance, when the template is $\forall I.t'[]$, it suffices to check $SMT(t'[\theta] \wedge \exists I.\neg t'[\theta]) \rightarrow UNSAT$ and $t'[]$ is well-formed with respect to θ. More importantly, well-formed templates allow us to infer the relation between hole-filling quantifier-free formulae.

Lemma 4. *Let A be a set of atomic propositions, $\theta_1 \in \mathsf{Prop}_A$, and $t[] \in \tau$ a well-formed template with respect to θ_1. For any $\theta_2 \in \mathsf{Prop}_A$, $t[\theta_1] \Rightarrow t[\theta_2]$ implies $\theta_1 \Rightarrow \theta_2$.*

By Lemma 4 and 2, we have $\mu \models \lambda$ from $\rho \Rightarrow \underline{\iota}$ (line 4) and the well-formedness of $t[]$ with respect to $\gamma^*(\mu)$. As in the case of the equivalence query resolution algorithm, incorrect models from SMT solvers (line 3) simply guide the CDNF algorithm to other quantified invariants. Note that Algorithm 2 also gives a random answer if a membership query cannot be resolved through invariant approximations. The correctness of generated invariants is ensured by SMT solvers in the equivalence query resolution algorithm (Algorithm 1).

5.3 Main Loop

Algorithm 3 shows our invariant generation algorithm. It invokes the CDNF algorithm in the main loop. Whenever a query is made, our algorithm uses one of the query resolution algorithms (Algorithm 1 or 2) to give an answer. In both query resolution algorithms, we use the strongest under-approximation δ and the weakest over-approximation $\kappa \vee \epsilon$ to resolve queries from the learning algorithm. Observe that the equivalence and membership query resolution algorithms give random answers independently. They may send inconsistent answers to the CDNF algorithm. When inconsistencies arise, the main loop forces the learning algorithm to restart (line 6). If the CDNF algorithm infers a Boolean formula $\lambda \in \mathsf{Bool}_{B(A)}$, the first-order formula $t[\gamma(\lambda)]$ is an invariant for the annotated loop in the form of the template $t[]$.

Algorithm 3. Main Loop

Input: $\{\delta\}$ `while` κ `do` S $\{\epsilon\}$: an annotated loop; $t[]$: a template
Output: an invariant in the form of $t[]$

```
1 ι̲ := δ;
2 ῑ := κ ∨ ϵ;
3 repeat
4     try
5         λ := call CDNF with query resolution algorithms (Algorithm 1 and 2)
6     when inconsistent → continue
7 until λ is defined ;
8 return t[γ(λ)];
```

In contrast to traditional deterministic algorithms, our algorithm gives random answers in both query resolution algorithms. Due to the undecidability of first-order theories in SMT solvers, verifying quantified invariants and comparing invariant approximations are not solvable in general. If we committed to a particular solution deterministically, we would be forced to address computability issues. Random answers simply divert the learning algorithm to search for other quantified invariants and try the limit of SMT solvers. They could not be effective if there were very few solutions. Our thesis is that there are sufficiently many invariants for any given annotated loop in practice. As long as our random answers are consistent with one verifiable invariant, the CDNF algorithm is guaranteed to generate an invariant for us.

Similar to other invariant generation techniques based on predicate abstraction, our algorithm is not guaranteed to generate invariants. If no invariant can be expressed by the template with a given set of atomic propositions, our algorithm will not terminate. Moreover, if no invariant in the form of the given template can be verified by SMT solvers, our algorithm does not terminate either. On the other hand, if there is one verifiable invariant in the form of the given template, there is a sequence of random answers that leads to the verifiable invariant. If sufficiently many verifiable invariants are expressible in the form of the template, random answers almost surely guide the learning algorithm to one of them. Since our algorithmic learning approach with random answers does not commit to any particular invariant, it can be more flexible and hence effective than traditional deterministic techniques in practice.

Table 1. Experimental Results.
AP : # of atomic propositions, MEM : # of membership queries, EQ : # of equivalence queries, MEM_R : fraction of randomly resolved membership queries to MEM, EQ_R fraction of randomly resolved equivalence queries to EQ, $ITER$: # of the CDNF algorithm invocations, and σ_{Time} : standard deviation of the running time.

case	Template	AP	MEM	EQ	MEM_R	EQ_R	$ITER$	Time (s)	σ_{Time}(s)
`max`	$\forall k.[]$	7	5,968	1,742	65%	26%	269	5.71	7.01
`selection_sort`	$\forall k_1.\exists k_2.[]$	6	9,630	5,832	100%	4%	1,672	9.59	11.03
`devres`	$\forall k.[]$	7	2,084	1,214	91%	21%	310	0.92	0.66
`rm_pkey`	$\forall k.[]$	8	2,204	919	67%	20%	107	2.52	1.62
`tracepoint1`	$\exists k.[]$	4	246	195	61%	25%	31	0.26	0.15
`tracepoint2`	$\forall k_1.\exists k_2.[]$	7	33,963	13,063	69%	5%	2,088	157.55	230.40

6 Experiments

We have implemented a prototype[2] in OCaml. In our implementation, we use YICES as the SMT solver to resolve queries (Algorithm 1 and 2). Table 1 shows experimental results. We took two cases from the ten benchmarks in [20] with the same annotation (`max` and `selection_sort`). We also chose four `for` statements from Linux 2.6.28. We translated them into our language and annotated pre- and post-conditions manually. Sets of atomic proposition are manually chosen from the program texts. Benchmark `devres` is from library, `tracepoint1` and `tracepoint2` are from kernel, and `rm_pkey` is from InfiniBand device driver. The data are the average of 500 runs and collected on a 2.66GHz Intel Core2 Quad CPU with 8GB memory running Linux 2.6.28.

`devres` from Linux Library. Figure 5(c) shows an annotated loop extracted from a Linux library.[3] In the postcondition, we assert that ret implies $tbl[i] = 0$, and every element in the array $tbl[]$ is not equal to $addr$ otherwise. Using the set of atomic propositions $\{tbl[k] = addr,\ i < n,\ i = n,\ k < i,\ tbl[i] = 0,\ ret\}$ and the simple template $\forall k.[]$, our algorithm finds following quantified invariants in different runs:

$$\forall k.(k < i \Rightarrow tbl[k] \neq addr) \wedge (ret \Rightarrow tbl[i] = 0) \text{ and } \forall k.(k < i) \Rightarrow tbl[k] \neq addr.$$

Observe that our algorithm is able to infer an arbitrary quantifier-free formula (over a fixed set of atomic propositions) to fill the hole in the given template. A simple template such as $\forall k.[]$ suffices to serve as a hint in our approach.

`selection_sort` from [20]. Consider the selection sort algorithm in Figure 5(b). Let $'a[]$ denote the content of the array $a[]$ before the algorithm is executed. The postcondition states that the contents of array $a[]$ come from its old contents. In this test case, we apply our invariant generation algorithm to compute an

[2] Available at `http://ropas.snu.ac.kr/aplas10/qinv-learn-released.tar.gz`

[3] The source code can be found in function `devres` of `lib/devres.c` in Linux 2.6.28.

(a) rm_pkey
$\{\ i = 0 \wedge key \neq 0 \wedge \neg ret \wedge \neg break\}$
1 while$(i < n\ \wedge\ \neg break)$ do
2   if$(pkeys[i] = key)$ then
3      $pkeyrefs[i]:=pkeyrefs[i] - 1;$
4   if$(pkeyrefs[i] = 0)$ then
5        $pkeys[i]:=0;\ ret:=true;$
6   break:=true;
7   else $i:=i + 1;$
8 done
$\{(\neg ret \wedge \neg break) \Rightarrow (\forall k.k < n \Rightarrow pkeys[k] \neq key)$
$\wedge(\neg ret \wedge break) \Rightarrow (pkeys[i] = key \wedge pkeyrefs[i] \neq 0)$
$\wedge\ ret \Rightarrow (pkeyrefs[i] = 0 \wedge pkeys[i] = 0)\ \}$

(c) devres
$\{\ i = 0 \wedge \neg ret\ \}$
1 while $i < n \wedge \neg ret$ do
2   if $tbl[i] = addr$ then
3      $tbl[i]:=0;\ ret:=true$
4   else
5      $i:=i + 1$
6 end
$\{(\neg ret \Rightarrow \forall k.\ k < n \Rightarrow tbl[k] \neq addr)$
$\wedge(ret \Rightarrow tbl[i] = 0)\ \}$

(b) selection_sort
$\{\ i = 0\ \}$
1 while $i < n - 1$ do
2   min:=i;
3    $j:=i + 1;$
4   while $j < n$ do
5   if $a[j] < a[min]$ then
6   min:=j;
7      $j:=j + 1;$
8   done
9   if $i\neq min$ then
10     $tmp:=a[i];$
11     $a[i]:=a[min];$
12     $a[min]:=tmp;$
13   $i:=i + 1;$
14 done
$\{(i \geq n - 1)$
$\wedge (\forall k_1.k_1 < n \Rightarrow$
$(\exists k_2.k_2 < n \wedge a[k_1] = {'}a[k_2]))\}$

Fig. 5. Benchmark Examples: (a) rm_pkey from Linux InfiniBand driver, (b) selection_sort from [20], and (c) devres from Linux library

invariant to establish the postcondition of the outer loop. For computing the invariant of the outer loop, we make use of the inner loop's specification.

We use the following set of atomic propositions: $\{k_1 \geq 0,\ k_1 < i,\ k_1 = i,$ $k_2 < n,\ k_2 = n,\ a[k_1] = {'}a[k_2],\ i < n - 1,\ i = min\}$. Using the template $\forall k_1.\exists k_2.[]$, our algorithm infers following invariants in different runs:

$$\forall k_1.(\exists k_2.[(k_2 < n \wedge a[k_1] = {'}a[k_2]) \vee k_1 \geq i]);\text{ and}$$
$$\forall k_1.(\exists k_2.[(k_1 \geq i \vee min = i \vee k_2 < n) \wedge (k_1 \geq i \vee (min \neq i \wedge a[k_1] =' a[k_2]))]).$$

Note that all membership queries are resolved randomly due to the alternation of quantifiers in array theory. Still a simple random walk suffices to find invariants in this example. Moreover, templates allow us to infer not only universally quantified invariants but also first-order invariants with alternating quantifications. Inferring arbitrary quantifier-free formulae over a fixed set of atomic propositions again greatly simplifies the form of templates used in this example.

rm_pkey from Linux InfiniBand Driver. Figure 5(a) is a while statement extracted from Linux InfiniBand driver.[4] The conjuncts in the postcondition represent (1) if the loop terminates without break, all elements of *pkeys* are not equal to *key* (line 2); (2) if the loop terminates with break but *ret* is false, then *pkeys[i]* is equal to *key* (line 2) but *pkeyrefs[i]* is not equal to zero (line 4); (3) if *ret* is true after the loop, then both *pkeyrefs[i]* (line 4) and *pkeys[i]* (line 5) are equal to zero. From the postcondition, we guess that an invariant

---

[4] The source code can be found in function rm_pkey of drivers/infiniband/hw/ ipath/ipath_mad.c in Linux 2.6.28.

can be universally quantified with k. Using the simple template $\forall k.[]$ and the set of atomic propositions $\{ret,\ break,\ i < n,\ k < i,\ pkeys[i] = 0,\ pkeys[i] = key,\ pkeyrefs[i] = 0,\ pkeyrefs[k] = key\}$, our algorithm finds following quantified invariants in different runs:

$$(\forall k.(k < i) \Rightarrow pkeys[k] \neq key) \wedge (ret \Rightarrow pkeyrefs[i] = 0 \wedge pkeys[i] = 0)$$
$$\wedge\ (\neg ret \wedge break \Rightarrow pkeys[i] = key \wedge pkeyrefs[i] \neq 0);\ \text{and}$$
$$(\forall k.(\neg ret \vee \neg break \vee (pkeyrefs[i] = 0 \wedge pkeys[i] = 0)) \wedge (pkeys[k] \neq key \vee k \geq i)$$
$$\wedge(\neg ret \vee (pkeyrefs[i] = 0 \wedge pkeys[i] = 0 \wedge i < n \wedge break))$$
$$\wedge\ (\neg break \vee pkeyrefs[i] \neq 0 \vee ret) \wedge (\neg break \vee pkeys[i] = key \vee ret)).$$

In spite of undecidability of first-order theories in YICES and random answers, each of the 3000 ($= 6 \times 500$) runs in our experiments infers an invariant successfully. Moreover, several quantified invariants are found in each case among 500 runs. This suggests that invariants are abundant. Note that the templates in the test cases `selection_sort` and `tracepoint2` have alternating quantification. Satisfiability of alternating quantified formulae is in general undecidable. That is why both cases have substantially more restarts than the others. Interestingly, our algorithm is able to generate a verifiable invariant in each run. Our simple randomized mechanism proves to be effective even for most difficult cases.

7 Related Work

Comparing with the work [15] of generating quantifier-free invariants, we develop the following technical extensions. First, we integrate potential counterexamples in resolving equivalence query algorithm (line 6 - 7 in Algorithm 1, and line 3 in Algorithm 2) instead of restarting. Due to the undecidability of satisfiability of quantified formulae, SMT solvers often give potential counterexamples. We exploit potential counterexamples to enhance our algorithm. Second, a new condition (Definition 1) to answer positively in resolving membership queries is proposed. Without this condition, we can answer negatively to membership queries.

In contrast to previous template-based approaches [20,9], our template is more general as it allows arbitrary hole-filling quantifier-free formulae. The templates in [20] can only be filled with formulae over conjunctions of predicates from a given set. Any disjunction must be explicitly specified as part of a template. In [9], the authors consider invariants of the form $E \wedge \bigwedge_{j=1}^{n} \forall U_j(F_j \Rightarrow e_j)$, where E, F_j and e_j must be quantifier free finite conjuctions of atomic facts.

Existing technologies can strengthen our framework. Firstly, its completeness can be increased by more powerful decision procedures [6,8,21] and theorem provers [18,1,19]. Moreover, our approach can be improved by using more accurate approximations from existing invariant generation techniques. The tool InvGen collects reached states satisfying the program invariants, and also computes a collection of invariants for efficient invariant generation [11]. They can be used as under- and over-approximations, respectively.

Regarding the generation of unquantified invariants, a constraint analysis approach is proposed in [10]. Invariants in the combined theory of linear arithmetic and uninterpreted functions are synthesized in [2], while InvGen [11] presents an efficient approach for linear arithmetic invariants. For quantified loop invariants, Skolemization is used for generating universally quantified invariants [7]. In [18], a paramodulation-based saturation prover is extended to generate universally quantified invariants by interpolation.

With respect to the analysis of properties of array contents, Halbwachs et al. [12] handle programs which manipulate arrays by sequential traversal, incrementing (or decrementing) their index at each iteration, and which access arrays by simple expressions of the loop index. A loop property generation method for loops iterating over multi-dimensional arrays is introduced in [13]. For inferring range predicates, Jhala and McMillan [14] described a framework that uses infeasible counterexample paths. As a deficiency, the prover may find proofs refuting short paths, but which do not generalize to longer paths. Due to this problem, this approach [14] fails to prove that an implementation of insertion sort correctly sorts an array.

8 Conclusions

By combining algorithmic learning, decision procedures, predicate abstraction, and templates, we present a technique for generating quantified invariants. The new technique searches for invariants in the given template form guided by query resolution algorithms. We exploit the flexibility of algorithmic learning by deploying a randomized query resolution algorithm. When there are sufficiently many invariants, random answers will not prevent algorithmic learning from inferring verifiable invariants. Our experiments show that our learning-based approach is able to infer non-trivial quantified invariants with this naïve randomized resolution for some loops extracted from Linux drivers.

Under- and over-approximations are presently derived from annotations provided by users. They can in fact be obtained by other techniques such as static analysis. For deciding the set of atomic propositions, it will be interesting whether existing techniques [4,17] are applicable. The integration of various refinement techniques for predicate abstraction will certainly be an important future work.

Acknowledgment. We are grateful to Wontae Choi, Suwon Jang, Will Klieber, Wonchan Lee, Ben Lickly, Bruno Oliveira, and Sungwoo Park for their detailed comments and helpful suggestions. We also thank Heejae Shin for implementing OCaml binding for Yices.

References

1. Bertot, Y., Castéran, P.: Interactive Theorem Proving and Program Development. Coq'Art: The Calculus of Inductive Constructions. Texts in Theoretical Computer Science. Springer, Heidelberg (2004)
2. Beyer, D., Henzinger, T.A., Majumdar, R., Rybalchenko, A.: Invariant synthesis for combined theories. In: Cook, B., Podelski, A. (eds.) VMCAI 2007. LNCS, vol. 4349, pp. 378–394. Springer, Heidelberg (2007)

3. Bshouty, N.H.: Exact learning boolean functions via the monotone theory. Information and Computation 123, 146–153 (1995)
4. Clarke, E.M., Grumberg, O., Jha, S., Lu, Y., Veith, H.: Counterexample-guided abstraction refinement. In: Emerson, E.A., Sistla, A.P. (eds.) CAV 2000. LNCS, vol. 1855, pp. 154–169. Springer, Heidelberg (2000)
5. David, C., Jung, Y., Kong, S., Wang, B.Y., Yi, K.: Inferring quantified invariants via algorithmic learning, decision procedure, and predicate abstraction. Technical Memorandum ROSAEC-2010-007, Research On Software Analysis for Error-Free Computing (2010)
6. Dutertre, B., Moura, L.D.: The Yices SMT solver. Technical report, SRI International (2006)
7. Flanagan, C., Qadeer, S.: Predicate abstraction for software verification. In: POPL, pp. 191–202. ACM, New York (2002)
8. Ge, Y., Moura, L.: Complete instantiation for quantified formulas in satisfiabiliby modulo theories. In: Bouajjani, A., Maler, O. (eds.) CAV 2009. LNCS, vol. 5643, pp. 306–320. Springer, Heidelberg (2009)
9. Gulwani, S., McCloskey, B., Tiwari, A.: Lifting abstract interpreters to quantified logical domains. In: POPL, pp. 235–246. ACM, New York (2008)
10. Gulwani, S., Srivastava, S., Venkatesan, R.: Constraint-based invariant inference over predicate abstraction. In: Jones, N.D., Müller-Olm, M. (eds.) VMCAI 2009. LNCS, vol. 5403, pp. 120–135. Springer, Heidelberg (2009)
11. Gupta, A., Rybalchenko, A.: Invgen: An efficient invariant generator. In: Bouajjani, A., Maler, O. (eds.) CAV 2009. LNCS, vol. 5643, pp. 634–640. Springer, Heidelberg (2009)
12. Halbwachs, N., Péron, M.: Discovering properties about arrays in simple programs. In: PLDI, pp. 339–348 (2008)
13. Henzinger, T.A., Hottelier, T., Kovács, L., Voronkov, A.: Invariant and type inference for matrices. In: Barthe, G., Hermenegildo, M. (eds.) VMCAI 2010. LNCS, vol. 5944, pp. 163–179. Springer, Heidelberg (2010)
14. Jhala, R., McMillan, K.L.: Array abstractions from proofs. In: Damm, W., Hermanns, H. (eds.) CAV 2007. LNCS, vol. 4590, pp. 193–206. Springer, Heidelberg (2007)
15. Jung, Y., Kong, S., Wang, B.Y., Yi, K.: Deriving invariants in propositional logic by algorithmic learning, decision procedure, and predicate abstraction. In: Barthe, G., Hermenegildo, M. (eds.) VMCAI 2010. LNCS, vol. 5944, pp. 180–196. Springer, Heidelberg (2010)
16. Kroening, D., Strichman, O.: Decision Procedures an algorithmic point of view. EATCS. Springer, Heidelberg (2008)
17. McMillan, K.L.: Lazy abstraction with interpolants. In: Ball, T., Jones, R.B. (eds.) CAV 2006. LNCS, vol. 4144, pp. 123–136. Springer, Heidelberg (2006)
18. McMillan, K.L.: Quantified invariant generation using an interpolating saturation prover. In: Ramakrishnan, C.R., Rehof, J. (eds.) TACAS 2008. LNCS, vol. 4963, pp. 413–427. Springer, Heidelberg (2008)
19. Nipkow, T., Paulson, L.C., Wenzel, M.T.: Isabelle/HOL. LNCS, vol. 2283. Springer, Heidelberg (2002)
20. Srivastava, S., Gulwani, S.: Program verification using templates over predicate abstraction. In: PLDI, pp. 223–234. ACM, New York (2009)
21. Srivastava, S., Gulwani, S., Foster, J.S.: VS3: SMT solvers for program verification. In: Bouajjani, A., Maler, O. (eds.) CAV 2009. LNCS, vol. 5643, pp. 702–708. Springer, Heidelberg (2009)

Relational Parametricity for a Polymorphic Linear Lambda Calculus

Jianzhou Zhao, Qi Zhang, and Steve Zdancewic

University of Pennsylvania
{jianzhou,qzh,stevez}@cis.upenn.edu

Abstract. This paper presents a novel syntactic logical relation for a polymorphic linear λ-calculus that treats all types as linear and introduces the constructor ! to account for intuitionistic terms, and System F°—an extension of System F that uses kinds to distinguish linear from intuitionistic types. We define a logical relation for open values under both open linear and intuitionistic contexts, then extend it for open terms with evaluation and open relation substitutions. Relations that instantiate type quantifiers are for open terms and types. We demonstrate the applicability of this logical relation through its soundness with respect to contextual equivalence, along with free theorems for linearity that are difficult to achieve by closed logical relations. When interpreting types on only closed terms, the model defaults to a closed logical relation that is both sound and complete with respect to contextual equivalence and is sufficient to reason about isomorphisms of type encodings. All of our results have been mechanically verified in Coq.

1 Introduction

In the polymorphic lambda calculus, System F [13], relational parametricity [18] is the essence of type abstraction. It asserts that a parametrically polymorphic function must use the same algorithm to compute its result, independently of the instantiated types.

Relational parametricity can be used to derive equivalences involving functional programs by observing solely the types of those programs, with no knowledge of the functions' actual definitions. Wadler [23] refers to these equivalences as the "free theorems" associated with particular types. For instance, we can conclude that there is no closed inhabitant of type $\forall\alpha.\alpha$ in a pure setting. If there were such a term, it must yield a value of any type at which it is instantiated, but there is no uniform algorithm to compute a value at any type. Therefore, $\forall\alpha.\alpha$ is an empty type. Given a closed polymorphic function B with type $\forall\alpha.\alpha \to \alpha \to \alpha$, for any type τ, $B[\tau]$ evaluates to a function F of type $\tau \to \tau \to \tau$. Since B is polymorphic, F cannot depend on its arguments. Given any closed values $V_1{:}\tau$, $V_2{:}\tau$, F must return one of the arguments directly or yield a term equivalent to one of the arguments. Therefore we can conclude that B must behave like one of $\Lambda\alpha.\ \lambda x{:}\alpha.\ \lambda y{:}\alpha.\ x$ or $\Lambda\alpha.\ \lambda x{:}\alpha.\ \lambda y{:}\alpha.\ y$.

Linearity and Parametricity. Bierman et al. [6] used $\top\top$-closed [17] logical relations for the parametricity principle of the programming language Lily—a dual intuitionistic linear lambda calculus [4] with polymorphic types and recursion. They proved isomorphisms of type encodings via relational parametricity properties. In the language without recursion, their model defaults to the standard logical relations (that interpret types

K. Ueda (Ed.): APLAS 2010, LNCS 6461, pp. 344–359, 2010.

with pairs of closed terms), while the free theorems obtained by the standard techniques do not tell the whole story because linearity changes the set of possible well-typed programs. Consider a *linear* variant of the Boolean type used above: $\forall\alpha.\alpha \multimap \alpha \multimap \alpha$. Here, $\multimap$ is a linear function type. The following standard parametricity holds:

Theorem 1 (Parametricity). *If $\Gamma; \Delta \vdash M{:}\tau$, then $\Gamma; \Delta \vdash M \simeq^{\star}_{\mathsf{log}} M \in \tau$.*

Here, $\simeq^{\star}_{\mathsf{log}}$ denotes a standard logical relation. As in the case for ordinary System F, this parametricity theorem implies that any closed term M with type $\forall\alpha.\alpha \multimap \alpha \multimap \alpha$ must behave like either $\Lambda\alpha.\lambda a_1{:}\alpha.\lambda a_2{:}\alpha.a_1$ or $\Lambda\alpha.\lambda a_1{:}\alpha.\lambda a_2{:}\alpha.a_2$. However, the linear variables a_1 and a_2 must be used exactly once in the body of M. Therefore, *neither* of these expressions is well-typed. More generally, the free theorem of this type should say that this is an *empty* type—there are no terms that inhabit it! On the other hand, the similar type $\forall\alpha.!\alpha \multimap !\alpha \multimap !\alpha$, in which ! constructs an intuitionistic term, is still isomorphic to the Booleans. Moreover, analogous examples can be constructed in System F$^{\circ}$ [16]—a variant of polymorphic linear lambda calculus that uses the kinds, instead of ! type constructor, to distinguish linear from intuitionistic types. These observations suggest that there might be a stronger linear parametricity that distinguishes these cases.

The key idea of this paper is that linearity properties can be properly taken into account by using *open* logical relations. There is a large body of work on logical relations that interprets types as relations R, which are sets of pairs of *closed* terms with *closed* types under empty contexts. Linear type systems, however, restrict the use of variables of linear types in a *non-empty* context. Intuitively, if logical relations interpret types by relations for *open* terms under non-empty linear contexts, the free theorem associated with the above type should show that it is void.

Suppose we apply M to open values V_1 and V_2 with type τ where V_1 and V_2 are logically related to themselves under disjoint linear contexts respectively. By the free theorem we have $M[\tau]\,V_1\,V_2 \longrightarrow^* V_1$ or $M[\tau]\,V_1\,V_2 \longrightarrow^* V_2$. But neither of the above evaluations is valid, because the set of free linear variables in a well-formed expression should be preserved under reduction; in other words, the evaluation should not consume the set of free linear variables from either V_1 or V_2. With this stronger logical relation, we can conclude that there is no such closed M of type $\forall\alpha.\alpha \multimap \alpha \multimap \alpha$. However, closed terms with type $\forall\alpha.!\alpha \multimap !\alpha \multimap !\alpha$ still behave like polymorphic boolean functions because the system ensures that intuitionistic values V_1 and V_2 cannot capture linear variables. Section 4.1 formally proves these results, and explains that the standard logical relations cannot distinguish them. Although Tait [21], Girard [13], Crary [10] and Hasegawa [14] developed logical relations for *open* terms, their works do not support both polymorphism and linearity. We discuss related work in Section 3.

The specific contributions of this paper include:

1. Section 2 gives the type system and operational semantics for PDILL that combines a term calculus for Plotkin's dual intuitionistic linear logic [4] with impredicative polymorphism. We then discuss related work, provide a novel syntactic logical relation that interprets types with pairs of open terms for PDILL in Section 3, and show that every well-typed expression is related to itself in the interpretation of its type by this logical relation. This logical relation is sound with respect to contextual equivalence, and therefore suitable for reasoning about program equivalence. When

interpreting types on only closed terms, it defaults to a standard logical relation that is both sound and complete with respect to contextual equivalence.
2. In Section 4 we give several applications of this logical relational model: free theorems for linearity that are difficult to achieve by standard logical relations, properties of contextual equivalence, and isomorphisms of type encodings.
3. The results for PDILL also carry over to System F$^\circ$ [16]. All of our results (including PDILL, System F$^\circ$ and System F) are available at `http://www.cis.upenn.edu/~jianzhou/parametricity4linf`, and are mechanically verified in Coq [9] and OTT [20]. We do not only view this formalization as supporting material, but also as an extensive formalization for polymorphic (linear) languages in Coq [3]. Section 5 briefly discusses the mechanical proofs and future work.

2 A Brief Introduction to PDILL

In programming languages, linear type systems check the ability to duplicate and to discard a resource. There are many variants on linear type systems to distinguish linear from intuitionistic variables [24]. PDILL combines a term calculus for Plotkin's dual intuitionistic linear logic [4] with impredicative polymorphism. Figure 1, 2 and 3 give the syntax, typing rules and evaluation relations for PDILL. Our typing rules take an intuitionistic context Γ — an ordered list of both type and intuitionistic term variables, and a linear context Δ that binds only linear term variables. Intuitionistic variables x that may be duplicated and discarded, and linear variables a that must be used exactly once are syntactically different. We encode intuitionistic lambda abstractions $\lambda x{:}\tau_1.M_2$ as $\lambda a{:}!\tau_1.\mathbf{let}\,!x = a\,\mathbf{in}\,M_2$ with type $!\tau_1 \multimap \tau_2$.

Typing rules can drop unused variables (weakening) or use a variable more than once (contraction) from an intuitionistic context Γ, but must use variables exactly once from a linear context Δ. Linear usage of Δ holds because T_IVAR allows only an empty Δ, and T_LVAR takes a linear context that consists of only the variable typechecked. Rules T_LVAR and T_IVAR permit weakening and contraction by allowing an arbitrary Γ at the leaves of typing derivations, while rule T_APP duplicates Γ but splits Δ. T_APP splits Δ using the operation $\uplus$, which allows type variables and intuitionistic expression variables to propagate to both sides of an application while restricting linear variables. We treat all types as linear, and use the ! constructor to account for terms that can be discarded or duplicated. A ! value cannot capture linear variables, and is used lazily. We have two distinct forms of pairs: (M_1, M_2) is a muplicative pair where

$$
\begin{array}{ll}
\text{Terms } M ::= x \mid a \mid \lambda a{:}\tau.M \mid M\,M' \mid \Lambda\alpha.M \mid M[\tau] \mid !M \mid \mathbf{let}\,!x = M\,\mathbf{in}\,M' \\
\qquad\qquad \mid \langle M, M'\rangle \mid M.1 \mid M.2 \mid (M, M') \mid \mathbf{let}\,(a, a') = M\,\mathbf{in}\,M' \\
\text{Values } V, U ::= \lambda a{:}\tau.M \mid \Lambda\alpha.M \mid !M \mid \langle M, M'\rangle \mid (V, V') \\
\text{Types } \tau, \sigma ::= \alpha \mid \tau \multimap \tau' \mid \forall\alpha.\tau \mid !\tau \mid \tau \& \tau' \mid \tau \otimes \tau' \\
\text{Intuitionistic contexts } \Gamma, G ::= \cdot \mid \Gamma, x{:}\tau \mid \Gamma, \alpha \qquad \text{Linear contexts } \Delta, D ::= \cdot \mid \Delta, a{:}\tau
\end{array}
$$

Fig. 1. Syntax for PDILL

$$\boxed{\vdash \Gamma}$$

$$\frac{}{\vdash \cdot} \qquad \frac{\vdash \Gamma \quad \Gamma \vdash \tau \quad x \notin dom(\Gamma)}{\vdash \Gamma, x{:}\tau} \qquad \frac{\vdash \Gamma \quad \alpha \notin dom(\Gamma)}{\vdash \Gamma, \alpha}$$

$$\boxed{\Gamma \vdash \Delta}$$

$$\frac{\vdash \Gamma}{\Gamma \vdash \cdot} \qquad \frac{\Gamma \vdash \Delta \quad \Gamma \vdash \tau \quad a \notin dom(\Delta)}{\Gamma \vdash \Delta, a{:}\tau}$$

$$\boxed{\Gamma \vdash \tau}$$

$$\frac{\vdash \Gamma \quad \alpha \in \Gamma}{\Gamma \vdash \alpha} \qquad \frac{\Gamma \vdash \tau_1 \quad \Gamma \vdash \tau_2}{\Gamma \vdash \tau_1 \multimap \tau_2} \qquad \frac{\Gamma, \alpha \vdash \tau}{\Gamma \vdash \forall\alpha.\tau}$$

$$\frac{\Gamma \vdash \tau}{\Gamma \vdash !\tau} \qquad \frac{\Gamma \vdash \tau \quad \Gamma \vdash \tau'}{\Gamma \vdash \tau \& \tau'} \qquad \frac{\Gamma \vdash \tau \quad \Gamma \vdash \tau'}{\Gamma \vdash \tau \otimes \tau'}$$

$$\boxed{\Gamma \vdash \Delta_1 \Cup \Delta_2 = \Delta}$$

$$\frac{\vdash \Gamma}{\Gamma \vdash \cdot \Cup \cdot = \cdot} \qquad \frac{\Gamma \vdash \tau \quad \Gamma \vdash \Delta_1 \Cup \Delta_2 = \Delta \quad a \notin \Gamma, \Delta}{\Gamma \vdash \Delta_1, a{:}\tau \Cup \Delta_2 = \Delta, a{:}\tau} \qquad \frac{\Gamma \vdash \tau \quad \Gamma \vdash \Delta_1 \Cup \Delta_2 = \Delta \quad a \notin \Gamma, \Delta}{\Gamma \vdash \Delta_1 \Cup \Delta_2, a{:}\tau = \Delta, a{:}\tau}$$

$$\boxed{\Gamma; \Delta \vdash M{:}\tau}$$

$$\frac{\Gamma \vdash (a{:}\tau)}{\Gamma; a{:}\tau \vdash a{:}\tau}\ \text{T\_LVAR} \qquad \frac{\vdash \Gamma \quad x{:}\tau \in \Gamma}{\Gamma; \cdot \vdash x{:}\tau}\ \text{T\_IVAR}$$

$$\frac{\Gamma \vdash \tau_1 \quad \Gamma; \Delta, a{:}\tau_1 \vdash M_2{:}\tau_2}{\Gamma; \Delta \vdash \lambda a{:}\tau_1.M_2{:}\tau_1 \multimap \tau_2}\ \text{T\_ABS} \qquad \frac{\Gamma; \Delta_1 \vdash M_1{:}\tau_{11} \multimap \tau_{12} \quad \Gamma; \Delta_2 \vdash M_2{:}\tau_{11} \quad \Gamma \vdash \Delta_1 \Cup \Delta_2 = \Delta_3}{\Gamma; \Delta_3 \vdash M_1\ M_2{:}\tau_{12}}\ \text{T\_APP}$$

$$\frac{\Gamma, \alpha; \Delta \vdash M_1{:}\tau}{\Gamma; \Delta \vdash \Lambda\alpha.M_1{:}\forall\alpha.\tau}\ \text{T\_TABS} \qquad \frac{\Gamma; \Delta \vdash M_1{:}\forall\alpha.\tau \quad \Gamma \vdash \tau_1}{\Gamma; \Delta \vdash M_1[\tau_1]{:}\tau\{\tau_1/\alpha\}}\ \text{T\_TAPP}$$

$$\frac{\Gamma; \cdot \vdash M{:}\tau}{\Gamma; \cdot \vdash !M{:}!\tau}\ \text{T\_BANG} \qquad \frac{\Gamma; \Delta_1 \vdash M_1{:}!\tau_1 \quad \Gamma, x{:}\tau_1; \Delta_2 \vdash M_2{:}\tau_2 \quad \Gamma \vdash \Delta_1 \Cup \Delta_2 = \Delta_3}{\Gamma; \Delta_3 \vdash \textbf{let}\,!x = M_1\ \textbf{in}\ M_2{:}\tau_2}\ \text{T\_LET}$$

$$\frac{\Gamma; \Delta \vdash M_1{:}\tau_1 \quad \Gamma; \Delta \vdash M_2{:}\tau_2}{\Gamma; \Delta \vdash \langle M_1, M_2\rangle{:}\tau_1 \& \tau_2}\ \text{T\_APAIR} \qquad \frac{\Gamma; \Delta \vdash M{:}\tau_1 \& \tau_2}{\Gamma; \Delta \vdash M.i{:}\tau_i}\ \text{T\_PROJI}$$

$$\frac{\Gamma; \Delta_1 \vdash M_1{:}\tau_1 \quad \Gamma; \Delta_2 \vdash M_2{:}\tau_2 \quad \Gamma \vdash \Delta_1 \Cup \Delta_2 = \Delta_3}{\Gamma; \Delta_3 \vdash (M_1, M_2){:}\tau_1 \otimes \tau_2}\ \text{T\_PPAIR} \qquad \frac{\Gamma; \Delta_1 \vdash M_1{:}\tau_1 \otimes \tau_2 \quad \Gamma; \Delta_2, a_1{:}\tau_1, a_2{:}\tau_2 \vdash M_2{:}\tau \quad \Gamma \vdash \Delta_1 \Cup \Delta_2 = \Delta_3}{\Gamma; \Delta_3 \vdash \textbf{let}\,(a_1, a_2) = M_1\ \textbf{in}\ M_2{:}\tau}\ \text{T\_PLET}$$

Fig. 2. Kinding and typing rules for PDILL

both components are used eagerly (eliminated via pattern matching using let), and the free linear variables of M_1 and M_2 are disjoint; $\langle M_1, M_2\rangle$ is an additive pair where only one component is used lazily (projected), and the free linear variables of M_1 and M_2 are identical. Lemma 1 states that linear contexts Δ contain exactly the free linear variables in a well-typed expression:

Lemma 1. *If $\Gamma; \Delta \vdash M{:}\tau$, then the set of free linear variables in M is* $\mathsf{dom}(\Delta)$.

By the preservation lemma and Lemma 1, we also have that the set of free linear variables in a well-typed term is preserved under reduction:

Lemma 2. *If $\Gamma; \Delta \vdash M{:}\tau$, and $M \longrightarrow^* M'$, then M and M' contain the same free linear variables.*

$$\text{Evaluation Contexts } E ::= \square \mid E\,M \mid V\,E \mid E[\tau] \mid E.1 \mid E.2 \mid (E, M) \mid (V, E) \mid \textbf{let}\,(a, a') = E\,\textbf{in}\,M \mid \textbf{let}\,!x = E\,\textbf{in}\,M$$

$$\boxed{M \longrightarrow M'}$$

$$\frac{M \longrightarrow M'}{E[M] \longrightarrow E[M']} \qquad \frac{}{(\Lambda\alpha.M)[\tau] \longrightarrow M\{\tau/\alpha\}} \qquad \frac{}{\textbf{let}\,!x = !M_1\,\textbf{in}\,M_2 \longrightarrow M_2\{M_1/x\}}$$

$$\frac{}{(\lambda a{:}\tau.M)\,V' \longrightarrow M\{V'/a\}} \qquad \frac{}{\textbf{let}\,(a_1, a_2) = (V_1, V_2)\,\textbf{in}\,M \longrightarrow M\{V_1/a_1\}\{V_2/a_2\}}$$

Fig. 3. Evaluation relations for PDILL

3 Parametricity for PDILL

This section presents the main contribution of this paper, namely a syntactic logical relation for PDILL. Proof by logical relations is a fundamental technique for proving properties of programming languages. This technique was first developed by Tait [21] to prove that the simply typed λ-calculus is strongly normalizing, and was adopted by Girard [13] to prove normalization for System F^ω.

Although their logical relations were for *open* terms via open substitutions, there are a large number of related works on logical relations that interpret types as relations for closed terms. Its basic idea is to first define an equivalence relation for closed values inductively on type structures. The case of arrow types is a typical case where two closed functions are logically related at the type $\tau_1 \rightarrow \tau_2$ if they evaluate to values that are logically related at τ_2 with closed arguments that are logically related at τ_1. Logical relations are extended to closed terms with evaluation, and then extended to open terms via closing substitutions. The fundamental theorem proves that any well-typed term, under those closing substitutions, is related to itself by the relation induced logically by its type. To build logical relations for recursive functions and quantified types, Pitts [17] developed logical relations based on the notion of $\top\top$-closed relations. Bierman et al. [6] also used $\top\top$-closed relations for the parametricity principle of the programming language Lily—a polymorphic intuitionistic/linear lambda calculus. Ahmed [1] proposed step-indexed logical relations for recursive and stateful types. Ahmed et al. [2], Birkedal et al. [8] extended step-indexed logical relations with possible "worlds" based on Kripke logical relations for increasingly realistic languages.

Crary [10] developed the technique of Kripke logical relations for *open* terms under open contexts to show the completeness of an equivalence algorithm for terms in a simply typed λ-calculus. To ensure that a relation holds by adding variables to the current context, the logical relation is required to be monotone with respect to contexts analogous to "worlds" in Kripke models. Hasegawa [14] developed a notion of Kripke logical predicates for two fragments of intuitionistic linear logic (MILL and DILL) in terms of their category-theoretic models. However these logical relations do not support both polymorphism and linearity.

Our logical relation first interprets types as relations for pairs of *open* values, then extends to logical relations for *open* terms with evaluation and *open* relation substitutions. Open relation substitutions map term variables to related open values, and type variables to relations for open terms. The fundamental theorem shows that a well-typed term, under open substitutions and evaluation, is related to itself in the interpretation of its type. Lemma 1 and 2 also prove that the set of the free linear variables in a well-typed term is equal to its linear context, and preserved under reduction. Section 4 illustrates how these properties and logical relations eliminate possible inhabitants for a type.

3.1 Definitions

Figure 4 gives a logical relation for PDILL. In the following sections, we shaded the difference in definitions, lemmas and proofs between our open logical relation and a closed one. Without shaded parts, the formalism defaults to the setting of a closed logical relation. We abbreviate $\Gamma;\Delta \vdash M{:}\tau \wedge \Gamma;\Delta \vdash M'{:}\tau$ to $\Gamma;\Delta \vdash M, M'{:}\tau$, and $\cdot;\cdot \vdash J$ to $\vdash J$. A type relation substitution, θ, maps type variables to relations R for pairs of open terms with type τ and τ'. We use θ_l and θ_r to denote relation type substitutions. γ and δ are intuitionistic and linear open value relation substitutions respectively. We also use γ_l, γ_r, δ_l, and δ_r to denote relation value substitutions.

Type Substitution Contexts	$\theta ::= \cdot \mid \theta, \alpha{\mapsto}(R, \tau, \tau')$
Intuitionistic Substitution Contexts	$\gamma ::= \cdot \mid \gamma, x{\mapsto}(V, V')$
Linear Substitution Contexts	$\delta ::= \cdot \mid \delta, a{\mapsto}(V, V')$

To simplify the definition of substitutions, we require that the domains of substitutions are disjoint from the free variables of types and values in the ranges of substitutions. Thus types and values in substitutions do not reuse any variable in their domains. We use Γ and Δ to typecheck the domains of substitutions, and G and D to denote contexts that typecheck types, relations, and terms in the ranges of θ, γ and δ. Our definitions force the variables of G and D to be disjoint from the variables of Γ and Δ. This simplification has been chosen since all parametricity reasoning in our experience involves only disjoint variables. We consider the definition of substitutions on types and values that can reuse variables in domains of substitutions in future work.

Two open PDILL values are related at type τ under a relation substitution θ, written $G;D \vdash V \sim V' \in \tau{:}\theta$ and defined inductively on type structures. An intuitionistic context G and a linear context D contain the free type and term variables in the values

$\boxed{G; D \vdash V \sim V' \in \tau{:}\theta}$ Related open values

$$G; D \vdash V \sim V' \in \alpha{:}\theta \triangleq \quad \text{OVR\_VAR}$$
$$\alpha{\mapsto}(R, \tau, \tau') \in \theta \wedge (V, V') \in R$$

$$G; D \vdash \lambda a{:}\tau_1.M \sim \lambda a{:}\tau_1.M' \in \tau_1 \multimap \tau_2{:}\theta \triangleq \quad \text{OVR\_ARR}$$
$$\forall (G; \boldsymbol{D_1} \vdash V{:}\theta_l(\tau_1) \wedge G; \boldsymbol{D_1} \vdash V'{:}\theta_r(\tau_1) \wedge$$
$$G; \boldsymbol{D_1} \vdash V \sim V' \in \tau_1{:}\theta \wedge G \vdash D, \boldsymbol{D_1}).$$
$$G; D, \boldsymbol{D_1} \vdash (\lambda a{:}\tau_1.M)\, V \simeq (\lambda a{:}\tau_1.M')\, V' \in \tau_2{:}\theta$$

$$G; D \vdash \Lambda\alpha.M \sim \Lambda\alpha.M' \in \forall\alpha.\tau{:}\theta \triangleq \quad \text{OVR\_ALL}$$
$$\forall (R \in \tau_2 \leftrightarrow \tau_2' \dashv \boldsymbol{G}).$$
$$G; D \vdash (\Lambda\alpha.M)[\tau_2] \simeq (\Lambda\alpha.M')[\tau_2'] \in \tau{:}(\theta, \alpha{\mapsto}(R, \tau_2, \tau_2'))$$

$$G; D \vdash !M \sim !M' \in !\tau{:}\theta \triangleq \quad \text{OVR\_BANG}$$
$$G; D \vdash M \simeq M' \in \tau{:}\theta$$

$$G; D \vdash \langle M_1, M_2 \rangle \sim \langle M_1', M_2' \rangle \in \tau_1 \& \tau_2{:}\theta \triangleq \quad \text{OVR\_WITH}$$
$$G; D \vdash M_1 \simeq M_1' \in \tau_1{:}\theta \wedge G; D \vdash M_2 \simeq M_2' \in \tau_2{:}\theta$$

$$G; D \vdash (V_1, V_2) \sim (V_1', V_2') \in \tau_1 \otimes \tau_2{:}\theta \triangleq \quad \text{OVR\_TENSOR}$$
$$\exists D_1\, D_2, G; D_1 \vdash V_1 \sim V_1' \in \tau_1{:}\theta \wedge G; D_2 \vdash V_2 \sim V_2' \in \tau_2{:}\theta$$
$$\wedge\, G \vdash D_1 \Cup D_2 = D$$

$\boxed{G; D \vdash M \simeq M' \in \tau{:}\theta}$ Related open terms

$$\frac{G; D \vdash M{:}\theta_l(\tau) \quad G; D \vdash M'{:}\theta_r(\tau) \quad M \longrightarrow^* V \quad M' \longrightarrow^* V' \quad G; D \vdash V \sim V' \in \tau{:}\theta}{G; D \vdash M \simeq M' \in \tau{:}\theta}$$

$\boxed{\Gamma; \Delta \vdash \theta|\gamma; \delta{:}G; D}$ Open relation substitutions

$$\frac{\vdash G}{\cdot; \cdot \vdash \cdot|\cdot; \cdot{:}G; \cdot} \qquad \frac{\Gamma; \Delta \vdash \theta|\gamma; \delta{:}G; D_1 \quad \Gamma \vdash \tau \quad G \vdash D_1, \boldsymbol{D_2} \quad G; \boldsymbol{D_2} \vdash V \sim V' \in \tau{:}\theta \quad a \notin \Gamma, \Delta, G, (D_1, \boldsymbol{D_2})}{\Gamma; \Delta, a{:}\tau \vdash \theta|\gamma; \delta, a{\mapsto}(V, V'){:}G; D_1, \boldsymbol{D_2}}$$

$$\frac{\Gamma; \Delta \vdash \theta|\gamma; \delta{:}G; D \quad \Gamma \vdash \tau \quad G; \cdot \vdash V \sim V' \in \tau{:}\theta \quad x \notin \Gamma, \Delta, G, D}{\Gamma, x{:}\tau; \Delta \vdash \theta|\gamma, x{\mapsto}(V, V'); \delta{:}G; D} \qquad \frac{\Gamma; \Delta \vdash \theta|\gamma; \delta{:}G; D \quad R \in \tau \leftrightarrow \tau' \dashv \boldsymbol{G} \quad \alpha \notin \Gamma, \Delta, G, D}{\Gamma, \alpha; \Delta \vdash \theta, \alpha{\mapsto}(R, \tau, \tau')|\gamma; \delta{:}G; D}$$

$\boxed{\Gamma; \Delta \vdash \theta|\gamma; \delta_1 \Cup \delta_2 = \delta{:}G; D_1 \Cup D_2 = D}$ Disjoint linear relation substitutions

$$\frac{\Gamma; \cdot \vdash \theta|\gamma; \cdot{:}G; \cdot}{\Gamma; \cdot \vdash \theta|\gamma; \cdot \Cup \cdot = \cdot{:}G; \cdot \Cup \cdot = \cdot}$$

$$\frac{\Gamma; \Delta \vdash \theta|\gamma; \delta_1 \Cup \delta_2 = \delta{:}G; D_1 \Cup D_2 = D_3 \quad \Gamma \vdash \tau \quad G; D' \vdash V \sim V' \in \tau{:}\theta \quad a \notin \Gamma, \Delta, G, (D_3, D')}{\Gamma; \Delta, a{:}\tau \vdash \theta|\gamma; (\delta_1, a{\mapsto}(V, V')) \Cup \delta_2 = (\delta, a{\mapsto}(V, V')){:}G; D_1, D' \Cup D_2 = D_3, D'}$$

$$\frac{\Gamma; \Delta \vdash \theta|\gamma; \delta_1 \Cup \delta_2 = \delta{:}G; D_1 \Cup D_2 = D_3 \quad \Gamma \vdash \tau \quad G; D' \vdash V \sim V' \in \tau{:}\theta \quad a \notin \Gamma, \Delta, G, (D_3, D')}{\Gamma; \Delta, a{:}\tau \vdash \theta|\gamma; \delta_1 \Cup (\delta_2, a{\mapsto}(V, V')) = (\delta, a{\mapsto}(V, V')){:}G; D_1 \Cup D_2, D' = D_3, D'}$$

Fig. 4. Related open values and terms for PDILL

V and V'. Type variables in indexed types τ are disjoint from the domains of G and D. θ maps variables in τ to relations with types under contexts G and D.

A relation for each type variable α is defined by looking up relations in substitution contexts θ. Two functions are related if and only if they map related inputs to related outputs. When testing equivalence on two open function values under a linear context D, OVR_ARR applies the two functions to arbitrary open related values under a linear context $\boldsymbol{D}_1$, which is disjoint from D, and tests if they can normalize to two related values under a merged linear context $D, \boldsymbol{D}_1$. A standard logical relation does not necessarily require related closed arguments to be well-typed in the arrow type case. However, the logical relation for PDILL allows only well-typed related open arguments at OVR_ARR because the invariant that reduction preserves the set of free linear variables is satisfied for only typechecked terms. PDILL ensures that a ! value cannot capture linear variables in its closure; thus we conclude that $\boldsymbol{D}_1 = \cdot$ if τ_1 is a ! type, since the arguments are well-typed.

The idea of the parametricity of polymorphism is that even when passed completely different type arguments, logically related type abstractions must behave uniformly, so they may not use different algorithms for different arguments by analyzing the type argument. To formalize the independence of type arguments, Reynolds' approach is to interpret a type quantifier as an (almost) arbitrary relation that relates two type arguments at which the type quantifier can be instantiated, although a relational interpretation needs to satisfy certain admissibility conditions [17]. Relational interpretations for type variables are stored in type relation substitutions θ that parameterize logical relations. At rule OVR_ALL, two type abstractions are related if and only if two type inputs, which are related by any well-formed relation, generate related outputs with type substitutions extended by that new relation for type variable α. $R \in \tau_2 \leftrightarrow \tau_2' \dashv \boldsymbol{G}$ defines a well-formed binary relation on open terms with types τ_2 and τ_2' respectively. τ_2 and τ_2' are under an intuitionistic context G.

In PDILL, the behavior of logically related type abstractions cannot depend on which linear contexts the arguments with polymorphic types will take, either. Suppose we have related values of type $\forall\alpha.\alpha \multimap \alpha$ under contexts G and D with an empty relation type substitution. Rule OVR_ALL maps α to $R \in \tau_2 \leftrightarrow \tau_2' \dashv \boldsymbol{G}$. At rule OVR_ARR, we must choose a pair of related values $\boldsymbol{G}; \boldsymbol{D}_1 \vdash V \sim V' \in \alpha{:}(\alpha{\mapsto}(R, \tau_2, \tau_2'))$ under an arbitrary fresh linear context D_1. Rule OVR_VAR requires that $(V, V') \in R$. If R is a relation that only takes the linear context D, we cannot choose the above V and V' for an arbitrary D_1. Therefore, $R \in \tau \leftrightarrow \tau' \dashv \boldsymbol{G}$ does not specify which linear context D to use. For any pair of terms related by R, it only requires that there exists a linear context that can typecheck them:

$$\boldsymbol{G} \vdash \tau \wedge \boldsymbol{G} \vdash \tau' \wedge \forall((M, M') \in R).\, \exists D, G; D \vdash M{:}\tau \wedge G; D \vdash M'{:}\tau'$$

Two values $!M$ and $!M'$ are logically related by type $!\tau$ if and only if the two suspended terms M and M' are related by type τ. Under a linear context D, two values are logically related by an additive product $\tau_1 \& \tau_2$ if and only if their components are logically related under D respectively; two values are logically related by a muplicative product $\tau_1 \otimes \tau_2$ if and only if D can be split into disjoint D_1 and D_2, and their components are related under D_1 and D_2 respectively.

$G; D \vdash M \simeq M' \in \tau{:}\theta$ extends logical relations on open values to well-typed open terms with evaluation.The well-formedness of open terms ensures that terms use linear expressions exactly once, and preserves the invariant that reduction does not consume free linear variables. A relation substitution θ also maps free variables in τ that are disjoint to the domains of G and D to relations with types under the context G.

$\Gamma; \Delta \vdash \theta|\gamma; \delta{:}G; D$ formalizes open relation substitutions. Relation substitutions θ, γ, and δ map type and term variables in Γ and term variables in Δ respectively to open types and values with free variables in G and D. The domains of Γ and Δ and the domains of G and D are disjoint. Related open values indexed by ! types must typecheck under an empty linear context and do not introduce free linear variables in D, not changing D. Adding relations with related types to relation substitutions does not change D either. However, related open values indexed by linear types can contain free linear variables, introducing new linear variables in D. When extending the existing linear context Δ with a variable a of type τ, we must add a pair of related values under a linear context $\boldsymbol{D}_2$ that is disjoint from D_1, extending D_1 to $D_1, \boldsymbol{D}_2$. The intuitionistic context G satisfies weakening and contraction properties.

Since linear variables in Δ must be used exactly once, the corresponding linear relation substitutions should satisfy a similar property. That is, a substitution on a linear variable must occur exactly once. Lemma 3 formalizes this idea, stating that, in a judgment $\Gamma; \Delta \vdash \theta|\gamma; \delta{:}G; D$, because only related values in δ can contain variables in D, given that Δ can be split into Δ_1 and Δ_2, we can split the linear relation substitution δ into two linear relation substitutions δ_1 and δ_2 under D_1 and D_2 respectively, where D must be split into D_1 and D_2. Figure 4 also defines the operation $\uplus$ on δ.

Lemma 3 (Split Linear Relation Substitutions). *If* $\Gamma \vdash \Delta_1 \uplus \Delta_2 = \Delta$, *and* $\Gamma; \Delta \vdash \theta|\gamma; \delta{:}G; D$, *then* $\exists \delta_1, \delta_2, D_1, D_2$. $\Gamma; \Delta \vdash \theta|\gamma; \delta_1 \uplus \delta_2 = \delta{:}G; D_1 \uplus D_2 = D$, $\Gamma; \Delta_1 \vdash \theta|\gamma; \delta_1{:}G; D_1$, *and* $\Gamma; \Delta_2 \vdash \theta|\gamma; \delta_2{:}G; D_2$.

$\Gamma; \Delta \vdash M \simeq_{\mathsf{log}} M' \in \tau$ defines that two well-typed terms with the same type are logically equivalent if they are related under all open relation substitutions. $\Gamma; \Delta \vdash M \simeq^{\star}_{\mathsf{log}} M' \in \tau$ defines closed logical equivalence:

$$\begin{aligned}
\Gamma; \Delta \vdash M \simeq_{\mathsf{log}} M' \in \tau \triangleq{}& \Gamma; \Delta \vdash M{:}\tau \wedge \Gamma; \Delta \vdash M'{:}\tau \wedge \\
& \forall(\Gamma; \Delta \vdash \theta|\gamma; \delta{:}G; D).\, G; D \vdash \theta_l(\gamma_l(\delta_l(M))) \simeq \theta_r(\gamma_r(\delta_r(M'))) \in \tau{:}\theta \\
\Gamma; \Delta \vdash M \simeq^{\star}_{\mathsf{log}} M' \in \tau \triangleq{}& \Gamma; \Delta \vdash M{:}\tau \wedge \Gamma; \Delta \vdash M'{:}\tau \wedge \\
& \forall(\Gamma; \Delta \vdash \theta|\gamma; \delta).\, \theta_l(\gamma_l(\delta_l(M))) \simeq \theta_r(\gamma_r(\delta_r(M'))) \in \tau{:}\theta
\end{aligned}$$

3.2 Fundamental Theorem

Theorem 2 shows parametricity, which states that, independent of open relation substitutions for terms, types and relations under contexts Γ and Δ, a well-typed term, via open substitutions, is related to itself under the same contexts Γ and Δ.

As usual, the proof of parametricity depends on a compositionality lemma (Lemma 4) for logical relations. Note that R contains a *family* of logical relations under different D''s, but not only the linear context D that σ takes.

Lemma 4 (Compositionality). $G; D \vdash V \sim V' \in \sigma{:}(\theta, \alpha {\mapsto} (R, \theta_l(\tau), \theta_r(\tau)))$ *iff* $G; D \vdash V \sim V' \in \sigma\{\tau/\alpha\}{:}\theta$ *where* $R \in \theta_l(\tau) \leftrightarrow \theta_r(\tau) \dashv G$ *is a relation such that* $(U, U') \in R$ *iff* $\exists D'$, $G; D' \vdash U \sim U' \in \tau{:}\theta$.

Theorem 2 (Parametricity). *If* $\Gamma; \Delta \vdash M{:}\tau$, *then* $\Gamma; \Delta \vdash M \simeq_{\mathsf{log}} M \in \tau$.

Proof. By induction on the typing derivation, case T_APP relies on Lemma 3, and case T_TAPP uses Lemma 4.

If the logical relation interprets types by relations for only closed terms, Theorem 2 degrades to Theorem 1. Thus Theorem 2 is a more general result than Theorem 1.

3.3 Soundness and Completeness

This section proves that the logical equivalence $\Gamma; \Delta \vdash M \simeq^{\star}_{\mathsf{log}} M \in \tau$, which interprets types on closed terms, is sound and complete with respect to contextual equivalence. We use these results to show the properties of contextual equivalence in Section 4. We also prove that the logical equivalence $\Gamma; \Delta \vdash M \simeq_{\mathsf{log}} M \in \tau$, which interprets types on open relations, is sound with respect to contextual equivalence. Here we state interesting aspects of the proofs. Further details are available online in our Coq scripts.

The definition of contextual equivalence [17] is based on identifying a type of *answers* that are observable outcomes of closed programs. To achieve this, we enrich the system with a base type, $\mathbf{Bool}$, containing two constants, $\mathbf{true}$ and $\mathbf{false}$, that serve as possible answers for a *complete computation* that is a closed expression of type $\mathbf{Bool}$. Two values are logically related with type $\mathbf{Bool}$ iff they are both $\mathbf{true}$ or both $\mathbf{false}$.

Kleene equivalence $M \simeq_{\mathsf{kleene}} M'$ is defined for complete computations M and M' by requiring that $M \longrightarrow^* \mathbf{true} \wedge M' \longrightarrow^* \mathbf{true}$ or $M \longrightarrow^* \mathbf{false} \wedge M' \longrightarrow^* \mathbf{false}$.

To define contextual equivalence, we define contexts C as expressions with a single hole $\Box$. Bierman [5] and Crole [11] showed how to define a program context in a linear setting without polymorphic types. We extend their definitions with polymorphic types.

Typing judgments for contexts have the form $\Gamma'; \Delta' \vdash C{:}(\Gamma; \Delta \rhd \tau) \leadsto \tau'$, where $\Gamma; \Delta \rhd \tau$ indicates the type of the hole. Most typing judgments for contexts are similar to the typing rules listed in Figure 5 and 6 at [25]. Plugging an expected expression into a well-formed context produces a well-typed term with type τ' under Γ' and Δ'.

Two well-formed expressions of the same type are contextually equivalent if, given any well-formed context C that is a complete computation when an expected expression is plugged into, $C[M]$ and $C[M']$ are Kleene equivalent:

$$\begin{aligned}\Gamma; \Delta \vdash M \simeq_{\mathsf{ctx}} M' \in \tau \triangleq\ & \Gamma; \Delta \vdash M{:}\tau \ \wedge\ \Gamma; \Delta \vdash M'{:}\tau \ \wedge \\ & \forall(\cdot;\cdot \vdash C{:}(\Gamma; \Delta \rhd \tau) \leadsto \mathbf{Bool}).C[M] \simeq_{\mathsf{kleene}} C[M']\end{aligned}$$

We first prove that logical equivalence is congruent with respect to contexts:

Lemma 5 (Logical Equivalence is Congruent). *If* $\Gamma; \Delta \vdash M \simeq_{\mathsf{log}} M' \in \tau$, *and* $\Gamma'; \Delta' \vdash C{:}(\Gamma; \Delta \rhd \tau) \leadsto \tau'$, *then* $\Gamma'; \Delta' \vdash C[M] \simeq_{\mathsf{log}} C[M'] \in \tau'$.

Theorem 3 (Soundness). *If* $\Gamma; \Delta \vdash M \simeq_{\mathsf{log}} M' \in \tau$, *then* $\Gamma; \Delta \vdash M \simeq_{\mathsf{ctx}} M' \in \tau$.

Proof. By Lemma 5, and that $\mathbf{true}$ and $\mathbf{false}$ are not related.

When interpreting relations for only closed terms:

Theorem 4. *If* $\Gamma; \Delta \vdash M \simeq^{\star}_{\mathsf{log}} M' \in \tau$, *then* $\Gamma; \Delta \vdash M \simeq_{\mathsf{ctx}} M' \in \tau$.

A typical approach [17] [1] to proving that a logical relation is complete with respect to contextual equivalence is via the notion of CIU-equivalence, introduced by Mason and Talcott [15]. Let evaluation contexts E be a subset of contexts C, and consist of only holes for closed terms. Two well-formed closed terms M and M' are CIU-equivalent if, given any context E, $E[M]$ and $E[M']$ are complete computations, and Kleene equivalent. Given any closing substitution $\Gamma;\Delta \vdash s|g;d$ where s maps type variables in Γ to closed types, g and d map intuitionistic and linear term variables typed in Γ and Δ to closed values respectively, we extend it to open terms as follows:

$$\begin{aligned}\Gamma;\Delta \vdash M \simeq_{\mathsf{ciu}} M' \in \tau \triangleq\ & \Gamma;\Delta \vdash M{:}\tau \wedge \Gamma;\Delta \vdash M'{:}\tau \wedge \\ & \forall(\Gamma;\Delta \vdash s|g;d \wedge \cdot;\cdot \vdash E{:}(\cdot;\cdot \rhd s(\tau)) \rightsquigarrow \mathbf{Bool}). \\ & E[s(g(d(M)))] \simeq_{\mathsf{kleene}} E[s(g(d(M')))]\end{aligned}$$

Given a term M with closing substitutions s, g and d, we can construct a context C such that when M is placed into the hole, $C[M]$ evaluates to the same value that $s(g(d(M)))$ can reduce to. We can use the context $(\cdots(\cdots(\cdots(\Lambda\alpha_1\cdots\alpha_n.\lambda x_1 : \tau_1\cdots x_m : \tau_m.\lambda a_1 : \tau_1'\cdots a_l : \tau_l'.\Box)\cdots[\sigma_i]\cdots)\cdots V_i\cdots)\cdots V_i'\cdots)$ where s maps α_i to closed type σ_i, g maps intuitionistic variables x_i with type τ_i to closed terms V_i, and d maps linear variables a_i with type τ_i' to closed terms V_i'. Therefore, we have:

Lemma 6 **($\simeq_{\mathsf{ctx}} \subseteq \simeq_{\mathsf{ciu}}$).** *If $\Gamma;\Delta \vdash M \simeq_{\mathsf{ctx}} M' \in \tau$, then $\Gamma;\Delta \vdash M \simeq_{\mathsf{ciu}} M' \in \tau$.*

To ensure that our closed logical relations are complete, we will restrict attention to a certain class of *admissible* binary relations R that respect CIU-equivalence [1]:

Definition 1 **(Admissibility).** *$R \in \tau_2 \leftrightarrow \tau_2'$ is admissible iff it satisfies that if $(M_1, M_2) \in R$, $\cdot;\cdot \vdash M_1 \simeq_{\mathsf{ciu}} M_1' \in \tau_2$, $\cdot;\cdot \vdash M_2 \simeq_{\mathsf{ciu}} M_2' \in \tau_2'$, then $(M_1', M_2') \in R$.*

Thus we prove that closed logical relations respect CIU-equivalence:

Lemma 7 **(Equivalence-Respecting).** *If $\Gamma;\Delta \vdash M_1 \simeq^{\star}_{\mathsf{log}} M_2 \in \tau$, $\Gamma;\Delta \vdash M_1 \simeq_{\mathsf{ciu}} M_1' \in \tau$, and $\Gamma;\Delta \vdash M_2 \simeq_{\mathsf{ciu}} M_2' \in \tau$, then $\Gamma;\Delta \vdash M_1' \simeq^{\star}_{\mathsf{log}} M_2' \in \tau$.*

By Theorem 1, Lemmas 6 and Lemma 7, we have:

Theorem 5 **(Completeness).** *If $\Gamma;\Delta \vdash M \simeq_{\mathsf{ctx}} M' \in \tau$, then $\Gamma;\Delta \vdash M \simeq^{\star}_{\mathsf{log}} M' \in \tau$.*

We have thus proved that the relations $\simeq^{\star}_{\mathsf{log}}$, $\simeq_{\mathsf{ctx}}$ and $\simeq_{\mathsf{ciu}}$ coincide with each other. It remains an open question as to whether $\simeq_{\mathsf{log}}$ is complete.

4 Examples

In this section we present applications of our method. Our reasoning about equivalence and definitions of relations in this section depends on properties of contextual equivalence that include reflexivity, symmetry, transitivity, $\beta\eta$-reduction, and congruence (see Figure 7 at [25]). Most of these properties are straightforward, following from the definition of contextual equivalence and Theorems 3, 4 and 5. With closed logical relation $\simeq^{\star}_{\mathsf{log}}$, we proved that τ is isomorphic to $\forall\alpha.(\tau \multimap \alpha) \multimap \alpha$, $\forall\alpha.(\tau_1 \multimap (\tau_2 \multimap \alpha)) \multimap \alpha$ encodes $\tau_1 \otimes \tau_2$, and other type encodings in [23] [7] [16]. This section is focused on novel applications that open logical relations can prove. We abbreviate $\Gamma;\Delta \vdash M \simeq_{\mathsf{ctx}} M' \in \tau \wedge \Gamma;\Delta \vdash M' \simeq_{\mathsf{ctx}} M'' \in \tau$ to $\Gamma;\Delta \vdash M \simeq_{\mathsf{ctx}} M' \simeq_{\mathsf{ctx}} M'' \in \tau$.

4.1 Polymorphic Boolean

A closed term M with type $\forall\alpha.\alpha \multimap \alpha \multimap \alpha$ does not exist, while a closed term with type $\forall\alpha.!\alpha \multimap !\alpha \multimap !\alpha$ must behave like a polymorphic boolean function.

Given $\cdot;\cdot \vdash M{:}\forall\alpha.\alpha \multimap \alpha \multimap \alpha$, Theorem 2 gives:

$$\begin{array}{l}\forall(R \in \tau \leftrightarrow \tau' \dashv \cdot).\forall(\cdot; D_1 \vdash V_1{:}\tau \wedge \cdot; D_1 \vdash V_1'{:}\tau' \wedge (V_1, V_1') \in R).\\ \forall(\cdot; D_2 \vdash V_2{:}\tau \wedge \cdot; D_2 \vdash V_2'{:}\tau' \wedge (V_2, V_2') \in R).\\ \quad M[\tau]\,V_1\,V_2 \longrightarrow^* V \wedge M[\tau']\,V_1'\,V_2' \longrightarrow^* V' \wedge (V, V') \in R\end{array}$$

Here D_1 and D_2 are disjoint. Consider $\cdot; D_1 \vdash V_1{:}\tau$ and $\cdot; D_2 \vdash V_2{:}\tau$; let R be a relation $\{(M, M') \mid \cdot; D_1 \vdash M \simeq_{\mathsf{ctx}} M' \simeq_{\mathsf{ctx}} V_1 \in \tau \vee \cdot; D_2 \vdash M \simeq_{\mathsf{ctx}} M' \simeq_{\mathsf{ctx}} V_2 \in \tau\}$. By the free theorem and properties of $\simeq_{\mathsf{ctx}}$, $\cdot; D_1 \vdash (M[\tau]\,V_1\,V_2) \simeq_{\mathsf{ctx}} V_1 \in \tau \vee \cdot; D_2 \vdash (M[\tau]\,V_1\,V_2) \simeq_{\mathsf{ctx}} V_2 \in \tau$. By regularity of $\simeq_{\mathsf{ctx}}$, we have
(1) $\cdot; D_1 \vdash M[\tau]\,V_1\,V_2{:}\tau \vee \cdot; D_2 \vdash M[\tau]\,V_1\,V_2{:}\tau$
However, by typing rules we can also derive
(2) $\cdot; D_1, D_2 \vdash M[\tau]\,V_1\,V_2{:}\tau$
By Lemma 1 on (1) and (2), $\mathsf{dom}(D_1) = \mathsf{dom}(D_1, D_2) \vee \mathsf{dom}(D_2) = \mathsf{dom}(D_1, D_2)$. In this case, D_1 and D_2 can be non-empty and must be disjoint from each other; this contradicts the above constraint. Thus we conclude that the type $\forall\alpha.\alpha \multimap \alpha \multimap \alpha$ is empty. The closed logical relation cannot show this contradiction because it requires that D_1 and D_2 must be empty. Similarly, we can prove that the types $\forall\alpha.\alpha \multimap \alpha \multimap (\alpha \& \alpha)$ and $\forall\alpha.\alpha \multimap (\alpha \otimes \alpha)$ do not have any closed inhabitant.

If a closed term M is of type $\forall\alpha.!\alpha \multimap !\alpha \multimap !\alpha$, its free theorem is:

$$\begin{array}{l}\forall(R \in \tau \leftrightarrow \tau' \dashv \cdot).\\ \forall(\cdot;\cdot \vdash M_1{:}\tau \wedge \cdot;\cdot \vdash M_1'{:}\tau' \wedge M_1 \longrightarrow^* V_1 \wedge M_1' \longrightarrow^* V_1' \wedge (V_1, V_1') \in R).\\ \forall(\cdot;\cdot \vdash M_2{:}\tau \wedge \cdot;\cdot \vdash M_2'{:}\tau' \wedge M_2 \longrightarrow^* V_2 \wedge M_2' \longrightarrow^* V_2' \wedge (V_2, V_2') \in R).\\ \quad M[\tau]\,!M_1\,!M_2 \longrightarrow^* !N \wedge M[\tau']\,!M_1'\,!M_2' \longrightarrow^* !N' \wedge\\ \quad N \longrightarrow^* V \wedge N' \longrightarrow^* V' \wedge (V, V') \in R\end{array}$$

which only allows us to reason about closed terms, because ! values do not capture any free linear variables. Given any $\cdot;\cdot \vdash !M_1, !M_2{:}!\tau$, by strong normalization (that is proved by Theorem 1) there exist values V_1 and V_2 such that $M_1 \longrightarrow^* V_1$ and $M_2 \longrightarrow^* V_2$. Let R be a relation $\{(M, M') \mid \cdot;\cdot \vdash M \simeq_{\mathsf{ctx}} M' \simeq_{\mathsf{ctx}} V_1 \in \tau \vee \cdot;\cdot \vdash M \simeq_{\mathsf{ctx}} M' \simeq_{\mathsf{ctx}} V_2 \in \tau\}$. The free theorem shows that $\cdot;\cdot \vdash (M[\tau]\,!M_1\,!M_2) \simeq_{\mathsf{ctx}} !M_1 \in !\tau$ or $\cdot;\cdot \vdash (M[\tau]\,!M_1\,!M_2) \simeq_{\mathsf{ctx}} !M_2 \in !\tau$, namely that M behaves like a polymorphic boolean function. We can also derive possible inhabitants of types $\forall\alpha.!\alpha \multimap !\alpha \multimap (!\alpha \& !\alpha)$ and $\forall\alpha.!\alpha \multimap (!\alpha \otimes !\alpha)$.

4.2 Multiplicative Selection

This section derives closed inhabitants of the type $\forall\alpha.\alpha \multimap \alpha \multimap (\alpha \otimes \alpha)$. By Theorem 2, this type gives:

$$\begin{array}{l}\forall(R \in \tau \leftrightarrow \tau' \dashv \cdot).\forall(\cdot; D_1 \vdash V_1 : \tau \wedge \cdot; D_1 \vdash V_1' : \tau' \wedge (V_1, V_1') \in R).\\ \forall(\cdot; D_2 \vdash V_2 : \tau \wedge \cdot; D_2 \vdash V_2' : \tau' \wedge (V_2, V_2') \in R).\\ \quad M[\tau]\,V_1\,V_2 \longrightarrow^* (V_3, V_4) \wedge M[\tau']\,V_1'\,V_2' \longrightarrow^* (V_3', V_4')\\ \quad \wedge (V_3, V_3') \in R \wedge (V_4, V_4') \in R\end{array}$$

Here D_1 and D_2 are disjoint. Consider $\cdot; D_1 \vdash V_1 : \tau$ and $\cdot; D_2 \vdash V_2 : \tau$; let R be a relation $\{(M, M') \mid \cdot; D_1 \vdash M \simeq_{\mathsf{ctx}} M' \simeq_{\mathsf{ctx}} V_1 \in \tau \vee \cdot; D_2 \vdash M \simeq_{\mathsf{ctx}} M' \simeq_{\mathsf{ctx}} V_2 \in \tau\}$. By the free theorem, $M[\tau]\, V_1\, V_2 \longrightarrow^* (V_3, V_4) \wedge (V_3, V_3) \in R \wedge (V_4, V_4) \in R$. By the definition of R, $\cdot; D_1 \vdash V_3 \simeq_{\mathsf{ctx}} V_1 \in \tau \vee \cdot; D_2 \vdash V_3 \simeq_{\mathsf{ctx}} V_2 \in \tau$ and $\cdot; D_1 \vdash V_4 \simeq_{\mathsf{ctx}} V_1 \in \tau \vee \cdot; D_2 \vdash V_4 \simeq_{\mathsf{ctx}} V_2 \in \tau$. By regularity of $\simeq_{\mathsf{ctx}}$,
(1) $\cdot; D_1 \vdash V_3 : \tau \vee \cdot; D_2 \vdash V_3 : \tau$ and $\cdot; D_1 \vdash V_4 : \tau \vee \cdot; D_2 \vdash V_4 : \tau$
By typing rules we also have,
(2) $\cdot; D_1, D_2 \vdash (V_3, V_4) : \tau \otimes \tau$
By Lemma 1 on (1) and (2),

$\cdot; D_1 \vdash V_3 \simeq_{\mathsf{ctx}} V_1 \in \tau \wedge \cdot; D_2 \vdash V_4 \simeq_{\mathsf{ctx}} V_2 \in \tau$ and $\mathsf{dom}(D_1, D_2) = \mathsf{dom}(D_1, D_2)$ or
$\cdot; D_2 \vdash V_3 \simeq_{\mathsf{ctx}} V_2 \in \tau \wedge \cdot; D_1 \vdash V_4 \simeq_{\mathsf{ctx}} V_1 \in \tau$ and $\mathsf{dom}(D_2, D_1) = \mathsf{dom}(D_1, D_2)$ or
$\cdot; D_1 \vdash V_3 \simeq_{\mathsf{ctx}} V_1 \in \tau \wedge \cdot; D_1 \vdash V_4 \simeq_{\mathsf{ctx}} V_1 \in \tau$ and $\mathsf{dom}(D_1, D_1) = \mathsf{dom}(D_1, D_2)$ or
$\cdot; D_2 \vdash V_3 \simeq_{\mathsf{ctx}} V_2 \in \tau \wedge \cdot; D_2 \vdash V_4 \simeq_{\mathsf{ctx}} V_2 \in \tau$ and $\mathsf{dom}(D_2, D_2) = \mathsf{dom}(D_1, D_2)$.

Because D_1 and D_2 can be non-empty in our case, M can only behave like one of $\Lambda\alpha.\lambda a_1 : \alpha.\lambda a_2 : \alpha.(a_1, a_2)$, and $\Lambda\alpha.\lambda a_1 : \alpha.\lambda a_2 : \alpha.(a_2, a_1)$. If M is of type $\forall\alpha.!\alpha \multimap\, !\alpha \multimap (!\alpha \otimes !\alpha)$, D_1 and D_2 must be empty. Therefore M can be equivalent to one of $\Lambda\alpha.\lambda x_1 : !\alpha.\lambda x_2 : !\alpha.(x_1, x_2)$, $\Lambda\alpha.\lambda x_1 : !\alpha.\lambda x_2 : !\alpha.(x_2, x_1)$, $\Lambda\alpha.\lambda x_1 : !\alpha.\lambda x_2 : !\alpha.(x_1, x_1)$, and $\Lambda\alpha.\lambda x_1 : !\alpha.\lambda x_2 : !\alpha.(x_2, x_2)$.

4.3 Natural Numbers

This section proves properties of type $\forall\alpha.(\alpha \multimap \alpha) \multimap \alpha \multimap \alpha$ and $\forall\alpha.!(\alpha \multimap \alpha) \multimap \alpha \multimap \alpha$. Given a closed term N of type $\forall\alpha.(\alpha \multimap \alpha) \multimap \alpha \multimap \alpha$. By Theorem 2, this type gives:

$$\forall(R \in \tau \leftrightarrow \tau' \dashv \cdot).\forall(\cdot; Dz \vdash Z : \tau \wedge \cdot; Dz \vdash Z' : \tau' \wedge (Z, Z') \in R).$$
$$\forall(\cdot; Ds \vdash S : \tau \multimap \tau \wedge \cdot; Ds \vdash S' : \tau' \multimap \tau' \wedge \cdot; Ds \vdash S \sim S' \in \alpha \multimap \alpha : \theta).$$
$$N[\tau]\, S\, Z \longrightarrow^* V \wedge N[\tau']\, S'\, Z' \longrightarrow^* V' \wedge (V, V') \in R$$

Here Ds and Dz are disjoint, and $\theta = \alpha \mapsto (R, \tau, \tau')$. Consider $\cdot; Ds \vdash S : \tau \multimap \tau$ and $\cdot; Dz \vdash Z : \tau$; let R be a relation $\{(N, N') \mid \exists n.\ \cdot; Ds^n, Dz \vdash N \simeq_{\mathsf{ctx}} N' \simeq_{\mathsf{ctx}} S^n\, Z \in \tau\}$. Here $S^0 = Id$, $S^{n+1} = \lambda a : \tau.(r_n(S))\,(S^n\, a)$, $\cdot; r_i(Ds) \vdash r_i(S) : \tau \multimap \tau$ and $Ds^n = r_1(Ds), \cdots, r_n(Ds)$, where r_i is a well-formed renaming that is a finite function from free linear variables to free linear variables. A renaming is well-formed if it is identical, or it is bijective from the domain of Ds to a range that is disjoint from Ds. We have $(Z, Z) \in R$ because n can be 0. Suppose $(V, V') \in R$, we have that there exists an n such that $\cdot; Ds^n, Dz \vdash V \simeq_{\mathsf{ctx}} V' \simeq_{\mathsf{ctx}} S^n\, Z \in \tau$ where (Ds^n, Dz) and Ds are disjoint. Let r_{n+1} to be identical, we have $\cdot; Ds, Ds^n, Dz \vdash S\, V \simeq_{\mathsf{ctx}} S\, V' \simeq_{\mathsf{ctx}} S\,(S^n\, Z) \in \tau$ for $n + 1$, namely $(S\, V, S\, V') \in R$. Therefore, we proved that $\cdot; Ds \vdash S \sim S' \in \alpha \multimap \alpha : \alpha \mapsto (R, \tau, \tau)$. By the free theorem, $N[\tau]\, S\, Z \longrightarrow^* V$ and $\cdot; Ds^n, Dz \vdash V \simeq_{\mathsf{ctx}} S^n\, Z \in \tau$ for some n. By regularity, we have $\mathsf{dom}(Ds, Dz) = \mathsf{dom}(Ds^n, Dz)$.

Because Ds can be non-empty, N can only behave like $\Lambda\alpha.\lambda S : \alpha \multimap \alpha.\lambda Z : \alpha.(S\, Z)$. If N is of type $\forall\alpha.!(\alpha \multimap \alpha) \multimap \alpha \multimap \alpha$, the free theorem proves that N encodes natural numbers (it is equivalent to $\Lambda\alpha.\lambda x : !(\alpha \multimap \alpha).\lambda Z : \alpha.\mathbf{let}\, !S = x\, \mathbf{in}\, S^n\, Z$) because Ds must be empty. We can also prove that the closed inhabitants of

$\forall\alpha.(\alpha \multimap \alpha) \multimap (\alpha \multimap \alpha) \multimap \alpha \multimap \alpha$ must behave like $\Lambda\alpha.\lambda F_1 : \alpha \multimap \alpha.\lambda F_2 : \alpha \multimap \alpha.\lambda a : \alpha.(F_1\ (F_2\ a))$ or $\Lambda\alpha.\lambda F_1 : \alpha \multimap \alpha.\lambda F_2 : \alpha \multimap \alpha.\lambda a : \alpha.(F_2\ (F_1\ a))$.

5 Discussion

Other formulations of linearity. All of these results presented here also carry through to System F° [16]—an extension of System F that uses kinds to distinguish linear from intuitionistic types. The online technical appendix [25] gives all formation rules. As expected, values with intuitionistic kind do not capture any linear variables. Open logical relations can easily adapt the definitions from PDILL. At the case of arrow types, when the well-formed open input values are with type of intuitionistic kind, they must be under empty linear contexts. We proved similar applications presented in Section 4.

Formalization. There have been several formalizations of logical relations in proof assistants. Schürmann and Sarnat illustrated how to use logical relation arguments in Twelf by assertion logic [19]. Donnelly and Xi proved strong normalization for System F using high-order abstract syntax in ATS/LF [12].Vytiniotis and Weirich formalized System F in Isabelle/HOL using the locally nameless representation [22].

We formalized all results (including PDILL, System F° [16] and System F) in Coq. The development uses the Coq metatheory libraries [3] that combined locally nameless representation of de Bruijn indices for the bound variables and cofinite quantification of free variable names in inductive definitions of relations. The whole development for PDILL represents approximately 75,000 lines (350,000 words) of Coq (excluding comments). The formalism comprises of 6% of the calculus of PDILL that is extended from the proofs of type soundness for System $F_{<:}$ [3], 10% of closed logical relations, 17% of open logical relations, 43% of properties for contextual equivalence and applications, and 24% of supporting definitions and lemmas for logical relations and contextual equivalence. Definitions account for 5% of the source, and infrastructure overhead accounts for 24% of the source. The size of the formalism for System F° is similar.

The logical relations are recursively defined by *Program Fixpoint* on the size of types (typ_size) indicated by the keyword *measure*:

$$\begin{array}{l}
\textit{Program Fixpoint } G; D \vdash V \sim V' \in \tau{:}\theta\ \{\textit{measure}\ \text{typ_size}\ \tau\} : \textit{Prop} := \\
\textit{match}\ \tau\ \textit{with} \\
\quad \ldots \\
\quad |\ \tau_1 \multimap \tau_2 \Rightarrow \exists L, \forall D_1 V_1 V_1',\ (L \sharp D_1 \wedge G; D_1 \vdash V_1{:}\theta_l(\tau_1) \wedge G; D_1 \vdash V_1'{:}\theta_r(\tau_1) \wedge \\
\qquad\qquad G; D_1 \vdash V_1 \sim V_1' \in \tau_1{:}\theta \wedge G \vdash D, D_1) \Rightarrow \\
\qquad\qquad\qquad G; D, D_1 \vdash V\,V_1 \simeq V'\,V_1' \in \tau_2{:}\theta \\
\textit{end}.
\end{array}$$

At the case of arrow types, to ensure that the domains of substitutions are disjoint from the free variables of types and values in the ranges of substitutions, we first choose an L that includes all the existing free variables in the domains of substitutions, and then pick a fresh linear context D_1 that is disjoint from the L.

Aydemir et al. [3] gave the case that renaming is necessary for proofs. The proof of Theorem 2 is by induction on the typing derivation. At T_APP, we have two induction hypotheses: $G; D_1 \vdash V \sim V' \in \tau_1 \multimap \tau_2{:}\theta$ and $G; D_2 \vdash V_1 \sim V_1' \in \tau_1{:}\theta$

where $G \vdash D_1 \uplus D_2 = D$. To conclude $G; D \vdash V\, V_1 \simeq V'\, V_1' \in \tau_2{:}\theta$, we need to apply the first hypothesis to the second one. However, we cannot show that D_2 is disjoint from the existential L in the first hypothesis. The proof goes like this: we first pick a fresh linear context D_2' that is disjoint from L and other existing free variables, constructing a bijective renaming r from D_2 to D_2'; by renaming lemmas we have $G; D_2' \vdash r(V_1) \sim r(V_1') \in \tau_1{:}\theta$; then induction hypotheses give that $G; D' \vdash V\,(r(V_1)) \simeq V'\,(r(V_1')) \in \tau_2{:}\theta$ where $G \vdash D_1 \uplus D_2' = D'$; finally renaming lemmas conclude $G; D \vdash V\, V_1 \simeq V'\, V_1' \in \tau_2{:}\theta$. In the intuitionistic setting, renaming lemmas may be derived from properties such as substitution and weakening, while in the linear setting that disallows weakening, renaming lemmas for each judgment that accounts for 5% of the source must be proved directly. In future work we would like to allow substitutions on types and values that can reuse variables in domains of substitutions. That would remove the L from the formalization of the logical relations, and simplify the proof, because we do not need renaming lemmas to apply induction hypotheses.

The proof of Lemma 4 requires that the relation such that $(U, U') \in R$ iff $\exists D, G; D \vdash U \sim U' \in \tau{:}\theta$ has the weakening property on θ. Suppose we extend θ to $(\theta, \alpha \mapsto (R, \tau_2, \tau_2'))$. Here α is free to existing variables. However, we do not know which D the relation takes before picking a free α that can be captured by D because R is defined for arbitrary linear contexts. α is a type variable, and the domain of D consists of only term variables. If type and term variables are in different name spaces, we can always pick an α that is free for D. The metatheory [3] does not support name spaces separation. We define axioms that assume separate name spaces between type and term variables. Adding this feature to metatheory libraries is our future work.

An important feature of contexts formalism is that holes are place-holders into which open terms may be placed, whose free variables may be captured. This capture feature is defined by *close* that turns free variable into de Bruijn indices, and *lift* that explicitly selects correct de Bruijn indices for bound variables. The infrastructure lemmas for *close* and *lift* account for 14% of the source.

Effects. As usual for parametricity properties, our results would need to be modified in the presence of effects. We expect we can adopt the TT-closed relations [6] in PDILL to support fixpoints. That paper defines TT-closed relations on closed terms with closed testing functions, to avoid explicit treatment of holes in contexts. However, to test open terms, we need testing contexts with holes that capture variables from those open terms. We also hope to apply open logical relations to other substructural type systems [24].

References

1. Ahmed, A.: Step-indexed syntactic logical relations for recursive and quantified types. In: Sestoft, P. (ed.) ESOP 2006. LNCS, vol. 3924, pp. 69–83. Springer, Heidelberg (2006)
2. Ahmed, A., Dreyer, D., Rossberg, A.: State-dependent representation independence. SIGPLAN Not. 44(1), 340–353 (2009)
3. Aydemir, B., Charguéraud, A., Pierce, B.C., Pollack, R., Weirich, S.: Engineering formal metatheory. In: POPL 2008: Proceedings of the 35th annual ACM SIGPLAN-SIGACT symposium on Principles of programming languages (2008)

4. Barber, A.: Linear Type Theories, Semantics and Action Calculi. PhD thesis, Edinburgh University (1997)
5. Bierman, G.M.: Program equivalence in a linear functional language. J. Funct. Program. 10(2), 167–190 (2000)
6. Bierman, G.M., Pitts, A.M., Russo, C.V.: Operational properties of lily, a polymorphic linear lambda calculus with recursion. In: Proc. of HOOTS. ENTCS, vol. 41. Elsevier, Amsterdam (2000)
7. Birkedal, L., Møgelberg, R.E., Petersen, R.L.: Linear Abadi and Plotkin logic. Logical Methods in Computer Science 2(5:1), 1–33 (2006)
8. Birkedal, L., Støvring, K., Thamsborg, J.: Relational parametricity for references and recursive types. In: TLDI 2009: Proceedings of the 4th International Workshop on Types in Language Design and Implementation, pp. 91–104. ACM, New York (2009)
9. The Coq Development Team. The Coq Proof Assistant Reference Manual, Version 8.2 (2009), `http://coq.inria.fr`
10. Crary, K.: Logical Relations and a Case Study in Equivalence Checking. In: Advanced Topics in Types and Programming Languages. MIT Press, Cambridge (2005)
11. Crole, R.L.: Completeness of bisimilarity for contextual equivalence in linear theories. Logic Jnl IGPL 9(1), 27–51 (2001)
12. Donnelly, K., Xi, H.: A formalization of strong normalization for simply-typed lambda-calculus and System F. Electron. Notes Theor. Comput. Sci. 174(5), 109–125 (2007)
13. Girard, J.-Y.: Interprétation fonctionnelle et élimination des coupures de l'arith mé tique d'ordre supérieur. Thèse d'état (1972); Summary in Fenstad, J.E. (ed.): Scandinavian Logic Symposium, pp. 63–92. North-Holland, Amsterdam (1971)
14. Hasegawa, M.: Logical predicates for intuitionistic linear type theories. In: Girard, J.-Y. (ed.) TLCA 1999. LNCS, vol. 1581, pp. 198–213. Springer, Heidelberg (1999)
15. Mason, I., Talcott, C.: Equivalence in functional languages with effects. J. Funct. Program. 1(3), 245–285 (1991)
16. Mazurak, K., Zhao, J., Zdancewic, S.: Lightweight linear types in system F. In: TLDI 2010: Proceedings of the 4th International Workshop on Types in Language Design and Implementation (2010)
17. Pitts, A.: Typed Operational Reasoning. In: Advanced Topics in Types and Programming Languages. MIT Press, Cambridge (2005)
18. Reynolds, J.C.: Types, abstraction, and parametric polymorphism. In: Mason, R.E.A. (ed.) Information Processing, pp. 513–523. Elsevier Science Publishers B.V., Amsterdam (1983)
19. Schürmann, C., Sarnat, J.: Towards a judgmental reconstruction of logical relation proofs. Technical report, Yale University (2006)
20. Sewell, P., Nardelli, F.Z., Owens, S., Peskine, G., Ridge, T., Sarkar, S., Strniša, R.: Ott: Effective Tool Support for the Working Semanticist. J. Funct. Program. 20(1), 71–122 (2010)
21. Tait, W.W.: Intensional interpretations of functionals of finite type I. Journal of Symbolic Logic 32(2), 198–212 (1967)
22. Vytiniotis, D., Weirich, S.: Free theorems and runtime type representations. Electron. Notes Theor. Comput. Sci. 173, 357–373 (2007)
23. Wadler, P.: Theorems for free! In: Proceedings of the 4th International Symposium on Functional Programming and Computer Architecture (September 1989)
24. Walker, D.: Substructural Type Systems. In: Advanced Topics in Types and Programming Languages. MIT Press, Cambridge (2005)
25. Zhao, J., Zhang, Q., Zdancewic, S.: Relational parametricity for a polymorphic linear lambda calculus. Technical report (2010), `http://www.cis.upenn.edu/~jianzhou/parametricity4linf`

A Certified Implementation of ML with Structural Polymorphism

Jacques Garrigue

Graduate School of Mathematical Sciences,
Nagoya University, Chikusa-ku, Nagoya 464-8602
garrigue@math.nagoya-u.ac.jp

Abstract. The type system of Objective Caml has many unique features, which make ensuring the correctness of its implementation difficult. One of these features is structurally polymorphic types, such as polymorphic object and variant types, which have the extra specificity of allowing recursion. We implemented in Coq a certified interpreter for Core ML extended with structural polymorphism and recursion. Along with type soundness of evaluation, soundness and principality of type inference are also proved.

1 Introduction

While many results have already been obtained in the mechanization of metatheory for ML [13,6,5,11,19] and pure type systems [3,1], Objective Caml [12] has unique features which are not covered by existing works. For instance, polymorphic object and variant types require some form of structural polymorphism [8], combined with recursive types, and both of them do not map directly to usual type systems. Among the many other features, let us just cite the relaxed valued restriction [9], which accommodates side-effects in a smoother way, first class polymorphism [10] as used in polymorphic methods, labeled arguments [7], structural and nominal subtyping (the latter obtained through private abbreviations). There is plenty to do, and we are interested not only in type safety, but also in the correctness of type inference, as it gets more and more involved with each added feature.

Since it seems difficult to ensure the correctness of the current implementation, it would be nice to have a fully certified reference implementation at least for a subset of the language, so that one could check how it is supposed to work. As a first step, we certified type inference and evaluation for Core ML extended with local constraints, a form of structural polymorphism which allows inference of recursive types, such as polymorphic variants or objects. The formal proofs cover soundness of evaluation, both through rewriting rules and using a stack-based abstract machine, and soundness and completeness of the type inference algorithm.

While we based our developments on the "Engineering metatheory" methodology [1], our interest is in working on a concrete type system, with advanced typing features, like in the mechanized metatheory of Standard ML [11]. We are not so much concerned about giving a full specification of the operational semantics, as in [15].

K. Ueda (Ed.): APLAS 2010, LNCS 6461, pp. 360–375, 2010.

The contribution of this paper is two-fold. First, the proofs presented here are original, and in particular it is to our knowledge the first proof of correctness of type inference for a type system containing recursive types, and even of type soundness for a system combining recursive types and a form of structural subsumption. Second, we have used extensively the techniques proposed in [1] to handle binding, and it is interesting to see how they fare in a system containing recursion, or when working on properties other than soundness. On the one hand we have been agreeably surprised by the compatibility of these techniques with explicit renaming (as necessary for type inference), but on the other hand one can easily get entangled in the plethora of quantifiers.

The Coq proof scripts and the extracted code can be found at:

```
http://www.math.nagoya-u.ac.jp/~garrigue/papers/#certint1009
```

Having them at hand while reading this paper should clarify many points. In particular, due to the size of some definitions, we could only include part of them in this paper, and we refer the reader to the proof scripts for all the missing details.

2 Structural Polymorphism

Structural polymorphism, embodied by polymorphic variants and objects, enriches types with both a form of width subsumption, and mutual recursive types. A type system for structural polymorphism was introduced in [8]. To help understand what we are working with, we repeat here the basic definitions, but please refer to the above paper for details.

Terms are the usual ones: variables, constants, functions, application and let-binding. We intend to provide all other constructs through constants and δ-rules.

$$e ::= x \mid c \mid \lambda x.e \mid e\ e \mid \mathsf{let}\ x = e\ \mathsf{in}\ e$$

Types are less usual.

$$\begin{array}{ll}
\tau ::= \alpha \mid \tau_1 \rightarrow \tau_2 & \text{type} \\
\kappa ::= \bullet \mid (C, \{l_1 \mapsto \tau_1, \ldots, l_n \mapsto \tau_n\}) & \text{kind} \\
\mathrm{K} ::= \alpha_1 :: \kappa_1, \ldots, \alpha_n :: \kappa_n & \text{kinding environment} \\
\sigma ::= \forall \bar{\alpha}.\mathrm{K} \triangleright \tau & \text{polytype}
\end{array}$$

A *type* is either a type variable or a function type. This may seem not expressive enough, but in this system type variables need not be abstract, as a *kinding environment* associates them with their respective *kinds*. When they are associated with a concrete kind, they actually denote structural types, like records or variants. Such types are described by a pair (C,R) of a local constraint C and a mapping[1] R from labels to types. On the other hand $\bullet$ just denotes an (abstract) type variable. As you can see, type variables may appear inside kinds, and since kinding environments are allowed to be recursive,

[1] In order to make type inference principal, this "mapping" is not always a function (*i.e.* the same l may, under some conditions, be related to several τ's), but this should not matter at the level of detail of this paper.

VARIABLE
$$\frac{\mathrm{K},\mathrm{K}_0 \vdash \theta : \mathrm{K} \quad \mathsf{dom}(\theta) \subset B}{\mathrm{K};\Gamma, x : \forall B.\mathrm{K}_0 \rhd \tau \vdash x : \theta(\tau)}$$

CONSTANT
$$\frac{\mathrm{K}_0 \vdash \theta : \mathrm{K} \quad \mathrm{Tconst}(c) = \mathrm{K}_0 \rhd \tau}{\mathrm{K};\Gamma \vdash c : \theta(\tau)}$$

ABSTRACTION
$$\frac{\mathrm{K};\Gamma, x : \tau \vdash e : \tau'}{\mathrm{K};\Gamma \vdash \lambda x.e : \tau \to \tau'}$$

APPLICATION
$$\frac{\mathrm{K};\Gamma \vdash e_1 : \tau \to \tau' \quad \mathrm{K};\Gamma \vdash e_2 : \tau}{\mathrm{K};\Gamma \vdash e_1\, e_2 : \tau'}$$

LET
$$\frac{\mathrm{K};\Gamma \vdash e_1 : \sigma \quad \mathrm{K};\Gamma, x : \sigma \vdash e_2 : \tau}{\mathrm{K};\Gamma \vdash \mathsf{let}\ x = e_1\ \mathsf{in}\ e_2 : \tau}$$

GENERALIZE
$$\frac{\mathrm{K};\Gamma \vdash e : \tau \quad B = \mathsf{FV}_{\mathrm{K}}(\tau) \setminus \mathsf{FV}_{\mathrm{K}}(\Gamma)}{\mathrm{K}|_{\mathrm{K}\setminus B};\Gamma \vdash e : \forall B.\mathrm{K}|_B \rhd \tau}$$

Fig. 1. Typing rules (original)

VARIABLE
$$\frac{\mathrm{K} \vdash \bar{\tau} :: \bar{\kappa}^{\bar{\tau}}}{\mathrm{K};\Gamma, x : \bar{\kappa} \rhd \tau_1 \vdash x : \tau_1^{\bar{\tau}}}$$

CONSTANT
$$\frac{\mathrm{K} \vdash \bar{\tau} :: \bar{\kappa}^{\bar{\tau}} \quad \mathrm{Tconst}(c) = \bar{\kappa} \rhd \tau_1}{\mathrm{K};\Gamma \vdash c : \tau_1^{\bar{\tau}}}$$

ABSTRACTION
$$\frac{\forall x \notin L \qquad \mathrm{K};\Gamma, x : \tau \vdash e^x : \tau'}{\mathrm{K};\Gamma \vdash \lambda e : \tau \to \tau'}$$

APPLICATION
$$\frac{\mathrm{K};\Gamma \vdash e_1 : \tau \to \tau' \quad \mathrm{K};\Gamma \vdash e_2 : \tau}{\mathrm{K};\Gamma \vdash e_1\, e_2 : \tau'}$$

LET
$$\frac{\mathrm{K};\Gamma \vdash e_1 : \sigma \quad \forall x \notin L \quad \mathrm{K};\Gamma, x : \sigma \vdash e_2^x : \tau}{\mathrm{K};\Gamma \vdash \mathsf{let}\ e_1\ \mathsf{in}\ e_2 : \tau}$$

GENERALIZE
$$\frac{\forall \bar{\alpha} \notin L \quad \mathrm{K}, \bar{\alpha} :: \bar{\kappa}^{\bar{\alpha}};\Gamma \vdash e : \tau^{\bar{\alpha}}}{\mathrm{K};\Gamma \vdash e : \bar{\kappa} \rhd \tau}$$

Fig. 2. Typing rules using cofinite quantification

we can use them to define recursive types (where the recursion must necessarily go through kinds.) Since type variables only make sense in presence of a kinding environment, *polytypes* have to include a kinding environment for the variables they quantify; *i.e.*, in $\forall \bar{\alpha}.\mathrm{K} \rhd \tau$, K is such that $\mathsf{dom}(\mathrm{K}) = \{\bar{\alpha}\}$, and the variables of $\bar{\alpha}$ may appear both inside the kinds of K and in τ. A good way to understand these definitions is to see types as directed graphs, where variables are just labels for nodes.

This type system is actually a framework, where the concrete definition of local constraints, and how they interact with types, is kept abstract. One can then apply this framework to an appropriate *constraint domain* to implement various flavours of polymorphic variants and records. A constraint domain $\mathscr{C}$ is a set of constraints combined with an entailment relation $\models$ on these constraints, and a predicate $\mathsf{unique}(C, l)$ telling whether l may map to several types, satisfying some properties. By extension we also use the notation $\kappa' \models \kappa$ for kinds, *i.e.* $(C', R') \models (C, R)$ iff $C' \models C$ and $R \subset R'$.

Kinding environments are used in two places: in polytypes where they associate kinds to quantified type variables, and in typing judgments, which are of the form $\mathrm{K};\Gamma \vdash e : \tau$, where the variables kinded in K may appear in both Γ and τ. The typing rules are given in Fig. 1. $\mathrm{K} \vdash \theta : \mathrm{K}'$ means that the substitution θ (defined as usual) preserves kinds between K and K′ (it is *admissible* between K and K′). Formally, if α has a concrete kind in K ($\alpha :: \kappa \in \mathrm{K},\ \kappa \neq \bullet$), then $\theta(\alpha) = \alpha'$ is a variable, and it has a more concrete kind in K′ ($\alpha' :: \kappa' \in \mathrm{K}'$ and $\kappa' \models \theta(\kappa)$). The main difference with Core ML is that GENERALIZE has to split the kinding environment into a generalized part, which contains the kinds associated to generalized type variables (denoted by $\mathrm{K}|_B$), and a non-generalized part for the rest (denoted by $\mathrm{K}|_{\mathrm{K}\setminus B}$). When determining which type

$$\text{R-ABS}\quad (\lambda e_1)\, v_2 \longrightarrow e_1^{v_2} \qquad \text{R-DELTA}\quad \frac{e = \mathsf{Delta.reduce}\; c\; [v_1;\ldots;v_n]}{c\; v_1\; \ldots\; v_n \longrightarrow e} \qquad \text{R-APP}_1\quad \frac{e_1 \longrightarrow e_1'}{e_1\, e_2 \longrightarrow e_1'\, e_2}$$

$$\text{R-LET}\quad \mathsf{let}\; v_1\; \mathsf{in}\; e_2 \longrightarrow e_2^{v_1} \qquad \text{R-LET}_1\quad \frac{e_1 \longrightarrow e_1'}{\mathsf{let}\; e_1\; \mathsf{in}\; e_2 \longrightarrow \mathsf{let}\; e_1'\; \mathsf{in}\; e_2} \qquad \text{R-APP}_2\quad \frac{e_2 \longrightarrow e_2'}{v_1\, e_2 \longrightarrow v_1\, e_2'}$$

Fig. 3. Reduction rules

variables can be generalized, we must be careful that for any type variable accessible from Γ, the type variables appearing in its kind (inside K) are also accessible. For this reason FV takes K as parameter; if $\alpha :: \kappa \in \mathrm{K}$, then $\mathsf{FV}_{\mathrm{K}}(\alpha) = \{\alpha\} \cup \mathsf{FV}_{\mathrm{K}}(\kappa)$.

It may be difficult to understand this type system in abstract form. Concrete constraint domains and constants are given in Fig. 6 and 7, and an example appears in Section 7 of this paper.

3 Type Soundness

The first step of our mechanical proof, using Coq [17], was to prove type soundness for the system described in the previous section, starting from Aydemir and others' proof for Core ML included in [1], which uses *locally nameless cofinite quantification*. This proof uses de Bruijn indices for local quantification inside terms and polytypes, and quantifies over an abstract avoidance set for avoiding name conflicts.

Fig. 2 contains the typing rules adapted to locally nameless cofinite quantification, and the reduction rules are in Fig. 3. They both use locally nameless terms and types.

$$\begin{array}{lll}
e & ::= n \mid x \mid c \mid \lambda e \mid e\; e \mid \mathsf{let}\; e\; \mathsf{in}\; e & \text{term} \\
\tau & ::= n \mid \alpha \mid \tau_1 \rightarrow \tau_2 & \text{type} \\
\kappa & ::= \bullet \mid (C, \{l_1 \mapsto \tau_1, \ldots, l_n \mapsto \tau_n\}) & \text{kind} \\
\sigma & ::= \bar{\kappa} \triangleright \tau & \text{polytype}
\end{array}$$

$\bar{\tau}$ and $\bar{\kappa}$ represent sequences of types and kinds. When we write $\bar{\alpha}$, we also assume that all type variables inside the sequence are distinct. Polytypes are now written $\bar{\kappa} \triangleright \tau$, where the length of $\bar{\kappa}$ is the number of generalized type variables, represented as de Bruijn indices $1 \ldots n$ inside types[2]. $\tau_1^{\bar{\tau}}$ is τ_1 where de Bruijn indices were substituted with types of $\bar{\tau}$, accessed by their position. Similarly $\bar{\kappa}^{\bar{\tau}}$ substitute all the indices inside the sequence $\bar{\kappa}$. e^x only substitutes x for the index 1. $\mathrm{K} \vdash \tau :: \kappa$ is true when either $\kappa = \bullet$, or $\tau = \alpha$, $\alpha :: \kappa' \in \mathrm{K}$ and $\kappa' \models \kappa$. $\mathrm{K} \vdash \bar{\tau} :: \bar{\kappa}$ enforces this for every member of $\bar{\tau}$ and $\bar{\kappa}$ at identical positions, which is just equivalent to our condition $\mathrm{K} \vdash \theta : \mathrm{K}'$ for the preservation of kinds.

$\forall x \notin L$ and $\forall \bar{\alpha} \notin L$ are cofinite quantifications, with scope the hypotheses on the right of the quantifier. Each L appearing in a derivation is existentially quantified (*i.e.* one chooses a concrete L when building the derivation), but has to be finite, to allow an infinite number of variables outside of L. At first, the rules may look very different from

[2] The implementation has indices starting from 0, but we will start from 1 in this explanation.

```
Module Type CstrIntf.
  Parameter cstr attr : Set.              (* types for abstract constraints and labels *)
  Parameter valid : cstr → Prop.                          (* validity of a constraint *)
  Parameter unique : cstr → attr → bool.                    (* uniqueness of a label *)
  Parameter ⊔ : cstr → cstr → cstr.                           (* least upper bound *)
  Parameter ⊨ : cstr → cstr → Prop.             (* entailment between constraints *)
  ...                                       (* some properties of these definitions *)
Module Type CstIntf.
  Parameter const : Set.                                             (* constants *)
  Parameter arity : const → nat.                                     (* their arity *)
```

Fig. 4. Interfaces for constraints and constants

those in Fig. 1, but they coincide if we instantiate L appropriately. For instance, if we use $\mathsf{dom}(\Gamma)$ for L in $\forall x \notin L$, this just amounts to ensuring that x is not already bound. Inside GENERALIZE, we could use $\mathsf{dom}(\mathrm{K}) \cup \mathsf{FV}_{\mathrm{K}}(\Gamma)$ for L to ensure that the newly introduced variables are locally fresh. This may not be intuitive, but this is actually a very clever way to encode naming constraints implicitly. Moreover, when we build a new typing derivation from an old one, we can avoid renaming variables by just enlarging the avoidance sets.

Starting from an existing proof was a tremendous help, but many new definitions were needed to accommodate kinds, and some existing ones had to be modified. For instance, in order to accommodate the mutually recursive nature of kinding environments, we need simultaneous type substitutions, rather than the iterated ones of the original proof. The freshness of individual variables (or sequences of variables: $\bar{\alpha} \notin L$) becomes insufficient, and we need to handle disjointness conditions on sets ($L_1 \cap L_2 = \emptyset$). As a result, the handling of freshness, which was almost fully automatized in the proof of Core ML, required an important amount of work with kinds, even after developing some tactics for disjointness.

We also added a formalism for constants and δ-rules, which are needed to give an operational semantics to structural types. Overall, the result was a doubling of the size of the proof, from 1000 lines to more than 2000, but the changes were mostly straightforward. This does not include the extra metatheory lemmas and set inclusion tactics that we use for all proofs.

The formalism of local constraints was defined as a framework, able to handle various flavours of variant and object types, just by changing the constraint part of the system. This was formalized through the use of functors. The signature for constraints and constants is in Fig. 4, and an outline of the module structure of the soundness proof (including the statements proved) is in Fig. 5. We omit here the definitions of terms, types, typing derivations, and reduction, as they just implement the locally nameless definitions we described above. A value is either a λ-abstraction, or a constant applied to a list of values of length less than its arity.

This approach worked well, but there are some drawbacks. One is that since some definitions depend on parameters of the framework, and some of the proofs required by the framework depend on those definitions, we need nested functors, and the instantiation of the framework with a *constraint domain* looks like a “dialogue”: we repeatedly

```
Module MkDefs (Cstr : CstrIntf) (Const : CstIntf).
 Inductive typ : Set := ...                                        (* our types *)
 Inductive type : typ → Prop := ...                        (* well-formed types *)
 Inductive trm : Set := ...                                        (* our terms *)
 ...
 Module Type DeltaIntf.
  Parameter type : Const.const → sch.                   (* types of constants *)
  Parameter reduce : ∀c el, (list_for_n value (1 + Const.arity c) el) → trm.   (* δ-rules *)
  ...                                                    (* 3 more properties *)
 Module MkJudge (Delta : DeltaIntf).
  Inductive ⊢ : kenv → env → trm → typ → Prop := ...     (* the typing judgment *)
  Inductive ⟶ : trm → trm → Prop := ...               (* the reduction relation *)
  Inductive value : trm → Prop := ...                               (* values *)
  ...
  Module Type SndHypIntf.
   Parameter delta_typed : ∀c el vl K Γ τ,
     (K;Γ ⊢ const_app c el : τ) → (K;Γ ⊢ Delta.reduce c el vl : τ).
  Module MkSound (SH : SndHypIntf).
   Theorem preservation : ∀K Γ e e' τ, (K;Γ ⊢ e : τ) → (e ⟶ e') → (K;Γ ⊢ e' : τ).
   Theorem progress : ∀K e τ, (K;∅ ⊢ e : τ) → (value e ∨ ∃e', e ⟶ e').
```

Fig. 5. Module structure

alternate domain-specific definitions, and applications of framework functors to those definitions, each new definition using the result of the previous functor application. The problem appears not so much with constraints themselves, but rather with constants and δ-rules. In order to obtain the definitions for typing judgments, one has to provide implementations for constraints and constants, extract the definition of types and terms, and use them to provide constant types and δ-rules. We enforce the completeness of δ-rules by requiring a function reduce which will be applied to a list of values of length $(1 + \text{Const.arity } c)$; through well-typedness they will be only used if Const.arity c is smaller than the arity of type c. Type soundness itself is another functor, that requires some lemmas whose proofs may use infrastructure lemmas on type judgments, and returns proofs of preservation and progress. The real structure is even more complex, because the proofs span several files, and each file must mimick this structure. The same problem is known to occur in programs using heavily ML functors, so this is not specific to Coq. But the level of stratification of definitions we see in this proof rarely occurs in programs.

This instantiation has been done for a constraint domain containing both polymorphic variants and records, and a fixpoint operator. We show the constraint domain in Fig. 6; we write $\langle\rangle$ for None, which denotes here the set of all possible labels. Constants and δ-rules are in Fig. 7, using the nameful syntax for types. You can see the duality between variants and records, at least for tag and get.

Both in the framework and domain proofs, cofinite quantification demonstrated its power, as no renaming of type or term variables was needed at all. It helped also in an indirect way: in the original rule for GENERALIZE, one has to close the set of free

```
Module Cstr.
  Definition attr := nat.
  Inductive ksort : Set := Ksum | Kprod | Kbot.
  Record cstr : Set := C {sort : ksort; low : list nat; high : option(list nat)}.
  Definition valid c := sort c ≠ Kbot ∧ (high c = ⟨⟩ ∨ low c ⊂ high c).
  Definition s1 ≤ s2 := s1 = Kbot ∨ s1 = s2.
  Definition c1 ⊨ c2 :=
    sort s2 ≤ sort s1 ∧ low c2 ⊂ low c1 ∧ (high c2 = ⟨⟩ ∨ high c1 ⊂ high c2).
  ...
```

Fig. 6. Constraint domain for polymorphic variants and records

$$\begin{aligned}
\mathsf{type}(\mathsf{tag}_l) &= \alpha :: (\langle \mathsf{Ksum}, \{l\}, \langle\rangle\rangle, \{l \mapsto \beta\}) \rhd \beta \to \alpha \\
\mathsf{type}(\mathsf{match}_{l_1 \ldots l_n}) &= \alpha :: (\langle \mathsf{Ksum}, \emptyset, \{l_1, \ldots, l_n\}\rangle, \{l_1 \mapsto \alpha_1, \ldots, l_n \mapsto \alpha_n\}) \\
&\quad \rhd (\alpha_1 \to \beta) \to \ldots \to (\alpha_n \to \beta) \to \alpha \to \beta \\
\mathsf{type}(\mathsf{record}_{l_1 \ldots l_n}) &= \alpha :: (\langle \mathsf{Kprod}, \emptyset, \{l_1, \ldots, l_n\}\rangle, \{l_1 \mapsto \alpha_1, \ldots, l_n \mapsto \alpha_n\}) \\
&\quad \rhd \alpha_1 \to \ldots \to \alpha_n \to \alpha \\
\mathsf{type}(\mathsf{get}_l) &= \alpha :: (\langle \mathsf{Kprod}, \{l\}, \langle\rangle\rangle, \{l \mapsto \beta\}) \rhd \alpha \to \beta \\
\mathsf{type}(\mathsf{recf}) &= ((\alpha \to \beta) \to (\alpha \to \beta)) \to (\alpha \to \beta)
\end{aligned}$$

$$\begin{aligned}
\mathsf{match}_{l_1 \ldots l_n}\ f_1\ \cdots\ f_n\ (\mathsf{tag}_{l_i}\ e) &\longrightarrow f_i\ e \\
\mathsf{get}_{l_i}\ (\mathsf{record}_{l_1 \ldots l_n}\ e_1\ \cdots\ e_n) &\longrightarrow e_i \\
\mathsf{recf}\ f\ e &\longrightarrow f\ (\mathsf{recf}\ f)\ e
\end{aligned}$$

Fig. 7. Types and δ-rules for constants

variables of a type with the free variables of their kinds; but the cofinite quantification takes care of that implicitly, without any extra definitions.

While cofinite quantification may seem perfect, there is a pitfall in this perfection itself. One forgets that some proof transformations intrinsically require variable renaming. Concretely, to make typing more modular, I added a rule that discards irrelevant kinds from the kinding environment. Fig. 8 shows both the normal and cofinite forms. Again one can see the elegance of the cofinite version, where there is no need to specify which kinds are irrelevant: just the ones whose names have no impact on typability. Proofs went on smoothly, until I realized that I needed the following inversion lemma, relating derivations using KIND GC, and those without it.

$$\forall \mathrm{K} \Gamma e \tau,\ (\mathrm{K}; \Gamma \vdash_{GC} e : \tau) \to \exists \mathrm{K}',\ (\mathrm{K}, \mathrm{K}'; \Gamma \vdash e : \tau)$$

Namely, by putting back the kinds we discarded, we shall be able to obtain a derivation that does not rely on KIND GC. This is very intuitive, but since this requires making KIND GC commute with GENERALIZE, we end up commuting quantifiers. And this is just impossible without a true renaming lemma. I got stuck there for a while, unable to see what was going wrong[3]. Even more confusing, the same problem occurs when we try to make KIND GC commute with ABSTRACTION, whereas intuitively the choice of names for term variables is independent of the choice of names for type variables.

[3] Thanks to Arthur Charguéraud for opening my eyes.

KIND GC
$$\frac{\mathrm{K},\mathrm{K}';\Gamma \vdash e : \tau \quad \mathsf{FV}_{\mathrm{K}}(\Gamma,\tau)\cap \mathsf{dom}(\mathrm{K}') = \emptyset}{\mathrm{K};\Gamma \vdash e : \tau}$$

CO-FINITE KIND GC
$$\frac{\forall \bar{\alpha} \notin L \quad \mathrm{K},\bar{\alpha} :: \bar{\kappa}^{\bar{\alpha}};\Gamma \vdash e : \tau}{\mathrm{K};\Gamma \vdash e : \tau}$$

Fig. 8. Kind discarding

Finally this lemma required about 1000 lines to prove it, including renaming lemmas for both term and type variables.

Lemma typing_rename : $\forall \mathrm{K}\,\Gamma\, x\, y\, \sigma\, \Gamma'\, e\, \tau,$
$\mathrm{K};\Gamma,x{:}\sigma,\Gamma' \vdash e : \tau \rightarrow y \notin \mathsf{dom}(\Gamma,\Gamma') \cup \{x\} \cup \mathsf{FV}(e) \rightarrow \mathrm{K};\Gamma,y{:}\sigma,\Gamma' \vdash [y/x]e : \tau.$
Lemma typing_rename_typ : $\forall \mathrm{K}\,\Gamma\,\bar{\kappa}\,\tau\,\bar{\alpha}\,\bar{\alpha}'\,e,$
$\bar{\alpha} \notin \mathsf{FV}(\Gamma) \cup \mathsf{FV}(\bar{\kappa} \triangleright \tau) \cup \mathsf{dom}\mathrm{K} \cup \mathsf{FV}(\mathrm{K})) \rightarrow \bar{\alpha}' \notin \mathsf{dom}\mathrm{K} \cup \{\bar{\alpha}\} \rightarrow$
$\mathrm{K},\bar{\alpha} :: \bar{\kappa}^{\bar{\alpha}};\Gamma \vdash e : \tau^{\bar{\alpha}} \rightarrow \mathrm{K},\bar{\alpha}' :: \bar{\kappa}^{\bar{\alpha}'};\Gamma \vdash e : \tau^{\bar{\alpha}'}.$

The renaming lemmas were harder to prove than expected (100 lines each). Contrary to what was suggested in [1], we found it rather difficult to prove these lemmas starting from the substitution lemmas of the soundness proof; while renaming for types used this approach, renaming for terms was proved by a direct induction, and they ended up being of the same length. On the other hand, one could argue that the direct proof was easy precisely thanks to cofinite quantification, which eschews the need for extra machinery.

Once the essence of the problem (*i.e.* commutation of quantifiers) becomes clear, one can see a much simpler solution: in most situations, it is actually sufficient to have KIND GC occur only just above ABSTRACTION and GENERALIZE, and the canonicalization lemma is just 100 lines, as it doesn't change the quantifier structure of the proof. This also raises the issue of how to handle several variants of a type system in the same proof. Here this was done by parameterizing the predicate $\vdash$ with the canonicity of the derivation, and whether KIND GC is allowed at this point. This gives 4 cases for the availability of KIND GC: allowed nowhere, allowed everywhere, or inside a canonical derivation where it is allowed or not at the current point. Functions gc_ok, gc_raise and gc_lower, which are used by the definitions themselves, allow to manipulate this state transparently.

4 Type Inference

The main goal of using local constraints was to keep the simplicity of unification-based type inference. Of course, unification has to be extended in order to handle kinding, but the algorithms for unification and type inference stay reasonably simple.

4.1 Unification

Unification has been a target of formal verification for a long time, with formal proofs as early as 1985 [16]. Here we just wrote down the algorithm in Coq, and proved

$[\bar{\alpha}]\tau = \tau_*$ such that $\tau_*^{\bar{\alpha}} = \tau$
and $\mathsf{FV}(\tau_*) \cap \bar{\alpha} = \emptyset$
$[\bar{\alpha}](\bar{\kappa} \triangleright \tau) = ([\bar{\alpha}]\bar{\kappa} \triangleright [\bar{\alpha}]\tau)$

Definition generalize$(\mathrm{K}, \Gamma, L, \tau) :=$
let $A = \mathsf{FV}_\mathrm{K}(\Gamma)$ and $B = \mathsf{FV}_\mathrm{K}(\tau)$ in
let $\mathrm{K}' = \mathrm{K}|_{\mathrm{K}\setminus A}$ in
let $\bar{\alpha} :: \bar{\kappa} = \mathrm{K}'|_B$ in
let $\bar{\alpha}' = B \setminus (A \cup \bar{\alpha})$ in
let $\bar{\kappa}' =$ map $(\lambda\_.\bullet)\ \bar{\alpha}'$ in
$\langle(\mathrm{K}|_A, \mathrm{K}'|_L), [\bar{\alpha}\bar{\alpha}'](\bar{\kappa}\bar{\kappa}' \triangleright \tau)\rangle$.

Definition typinf$(\mathrm{K}, \Gamma, \text{let } e_1 \text{ in } e_2, \tau, \theta, L) :=$
let $\alpha =$ fresh(L) in
match typinf$(\mathrm{K}, \Gamma, e_1, \alpha, \theta, L \cup \{\alpha\})$ with
| $\langle \mathrm{K}', \theta', L' \rangle \Rightarrow$
let $\mathrm{K}_1 = \theta'(\mathrm{K}')$ and $\Gamma_1 = \theta'(\Gamma)$ in
let $L_1 = \theta'(\mathsf{dom}(\mathrm{K}))$ and $\tau_1 = \theta'(\alpha)$ in
let $\langle \mathrm{K}_A, \sigma \rangle =$ generalize$(\mathrm{K}_1, \Gamma_1, L_1, \tau_1)$ in
let $x =$ fresh$(\mathsf{dom}(\Gamma) \cup \mathsf{FV}(e_1) \cup \mathsf{FV}(e_2))$ in
typinf$(\mathrm{K}_A, (\Gamma, x:\sigma), e_2^x, \tau, \theta', L')$
| $\langle\rangle \Rightarrow \langle\rangle$
end.

Fig. 9. Type inference algorithm

both partial-correctness and completeness. A rule-based version of the algorithm can be found in [8]. The following statements were proved:

Definition unifies $\theta\ l := \forall \tau_1 \tau_2, \mathsf{In}\ (\tau_1, \tau_2)\ l \rightarrow\ \theta(\tau_1) = \theta(\tau_2)$.

Theorem unify_types : $\forall h l \mathrm{K} \theta$, unify $h\ l\ \mathrm{K}\ \theta = \langle \mathrm{K}', \theta' \rangle \rightarrow$ unifies $\theta'\ l$.

Theorem unify_kinds : $\forall h l \mathrm{K} \theta$,
unify $h\ l\ \mathrm{K}\ \theta = \langle \mathrm{K}', \theta' \rangle \rightarrow \mathsf{dom}(\theta) \cap \mathsf{dom}(\mathrm{K}) = \emptyset \rightarrow$
$\mathrm{K} \vdash \theta' : \theta'(\mathrm{K}') \wedge \mathsf{dom}(\theta') \cap \mathsf{dom}(\mathrm{K}') = \emptyset$.

Theorem unify_mgu : $\forall h l \mathrm{K}_0 \mathrm{K} \theta$,
unify $h\ l\ \mathrm{K}_0$ id $= \langle \mathrm{K}, \theta \rangle \rightarrow$ unifies $\theta'\ l \rightarrow \mathrm{K}_0 \vdash \theta' : \mathrm{K}' \rightarrow \theta' \sqsupseteq \theta \wedge \mathrm{K} \vdash \theta : \mathrm{K}'$.

Theorem unify_complete : $\forall \mathrm{K} \theta \mathrm{K}_0 l h$,
unifies $\theta\ l \rightarrow \mathrm{K}_0 \vdash \theta : \mathrm{K} \rightarrow$ size_pairs id $\mathrm{K}_0\ l < h \rightarrow$ unify $h\ l\ \mathrm{K}_0$ id $\neq \langle\rangle$.

The first argument to unify is the number of type variables, which is used to enforce termination. Then come a list of type pairs to unify and the original kinding environment. Last is a starting substitution, so that the algorithm is tail-recursive. To keep the statement clear, well-formedness conditions are omitted here. The proof is rather long, as kinds need particular treatment, but there was no major stumbling block. The proof basically follows the algorithms, but there are two useful tricks. One concerns substitutions. Rather than using the relation "θ is more general than θ'" ($\exists \theta_1,\ \theta' = \theta_1 \circ \theta$), we used the more direct "θ' extends θ" ($\forall \alpha,\ \theta'(\theta(\alpha)) = \theta'(\alpha)$). In the above theorem it is noted $\theta' \sqsupseteq \theta$. When θ is idempotent, the two definitions are equivalent, but the latter can be used directly through rewriting. The other idea was to define a special induction lemma for successful unification, which uses symmetries to reduce the number of cases to check. Unification being done on first-order terms, the types we are unifying shall contain no de Bruijn indices, but only global variables. Since we started with a representation allowing both kinds of variables, there was no need to change it.

4.2 Inference

The next step is type inference itself. Again, correctness has been proved before for Core ML [13,6,19], but to our knowledge never for a system containing equi-recursive types.

$$\begin{array}{l}\mathsf{Theorem\ soundness} : \forall \mathrm{K}\,\Gamma\, e\, \tau\, \theta\, L\, \mathrm{K}'\, \theta'\, L',\\ \quad \mathsf{typinf}(\mathrm{K},\Gamma,e,\tau,\theta,L) = \langle \mathrm{K}',\theta',L'\rangle \rightarrow\\ \quad \mathsf{dom}(\theta) \cap \mathsf{dom}(\mathrm{K}) = \emptyset \rightarrow\\ \quad \mathsf{FV}(\theta,\mathrm{K},\Gamma,\tau) \subset L \rightarrow\\ \quad \theta'(\mathrm{K}');\theta'(\Gamma) \vdash e : \theta'(\tau) \wedge\\ \quad \mathrm{K} \vdash \theta' : \theta'(\mathrm{K}') \wedge \theta' \sqsupseteq \theta \wedge\\ \quad \mathsf{FV}(\theta',\mathrm{K}',\Gamma) \cup L \subset L' \wedge\\ \quad \mathsf{dom}(\theta') \cap \mathsf{dom}(\mathrm{K}') = \emptyset.\end{array}$$

$$\begin{array}{l}\mathsf{Theorem\ principality} : \forall \mathrm{K}\,\Gamma\, e\, \tau\, \theta\, \mathrm{K}_1\, \theta_1\, L,\\ \quad \mathrm{K};\theta(\Gamma) \vdash e : \theta(\tau) \rightarrow \mathrm{K}_1 \vdash \theta : \mathrm{K} \rightarrow\\ \quad \theta \sqsupseteq \theta_1 \rightarrow \mathsf{dom}(\theta_1) \cap \mathsf{dom}(\mathrm{K}_1) = \emptyset \rightarrow\\ \quad \mathsf{dom}(\theta) \cup \mathsf{FV}(\theta_1,\mathrm{K}_1,\Gamma,\tau) \subset L \rightarrow\\ \quad \exists \mathrm{K}'\theta' L',\\ \quad\ \mathsf{typinf}(\mathrm{K}_1,\Gamma,e,\tau,\theta_1,L) = \langle \mathrm{K}',\theta',L'\rangle \wedge\\ \quad\ \exists \theta'', \mathrm{K}' \vdash \theta\theta'' : \mathrm{K} \wedge \theta\theta'' \sqsupseteq \theta' \wedge\\ \quad\quad\quad \mathsf{dom}(\theta'') \subset L' \setminus L.\end{array}$$

Fig. 10. Properties of type inference

Proving both soundness and principality was rather painful. This time one problem was the complexity of the algorithm itself, in particular the behaviour of type generalization. The usual behaviour for ML is just to find the variables that are not free in the typing environment and generalize them, but with a kinding environment several extra steps are required. First, the free variables should be closed transitively using the kinding environment. Then, the kinding environment also should be split into generalizable and non-generalizable parts. Last, some generalizable parts of the kinding environment need to be duplicated, as they might be used independently in some other parts of the typing derivation. The definitions for generalize and the let case of typinf are shown in Fig. 9. $[\bar{\alpha}]\tau$ stands for the generalization of τ with respect to $\bar{\alpha}$, obtained by replacing the occurrences of variables of $\bar{\alpha}$ in τ by their indices.

Due to the large number of side-conditions required, the statements for the inductive versions of soundness of principality become very long. In Fig. 10 we show slightly simplified versions, omitting well-formedness properties. These statements can be proved directly by induction. From those, we can derive the following corollaries for a simplified version of typinf, taking only a term and a closed environment as arguments.

$$\begin{array}{l}\mathsf{Corollary\ soundness'}\ : \forall \mathrm{K}\,\Gamma\, e\, \tau,\ \mathsf{FV}(\Gamma) = \emptyset \rightarrow \mathsf{typinf'}\ \Gamma\ e = \langle \mathrm{K},\tau\rangle \rightarrow \mathrm{K};\Gamma \vdash e : \tau.\\ \mathsf{Corollary\ principality'} : \forall \mathrm{K}\,\Gamma\, e\, \tau,\ \mathsf{FV}(\Gamma) = \emptyset \rightarrow \mathrm{K};\Gamma \vdash e : \tau \rightarrow\\ \qquad\qquad \exists \mathrm{K}', \exists T', \mathsf{typinf'}\ \Gamma\ e = \langle \mathrm{K}',T'\rangle \wedge \exists \theta, \mathrm{K}' \vdash \theta : \mathrm{K} \wedge \tau = \theta(\tau').\end{array}$$

As usual, the proof of principality requires the following lemma, which states that if a term e has a type τ under an environment Γ, then we can give it the same type under a more general environment Γ_1.

$$\mathsf{Lemma\ typing\_moregen} : \forall \mathrm{K}\,\Gamma\,\Gamma_1\, e\, \tau,\ \mathrm{K};\Gamma \vdash e : \tau \rightarrow \mathrm{K} \vdash \Gamma_1 \leq \Gamma \rightarrow \mathrm{K};\Gamma_1 \vdash e : \tau.$$

$\mathrm{K} \vdash \Gamma_1 \leq \Gamma$ means that the polytypes of Γ are instances of those in Γ_1. Due to the presence of kinds, the definition of the instantiation order gets a bit complicated.

$$\mathrm{K} \vdash \bar{\kappa}_1 \triangleright \tau_1 \leq \bar{\kappa} \triangleright \tau \stackrel{\mathrm{def}}{=} \forall \bar{\alpha}, \mathsf{dom}(\mathrm{K}) \cap \bar{\alpha} = \emptyset \rightarrow \exists \bar{\tau},\ \mathrm{K}, \bar{\alpha} :: \bar{\kappa}^{\bar{\alpha}} \vdash \bar{\tau} :: \bar{\kappa}_1^{\bar{\tau}} \wedge \tau_1^{\bar{\tau}} = \tau^{\bar{\alpha}}.$$

It may be easier to consider the version without de Bruijn indices.

$$\mathrm{K} \vdash \forall \bar{\alpha}_1.\mathrm{K}_1 \triangleright \tau_1 \leq \forall \bar{\alpha}_2.\mathrm{K}_2 \triangleright \tau_2 \stackrel{\mathrm{def}}{=} \exists \theta,\ \mathsf{dom}(\theta) \subset \bar{\alpha}_1\ \wedge \mathrm{K},\mathrm{K}_1 \vdash \theta : \mathrm{K},\mathrm{K}_2 \wedge \theta(\tau_1) = \tau_2.$$

Another difficulty is that, since we are building a derivation, cofinite quantification appears as a requirement rather than a given, and we need renaming for both terms and

```
Inductive clos : Set :=
  | clos_abs   : trm → list clos → clos
  | clos_const : Const.const → list clos → clos.
Fixpoint clos2trm(c : clos) : trm :=
  match c with
  | clos_abs e l    ⇒ trm_inst (λe) (map clos2trm l)
  | clos_const c l ⇒ const_app c (map clos2trm l)
  end.
Record frame : Set := Frame {frm_benv : list clos; frm_app : list clos; frm_trm : trm}.
Inductive eval_res : Set :=
  | Result : nat → clos → eval_res
  | Inter   : list frame → eval_res.
Fixpoint eval (h : nat) (benv : list clos) (app : list clos) (e : trm) (stack : list frame)
   {struct h} : eval_res := ...
Theorem eval_sound : ∀h K e τ,
   (K;Γ ⊢ e : τ) → (K;Γ ⊢ res2trm (eval h nil nil t nil) : τ).
Theorem eval_complete : ∀K e e' τ,
   (K;Γ ⊢ e : τ) → (e −*→ e') → value e' →
   ∃h, ∃cl, eval h nil nil t nil = Result 0 cl ∧ e' = clos2trm cl.
```

Fig. 11. Definitions and theorems for stack-based evaluation

types in many places. This is true both for soundness and principality, since in the latter the type variables of the inferred derivation and of the provided derivation are different. As a result, while we could finally avoid using the renaming lemmas for type soundness, they were ultimately needed for type inference.

5 Interpreter

Type soundness ensures that evaluation according to a set of source code rewriting rules cannot go wrong. However, programming languages do not evaluate a program by rewriting it, but rather interpreting it with a virtual machine. We defined a stack-based abstract machine, and proved that at every step the state of the abstract machine could be converted back to a term whose typability was a direct consequence of the typability of the reduced program. This ensures that evaluation cannot go wrong, and the final result, if reached, shall be either a constant or a function closure. Once the relation between program and state was properly specified, the proof was mostly straightforward.

The basic definitions and the statements for soundness and completeness are in Fig. 11. We omit here the concrete definition of eval for lack of space. A closure is either a function body paired with its environment, or a partially applied constant. clos2trm converts back a closure to an equivalent term, trm_inst intantiating all de Bruijn indices at once with a list of terms, and const_app building the curried application of c to a list of terms. Since evaluation may not terminate, eval takes as argument the number h of reduction steps to compute. The remaining arguments are the environment *benv*, accessed through de Bruijn indices, the application stack *app* which contains the arguments to the term being evaluated, the term e itself, which provides an efficient representation of code thanks to de Bruijn indices, and the control stack *stack*. Here the nameless representation of terms was handy, as it maps naturally to a stack machine. The result of eval is either a closure, with the number of evaluation steps remaining, or the current state of the machine.

We also proved completeness with respect to the rewriting rules, *i.e.* if the rewriting based evaluation reaches a normal form, then evaluation by the abstract machine terminates with the same normal form. This required building a bisimulation between the two evaluations, and was trickier than expected. Namely we need to prove the following lemma:

$$\text{Definition inst } t\ benv := \text{trm\_inst } t\ (\text{map clos2trm } benv).$$

$$\begin{aligned}&\text{Lemma complete\_rec} : \forall args\, args'\, fl\, fl'\, e\, e'\, benv\, benv'\, \tau,\\ &\quad args \equiv args' \rightarrow fl \equiv fl' \rightarrow (\text{inst } e\ benv \longrightarrow \text{inst } e'\ benv') \rightarrow\\ &\quad K;\Gamma \vdash \text{stack2trm } (\text{app2trm } (\text{inst } e\ benv)\ args)\ fl\ : \tau \rightarrow\\ &\quad \exists h, \exists h', \text{eval } h\ benv\ args\ e\ fl \equiv \text{eval } h'\ benv'\ args'\ e'\ fl'.\end{aligned}$$

where $\equiv$ denotes the equality of closures after substitution by their environment, *i.e.* $\text{clos\_abs } e\ benv \equiv \text{clos\_abs } e'\ benv'$ iff $\text{inst } (\lambda e)\ benv = \text{inst } (\lambda e')\ benv'$. Proving this by case analysis on e and e' ended up being very time consuming. The proofs being rather repetitive, they may profit from better lemmas.

6 Dependent Types

As we pointed in section 4, the statements of many lemmas and theorems include lots of well-formedness properties, which are expected to be true of any value of a given type. For instance, substitutions should be idempotent, environments should not bind the same variable twice, de Bruijn indices should not escape, kinds should be valid, *etc.*.. A natural impulse is to use dependent types to encode these properties. Yet proofs from [1] only use dependent types for the generation of fresh variables. The reason is simple enough: as soon as a value is defined as a dependent sum, using rewriting on it becomes much more cumbersome. I attempted using it for the well-formedness of polytypes, but had to abandon the idea because there were too many things to prove upfront. On the other hand, using dependent types to make sure that kinds are valid and coherent was not so hard, and helped to streamline the proofs. This is probably due to the abstract nature of constraint domains, which limits interactions between kinds and other features. The definition of kinds becomes:

$$\begin{aligned}&\text{Definition coherent } kc\ kr := \forall x\, (\tau\, \tau' : \text{typ}),\\ &\quad \text{Cstr.unique } kc\ x = \text{true} \rightarrow \text{In } (x,\tau)\ kr \rightarrow \text{In } (x,\tau')\ kr \rightarrow \tau = \tau'.\end{aligned}$$

$$\begin{aligned}&\text{Record ckind : Set} := \text{Kind}\{\\ &\quad \text{kind\_cstr : Cstr.cstr; kind\_valid : Cstr.valid kind\_cstr;}\\ &\quad \text{kind\_rel : list (Cstr.attr} \times \text{typ); kind\_coherent : coherent kind\_cstr kind\_rel}\}.\end{aligned}$$

We still need to apply substitutions to kinds, but this is not a problem as substitutions do not change the constraint, and preserve the coherence. We just need the following function.

$$\text{Definition ckind\_map\_spec} : \forall (f : \text{typ} \rightarrow \text{typ})(k : \text{ckind}),$$
$$\{k' : \text{ckind} \mid \text{kind\_cstr } k = \text{kind\_cstr } k' \wedge \text{kind\_rel } k' = \text{map\_snd } f \text{ (kind\_rel } k)\}.$$

We also sometimes have to prove the equality of two kinds obtained independently. This requires the following lemma, which can be proved using proof irrelevance[4].

$$\text{Lemma ckind\_pi} : \forall k k' : \text{ckind},$$
$$\text{kind\_cstr } k = \text{kind\_cstr } k' \rightarrow \text{kind\_rel } k = \text{kind\_rel } k' \rightarrow k = k'.$$

Another application of dependent types is ensuring termination for the unification and type inference algorithms. In Coq all functions must be complete. Originally, this was ensured by adding a step counter, and proving separately that one can choose a number of steps sufficient to obtain a result. This is the style used in section 4.1. This approach is simple, but this extra parameter stays in the extracted code. In a first version of the proof, the parameter was so big that the unification algorithm would just take forever trying to compute the number of steps it needed. I later came up with a smaller value, but it would be better to have it disappear completely. This is supported in Coq through well-founded recursion. In practice this works by moving the extra parameter to the universe of proofs (Prop), so that it will disappear during extraction. The Function command automates this, but there is a pitfall: while it generates dependent types, it doesn't support them in its input. The termination argument for unification being rather complex, this limitation proved problematic. Attempts with Program Fixpoint didn't succeed either. Finally I built the dependently typed function by hand. While this requires a rather intensive use of dependent types, the basic principle is straightforward, and it makes the proof of completeness simpler. As a result the overall size of the proof for unification didn't change. However, since the type inference algorithm calls unification, it had to be modified too, and its size grew by about 10%. An advantage of building our functions by hand is that we control exactly the term produced; since rewriting on dependently typed terms is particularly fragile, this full control proves useful.

7 Program Extraction

Both the type checker and interpreter can be extracted to Objective Caml code. This lets us build a fully certified[5] implementation for a fragment of Objective Caml's type system. Note that there is no parser or read-eval-print loop yet, making it just a one-shot interpreter for programs written directly in abstract syntax. Moreover, since Coq requires all programs to terminate, one has to indicate the number of steps to be evaluated explicitly. Well-founded recursion cannot be used here, as our language is Turing-complete. (Actually, Objective Caml allows one to define cyclic constants, so that we can build a value representing infinity, and remove the need for an explicit number of steps. However, this is going around the soundness of Coq.)

Here is an example of program written in abstract syntax (with a few abbreviations), and its inferred type (using lots of pretty printing).

---

[4] Since both validity and coherence are decidable, proof irrelevance could be avoided here by slightly changing definitions.

[5] The validity of our certification relies on the correctness of Coq and Objective Caml, which are rather strong assumptions.

```
# let rev_append =
  recf (abs (abs (abs
  (matches [0;1]
   [abs (bvar 1);
    abs (apps (bvar 3) [sub 1 (bvar 0); cons (sub 0 (bvar 0)) (bvar 1)]);
    bvar 1])))) ;;
val rev_append : trm = ...
# typinf2 Nil rev_append;;
- : (var * kind) list * typ =
  ([(10, <Ksum, {}, {0; 1}, {0 => tv 15; 1 => tv 34}>);
    (29, <Ksum, {1}, any, {1 => tv 26}>);
    (34, <Kprod, {1; 0}, any, {0 => tv 30; 1 => tv 10}>);
    (30, any);
    (26, <Kprod, {}, {0; 1}, {0 => tv 30; 1 => tv 29}>);
    (15, any)],
   tv 10 @> tv 29 @> tv 29)
```

Here recf is an extra constant which implements the fixpoint operator. Our encoding of lists uses 0 and 1 as labels for both variants and records, but we could have used any other natural numbers: their meaning is not positional, but associative. Since de Bruijn indices can be rather confusing, here is a version translated to a syntax closer to Objective Caml, with meaningful variable names and labels.

```
let rec rev_append l1 l2 =
  match l1 with
  | `Nil _ -> l2
  | `Cons c ->
    rev_append c.tl (`Cons {hd=c.hd; tl=l2})
val rev_append :
  ([< `Nil of '15 | `Cons of {hd:'30; tl:'10; ..}] as '10) ->
  ([> `Cons of {hd:'30; tl:'29}] as '29) -> '29
```

8 Related Works

The mechanization of type safety proofs for programming languages has been extensively studied. Existing works include Core ML using Coq [5], Java using Isabelle/HOL [14], and more recently full specification of OCaml light using HOL-4 [15] and Standard ML using Twelf [11,4]. The main difference in our system is the presence of structural polymorphism and recursion. In particular, among the above works, only [11] handles inclusion problems for iso-recursive types (in a simpler setting than ours, since when checking signature subtyping no structural polymorphism is allowed). It is also the work closest to our goal of handling advanced type features (it already handles fully Standard ML). OCaml-light rather focuses on subtle points in the dynamic semantics of the language. Typed Scheme [18] has a type system remarkably similar to ours, and part of the soundness proof was mechanized in Isabelle/HOL, but the mechanized part does not contain recursive types.

Concerning unification and type inference, we have already mentioned the works of Paulson in LCF [16], Dubois and Ménissier-Morain in Coq [6], and Naraschewski and Nipkow in Isabelle [13], and the more recent Isabelle/Nominal proof by Urban and Nipkow [19]. The main difference is the introduction of structural polymorphism,

Table 1. Components of the proof

File	Lines	Contents
Lib_*	1706	Auxiliary lemmas and tactics from [1]
Metatheory	1376	Metatheory lemmas and tactics from [1]
Metatheory_SP	1304	Additional lemmas and tactics
Definitions	458	Definition of the type system
Infrastructure	1152	Common lemmas
Soundness	633	Soundness proof
Rename	985	Renaming and inversion lemmas
Eval	2935	Stack-based evaluation
Unify	1832	Unification
Inference	3159	Type inference
Domain	1085	Constraint domain specific proofs
Unify_wf	1827	Unification using dependent measure
Inference_wf	3443	Inference using dependent measure

which results in much extended statements to handle admissible substitutions. Even in the absence of structural polymorphism, just handling equi-recursive types makes type inference more complex, and we are aware of no proof of principality including them. It might be interesting to compare these different proofs of W in more detail, as the first two use de Bruijn indices [6,13], the latter nominal datatypes [19], and ours cofinite quantification. However, as Urban and Nipkow already observed, while there are clear differences between the different approaches, in the case of type inference lots of low-level handling of type variables has to be done, and as a result clever encodings do not seem to be that helpful.

More generally, all the litterature concerning the PoplMark challenge [2] can be seen as relevant here, at least for the type soundness part. In particular, one could argue that structural polymorphism being related to structural subtyping, challenges 1B and 2B (transitivity of subtyping with records, and type safety with records and pattern matching) should be relevant. However, in the case of structural polymorphism, the presence of recursive types requires the use of a graph structure to represent types, which does not seem to be necessary for those challenges, where trees are sufficient. We believe that this changes the complexity of the proof.

9 Conclusion

We have reached our first goal, providing a fully certified type checker and interpreter. We show the size and contents of the various components of the proof in table 1. While this is a good start, it currently handles only a very small subset of Objective Caml. The next goal is of course to add new features. A natural next target would be the addition of side-effects, with the relaxed value restriction. Note that since the value restriction relies on subtyping, it would be natural to also add type constructors, with variance annotations, at this point. Considering the difficulties we have met up to now, we do not expect it to be an easy task.

Acknowledgments. I wish to thank the anonymous reviewers for their detailed and helpful comments.

References

1. Aydemir, B., Charguéraud, A., Pierce, B.C., Pollack, R., Weirich, S.: Engineering formal metatheory. In: Proc. ACM Symposium on Principles of Programming Languages, pp. 3–15 (2008)
2. Aydemir, B.E., Bohannon, A., Fairbairn, M., Foster, J.N., Pierce, B.C., Sewell, P., Vytiniotis, D., Washburn, G., Weirich, S., Zdancewic, S.: Mechanized metatheory for the masses: The PoplMark challenge. In: Hurd, J., Melham, T. (eds.) TPHOLs 2005. LNCS, vol. 3603, pp. 50–65. Springer, Heidelberg (2005)
3. Barras, B.: Auto-validation d'un système de preuves avec familles inductives. Thèse de doctorat, Université Paris 7 (November 1999)
4. Crary, K., Harper, B.: Mechanized definition of Standard ML alpha release. Twelf proof scripts (August 2009)
5. Dubois, C.: Proving ML type soundness within Coq. In: Aagaard, M.D., Harrison, J. (eds.) TPHOLs 2000. LNCS, vol. 1869, pp. 126–144. Springer, Heidelberg (2000)
6. Dubois, C., Ménissier-Morain, V.: Certification of a type inference tool for ML: Damas-Milner within Coq. Journal of Automated Reasoning 23(3), 319–346 (1999)
7. Furuse, J.P., Garrigue, J.: A label-selective lambda-calculus with optional arguments and its compilation method. RIMS Preprint 1041, Research Institute for Mathematical Sciences, Kyoto University (October 1995)
8. Garrigue, J.: Simple type inference for structural polymorphism. In: The Ninth International Workshop on Foundations of Object-Oriented Languages, Portland, Oregon (2002)
9. Garrigue, J.: Relaxing the value restriction. In: Kameyama, Y., Stuckey, P.J. (eds.) FLOPS 2004. LNCS, vol. 2998, Springer, Heidelberg (2004)
10. Garrigue, J., Rémy, D.: Extending ML with semi-explicit higher order polymorphism. Information and Computation 155, 134–171 (1999)
11. Lee, D.K., Crary, K., Harper, R.: Towards a mechanized metatheory of standard ML. In: Proc. ACM Symposium on Principles of Programming Languages, pp. 173–184 (January 2007)
12. Leroy, X., Doligez, D., Garrigue, J., Rémy, D., Vouillon, J.: The Objective Caml system release 3.11, Documentation and user's manual. Projet Gallium, INRIA (November 2008)
13. Naraschewski, W., Nipkow, T.: Type inference verified: Algorithm W in Isabelle/HOL. Journal of Automated Reasoning 23, 299–318 (1999)
14. Oheimb, D.v., Nipkow, T.: Machine-checking the Java specification: Proving type-safety. In: Alves-Foss, J. (ed.) Formal Syntax and Semantics of Java. LNCS, vol. 1523, pp. 119–156. Springer, Heidelberg (1999)
15. Owens, S.: A sound semantics for OCaml light. In: Drossopoulou, S. (ed.) ESOP 2008. LNCS, vol. 4960, pp. 1–15. Springer, Heidelberg (2008)
16. Paulson, L.: Verifying the unification algorithm in LCF. Science of Computer Programming 5, 143–169 (1985)
17. The Coq Team. The Coq Proof Assistant, Version 8.2. INRIA (2009)
18. Tobin-Hochstadt, S., Felleisen, M.: The design and implementation of typed scheme. In: Proc. ACM Symposium on Principles of Programming Languages (2008)
19. Urban, C., Nipkow, T.: Nominal verification of algorithm W. In: Huet, G., Lévy, J.-J., Plotkin, G. (eds.) From Semantics to Computer Science. Essays in Honour of Gilles Kahn, pp. 363–382. Cambridge University Press, Cambridge (2009)

Type Inference for Sublinear Space Functional Programming

Ugo Dal Lago[1,⋆] and Ulrich Schöpp[2,⋆⋆]

[1] University of Bologna, Italy
[2] LMU Munich, Germany

Abstract. We consider programming language aspects of algorithms that operate on data too large to fit into memory. In previous work we have introduced IntML, a functional programming language with primitives that support the implementation of such algorithms. We have shown that IntML can express all LOGSPACE functions but have left open the question how easy it is in practice to program typical LOGSPACE algorithms in IntML. In this paper we develop algorithms for IntML type inference. We show that with type inference one can handle programs that could not be reasonably manipulated by hand. We do so by implementing in IntML a typical LOGSPACE algorithm, a test for acyclicity of undirected graphs. Thus we show that with type inference IntML can express typical algorithmic patterns of LOGSPACE easily and in a natural way.

The study of algorithms operating on data too large to fit into memory has a long tradition in complexity theory; it comprises in particular the complexity classes LOGSPACE and NLOGSPACE of algorithms with logarithmic space usage. By comparison, questions about the programming language aspects of these classes have received little study. What is a good way of programming LOGSPACE algorithms in, say, a functional language? How should one represent values that do not fit in memory and that can only be accessed piece by piece from some external store, such as the input and output of a LOGSPACE function?

To approach such questions, we have recently introduced the functional programming language IntML with support for working with externally stored data [6]. As a first test of the expressive power of IntML, we have shown that each LOGSPACE-function can be expressed in IntML. However, since this result is obtained by encoding Turing Machines, it is not very informative about whether or not it is possible to program such functions easily and in a natural way. In this paper we ask how easy it is to express well-known algorithms with logarithmic space usage in IntML. We take a typical LOGSPACE-algorithm, Cook & McKenzie's test for acyclicity in undirected graphs [5], and show that it can be programmed in IntML in a natural way.

The main contribution of this paper is the development of type inference algorithms for IntML, which make programming such typical LOGSPACE-algorithms in IntML practical. Type inference is particularly important, as the IntML type system allows one to

⋆ The author is partially supported by PRIN project "CONCERTO" and FIRB grant RBIN04M8S8, "Intern. Inst. for Applicable Math."

⋆⋆ Part of this work was carried out while the author was supported by the Institute of Advanced Studies at the University of Bologna.

K. Ueda (Ed.): APLAS 2010, LNCS 6461, pp. 376–391, 2010.

read off bounds on the space-usage of programs directly from a typing derivation, which means that writing out all type information fully will soon become unmanageable. In this paper we show that much of this information can be reconstructed automatically using a type inference algorithm. While type inference has been shown to be possible for languages capturing PTIME [2,4], in the context of languages for sublinear space the possibility of type inference has not been investigated.

1 Programming with Bidirectional Data Flow

The definition of IntML can be summarised as follows: start with a standard functional programming language and extend it with primitives for writing programs with bidirectional data flow. Bidirectional data flow is an important property of computation with external data that may not fit into memory. An input that is too large to be stored cannot be read all at once; it can only be queried piece-by-piece during the course of the computation. Thus, information flows not just from the input to a program but in the form of queries also in the opposite direction. We believe that providing a good account for this kind of bidirectional data flow should be a central goal in the construction of programming languages for computation with external data.

The construction of IntML starts with a very simple language having just polynomial types α, 1, $A + A$ and $A \times A$. It has the usual terms for these types and also a loop construct for possibly nonterminating iteration. More details are not needed for now (but they appear below). Richer languages are possible, but this one is suitable for capturing LOGSPACE. We consider this language as a model of computation with unidirectional data flow. A term $c{:}A \vdash f\colon B$ represents a function from values of type A to values of type B, which can be computed by substituting an input for c and subsequent reduction.

Suppose now that there is some externally stored data that we can query piece-by-piece. Its interface is given by a pair of types (X^-, X^+). The type X^- consists of the queries that may be sent to the datum and the type X^+ encodes possible answers. For example, to represent binary words that can be queried character-by-character, one may take X^- to be a type that can represent the position of characters in the word and one may take X^+ to be a type that can encode the characters themselves. We may take X^+ to be $1 + 1$ and it is reasonable to use a binary encoding for the character positions, i.e. take $X^- = (1 + 1) \times \cdots \times (1 + 1)$ (k times). With this interface we can represent words of length up to 2^k, so we can note here already that the size of the values of type X^- and X^+ is logarithmic in the length of the words that can be represented.

A program with bidirectional data flow can now be considered as a message passing node with a number of input and output wires, e.g. Fig. 1. Each wire has a direction and is labelled with a pair of types $X = (X^-, X^+)$. The intention is that values of type X^+ can flow as messages in the direction of the wire, and values of type X^- can flow in the opposite direction, see Fig. 2. Message passing nodes are stateless and may react to messages arriving (one at a time) at one of the wires connected to them. When a message arrives, the node uses it as input in order to compute an output message that it may then pass along one of the wires connected to it. We emphasise that wires are bidirectional and that messages can be passed in *both* directions on all wires. The direction of the wire merely determines which type of message can be passed in each direction. It would

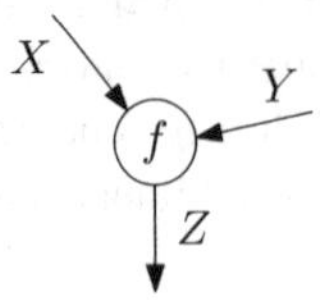

Fig. 1. A node

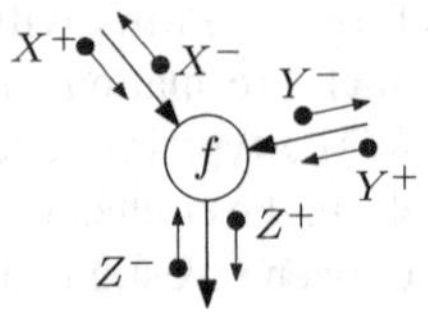

Fig. 2. Types of messages

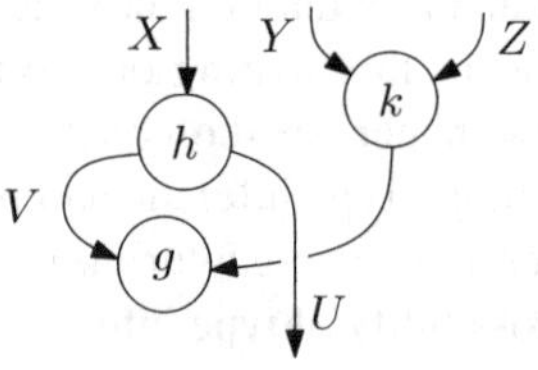

Fig. 3. A circuit

make no difference if we reversed an edge labelled with $Z = (Z^-, Z^+)$ and changed the label to $Z^* = (Z^+, Z^-)$.

Several such message passing nodes can be combined easily, simply by connecting matching wires to form message passing circuits. For example, in the example circuit in Fig. 3, a value of type U^- may be passed to h against the direction of the output wire. With this input, the node h may then perhaps decide to pass a value of type V^+ along the wire to g or to return a value of type X^- to the environment. It may also decide not to do anything, in which case the whole computation will be blocked. Also, message passing inside the network may go on indefinitely in an infinite loop.

We have found that this way of modelling bidirectional computation by message passing nodes is useful for constructing programs that access externally stored data by means of message passing. This model accounts for sublinear space computation, as the accessed data may be much larger than the messages used to access it.

For the definition of IntML it is important to notice that the message passing circuits can be implemented in the simple functional language that we started with. The node f shown in Fig. 1 can be implemented by a term that takes as input a value of type $Z^- + (X^+ + Y^+)$ and that gives as output a value of type $Z^+ + (X^- + Y^-)$. If a message z of type Z^- arrives at the node, we give $\mathsf{inl}(z)$ as an input to this term and evaluate the result. If the result is $\mathsf{inr}(\mathsf{inl}(x))$, say, then we pass on x along the edge labelled with X. It is not hard to see, even with minimal assumptions about the language, that if all the nodes in a circuit can be implemented thus, then so can the whole circuit. For instance, the circuit in Fig. 3 can be implemented by a term $c\colon U^- + X^+ + Y^+ + Z^+ \vdash u\colon U^+ + X^- + Y^- + Z^-$ that takes as input a message that may arrive at one of the ports of the circuit and that returns the message that will come out of the circuit. Thus, we may think of the circuits as a tool for writing programs with bidirectional data flow in the simple programming language. However, writing such programs for circuits can be quite awkward. Try, for example, to write out a program (in OCaml or Haskell, say) for the circuit in Fig. 3 from given programs for g, h and k.

IntML provides programming language primitives for a more convenient construction and manipulation of such circuits. These primitives are not just a textual representation of circuits; they take the form of well-established programming language constructs like pairs and functions. The new primitives are a conservative extension of the original language; they can only be used to program circuits that could have been programmed directly as well.

$$\frac{}{\Sigma,\, c{:}A \vdash c\colon A} \qquad \frac{}{\Sigma \vdash min_A\colon A} \qquad \frac{\Sigma \vdash f\colon A}{\Sigma \vdash succ_A(f)\colon A} \qquad \frac{\Sigma \vdash f\colon A \qquad \Sigma \vdash g\colon A}{\Sigma \vdash eq_A(f,g)\colon 1+1}$$

$$\frac{}{\Sigma \vdash *\colon 1} \qquad \frac{\Sigma \vdash f\colon A \qquad \Sigma \vdash g\colon B}{\Sigma \vdash \langle f,g\rangle\colon A\times B} \qquad \frac{\Sigma \vdash f\colon A\times B}{\Sigma \vdash \mathsf{fst}(f)\colon A} \qquad \frac{\Sigma \vdash f\colon A\times B}{\Sigma \vdash \mathsf{snd}(g)\colon B}$$

$$\frac{\Sigma \vdash f\colon A}{\Sigma \vdash \mathsf{inl}(f)\colon A+B} \qquad \frac{\Sigma \vdash f\colon A+B \qquad \Sigma,\, c{:}A \vdash g\colon C \qquad \Sigma,\, d{:}B \vdash h\colon C}{\Sigma \vdash \mathsf{case}\ f\ \mathsf{of}\ \mathsf{inl}(c) \Rightarrow g \mid \mathsf{inr}(d) \Rightarrow h\colon C}$$

$$\frac{\Sigma \vdash f\colon B}{\Sigma \vdash \mathsf{inr}(f)\colon A+B} \qquad \frac{\Sigma,\, c{:}A \vdash f\colon A+B \quad \Sigma \vdash g\colon A}{\Sigma \vdash \mathsf{loop}(c.\,f)(g)\colon B} \qquad \frac{\Sigma \mid - \vdash t\colon [A]}{\Sigma \vdash \mathsf{unbox}(t)\colon A}$$

Fig. 4. Working Class Typing Rules

2 IntML

IntML has two classes of terms and types, one corresponding to the functional programming language that we start with and one for working with circuits over this language. We call the former the *working class* and the latter the *upper class*. This terminology reflects that all computation will be done by working class terms. Upper class terms merely represent message passing circuits; the actual message passing will be done by the working class terms implementing the circuits.

For completeness we include a definition of the working class calculus. Its types are

$$A ::= \alpha \mid 1 \mid A+A \mid A\times A$$

and the typing rules are given in Fig. 4. This language is a fairly standard call-by-value language. For convenience we include constants min_A, $succ_A$ and eq_A for any type, including types with variables. These constants provide a total ordering on any type generically. For example, min_{1+1} is $\mathsf{inl}(*)$ and its successor is $\mathsf{inr}(*)$. The constant loop is a simple way of including iteration in the language. The intended operational semantics is $\mathsf{loop}(c.f)(v) \longrightarrow \mathsf{case}\ f[v/c]\ \mathsf{of}\ \mathsf{inl}(d) \Rightarrow \mathsf{loop}(c.f)(d) \mid \mathsf{inr}(d) \Rightarrow d$.

The upper class part of IntML is a calculus of circuits over working class terms. Upper class terms denote circuits and the types denote the labels of the wires going in and coming out of such circuits.

The upper class types in IntML are formed by the following grammar

$$X ::= \beta \mid [A] \mid X\otimes X \mid A\cdot X \multimap X$$

in which A ranges over working class types. The type $[A]$ is intended to denote a wire with $[A]^- = 1$ and $[A]^+ = A$. It represents an interface of a thunk: we may send the unique element of 1 as a signal to start some computation, whose result of type A we expect to arrive from the same wire. A thunk node $[f]$, as shown below, can be implemented by a working class term $c{:}1 \vdash f\colon A$. The type $X\otimes Y$ represents a bundle of a wire of type X and a wire of type Y. Such a bundle can be implemented as a single wire with $(X\otimes Y)^- = X^- + Y^-$ and $(X\otimes Y)^+ = X^+ + Y^+$. It is straightforward to implement message passing nodes for the packing and unpacking of such bundles:

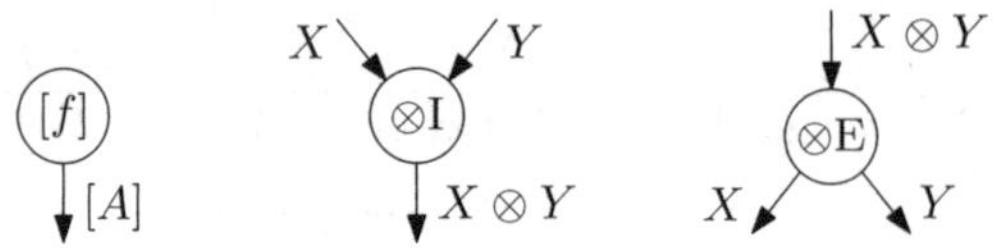

The type $A \cdot X \multimap Y$, in which A is a working class type, represents a function space. One should read $A \cdot X$ as an A-fold copy of X, one copy for each value of type A. Thus, the type $A \cdot X \multimap Y$ denotes functions from X to Y, in which the argument can be used A-many times. We use a type A instead of natural numbers or polynomials, since we usually want to use working class values to address the particular copies of X and it would be awkward to have to encode and decode them as numbers in the language. We call A the *index type* of the function.

In terms of circuit wires, the type $A \cdot X \multimap Y$ is implemented by $(A \cdot X \multimap Y)^- = A \times X^+ + Y^-$ and $(A \cdot X \multimap Y)^+ = A \times X^- + Y^+$. This definition captures functions in a way familiar from game semantics, see e.g. [1]. When one asks a function for its result (sends a query in Y^-), it may come back with an answer (a message in Y^+) or with a request for its argument (a message in X^-). The argument circuit may send its answer (of type X^+) along the same channel as the original question. The A-fold replication of the argument is implemented by adding to the message a component $A \times -$ that indicates the copy that we are communicating with.

The terms of the upper class calculus represent circuits. The typing sequents have the form

$$\Sigma \mid x_1 : A_1 \cdot X_1, \ldots, x_n : A_n \cdot X_n \vdash t \colon Y \ ,$$

where Σ is a working class context. In this sequent each upper class variable x_i is assigned an upper class type X_i and appears with a multiplicity given by an *index type* A_i, which is a working class type. The term t in this sequent represents a circuit with one outgoing wire labelled Y and with n incoming wires labelled with $A_1 \cdot X_1$, $\ldots$, $A_n \cdot X_n$, where $A_i \cdot X_i = (A_i \times X_i^-, A_i \times X_i^+)$. This circuit is implemented by a working class program that may refer to the variables from Σ.

The upper class calculus appears in Fig. 5. In these rules we write $A \cdot \Gamma$ for the context obtained by replacing each declaration $x : B \cdot X$ in Γ with $x : (A \times B) \cdot X$.

The upper class terms represent a number of constructions on circuits. For example, the term $\langle s, t \rangle$ in rule (⊗I) corresponds to taking the two circuits for s and t and joining their output wires with the node ⊗I shown above.

Note that all rules are additive in the context Σ, so that in particular the variables from this context can be used more than once. That this is very useful can be seen in the examples in Sect. 3, where working-class variables are often used more than once. The only upper class rule that modifies the context Σ is ([ ]E). Informally the let-term in this rule first requests the output from the circuit for s. Upon receipt of this value (of type A), it then binds c to this value and requests the value of circuit t.

The structural rule (STRUCT) has a side condition $A \precsim B$, which informally states that any value of type A can be encoded as a value of type B. The rule is sound whenever A is a retract of B, which means that there are working class terms $c{:}A \vdash f \colon B$ and $d{:}B \vdash g \colon A$ such that for any closed value $v{:}A$, the term $g[f[v/c]/d]$ reduces to v.

$$\text{(VAR)}\ \frac{}{\Sigma \mid \Gamma,\, x\colon 1\cdot X \vdash x\colon X} \qquad \text{(STRUCT)}\ \frac{\Sigma \mid \Gamma,\, x\colon A\cdot X \vdash s\colon Y}{\Sigma \mid \Gamma,\, x\colon B\cdot X \vdash s\colon Y}\ A \precsim B$$

$$\text{(WEAK)}\ \frac{\Sigma \mid \Gamma \vdash s\colon Y}{\Sigma \mid \Gamma,\, x\colon A\cdot X \vdash s\colon Y} \qquad \text{(EXCH)}\ \frac{\Sigma \mid \Gamma,\, x\colon A\cdot X,\, y\colon B\cdot Y,\, \Delta \vdash s\colon Z}{\Sigma \mid \Gamma,\, y\colon B\cdot Y,\, x\colon A\cdot X,\, \Delta \vdash s\colon Z}$$

$$(\otimes\text{I})\ \frac{\Sigma \mid \Gamma \vdash s\colon X \qquad \Sigma \mid \Delta \vdash t\colon Y}{\Sigma \mid \Gamma,\, \Delta \vdash \langle s,t\rangle\colon X \otimes Y}$$

$$(\otimes\text{E})\ \frac{\Sigma \mid \Gamma \vdash s\colon X \otimes Y \qquad \Sigma \mid \Delta,\, x\colon A\cdot X,\, y\colon A\cdot Y \vdash t\colon Z}{\Sigma \mid \Delta,\, A\cdot\Gamma \vdash \mathsf{let}\ s\ \mathsf{be}\ \langle x,y\rangle\ \mathsf{in}\ t\colon Z}$$

$$(\multimap\text{I})\ \frac{\Sigma \mid \Gamma,\, x\colon A\cdot X \vdash s\colon Y}{\Sigma \mid \Gamma \vdash \lambda x.\, s\colon A\cdot X \multimap Y} \qquad (\multimap\text{E})\ \frac{\Sigma \mid \Gamma \vdash s\colon A\cdot X \multimap Y \qquad \Sigma \mid \Delta \vdash t\colon X}{\Sigma \mid \Gamma,\, A\cdot\Delta \vdash s\,t\colon Y}$$

$$\text{(CONTR)}\ \frac{\Sigma \mid \Gamma \vdash s\colon X \qquad \Sigma \mid \Delta,\, x\colon A\cdot X,\, y\colon B\cdot X \vdash t\colon Y}{\Sigma \mid \Delta,\, (A+B)\cdot\Gamma \vdash \mathsf{copy}\ s\ \mathsf{as}\ x,y\ \mathsf{in}\ t\colon Y}$$

$$\text{(CASE)}\ \frac{\Sigma \vdash f\colon A+B \qquad \Sigma,\, c{:}A \mid \Gamma \vdash s\colon X \qquad \Sigma,\, d{:}B \mid \Gamma \vdash t\colon X}{\Sigma \mid \Gamma \vdash \mathsf{case}\ f\ \mathsf{of}\ \mathsf{inl}(c) \Rightarrow s \mid \mathsf{inr}(d) \Rightarrow t\colon X}$$

$$([\,]\text{I})\ \frac{\Sigma \vdash f\colon A}{\Sigma \mid - \vdash [f]\colon [A]} \qquad ([\,]\text{E})\ \frac{\Sigma \mid \Gamma \vdash s\colon [A] \qquad \Sigma,\, c{:}A \mid \Delta \vdash t\colon [B]}{\Sigma \mid \Gamma,\, A\cdot\Delta \vdash \mathsf{let}\ s\ \mathsf{be}\ [c]\ \mathsf{in}\ t\colon [B]}$$

$$\text{(HACK)}\ \frac{\Sigma,\, c{:}X^- \vdash f\colon X^+}{\Sigma \mid - \vdash \mathsf{hack}_X(c.f)\colon Y}\ \begin{array}{l} X \precsim Y, \\ X \text{ and } Y \text{ contain no upper class type variables}\end{array}$$

Fig. 5. Upper Class Typing Rules

Here we choose for $\precsim$ the following syntactic approximation of retraction. Let *structural congruence* $\cong$ be the smallest congruence on working class types that satisfies:

$$A \times 1 \cong A \qquad\qquad 1 \times A \cong A \qquad \text{(U)}$$

$$A \times (B + C) \cong A \times B + A \times C \qquad (B + C) \times A \cong B \times A + C \times A \qquad \text{(D)}$$

Let $\leq$ be the the least reflexive, transitive relation that satisfies $A \leq A+B$, $B \leq A+B$, $A \leq A \times B$ and $B \leq A \times B$, and that is compatible with all type operations, in the sense that $A \leq B$ implies $C[A/\alpha] \leq C[B/\alpha]$ for all C. We then define

$$A \precsim B \iff \exists C.\, A \leq C \cong B\ .$$

We remark that $A \precsim B$ is also equivalent to $\exists C, D.\, A \cong C \leq D \cong B$ and moreover that $\precsim$ is transitive. It can also be shown that $A \precsim B$ and $B \precsim A$ imply $A \cong B$.

We include the rule (STRUCT) to make index types more flexible. The unit laws (U) allow us to give the composition $\lambda x.\, f\ (g\ x)$ of two upper class functions $f\colon 1\cdot X \multimap Y$ and $g\colon 1\cdot Y \multimap Z$ the type $1\cdot X \multimap Z$. Otherwise this term could only be given type

$(1 \times 1) \cdot X \multimap Z$. Distributivity (D) is useful to type the terms $s\ (\mathsf{copy}\ x\ \mathsf{as}\ x_1, x_2\ \mathsf{in}\ t)$ and $\mathsf{copy}\ x\ \mathsf{as}\ x_1, x_2\ \mathsf{in}\ (s\ t)$ in the same context. Without distributivity we only have:

$$\Sigma \mid \Gamma,\ x\colon (A \times (C + D)) \cdot X \vdash s\ (\mathsf{copy}\ x\ \mathsf{as}\ x_1, x_2\ \mathsf{in}\ t)\colon Z$$
$$\Sigma \mid \Gamma,\ x\colon (A \times C + A \times D) \cdot X \vdash \mathsf{copy}\ x\ \mathsf{as}\ x_1, x_2\ \mathsf{in}\ (s\ t)\colon Z$$

Finally, the inequalities $\leq$ are often useful in conjunction with rule ($\otimes$E). The right premise of ($\otimes$E) demands that the index types of x and y are the same and the inequalities can be used to satisfy that demand.

The upper class rules are completed by the rule (HACK). With this rule a programmer can implement message passing nodes directly by providing a working class term. This rule can be used to define constants of complex types that would otherwise not be definable. We like to think of (HACK) as an analogue of inline assembly in C.

An important use of (HACK) is for the definition of an iteration combinator [6]:

$$\texttt{loop}\colon \alpha \cdot (\gamma \cdot [\alpha] \multimap [\alpha + \beta]) \multimap [\alpha] \multimap [\beta]$$

Informally, the first argument of `loop` is the step function and the second argument is the initial value. The return value of the step function is either the final result (of type β) or the value for the next application of the step function: $\texttt{loop}\ s\ t = [w]$ if $s\ t = [\mathsf{inr}(w)]$ and $\texttt{loop}\ s\ t = \texttt{loop}\ s\ [w]$ if $s\ t = [\mathsf{inl}(w)]$. To make loops easier to read, we use $\mathsf{return}(w)$ and $\mathsf{continue}(w)$ as abbreviations for $\mathsf{inr}(w)$ and $\mathsf{inl}(w)$ respectively.

We formulate the rule (HACK) so that the type of $\mathsf{hack}_X(c.f)$ is closed under structural manipulation analogous to rule (STRUCT). We may extend structural congruence to upper class types by defining $\precsim$ to be the least reflexive relation satisfying:

$$(X \precsim Z) \wedge (Y \precsim U) \implies (X \otimes Y) \precsim (Z \otimes U)$$
$$(B \precsim A) \wedge (Z \precsim X) \wedge (Y \precsim U) \implies (A \cdot X \multimap Y) \precsim (B \cdot Z \multimap U)$$

Without terms of the form $\mathsf{hack}_X(c.f)$, the type system has the property that $\Sigma \mid \Gamma \vdash t\colon X$ and $X \precsim Y$ implies $\Sigma \mid \Gamma \vdash t\colon Y$. A derivation of $\Sigma \mid \Gamma \vdash t\colon X$ can be turned into one of $\Sigma \mid \Gamma \vdash t\colon Y$ by inserting applications of rule (STRUCT). To maintain this typing property in the presence of hack-terms, we allow $\mathsf{hack}_X(c.f)$ to have any type Y with $X \precsim Y$.

For details about the translation of upper class terms to circuits we refer to [6]. For the practical use of the upper class language, it is not important to know the technical details of the translation. The upper class terms may be understood in terms of a simple operational semantics with reductions such as $(\lambda x.\, s)\ t \longrightarrow s[t/x]$ and $(\mathsf{let}\ [v]\ \mathsf{be}\ [c]\ t) \longrightarrow t[v/c]$ and the translation to circuits is a sound (and space efficient!) implementation of this operational semantics [6].

Nevertheless, we should outline how the translation to circuits can be used to obtain space bounds for IntML programs. An upper class IntML-term is compiled to a circuit in which each wire is annotated with a pair of working class types. The working class types that thus appear in the compiled circuits can be read-off from a typing derivation of the term. Now, in the evaluation of a circuit, at any time one needs to store only the message that is just being passed along some edge together with its position. Hence, the space needed to evaluate a circuit depends only on the size of the circuit and the maximum size of a message that can be passed along one of its edges. The size of the circuit is constant and a bound on the size of messages can be found simply by looking at the types that are written on the various wires. Due to the simplicity of the working class calculus, it is quite easy to give bounds on the size of values of given working class types. In this way, we obtain useful bounds on the space usage of IntML programs simply by looking at the types that appear in the circuits of upper class programs.

3 Application: Graph Algorithms

To illustrate that algorithms with external data can be expressed quite naturally in IntML and to show how interesting space bounds can be read off from a typing derivation, we present an implementation of a classic LOGSPACE graph algorithm in IntML. We implement the test of acyclicity in undirected graphs due to Cook & McKenzie [5]. Of course, IntML is LOGSPACE-complete [6], so we already know that a program for this problem can be written in IntML, just as in any other LOGSPACE-complete language. The particular implementation in this section shows that the known algorithm can be programmed in IntML in a fairly natural way, which does not follow from LOGSPACE-completeness. The example also provides good motivation for studying type inference.

In the implementation of graph algorithms we use a higher-order representation of graphs, where a graph is given by two predicates on a carrier type. The first predicate is unary and tells which elements of the carrier represent graph nodes; the second predicate is binary and encodes the edge predicate. In IntML such a pair of predicates can be represented by the upper class type below. Therein, α is the carrier and β and γ are parameters (which we will usually elide) and the type $2 = 1 + 1$ represents booleans.

$$\mathit{Graph}_{\beta,\gamma}(\alpha) = (\beta \cdot [\alpha] \multimap [2]) \otimes (\gamma \cdot [\alpha \times \alpha] \multimap [2])$$

Since in IntML each working class type comes with a total ordering, we do not need to choose up front a type for α and can just use the total ordering on this type variable α.

Leaving α to be a type variable is important also in order to handle input graphs of arbitrary size. Suppose we have a program of polymorphic type $A \cdot \mathit{Graph}(\alpha) \multimap [2]$ and we have a (large, externally stored) graph of size n that we would like to give as input to that program. The graph may be given in any reasonable encoding, e.g. by a textual encoding of adjacency list on a tape as for Turing Machines. To evaluate the program with this graph as input we choose for α a type N large enough to encode all the nodes of the graph. The interface between the program and the graph is then given in terms of the messages that are being passed along the edge with label $(A[N/\alpha]) \cdot \mathit{Graph}(N)$. To start the evaluation of the program, we send it the request for its result value of type $[2]$. Now, the program may reply with a request to the graph of type $((A[N/\alpha]) \cdot \mathit{Graph}(N))^-$. In this event we interpret the request on the particular input graph, pack up the answer as a value of type $((A[N/\alpha]) \cdot \mathit{Graph}(N))^+$ and pass it back to the program. We continue thus until the program returns its final answer of type $[2]$.

The choice of graph representation is not only quite natural, it also allows us to obtain logarithmic space bounds easily [6]. If for α we choose the type $2 \times \cdots \times 2$ (k times), then $\mathit{Graph}(\alpha)$ can represent graphs with up to 2^k nodes. On the other hand, the values of type $\mathit{Graph}(\alpha)^-$ and $\mathit{Graph}(\alpha)^+$ have size $O(k)$, as is easily seen directly.

The algorithm of Cook & McKenzie for checking acyclicity of undirected graphs can be explained using the notion of a right-hand walk. A right-hand walk is like a walk in a labyrinth where one always keeps his right hand on the wall. One imagines the graph edges to be corridors and the nodes to be junctions. The edges connected to each node are ordered as if the node were a junction of the arriving corridors. Cook & McKenzie's observation then is that an undirected graph is acyclic if and only if any right-hand walk will return to its starting point by traversing the edge over which it has left this point in the opposite direction. This observation leads to a LOGSPACE algorithm, since this property can be checked by following right-hand walks, and for this one needs to keep in memory just a few graph nodes.

To present an implementation of this algorithm in IntML, we introduce a few notational abbreviations. First, when programming in IntML it is usually not necessary to think about the index types. We will therefore hide them and write just $X \to Y$ instead of $A \cdot X \multimap Y$, with the understanding that A is still there, it is just not shown.

For accessing the node and edge predicates of a given graph we use functions $\mathit{node} = \lambda \mathit{graph}.\, \mathsf{let}\ \mathit{graph}\ \mathsf{be}\ \langle n, e\rangle\ \mathsf{in}\ n$ and $\mathit{egde} = \lambda \mathit{graph}.\, \mathsf{let}\ \mathit{graph}\ \mathsf{be}\ \langle n, e\rangle\ \mathsf{in}\ e$. We also write *src* and *dst* as abbreviations for fst and snd when they are used on pairs in $\alpha \times \alpha$ that represent edges.

We use 2 as a type of boolean values and define $\mathit{true} = \mathsf{inl}(*)$ and $\mathit{false} = \mathsf{inr}(*)$. Upper class case distinction $\mathit{if}\colon [2] \to X \to X \to X$ can for arbitrary X be defined by $\lambda b.\, \lambda x.\, \lambda y.\, \mathsf{let}\ b\ \mathsf{be}\ [c]\ \mathsf{in}\ \mathsf{case}\ c\ \mathsf{of}\ \mathsf{inl}(t) \Rightarrow x \mid \mathsf{inr}(f) \Rightarrow y$. We also use a similarly defined function $\mathit{and}\colon [2] \to [2] \to [2]$.

With these definitions, we can implement an algorithm for checking acyclicity. In order to implement right-hand walks, we first need a function

$$\mathit{nextEdge}_\alpha\colon \mathit{Graph}(\alpha) \to [\alpha \times \alpha] \to [\alpha \times \alpha]$$

that takes an edge $\langle s, d\rangle$ and returns the next edge $\langle s, e\rangle$ emanating from the same source. It does so by repeatedly applying succ_α to the second component of the pair, wrapping around to min_α if the maximum element is reached, until an edge is found. Recall that all working class types come with a total ordering.

We can then write a function $\mathit{checkpath}_\alpha$, which follows a right-hand-rule walk starting from some given edge and checks if this walk returns to its origin by walking the given edge in the opposite direction.

$$
\begin{aligned}
&\mathit{checkpath}_\alpha\colon \mathit{Graph}(\alpha) \to [\alpha \times \alpha] \to [2] \;=\\
&\quad \lambda \mathit{graph}.\, \lambda \mathit{inputedge}.\ \mathsf{copy}\ \mathit{graph}\ \mathsf{as}\ \mathit{graph1}, \mathit{graph2}\ \mathsf{in}\\
&\qquad\qquad \mathsf{let}\ \mathit{inputedge}\ \mathsf{be}\ [e]\ \mathsf{in}\\
&\qquad\qquad \mathit{if}\,(\mathit{edge}\ \mathit{graph1}\ [e])\\
&\qquad\qquad\quad (\mathtt{loop}\ (\lambda w.\, \mathsf{let}\ w\ \mathsf{be}\ [p]\ \mathsf{in}\\
&\qquad\qquad\qquad\qquad \mathit{if}\,[\mathit{eq}_\alpha(\mathit{dst}\ p, \mathit{src}\ e)]\\
&\qquad\qquad\qquad\qquad\quad [\mathsf{return}(\mathit{eq}_\alpha(\mathit{src}\ p, \mathit{dst}\ e))]\\
&\qquad\qquad\qquad\qquad\quad (\mathsf{let}\ \mathit{nextEdge}_\alpha\ \mathit{graph2}\ [\langle \mathit{dst}\ p, \mathit{src}\ p\rangle]\\
&\qquad\qquad\qquad\qquad\qquad \mathsf{be}\ [d]\ \mathsf{in}\ [\mathsf{continue}(d)])))\ [e])\\
&\qquad\qquad\quad [\mathit{true}]
\end{aligned}
$$

Now, writing a function $checkcycle_\alpha$ for testing acyclicity of undirected graphs it a simple matter of applying $checkpath_\alpha$ to all edges in the graph and combining the results using *and*. We can do this by using a combinator $fold_\beta$, which is such that $fold_\beta\ f\ y$ computes $f\ x_n\ (\dots (f\ x_1\ (f\ x_0\ y)))$, where $x_0 = min_\beta$ and $x_{i+1} = succ_\beta(x_i)$ and x_n is the maximum element of β, i.e. the element with $x_n = succ_\beta(x_n)$. The combinator $fold_\beta$ is not hard to define, see [6].

$$
\begin{array}{l}
checkcycle_\alpha : Graph(\alpha) \to [2] = \\
\quad \lambda graph.\ \mathsf{copy}\ graph\ \mathsf{as}\ graph1, graph2\ \mathsf{in} \\
\qquad fold_{\alpha\times\alpha}\ (\lambda vertexpair.\ \lambda acyclic. \\
\qquad\qquad\qquad \mathsf{let}\ vertexpair\ \mathsf{be}\ [e]\ \mathsf{in} \\
\qquad\qquad\qquad and\ acyclic \\
\qquad\qquad\qquad\quad (if\ (edge\ graph1\ [e]) \\
\qquad\qquad\qquad\qquad (checkpath_\alpha\ graph2\ [e]) \\
\qquad\qquad\qquad\qquad [true])) \\
\qquad\qquad [true]
\end{array}
$$

Above we have hidden the index types in the type of $checkcycle_\alpha$. Fully spelt out, this function may be given the type

$$A \cdot ((\beta \cdot [\alpha] \multimap [2]) \otimes (\gamma \cdot [\alpha \times \alpha] \multimap [2])) \multimap [2],$$

where A is the working class type $(\alpha \times \alpha \times 2 \times (\alpha \times \alpha \times 2) \times (\alpha \times \alpha \times 2) + \alpha \times \alpha \times 2 \times (\alpha \times \alpha \times 2) \times (\alpha \times \alpha \times (2 \times (2 \times ((\alpha \times \alpha + \alpha \times \alpha \times (2 \times (\alpha \times \alpha \times (\alpha \times \alpha \times (2 \times (\alpha \times \alpha \times (\alpha \times \alpha \times (\alpha \times \alpha))))))))))))$. The program may therefore use A-many copies of the input graph, one for each value of type A. The type variables β and γ indicate that the program does not impose constraints on how often the node- and edge-predicates may use their argument. However, without loss of generality β and γ could be instantiated to 1, since by the rule ([−]-E) there is no need to use arguments of thunk-type more than once.

The index type A may look complicated, but we did not have to consider it when writing the function above. It was computed by a type inference algorithm only *after* the program was already written.

The type A tells us something about the space usage of the program. Whenever the program sends a request to the graph, such as whether a pair of type $\alpha \times \alpha$ is an edge, it encodes its internal state as a value of type A, so that it can resume work when an answer arrives. Examining A, we see that storing one of its elements needs about as much space to store 20 elements of type α, which here represent graph nodes.

By considering all the edges in the circuit for $checkcycle_\alpha$ in this way, we can read off from the circuit how many graph nodes this function needs to store and thus obtain an upper bound on its space usage. In this example, our prototype implementation obtains a space bound of $20x + 1460$, where x is an upper bound on the size of the values in α. In other words, the program needs to store 20 nodes and it needs some constant space of size 1460. Here, we use the standard size of values, e.g. $|\langle f, g\rangle| = 1 + |f| + |g|$ and $|\mathsf{inl}(f)| = 1 + |f|$. For a given input graph with n nodes, we can take α to be

$2 \times \cdots \times 2$ ($\lceil \log n \rceil$ times), so that simply by looking at the types of the circuits we obtain a logarithmic space bound for the overall program.

4 Type Inference

The graph algorithm example shows that it is not hard to understand which type an upper class term has, so long as we hide the index types. We have found that the types are not generally a hindrance when writing upper class programs. However, the example also shows that the index types quickly become too complicated to be handled by hand. The practicability of IntML depends on useful type inference algorithms. In this section we analyse the problem of type inference and develop the simple algorithm that we have used to infer the types of the above example.

Type inference is essential to making IntML programming practical: IntML programs have minimal type annotations, but once they have been typed, space bounds for their evaluation can be read off from the types, as explained above for graph algorithms. Thus, type inference amounts to inference of space bounds and we cannot expect a programmer to calculate such bounds by hand.

4.1 Constraint-Based Type Inference

As is standard, see e.g. [9], we separate the type inference algorithms into two parts: finding a set of constraints that needs to be solved in order for a term to be typed and solving the constraint set.

Definition 1. *A* constraint *is either an equality $X = Y$ between upper class types or an equality $A = B$, a structural inequality $A \precsim B$ or a congruence $A \cong B$ between working class types.*

Although $A \cong B$ can be expressed by $\{A \precsim B,\ B \precsim A\}$, we include $\cong$-constraints for technical convenience.

For a type substitution σ, i.e. a finite mapping from upper class type variables to upper class types and working class type variables to working class types, and a set of constraints C, we write $\sigma \models C$ if applying σ to all the types in C makes all the constraints therein true (in the evident sense). We say that σ *is a solution of* C.

We define two partial type inference functions $\mathcal{T}(\Sigma, f)$ and $\mathcal{T}(\Sigma \mid \Gamma, t)$. The first returns a pair (A, C) of a working-class type and a set of constraints, and the second returns a pair (X, C) of an upper class type and a set of constraints. These functions compute principal types in the following sense:

Proposition 1 (Soundness)

1. *If $\mathcal{T}(\Sigma, f) = (A, C)$ and $\sigma \models C$ then $\Sigma\sigma \vdash f\sigma\colon A\sigma$.*
2. *If $\mathcal{T}(\Sigma \mid \Gamma, t) = (X, C)$ and $\sigma \models C$ then $\Sigma\sigma \mid \Gamma\sigma \vdash t\sigma\colon X\sigma$.*

Proposition 2 (Completeness)

1. *If $\Sigma\sigma \vdash f\sigma\colon A\sigma$ then there exist B and C with $\mathcal{T}(\Sigma, f) = (B, C)$ such that σ can be extended to a type substitution ρ satisfying $A\sigma = B\rho$ and $\rho \models C$.*

$$\frac{\Gamma \text{ contains } x : A{\cdot}X}{\mathcal{T}(\Sigma \mid \Gamma, x) = (X, \{1 \precsim A\})} \qquad \frac{\mathcal{T}(\Sigma \mid (\Gamma,\, x : \alpha{\cdot}\beta), s) = (X, C) \qquad \alpha, \beta \text{ fresh}}{\mathcal{T}(\Sigma \mid \Gamma, \lambda x.\, s) = (\alpha \cdot \beta \multimap X, C)}$$

$$\frac{\begin{array}{ll} \mathcal{T}(\Sigma \mid \Gamma|_s, s) = (Y_1, C_1) & \vec{\alpha}, \beta, \gamma, \delta \text{ fresh} \\ \Gamma|_t = (x_1 : A_1{\cdot}X_1, \ldots, x_n : A_n{\cdot}X_n) & FV(s) \cap FV(t) = \emptyset \\ \mathcal{T}(\Sigma \mid (x_1 : \alpha_1{\cdot}X_1, \ldots, x_n : \alpha_n{\cdot}X_n), t) = (Y_2, C_2) & C = C_1 \cup C_2 \end{array}}{\mathcal{T}(\Sigma \mid \Gamma, s\, t) = (\beta, C \cup \{Y_1 = \delta \cdot \gamma \multimap \beta, Y_2 = \gamma\} \cup \{\delta \times \alpha_i \precsim A_i \mid 1 \leq i \leq n\}))}$$

$$\frac{\begin{array}{ll} \Gamma|_s = (x_1 : A_1{\cdot}X_1, \ldots, x_n : A_n{\cdot}X_n) & \vec{\alpha}, \beta, \gamma, \delta \text{ fresh} \\ \mathcal{T}(\Sigma \mid (x_1 : \alpha_1{\cdot}X_1, \ldots, x_n : \alpha_n{\cdot}X_n), s) = (Y_1, C_1) & FV(s) \cap FV(t) = \emptyset \\ \mathcal{T}(\Sigma \mid (\Gamma|_t,\, x : \delta{\cdot}\gamma,\, x : \beta{\cdot}\gamma), t) = (Y_2, C_2) & C = C_1 \cup C_2 \end{array}}{\mathcal{T}(\Sigma \mid \Gamma, \mathsf{copy}\ s\ \mathsf{as}\ x, y\ \mathsf{in}\ t) = (Y_2, C \cup \{Y_1 = \gamma\} \cup \{(\delta + \beta) \times \alpha_i \precsim A_i \mid 1 \leq i \leq n\})}$$

$$\frac{\mathcal{T}(\Sigma, f) = (A, C)}{\mathcal{T}(\Sigma \mid \Gamma, [f]) = ([A], C)}$$

$$\frac{\begin{array}{ll} \mathcal{T}(\Sigma \mid \Gamma|_s, s) = (Y_1, C_1) & \vec{\alpha}, \beta \text{ fresh} \\ \Gamma|_t = (x_1 : A_1{\cdot}X_1, \ldots, x_n : A_n{\cdot}X_n) & FV(s) \cap FV(t) = \emptyset \\ \mathcal{T}((\Sigma,\, c{:}\beta) \mid (x_1 : \alpha_1{\cdot}X_1, \ldots, x_n : \alpha_n{\cdot}X_n), t) = (Y_2, C_2) & C = C_1 \cup C_2 \end{array}}{\mathcal{T}(\Sigma \mid \Gamma, \mathsf{let}\ s\ \mathsf{be}\ [c]\ \mathsf{in}\ t) = (Y_2, C \cup \{Y_1 = [\beta]\} \cup \{\beta \times \alpha_i \precsim A_i \mid 1 \leq i \leq n\})}$$

Fig. 6. Upper Class Type Inference Rules (selection)

2. *If* $\Sigma\sigma \mid \Gamma\sigma \vdash t\sigma \colon X\sigma$ *then there exist* Y *and* C *with* $\mathcal{T}(\Sigma \mid \Gamma, t) = (Y, C)$ *such that* σ *can be extended to a type substitution* ρ *satisfying* $X\sigma = Y\rho$ *and* $\rho \models C$.

In Fig. 6 we give a selection of typical rules for $\mathcal{T}(\Sigma \mid \Gamma, t)$. These rules formalise a definition of $\mathcal{T}(\Sigma \mid \Gamma, t)$ by structural recursion over t. In the rules we write $\Gamma|_s$ for the subcontext of Γ, in which only the free (term)-variables that appear freely in s are being declared. It is easy to see that (up to the choice of fresh names) these rules define a partial function, which is easy to compute. We omit standard rules for $\mathcal{T}(\Sigma, f)$.

Propositions 1 and 2 can then be proved in a standard way by induction on the derivations of $\mathcal{T}(\Sigma, f) = (A, C)$ and $\mathcal{T}(\Sigma \mid \Gamma, t) = (X, C)$ respectively.

4.2 Solving Constraints

Having reduced type inference to constraint solving, it remains to study how constraint sets can be solved.

Reducing Constraints to E-Unification. First we note that because equality up to congruence $A \cong B$ is a constraint, constraint solving must be at least as hard as E-unification, the problem of unification up to some given equational theory. E-unification is a well-studied problem and there are results for a wide range of equational theories, see [3,8] for an overview.

Constraint solving can be reduced to E-unification. Equality constraints can be removed up front by standard unification, leaving us with constraints of the form $A \cong B$ and $A \precsim B$. To eliminate the latter, we recall that $A \precsim B$ is equivalent to $\exists C, D.\, A \cong C \leq D \cong B$. This suggests a simple nondeterministic algorithm for reducing constraint solving to E-unification. For any structural constraint $A \precsim B$, we guess type C and D with $C \leq D$ and replace the $A \precsim B$ by $A \cong C$ and $D \cong B$. Now we can use E-unification to solve the remaining constraints.

The efficiency of this approach depends on the maximum size that needs to be taken into account for C and D as well as the efficiency of an E-unification procedure. Constraints like $C \leq D$ can be verified easily, e.g. using dynamic programming.

For IntML-type inference, we need to solve E-unification problems for the theory of the unit laws (U) and the distributivity laws (D), recall their definition in Sec. 2. Unfortunately, to the best of our knowledge, the problem of E-unification for this theory is still open. Moreover, even if we could find an algorithm for this problem, it would most likely be unpractical for IntML type inference. At the very least it would be NP-hard [10], although it might be much worse.

That constraint solving is hard does not immediately imply the same for IntML type inference. One could hope that in type inference only certain kinds of constraint sets can arise, which are easier to solve. However, this is not the case:

Proposition 3. *Solving the constraint sets that arise in* IntML *type inference is at least as hard as equational unification for (U)+(D).*

Avoiding Distributivity. One choice in the definition of IntML that makes type checking hard is the inclusion of distributivity laws in rule (STRUCT), since in conjunction with the unit laws this appears to make equational unification hard. This leads us to reconsidering the definition of structural congruence. Our motivation for introducing the distributivity laws was to be able to commute copy with other operators without having to change index types in the context, as explained in Sec. 2.

With a reasonable restriction to the IntML type system, we can obtain a similar property without the distributivity laws. We may weaken the contraction rule as follows:

$$(\text{CONTR2})\ \frac{\Sigma \mid \Gamma \vdash s\colon X \qquad \Sigma \mid \Delta,\, x\colon A{\cdot}X,\, y\colon A{\cdot}X \vdash t\colon Y}{\Sigma \mid \Delta,\, (2 \times A)\cdot \Gamma \vdash \mathsf{copy}\ s\ \mathsf{as}\ x, y\ \mathsf{in}\ t\colon Y}$$

This rule is derivable with the distributivity and unit laws, but (CONTR) is not derivable from (CONTR2). With (CONTR2) the two problematic copy-terms can be typed as:

$$\Sigma \mid \Gamma,\, x\colon A \times (2 \times B){\cdot}X \vdash s\ (\mathsf{copy}\ x\ \mathsf{as}\ x_1, x_2\ \mathsf{in}\ t)\colon Y$$
$$\Sigma \mid \Gamma,\, x\colon 2 \times (A \times B){\cdot}X \vdash \mathsf{copy}\ x\ \mathsf{as}\ x_1, x_2\ \mathsf{in}\ (s\ t)\colon Y$$

Therefore, with the weaker version of contraction, we may use the associativity (A) and commutativity (C) laws for $\times$ to achieve the same effect as with the distributivity laws for the general contraction rule. The working class type system remains unchanged.

Since E-unification up to the theory (A)+(C)+(U) is known to be NP-complete [8], we obtain the following hardness result.

Proposition 4. *Type inference for the variant of* IntML *obtained by replacing* (CONTR) *with* (CONTR2) *and by letting* $\cong$ *be defined by (A)+(C)+(U) is NP-hard.*

We do not know if type inference for this variant of IntML is also in NP; it is unclear how to reduce $\precsim$-constraints to $\cong$-constraints in general.

We side-step the difficulty of reducing $\precsim$ to $\cong$ by noticing that the relation $\precsim$ is larger than it needs to be in order to obtain the properties discussed in Sec. 2, which were the original reasons for introducing $\precsim$ into the type system. In the IntML-variant with (CONTR2), it would suffice to be able to treat index types of the form $A_1 \times \cdots \times A_n$ as if they were multisets $\{A_1, \ldots, A_n\}$. The relation $\precsim$ does more than that.

For any working class type A define the multiset $M(A)$ represented by it inductively as follows: $M(1) = \emptyset$, $M(\alpha) = \{\alpha\}$, $M(A + B) = \{A + B\}$ and $M(A \times B) = M(A) \cup M(B)$.

We define $\precsim_M$ such that $A \precsim_M B$ holds if and only if $M(A)$ is a sub-multiset of $M(B)$ in the sense that there exists a multiset E with $M(B) = M(A) \cup E$. Syntactic congruence is then defined by $A \cong_M B$ if and only if $M(A) = M(B)$.

With this definition of $\precsim_M$ and $\cong_M$, the variant of IntML with $\precsim_M$ instead of $\precsim$ is not only well-behaved, its type inference constraints can also easily be reduced to E-unification up to (A)+(C)+(U). First, any constraint $A \precsim_M B$ may equivalently be replaced by $A \times \alpha \cong_M B$ for some fresh variable α. Then, solving $A \cong_M B$ amounts to unifying A and B up to (A)+(C)+(U), where each type of the form $C + D$ is considered a constant. Thus, type inference is equally hard as unification of terms over $(\times, 1)$ up to (A)+(C)+(U) and infinitely many constants, an NP-complete problem [3]:

Proposition 5. *Type inference for the variant of* IntML *obtained by replacing* (CONTR) *with* (CONTR2) *and by using* $\precsim_M$ *in rule* (STRUCT) *is NP-complete.*

Quick and Simple Constraint Solving. For use in practice, an NP-complete algorithm for type inference may still be too complex, with regard to running time and to implementation effort. Here we present a quick and simple algorithm for type inference that we have found to be practically useful (it handles all the applications we know), even though it does not handle the full the type system or find most general types.

For this algorithm we take the congruence $\cong$ to be syntactic equality, i.e. we consider ordinary unification instead of E-unification. In this case the relations $\leq$ and $\precsim$ coincide, so we will write $A \leq B$ for $A \precsim B$ in the rest of this section.

The restriction to syntactic equality alone is not enough to make type inference easy. We must also restrict the context Γ in the type inference problem $\mathcal{T}(\Sigma \mid \Gamma, t)$. We will consider here contexts that do not impose any constraints on index types. Such a restriction not only reflects the typical use of type inference in practice, where one does not have information about index types and would like to have them inferred. It also makes type inference significantly easier. If we do not impose such a restriction then type inference remains NP-hard, even when $\cong$ is syntactic equality.

Proposition 6. *Even if we let the congruence relation* $\cong$ *be syntactic equality, it is NP-hard to decide if a constraint set returned by the type inference function has a solution.*

We now identify a class of type inference problems $\mathcal{T}(\Sigma \mid \Gamma, t)$ that are useful in practice and that can be solved easily. We obtain this class by restricting Γ to be an *unconstrained context*, which does not impose restrictions on index types, and by restricting t to contain only instances of $\mathsf{hack}_X(c.f)$ where the index types in positive positions in X are all type variables.

We next formulate the restrictions precisely. To allow for a compact formulation of freshness assumptions, we choose a partition of the set of type variables into two (arbitrary) disjoint infinite subsets Var and $IdxVar$.

A *positively (resp. negatively) unconstrained type* is an upper class type in which all index types in positive (resp. negative) position are variables from $IdxVar$, and variables from $IdxVar$ may only appear as index types. Formally, the positively and negatively unconstrained types are defined by the grammar below, in which A ranges over working class types with variables in Var, α ranges over Var and β over $IdxVar$.

$$\text{positively unconstrained:} \qquad P ::= \alpha \mid [A] \mid P \otimes P \mid A \cdot N \multimap P$$
$$\text{negatively unconstrained:} \qquad N ::= \alpha \mid [A] \mid N \otimes N \mid \beta \cdot P \multimap N$$

An *unconstrained type* is a type that is both positively and negatively unconstrained, i.e. in which all index types are variables from $IdxVar$.

A *unconstrained context* is a context of the form $x_1 : \alpha_1{\cdot}X_1, \dots, x_n : \alpha_n{\cdot}X_n$, where all α_i are variables from $IdxVar$ and all X_i are unconstrained types.

We can now formulate conditions that make type inference easy.

Proposition 7. *Let $\cong$ be syntactic equality. Let Σ be a working class context containing only type variables from Var, let Γ be an unconstrained context, and let t be a term that may contain* $\mathsf{hack}_X(c.f)$ *as a subterm only if X is a positively unconstrained type. For such Σ, Γ and t we can compute in polynomial time either a type X and a substitution σ with $\Sigma\sigma \mid \Gamma\sigma \vdash t\sigma \colon X\sigma$; or reject if no such X and σ exist.*

We believe that this proposition captures a practically useful class of type inference problems. It contains all the practical examples we know, including the graph algorithm example from the previous section. Restricting to unconstrained contexts seems reasonable, since the index types capture information about the space usage of programs but are not important for understanding the meaning of programs. One would like to not worry about the index types and leave it to the type inference to fill them in.

For the proof of Prop. 7 we may use the following simple algorithm:

1. Compute $\mathcal{T}(\Sigma \mid \Gamma, t)$, which gives a pair (X, C).
2. Compute the most general unifier σ of all equations in C (ignoring the inequations) and set $I = \{A\sigma \leq B\sigma \mid (A \leq B) \in C\}$. Reject if the equations are not unifiable.
3. While possible, choose from I two inequalities $A \leq C$ and $B \leq C$ with the same upper bound C and replace them with $A + B \leq C$.
4. Compute the most general unifier τ of the set $\{A = B \mid (A \leq B) \in I\}$.
5. Return X and $\sigma; \tau$ as the final result.

We cannot hope for this algorithm to compute most general solutions, simply because the constraint set C may be infinitary. This means that in general there does not exist a finite set S of substitutions that solves a given constraint set C in the sense that any solution of C is an instance of one of the substitutions in S.

Proposition 8. *If we let the congruence relation $\cong$ be syntactic equality, then the constraint solving problem is infinitary.*

Although the simple algorithm above does not in general find most general types, practical experiments indicate that it finds useful typings. In our experience with a prototype implementation, the fact that the algorithm does not compute most general types means that the index types are a little larger than they need to be. The effect of this is an increased space usage of IntML-programs, since the index types appear in the types of messages that are being stored during the computation. In examples like those from Sec. 3, the space usage nevertheless quite reasonable.

5 Conclusion

The usefulness of a type system for a programming language depends on how well it strikes a balances between the benefits gained by types and the overhead of dealing with types when writing programs. Here we have shown that the overhead of the IntML type system can be reduced substantially by means of type inference. With its index types, the IntML type system is precise enough to guarantee space bounds on IntML-programs, and so it is not a surprise that full type inference turns out to be quite hard. Nevertheless, we were able to identify a class of type inference instances that can be solved quickly and easily and that still appears to be useful in practice. To substantiate this claim, we have expressed a typical LOGSPACE-graph algorithm in IntML. With type inference it could be programmed with surprisingly little overhead due to the type system.

References

1. Abramsky, S., Jagadeesan, R., Malacaria, P.: Full Abstraction for PCF. Inf. Comput. 163(2), 409–470 (2000)
2. Atassi, V., Baillot, P., Terui, K.: Verification of ptime reducibility for system F terms: Type inference in dual light affine logic. Logical Methods in Computer Science 3(4) (2007)
3. Baader, F., Snyder, W.: Unification theory. In: Robinson, J.A., Voronkov, A. (eds.) Handbook of Automated Reasoning, pp. 445–532. Elsevier and MIT Press (2001)
4. Burrell, M.J., Cockett, R., Redmond, B.F.: Pola: a language for PTIME programming. In: Workshop on Logic and Computational Complexity, LCC (2009)
5. Cook, S., McKenzie, P.: Problems complete for deterministic logarithmic space. Journal of Algorithms 8(3), 385–394 (1987)
6. Dal Lago, U., Schöpp, U.: Functional programming in sublinear space. In: Gordon, A.D. (ed.) Programming Languages and Systems. LNCS, vol. 6012, pp. 205–225. Springer, Heidelberg (2010)
7. Hermann, M., Kolaitis, P.G.: Computational complexity of simultaneous elementary matching problems. J. Autom. Reasoning 23(2), 107–136 (1999)
8. Kapur, D., Narendran, P.: Complexity of unification problems with associative-commutative operators. J. Autom. Reasoning 9(2), 261–288 (1992)
9. Pottier, F., Rémy, D.: The essence of ML type inference. In: Pierce, B.C. (ed.) Advanced Topics in Types and Programming Languages, pp. 389–489. MIT Press, Cambridge (2005)
10. Tidén, E., Arnborg, S.: Unification problems with one-sided distributivity. J. Symb. Comput. 3(1/2), 183–202 (1987)

Liveness of Communicating Transactions* (Extended Abstract)

Edsko de Vries, Vasileios Koutavas, and Matthew Hennessy

Trinity College Dublin
{Edsko.de.Vries,Vasileios.Koutavas,Matthew.Hennessy}@cs.tcd.ie

Abstract. We study liveness and safety in the context of CCS extended with *communicating transactions*, a construct we recently proposed to model automatic error recovery in distributed systems. We show that fair-testing and may-testing capture the right notions of liveness and safety in this setting, and argue that must-testing imposes too strong a requirement in the presence of transactions. We develop a sound and complete theory of fair-testing in terms of CCS-like tree failures and show that, compared to CCS, communicating transactions provide increased distinguishing power to the observer. We also show that weak bisimilarity is a sound, though incomplete, proof technique for both may- and fair-testing. To the best of our knowledge this is the first semantic treatment of liveness in the presence of transactions. We exhibit the usefulness of our theory by proving illuminating liveness laws and simple but non-trivial examples.

1 Introduction

The correctness of distributed systems can to a large extent be specified in terms of its safety and liveness properties. In the presence of some form of built-in fault tolerance, such as support for transactions, the verification of safety properties is simplified but the verification of liveness properties becomes more subtle.

In previous work [22] we defined the novel language construct of *communicating transactions*, which drops the isolation requirement of classical transactions and models automatic error recovery of distributed communicating systems. We gave a high-level semantics of communicating transactions in a calculus called TransCCS, an extension of CCS, and developed a compositional theory for this calculus based on may-testing preorder.

May-testing can be used to reason about safety [14]. The intuition of safety is that "nothing bad will happen" [18]. A safety property can be formulated as a safety test T^{ϖ} which detects and reports the bad behaviour on a channel ϖ. We say that a process P *passes* a safety test if $(P \mid T^{\varpi})$ cannot report on ϖ. An implementation I then preserves the safety properties of a specification S if I passes all the safety tests of S (i.e. $S \sqsupseteq_{\text{may}} I$).

* This research was supported by SFI project SFI 06 IN.1 1898.

K. Ueda (Ed.): APLAS 2010, LNCS 6461, pp. 392–407, 2010.

Let us briefly consider in a value-passing version of TransCCS a simple distributed communication system *Sys* that implements the specification

$$Spec_{rec,del} = rec(x).\overline{del}\langle x\rangle.\mathbb{0}$$

The implementation uses restarting communicating transactions. A restarting transaction is written as $\mu X. [\![P \rhd_k X]\!]$ and executes its *default* P until P commits the transaction by executing a $\mathtt{co}\ k$ or the runtime non-deterministically aborts the transaction. P can communicate with the environment of the transaction, but these effects are rolled back automatically in the case of an abort.

$$\begin{aligned}
Sys_{rec,del} &= \nu q.\nu s.\left(Src_{rec,s,q} \mid Trg_{del,s,q} \mid \overline{s}\langle 0\rangle\right)\\
Src_{rec,s,q} &= \mu X\ [\![s(x).\mathtt{if}\ x = 0\ \mathtt{then}\ rec(y).(\overline{q}\langle y\rangle \mid \overline{s}\langle 1\rangle \mid \mathtt{co}\ k)\ \mathtt{else}\ \mathbb{0} \rhd_k X]\!]\\
Trg_{del,s,q} &= \mu X\ [\![s(x).\mathtt{if}\ x = 1\ \mathtt{then}\ q(y).(\overline{del}\langle y\rangle \mid \overline{s}\langle 0\rangle \mid \mathtt{co}\ l)\ \mathtt{else}\ \mathbb{0} \rhd_l X]\!]
\end{aligned}$$

The system uses a one-place queue, with *Src* storing the value received on *rec* as an output on q, if the current size of the queue, stored in s, is 0; *Trg* conveys the value from q to $\overline{del}$, if the queue is not empty. Both *Src* and *Trg* rely on an abort to undo the input on s if their condition is not satisfied.

As discussed, *Sys* is a safe implementation of *Spec* if $Spec \sqsupseteq_{\text{may}} Sys$. This would guarantee that an observer testing for a violation of the safety property that the received and delivered values match,

$$T^{\varpi} = \overline{rec}\langle v\rangle.del(x).\mathtt{if}\ x = v\ \mathtt{then}\ \mathbb{0}\ \mathtt{else}\ \varpi$$

can not report ϖ with *Sys* because it can not report this with *Spec*.

The intuition of *liveness* is that "something good will eventually happen". As for safety properties, a liveness property can be formulated as a liveness test T^{ω} which detects and reports the good behaviour on a channel ω. For example,

$$T^{\omega} = \omega + \overline{rec}\langle v\rangle.del(x).\omega$$

tests for the property that *if* an input is received on *rec* we eventually get an output on *del* (ω appears twice in the test because the implication can be satisfied in two ways). The definition of *passing* a liveness test however is delicate.

One possibility, corresponding to *must-testing* [11], is to require that every computation of $(Sys \mid T^{\omega})$ reports success. A restarting transaction can however be aborted by the runtime system infinitely often, even though at every point in the computation the transaction can follow a path to a commit. Under such, admittedly pathological, schedules no restarting transaction can guarantee liveness: in $(Sys \mid T^{\omega})$, after the value is received on *rec*, infinite aborts of *Trg* will prevent the value from being delivered on *del*, and the test will not succeed along this schedule. Indeed, under this scheme there would be no difference between *Sys* and the process $\mu X.\tau.X$, as neither can guarantee any liveness properties.

A more useful definition assumes a notion of fairness, and considers only schedules where *every transaction that gets a chance to commit infinitely often will eventually do so* [8]. We say that a process P passes a liveness test T^{ω} if

$(P \mid T^\omega)$ *should* report success on ω: $(P \mid T^\omega)$ will eventually ring under a fair scheduler. This definition of passing a liveness test leads to fair-testing [21].

With that definition we can show that *Sys* is a live implementation of *Spec*: *Sys* passes all the liveness tests of *Spec* (i.e. $\mathit{Spec} \sqsubseteq_{\text{fair}} \mathit{Sys}$). This is a non-trivial property of *Sys* which implies, among others, that relying on the abort of the transactions to restore the output on s when the conditions of *Src* and *Trg* are not satisfied does not introduce any deadlocks.

We make the following contributions in this paper:

1. We study liveness and safety in a concurrent language with communicating transactions and show that these notions are captured respectively by fair-testing and may-testing. To the best of our knowledge this is the first semantic treatment of liveness in the presence of transactions.
2. We give a characterization of liveness preservation in TransCCS in terms of so-called *clean tree failures*. This builds on previous results about clean traces (traces that contain only actions that will be committed), as well as newly proved properties of communicating transactions and the identification of characteristic TransCCS liveness tests.
3. We show that transactions add observational power to the observer with respect to liveness preservation and explain this through examples.
4. We define a variation on weak bisimilarity over clean traces and show that this is a sound but incomplete proof technique for safety and liveness.
5. We exhibit the usefulness of our theory by illuminating laws and examples.

2 Syntax and Reduction Semantics of TransCCS

The syntax and the reduction semantics of TransCCS are shown in Fig. 2; as usual a ranges over a set of actions Act on which is defined a bijective function $(\bar{\cdot}) : Act \to Act$, used to formalize communication, and μ ranges over Act_τ, the set Act augmented with a new action τ, used to represent internal activity. We use the standard abbreviations for CCS terms.

TransCCS extends CCS with the constructs $[\![P \rhd_k Q]\!]$ which denotes a transaction, and $\mathsf{co}\ k$ which commits transaction k. The transaction runs its *default* P, which replaces the transaction in the case of a commit. The *alternative* Q replaces the transaction in the case of a non-deterministic abort. The occurrences of k in P are bound by the transaction; after a commit any remaining free $\mathsf{co}\ k$ behave as the nil process. Fig. 1 shows some simple examples of transactions. We will refer to these examples throughout the paper.

$$S_{ab} = \mu X.\, [\![a.b.\mathsf{co}\ k \rhd_k X]\!]$$

$$I_1 = [\![a.b.\mathsf{co}\ k \rhd_k \mathbb{0}]\!] \qquad I_3 = \mu X.\, [\![a.b.\mathsf{co}\ k + \overline{err} \rhd_k X]\!]$$

$$I_2 = \mu X.\, [\![a.b.\mathbb{0} \rhd_k X]\!] \qquad I_4 = \mu X.\, [\![a.b.\mathsf{co}\ k \mid \overline{err} \rhd_k X]\!]$$

Fig. 1. Example Transactions

Syntax

$$\begin{array}{llll} P, Q ::= \sum \mu_i.P_i & \text{prefix} & \mid [\![P \rhd_k Q]\!] & \text{transaction } (k \text{ bound in } P) \\ \quad \mid (P \mid Q) & \text{parallel} & \mid \mathsf{co}\ k & \text{commit} \\ \quad \mid \nu a.P & \text{hiding} & \mid \mu X.P & \text{recursion} \end{array}$$

Reduction Rules ($\rightarrow$) is the least relation that satisfies

R-Comm
$$\frac{a_i = \overline{a}_j}{\sum_{i \in I} a_i.P_i \mid \sum_{j \in J} a_j.Q_j \rightarrow P_i \mid Q_j}$$

R-Emb
$$\frac{k \notin R}{[\![P \rhd_k Q]\!] \mid R \rightarrow [\![P \mid R \rhd_k Q \mid R]\!]}$$

R-Tau
$$\frac{\mu_i = \tau}{\sum_{i \in I} \mu_i.P_i \rightarrow P_i}$$

R-Co
$$\frac{}{[\![P \mid \mathsf{co}\ k \rhd_k Q]\!] \rightarrow P}$$

R-Ab
$$\frac{}{[\![P \rhd_k Q]\!] \rightarrow Q}$$

R-Rec
$$\frac{}{\mu X.P \rightarrow P[X := \mu X.P]}$$

R-Str
$$\frac{P \equiv P' \rightarrow Q' \equiv Q}{P \rightarrow Q}$$

and is closed under the contexts $C ::= [] \mid (C \mid Q) \mid [\![C \rhd_k Q]\!] \mid \nu a.C$.
Structural equivalence ($\equiv$) contains the usual rules for parallel and hiding.

Fig. 2. Language Definition

A transaction can communicate with a process R in its environment by *embedding* R in its default and alternative (R-Emb). This simple but important operation allows the default of the transaction to interact with R.

Example 1. Consider transaction S_{ab} in parallel with the test $T^{\omega}_{ab} = \overline{a}.\overline{b}.\omega$. After an embedding step, the transaction can communicate with the process; both will be restored to their original state in the case of an abort. The possible traces are summarized in the following graph.

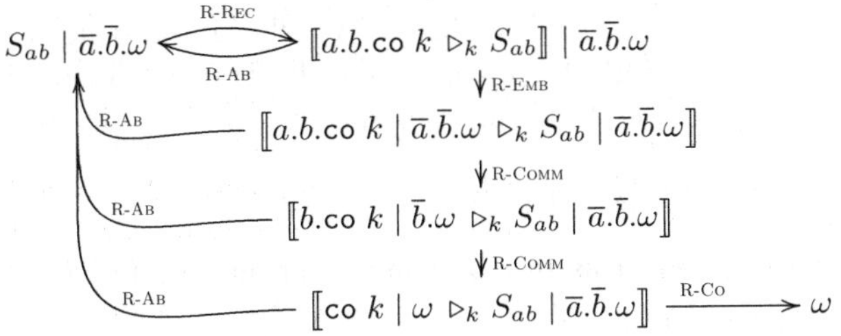

□

3 Liveness

We now formalize liveness as described in the introduction. A process P (typically the parallel composition of a test and a process-under-test) can output on a channel ω, written $P{\Downarrow_\omega}$ if it can reach a top-level ω after some internal steps:

Definition 1. $P\Downarrow_\omega$ iff there exist P' such that $P \to^* \omega \mid P'$.

We are interested only in top-level occurrences of ω, because an output that is still inside a transaction may still be undone.

A process P passes a liveness test T^ω if it cannot reach a state from which the test cannot detect the good behaviour.

Definition 2 (Passing Liveness Tests). *A process P passes a liveness test T^ω, written $P\,\mathrm{shd}\,T^\omega$, when $\forall R.$ if $P \mid T^\omega \to^* R$ then $R \Downarrow_\omega$.*

Example 2. Transaction S_{ab} passes the liveness test $T^\omega_{ab} = \bar{a}.\bar{b}.\omega$ even though it may keep aborting. S_{ab} would *not* pass this test with the stronger definition of liveness (must-testing [11]), which would not ignore this pathological schedule.

The reduction graph of $S_{ab} \mid T^\omega_{ab}$ was shown in Ex. 1. Although there are infinite aborting paths, at no point does the system reach a state in which communication on a and b has become impossible. This is not true for I_1:

$$I_1 \mid T^\omega_{ab} \xrightarrow{\text{R-AB}} \mathbf{0} \mid T^\omega_{ab}\not\Downarrow_\omega$$

Transaction I_2 also fails the liveness test since the transaction never commits and the output on ω by the test therefore never becomes top-level. $\qquad\square$

Given a specification S, an implementation I preserves the liveness properties of S if every successful liveness test of S is also a successful liveness test of I. This naturally leads us to the standard definition of *fair-testing* [21] which here we call *liveness preservation*.

Definition 3 (Liveness Preservation). *I preserves the liveness properties of S, written $S \sqsubseteq_{\text{live}} I$, when for all liveness tests T^ω, if $S\,\mathrm{shd}\,T^\omega$ then $I\,\mathrm{shd}\,T^\omega$. We write $S \approx_{\text{live}} I$ if $S \sqsubseteq_{\text{live}} I$ and $I \sqsubseteq_{\text{live}} S$.*

Example 3. We saw in Ex. 2 that S_{ab} passes the test T^ω_{ab} and that neither I_1 nor I_2 does. It follows immediately that $S_{ab} \not\sqsubseteq_{\text{live}} I_1$ and $S_{ab} \not\sqsubseteq_{\text{live}} I_2$. $\qquad\square$

Example 4. We will formally prove $S_{ab} \sqsubseteq_{\text{live}} I_3$ after we develop our theory of liveness. Here we note only that $I_3\,\mathrm{shd}\,T^\omega_{ab}$, which is easy to see from the reduction graph of $I_3 \mid T^\omega_{ab}$ (which is almost identical to the graph shown in Ex. 1). $\qquad\square$

Example 5 (Transactional Liveness Tests). Another interesting case are the processes $P = a.(b.c + b.d)$ and $Q = a.b.c + a.b.d$. In TransCCS (unlike in CCS) we have that $P \not\sqsubseteq_{\text{live}} Q$. To see that consider the transactional liveness test

$$T^\omega = \omega + a.\Big(\mu X.\, [\![b.c.(\omega \mid \mathrm{co}\ k) \rhd_k X]\!] \Big)$$

We can see that P passes this test by the reduction graph of $P \mid T^\omega_{(a,bd)}$:

$$\Big(a.(b.c + b.d)\Big) \mid \Big(\omega + a.\big(\mu X.\, [\![b.c.(\omega \mid \mathrm{co}\ k) \rhd_k X]\!]\big)\Big)$$

$\downarrow$ R-COMM

$(b.c + b.d) \mid \mu X.\, [\![b.c.(\omega \mid \mathrm{co}\ k) \rhd_k X]\!] \underset{\text{R-AB}}{\overset{\text{R-REC}}{\rightleftarrows}} (b.c + b.d) \mid [\![b.c.(\omega \mid \mathrm{co}\ k) \rhd_k T^\omega]\!]$

$\downarrow$ R-EMB

R-AB $\longrightarrow [\![b.c.(\omega \mid \mathrm{co}\ k) \mid (b.c + b.d) \rhd_k T^\omega \mid (b.c + b.d)]\!]$

$\downarrow$ R-COMM^2

R-AB $\longrightarrow [\![\omega \mid \mathrm{co}\ k \rhd_k T^\omega \mid (b.c + b.d)]\!] \xrightarrow{\text{R-CO}} \omega$

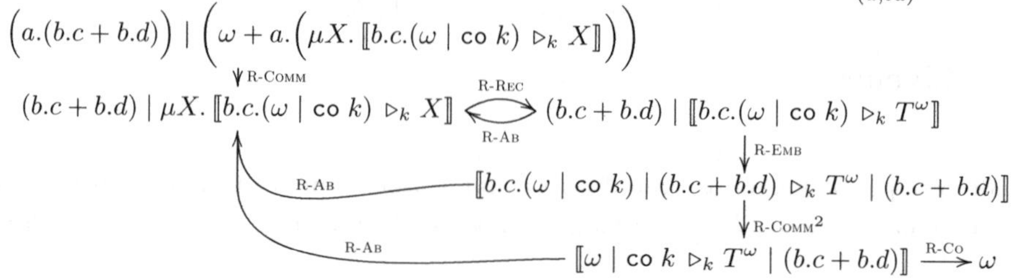

The restarting transaction makes it possible to restore the choice $b.c + b.d$ if the wrong branch of P communicates on b. However, Q does not pass this test:

$$(a.b.c + a.b.d) \mid \omega + a.\Big(\mu X.\, [\![b.c.(\omega \mid \mathsf{co}\ k) \rhd_k X]\!]\Big)$$
$$\xrightarrow{\text{R-COMM}} b.d \mid \mu X.\, [\![b.c.(\omega \mid \mathsf{co}\ k) \rhd_k X]\!] \not\Downarrow_\omega \qquad \square$$

Proposition 1. *If* $\mathsf{co}\ k \notin R$ *then*

$$[\![P + R \rhd_k Q]\!] \eqsim_{\text{live}} [\![P \rhd_k Q]\!] \qquad \mu X.\, [\![P + R \rhd_k X]\!] \eqsim_{\text{live}} \mu X.\, [\![P \rhd_k X]\!]$$
$$[\![P \rhd_k Q]\!] \gtrsim_{\text{live}} \tau.P + \tau.Q \qquad \mu X.\, [\![P \mid \mathsf{co}\ k \rhd_k X]\!] \eqsim_{\text{live}} P$$

In TransCCS, unlike CCS, the point of internal choice is important with respect to liveness preservation.

Proposition 2 (Choice). $\tau.a.P + \tau.a.Q \sqsubseteq_{\text{live}} a.P + a.Q \eqsim_{\text{live}} a.(\tau.P + \tau.Q)$.

To see that $\tau.a.P+\tau.a.Q \not\sqsupseteq_{\text{live}} a.P+a.Q$ consider the processes $R_1 = \tau.a.c+\tau.a.d$ and $R_2 = a.c + a.d$ and the liveness test $T^\omega = \mu X.\, [\![\overline{a}.\overline{c}.(\omega \mid \mathsf{co}\ k \rhd_k X]\!])$. R_2 passes this test but R_1 does not (*cf.* Ex. 5).

Proposition 3 (Compositionality Laws). *If* $P \sqsubseteq_{\text{live}} P'$ *and* $Q \sqsubseteq_{\text{live}} Q'$ *then:*

$$a.P \sqsubseteq_{\text{live}} a.P' \qquad P \mid Q \sqsubseteq_{\text{live}} P' \mid Q' \qquad a.P + b.Q \sqsubseteq_{\text{live}} a.P' + b.Q'$$

These laws can be proven using our characterization of liveness preservation in Sect. 6. As in CCS [21], however, recursive contexts do *not* preserve ($\sqsubseteq_{\text{live}}$), as illustrated in the next example.

Example 6 (Fault tolerance). Consider the processes $P = a + \tau$ and $Q = \mathbf{0}$. P can be thought of as a process with a fault: it may do an a action or it may get stuck. Any liveness test that P passes can therefore not rely on the a action, and hence we have $P \sqsubseteq_{\text{live}} Q$. However, consider the context

$$C = \nu a.\mu X.\, [\![\overline{a}.(b \mid \mathsf{co}\ k) \mid [\,] \rhd_k X]\!]$$

This context adds fault tolerance: if P faults in $C[P]$, the transaction can abort and try again, so that $C[P]$ will pass the liveness test $T_b^\omega = \overline{b}.\omega$. However, Q *never* does the a action, so the addition of fault tolerance makes no difference; in particular, $C[Q]$ does not pass T_b^ω. Hence, $C[P] \not\sqsubseteq_{\text{live}} C[Q]$. $\square$

4 Safety

As discussion in the introduction, a safety test T^ϖ is a process that tests and reports "bad" behaviour on a channel ϖ; a process P *passes* the test if $P \mid T^\varpi$ cannot output on ϖ:

Definition 4 (Passing Safety Tests). *A process P passes a safety test T^ϖ, written $P\,\text{cannot}\,T^\varpi$, when $P \mid T^\varpi \not\Downarrow_\varpi$.*

Given a specification S, an implementation I preserves the liveness properties of S if every successful safety test of S is also a successful safety test of I. This leads us to the definition of *safety preservation*, which amounts to the inverse of the standard definition of *may-testing* [11].

Definition 5 (Safety Preservation). *I preserves the safety properties of S, and we write $S \sqsubseteq_{\text{safe}} I$, if for every safety test T^{ϖ} if $S\,\text{cannot}\,T^{\varpi}$ then $I\,\text{cannot}\,T^{\varpi}$.*

Example 7. Consider the safety test $T^{\varpi}_{ab} = err.\varpi \mid \bar{a}.\bar{b}$. Transaction I_3 passes this test, because there is no possibility of reaching a top-level output on ϖ:

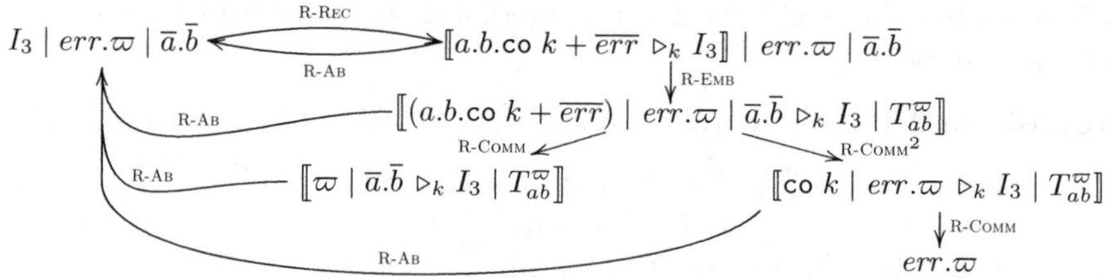

$I_3 \mid err.\varpi \mid \bar{a}.\bar{b}$
R-Rec
R-Ab
$[\![a.b.\mathsf{co}\ k + \overline{err} \rhd_k I_3]\!] \mid err.\varpi \mid \bar{a}.\bar{b}$
R-Emb
$[\![(a.b.\mathsf{co}\ k + \overline{err}) \mid err.\varpi \mid \bar{a}.\bar{b} \rhd_k I_3 \mid T^{\varpi}_{ab}]\!]$
R-Ab
R-Comm
R-Comm^2
R-Ab
$[\![\varpi \mid \bar{a}.\bar{b} \rhd_k I_3 \mid T^{\varpi}_{ab}]\!]$
$[\![\mathsf{co}\ k \mid err.\varpi \rhd_k I_3 \mid T^{\varpi}_{ab}]\!]$
R-Comm
R-Ab
$err.\varpi$

At no point do we have a top-level output on ϖ, so that I_3 passes this test. In fact, we have that $S_{ab} \sqsubseteq_{\text{safe}} I_3$ (we prove this formally in Ex. 12). I_4 however is not a safe implementation of S_{ab} because it does not pass this test:

$$I_4 \mid \bar{a}.\bar{b}.err.\varpi \xrightarrow{\text{R-Rec}}\xrightarrow{\text{R-Emb}} [\![(a.b.\mathsf{co}\ k \mid \overline{err}) \mid \bar{a}.\bar{b}.err.\varpi \rhd_k I_4 \mid T^{\varpi}_{ab}]\!]$$
$$\xrightarrow{\text{R-Comm}^3} [\![\mathsf{co}\ k \mid \varpi \rhd_k I_4 \mid T^{\varpi}_{ab}]\!] \xrightarrow{\text{R-Co}} \varpi \qquad \square$$

As we will prove by Thm. 3 in Sect. 6, liveness preservation implies safety preservation. Thus, to show that an implementation I preserves both the liveness and safety properties of a specification S, it suffices to show that $S \sqsubseteq_{\text{live}} I$.

5 Clean Traces and Safety

We give an overview of the definitions and results we reuse from previous work [22,23]. These involve the definition of a Labelled Transition System (LTS) that describes the traces of processes, the definition of clean traces over this LTS, and a rephrasing of results about may-testing in terms of safety.

5.1 Labelled Transition System

The LTS (Fig(s). 3 and 4) is defined over an extension called TransCCS°, ranged over by $\mathcal{P}, \mathcal{Q}$. Transactions in TransCCS° are distributed as a primary transaction, denoted by $[\![\mathcal{P} \rhd_k \mathcal{Q}]\!]$, and zero or more secondary transactions, denoted by $[\![\mathcal{P} \rhd_k \mathcal{Q}]\!]^{\circ}$ which correspond to embedded processes. This simulates embedding in the reduction semantics while keeping processes separate, supporting compositional reasoning. Internal actions in the LTS correspond to reduction steps up to this distribution of transactions; this is made precise in [22].

$$\text{L-ACT}\quad \frac{}{\sum \mu_i.P_i \xrightarrow{\mu_i} P_i} \qquad \text{L-PAR}\quad \frac{\mathcal{P} \xrightarrow{\tilde{k}(\mu)} \mathcal{P}'}{\mathcal{P} \mid \mathcal{Q} \xrightarrow{\tilde{k}(\mu)} \mathcal{P}' \mid \mathcal{Q}} \qquad \text{L-TRANS}\quad \frac{\mathcal{P} \xrightarrow{\tilde{l}(\mu)} \mathcal{P}'}{[\![\mathcal{P} \rhd_k \mathcal{Q}]\!] \xrightarrow{k(\tilde{l}(\mu))} [\![\mathcal{P}' \rhd_k \mathcal{Q}]\!]}$$

$$\text{L-REC}\quad \frac{}{\mu X.\mathcal{P} \xrightarrow{\tau} \mathcal{P}[X := \mu X.\,\langle \mathcal{P} \rangle]} \qquad \text{L-HIDE}\quad \frac{\mathcal{P} \xrightarrow{\mu} \mathcal{P}' \qquad a \notin \mu}{\nu a.\mathcal{P} \xrightarrow{\mu} \nu a.\mathcal{P}'} \qquad \text{L-COMM}\quad \frac{\mathcal{P} \xrightarrow{\tilde{k}(a)} \mathcal{P}' \qquad \mathcal{Q} \xrightarrow{\tilde{k}(\overline{a})} \mathcal{Q}'}{\mathcal{P} \mid \mathcal{Q} \xrightarrow{\tilde{k}(\tau)} \mathcal{P}' \mid \mathcal{Q}'}$$

(eliding L-TRANS for secondary transactions)

Fig. 3. LTS: Standard Actions

As an example, consider the trace starting with $I_3 \mid \overline{a}.\overline{b}.\omega$:

$$\begin{aligned} &\mu X.\,[\![a.b.\mathsf{co}\ k + \overline{err}.\mathbb{0} \rhd_k X]\!] \mid \overline{a}.\overline{b}.\omega \\ \xrightarrow{\tau}\xrightarrow{\mathsf{emb}\ k}\ &[\![a.b.\mathsf{co}\ k + \overline{err}.\mathbb{0} \rhd_k I_3]\!] \mid [\![\overline{a}.\overline{b}.\omega \rhd_k \overline{a}.\overline{b}.\omega]\!]^{\circ} \\ \xrightarrow{k(\tau)}\xrightarrow{k(\tau)}\ &[\![b.\mathsf{co}\ k \rhd_k I_3]\!] \mid [\![\overline{b}.\omega \rhd_k \overline{a}.\overline{b}.\omega]\!]^{\circ} \xrightarrow{\mathsf{co}\ k} \omega \end{aligned}$$

Notice how (after unfolding the transaction once) the test is embedded and becomes a secondary transaction $[\![\overline{a}.\overline{b}.\omega \rhd_k \overline{a}.\overline{b}.\omega]\!]^{\circ}$. Actions in the LTS are marked with the transactions that execute them (rule L-TRANS); a primary and secondary k-transaction can communicate and therefore the action $k(a)$ of the primary k-transaction is matched by the action $k(\overline{a})$ of the secondary k-transaction (L-COMM), resulting in a $k(\tau)$ action.

Consider also the trace starting with $I_3 \mid T^{\varpi}_{ab}$ (*cf.* Ex. 7):

$$\begin{aligned} &\mu X.\,[\![a.b.\mathsf{co}\ k + \overline{err}.\mathbb{0} \rhd_k X]\!] \mid err.\varpi \mid \overline{a}.\overline{b} \\ \xrightarrow{\tau}\xrightarrow{\mathsf{emb}\ k}\ &[\![a.b.\mathsf{co}\ k + \overline{err}.\mathbb{0} \rhd_k I_3]\!] \mid [\![err.\varpi \mid \overline{a}.\overline{b} \rhd_k err.\varpi \mid \overline{a}.\overline{b}]\!]^{\circ} \\ \xrightarrow{k(\tau)}\ &[\![\mathbb{0} \rhd_k I_3]\!] \mid [\![\varpi \mid \overline{a}.\overline{b} \rhd_k err.\varpi \mid \overline{a}.\overline{b}]\!]^{\circ} \end{aligned}$$

At this point, the transaction can only abort:

$$\xrightarrow{\mathsf{ab}\ k} \mu X.\,[\![a.b.\mathsf{co}\ k + \overline{err}.\mathbb{0} \rhd_k X]\!] \mid err.\varpi \mid \overline{a}.\overline{b}$$

As in the reduction semantics, no trace of $I_3 \mid T^{\varpi}_{ab}$ leads to a top-level ϖ.

5.2 Clean Traces

There is an essential difference between the two traces of the previous section:

$$I_3 \mid T^{\omega}_{ab} \xrightarrow{\tau,\mathsf{emb}\ k,k(\tau),k(\tau),\mathsf{co}\ k} \omega \qquad\qquad I_3 \mid T^{\varpi}_{err} \xrightarrow{\tau,\mathsf{emb}\ k,k(\tau),\mathsf{ab}\ k} I_3 \mid T^{\varpi}_{err}$$

In the first, every action performed inside a transaction is eventually committed; in the second trace, however, the embedding step into the k transaction and the internal step within the k transaction are subsequently aborted and undone.

$$\text{B-CoPri}\ \frac{\mathcal{P} \equiv \mathcal{P}' \mid \mathsf{co}\ k}{[\![\mathcal{P} \rhd_k \mathcal{Q}]\!] \xrightarrow{\mathsf{co}\ k} \mathcal{P}'} \qquad \text{B-CoSec}\ \frac{}{[\![\mathcal{P} \rhd_k \mathcal{Q}]\!]^{\circ} \xrightarrow{\mathsf{co}\ k} \mathcal{P}} \qquad \text{B-Ab}\ \frac{}{[\![\mathcal{P} \rhd_k \mathcal{Q}]\!] \xrightarrow{\mathsf{ab}\ k} \mathcal{Q}}$$

$$\text{B-Emb}\ \frac{}{\mathcal{P} \xrightarrow{\mathsf{emb}\ k} [\![\mathcal{P} \rhd_k \langle\mathcal{P}\rangle]\!]^{\circ}} \qquad \text{B-Trans}\ \frac{\mathcal{P} \xrightarrow{\beta} \mathcal{P}' \quad \beta \neq \mathsf{co}\ k, \mathsf{ab}\ k}{[\![\mathcal{P} \rhd_k \mathcal{Q}]\!] \xrightarrow{\beta} [\![\mathcal{P}' \rhd_k \mathcal{Q}]\!]} \qquad \text{B-Par}\ \frac{\mathcal{P} \xrightarrow{\beta} \mathcal{P}' \quad \mathcal{Q} \xrightarrow{\beta} \mathcal{Q}'}{\mathcal{P} \mid \mathcal{Q} \xrightarrow{\beta} \mathcal{P}' \mid \mathcal{Q}'}$$

$$\text{B-Rec}\ \frac{}{\mu X.P \xrightarrow{\beta} \mu X.P} \qquad \text{B-Act}\ \frac{}{\sum \mu_i.P_i \xrightarrow{\beta} \sum \mu_i.P_i} \qquad \text{B-Co}\ \frac{}{\mathsf{co}\ k \xrightarrow{\beta} \mathsf{co}\ k} \qquad \text{B-Hide}\ \frac{\mathcal{P} \xrightarrow{\beta} \mathcal{P}'}{\nu a.\mathcal{P} \xrightarrow{\beta} \nu a.\mathcal{P}'}$$

(eliding B-Ab and B-Trans for secondary transactions)

Fig. 4. LTS: Broadcast actions

$$\frac{\mathcal{P} \xrightarrow{\widetilde{k}(\mu)} \mathcal{P}'' \xrightarrow{t}_{\Delta} \mathcal{P}' \quad \widetilde{k} \subseteq \Delta}{\mathcal{P} \xrightarrow{\mu,t}_{\Delta} \mathcal{P}'}\text{C-Act} \qquad \frac{\mathcal{P} \xrightarrow{\mathsf{ab}\ k} \mathcal{P}'' \xrightarrow{t}_{\Delta} \mathcal{P}' \quad k \notin \Delta}{\mathcal{P} \xrightarrow{t}_{\Delta} \mathcal{P}'}\text{C-Ab}$$

$$\frac{\mathcal{P} \xrightarrow{\mathsf{emb}\ k} \mathcal{P}'' \xrightarrow{t}_{\Delta} \mathcal{P}' \quad k \in \Delta}{\mathcal{P} \xrightarrow{t}_{\Delta} \mathcal{P}'}\text{C-Emb} \qquad \frac{\mathcal{P} \xrightarrow{\mathsf{co}\ \Delta} \mathcal{P}'}{\mathcal{P} \xrightarrow{\epsilon}_{\Delta} \mathcal{P}'}\text{C-Co}$$

Fig. 5. Clean Traces

Clean traces are CCS traces that correspond to raw traces in the LTS where all transactions performing actions are eventually committed at the end of the trace. Formally, clean traces are specified by the relation $\mathcal{P} \xrightarrow{t}_{\Delta} \mathcal{P}'$, given in Fig. 5. The parameter Δ is used to record which transactions will commit, and hence which actions are allowed inside the trace.

Example 8. The clean trace $I_3 \mid T^{\omega}_{ab} \xrightarrow{\tau,\tau,\tau}_{\{k\}} \omega$ corresponds to the first trace above. In isolation, I_3 has the clean traces $I_3 \xrightarrow{\epsilon}_{\emptyset} I_3$ and $I_3 \xrightarrow{ab}_{\{k\}} \mathbf{0}$, but not the singleton trace a: we need $k \in \Delta$ to do the a action inside the transaction, but we cannot derive $I_3 \xrightarrow{a}_{\{k\}}$ since the transaction cannot yet commit having done only the a action. Clean traces are hence not prefix closed. □

Usually, we care only that there is *some* Δ for which $\mathcal{P} \xrightarrow{t}_{\Delta} \mathcal{P}'$ can be derived, which motivates the following definition:

Definition 6. *We write $\mathcal{P} \xrightarrow{t}_{CL}$ iff t is a clean trace of $\mathcal{P}$, that is $\exists \Delta, \mathcal{P}'$ such that $\mathcal{P} \xrightarrow{t}_{\Delta} \mathcal{P}'$. We write $\mathcal{P} \stackrel{t}{\Rightarrow}_{CL}$ to denote that t is a weak clean trace of $\mathcal{P}$.*

5.3 Characterization of Safety as Clean Trace Inclusion

Safety preservation is characterized by clean trace inclusion [22].

Definition 7 (Language). *The language of a process $\mathcal{P}$ is the set of weak clean traces it can do:*

$$\mathcal{L}(\mathcal{P}) \stackrel{\text{def}}{=} \{t \mid \mathcal{P} \stackrel{t}{\Rightarrow}_{CL}\}$$

Theorem 1 (Safety preservation). $P \sqsubset\!\!\!\sim_{\text{safe}} Q$ *iff* $\mathcal{L}(P) \supseteq \mathcal{L}(Q)$.

6 Characterization of Liveness as Clean Tree Failures

We now proceed with the main technical result of this paper: a sound and complete characterization of liveness preservation in terms of *clean tree failures*. In this section we present the model, give a number of examples, and state the main results. The proof of soundness and completeness is summarized in Sect. 8.

The intuition of our model is that $\mathcal{P}$ has a clean tree failure (t, Ref) iff $\mathcal{P}$ can do a clean trace to $\mathcal{P}'$ and $\mathcal{P}'$ cannot do any of the clean traces in the set Ref.

Definition 8 (Tree failures). *Tree failures are defined as*

$$\mathcal{F}(\mathcal{P}) \stackrel{\text{def}}{=} \{(t, \mathit{Ref}) \mid \exists \mathcal{P}'.\ \mathcal{P} \stackrel{t}{\Rightarrow}_{CL} \mathcal{P}' \text{ and } \mathcal{L}(\mathcal{P}') \cap \mathit{Ref} = \emptyset\}$$

Theorem 2 (Liveness Preservation). $P \sqsubset\!\!\!\sim_{\text{live}} Q$ *iff* $\mathcal{F}(P) \supseteq \mathcal{F}(Q)$.

Example 9. Consider the transactions S_{ab} and I_3 from Fig. 1. The only clean traces either of these processes can do is the empty trace ϵ and the trace ab; moreover, for either process, the only clean trace that they cannot refuse after the empty trace is the trace ab, and both can refuse all clean traces after the trace ab. Hence, the set of failures for both processes is

$$\{(\epsilon, \mathit{Ref}) \mid ab \notin \mathit{Ref}\} \cup \{(ab, \mathit{Ref}) \mid \text{any } \mathit{Ref}\}$$

so that by Thm. 2 we have $S_{ab} \eqsim_{\text{live}} I_3$. □

Our model is simpler than the model of liveness preservation in CCS [21]. This is due to the existence of transactional tests that do not allow processes to deadlock while they communicate with these tests, as shown in Ex. 5.

As in CCS, liveness preservation implies safety preservation.

Theorem 3 (Liveness implies safety). *If* $P \sqsubset\!\!\!\sim_{\text{live}} Q$ *then* $P \sqsubset\!\!\!\sim_{\text{safe}} Q$.

Proof. By Thm. 1 it suffices to prove that if t is a clean trace of Q then it is a clean trace of P. Let t be a clean trace of Q; then $(t, \emptyset) \in \mathcal{F}(Q)$ and by Thm. 2, $(t, \emptyset) \in \mathcal{F}(P)$. Thus t is a clean trace of P. □

7 Canonical Tests

We identify a class of canonical liveness tests that encode sufficient power to distinguish any processes P and Q for which $P \not\sqsubset\!\!\!\sim_{\text{live}} Q$. We use these tests in the definition of a restricted form of liveness preservation, which we will show by Prop. 8 in the following section implies inverse failure inclusion. This result is crucial to show completeness of our characterization, but also implies that restricted liveness coincides with standard liveness.

Definition 9 (T^{ω}_{Ref})**.** *If Ref is a set of clean traces, we define the liveness test*

$$T^{\omega}_{Ref} \stackrel{\text{def}}{=} \mu X. \left[\!\left[\sum_{t \in Ref} \tau.\bar{t}.(\mathsf{co}\ k \mid \omega) \rhd_k X \right]\!\right]$$

Definition 10 ($T^{\omega}_{(t,Ref)}$)**.** *If t is a clean trace and Ref a set of clean traces, we define the liveness test $T^{\omega}_{(t,Ref)}$ by induction on t:*

$$T^{\omega}_{(\epsilon,Ref)} \stackrel{\text{def}}{=} T^{\omega}_{Ref} \qquad T^{\omega}_{(at,Ref)} \stackrel{\text{def}}{=} \omega + \bar{a}.T^{\omega}_{(t,Ref)}$$

These tests are interesting because (as we will show in Sect. 8) a process P passes the liveness test $T^{\omega}_{(t,Ref)}$ exactly if (t, Ref) is not a failure of P. Note that P fails the liveness test $T^{\omega}_{(t,Ref)}$ only if it can do a clean trace t and then refuse to do all the traces of Ref.

Example 10. The liveness test T^{ω} we considered in Ex. 5 is exactly the test $T^{\omega}_{(a,\{bc\})}$. We saw that $P = a.(b.c + b.d)$ passes this test, but $Q = a.b.c + a.b.d$ does not. Hence, $(a, \{bc\})$ is a failure of Q but not of P. □

Definition 11 (Restricted Liveness Preservation ($\hat{\sqsubseteq}_{\text{live}}$))

$$P \mathrel{\hat{\sqsubseteq}_{\text{live}}} Q \stackrel{\text{def}}{=} \forall t, Ref.\ \ \textit{if}\ P\,\text{shd}\,T^{\omega}_{(t,Ref)}\ \ \textit{then}\ Q\,\text{shd}\,T^{\omega}_{(t,Ref)}$$

Theorem 4. $(\sqsubseteq_{\text{live}}) = (\hat{\sqsubseteq}_{\text{live}})$.

Proof. Follows by Prop. 6 (soundness) and Prop. 8 in the following section. □

8 Soundness and Completeness

We now outline the proof that the characterization of the fair-testing preorder in terms of clean tree failures is sound and complete. This proof makes use of the ability to zip and unzip clean traces, proved in [22,23], which means that processes can communicate independently of their transaction structure.

Proposition 4 (Clean unzipping). *If $P \mid Q \stackrel{\epsilon}{\Rightarrow}_{CL} \mathcal{R}$ then there exist t, $\mathcal{P}'$, and $\mathcal{Q}'$ such that $P \stackrel{t}{\Rightarrow}_{CL} \mathcal{P}'$ and $Q \stackrel{\bar{t}}{\Rightarrow}_{CL} \mathcal{Q}'$ and $\mathcal{R}$ is equal up to merging of distributed transactions with $\mathcal{P}' \mid \mathcal{Q}'$.*

Proposition 5 (Clean zipping). *If $P \stackrel{t}{\Rightarrow}_{CL} \mathcal{P}'$ and $Q \stackrel{\bar{t}}{\Rightarrow}_{CL} \mathcal{Q}'$ then there exists an $\mathcal{R}$ such that $P \mid Q \stackrel{\epsilon}{\Rightarrow}_{CL} \mathcal{R}$ and $\mathcal{R}$ is equal up to merging of distributed transactions with $\mathcal{P}' \mid \mathcal{Q}'$.*

The following theorem is key in the proof of soundness and completeness, and states that we can construct clean traces from raw traces:

Theorem 5 (Clean trace construction). *If $\mathcal{P} \stackrel{\epsilon}{\Rightarrow} \mathcal{R}$ then there exists $\mathcal{R}'$ such that $\mathcal{P} \stackrel{\epsilon}{\Rightarrow}_{CL} \mathcal{R}'$ and*

1. *If $\mathcal{R}\downarrow_{\omega}$ then $\mathcal{R}'\downarrow_{\omega}$ (success is preserved)*
2. *If $\mathcal{R}\not\Downarrow_{\omega}$ then $\mathcal{R}'\not\Downarrow_{\omega}$ (failure is preserved)*

This theorem strengthens an earlier result [22], where we proved (1) but not (2); the proof is however significantly different. Intuitively, the construction of the clean trace postpones all commits to the end of the trace and aborts all actions that are never committed in the raw trace.

Definition 12. $\mathcal{L}^{\omega}(\mathcal{P}) \stackrel{\text{def}}{=} \{t \mid \mathcal{P} \stackrel{t}{\Rightarrow}_{CL}, \omega \notin t\}$

The proof of soundness is based on the construction of a clean trace from a raw trace, and zipping and unzipping of clean traces.

Proposition 6 (Soundness). *If $\mathcal{F}(P) \supseteq \mathcal{F}(Q)$ then $P \sqsubseteq_{\text{live}} Q$.*

Proof. Assume $\mathcal{F}(P) \supseteq \mathcal{F}(Q)$. We prove the contrapositive of $P \sqsubseteq_{\text{live}} Q$: suppose $\neg(Q \,\text{shd}\, T)$ for some test T; we have to show that $\neg(P \,\text{shd}\, T)$.

Since $\neg(Q \,\text{shd}\, T)$, there exists an $\mathcal{R}$ such that $Q \mid T \stackrel{\epsilon}{\Rightarrow} \mathcal{R}\not\Downarrow_{\omega}$. Hence by Thm. 5, there exists $\mathcal{R}'$ such that $Q \mid T \stackrel{\epsilon}{\Rightarrow}_{\text{CL}} \mathcal{R}'\not\Downarrow_{\omega}$. By Prop. 4, there exist $t, \mathcal{Q}', \mathcal{T}'$ such that $Q \stackrel{t}{\Rightarrow}_{\text{CL}} \mathcal{Q}'$ and $T \stackrel{\bar{t}}{\Rightarrow}_{\text{CL}} \mathcal{T}'$, where $\mathcal{R}'$ is equal to $\mathcal{Q}' \mid \mathcal{T}'$ up to distribution of transactions. Define $\mathit{Ref} = \{t' \mid \mathcal{T}' \stackrel{\bar{t}'}{\Rightarrow}_{\text{CL}} \mathcal{T}'' \mid \omega\}$. Then $\mathcal{L}(\mathcal{Q}') \cap \mathit{Ref}$ must be empty, because otherwise $\mathcal{R}'\Downarrow_{\omega}$ by zipping the clean traces. Hence $(t, \mathit{Ref}) \in \mathcal{F}(\mathcal{Q})$ and therefore $(t, \mathit{Ref}) \in \mathcal{F}(\mathcal{P})$. It follows that exists $\mathcal{P}'$ such that $P \stackrel{t}{\Rightarrow}_{\text{CL}} \mathcal{P}'$ and $\mathcal{L}(\mathcal{P}') \cap \mathit{Ref} = \emptyset$. By Prop. 5, $P \mid T \stackrel{t'}{\Rightarrow}_{\text{CL}} \mathcal{P}' \mid \mathcal{T}'$ where $\mathcal{P}' \mid \mathcal{T}'\not\Downarrow_{\omega}$ since $\mathcal{L}(\mathcal{P}') \cap \mathit{Ref} = \emptyset$. Therefore $\neg(P \,\text{shd}\, T)$. □

The proof of completeness makes essential use of the canonical tests (Sect. 7).

Lemma 1. $\mathcal{L}^{\omega}(\mathcal{T}_{\mathit{Ref}}) = \overline{\mathit{Ref}}$

Proof. By definition of $\mathcal{L}^{\omega}()$ and $\mathcal{T}_{\mathit{Ref}}$. Note that $\mathcal{L}^{\omega}(\mathcal{T}_{\mathit{Ref}})$ is not the prefix closure of Ref because we used a transactional $\mathcal{T}_{\mathit{Ref}}$. □

Lemma 2. $\mathcal{L}(\mathcal{P}) \cap \mathit{Ref} = \emptyset$ *iff* $(\mathcal{P} \mid \mathcal{T}_{\mathit{Ref}})\not\Downarrow_{\omega}$.

Proof. (Only if) By contradiction: Assume $(\mathcal{P} \mid \mathcal{T}_{\mathit{Ref}})\Downarrow_{\omega}$, i.e. $\mathcal{P} \mid \mathcal{T}_{\mathit{Ref}} \stackrel{\epsilon}{\Rightarrow} \mathcal{R}\downarrow_{\omega}$. Then by Thm. 5 there exists $\mathcal{R}'$ such that $\mathcal{P} \mid \mathcal{T}_{\mathit{Ref}} \stackrel{\epsilon}{\Rightarrow}_{\text{CL}} \mathcal{R}'\downarrow_{\omega}$. We can therefore apply Prop. 4 to get a clean trace $t \in \mathcal{L}(\mathcal{P})$ and $\bar{t} \in \mathcal{L}^{\omega}(\mathcal{T}_{\mathit{Ref}})$. Hence by Lem. 1 we must have $t \in \mathit{Ref}$, contradicting the assumption that $\mathcal{L}(\mathcal{P}) \cap \mathit{Ref} = \emptyset$.

(If) By contradiction: Assume there exists $t \in \mathcal{L}(\mathcal{P}) \cap \mathit{Ref}$. Then we can apply Prop. 5 to get $\mathcal{P} \mid \mathcal{T}_{\mathit{Ref}} \stackrel{\epsilon}{\Rightarrow}_{\text{CL}} \mathcal{P}'\downarrow_{\omega}$ contradicting $(\mathcal{P} \mid \mathcal{T}_{\mathit{Ref}})\not\Downarrow_{\omega}$. □

Lemma 3. $\mathcal{L}^{\omega}(\mathcal{T}_{(t,\mathit{Ref})}) = \{\bar{t}_1 \mid \exists t_2.\ t = t_1 t_2\} \cup \{\bar{t}t' \mid t' \in \mathcal{L}^{\omega}(\mathcal{T}_{\mathit{Ref}})\}$

Proof. By definition of $\mathcal{L}^{\omega}()$ and $\mathcal{T}_{(t,\mathit{Ref})}$. □

A process fails a canonical liveness test iff it has the corresponding tree failure.

Proposition 7 (Tests and Failures). $(t, \mathit{Ref}) \in \mathcal{F}(P)$ *iff* $\neg(P \,\text{shd}\, T_{(t,\mathit{Ref})})$.

Proof. (Only if) Let $(t, \mathit{Ref}) \in \mathcal{F}(P)$, i.e. $\exists \mathcal{P}'.\ P \stackrel{t}{\Rightarrow}_{\text{CL}} \mathcal{P}'$ and $\mathcal{L}(\mathcal{P}') \cap \mathit{Ref} = \emptyset$. Clearly $T_{(t,\mathit{Ref})} \stackrel{\bar{t}}{\Rightarrow}_{\text{CL}} T_{\mathit{Ref}}$ so that, by Prop. 5, $P \mid T_{(t,\mathit{Ref})} \stackrel{\epsilon}{\Rightarrow}_{\text{CL}} \mathcal{R}$ equal up to merging of transactions to $\mathcal{P}' \mid T_{Ref}$. It follows from Lem. 2 that success is not reachable from this state.

(If) Since $\neg(P \operatorname{shd} T_{(t,Ref)})$ it follows that $\exists \mathcal{R}.\ P \mid T_{(t,Ref)} \stackrel{\epsilon}{\Rightarrow} \mathcal{R}\not\Downarrow_\omega$. Then by Thm. 5, $\exists \mathcal{R}'.\ P \mid T_{(t,Ref)} \stackrel{\epsilon}{\Rightarrow}_{\mathrm{CL}} \mathcal{R}'\not\Downarrow_\omega$. By Prop. 4, there exist $t', \mathcal{P}', \mathcal{T}'$ such that $P \stackrel{t'}{\Rightarrow}_{\mathrm{CL}} \mathcal{P}'$ and $T_{(t,Ref)} \stackrel{\overline{t}'}{\Rightarrow}_{\mathrm{CL}} \mathcal{T}'$, and $\mathcal{P}' \mid \mathcal{T}'\not\Downarrow_\omega$. Thus, $t' \in \mathcal{L}(P)$ and by Lem. 3

$$\overline{t}' \in \mathcal{L}^\omega(T_{(t,Ref)}) = \{\overline{t}_1 \mid \exists t_2.\ t = t_1\, t_2\} \cup \{\overline{t}\, t_2 \mid t_2 \in \mathcal{L}^\omega(\mathcal{T}_{Ref})\}$$

We take cases on $\overline{t}' \in \mathcal{L}^\omega(\mathcal{T}_{(t,Ref)})$:

1. $\overline{t}' = \overline{t}t_2$ for some $t_2 \in \mathcal{L}^\omega(T_{Ref})$. Not possible, because then $\mathcal{T}' = \omega\downarrow_\omega$.
2. $\overline{t}' = \overline{t_1}$ for some $t_1 t_2 = t$ with t_2 non-empty; again, not possible because then $\mathcal{T}' = \omega + \mathcal{T}''\downarrow_\omega$.
3. $\overline{t}' = \overline{t}$. Then $\mathcal{T}' = T_{Ref}$ and by Lem. 2 $\mathcal{L}(\mathcal{P}') \cap Ref = \emptyset$. Hence $(t, Ref) \in \mathcal{F}(\mathcal{P})$. □

Restricted liveness preservation implies inverse failure inclusion.

Proposition 8. *If $P \mathrel{\hat{\sqsubseteq}}_{\mathrm{live}} Q$ then $\mathcal{F}(P) \supseteq \mathcal{F}(Q)$.*

Proof. Let $(t, Ref) \in \mathcal{F}(Q)$. By Prop. 7 we have $\neg(Q \operatorname{shd} T_{(t,Ref)})$, therefore $\neg(P \operatorname{shd} T_{(t,Ref)})$ since $P \mathrel{\hat{\sqsubseteq}}_{\mathrm{live}} Q$, and finally $(t, Ref) \in \mathcal{F}(P)$ by Prop. 7. □

Corollary 1 (Completeness). *If $P \sqsubseteq_{\mathrm{live}} Q$ then $\mathcal{F}(P) \supseteq \mathcal{F}(Q)$.*

Proof. By the definitions of $(\sqsubseteq_{\mathrm{live}})$ and $(\hat{\sqsubseteq}_{\mathrm{live}})$ and Prop. 8. □

9 Weak Clean-Trace Bisimilarity

In this section we present a convenient coinductive proof technique for liveness preservation, which is based on weak bisimilarity over clean traces. We show that this technique is sound but not complete with respect to liveness preservation, and use it to prove liveness and safety preservation.

Definition 13 (Weak Clean-Trace Bisimulation). *Θ is a weak clean-trace bisimulation if whenever $(\mathcal{P}, \mathcal{Q}) \in \Theta$ the following two conditions are satisfied.*

1. *$\forall t, \mathcal{P}'.\ \mathcal{P} \stackrel{t}{\Rightarrow}_{CL} \mathcal{P}'$ we have $\exists \mathcal{Q}'$ such that $\mathcal{Q} \stackrel{t}{\Rightarrow}_{CL} \mathcal{Q}'$ and $(\mathcal{P}', \mathcal{Q}') \in \Theta$,*
2. *$\forall t, \mathcal{Q}'.\ \mathcal{Q} \stackrel{t}{\Rightarrow}_{CL} \mathcal{Q}'$ we have $\exists \mathcal{P}'$ such that $\mathcal{P} \stackrel{t}{\Rightarrow}_{CL} \mathcal{P}'$ and $(\mathcal{P}', \mathcal{Q}') \in \Theta$.*

Weak clean-trace bisimilarity, denoted by $\approx$, is the largest weak clean-trace bisimulation.

Weak clean-trace bisimilarity is sound with respect to both liveness and safety.

Theorem 6 (Soundness of $(\approx)$). *If $\mathcal{P} \approx \mathcal{Q}$ then $\mathcal{P} \eqsim_{\mathrm{live}} \mathcal{Q}$ and $\mathcal{P} \eqsim_{\mathrm{safe}} \mathcal{Q}$.*

Proof. Since $\approx$ is commutative, it suffices to prove that $\mathcal{P} \sqsubseteq_{\mathrm{live}} \mathcal{Q}$ and hence by Thm. 2 that $\mathcal{F}(\mathcal{P}) \supseteq \mathcal{F}(\mathcal{Q})$. Let $(t, S) \in \mathcal{F}(\mathcal{Q})$, i.e. $\mathcal{P} \stackrel{t}{\Rightarrow}_{\mathrm{CL}} \mathcal{P}'$ where $\mathcal{L}(\mathcal{P}') \cap S = \emptyset$.

Since $\mathcal{P} \approx \mathcal{Q}$, $\exists \mathcal{Q}'$ such that $\mathcal{Q} \overset{t}{\Rightarrow}_{\mathrm{CL}} \mathcal{Q}'$ where $\mathcal{P}' \approx \mathcal{Q}'$. It remains to show that $\mathcal{L}(\mathcal{Q}') \cap S = \emptyset$. We proceed by contradiction. Suppose that $\exists t' \in \mathcal{L}(\mathcal{Q}') \cap S$. Then $\exists \mathcal{Q}''$ such that $\mathcal{Q}' \overset{t'}{\Rightarrow}_{\mathrm{CL}} \mathcal{Q}''$. But then since $\mathcal{P}' \approx \mathcal{Q}'$, $\exists \mathcal{P}''$ such that $\mathcal{P}' \overset{t'}{\Rightarrow}_{\mathrm{CL}} \mathcal{P}''$, contradicting the assumption that $\mathcal{L}(\mathcal{P}') \cap S = \emptyset$. □

The following example shows that weak clean-trace bisimilarity is not complete with respect to liveness and safety.

Example 11. Consider the processes $P = a.(\tau.b + \tau.c)$ and $Q = a.b + a.c$. The two processes are not bisimilar: P can do a clean trace $P \overset{a}{\Rightarrow}_{\mathrm{CL}} (\tau.b + \tau.c)$ and Q can only follow it by $Q \overset{a}{\Rightarrow}_{\mathrm{CL}} b$ or $Q \overset{a}{\Rightarrow}_{\mathrm{CL}} c$. Neither b nor c are bisimilar to $(\tau.b + \tau.c)$. It is not difficult to show, however, that $P \eqsim_{\text{live}} Q$ (and thus, by Thm. 3, $P \eqsim_{\text{may}} Q$) by observing that any tree failure $(t, S) \in \mathcal{F}(P)$ is a tree failure of Q and vice versa. □

The next result simplifies reasoning about weak clean-trace bisimilarity by allowing us to consider a single unfolding of recursive transactions.

Proposition 9. *If* $[\![P \rhd_k \mathbb{0}]\!] \approx [\![Q \rhd_k \mathbb{0}]\!]$ *then* $\mu X. [\![P \rhd_k X]\!] \approx \mu X. [\![Q \rhd_k X]\!]$.

Proof. By enumeration of the clean traces of the restarting transactions, which start with a number of aborts and continue with a clean trace of the non-restarting transactions. □

We use weak clean-trace bisimilarity to give simple coinductive proofs of liveness and safety preservation for the examples of the introduction and Fig. 1.

Example 12. Recall once more transactions S_{ab} and I_3 (Fig. 1). We prove that $S_{ab} \eqsim_{\text{live}} I_3$ and $S_{ab} \eqsim_{\text{may}} I_3$ by showing $S_{ab} \approx I_3$. By Prop. 9 it suffices to show $[\![a.b.\mathsf{co}\ k \rhd_k \mathbb{0}]\!] \approx [\![a.b.\mathsf{co}\ k + \overline{err}.\mathbb{0} \rhd_k \mathbb{0}]\!]$, which can be easily proved by showing that the relation containing the two transactions and $(\mathbb{0}, \mathbb{0})$ is a bisimulation. □

Example 13. We now turn our attention to the example of the introduction. We show that the implementation *Sys* preserves both the liveness and safety properties of the specification *Spec*. In fact, we prove the stronger results that $\mathit{Spec} \eqsim_{\text{live}} \mathit{Sys}$ and $\mathit{Spec} \eqsim_{\text{safe}} \mathit{Sys}$ by showing that $\mathit{Spec} \approx \mathit{Sys}$. Consider the relation $\Theta = \{(\mathit{Spec}, \mathit{Sys})\} \cup \{ (\overline{rec}\langle v \rangle,\ \nu q.\nu s. (\mathit{Trg}_{del,s,q} \mid \overline{q}\langle v \rangle \mid \overline{s}\langle 1 \rangle)) \mid \exists v\} \cup \{(\mathbb{0}, \mathbb{0})\}$. It is easy to verify that Θ is a weak clean-trace bisimulation. □

10 Related Work

The study of safety and liveness in concurrent languages goes back thirty years [18,19], but although there are many studies of (isolated) transactions in concurrent languages [1,2,3,4,5,6,9,12,15,17] none of them study liveness.

There is much less research on *communicating* transactions. We are aware of only three other studies: Committed π [7], RCCS [10], and Transactors [13], none of which discuss safety or liveness properties of transactions.

Most closely related is the Committed π calculus where, like in TransCCS, transactions must be combined before they can communicate. However, they are merged rather than embedded: $[\![P_1 \rhd Q_1]\!] \mid [\![P_2 \rhd Q_2]\!] \to [\![P_1 \mid P_2 \rhd Q_1 \mid Q_2]\!]$. This leads to pessimistic rollback behaviour: when transactions communicate and a failure happens, *all* transactions must be rolled back to their initial state. Moreover, Committed π includes an explicit abort construct, which makes uncommitted actions observable [22]. For example, the transaction $[\![a.\mathbb{0} \rhd \mathbb{0}]\!]$ can be distinguished from $\mathbb{0}$ by $[\![\overline{a}.\mathtt{ab} \rhd \omega]\!]$.

Reversible CCS extends CCS with reversible actions which can be rolled back and irreversible actions which act as a commit. The most important difference with TransCCS is that in RCCS a commit by a single transaction will cause the commit of all transactions it has communicated with. For example, the RCCS transaction $[\![a.\mathbb{0} \rhd_k \mathbb{0}]\!]$ can be distinguished from $\mathbb{0}$ by $[\![\overline{a}.(\mathtt{co}\ l \mid \omega) \rhd_l \mathbb{0}]\!]$.

Finally, Transactors is an extension of the actors model with communicating transactions. It is a much lower level language than TransCCS with a more complicated semantics, but it is similar in intent: for instance, $[\![a.\mathbb{0} \rhd_k \mathbb{0}]\!]$ seems indistinguishable from $\mathbb{0}$, although in the absence of a behavioural theory for the language this is difficult to show.

We studied liveness properties of communicating transactions under an assumption of fairness, which must be guaranteed by potential implementations of the language. There is some work that investigates the fairness guarantees that can be offered by implementations of isolated transactions [16,20]; an extension of those studies to communicating transactions would be worthwhile.

11 Conclusions

We studied liveness and safety in TransCCS; to the extent of our knowledge, this is the first semantic study of liveness in the presence of transactions. We showed that fair-testing and may-testing capture the right notions of liveness and safety and gave numerous examples to build useful intuitions. We developed a sound and complete characterization of liveness preservation in terms of clean tree failures, extending our earlier work on clean traces. This characterization is simpler than the characterization of liveness preservation in CCS, made possible by the additional distinguishing power added by transactions. We also gave a coinductive proof technique for liveness preservation based on weak clean trace bisimulation, which we proved to be sound but incomplete. We used the characterization and the bisimulation in example proofs of liveness preservation.

Further study of weak bisimulation and other proof techniques is future work. For instance, it is unclear at present whether bisimilarity preserves all contexts and what its characterization is. We also plan to extend TransCCS to the π-calculus. Finally, we intend to investigate the usefulness of the construct of communicating transactions in a more realistic programming language.

References

1. Acciai, L., Boreale, M., Zilio, S.D.: A concurrent calculus with atomic transactions. In: De Nicola, R. (ed.) ESOP 2007. LNCS, vol. 4421, pp. 48–63. Springer, Heidelberg (2007)

2. Black, A.P., Cremet, V., Guerraoui, R., Odersky, M.: An equational theory for transactions. In: Pandya, P.K., Radhakrishnan, J. (eds.) FSTTCS 2003. LNCS, vol. 2914, pp. 38–49. Springer, Heidelberg (2003)
3. Bocchi, L.: Compositional nested long running transactions. In: Wermelinger, M., Margaria-Steffen, T. (eds.) FASE 2004. LNCS, vol. 2984, pp. 194–208. Springer, Heidelberg (2004)
4. Bruni, R., Laneve, C., Montanari, U.: Orchestrating transactions in join calculus*. In: Brim, L., Jančar, P., Křetínský, M., Kucera, A. (eds.) CONCUR 2002. LNCS, vol. 2421, pp. 321–544. Springer, Heidelberg (2002)
5. Bruni, R., Melgratti, H., Montanari, U.: Theoretical foundations for compensations in flow composition languages. In: POPL, pp. 209–220. ACM, New York (2005)
6. Bruni, R., Melgratti, H., Montanari, U.: Nested commits for mobile calculi: extending Join. In: IFIP-TCS, pp. 569–582. Kluwer Academic Publishers, Dordrecht (2004)
7. Buscemi, M.G., Melgratti, H.: Transactional service level agreement. In: Kaklamanis, C., Nielson, F. (eds.) TGC 2008. LNCS, vol. 5474, pp. 124–139. Springer, Heidelberg (2009)
8. Cacciagrano, D., Corradini, F., Palamidessi, C.: Explicit fairness in testing semantics. Logical Methods in Computer Science 5(2) (2009)
9. Caires, L., Ferreira, C., Vieira, H.T.: A process calculus analysis of compensations. In: Kaklamanis, C., Nielson, F. (eds.) TGC 2008. LNCS, vol. 5474, pp. 87–103. Springer, Heidelberg (2009)
10. Danos, V., Krivine, J.: Transactions in RCCS. In: Abadi, M., de Alfaro, L. (eds.) CONCUR 2005. LNCS, vol. 3653, pp. 398–412. Springer, Heidelberg (2005)
11. De Nicola, R., Hennessy, M.C.B.: Testing equivalences for processes. Theoretical Computer Science 34(1-2), 83–133 (1984)
12. Elmas, T., Qadeer, S., Tasiran, S.: A calculus of atomic actions. In: POPL, pp. 2–15 (2009)
13. Field, J., Varela, C.A.: Transactors: a programming model for maintaining globally consistent distributed state in unreliable environments. In: POPL, pp. 195–208 (2005)
14. van Glabbeek, R.: The linear time–branching time spectrum after 20 years. Celebration of 20 years of CONCUR (2009)
15. Gorrieri, R., Marchetti, S., Montanari, U.: A^2CCS: atomic actions for CCS. Theor. Comp. Sci. 72(2-3), 203–223 (1990)
16. Guerraoui, R., Kapalka, M.: How Live Can a Transactional Memory Be? Tech. rep., EPFL (2009)
17. Harris, T., Marlow, S., Peyton-Jones, S., Herlihy, M.: Composable memory transactions. In: PPoPP, pp. 48–60. ACM, New York (2005)
18. Lamport, L.: Proving the correctness of multiprocess programs. IEEE Trans. Softw. Eng. 3(2), 125–143 (1977)
19. Owicki, S., Lamport, L.: Proving liveness properties of concurrent programs. ACM Trans. Program. Lang. Syst. 4(3), 455–495 (1982)
20. Pedone, F., Guerraoui, R.: On transaction liveness in replicated databases. In: PRFTS, p. 104 (1997)
21. Rensink, A., Vogler, W.: Fair testing. Inf. and Comp. 205(2), 125–198 (2007)
22. de Vries, E., Koutavas, V., Hennessy, M.: Communicating Transactions. In: CONCUR 2010 (to appear, 2010)
23. de Vries, E., Koutavas, V., Hennessy, M.: Communicating transactions—technical appendix (April 2010), `http://www.scss.tcd.ie/Edsko.de.Vries`

Model Independent Order Relations for Processes*

Chaodong He**

BASICS***, Department of Computer Science
Shanghai Jiaotong University, Shanghai 200240, China
hechaodong1130@gmail.com

Abstract. Semantic preorders between processes are usually applied in practice to model approximation or implementation relationships. For interactive models these preorders depend crucially on the observational behaviours of processes as well as on the observing power of environments. The paper aims at a model independent observational theory of the semantic preorders for interactive models. Depending on whether environments change dynamically or not, two classes of model independent preorders are formalized. These formalizations are intensively studied in the framework of CCS. Operational characterizations of these preorders are investigated, and the relationships between them are revealed. Several new preorders for CCS are proposed along the way. Behavioural properties are discussed in a model independent manner as far as possible.

1 Introduction

Observational theory is an old and fruitful area of fundamental research in process calculi, which studies behavioural equivalences and preorders between processes. The starting point is to give clear criteria when one process is a correct implementation or an approximation of the other. It is realized from the very beginning [5,15] that equivalences or preorders for processes ought to be 'observational' since it is the effect that processes place on environments that really matter. However, one of the insights that has been gained in the past three decades is that there does not really exist the canonical notion of 'observable behaviour'. Depending on different formalizations of observability, many different notions of behavioural equivalences or preorders come out. The readers may consult Van Glabbeek [17,18] for an overview.

A preorder and its inverse can be combined into an equivalence. Apart from this, preorders on processes have significance of there own. In practice, to build a

* The full version of this paper which contains more proof details is available at http://basics.sjtu.edu.cn/~chaodong/.

** The work is supported by the National Nature Science Foundation of China (60873034, 61011140074, 61003013, 61033002).

*** Laboratory for Basic Studies in Computing Science (http://basics.sjtu.edu.cn).

K. Ueda (Ed.): APLAS 2010, LNCS 6461, pp. 408–423, 2010.

system, we have a specification, say P, which is described as a process in a certain language. Then, this specification is usually implemented as a process, say Q, in the same language. A question one may raise is whether the implementation Q is favourable for the specification P. On such occasions, symmetry is less important. The answer is to find a proper preorder and checking whether P is less than Q.

Historically, there are two families of preorders which turn out to be very successful under two different presumptions on the observation power of environments. They are the testing preorders and the bisimulation equivalences.

In the philosophy of testing theory developed by De Nicola and Hennessy [11], the behaviours of processes are investigated by a series of tests. The preorder between two processes is formulated in terms of their capability to respond to a test. The proposed implementation Q will be considered less than the given specification P whenever Q has all the concerned capabilities that P has. According to two different meanings of 'capability', *may-testing* and *must-testing* preorders are defined respectively. The presumption in the testing approach is the 'static' environments, which means that a test is performed by a single tester in an exclusive manner. Under this presumption, the only thing to concern is the results of tests — success or failure. It does not matter what a process will turn into after a test. Consequently, testing approach will not cope with dynamically changed environments.

In 'dynamic' environments, a process could be subject to interference a potentially unbounded number of observers in an interleaving manner. 'Dynamic' here means that the testers can be dynamically changed during a single test. This scenario usually happens in distributed systems. In this situation, the appropriate process preorders are bisimilarities [13,5,6,19], for the 'bisimulation property' not only cares about testing results, but imposes additional restraints to intermediate states as well. These additional restraints can be conceived as the additional requirements whenever testers are changed. According to the philosophy of bisimilarity, environments also have the power to exchange the roles of processes for comparison. Such a strong assumption on the power of environments is sometimes considered a shortcoming of the bisimulation approach by some researchers.

This paper is devoted to create a unified observational theory for interactive models, highlighting approximation or implementation relationships, concentrated on two preassumptions about observing power of environments mentioned above. Before further exploration, two beneficial questions ought to be answered at first, from which some important notions are introduced which will be crucial to the characterizations of preorders throughout this article.

The first question is the reasons behind the great success of the testing and the bisimulation approaches. In the opinion of the author, there are two important reasons. The first reason is that the preorders defined in these two approaches support the way of comparing processes in a modular fashion. Intuitively, whenever Q is an approximation of P and they are treated as certain component of an environment $\mathbf{C}[\_]$, a desired property is $\mathbf{C}[Q]$ being an approximation of

$\mathbf{C}[P]$. This property is called *extensionality*. It turns out that testing preorders and bisimilarities are all extensional preorders. The second reason, which is more important, is that these preorders can be characterized without depending on the features of special models such as the existence of *labeled transition semantics*. Preorders with this property are called having *model-independent characterizations*. To clarify the precise meaning of 'model-independent' here, we have the following basic requirements on every interaction models. Firstly, every models are supposed to support computations and observations. The formers are formalized via reductions or τ-transitions, while the latters are made only by interactions, which are conducted via *interfaces* formalized as *names*. Secondly, in order to support observation, the *composition* $\_|\_$ and *localization* $(a)(\_)$ operations are indispensable. Composition operation enables observations while localization operation disables observations. Model-independent characterization is motivated to give a profound understanding of observational preorders. With this crucial property, some preorders can be immediately generalized to other interactive models such as name-passing calculi (like π-calculus [7,8]), value-passing calculi (like value-passing CCS [6]), and process-passing (or higher order) calculi (like CHOCS [16], HOπ-calculus [14]).

Behavioural preorders reflect approximating or implementing relations, therefore some 'capabilities' need to be preserved by preorders. Depending on different meanings of approximation or implementation, different notions of 'capabilities' should be concerned, which ultimately lead to different preorders. In this paper, the definitions of preorders are based on preservations of 'capabilities', which leads to the second question: how will 'capabilities' be chosen? We will take the very simple answer: all involved capabilities must be composed from the following four basic ones.

1. $\Diamond$-*capability*: possibly interacting with environment;
2. $\blacksquare$-*capability*: possibly not interacting with environment;
3. $\blacklozenge$-*capability*: impossibly interacting with environment;
4. $\Box$-*capability*: inevitably interacting with environment.

These four basic capabilities will prove powerful enough to produce the most significant preorders. In fact, $\Diamond$-capability and $\Box$-capability are the simplified and model-independent versions for may-testing and must-testing, while $\blacklozenge$-capability and $\blacksquare$-capability are the negations. These four capabilities can be composed arbitrarily to obtain totally 2^4=16 combinations. Following the idea of testing approach, every combination of capabilities will lead to a preorder (not necessarily different). Following the idea of bisimulation approach, however, all these combinations appear redundant, since the bisimulation property covers all four basic capabilities. However, there is another well-known preorder in literatures which lies between bisimilarity and may-testing preorder named *similarity*, which merely preserves $\Diamond$-capability. One can expect the existence of some other simulation-like preorders which preserve more capabilities above.

In the present paper, a number of preorders will be formalized. These preorders are defined and studied in a model-independent manner at first. Then the corresponding operational counterparts of all these preorders are investigated in the framework of CCS [5,6]. The preorders for static environments turn out to be variants of testing preorders. Amongst them, failure preorder is redefined so as to cater for the model-independent counterpart, which have more favourable properties. For dynamic environments, it becomes more interesting that the traditional similarity can not be obtained, instead several new simulation-like preorders are discovered during the exploration of operational counterparts, especially t-conserving similarity and f-conserving similarity. The separation results for all these preorders are established for CCS. Moreover, behavioural properties such as stuttering-property, X-property, and computation property are redefined and studied for preorders. Unlike the case for equivalences, stuttering-property and X-property for preorders stress different aspects of process behaviours and they are not able to derive each other.

The rest of the paper is organized as follows. Section 2 lays down the prerequisites of CCS and basic notions for model-independent characterization. Section 3 expounds model-independent characterization of preorders with their behavioural properties and the operational definitions for CCS under the assumption of static environments. Section 4 works in the same framework under the assumption of dynamic environments. Section 5 is the conclusion.

2 Basic Definitions and Notations

2.1 CCS

We begin with the syntax and semantics of CCS. To describe the interactions between systems, we need *names*. The set of the names $\mathcal{N}$ is ranged over by a, b, c, d, e. The set of the names and the conames $\mathcal{L} = \mathcal{N} \cup \overline{\mathcal{N}}$ is ranged over by l and satisfies the identity $\overline{\overline{a}} = a$. The set of finite string of names and conames, $\mathcal{L}^*$, is ranged over by u, v, w, s, t, r, and satisfies the identity $\overline{u \cdot v} = \overline{u} \cdot \overline{v}$. To define the operational semantics, we need *action labels*. The set of the action labels $\mathcal{A} = \mathcal{L} \cup \{\tau\}$ is ranged by λ. To introduce infinite behaviours of systems, we introduce the set $\mathcal{C}$ of *constant processes* which is ranged over by A, B, C.

The set $\mathcal{P}$ of CCS processes, ranged over by P, Q, R, M, N, is generated inductively by the following grammar.

$$P \ ::= \ \mathbf{0} \mid \lambda.P \mid P \,|\, P' \mid (a)P \mid P + P' \mid \mathbf{rec}_{C_n}\{C_i \stackrel{\text{def}}{=} P_i\}_{i \in I}$$

We have left out the relabeling operation for two reasons. One interest in CCS is that it is the core language such that the results obtained in CCS can be easily transferred to other interactive models, such as π-calculus. For that purpose the relabeling operation is not necessary. In additional, adding relabeling operator would not make CCS more expressive if infinite behaviours of processes are specified by *constant definition*, see [3] for more on expressiveness of CCS. The binary choice $P + P'$ will be used in its guarded form, meaning that both P and P' are in prefix form. The guardedness guarantees the finite branching property. A name a in localization form $(a)P$ is *local*. A name is *global* if it is not local.

$$\text{Prefix}\ \frac{}{\lambda.E \xrightarrow{\lambda} E} \qquad \text{Localization}\ \frac{E \xrightarrow{\lambda} E' \quad a \text{ does not appear in } \lambda}{(a)E \xrightarrow{\lambda} (a)E'}$$

$$\text{Choice}\ \frac{E \xrightarrow{\lambda} E'}{E + F \xrightarrow{\lambda} E'} \qquad \text{Composition}\ \frac{E \xrightarrow{\lambda} E'}{E \,|\, F \xrightarrow{\lambda} E' \,|\, F} \quad \frac{E \xrightarrow{l} E' \quad F \xrightarrow{\bar{l}} F'}{E \,|\, F \xrightarrow{\tau} E' \,|\, F'}$$

$$\text{Constant}\ \frac{P_n\{(\mathbf{rec}_{C_j}\{C_i \stackrel{\text{def}}{=} P_i\}_{i\in I})/C_j\}_{j\in I} \xrightarrow{\lambda} P'}{\mathbf{rec}_{C_n}\{C_i \stackrel{\text{def}}{=} P_i\}_{i\in I} \xrightarrow{\lambda} P'}$$

Fig. 1. The Semantics for CCS

The notation $\mathsf{gn}(\_)$ ($\mathsf{ln}(\_)$) stands for a function that returns the set of global names (local names). In the form of constant definition $\mathbf{rec}_{C_n}\{C_i \stackrel{\text{def}}{=} P_i\}_{i\in I}$, every constant process in P_i are required to be C_j for some $j \in I$.

The standard semantics of CCS is given by the *labeled transition system* $(\mathcal{P}, \mathcal{A}, \longrightarrow)$. The relation $\longrightarrow \subseteq \mathcal{P} \times \mathcal{A} \times \mathcal{P}$ is the *transition* relation. The membership $(P, \lambda, P') \in \longrightarrow$ is always indicated by $P \xrightarrow{\lambda} P'$. The relation $\longrightarrow$ is generated inductively by the rules defined in Fig. 1.

The *weak transition* $\Longrightarrow \subseteq \mathcal{P} \times \mathcal{A} \times \mathcal{P}$ is defined as usual: $P \stackrel{\lambda}{\Longrightarrow} P'$ if $P \xrightarrow{\tau}^* \xrightarrow{\lambda} \xrightarrow{\tau}^* P'$. In the following, both $\longrightarrow$ and $\Longrightarrow$ are lifted as a subset of $\mathcal{P} \times \mathcal{A}^* \times \mathcal{P}$. $P \stackrel{\epsilon}{\Longrightarrow} P'$, namely $P \xrightarrow{\tau}^* P'$, is usually abbreviated as $P \Longrightarrow P'$. The mapping $\widehat{\cdot} : \mathcal{A}^* \to \mathcal{L}^*$ is defined by $\widehat{l} = l$, $\widehat{\tau} = \epsilon$, and $\widehat{u \cdot v} = \widehat{u} \cdot \widehat{v}$. We write $P \stackrel{u}{\Longrightarrow}$ if $P \stackrel{u}{\Longrightarrow} P'$ for some P', and write $P \Downarrow$ if $P \stackrel{l}{\Longrightarrow}$ for some l.

2.2 Basic Notions for Model-Independent Characterization

In Section 1, it is suggested that a process preorder need to be extensional.

Definition 1 (extensionality). *A binary relation $\mathcal{R}$ is* extensional *if both the following two statements are valid:*

- *If $M\mathcal{R}N$ and $P\mathcal{R}Q$ then $(M \,|\, P)\mathcal{R}(N \,|\, Q)$;*
- *If $P\mathcal{R}Q$ then $(a)P\mathcal{R}(a)Q$.*

The first statement tells us that, if M is an approximation of N and P is an approximation of Q, then the result of M observing P should be an approximation of the result of N observing Q. The second property confirms that, if P is an approximation of Q, then the approximation relationship is preserved when observation through some ports are prohibited.

Extensionality defined in Definition 1 is to some extent close to a notion called *pre-congruence* in some literatures. We use extensionality to emphasize on the aspects of observation or interaction, while pre-congruence stress the algebraic aspects. The former is model-independent while the latter is model-dependent. By the way, bisimilarity is extensional yet not a pre-congruence for CCS.

Extensionality suggests that, approximation relationship will be preserved when the related processes are put into a certain environment.

Definition 2 (environment). *An environment* $\mathbf{C}[\_]$ *is either* $[\_]$, *or* $(c)\mathbf{C}'[\_]$, *or* $P \mid \mathbf{C}'[\_]$, *or* $\mathbf{C}'[\_] \mid P$, *where* $c \in \mathcal{N}$, $P \in \mathcal{P}$ *and* $\mathbf{C}'[\_]$ *is an environment.*

Lemma 1. *If* $\mathcal{R}$ *is reflexive and extensional, then* $\mathbf{C}[P]\mathcal{R}\mathbf{C}[Q]$ *for every environment* $\mathbf{C}[\_]$ *whenever* $P\mathcal{R}Q$.

As is discussed in Section 1, a process preorder may preserve several capabilities. Four basic capabilities are formalized as follows.

Definition 3 (capabilities). *Let* P *be a process.*

1. P *has* $\Diamond$-capability *if* $P \Downarrow$.
2. P *has* $\blacksquare$-capability *if for some* P', $P \Longrightarrow P'$ *and* $P' \not\Downarrow$.
3. P *has* $\blacklozenge$-capability *if* P *does not have* $\Diamond$*-capability.*
4. P *has* $\Box$-capability *if* P *does not have* $\blacksquare$*-capability.*

The preservation of capabilities is defined automatically.

Definition 4 (capability-preservation). *Let* $M \subseteq \{\Diamond, \blacksquare, \blacklozenge, \Box\}$ *be a set of basic capabilities. A binary relation* $\mathcal{R}$ *is* M-preserving *if for every* $\bullet \in M$, Q *has* $\bullet$*-capability whenever* $P\mathcal{R}Q$ *and* P *has* $\bullet$*-capability.*

$\mathcal{R}$ *is* M-equipollent *if whenever* $P\mathcal{R}Q$, Q *has* $\bullet$*-capability if and only if* P *has* $\bullet$*-capability for every* $\bullet \in M$.

In views of Definition 3, $\blacklozenge$ (or $\Box$) is called *duality* of $\Diamond$ (or $\blacksquare$), and vice versa. Let $M \subseteq \{\Diamond, \blacksquare, \blacklozenge, \Box\}$. The duality of M, denoted M^D, is the set of members whose dualities are in M.

Some simple inferences following Definition 3 and Definition 4 are listed as the following lemma.

Lemma 2. *Let* R *be a binary relation.* $M \subseteq \{\Diamond, \blacksquare, \blacklozenge, \Box\}$.

1. $\mathcal{R}$ *is* M*-preserving if and only if* $\mathcal{R}^{-1}$ *is* M^D*-preserving.*
2. $\mathcal{R}$ *is* M*-equipollent (or equivalently* M^D*-equipollent) if and only if* R *is both* M*-preserving and* M^D*-preserving.*

3 Orders for Static Environments

3.1 Model-Independent Definition of Orders

When environment is static, the model-independent preorders are defined merely via the properties of extensionality and some forms of capability-preservation.

Definition 5 (capability-preserving preorders). *Let* $M \subseteq \{\Diamond, \blacksquare, \blacklozenge, \Box\}$. *The* M-preserving preorder $\leqq_M$ *is the largest relation that is reflexive, extensional and* M*-preserving.*

The M-equipollent preorder *is the largest relation that is reflexive, extensional and* M*-equipollent, which equals to* $\leqq_{M \cup M^D}$.

The M-preserving equality, $=_M$, *is defined as* $\leqq_M \cap \leqq_M^{-1}$.

Definition 5 may look cumbersome at first glance. Firstly, one can check that 'largest' always makes sense. In additional, from Lemma 3, $\leqq_M$ is reflexive and transitive. The transitivity is ensured by the fact that the property of M-preserving is preserved under relational composition. Secondly, under static environments, only the preorders $\leqq_M$ need to focus on. Both M-equipollent preorders and M-preserving equalities are redundant, which is ensured by Lemma 4. These two notions are introduced here for the reason that they are necessary under dynamic environments. Thirdly, a direct inference from Definition 5 is $\leqq_M \subseteq \leqq_{M'}$ whenever $M' \subseteq M$. Lemma 4 even confirms stronger results.

Lemma 3. *Let $M \subseteq \{\Diamond, \blacksquare, \blacklozenge, \Box\}$. If $\{\mathcal{R}_i\}_{i \in I}$ is a family of reflexive, extensional, and M-preserving relations, then $(\bigcup_{i \in I} \mathcal{R}_i)^*$ is also a reflexive, extensional, and M-preserving relation.*

Lemma 4. *Let $M, M_1, M_2 \subseteq \{\Diamond, \blacksquare, \blacklozenge, \Box\}$.*

1. *$\leqq_{M^D}$ coincides with $\leqq_M^{-1}$.*
2. *$\leqq_{M_1 \cup M_2}$ coincides with $\leqq_{M_1} \cap \leqq_{M_2}$.*
3. *$\leqq_{M \cup M^D}$ coincides with $=_M$.*

When all the subsets of $\{\Diamond, \blacksquare, \blacklozenge, \Box\}$ are exhausted, a complete lattice containing at most 16 preorders are produced. Lemma 4 confirms that there is no need to explore each of them one by one. For every nonempty M, $\leqq_M$ can be obtained by taking a few steps of conjunction or inversion from $\leqq_\Diamond$ and $\leqq_\blacksquare$. In view of this, as well as the trivial fact that $\leqq_\emptyset = \mathcal{P}^2$, we shall concentrate on $\leqq_\Diamond$ and $\leqq_\blacksquare$ in the following of this section.

3.2 Behavioural Properties

This part aims to study the behavioural properties of $\leqq_M$. The stuttering property, X-property, and computation property for process equivalences are widely known. The X-property is initially described by De Nicola, Montanari and Vaandrager in [12]. The stuttering property can be found in [19]. These fundamental properties are generalized for process preorders in the following definition.

Definition 6 (stuttering property, X-property and computation property). *Let $\leqq$ be a binary relation on $\mathcal{P}$. Let $=$ be $\leqq \cap \leqq^{-1}$.*

1. *$\leqq$ has* stuttering property *if the followings hold: (1) whenever $Q_0 \xrightarrow{\tau} Q_1 \xrightarrow{\tau} \cdots \xrightarrow{\tau} Q_n$, $P \leqq Q_0$ and $P \leqq Q_n$, then $P \leqq Q_i$ for every $0 \leq i \leq n$. (2) whenever $P_0 \xrightarrow{\tau} P_1 \xrightarrow{\tau} \cdots \xrightarrow{\tau} P_m$, $P_0 \leqq Q$, $P_m \leqq Q$, then $P_j \leqq Q$ for every $0 \leq j \leq m$.*
2. *$\leqq$ has* X-property *if $P \Longrightarrow \leqq^{-1} Q$ and $Q \Longrightarrow \leqq^{-1} P$ imply $P = Q$.*
   $\leqq$ has inverted X-property *if $P \Longrightarrow \leqq Q$ and $Q \Longrightarrow \leqq P$ imply $P = Q$.*
3. *$\leqq$ has* computation property *if the following holds: whenever $P_0 \xrightarrow{\tau} P_1 \xrightarrow{\tau} \cdots \xrightarrow{\tau} P_m$ and $P_0 \leqq P_m$, then $P_0 = P_1 = \cdots = P_m$.*
   $\leqq$ has inverted computation property *if the following holds: whenever $P_0 \xrightarrow{\tau} P_1 \xrightarrow{\tau} \cdots \xrightarrow{\tau} P_m$ and $P_m \leqq P_0$, then $P_0 = P_1 = \cdots = P_m$.*

Stuttering property for preorder is motivated from the following intuition. If both Q_0 and Q_n have the capabilities of P, and Q_0 can evolve to Q_n by finite steps of computation, then all the intermediate states between Q_0 and Q_n are deemed to have such capabilities. On the other hand, if Q has the capabilities of both P_0 and P_m, and P_0 can evolve to P_m by a finite number of steps of computation, then Q also has the capabilities of all the intermediate states between P_0 and P_m. Stuttering property is quite natural that every eligible observational preorder should satisfy it.

Computation property for preorder is motivated from the following intuition. During the computation from P_0 to P_m, P_m may lose some capabilities of P_0. If, however, P_m indeed has all the concerned capabilities that P_0 has, then all the intermediate states are deemed to be equal. Computation property has the inverted version because it is possible that, during the computation from P_0 to P_m, P_m may acquire some new capabilities. If this happens, and P_0 has all the concerned capabilities that P_m has, then all the intermediate states are equal. In line with the above, computation property (or its inverted version) does not hold automatically for every preorder. Whether computation property holds or not for a given preorder will depend on the capabilities being concerned. Finally, X-property is a generalized version of computation property.

When considering equivalences only, computation property is a special case of stuttering property. For preorders, however, stuttering property and computation property focus on different aspects. They do not imply each other.

Lemma 5. *Let* $M_1, M_2 \subseteq \{\Diamond, \blacksquare, \blacklozenge, \Box\}$.

1. *If stuttering property holds for* $\leqq_{M_1}$ *and* $\leqq_{M_2}$*, then it also holds for* $\leqq_{M_1 \cup M_2}$ *and* $\leqq_{M_1^D}$.
2. *If X-property (or computation property) holds for* $\leqq_{M_1}$ *and* $\leqq_{M_2}$*, then it also holds for* $\leqq_{M_1 \cup M_2}$*. If X-property (or computation property) holds for* $\leqq_{M_1}$*, then it also holds for* $=_{M_1}$*. X-property (or computation property) holds for* $\leqq_{M_1}$ *if and only if inverted X-property (or inverted computation property) holds for* $\leqq_{M_1^D}$.

Lemma 5 confirms that behaviour properties of $\leqq_M$ may be derived from those of $\leqq_\Diamond$ and $\leqq_\blacksquare$, which is established in Proposition 1.

Proposition 1. *Stuttering property, X-property, and computation property hold for* $\leqq_\Diamond$ *and* $\leqq_\blacksquare$.

Corollary 1. $\leqq_M$ *has stuttering property for every* $M \subseteq \{\Diamond, \blacksquare, \blacklozenge, \Box\}$.

3.3 Operational Counterparts of Orders

This part aims to discover the operational counterparts of $\leqq_\Diamond$ and $\leqq_\blacksquare$ for CCS. As a result, $\leqq_\Diamond$ happens to be trace preorder while $\leqq_\blacksquare$ turns out to be an improved variant of failure preorder which we call potential failure preorder.

Definition 7 (trace preorder). *The* trace set *of P, denoted* $\mathbf{TR}(P)$, *is the set* $\{u \in \mathcal{L}^* \mid P \stackrel{u}{\Longrightarrow}\}$. *We say* $P \precsim_{\mathrm{Tr}} Q$, *if* $Q \stackrel{u}{\Longrightarrow}$ *whenever* $P \stackrel{u}{\Longrightarrow}$. $\precsim_{\mathrm{Tr}}$ *is called the* trace preorder. *That is,* $P \precsim_{\mathrm{Tr}} Q$ *if and only if* $\mathbf{TR}(P) \subseteq \mathbf{TR}(Q)$. *The* trace equivalence, $\approx_{\mathrm{Tr}}$, *is defined as* $\precsim_{\mathrm{Tr}} \cap \precsim_{\mathrm{Tr}}^{-1}$.

To obtain the first main result that $\precsim_{\mathrm{Tr}}$ coincides with $\leqq_{\Diamond}$, we need two-side inclusions. $\precsim_{\mathrm{Tr}} \subseteq \leqq_{\Diamond}$ is ensured by checking $\precsim_{\mathrm{Tr}}$ reflexive, extensional, and $\Diamond$-preserving. The reversed inclusion is proved by making use of observing power of CCS.

Lemma 6. $\precsim_{\mathrm{Tr}}$ *is reflexive, extensional, and* $\Diamond$*-preserving.*

Theorem 1. *For* CCS, $\leqq_{\Diamond} = \precsim_{\mathrm{Tr}}$. *Therefore,* $\leqq_{\blacklozenge} = \precsim_{\mathrm{Tr}}^{-1}$ *and* $=_{\Diamond} = \approx_{\mathrm{Tr}}$.

Proof. By Lemma 6 and Definition 5, $\precsim_{\mathrm{Tr}} \subseteq \leqq_{\Diamond}$ holds. To prove $\leqq_{\Diamond} \subseteq \precsim_{\mathrm{Tr}}$, suppose that $P \leqq_{\Diamond} Q$, and let $u = l_1 l_2 \ldots l_n \in \mathbf{TR}(P)$. We will show $u \in \mathbf{TR}(Q)$. Construct environment $\mathbf{C}[\_] = (\widetilde{a})(\_ \mid \overline{l_1}.\overline{l_2}.\ldots.\overline{l_n}.d)$, in which $\widetilde{a}$ indicates all names in $\mathsf{gn}(P) \cup \mathsf{gn}(Q)$ and $d \notin \mathsf{gn}(P) \cup \mathsf{gn}(Q)$ is a fresh name. By extensionality of $\leqq_{\Diamond}$ and Lemma 1, $\mathbf{C}[P] \leqq_{\Diamond} \mathbf{C}[Q]$. Since $P \stackrel{l_1 l_2 \ldots l_n}{\Longrightarrow}$, $\mathbf{C}[P] \stackrel{d}{\Longrightarrow}$, which means $\mathbf{C}[P] \Downarrow$. By $\Diamond$-preserving, $\mathbf{C}[Q] \Downarrow$, which can only be caused by $Q \stackrel{u}{\Longrightarrow}$. Therefore, $u \in \mathbf{TR}(Q)$.

The second main result is that $\leqq_{\blacksquare}$ coincides with a refined version of failure preorder. To give the operational definition precisely, some additional notations are introduced in advance. Let $V \subseteq \mathcal{L}^*$. The *prefix closure* of V, denoted $\downarrow V$, is the set $\{w \in \mathcal{L}^* \mid wv \in V \text{ for some } v\}$. The *first label* of V, denoted $\mathsf{First}(V)$, is $\{l \in \mathcal{L} \mid lv \in V \text{ for some } v\}$. Let $v \in \downarrow V$, the *remainder* of V after v, denoted $v^{-1}V$, is the set$\{w \in \mathcal{L}^* \mid vw \in V\}$.

Definition 8 (potential failure preorder). *Let* $u \in \mathcal{L}^*$ *and* $V \subseteq \mathcal{L}^*$. (u, V) *is called a* potential failure pair *of P, if there exists* $w \in \downarrow V$ *and* $P \stackrel{uw}{\Longrightarrow} P'$ *for some P' such that* $P' \stackrel{v}{\not\Longrightarrow}$ *for every* $v \in w^{-1}V$. *In potential failure pair* (u, V), *u is called the* trace part, *while V is called the* refusal part.

The set of all potential failure pairs of P is denoted by $\mathbf{FL}(P)$. $P \precsim_{\mathrm{Fl}} Q$ *if and only if* $\mathbf{FL}(P) \subseteq \mathbf{FL}(Q)$. $P \approx_{\mathrm{Fl}} Q$ *if and only if* $\mathbf{FL}(P) = \mathbf{FL}(Q)$. $\precsim_{\mathrm{Fl}}$ *is called* potential failure preorder. $\approx_{\mathrm{Fl}}$ *is called* potential failure equivalence.

Intuitively, the meaning of potential failure pair (u, V) of P can be understood in the following way. At first P reaches a state P'' by performing u. After that, an execution of P'' is considered successful if P'' performs a trace in V. What the refusal part V affirms is the existence of a trap state P', such that P'' may go into the trap state by performing w, a prefix of some trace in V, and this starting of P'' has no way to be extended to any successful executions.

For more understanding about potential failures, some special cases are studied in the following. In the case $V = \emptyset$, $(u, \emptyset) \in \mathbf{FL}(P)$ if and only if $u \in \mathbf{TR}(P)$. In the case $\epsilon \in V$, $(u, V) \notin \mathbf{FL}(P)$ for every P. In the case $V \subseteq \mathcal{L}$, the traditional failure pairs and failure preorders are obtained.

It needs to be pointed out that the traditional failure preorder is not extensional, and another version of failure equivalence defined in Sect. 9.4 of [6] does not satisfy the property $\mathbf{TR}(P) = \{u \mid (u, \emptyset) \in \mathbf{FL}(P)\}$. These two versions, as well as the one in Definition 8, coincide for finite processes. For infinite processes, however, only potential failure preorder enjoys both the properties. It is worth noting that for CCS, potential failure preorder coincides with *fair testing equivalence* [10] or *should testing equivalence* [2].

An important property of potential failure pairs is stated in the next lemma.

Lemma 7. *If* $(uw, V) \in \mathbf{FL}(P)$, *then* $(u, wV) \in \mathbf{FL}(P)$.

We are now in a position to establish the second main result which confirms $\precsim_{\mathrm{Fl}}$ coincident with $\leqq_{\blacksquare}$. To show $\precsim_{\mathrm{Fl}} \subseteq \leqq_{\blacksquare}$, it is enough to check $\precsim_{\mathrm{Fl}}$ being reflexive, extensional, and $\blacksquare$-preserving. The reversed inclusion is also proved by taking advantage of the observing power of CCS.

Lemma 8. $\precsim_{\mathrm{Fl}}$ *is reflexive, extensional, and* $\blacksquare$*-preserving.*

The only difficulty in proving Lemma 8 is the extensionality. It really can be shown indirectly by proving $\precsim_{\mathrm{Fl}}$ coincident with should-testing preorder in [2], whose extensionality is easier to show. However, a direct proof is more desirable. In view of the requirements of additional technical lemmas, the proof is not given here. Readers may consult the extended version [4].

Theorem 2. *For* CCS, $\leqq_{\blacksquare} = \precsim_{\mathrm{Fl}}$. *Therefore,* $\leqq_{\square} = \precsim_{\mathrm{Fl}}^{-1}$ *and* $=_{\blacksquare} = \approx_{\mathrm{Fl}}$.

Proof. By Lemma 8 and Definition 5, $\precsim_{\mathrm{Fl}} \subseteq \leqq_{\blacksquare}$ holds. To prove $\leqq_{\blacksquare} \subseteq \precsim_{\mathrm{Fl}}$, suppose that $P \leqq_{\blacksquare} Q$, and let $(u, V) \in \mathbf{FL}(P)$. We will show $(u, V) \in \mathbf{FL}(Q)$. Let d be a name not in $\mathsf{gn}(P) \cup \mathsf{gn}(Q)$. Define processes $R_{u,V,d}$ recursively as follows:

$$R_{u,V,d} = \begin{cases} d + R_{u,V-\{\epsilon\},d} & \text{if } u = \epsilon, \epsilon \in V \\ \sum_{l \in \mathsf{First}(V)} \bar{l}.R_{\epsilon,l^{-1}V,d} & \text{if } u = \epsilon, \epsilon \notin V \\ d + \bar{l}.R_{u',V,d} & \text{if } u = lu' \end{cases}$$

Construct environment $\mathbf{C}[\_] = (\widetilde{a})(\_ \mid R_{u,V,d})$, $\widetilde{a}$ indicating all names in $\mathsf{gn}(P) \cup \mathsf{gn}(Q) \cup \mathsf{gn}(R_{u,V,d}) - \{d\}$. By extensionality of $\leqq_{\blacksquare}$ and Lemma 1, $\mathbf{C}[P] \leqq_{\blacksquare} \mathbf{C}[Q]$. Since $(u, V) \in \mathbf{FL}(P)$, we have $P \stackrel{u}{\Longrightarrow} P' \stackrel{w_1}{\Longrightarrow} P''$ for some w_1, P', P'' such that $P'' \stackrel{v}{\not\Longrightarrow}$ for every $v \in w_1^{-1}V$. Now, $\mathbf{C}[P] \equiv (\widetilde{a})(P \mid R_{u,V,d}) \Longrightarrow (\widetilde{a})(P' \mid R_{\epsilon,V,d}) \Longrightarrow (\widetilde{a})(P'' \mid R_{\epsilon,w_1^{-1}V,d})$. According to the definition of $R_{u,V,d}$, $P'' \stackrel{v}{\Longrightarrow}$ if and only if $(\widetilde{a})(P'' \mid R_{\epsilon,w_1^{-1}V,d}) \Downarrow$. Since already $P'' \stackrel{v}{\not\Longrightarrow}$, we have $(\widetilde{a})(P'' \mid R_{\epsilon,w_1^{-1}V,d}) \not\Downarrow$. In summary, $\mathbf{C}[P] \Longrightarrow \not\Downarrow$. Now, by $\blacksquare$-preserving of $\leqq_{\blacksquare}$, $\mathbf{C}[Q] \Longrightarrow \not\Downarrow$. To make this happen, there must be some Q', Q'' and w_2 such that $\mathbf{C}[Q] \equiv (\widetilde{a})(P \mid R_{u,V,d}) \Longrightarrow (\widetilde{a})(Q' \mid R_{\epsilon,V,d}) \Longrightarrow (\widetilde{a})(Q'' \mid R_{\epsilon,w_2^{-1}V,d}) \not\Downarrow$. This computation can only be caused by $Q \stackrel{u}{\Longrightarrow} Q' \stackrel{w_2}{\Longrightarrow} Q''$ with $Q'' \stackrel{v}{\not\Longrightarrow}$ for every $v \in w_2^{-1}V$, which means $(u, V) \in \mathbf{FL}(Q)$.

By Theorem 1, Theorem 2, and Lemma 4, every preorder defined model independently in Defintion 5 has its operational counterpart for CCS. By the fact that $\precsim_{\mathrm{Fl}} \subseteq \precsim_{\mathrm{Tr}}$, we have the following.

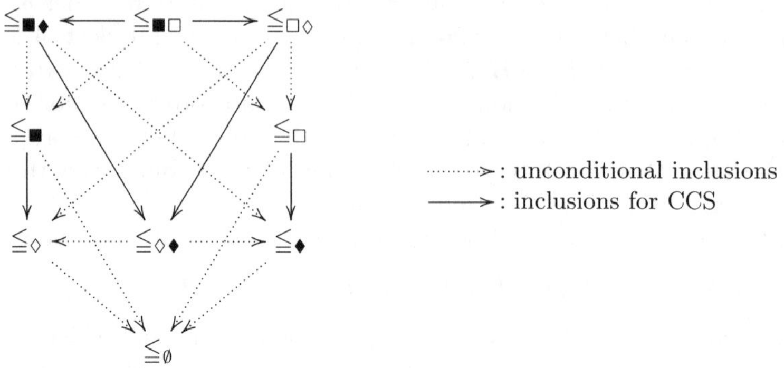

Fig. 2. Model-independent Order Spectrum for CCS: Static Environment

Lemma 9. *For* CCS, $\leqq_{\blacksquare} \subseteq \leqq_{\Diamond}$.

By Lemma 9 and Lemma 4, all the preorders defined in Definition 5 have been studied in the framework of CCS. They are summarized in the diagram of Fig. 2.

Proposition 2. *All the inclusions in Fig. 2 are strict for* CCS.

Proof. Only consider a few inclusions in the left half. To show $\leqq_{\blacksquare} \subsetneq \leqq_{\Diamond}$ and $\leqq_{\blacksquare\blacklozenge} \subsetneq \leqq_{\Diamond\blacklozenge}$, notice $a + \tau \leqq_{\Diamond\blacklozenge} a$ but $a + \tau \not\leqq_{\blacksquare} a$. To show $\leqq_{\blacksquare\blacklozenge} \subsetneq \leqq_{\blacksquare}$, notice $\tau \leqq_{\blacksquare} \tau + \tau.a$ but $\tau \not\leqq_{\blacksquare\blacklozenge} \tau + \tau.a$. To show $\leqq_{\blacksquare\Box} \subsetneq \leqq_{\blacksquare\blacklozenge}$, notice $a \leqq_{\blacksquare\blacklozenge} a + \tau$ but $a \not\leqq_{\blacksquare\Box} a + \tau$.

Finally, we point out that for CCS, X-property and computation property do not hold for some preorders in Fig 2.

Proposition 3. *For* CCS, *X-property and computation property hold for all the preorders in Fig. 2 except for* $\leqq_{\blacklozenge}$, $\leqq_{\Box}$, *and* $\leqq_{\Box\Diamond}$.

Proof. The positive results are all inferences of Lemma 5 and Proposition 1. As to the negative results, we select to prove the computation property not holding for $\leqq_{\Box\Diamond}$. Let $P_0 \equiv \tau.a + \tau \xrightarrow{\tau} a \equiv P_1$. We have$P_0 \leqq_{\Box\Diamond} P_1$ but $P_0 \not\leqq_{\blacksquare\blacklozenge} P_1$.

4 Orders for Dynamic Environments

In distributed systems, the environment tends to change dynamically. In these situations, additional stronger constraints other than extensionality and some forms of capability-preservation will be imposed on preorders. The constraints concerned in this paper are *simulation property* and *weak simulation property.* For the lack of space, only major definitions and results are stated here. The readers may consult [4] for details.

Definition 9 (simulation). *A binary relation* $\mathcal{R}$ *is a* simulation *if it validates the following* simulation property*: Whenever* $P\mathcal{R}Q$ *and* $P \xrightarrow{\tau} P'$, *then one of the following statements is valid:*

- $Q \Longrightarrow Q'$ *for some* Q' *such that* $P\mathcal{R}Q'$ *and* $P'\mathcal{R}Q'$.
- $Q \Longrightarrow Q'' \xrightarrow{\tau} Q'$ *for some* Q'', Q' *such that* $P\mathcal{R}Q''$ *and* $P'\mathcal{R}Q'$.

A binary relation $\mathcal{R}$ is a weak simulation *if it validates the following* weak simulation property*: Whenever $P\mathcal{R}Q$ and $P \xrightarrow{\tau} P'$, then:*

- *$Q \Longrightarrow Q'$ for some Q' such that $P'\mathcal{R}Q'$.*

A binary relation $\mathcal{R}$ is a (weak) bisimulation *if both $\mathcal{R}$ and $\mathcal{R}^{-1}$ are (weak) simulations. $\mathcal{R}$ has* (weak) bisimulation property *if both $\mathcal{R}$ and $\mathcal{R}^{-1}$ has (weak) simulation property.*

By means of extensionality, simulation, and some forms of capability-preservation, a set of preorders can be defined model-independently.

Definition 10 (capability preserving simulation preorders). *Let $M \subseteq \{\Diamond, \blacksquare, \blacklozenge, \Box\}$. The M-*preserving (weak) simulation preorder *$\leqq^{\mathrm{s}}_M$ ($\leqq^{\mathrm{ws}}_M$) is the largest (weak) simulation that is reflexive, extensional and M-preserving.*

*The M-*equipollent (weak) simulation preorder *is the largest (weak) simulation that is reflexive, extensional and M-equipollent, which equals to $\leqq^{\mathrm{s}}_{M\cup M^D}$ ($\leqq^{\mathrm{ws}}_{M\cup M^D}$).*

*The M-*preserving (weak) simulation equality*, $=^{\mathrm{s}}_M$ ($=^{\mathrm{ws}}_M$), is defined as $\leqq^{\mathrm{s}}_M \cap {\leqq^{\mathrm{s}}_M}^{-1}$ ($\leqq^{\mathrm{ws}}_M \cap {\leqq^{\mathrm{ws}}_M}^{-1}$).*

We point out that all the relations defined in Definition 10 are indeed preorders. Unlike the situation of static environments, there is no counterpart of Lemma 4 now. What we exactly know is $\leqq^{\mathrm{s}}_M \subseteq \leqq^{\mathrm{s}}_{M'}$ ($\leqq^{\mathrm{ws}}_M \subseteq \leqq^{\mathrm{ws}}_{M'}$) whenever $M' \subseteq M$, and $\leqq^{\mathrm{s}}_M \subseteq \leqq^{\mathrm{ws}}_M \subseteq \leqq_M$. It would be cumbersome to study every $\leqq^{\mathrm{s}}_M$ ($\leqq^{\mathrm{ws}}_M$) separately. Fortunately, this terrible situation can be greatly improved by the following results.

Lemma 10. $\leqq^{\mathrm{s}}_{\Diamond} = \leqq^{\mathrm{ws}}_{\Diamond} = \leqq_{\Diamond}$. $\leqq^{\mathrm{s}}_{\blacksquare} = \leqq^{\mathrm{ws}}_{\blacksquare} = \leqq_{\blacksquare}$.

Lemma 11. *$\leqq^{\mathrm{s}}_{\blacklozenge}$ ($\leqq^{\mathrm{ws}}_{\blacklozenge}$) is $\blacksquare$-preserving. Consequently, $\leqq^{\mathrm{s}}_{\blacklozenge} \subseteq \leqq^{\mathrm{s}}_{\blacksquare}$ ($\leqq^{\mathrm{ws}}_{\blacklozenge} \subseteq \leqq^{\mathrm{ws}}_{\blacksquare}$).*

Lemma 12. *For* CCS, *$\leqq^{\mathrm{s}}_{\blacksquare} = \leqq^{\mathrm{s}}_{\Diamond\blacksquare}$ ($\leqq^{\mathrm{ws}}_{\blacksquare} = \leqq^{\mathrm{ws}}_{\Diamond\blacksquare}$), $\leqq^{\mathrm{s}}_{\blacklozenge} = \leqq^{\mathrm{s}}_{\Diamond\blacksquare\blacklozenge}$ ($\leqq^{\mathrm{ws}}_{\blacklozenge} = \leqq^{\mathrm{ws}}_{\Diamond\blacksquare\blacklozenge}$), and $\leqq^{\mathrm{s}}_{\Box} = \leqq^{\mathrm{s}}_{\Diamond\blacksquare\blacklozenge\Box}$ ($\leqq^{\mathrm{ws}}_{\Box} = \leqq^{\mathrm{ws}}_{\Diamond\blacksquare\blacklozenge\Box}$). Consequently, for* CCS, *$\leqq^{\mathrm{s}}_{\Diamond} \subseteq \leqq^{\mathrm{s}}_{\blacksquare} \subseteq \leqq^{\mathrm{s}}_{\blacklozenge} \subseteq \leqq^{\mathrm{s}}_{\Box}$ ($\leqq^{\mathrm{ws}}_{\Diamond} \subseteq \leqq^{\mathrm{ws}}_{\blacksquare} \subseteq \leqq^{\mathrm{ws}}_{\blacklozenge} \subseteq \leqq^{\mathrm{ws}}_{\Box}$).*

Lemma 10 and Lemma 12 tell us that only $\leqq^{\mathrm{s}}_{\blacklozenge}$ ($\leqq^{\mathrm{ws}}_{\blacklozenge}$) and $\leqq^{\mathrm{s}}_{\Box}$ ($\leqq^{\mathrm{ws}}_{\Box}$) require further exploration.

The operational definitions for $\leqq^{\mathrm{s}}_{\blacklozenge}$ ($\leqq^{\mathrm{ws}}_{\blacklozenge}$) and $\leqq^{\mathrm{s}}_{\Box}$ ($\leqq^{\mathrm{ws}}_{\Box}$) are explored below.

Definition 11 (external simulation). *A binary relation $\mathcal{R}$ over $\mathcal{P}$ is an* external simulation *if whenever $P\mathcal{R}Q$ and $P \xrightarrow{\lambda} P'$, then one of the following statements is valid:*

- *$\lambda = \tau$ and $Q \Longrightarrow Q'$ for some Q' such that $P\mathcal{R}Q'$ and $P'\mathcal{R}Q'$.*
- *$Q \Longrightarrow Q'' \xrightarrow{\lambda} Q'$ for some Q'', Q' such that $P\mathcal{R}Q''$ and $P'\mathcal{R}Q'$.*

A binary relation $\mathcal{R}$ *over* $\mathcal{P}$ *is an* external weak simulation *if whenever* $P\mathcal{R}Q$ *and* $P \xrightarrow{\lambda} P'$, *then*

– $Q \stackrel{\widehat{\lambda}}{\Longrightarrow} Q'$ *for some* Q' *such that* $P'\mathcal{R}Q'$.

Definition 12 (t-conserving similarity). *A binary relation* $\mathcal{R}$ *over* $\mathcal{P}$ *is a* t-conserving external (weak) simulation *if* $\mathcal{R}$ *is an external (weak) simulation, and moreover* $\mathbf{TR}(P) = \mathbf{TR}(Q)$ *whenever* $P\mathcal{R}Q$.

The t-conserving (weak) similarity, $\precsim^{\mathrm{s}}_{\mathrm{T=}}$ $(\precsim^{\mathrm{ws}}_{\mathrm{T=}})$, *is the largest t-conserving external (weak) simulation. The* t-conserving external (weak) simulation equivalence, $\approx^{\mathrm{s}}_{\mathrm{T=}}$ $(\approx^{\mathrm{ws}}_{\mathrm{T=}})$, *is defined as* $\precsim^{\mathrm{s}}_{\mathrm{T=}} \cap {\precsim^{\mathrm{s}}_{\mathrm{T=}}}^{-1}$ $(\precsim^{\mathrm{ws}}_{\mathrm{T=}} \cap {\precsim^{\mathrm{ws}}_{\mathrm{T=}}}^{-1})$.

The first main result in this section is that $\precsim^{\mathrm{s}}_{\mathrm{T=}}$ $(\precsim^{\mathrm{ws}}_{\mathrm{T=}})$ coincides with $\leqq^{\mathrm{s}}_{\blacklozenge}$ $(\leqq^{\mathrm{ws}}_{\blacklozenge})$.

Theorem 3. *For* CCS, $\leqq^{\mathrm{s}}_{\blacklozenge} = \precsim^{\mathrm{s}}_{\mathrm{T=}}$ $(\leqq^{\mathrm{ws}}_{\blacklozenge} = \precsim^{\mathrm{ws}}_{\mathrm{T=}})$, *hence* $=^{\mathrm{s}}_{\blacklozenge} = \approx^{\mathrm{s}}_{\mathrm{T=}}$ $(=^{\mathrm{ws}}_{\blacklozenge} = \approx^{\mathrm{ws}}_{\mathrm{T=}})$.

Definition 13 (f-conserving similarity). *A binary relation* $\mathcal{R}$ *over* $\mathcal{P}$ *is a* f-conserving external (weak) simulation *if* $\mathcal{R}$ *is an external (weak) simulation, and moreover* $\mathbf{FL}(P) = \mathbf{FL}(Q)$ *whenever* $P\mathcal{R}Q$.

The f-conserving (weak) similarity, $\precsim^{\mathrm{s}}_{\mathrm{F=}}$ $(\precsim^{\mathrm{ws}}_{\mathrm{F=}})$, *is the largest f-conserving external (weak) simulation. The* f-conserving external (weak) simulation equivalence, $\approx^{\mathrm{s}}_{\mathrm{F=}}$ $(\approx^{\mathrm{ws}}_{\mathrm{F=}})$, *is defined as* $\precsim^{\mathrm{s}}_{\mathrm{F=}} \cap {\precsim^{\mathrm{s}}_{\mathrm{F=}}}^{-1}$ $(\precsim^{\mathrm{ws}}_{\mathrm{F=}} \cap {\precsim^{\mathrm{ws}}_{\mathrm{F=}}}^{-1})$.

The second main result in this section is that $\precsim^{\mathrm{s}}_{\mathrm{F=}}$ $(\precsim^{\mathrm{ws}}_{\mathrm{F=}})$ coincides with $\leqq^{\mathrm{s}}_{\Box}$ $(\leqq^{\mathrm{ws}}_{\Box})$.

Theorem 4. *For* CCS, $\leqq^{\mathrm{s}}_{\Box} = \precsim^{\mathrm{s}}_{\mathrm{F=}}$ $(\leqq^{\mathrm{ws}}_{\Box} = \precsim^{\mathrm{ws}}_{\mathrm{F=}})$, *hence* $=^{\mathrm{s}}_{\Box} = \approx^{\mathrm{s}}_{\mathrm{F=}}$ $(=^{\mathrm{ws}}_{\Box} = \approx^{\mathrm{ws}}_{\mathrm{F=}})$.

By Theorem 3, Theorem 4, Lemma 10, and Lemma 12, every preorder defined model independently in Defintion 10 has its operational counterpart for CCS.

For behaviour properties about preorders discussed in this section, we have the following.

Proposition 4. *For* CCS, *stuttering property, X-property and computation property hold for* $\leqq^{\mathrm{s}}_{M}$ $(\leqq^{\mathrm{ws}}_{M})$ *whenever* $M \subseteq \{\Diamond, \blacksquare, \blacklozenge, \Box\}$.

By the way, when (weak) simulation property is further strengthened to (weak) bisimulation property. We can define *(weak) bisimulation equality* $=^{\mathrm{bis}}$ $(=^{\mathrm{wbis}})$ to be the largest (weak) bisimulation that is reflexive, extensional and M-equipollent. (Weak) Bisimulation equality is an equivalence relation, and it has nothing to do with M provided that $M \neq \emptyset$. For CCS, $=^{\mathrm{bis}}$ $(=^{\mathrm{wbis}})$ coincides with *branching bisimilarity (weak bisimilarity)*.

The classification of all preorders in this paper for CCS is summarized in the diagram of Fig. 3.

Proposition 5. *All the inclusions in Fig. 3 are strict for* CCS.

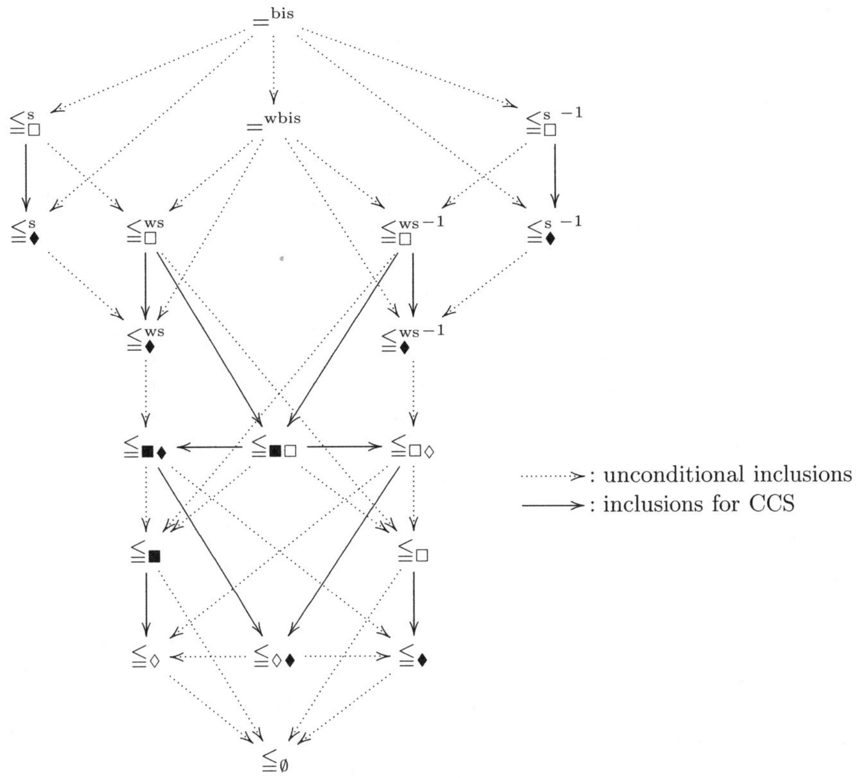

Fig. 3. Model-independent Order Spectrum for CCS

5 Conclusion

The most significant achievement of this paper is the establishment of a general setting to characterize process preorders model-independently.

Two prototypes of model-independent characterization are *testing equivalences* [11], presented by R.De Nicola and M.Hennessy, and *barbed bisimilarity*, presented by R.Milner and D.Sangiorgi [9]. For CCS, testing equivalences coincide with trace equivalence and failure equivalence (in Sect. 9.4 of [6]), while barbed bisimilarity coincide with weak bisimilarity for CCS. These two kinds of equivalences have been generalized to π-calculus by Boreale and De Nicola [1] and Sangiorgi [14]. For years, these two kinds of equivalences only act as two special ways for defining equivalences observationally. Based on the setting developed in this paper, all these equivalences and preorders are defined uniformly. Moreover, some interrelationships between them are revealed, and some other useful preorders are discovered.

Further studies on model-independent characterization may stretch in the following four directions.

The first direction is to give model-independent characterizations for more preorders. Preorders in linear-time branching-time spectrum [17] were presented at one time as semantic preorders for LTS. These preorders behave well for reactive systems without internal moves, and they are generalized to processes with internal moves in several different manners by Glabbeek [18]. It seems that some of these preorders are not adequate for interactive models. The crux is that some robust properties for reactive systems, such as *stability* and *convergence*, become vulnerable for interactive systems. The composition of two stable or convergent processes could be unstable or divergent. For this reason, imposing additional conditions to the states which have these vulnerable properties would be not very helpful. The equivalences which depend on these properties include *ready equivalence*, *ready trace equivalence*, *ready simulation equivalence*, and *stable bisimilarity*. These kinds of equivalences seem unlikely to have model-independent generalization in the sense of this paper. However, properties such as *unstability* and *divergence* are still robust. Accordingly, imposing additional conditions to unstable or divergent states are permitted. When restraints such as *codivergence* or *divergence preserving* are added as auxiliary conditions, a set of useful preorders will emerge. The current picture in Fig. 3 will be expanded accordingly.

The second direction is to re-depict Fig. 3 for some subcalculi of CCS. In [3], the expressiveness of different fragments of CCS are studied. The definition of CCS in this paper is the most general one, which has the strongest observational behaviour as well as the strongest observing power. The observing power is required in showing a preorder defined model-independently contained in the one defined operationally, while observational behaviour is required in showing the other direction. Since the subcalculi may weaken both observational behaviour and observing power simultaneously, the results depicted in Fig. 3 will vary according to the model being concerned. For example, in the proof of Theorem 2, guarded choice are used. If the concerned model did not support guarded choice, Theorem 2 and the inclusion $\leqq_{\Diamond}\subseteq\leqq_{\blacksquare}$ would no longer hold. When this happened, the substitute of Definition 8 should be found. The proof of Theorem 2 also makes use of constant definition. An interesting question is whether Theorem 2 holds if constant definition are replaced with μ-operator, or replication operator.

The third direction is to investigate these preorders in the framework of more general interactive models. Such models include different variations of π-calculus, value passing CCS, and CHOCS, HOπ-calculus. It is controversial which preorders or equivalences are best for these kinds of models. By taking the general setting introduced in this paper, preorders and equivalences can be explored accordingly. Then, operation definitions for them need to study carefully. Works in this direction will shed light on different observational behaviour, different observing power, and different expressiveness for different models.

The fourth direction is to create proof systems for the preorders in the paper. For finite processes, the objective is to establish a uniform setting of proof systems for all reasonable preorders. In addition, the author conjectures that both $\leqq^{s}_{\blacklozenge}$ and $\leqq^{s}_{\Box}$ can not be finitely axiomatized. For finite state processes, finding a proof system for $=_{\blacksquare}$ is actually a long standing open problem.

Acknowledgements. The author would like to thank Yuxi Fu for many helpful advices on this paper, to thank Mingzhang Huang for checking some of the proofs, to greatly thank the anonymous referees of APLAS'2010 for their detailed comments and suggestions on this paper.

References

1. Boreale, M., De Nicola, R.: Testing equivalence for mobile processes. Inf. Comput. 120(2), 279–303 (1995)
2. Brinksma, E., Rensink, A., Vogler, W.: Fair testing. In: Lee, I., Smolka, S.A. (eds.) CONCUR 1995. LNCS, vol. 962, pp. 313–327. Springer, Heidelberg (1995)
3. Fu, Y., Lu, H.: On the expressiveness of interaction. Theor. Comput. Sci. 411(11-13), 1387–1451 (2010)
4. He, C.: Model independent order relations for processes (2010), `http://basics.sjtu.edu.cn/~chaodong/`
5. Milner, R.: A Calculus of Communication Systems. LNCS, vol. 92. Springer, Heidelberg (1980)
6. Milner, R.: Communication and Concurrency. Prentice-Hall, Inc., Upper Saddle River (1989)
7. Milner, R., Parrow, J., Walker, D.: A calculus of mobile processes, i. Inf. Comput. 100(1), 1–40 (1992)
8. Milner, R., Parrow, J., Walker, D.: A calculus of mobile processes, ii. Inf. Comput. 100(1), 41–77 (1992)
9. Milner, R., Sangiorgi, D.: Barbed bisimulation. In: Kuich, W. (ed.) ICALP 1992. LNCS, vol. 623, pp. 685–695. Springer, Heidelberg (1992)
10. Natarajan, V., Cleaveland, R.: Divergence and fair testing. In: Fülöp, Z., Gecseg, F. (eds.) ICALP 1995. LNCS, vol. 944, pp. 648–659. Springer, Heidelberg (1995)
11. De Nicola, R., Hennessy, M.: Testing equivalences for processes. Theor. Comput. Sci. 34, 83–133 (1984)
12. De Nicola, R., Montanari, U., Vaandrager, F.W.: Back and forth bisimulations. In: Baeten, J.C.M., Klop, J.W. (eds.) CONCUR 1990. LNCS, vol. 458, pp. 152–165. Springer, Heidelberg (1990)
13. Park, D.M.R.: Concurrency and automata on infinite sequences. Theoretical Computer Science, 167–183 (1981)
14. Sangiorgi, D.: Expressing Mobility in Process Algebras: First-Order and Higher-Order Paradigms. PhD thesis, Department of Computer Science, University of Edinburgh (1992)
15. Sangiorgi, D.: On the origins of bisimulation and coinduction. ACM Trans. Program. Lang. Syst. 31(4) (2009)
16. Thomsen, B.: Plain chocs: A second generation calculus for higher order processes. Acta Inf. 30(1), 1–59 (1993)
17. van Glabbeek, R.J.: The linear time-branching time spectrum (extended abstract). In: Baeten, J.C.M., Klop, J.W. (eds.) CONCUR 1990. LNCS, vol. 458, pp. 278–297. Springer, Heidelberg (1990)
18. van Glabbeek, R.J.: The linear time - branching time spectrum ii. In: Best, E. (ed.) CONCUR 1993. LNCS, vol. 715, pp. 66–81. Springer, Heidelberg (1993)
19. van Glabbeek, R.J., Weijland, W.P.: Branching time and abstraction in bisimulation semantics. J. ACM 43(3), 555–600 (1996)

Concurrency Can't Be Observed, Asynchronously*

Paolo Baldan[1], Filippo Bonchi[2],
Fabio Gadducci[3], and Giacoma Valentina Monreale[3]

[1] Dipartimento di Matematica Pura e Applicata, Università Padova
[2] Laboratoire de l'Informatique du Parallélisme, ENS Lyon
[3] Dipartimento di Informatica, Università di Pisa

Abstract. The paper is devoted to an analysis of the concurrent features of asynchronous systems. A preliminary step is represented by the introduction of a non-interleaving extension of barbed equivalence. This notion is then exploited in order to prove that *concurrency cannot be observed* through asynchronous interactions, i.e., that the interleaving and concurrent versions of a suitable asynchronous weak equivalence actually coincide. The theory is validated on two case studies, related to nominal calculi (π-calculus) and visual specification formalisms (Petri nets).

1 Introduction

Since the introduction of process calculi, one of the richest sources of foundational investigations stemmed from the analysis of behavioural equivalences. The rationale is that in any formalism, specifications which are syntactically different may intuitively denote the same system, and it is then pivotal to be able to equate different specifications at the right level of abstraction.

By now classical, one of the most influential synthesis on the issue is offered by the taxonomy proposed in the so-called *linear time/branching time spectrum* [20]. Since then, a major dichotomy among equivalences was established between *interleaving* and *truly concurrent* semantics, according to the possibility of capturing the parallel composition of two systems by means of a non-deterministic selection. Concretely, adopting a CCS-like syntax, the system represented by the specification $a \mid b$ either coincides with (interleaving) or differs from (truly concurrent) the system represented by $a.b + b.a$.

Behavioural equivalences for process calculi often rely on *labelled transitions*: each evolution step of a system is tagged by some information aimed at capturing the possible interactions of the system with the environment. Nowadays, though, the tendency is to adopt operational semantics based on *unlabelled transitions*. This is due to the intricacies of the intended behaviour of a system, especially in the presence of topological or transactional features (see, e.g., foundational calculi such as Mobile Ambients [14] or Join [18]).

* Research partially supported by the EU FP7-ICT IP `ASCEns`, by the MIUR PRIN `SisteR` and by the University of Padova project `AVIAMo`.

K. Ueda (Ed.): APLAS 2010, LNCS 6461, pp. 424–438, 2010.

This paradigmatic shift stimulated the adoption of *barbed congruence* [33], a behavioural equivalence based on a family of predicates over the states of a system, called *barbs*, intended to capture the ability of a system of performing an *interaction* with the environment. For instance, in the calculus of Mobile Ambients [14], barb n verifies the occurrence of an ambient named n at top level [30]; in CCS [31], a process satisfies barb a if it may input on channel a [33].

Assuming that systems interact with a form of synchronous communication, barbs can be explained by a scenario where a system is just a black box with several buttons, one for each possible interaction with the environment. An observer can push a button only if the system is able to perform the corresponding interaction. In this scenario, barbs check if buttons can be pushed. Similarly, an asynchronous system is a black box equipped with several bags (unordered buffers) that are used to exchange messages with the environment. At any time the observer can insert a message in a bag or remove one, whenever present. In this case, barbs check the presence of messages inside bags. Moreover, in order to properly capture the scenario outlined above, for an observer internal steps should not be visible: we thus focus on weak equivalences.

So far, barbed congruences included no concurrent feature, abstractly characterized as the possibility of performing *simultaneously* more than one single interaction. However, in the synchronous scenario, systems $a.b + b.a$ and $a \mid b$ could be distinguished by an observer able to push two buttons at the same time, since only $a \mid b$ allows for the simultaneous pressing of buttons a and b.

The situations is less clearly-cut for asynchronous systems. Indeed, one of the assumptions of this communication style is that message sending is non-blocking: a system may send a message with no agreement with the receiver, and then continue its execution. Hence, an observer interacting with a system by message exchanges cannot know if or when a message has been received and thus message reception is deemed unobservable. And since message sending is non-blocking, a system which may emit a sequence of messages can also hold them, proceed with internal computation and make them available at once at a later time. So, the simultaneous observation of many sendings seems to add no discriminating power to the observer. Concretely, systems $a.b + b.a$ and $a \mid b$ should be equated in an asynchronous setting, even if observing concurrent barbs.

Moving from this intuition, we propose a formal framework where the slogan *concurrency can't be observed, asynchronously* is formalised. We work in a setting where we only assume the availability of an operator for parallel composition, used for defining the notions of *concurrent barb* and concurrent barbed congruence: a system exhibits a concurrent barb $a_1 \otimes a_2$ if it is decomposable into two components exhibiting barbs a_1 and a_2, respectively. We then identify a set of axioms which are intended to capture essential features of asynchronous systems in a barbed setting, showing that for any formalism satisfying them barbed congruence and its concurrent variant coincide. The appropriateness of the axioms is checked by proving that they are satisfied by concrete asynchronous formalisms, like the asynchronous π-calculus [25,9] and open Petri nets [27], as well as by the (output-buffered) asynchronous systems as characterised in [38].

Synopsis. Section 2 introduces our framework: the notion of concurrent barb, the corresponding behavioural equivalence and Theorem 1, stating the unobservability of concurrency through asynchronous interactions. Sections 3 and 4 show how our theory captures asynchronous π-calculus and open Petri nets, respectively. In the latter case the new concurrent equivalence is shown to coincide with standard step semantics. Section 5 proves that systems deemed as (output-buffered) asynchronous in [38] fall into our theory. Section 6 draws some conclusions, discusses related works and outlines directions for further research.

2 A Theory of Concurrent Barbs and Asynchrony

This section introduces a notion of equivalence based on *concurrent* barbs. It is then argued that, for a reasonable notion of asynchronous system, the possibility of observing concurrent barbs does not add any discriminating power.

2.1 Transition Systems and Barbs

Let $\mathcal{P}$ be a set of *systems* (ranged over by p, q ...) and $\rightarrow \subseteq \mathcal{P} \times \mathcal{P}$ a *transition relation*: we write $p \rightarrow q$ for $\langle p, q \rangle \in \rightarrow$, and we denote by $\rightarrow^*$ the reflexive and transitive closure of $\rightarrow$.

A *barb* is a predicate over the set $\mathcal{P}$ representing a minimal observation on any system. The set of barbs, ranged over by a, b, x, y ..., is denoted $\mathcal{B}$ and we write $p{\downarrow_a}$ if the system p *satisfies* the barb a. For each barb $a \in \mathcal{B}$, we say that p *weakly satisfy* a, written $p{\Downarrow_a}$, if $p \rightarrow^* p'$ and $p'{\downarrow_a}$. Moreover, we write $p\Box{\downarrow_a}$ if $p'{\downarrow_a}$ holds $\forall p'$ such that $p \rightarrow^* p'$. The weak version $p\Box{\Downarrow_a}$ is defined analogously.

We finally assume to have a commutative and associative *parallel composition* operator on systems $| : \mathcal{P} \times \mathcal{P} \rightarrow \mathcal{P}$, satisfying the axioms below

$$\text{(P1)} \quad \frac{p \rightarrow p'}{p|q \rightarrow p'|q} \qquad\qquad \text{(P2)} \quad \frac{p{\downarrow_a}}{p|r{\downarrow_a}}$$

In other terms, the parallel operator must preserve the barbs and the transition relation: the requirement concerning its associativity and commutativity would not be essential for our theory, but it simplifies the presentation.

With these ingredients we can define a behavioural equivalence which equates two systems if these cannot be distinguished by an observer that can add components in parallel and observe the barbs which are exposed. In the paper we focus only on weak equivalences, hence the qualification "weak" is omitted.

Definition 1 (saturated barbed bisimilarity). *A symmetric relation $R \subseteq \mathcal{P} \times \mathcal{P}$ is a saturated barbed bisimulation if whenever pRq then $\forall r \in \mathcal{P}$*

- $\forall a \in \mathcal{B}$, *if* $p|r{\Downarrow_a}$ *then* $q|r{\Downarrow_a}$
- *if* $p|r \rightarrow^* p'$ *then* $q|r \rightarrow^* q'$ *and* $p'Rq'$

We say that p and q are saturated barbed bisimilar (written $p \sim q$) if there exists a saturated barbed bisimulation relating them.

SYNCHRONOUS	ASYNCHRONOUS
$p ::= m, p_1 \mid p_2, \mathbf{0}$	$p ::= m, p_1 \mid p_2, \mathbf{0}, \bar{a}$
$m ::= \tau.p, a.p, \bar{a}.p, m_1 + m_2$	$m ::= \tau.p, a.p, m_1 + m_2$
$(\text{SYN})\ a.p + m \mid \bar{a}.q + n \rightarrow p \mid q$	$(\text{ASYN})\ a.p + m \mid \bar{a} \rightarrow p$

$$(\text{TAU})\ \tau.p + m \rightarrow p \qquad (\text{PAR})\ \frac{p \rightarrow q}{p \mid r \rightarrow q \mid r}$$

$$p \mid q \equiv q \mid p \quad p \mid (q \mid r) \equiv (p \mid q) \mid r \quad p \mid \mathbf{0} \equiv p$$
$$m + n \equiv n + m \quad m + (n + o) \equiv (m + n) + o$$

Fig. 1. The syntax and the reduction semantics of SCCS and ACCS

Note that $\sim$ is, by definition, a congruence with respect to the parallel composition operator[1]. It differs from *barbed congruence* [33] since in the latter the observer is allowed to add a parallel component only at the beginning of the computation and not at any step. Hence, in general, barbed congruence is coarser than saturated barbed bisimilarity, although in many cases the two definitions coincide (as e.g. in the asynchronous π-calculus [19]).

As a running example for illustrating our theory we use a finite fragment of CCS [31] and its asynchronous counterpart, with the reduction semantics in [32], but our considerations would trivially extend to the full calculus. A set of *names* $\mathcal{N}$ is fixed (ranged over by a, b ...) with $\tau \notin \mathcal{N}$. The syntax of synchronous CCS (SCCS) processes is defined by the grammar on the left of Figure 1, while asynchronous CCS (ACCS) processes are defined by the grammar on the right. In both cases processes are considered up to structural congruence $\equiv$. The transition relation $\rightarrow$ for SCCS is defined by rules SYN, TAU, and PAR. For ACCS, rule SYN is replaced by ASYN: the occurrence of an unguarded $\bar{a}$ indicates a message that is available on some communication media named a. The message disappears after its reception. Note that output prefixes $\bar{a}.p$ are absent in ACCS.

The definition of the "right" notion of barb is not a trivial task. For SCCS both input and output barbs are considered (see e.g. [33]). Intuitively, a process has an input (output) barb on a if it is ready to perform an input (output) on a. Formally, if $\alpha = a$ or $\alpha = \bar{a}$, then $p{\downarrow_\alpha}$ when $p \equiv \alpha.p_1 + m \mid p_2$ for processes p_1, p_2, m. Following [1], for ACCS only output barbs are considered, defined by $p{\downarrow_{\bar{a}}}$ when $p \equiv \bar{a} \mid p_1$ for a process p_1. The idea is that, since message sending is non-blocking, an external observer can just send messages without knowing if they will be received or not. Hence inputs are deemed unobservable.

Several works (e.g. [36,26,7]) have proposed abstract criteria for defining "good" barbs independently from the formalism at hand. Here, inspired by [36], we propose to formalise the intuition that barbs should capture the possibility of exhibiting an observable behaviour by introducing a notion of *test*.

[1] Requiring $\sim$ to be closed under all unary contexts, instead of just $-|r$ (see [26,30]), would not substantially change our theory, yet make its presentation more complex.

Definition 2 (barbs witnessed by a test). *A* test *is a family t of systems indexed by barbs, i.e., $t = \{t_x \mid x \in \mathcal{B}\}$. Given a barb $a \in \mathcal{B}$ and a system $p \in \mathcal{P}$, an element $t_x \in t$ is called a* concrete test for a on p *if whenever $p \rightarrow^* p'$*

$$p' \downarrow_a \qquad \textit{iff} \qquad p'|t_x \rightarrow p'' \textit{ and } p''\Box\downarrow_x.$$

A barb a is witnessed *by a test t if for all systems $p, q \in \mathcal{P}$ there exists a barb $x \in \mathcal{B}$ such that $t_x \in t$ is a concrete test for a on both p and q.*

Intuitively, a concrete test for a barb a on a process p is a process t_x capable of exposing a barb x, which is instead never observable in the evolution of p. Process t_x releases a (permanent) barb x only after interacting with a process exposing barb a. Since x can never be generated by p, observing x in the evolution of $p' \mid t_x$, where p' is a reduct of p, witnesses that p' has exposed the barb a.

Note that the notion of witness is defined by considering pairs of processes: this is motivated by the fact that tests witnessing a barb will be used when comparing processes in the bisimulation game.

Hereafter, we assume that any barb is always witnessed by some test.

(B) For any $a \in \mathcal{B}$ there exists a test witnessing a. We denote t^a a chosen test that witnesses barb a.

The assumption above holds for any calculus endowed with reduction semantics and barbs that we are aware of (see e.g. [32,1,14,18]). For instance, in ACCS each output barb $\bar{a}$ is witnessed by the test $t^{\bar{a}} = \{a.\bar{x} \mid x \in \mathcal{N}\}$. Indeed, for all processes p, q, a concrete test for $\bar{a}$ on p and q can be $t^{\bar{a}}_x = a.\bar{x}$, for $x \in \mathcal{N}$ a name that syntactically occurs neither in p nor in q. Note that input barbs cannot be witnessed by any test in ACCS, since there are no output prefixes. In SCCS, instead, for the presence of both input and output prefixes, an input barb a is witnessed by the test $\{\bar{a}.\bar{x} \mid x \in \mathcal{N}\}$.

Axiom (B) is pivotal in Section 2.3: the chosen witness for a barb is needed in the formulation of our axiom of asynchrony (AA), which abstractly characterizes a basic feature of asynchronous systems with reduction semantics and barbs.

2.2 Concurrent Barbs and Non-interleaving Semantics

Most semantics for interactive systems are *interleaving*, meaning that parallelism is reduced to non-determinism, or, in terms of processes, $a.b + b.a \sim a|b$. Here we propose a non-interleaving semantics based on barbs. For this, we first need a *concurrent transitions relation* on systems $\rightsquigarrow \subseteq \mathcal{P} \times \mathcal{P}$, for which we assume

$$\text{(C)} \quad \rightarrow \subseteq \rightsquigarrow \subseteq \rightarrow^*$$

and thus $\rightsquigarrow^* = \rightarrow^*$. The assumption is quite natural: it just means that (1) each non-concurrent transition is also a concurrent one and (2) each concurrent transition $p \rightsquigarrow q$ is simulated by a sequence of non-concurrent ones $p \rightarrow \ldots \rightarrow q$.

For both SCCS and ACCS the relation $\rightsquigarrow$ can be defined by the rules in Figure 2. Alternative definitions could be given, in order e.g. to avoid several concurrent

$$\frac{p \to p'}{p \leadsto p'} \qquad \frac{p \leadsto p' \quad q \leadsto q'}{p \mid q \leadsto p' \mid q'}$$

Fig. 2. Parametric rules for a concurrent transition relation

communications on the same channel. This is irrelevant here as our theory abstracts from the actual definition of $\leadsto$ and only relies on property (C) above.

As a second ingredient, we introduce concurrent barbs. For a set X, let $X^{\otimes}$ denote the free commutative monoid over X, whose elements are called *multisets*.

Definition 3 (concurrent barbs). *The set of* concurrent barbs $\mathcal{CB}$ *is the free monoid* $\mathcal{B}^{\otimes}$*, ranged over by* A, B, X, Y... *We write* $p{\downarrow}^c_A$ *to mean that* p *satisfies the concurrent barb* ${\downarrow}^c_A$*. The satisfaction relation is defined by the rules*

$$\frac{p{\downarrow}_a}{p{\downarrow}^c_a} \qquad \frac{p{\downarrow}^c_A \text{ and } q{\downarrow}^c_B}{p|q{\downarrow}^c_{A\otimes B}}$$

Weak concurrent barbs are defined as $p{\Downarrow}^c_A$ *if* $p \leadsto^* p'$ *and* $p'{\downarrow}^c_A$*.*

A more abstract theory could be defined relying on general, non necessarily free monoids of barbs. We defer this proposal to the full version of the paper.

Definition 4 (concurrent saturated barbed bisimilarity). *We define* concurrent saturated barbed bisimilarity*, denoted by* $\sim^c$*, by replacing* $\to$ *with* $\leadsto$ *and* ${\Downarrow}_a$ *with* ${\Downarrow}^c_A$ *in Definition 1.*

Note that for general, possibly synchronous languages, the concurrent equivalence can distinguish processes that are identical in the interleaving semantics. For example, in SCCS $a.b+b.a \not\sim^c a \mid b$ since $a.b+b.a$ does not satisfy ${\Downarrow}^c_{a\otimes b}$, while $a|b$ does. Instead, if we consider ACCS, where only output barbs are available, it is easy to see that the two processes are equivalent with respect to $\sim^c$.

2.3 Concurrency Can't Be Observed, Asynchronously

This section focus on the observability of concurrency through asynchronous interactions, arguing that $\sim^c = \sim$ in formalisms with asynchronous communication.

As a first step we require that assumption (B) actually holds for *concurrent* barbs, a property denoted as (CB). Formally, the witness property is defined as in Definition 2 by replacing $\mathcal{B}$ with $\mathcal{CB}$, $\to$ with $\leadsto$ and ${\downarrow}_a$ with ${\downarrow}^c_A$.

A further assumption is now needed, relating concrete tests for concurrent barbs and reduction sequences. Since it is intended to capture an essential feature of asynchronous communication, it is referred to as the *Axiom of Asynchrony*

(AA) Let A be a concurrent barb, p a system, t^A_X a concrete test for A on p with $X = \bigotimes_{i=1}^n x_i$. If $p|t^A_X \to^* p_1{\downarrow}_{x_1} \to^* \ldots \to^* p_n{\downarrow}_{x_n}$ then $p{\Downarrow}^c_A$.

$$p ::= \bar{a}b,\ p_1|p_2,\ (\nu a)p,\ !m,\ m \qquad m ::= \mathbf{0},\ \alpha.p,\ m_1 + m_2 \qquad \alpha ::= a(b),\ \tau$$

$p\|q \equiv q\|p$	$(p\|q)\|r \equiv p\|(q\|r)$	$p\|\mathbf{0} \equiv p$
$m + n \equiv n + m$	$(m+n)+o \equiv m+(n+o)$	$m+\mathbf{0} \equiv m$
$(\nu a)(\nu b)p \equiv (\nu b)(\nu a)p$	$(\nu a)(p\|q) \equiv p\|(\nu a)q$ if $a \notin fn(p)$	$(\nu a)\mathbf{0} \equiv \mathbf{0}$
$(\nu a)p \equiv (\nu b)(p\{^b/_a\})$ if $b \notin fn(p)$	$a(b).p \equiv a(c).(p\{^c/_b\})$ if $c \notin fn(p)$	$!p \equiv p\|!p$

$$\bar{a}b|(a(c).p + m) \rightarrow p\{^b/_c\} \qquad \tau.p + m \rightarrow p \qquad \frac{p \rightarrow q}{(\nu a)p \rightarrow (\nu a)q} \qquad \frac{p \rightarrow q}{p|r \rightarrow q|r}$$

Fig. 3. Syntax, structural congruence and reduction relation of the asynchronous π

Informally, the axiom can be explained as follows. We can think that A is a multiset of output messages. The fact that t_X^A is a concrete test for A on p and that $p|t_X^A \rightarrow^* p_1{\downarrow_{x_1}} \rightarrow^* \ldots \rightarrow^* p_n{\downarrow_{x_n}}$ means that p can emit the messages in A one after the other. Then the intuition is that, if the system is asynchronous and thus sending is non-blocking, the messages can be also kept internally and made all available concurrently at the end.

As for our running examples, axiom (AA) holds in ACCS, but not in SCCS. In fact, take the SCCS process $p = \bar{a}.\bar{b}$. A concrete test for the concurrent barb $A = \bar{a} \otimes \bar{b}$ could be $t_X^A = a.\bar{x_1} \mid b.\bar{x_2}$ with $X = \bar{x_1} \otimes \bar{x_2}$. Yet, $p|t_X^A \rightarrow \bar{b} \mid \bar{x_1} \mid b.\bar{x_2} \rightarrow \bar{x_1} \mid \bar{x_2}$ but $p \not\Downarrow_A^c$.

Relying on the assumptions made so far, we can prove the desired theorem.

Theorem 1 (concurrency can't be observed, asynchronously). *For any formalism satisfying axioms (P1), (P2), (CB), (C), and (AA), concurrent saturated barbed bisimilarity and saturated barbed bisimilarity coincide, i.e.,* $\sim = \sim^c$.

3 Asynchronous π-Calculus

This section shows that the asynchronous π-calculus fits in the theory of Section 2, and thus saturated barbed congruence (which coincides with barbed congruence [1]) and its concurrent version coincide.

Asynchronous π-calculus has been introduced in [25] as a model of distributed systems interacting via asynchronous message passing. Its syntax is shown in Figure 3: we assume an infinite set $\mathcal{N}$ of *names*, ranged over by $a, b \ldots$, with $\tau \notin \mathcal{N}$, and we let $p, q \ldots$ range over the set $\mathcal{P}_\pi$ of processes. *Free names* of a process p (denoted by $fn(p)$) are defined as usual. Processes are taken up to a *structural congruence*, axiomatised in Figure 3 and denoted by $\equiv$. The *reduction relation*, denoted by $\rightarrow$, describes process evolution: it is the least relation $\rightarrow \subseteq \mathcal{P}_\pi \times \mathcal{P}_\pi$ closed under $\equiv$ and inductively generated by the axioms and rules in Figure 3.

As for ACCS (Section 2), barbs account only for outputs. So, for an output $\bar{a}$, $p{\downarrow_{\bar{a}}}$ if $p \equiv (\nu a_1)\ldots(\nu a_k)(\bar{a}b|q)$ and $\forall i,\ a \neq a_i$ [1]. Concurrent barbs are multisets of outputs, and they check the presence of several parallel outputs.

A non-interleaving semantics for the calculus is obtained by introducing a concurrent transition relation $\rightsquigarrow$, as defined in Figure 2. Multiple synchronizations over the same channel are thus allowed, as in the semantics proposed in [12,34]. Different approaches are conceivable, see e.g. [28], yet they could still be accommodated in our theory.

Now, let $\sim_\pi$ denote saturated barbed bisimilarity for the asynchronous π-calculus and let $\sim_\pi^c$ denote the concurrent one. It is worth remarking that $\sim_\pi$ coincides with the standard semantics for the calculus, namely, *asynchronous bisimilarity* [1], as shown in [19]. Then we have the following result.

Corollary 1 (concurrency can't be observed in asynchr. π). $\sim_\pi = \sim_\pi^c$.

This follows from Theorem 1. Indeed, axioms (P1), (P2), and (C) clearly hold. Concerning (CB), a test witnessing the concurrent barb $A = \bigotimes_{i=1}^n \overline{a}_i$ is $t^A = \{t_C^A \mid C = \bigotimes_{i=1}^n \overline{c_i} \wedge t_C^A = a_1(b_1).\overline{c_1}d| \dots |a_n(b_n).\overline{c_n}d \wedge \forall i. b_i \neq c_i\}$: for processes p, q, we obtain a concrete test t_C^A for A on p and q by taking a C containing only names syntactically occurring neither in p nor q. With the above definition, it is easy to prove that also the Axiom of Asynchrony (AA) holds.

4 Open Petri Nets

Open Petri nets [27,37,3] are a reactive extension of ordinary P/T nets, equipped with a distinguished set of *open places* that represent the interfaces through which the environment interacts with a net. This kind of interactions is inherently asynchronous (see e.g. [2]) and thus it represents an ideal testbed.

This section shows that indeed the interleaving and concurrent equivalences defined in the literature (see e.g. [3]) are instances of $\sim$ and $\sim^c$, respectively. Then, since all the axioms of our theory are satisfied, these equivalences coincide.

Definition 5 (open nets). *An* open net *is a tuple $\hat{N} = (S, T, {}^\bullet(.), (.)^\bullet, O)$ for S a set of places, T a set of transitions, ${}^\bullet(.), (.)^\bullet : T \to S^\otimes$ functions mapping each transition to its pre- and post-set, and $O \subseteq S$ a set of* open places. *A marked (open) net is a pair $N = \langle \hat{N}, m \rangle$ for $\hat{N}$ an open net and $m \in S^\otimes$ a marking.*

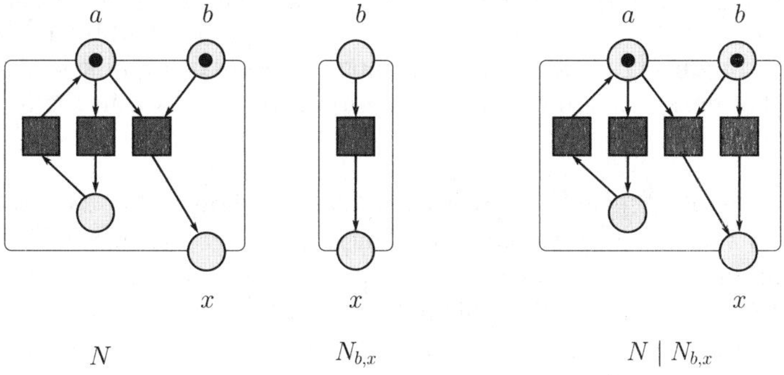

Fig. 4. Marked open nets and their parallel composition

Examples of marked nets can be found in Figure 4. As usual, circles represent places and rectangles transitions. Arrows from places to transitions represent function $^\bullet(.)$, arrows from transitions to places represent $(.)^\bullet$. An open net is enclosed in a box and open places are on the border of such a box.

We assume a fixed infinite set $\mathcal{S}$ of place names. The set of *interactions* (ranged over by i) is $\mathcal{I}_\mathcal{S} = \{s^+, s^- \mid s \in \mathcal{S}\}$. The set of *labels* (ranged over by l) consists in $\{0\} \uplus \mathcal{I}_\mathcal{S}$. The firing (interleaving) semantics of open nets is expressed by the rules on the top of Figure 5, where we write $^\bullet t$ and $t^\bullet$ instead of $^\bullet(t)$ and $(t)^\bullet$. The rule (TR) is the standard rule of P/T nets (seen as multiset rewriting) modelling internal transitions, which are labelled with 0 for subsequent use. The other two rules model interactions with the environment: at any moment a token can be inserted in (rule (IN)) or removed from (rule (OUT)) an open place.

Weak transitions are defined as usual, i.e., $\stackrel{0}{\Rightarrow}$ denotes the reflexive and transitive closure of $\stackrel{0}{\rightarrow}$ and $\stackrel{i}{\Rightarrow}$ denotes $\stackrel{0}{\Rightarrow}\stackrel{i}{\rightarrow}\stackrel{0}{\Rightarrow}$. We write $N \stackrel{i}{\Rightarrow} N'$ when $N = \langle \hat{N}, m\rangle$, $N' = \langle \hat{N}, m'\rangle$ and $m \stackrel{i}{\Rightarrow} m'$.

Definition 6 (firing bisimilarity). *A symmetric relation R over marked nets is a* firing bisimulation *if whenever $N_1 R N_2$, if $N_1 \stackrel{l}{\Rightarrow} N_1'$ then $N_2 \stackrel{l}{\Rightarrow} N_2'$ and $N_1' R N_2'$. We say that N_1 and N_2 are firing bisimilar (written $N_1 \approx N_2$) if there exists a firing bisimulation R such that $N_1 R N_2$.*

In order to ease the intuition, nets can be thought of as black boxes, where only the interfaces are visible. Two nets are bisimilar if they cannot be distinguished by an observer that may only insert and remove tokens in open places.

Steps of open nets ($\rightsquigarrow$) are defined in Figure 5, bottom. Step labels (ranged over by $c, c_1, c_2 \ldots$) are multisets of interactions $\mathcal{I}_N$. By rule (CFIR), each firing is also a step and, in particular, the label 0 is interpreted as the empty multiset. Rule (CSTEP) allows to construct concurrent steps. *Weak transitions* are defined as usual: $\stackrel{0}{\mapsto}$ denotes the reflexive and transitive closure of $\stackrel{0}{\rightsquigarrow}$ and $\stackrel{c}{\mapsto}$ denotes $\stackrel{0}{\mapsto}\stackrel{c}{\rightsquigarrow}\stackrel{0}{\mapsto}$. *Step bisimilarity* ($\approx^c$) is defined by replacing $\Rightarrow$ with $\mapsto$ in Definition 6.

We now show that $\approx$ and $\approx^c$ are instances of $\sim$ and $\sim^c$, respectively. The *parallel composition* $N_1|N_2$ of open nets N_1, N_2 is obtained by gluing them on their open places. More precisely, $N_1|N_2$ is the marked net obtained by taking the disjoint union of the nets, merging open places with the same name and summing the markings. An example of composition is shown in Figure 4.

$$(\textsc{tr})\ \frac{m = {}^\bullet t \otimes m' \quad t \in T}{m \stackrel{0}{\rightarrow} t^\bullet \otimes m'} \qquad (\textsc{in})\ \frac{s \in O}{m \stackrel{s^+}{\rightarrow} m \otimes s} \qquad (\textsc{out})\ \frac{m = m' \otimes s \quad s \in O}{m \stackrel{s^-}{\rightarrow} m'}$$

$$(\textsc{cfir})\ \frac{m \stackrel{\ell}{\rightarrow} m'}{m \stackrel{\ell}{\rightsquigarrow} m'} \qquad (\textsc{cstep})\ \frac{m = m_1 \otimes m_2 \quad m_1 \stackrel{c_1}{\rightsquigarrow} m_1' \quad m_2 \stackrel{c_2}{\rightsquigarrow} m_2'}{m \stackrel{c_1 \otimes c_2}{\rightsquigarrow} m_1' \otimes m_2'}$$

Fig. 5. Firing and step semantics for open nets

Transitions $\xrightarrow{0}$ of marked nets correspond to transitions $\rightarrow$ in the theory of Section 2, and $\overset{0}{\rightsquigarrow}$ corresponds to $\rightsquigarrow$. *Barbs* check the presence of tokens in open places. Formally, if we write $m \subseteq n$ for $m, n \in S^{\otimes}$ whenever $m = n \otimes n'$ for some $n' \in S^{\otimes}$, the marked net $N = \langle \hat{N}, m \rangle$ satisfies the barb b, denoted $N{\downarrow_b}$, if $b \in O$ (i.e., b is an open place of $\hat{N}$) and $b \subseteq m$. *Concurrent barbs* check the presence of multisets of tokens: for $m' \in \mathcal{S}^{\otimes}$, $N{\downarrow^c_{m'}}$ if $m' \in O^{\otimes}$ and $m' \subseteq m$.

With these definitions it is possible to prove that firing (step) bisimilarity coincides with (concurrent) saturated barbed bisimilarity.

Proposition 1. *Let N_1, N_2 be two marked nets. Then $N_1 \approx N_2$ iff $N_1 \sim N_2$ and $N_1 \approx^c N_2$ iff $N_1 \sim^c N_2$.*

In order to apply Theorem 1, we finally need to prove that all the axioms are satisfied. This is immediate for (P1), (P2), and (C). Instead, concerning (CB), a test witnessing a barb $b \in \mathcal{S}$ is given by $t^b = \{t^b_x \mid x \in \mathcal{S}\}$, where $t^b_x = N_{b,x}$ is the net in Figure 4, middle. For a concurrent barb $B = b_1 \otimes \cdots \otimes b_n \in \mathcal{S}^{\otimes}$ a test is given by $t^B = \{t^B_X \mid X = \bigotimes_{i=1}^n x_i \wedge t^B_X = t^{b_1}_{x_1} | \ldots | t^{b_n}_{x_n}\}$. With this definition of test, also the Axiom of Asynchrony (AA) can be easily shown to hold. Hence, as a corollary of Theorem 1 we get the following result.

Corollary 2 (concurrency can't be observed in open nets). $\approx = \approx^c$.

5 On Selinger's Axiomatization

An axiomatization of different classes of systems with asynchronous communication has been proposed in [38]. Roughly speaking, a system is said to be asynchronous if its observable behaviour is not changed by filtering its input and/or output through a suitable communication medium, which can store messages and release them later on. Different choices of the medium (queues, unordered buffers) are shown to lead to different notions of asynchrony, and suitable sets of axioms are then identified which are shown to precisely capture the various classes of asynchronous systems.

In order to further check the appropriateness of our framework, here we prove that the class of systems characterised as asynchronous in [38] satisfy the requirements in Section 2. More precisey, we focus on so-called *out-buffered asynchrony with feedback* [38, Section 3.2], where output is asynchronous, the order of messages is not preserved and the output of a process can be an input for the process itself (feedback). The corresponding axioms [38, Table 3] are listed in Figure 6. They are given for labelled transition systems, with labels $in\,a$, $out\,a$ and τ denoting input, output and internal transitions, respectively.

In order to bring the correspondence to a formal level, we must overcome two problems. Firstly, the theory in [38] is developed for a labelled semantics, while we are concerned with barbed reduction semantics, and secondly, the theory in [38] does not consider concurrent transitions, which are pivotal in our setting.

The first issue is solved by taking as reductions $p \rightarrow p'$ the τ-transitions $p \xrightarrow{\tau} p'$ and by defining (output) barbs $p{\downarrow_a}$ if $p \xrightarrow{out\,a}$.

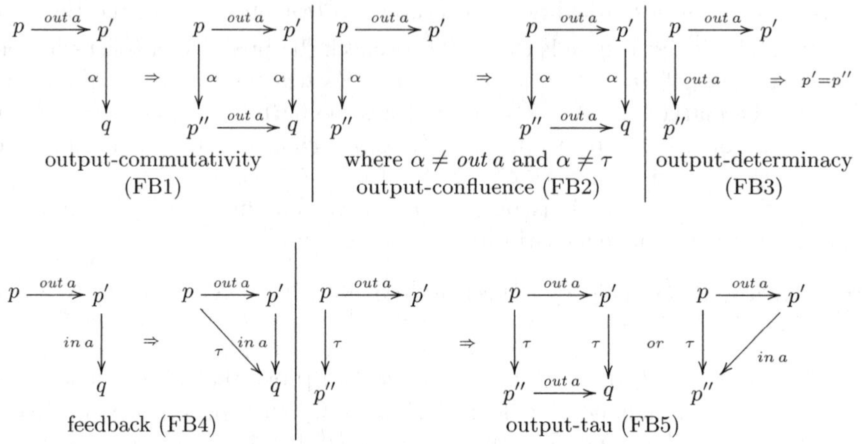

Fig. 6. Axioms for out-buffered agents with feedback

As a parallel operator for out-buffered agents with feedback, we use the parallel composition with interaction defined in [38, Section 3.1] and given by[2]

$$\frac{p \xrightarrow{\alpha} p'}{p|q \xrightarrow{\alpha} p'|q} \qquad \frac{q \xrightarrow{\alpha} q'}{p|q \xrightarrow{\alpha} p|q'} \qquad \frac{p|q \xrightarrow{out\, a} \xrightarrow{\tau}{}^{*} \xrightarrow{in\, a} r}{p|q \xrightarrow{\tau} r}$$

As far as concurrent barbs are concerned, we define $p{\downarrow}^c_A$, where $A = \bigotimes_{i=1}^n a_i$ whenever $p \xrightarrow{out\, a_1} \ldots \xrightarrow{out\, a_n}$. This is motivated by the fact that, by axiom (FB1), this implies that the same outputs can be performed by p in *any* order (in particular $p \xrightarrow{a_i}$ for any $i \in \{1, \ldots, n\}$). In words, although the labelled transition system does not provide any information on concurrency, we assume that outputs which can be observed in any order are generated concurrently.

Moreover, $\mathcal{A}(p)$ denotes the *acceptance set of* p defined as $\mathcal{A}(p) = \{a \mid \exists p' : p \rightarrow^* p' \textit{ and } p'{\downarrow}_a\}$, and we stick to systems p such that the set $\mathcal{A}(p)$ is finite.[3]

With the above definitions, it is easy to see that axiom (B) holds.

Lemma 1. *A barb a is witnessed by test $t^a = \{t^a_x \mid t^a_x \xrightarrow{in\, a} \xrightarrow{out\, x}\}$. In particular, for p, q, if $x \notin \mathcal{A}(p) \cup \mathcal{A}(q)$, the system t^a_x is a concrete test for a on p and q.*

Concurrent reductions can now be defined as in Figure 2. With this definition it is not difficult to see that assumptions (P1), (P2), (C) hold, and that (CB) is an immediate consequence of (B). In fact the test witnessing a concurrent barb $A = \bigotimes_{i=1}^n a_i$ can be $t^A = \{t^A_X \mid X = \bigotimes_{i=1}^n x_i \wedge t^{a_i}_{x_i} \in t^{a_i} \wedge t^A_X = t^{a_1}_{x_1}| \ldots |t^{a_n}_{x_n}\}$.

With this set up we can finally prove that also the Axiom of Asynchrony (AA) holds for any out-buffered system p with feedback.

[2] Actually, this operator is associative and commutative only up-to isomorphism of the underlying transition space of the system, which is implicitly assumed here.

[3] This requirement is far from restrictive. For instance, it holds in the π-calculus since for all processes p, q such that $p \rightarrow^* q$ we have $\mathrm{fn}(q) \subseteq \mathrm{fn}(p)$.

Lemma 2. *Let* $A = \bigotimes_{i=1}^{n} a_i$ *be a concurrent barb, let* p *be a system satisfying the axioms in Figure 6, and let* t_X^A *be a concrete test for* A *on* p *with* $X = \bigotimes_{i=1}^{n} x_i$*. If* $p|t_X^A \to^* p_1{\downarrow_{x_1}} \to^* \ldots \to^* p_n{\downarrow_{x_n}}$ *then* $p{\Downarrow}_A^c$*.*

6 Conclusions, Related and Future Works

Building on the notion of concurrent barbs, we introduced a non interleaving observational congruence for systems, and we proved that our slogan holds in a rather general fashion: whenever the observer is only able to check the possible interactions of a system with the environment, and the system can interact only through an unordered buffer (corresponding to the *out-buffered systems with feedback* of [38]), then concurrency cannot be observed, i.e., concurrent barbs add no observational power.

As case studies, we considered open Petri nets and the asynchronous π-calculus, showing that they fall in our framework. In particular, for nets we recovered the ordinary firing and step semantics (as defined in [3]); while for the π-calculus the well-known asynchronous bisimilarity [1]. Our result holds for other interesting formalisms as well, such as the Join calculus [18]. Indeed, the latter is an instance of [38] and thus, see Section 5, our theory applies.

The non-interleaving equivalence we introduced intuitively corresponds to *step semantics*. This has been shown for the concrete case of open Petri nets, even if it seems hard to raise the correspondence at an abstract level. Some idea could come from the observation that steps naturally arise from the *theory of reactive systems* [29] when replacing $\to$ with $\leadsto$. Since $p \xrightarrow{a} q$ means that $-|\bar{a}$ is the smallest context $c[-]$ such that $c[p] \to q$, analogously the step $p \xrightarrow{a\otimes b} q$ would mean that $-|\bar{a}|\bar{b}$ is the smallest $c[-]$ such that $c[p] \leadsto q$. As a side remark, note that one of the compelling arguments against step semantics (i.e., that it is not preserved by *action refinement* [21]) is weakened in the paradigm of reduction systems and barbed equivalences, since actions (labels) disappear.

As far as *ST-equivalences* [23] are concerned, it seems conceivable to develop an ST-operational semantics in an asynchronous setting, making production and consumption of messages (tokens) not instantaneous (see, e.g., [22] for a net model where token consumption is non-instantaneous and [13] for a similar study on Linda-like languages) and we conjecture that unobservability of concurrency would hold true also in this setting.

Close to our spirit are also *equivalences with localities* [10], that distinguish (interleaving equivalent) processes by observing the locations where interactions occur. We chose of not adopting this kind of equivalence for two main reasons: (1) localities are usually structured as trees, but this does not make much sense either in a calculus featuring joins (e.g. [18]) or in a graphical formalism such as open Petri nets; (2) equivalence with localities have never been defined for reduction semantics and, more importantly, for asynchronous formalisms.

It can be shown that equivalences with localities are incomparable with ours. Still we conjecture that our slogan "concurrency can't be observed, asynchronously" still holds for equivalences with localities. Indeed, since in the asynchronous case inputs are not observable, also their locations should not be observable. Therefore, only the locations of outputs could be observed, but these are all independent (since outputs have no continuations). A formal study of equivalences with localities for asynchronous systems is left as future work.

Our proposal is quite far from other non-interleaving semantics, such as those proposed in e.g. [16,17,21]: these consider *causal properties* of the systems, either by direct inspection of the state structure or by suitably enriching the labels of the transition steps, thus being of a more extensional nature. For these semantics, the fact that the internals of the systems are directly inspected, clearly implies that the unobservability of concurrency will not hold.

It would be interesting to investigate the possibility of extending our results to other classes of languages. This could include asynchronous calculi with bounded capacity channels, where a bounded number of messages can be transmitted simultaneously along the same channel. We would also like to study notions of asynchrony based on buffers which are not just unordered bags, but ordered structures like queues (see e.g. [5,6,38,4]). A preliminary investigation on the calculi $\pi_{\mathfrak{Q}}$ and $\pi_{\mathfrak{S}}$ in [4] (where buffers are, respectively, queues and stacks) seems to suggest that our results on the unobservability of concurrency should extend also to "ordered asynchrony". Intuitively, a key difference would be that in these calculi concurrent barbs should be *sets* of barbs instead of multisets, since these ordered buffers should not allow concurrent operations. Finally, another appealing case study could concern Linda-like languages, where the presence of test-and-check operators might allow an observer to verify not only the presence but also the absence of messages. In the same class would then end up also nets with inhibitor arcs.

The different distinguishing power of concurrent equivalences in the synchronous and asynchronous case could also be inspiring for the development of additional separation results between the two paradigms, along the style of [35]. In more general terms, integrating our framework with the one proposed in [24] seems to represent a promising direction for future investigations.

So far, few papers (such as e.g. [8,15,11]) tackled the study of the concurrency features of asynchronous systems. And to the best of our knowledge our result, albeit quite intuitive, has never been shown on any specific formalism, let alone for a general framework as in our paper. Indeed, besides the catchy slogan, we do believe that our work unearthed some inherent features of asynchronous systems that should hopefully shed some further light on the issue. That is, it should represent a further step towards a complete characterisation of the still fuzzy synchronous/asynchronous dichotomy.

Acknowledgments. The authors would like to thank Catuscia Palamidessi for the helpful discussions and the pointers to the literature.

References

1. Amadio, R.M., Castellani, I., Sangiorgi, D.: On bisimulations for the asynchronous π-calculus. In: Sassone, V., Montanari, U. (eds.) CONCUR 1996. LNCS, vol. 1119, pp. 147–162. Springer, Heidelberg (1996)

2. Baldan, P., Bonchi, F., Gadducci, F.: Encoding asynchronous interactions using open Petri nets. In: Bravetti, M., Zavattaro, G. (eds.) CONCUR 2009. LNCS, vol. 5710, pp. 99–114. Springer, Heidelberg (2009)
3. Baldan, P., Corradini, A., Ehrig, H., Heckel, R.: Compositional semantics for open Petri nets based on deterministic processes. Math. Str. in Comp. Sci 15(1), 1–35 (2005)
4. Beauxis, R., Palamidessi, C., Valencia, F.D.: On the asynchronous nature of the asynchronous π-calculus. In: Degano, P., De Nicola, R., Meseguer, J. (eds.) Concurrency, Graphs and Models. LNCS, vol. 5065, pp. 473–492. Springer, Heidelberg (2008)
5. Bergstra, J.A., Klop, J.W., Tucker, J.V.: Process algebra with asynchronous communication mechanisms. In: Brookes, S., Roscoe, A.W., Winskel, G. (eds.) Seminar on Concurrency. LNCS, vol. 197, pp. 76–95. Springer, Heidelberg (1985)
6. de Boer, F.S., Klop, J.W., Palamidessi, C.: Asynchronous communication in process algebra. In: LICS 1992, pp. 137–147. IEEE Computer Society, Los Alamitos (1992)
7. Bonchi, F., Gadducci, F., Monreale, G.V.: On barbs and labels in reactive systems. In: Klin, B., Sobociński, P. (eds.) SOS 2009. EPTCS, vol. 18, pp. 46–61 (2010)
8. Boreale, M., Sangiorgi, D.: Some congruence properties for π-calculus bisimilarities. Theor. Comp. Sci. 198(1-2), 159–176 (1998)
9. Boudol, G.: Asynchrony and the π-calculus. Tech. Rep. 1702, INRIA (1992)
10. Boudol, G., Castellani, I., Hennessy, M., Kiehn, A.: Observing localities. In: Tarlecki, A. (ed.) MFCS 1991. LNCS, vol. 520, pp. 93–102. Springer, Heidelberg (1991)
11. Bruni, R., Melgratti, H.C., Montanari, U.: Event structure semantics for dynamic graph grammars. ECEASST 2 (2006)
12. Busi, N., Gorrieri, R.: A Petri net semantics for π-calculus. In: Lee, I., Smolka, S.A. (eds.) CONCUR 1995. LNCS, vol. 962, pp. 145–159. Springer, Heidelberg (1995)
13. Busi, N., Gorrieri, R., Zavattaro, G.: Comparing three semantics for linda-like languages. Theor. Comp. Sci. 240(1), 49–90 (2000)
14. Cardelli, L., Gordon, A.D.: Mobile ambients. Theor. Comp. Sci. 240(1), 177–213 (2000)
15. Crafa, S., Varacca, D., Yoshida, N.: Compositional event structure semantics for the internal π-calculus. In: Caires, L., Vasconcelos, V.T. (eds.) CONCUR 2007. LNCS, vol. 4703, pp. 317–332. Springer, Heidelberg (2007)
16. Darondeau, P., Degano, P.: Causal trees. In: Ronchi Della Rocca, S., Ausiello, G., Dezani-Ciancaglini, M. (eds.) ICALP 1989. LNCS, vol. 372, pp. 234–248. Springer, Heidelberg (1989)
17. Degano, P., Nicola, R.D., Montanari, U.: Partial orderings descriptions and observations of nondeterministic concurrent processes. In: de Bakker, J.W., de Roever, W.-P., Rozenberg, G. (eds.) REX Workshop. LNCS, vol. 354, pp. 438–466. Springer, Heidelberg (1989)
18. Fournet, C., Gonthier, G.: The reflexive CHAM and the Join-calculus. In: POPL 1996, pp. 372–385. ACM Press, New York (1996)
19. Fournet, C., Gonthier, G.: A hierarchy of equivalences for asynchronous calculi. J. Log. Algebr. Program. 63(1), 131–173 (2005)
20. van Glabbeek, R.J.: The linear time-branching time spectrum. In: Baeten, J.C.M., Klop, J.W. (eds.) CONCUR 1990. LNCS, vol. 458, pp. 278–297. Springer, Heidelberg (1990)

21. van Glabbeek, R.J., Goltz, U.: Equivalence notions for concurrent systems and refinement of actions. In: Kreczmar, A., Mirkowska, G. (eds.) MFCS 1989. LNCS, vol. 379, pp. 237–248. Springer, Heidelberg (1989)
22. van Glabbeek, R.J., Goltz, U., Schicke, J.W.: Symmetric and asymmetric asynchronous interaction. In: Bonchi, F., Grohmann, D., Spoletini, P., Troina, A., Tuosto, E. (eds.) ICE 2008. ENTCS, vol. 229(3), pp. 77–95. Elsevier, Amsterdam (2009)
23. van Glabbeek, R.J., Vaandrager, F.W.: Petri net models for algebraic theories of concurrency. In: de Bakker, J.W., Nijman, A.J., Treleaven, P.C. (eds.) PARLE 1987. LNCS, vol. 259, pp. 224–242. Springer, Heidelberg (1987)
24. Gorla, D.: Towards a unified approach to encodability and separation results for process calculi. In: van Breugel, F., Chechik, M. (eds.) CONCUR 2008. LNCS, vol. 5201, pp. 492–507. Springer, Heidelberg (2008)
25. Honda, K., Tokoro, M.: An object calculus for asynchronous communication. In: America, P. (ed.) ECOOP 1991. LNCS, vol. 512, pp. 133–147. Springer, Heidelberg (1991)
26. Honda, K., Yoshida, N.: On reduction-based process semantics. Theor. Comp. Sci. 151(2), 437–486 (1995)
27. Kindler, E.: A compositional partial order semantics for Petri net components. In: Azéma, P., Balbo, G. (eds.) ICATPN 1997. LNCS, vol. 1248, pp. 235–252. Springer, Heidelberg (1997)
28. Lanese, I.: Concurrent and located synchronizations in π-calculus. In: van Leeuwen, J., Italiano, G.F., van der Hoek, W., Meinel, C., Sack, H., Plášil, F. (eds.) SOFSEM 2007. LNCS, vol. 4362, pp. 388–399. Springer, Heidelberg (2007)
29. Leifer, J.J., Milner, R.: Deriving bisimulation congruences for reactive systems. In: Palamidessi, C. (ed.) CONCUR 2000. LNCS, vol. 1877, pp. 243–258. Springer, Heidelberg (2000)
30. Merro, M., Nardelli, F.Z.: Bisimulation proof methods for mobile ambients. In: Baeten, J.C.M., et al. (eds.) ICALP 2003. LNCS, vol. 2719, pp. 584–598. Springer, Heidelberg (2003)
31. Milner, R.: Communication and Concurrency. Prentice Hall, Englewood Cliffs (1989)
32. Milner, R.: Communicating and Mobile Systems: the π-Calculus. Cambridge University Press, Cambridge (1999)
33. Milner, R., Sangiorgi, D.: Barbed bisimulation. In: Kuich, W. (ed.) ICALP 1992. LNCS, vol. 623, pp. 685–695. Springer, Heidelberg (1992)
34. Montanari, U., Pistore, M.: Concurrent semantics for the π-calculus. In: Brookes, S., Main, M., Melton, A., Misolve, M. (eds.) MFPS 1995. ENTCS, vol. 1, Springer, Heidelberg (1995)
35. Palamidessi, C.: Comparing the expressive power of the synchronous and asynchronous π-calculi. Math. Str. in Comp. Sci. 13(5), 685–719 (2003)
36. Rathke, J., Sassone, V., Sobociński, P.: Semantic barbs and biorthogonality. In: Seidl, H. (ed.) FOSSACS 2007. LNCS, vol. 4423, pp. 302–316. Springer, Heidelberg (2007)
37. Sassone, V., Sobociński, P.: A congruence for Petri nets. In: Ehrig, H., Padberg, J., Rozenberg, G. (eds.) PNGT 2004. ENTCS, vol. 127(2), pp. 107–120. Elsevier, Amsterdam (2005)
38. Selinger, P.: First-order axioms for asynchrony. In: Mazurkiewicz, A., Winkowski, J. (eds.) CONCUR 1997. LNCS, vol. 1243, pp. 376–390. Springer, Heidelberg (1997)

A Logical Mix of Approximation and Separation

Aquinas Hobor[1], Robert Dockins[2], and Andrew W. Appel[2]

[1] National University of Singapore
hobor@comp.nus.edu.sg
[2] Princeton University
{rdockins,appel}@cs.princeton.edu

Abstract. We extract techniques developed in the Concurrent C minor project to build a framework for constructing logics that contain approximation and/or separation. Approximation occurs when the naïve semantic definitions contain a contravariant circularity (*e.g.*, invariants of first-class locks), while separation occurs when one wishes to track resource accounting. We show how these two features can be mixed together in a modular way. Our work is machine checked in Coq and available as part of the Mechanized Semantic Library.

1 Introduction

The Concurrent C minor (CCM) project has been developing mechanized semantic models for concurrency, higher-order stores, separation, and program logics [HAZ08]. To Xavier Leroy's C minor language, which is a large industrial-strength C-like language (*e.g.*, complex local control flow and a sophisticated memory model) [Ler06], we have added first-class locks and threads to make Concurrent C minor. As a result of the scale and goals of our project we have been forced to redesign our semantic models in increasingly sophisticated and modular ways [DAH08, DHA09, HDA10].

Our focus here is an intimately related issue: the modular construction of a logic on top of our basic semantic models in a mechanization-friendly way. We are particularly interested in integrating two very useful features of our logic: approximation and separation. Approximation, in the sense that we use the term, is commonly associated with "step-indexing," [Ahm04, DAB09, HDA10] a useful technique for reasoning about certain kinds of recursion involving mutable state. In the CCM project we use step-indexing to model the invariants of first-class locks and threads, but it also occurs in, *e.g.*, ML references. Separation is an orthogonal feature which helps reasoning about an addressable memory, such as pointer aliasing. In the CCM project we are particularly interested in using separation to reason about concurrency.

We are able to smoothly integrate the features of approximation and separation by carefully building a framework where both can coexist peacefully. We model the assertion language of the program logic semantically via a Kripke semantics. That is, formulae of the assertion language are identified with metalogic propositions over a set of *worlds*, which are some abstraction of the program states. This is a common approach when mechanizing program logics, [Nip02] even among researchers who choose to model the judgments of the program logic syntactically.

When defining a program logic, the choice of which worlds to use in the assertion semantics depends strongly on the problem domain, *i.e.*, the particular language being

K. Ueda (Ed.): APLAS 2010, LNCS 6461, pp. 439–454, 2010.

modeled. The worlds contain most or all of the data in a program state in addition to certain metadata. Much previous work has focused on constructing complicated worlds for expressive languages and using the derived logic to prove some theorem of interest (often a soundness result) [HDA10, Ahm04, DHA09, COY07]. However, the important step of building the logic on top of the worlds is often given short shrift. A reader is left with the general impression that once the underlying model is in place, building the logic on top is straightforward. Unfortunately, this is not always the case.

Here we fill in the missing piece by explaining how to build sophisticated logics on top of clean axiomatizations. We construct a general framework for defining assertion languages containing approximation and separation—that is, a logic for worlds that contain approximation and substructure. Throughout this paper we largely abstract away from the details of any particular language, and thus we hold the choice of worlds abstract as well. Instead, we will focus on axiomatizing what features worlds must have in order to support approximation and separation, and showing how one can then build a powerful assertion logic containing both these features.

We combine approximation with separation by using a "stacked" approach in which we first axiomatize how our worlds become more approximate in §2, and show how to satisfy our axioms for settings wherein our worlds have meaningful approximation. If the domain of interest does not have any interesting approximation behavior (*e.g.*, a basic type system or separation logic), then we give methods for adding trivial approximation behavior so that the rest of our framework will still work. After defining the basic operators of our logic in §2.4, we define a multimodal layer on top in §3 to build smooth and modular logical framework for reasoning in the presence of approximation. In §4 we explain how to model and use the equirecursive operator μ.

Once we have specified how approximation should be handled, we specify the substructural properties of our worlds by forming a separation algebra in §5 as in [DHA09, COY07]. If our worlds have no interesting separation structure, this step can be omitted, or we can alternately provide a dummy implementation.

Our primary interest is in settings that combine both approximation and separation. In §6 we characterize the relationship between these properties and prove that the standard connectives of separation logic mix well with our logic of approximation. In §7, we show how one can use indirection theory to satisfy all of our approximation and separation axioms simultaneously in a nontrivial context.

Implementation. Our constructions and proofs are machine-checked in Coq, and made freely available as part of the Mechanized Semantic Library. Our mechanization contains a certain amount of "black magic Coqery" (*e.g.*, typeclasses, implicit coercions) to ensure that it slides together smoothly and works cleanly from the perspective of using the logic. From time to time we will mention a few design choices that enable simpler mechanical definitions/proofs, but readers particularly interested in this aspect of the result should consult the mechanization. Our results are available at:

`http://msl.cs.princeton.edu/`

Numbering convention. In this presentation we present three classes of equations: *definitions*, numbered with roman numerals; Coq-verified *theorems*, which we enumerate with arabic numerals; and *axioms in a given interface*, enumerated with letters. Many models can satisfy a given interface; one must prove the axioms from its construction.

2 A Logic of Approximation

Here we present the framework of our Gödel-Löb logic of approximation. The formulae of the logic will be identified with predicates on worlds that are *hereditary* with respect to an approximation relation. This simple base will allow us to build a powerful intuitionistic logic into which we can later fit the modal and substructural features.

2.1 Hereditary Scaffolding

We assume the existence of a set of *worlds* $\mathbb{W}$, whose precise construction depends on the domain of interest; see [HDA10, §2] for seven examples drawn from various program logics. Given a function P from worlds $\mathbb{W}$ to truth values $\mathbb{T}$ (*e.g.*, $\mathbb{T} \equiv \texttt{Prop}$ in Coq) and a relation R between worlds, we say that P is *hereditary over* R when, if P holds on some world w, then it also holds on all worlds reachable from w through R:

$$\mathsf{hereditary}(P, R) \quad \equiv \quad \forall w, w'.\ P(w) \rightarrow (wRw') \rightarrow P(w') \tag{i}$$

We assume that our worlds come with two operations for axiomatizing approximation: "level" $|w| : \mathbb{W} \rightarrow \mathbb{N}$ and "approximate" $w \leadsto w' : \mathbb{W} \rightharpoonup \mathbb{W}$. The intuition is that $|w| = n$ quantifies the "amount of information" in the world w, and approximating w into w' erases (*i.e.*, approximates) some information in w to make it "fit" into level $n - 1$. The level of a world $|w|$ counts the number of times the world can pass through the $\leadsto$ operation (emphasis: $\leadsto$ is partial). A predicate $P \in \mathbb{P}$ is a function from worlds to truth values $\mathbb{T}$ that is hereditary over the approximation relation:

$$\mathbb{P} \quad \equiv \quad \{P \in \mathbb{W} \rightarrow \mathbb{T} \mid \mathsf{hereditary}(P, \leadsto)\} \tag{ii}$$

In Coq, we define this type as a dependent pair and use implicit coercions that allow us to use the pair as a function when desired. We introduce the notation $w \models P$ when we wish to emphasize that we are thinking of P as an assertion rather than a function:

$$w \models P \qquad \equiv \qquad P(w) \tag{iii}$$

We say P entails Q, written $P \vdash Q$, when the truth of P forces the truth of Q:

$$P \vdash Q \qquad \equiv \qquad \forall w.\ (w \models P) \rightarrow (w \models Q) \tag{iv}$$

We write $\leadsto^*$ and $\leadsto^+$ for the reflexive and irreflexive transitive closure of the approximate relation, respectively. We say that two worlds w and w' are *fashionable**, written $w \sim w'$, if they contain the same amount of information, *i.e.*, if $|w| = |w'|$.

[⋆] The name "fashionable" is a play on words from when we used a time-based analogy for levels. A predicate P which holds fashionably is true on every world "now," but maybe not tomorrow.

Connection to intuitionistic logic. Our framework has much in common with Kripke models of intuitionistic logic in that predicates are hereditary over a relation between worlds. We develop this connection further in, *e.g.*, our model for implication in §2.4.

2.2 Axiomatization of Approximation

What kinds of properties do we require the approximation operations $\rightsquigarrow$ and $|\cdot|$ to have? In fact, our categorization for approximation is quite simple:**

Level of bottom:	$(\nexists w'.\ w \rightsquigarrow w') \rightarrow\ \ |w| = 0$	(a)
Level of approximation:	$(w \rightsquigarrow w')\ \ \rightarrow\ \ |w| = |w'| + 1$	(b)
Weak unapproximation:	$(\exists w.\ |w| = |w'| + 1)\ \rightarrow\ \exists w.\ w \rightsquigarrow w'$	(c)

If the world w cannot be further approximated, the level of w must be 0 (a). If the world w is approximated to w' then the level of w must be 1 larger than the level of w' (b). Finally, we sometimes wish to "unapproximate"—that is, given some world w', we would like to find a world w such that $w \rightsquigarrow w'$; an unapproximation to a given w' only exists if there is some world containing more information than w'. This unapproximation axiom allows us to obtain stronger equations relating to the approximation relation (see §3).

Three of the most important consequences of axioms (a)–(c) are the following:

Can't approximate:	$|w| = 0\ \rightarrow\ (\nexists w'.\ w \rightsquigarrow w')$	(1)
Can approximate:	$(|w| > 0)\ \rightarrow\ \exists w'.\ w \rightsquigarrow w'$	(2)
Well founded:	$(\forall w.\ (\forall w'.\ (w \rightsquigarrow w') \rightarrow w' \models P) \rightarrow w \models P) \rightarrow \forall w.\ w \models P$	(3)

That is, worlds of level 0 cannot be approximated further; but any world of level greater than 0 can be approximated. Moreover, the approximate relation is well-founded and thus allows proofs by induction over the action of approximation.

2.3 Models

A model is a triple $(\mathbb{W}, \rightsquigarrow, |\cdot|)$ of a set of worlds, an approximate operation, and a level operation such that axioms (a)–(c) hold. We present a simple model to give intuition and then a series of *generators* that build complex models from simpler components. We conclude with a nontrivial model generated by *indirection theory*.

Naturals. A very simple model is the naturals, $(\mathbb{N}, \rightsquigarrow_{\mathbb{N}}, |\cdot|_{\mathbb{N}})$, *i.e.*, $\mathbb{W} \equiv \mathbb{N}$. It is simple to define the approximation operations in this setting as follows: $n \rightsquigarrow_{\mathbb{N}} n' \equiv n = n' + 1$ and $|n|_{\mathbb{N}} \equiv n$. Axioms (a)–(c) follow directly from these definitions.

** To avoid clutter in our presentation, when we write an interface axiom we omit universal quantifications for variables scoped over the entire equation; *e.g.*, axiom (c) is actually:

$$\forall w'.\ ((\exists w.\ |w| = |w'| + 1)\ \rightarrow\ \exists w.\ w \rightsquigarrow w')$$

Generators. Showing that a particular model satisfies a collection of axioms is not always easy. A generator for a collection of axioms such as (a)–(c) is a method for constructing models for those axioms in a modular way by combining previous models in well-behaved ways. This is a particularly valuable technique in mechanized frameworks wherein small changes to the definitions can require significant amount of repair work. We use generators over a variety of axiom sets to allow rapid construction of models. From time to time we discover we are in some new setting and in that case our first task is to define a new generator so that if we encounter that setting again we can apply our new generator immediately. Our generators for the approximation axioms are:

- *Trivial.* Given a set of worlds $\mathbb{W}$, we can define the *trivial model* $(\mathbb{W}, \rightsquigarrow_0, |\cdot|_0)$ by setting and $|w|_0 \equiv 0$ and making the $\rightsquigarrow_0$ function undefined everywhere. We stated axiom (c) delicately to enable the trivial model, since we want neither approximation nor unapproximation. All predicates are automatically hereditary.
- *Semiproduct.* Given a model $(\mathbb{W}, \rightsquigarrow, |\cdot|)$ and some other set S, we can define the *semiproduct model* $(\mathbb{W} \times S, \rightsquigarrow_{\mathbb{W}\times S}, |\cdot|_{\mathbb{W}\times S})$ by defining approximate and level as:

$$(w, s) \rightsquigarrow_{\mathbb{W}\times S} (w', s') \quad \equiv \quad (s = s') \wedge (w \rightsquigarrow w') \quad \text{and} \quad |(w, s)|_{\mathbb{W}\times S} \quad \equiv \quad |w|.$$

- *Bijection.* Given a model $(\mathbb{W}, \rightsquigarrow, |\cdot|)$, some other set S, and a bijection $f : \mathbb{W} \to S$, we can define the *bijection model* $(S, \rightsquigarrow_f, |\cdot|_f)$ by setting

$$s \rightsquigarrow_f s' \quad \equiv \quad f^{-1}(s) \rightsquigarrow f^{-1}(s') \quad \text{and} \quad |s|_f \quad \equiv \quad |f^{-1}(s)|.$$

Although we only define a few generators here, we have found that they are sufficient for a large number of settings. One typically splits worlds into parts with trivial and nontrivial approximation behavior and combines the two using the semiproduct constructor, perhaps defining a bijection to a form more convenient for the remainder of one's proof. The trivial model is useful in most cases when the set of worlds does not have interesting approximation behavior; the exception is when one wishes to use the recursion operator μ defined in §4 since μ requires nontrivial approximation. In this case, semiproduct is useful in conjunction with the above model for the naturals $(\mathbb{N}, \rightsquigarrow_{\mathbb{N}}, |\cdot|_{\mathbb{N}})$ to add *non-trivial* approximation behavior to a set of worlds $\mathbb{W}$.

Indirection theory. The flagship non-trivial model for our approximation axioms is given by indirection theory [HDA10]. Indirection theory produces approximate solutions to a class of recursive domain equations defined by the pseudoequation:

$$K \qquad \approx \qquad F((K \times O) \to \mathbb{T})$$

Here F is a covariant functor (a type function together with an operation fmap satisfying the functor laws), O is some "other" noncircular data, and K is the object one wishes to model. A cardinality argument shows that this pseudoequation has no solutions in set theory. Indirection theory approximates a solution by constructing a type K (called the *knot*) and a model $(K, \rightsquigarrow_K, |\cdot|_K)$ that satisfies axioms (a)–(c). Our current construction of K is similar to the one given in [HDA10, §8] but we have enhanced it so that all predicates contained in a knot are hereditary [ADH10, `knot_hered.v`]. We use the product constructor to build the related model $(K \times O, \rightsquigarrow_{K\times O}, |\cdot|_{K\times O})$ and define $\mathbb{P}$ as the set of hereditary functions over $\rightsquigarrow_{K\times O}$ as in definition (*ii*).

Indirection theory also constructs two functions, $\mathsf{squash} : \mathbb{N} \times F(\mathbb{P}) \to K$ and $\mathsf{unsquash} : K \to \mathbb{N} \times F(\mathbb{P})$ whose behavior is given by the following set of equivalences:

$$\begin{array}{lcl} \mathsf{squash}(\mathsf{unsquash}(k)) & = & k \\ \mathsf{unsquash}(\mathsf{squash}(n, \mathcal{F})) & = & (n, \mathsf{fmap}\ \mathsf{approx}_n\ \mathcal{F}) \end{array}$$

That is, $\mathsf{squash} \circ \mathsf{unsquash}$ is the identity function, and $\mathsf{unsquash} \circ \mathsf{squash}$ is a kind of approximation function. The fmap function transforms $\mathcal{F} : F(\mathbb{P})$ by locating all of the predicates P inside $\mathcal{F}$ and replacing them with $\mathsf{approx}_n(P)$, defined as:

$$\mathsf{approx}_n(P) \in \mathbb{P} \quad \equiv \quad \lambda w. \begin{cases} P(w) & |w|_{K \times O} < n \\ \bot & |w|_{K \times O} \geq n \end{cases}$$

The relationship between squash-unsquash and $(K, \leadsto_K, |\cdot|_K)$ is given by:

$$\begin{array}{lcl} |k| & = & (\mathsf{unsquash}(k)).1 \\ k \leadsto k' & \leftrightarrow & \mathsf{let}\ (n, \mathcal{F}) = \mathsf{unsquash}(k)\ \ \mathsf{in}\ \ (n > 1) \wedge k' = \mathsf{squash}(n-1, \mathcal{F}) \end{array}$$

The level of k is equal to the first projection of k's unsquashing and approximation is equivalent to unsquashing and then resquashing to the next lower level. Axioms (a)–(b) follow directly; for (c), unsquash and then resquash to the next *higher* level.

We have used indirection theory to reason about first-class locks in a concurrent program [Hob08]; mutable references in the polymorphic λ-calculus; and program termination in a setting with function pointers and semantic `assert` statements [DH10].

2.4 Hereditary Base Logic

Truth constant:	$w \models \top$	$\equiv$	$\top$	*(v)*
Falsehood constant:	$w \models \bot$	$\equiv$	$\bot$	*(vi)*
Conjunction:	$w \models P \wedge Q$	$\equiv$	$(w \models P) \wedge (w \models Q)$	*(vii)*
Disjunction:	$w \models P \vee Q$	$\equiv$	$(w \models P) \vee (w \models Q)$	*(viii)*
Impredicative universal:	$w \models \forall x : \tau.\ P(x)$	$\equiv$	$\forall x : \tau.\ w \models P(x)$	*(ix)*
Impredicative existential:	$w \models \exists x : \tau.\ P(x)$	$\equiv$	$\exists x : \tau.\ w \models P(x)$	*(x)*
Implication:	$w \models P \Rightarrow Q$	$\equiv$	$\boxed{\begin{array}{l}\forall w'.\ (w \leadsto^* w') \to \\ \quad (w' \models P) \to (w' \models Q)\end{array}}$	*(xi)*
Negation:	$\neg P$	$\equiv$	$P \Rightarrow \bot$	*(xii)*

Given a model of approximation, we can now give semantic definitions for the operators of our base intuitionistic logic, which includes the usual propositional connectives as well as powerful higher-order quantification. Except for implication, each definition consists of a direct lifting of the underlying metalogic operator and can be proved hereditary easily from the assumption that the subformulae are hereditary. In contrast, implication requires that the hereditary assumption be baked in. The resulting model is exactly a Kripke model of intuitionistic logic and the standard intuitionistic proof theory (introduction and elimination rules) can be proved as lemmas from these definitions.

It is worth noting that the τ occurring above in the definitions of universal and existential quantification is allowed to range over all the types of the metalogic, including the type predicate itself; this makes the quantifiers *impredicative*. In contrast, a predicative quantifier would only be allowed to quantify over objects that are smaller according to some stratification, which turns out to be a significant technical restriction. Modeling certain programming language features, such as function closures, requires the stronger impredicative style of quantification that we provide.

3 The Very Model of a Modern Multimodal Logic

Appel *et al.* [AMRV07] showed how to reason about the action of approximation using modal logic; we go further using the *multimodal* approach outlined in [DAH08]. A *modality* $M \in \mathbb{M}$ is a binary relation that commutes with the approximation relation $\leadsto$:

$$\mathbb{M} \equiv \Big\{ M \in \mathcal{W} \to \mathcal{W} \to \mathbb{T} \;\Big|\; \forall w\, w''.\ \big(\exists w'.(w \leadsto w') \wedge (w' M w'')\big) \leftrightarrow \big(\exists w'.(w M w') \wedge (w' \leadsto w'')\big) \Big\} \qquad (xiii)$$

This condition on modalities is used to guarantee that the modal operators below are hereditary. Most "reasonable" relations one would like to define are modalities. We have seen four approximation relations: approximate $\leadsto$ and its reflexive $\leadsto^*$ and irreflexive $\leadsto^+$ transitive closures, and the same-level relation fashionably $\sim$; all are modalities:

$$\{\leadsto, \leadsto^*, \leadsto^+, \sim\} \;\subset\; \mathbb{M} \qquad (4)$$

The point of characterizing modalities is that we can then define modal operators parameterized by various modalities.

$$\begin{array}{llcll} \text{Necessarily:} & w \models \Box_M\, P & \equiv & \forall w'.\, (w M w') \to (w' \models P) & (xiv) \\ \text{Hypothetically:} & w \models \Diamond_M\, P & \equiv & \exists w'.\, (w' M w) \wedge (w' \models P) & (xv) \end{array}$$

Note we use the standard definition of the universal modality $\Box_M$, but our definition of the existential modality $\Diamond_M$ is backwards from what one might expect; indeed, we use the "proof-theoretic" dual discussed by Restall [Res00] as opposed to the more familiar boolean dual. We work with this proof-theoretic dual because it is immediately definable given the commutativity restrictions from definition (*xiii*) (whereas the boolean dual requires a different condition).

One of the major advantages of identifying and using modal operators is that there are a variety of useful rules and equations that apply to all modal operators. A few of these are listed below.

$$\begin{array}{rcll} {}_M P \vdash Q & \leftrightarrow & P \vdash \Box_M Q & (5) \\ \Box_M\, (P \Rightarrow Q) & \vdash & \Box_M\, P \Rightarrow \Box_M Q & (6) \\ \Box_M\, (P \wedge Q) & = & \Box_M\, P \wedge \Box_M\, Q & (7) \\ \Diamond_M\, (P \vee Q) & = & \Diamond_M\, P \vee \Diamond_M\, Q & (8) \\ \Box_M \big(\forall x : \tau.\ P(x)\big) & = & \forall x : \tau.\, \Box_M\, P(x) & (9) \\ \Diamond_M \big(\exists x : \tau.\ P(x)\big) & = & \exists x : \tau.\, \Diamond_M\, P(x) & (10) \end{array}$$

Lemma (5) gives the characteristic relationship between the $\Box$ modality and its associated dual $\Diamond$ modality. Readers familiar with modal logics will recognize (6) as axiom K, which is characteristic the "normal" modal logics.

Given the data we have about worlds and approximation at this point, we can define two important modal operators which capture some of the important aspects of the approximation model.

$$\text{Approximately:} \quad \rhd P \equiv \Box_{\leadsto^+} P \qquad (xvi)$$

$$\text{Fashionably:} \quad \bigcirc P \equiv \Box_{\sim} P \qquad (xvii)$$

The approximation modality $\rhd$ is especially important because it mediates the action of approximation. It interacts in a significant way with both the key Gödel-Löb induction rule (below) and with the recursion operator described in §4. The fashionability modality also interacts in a strong way with recursion. Because of the special relationship $\leadsto$ has with all the formulae of the logic, $\rhd$ enjoys some additional properties.

$$\rhd (\Box_M P) = \Box_M (\rhd P) \qquad (11)$$

$$\rhd (P \Rightarrow Q) = \rhd P \Rightarrow \rhd Q \qquad (12)$$

$$\rhd (P \vee Q) = \rhd P \vee \rhd Q \qquad (13)$$

$$Q \wedge \rhd P \vdash P \rightarrow Q \vdash P \qquad (14)$$

Lemma (11) shows that $\rhd$ commutes with every $\Box$ modality; this is a consequence of the validity condition for modal operators. Lemma (12) shows that $\rhd$ enjoys a stronger form of (6). Lemma (14), called the Löb rule, is especially notable because it embodies a kind of induction principle. It says that we can prove that Q entails P if we can show the (apparently) weaker statement that $Q \wedge \rhd P$ entails P; here $\rhd P$ is the induction hypothesis. The Löb rule follows from (3).

Note that (12) is a strengthened version of (6) with an equality rather than an entailment. We prefer equalities (when they can be achieved) to entailments because they allow us to use substitution tactics in mechanized proofs, (*e.g.*, `rewrite` in Coq) which is significantly more convenient than introducing a cut.

4 Recursion

In addition to its other benefits, the approximation structure baked into our logic gives us a powerful way to define recursive predicates. Suppose we have a predicate function F : predicate $\rightarrow$ predicate; then we can construct the recursive predicate μF : predicate satisfying the usual fixpoint equation $\mu F = F(\mu F)$ provided that F is *contractive*. Before we can formally define contractiveness we need a few additional definitions.

Recall from above the "fashionably" modality $\bigcirc P \equiv \Box_{\sim} P$. The underlying relation $w \sim w'$ holds iff $|w| = |w'|$, so $\bigcirc P$ holds when P holds in all worlds of the same level. Using $\bigcirc$, we define a stronger form of implication called "subtyping."

$$P \subseteq Q \equiv \bigcirc (P \Rightarrow Q) \qquad (xviii)$$

Subtyping is quite a bit stronger than regular implication because the only information it can "see" is the level of the current world. However, it is somewhat weaker than unconditional entailment. That is, if $w \models P \subseteq Q$ it might not be the case that $P \vdash Q$.

We say that P and Q are *equivalent* and write $P \cong Q$ iff $P \subseteq Q$ and $Q \subseteq P$. The intuition is that $w \models P \cong Q$ holds if P and Q are indistinguishable on worlds of level w and smaller. Any world that separates P from Q must have a level greater than $|w|$.

We say that F is contractive iff:

$$\forall P, Q.\ \ \triangleright (P \cong Q) \vdash F(P) \cong F(Q) \qquad (xix)$$

What does this mean? Every time you iterate the predicate function F, it "consumes" one level of approximation before using its argument. Usually, this means that the definition of F contains a $\triangleright$ operator guarding the occurrence of its argument.

What all this means is that we can define μ as a finite number of iterations of F:

$$w \models \mu F \qquad \equiv \qquad w \models F^{|w|}(\bot) \qquad (xx)$$

Here F^n means F iterated n times. The key point is that as long as F is contractive then we can prove the defining fixpoint theorem for μ:

$$\mu F \qquad = \qquad F(\mu F) \qquad (15)$$

Note that in the end we get a strong fixpoint theorem such that μF is simply *equal* to its one-step unfolding, which makes this a form of *equirecursion*. In contrast, systems with *isorecursion* typically require some computational step to allow the folding and unfolding of recursive definitions. Equirecursion is more convenient for our purposes because it allows us to use the rewriting facilities of the proof assistant, and also because it helps to decouple the semantics of the assertion logic from the (typically operational) semantics of the language. Furthermore, using the Löb induction rule and the fact that F is contractive, we can easily show that μF is the *unique* fixpoint of F [Ric10, §5].

5 Separation Algebras

Separation algebras are mathematical structures used to model separation logic. They provide the notion of disjoint merging that is central to the meaning of the operators of separation logic. We use a variant called a disjoint multi-unit separation algebra (hereafter just "DSA") [DHA09]. Briefly, a DSA is a set S and an associated three-place partial *join relation* $\oplus$, written $x \oplus y = z$, such that the join relation satisfies:

Functional:	$(x \oplus y = z_1) \ \rightarrow\ (x \oplus y = z_2) \ \rightarrow\ z_1 = z_2$	(d)
Commutative:	$x \oplus y \ = \ y \oplus x$	(e)
Associative:	$x \oplus (y \oplus z) \ = \ (x \oplus y) \oplus z$	(f)
Cancellative:	$(x_1 \oplus y = z) \ \rightarrow\ (x_2 \oplus y = z) \ \rightarrow\ x_1 = x_2$	(g)
Units:	$\forall x.\ \exists u_x.\ x \oplus u_x = x$	(h)
Disjointness:	$(x \oplus x = y) \ \rightarrow\ x = y$	(i)

These axioms define a structure that is like a commutative monoid in many ways, except that $\oplus$ is allowed to be a partial operation. The partiality is important, because it encodes disjointness. If $x \oplus y = z$, then x and y are disjoint, by definition.

Hidden in these axioms is the idea of an *identity*. We say x is an identity if whenever $x \oplus y = z$, then $y = z$. One fundamental property of identities is that x an identity if and only if $x \oplus x = x$. The units axiom (h) asserts the existence of (possibly many) identities. It is a consequence of the axioms that each element must have a *unique* identity associated with it.

In the following section we shall see how to use a separation algebra to build a separation logic. For the remainder of this section, we will briefly touch on some example DSAs and constructions for building more complicated ones.

5.1 Models

A model of a separation algebra is a set of worlds $\mathbb{W}$ together with a join relation $\oplus$ satisfying axioms (d)–(i). We give two trivial examples, followed by a series of simple generators, and conclude with some nontrivial generators and examples.

Examples and generators. The DSA axioms are well-behaved in the sense that they are easily propagated across a variety of useful constructions. In our work we have used the following, all of which are already implemented in Coq to enable rapid development:

- *Discrete.* Given a set S, define the *discrete DSA* $(S, \oplus_=)$ by defining

$$s_1 \ \oplus_= \ s_2 \ = \ s_3 \qquad \equiv \qquad s_1 \ = \ s_2 \ = \ s_3$$

  Every element joins only with itself and is an identity. Axioms (d)–(i) follow.
- *Option.* Given a set S, define the *option DSA* $(S_?, \oplus_?)$ by setting $S_? \equiv \mathsf{None} + \mathsf{Some}(s)$ and the join relation $\oplus_?$ as the least relation satisfying (where $s_? \in S_?$):

$$\begin{array}{rcccl} \mathsf{None} & \oplus_? & s_? & = & s_? \\ s_? & \oplus_? & \mathsf{None} & = & s_? \end{array}$$

  The $\oplus_?$ relation includes $\mathsf{None} \oplus_? \mathsf{None} = \mathsf{None}$. Axioms (d)–(i) follow easily.
- *Products.* If we are given two DSAs $(A, \oplus_A)$ and $(B, \oplus_B)$, we can define the *product DSA* $(A \times B, \oplus_{A \times B})$ componentwise by setting:

$$(a_1, b_1) \ \oplus_{A \times B} \ (a_2, b_2) \ = \ (a_3, b_3) \ \equiv \ (a_1 \oplus_A a_2 = a_3) \wedge (b_1 \oplus_B b_2 = b_3)$$

  Axioms (d)–(i) follow directly from the same axioms on A and B.
- *Functions.* Given a set A and a DSA $(B, \oplus_B)$, we can define the *function DSA* $(A \to B, \oplus_{A \to B})$ by lifting the DSA on B pointwise as follows:

$$f \ \oplus_{A \to B} \ g \ = \ h \qquad \equiv \qquad \forall a. \ \big(f(a) \ \oplus_B \ g(a) \ = \ h(a)\big)$$

  Axioms (d)–(i) follow directly from the axioms on B.
- *Bijection.* Given a DSA $(A, \oplus_A)$, a set B, and a bijection $f : A \to B$, we can define the *bijection DSA* $(B, \oplus_f)$ by setting

$$b_1 \ \oplus_f \ b_2 \ = \ b_3 \qquad \equiv \qquad f^{-1}(b_1) \ \oplus_A \ f^{-1}(b_2) \ = \ f^{-1}(b_3)$$

  Axioms (d)–(i) follow because f is a bijection and the axioms hold on A.

The previous generators are simple but very useful. For example, if A is a set of addresses and V a set of values, then the archetypical example of partial program heaps is given by the DSA $(A \rightarrow (V?), \oplus_{A\rightarrow(V?)})$, using the function and option generators. We have a large number of other generators in our toolkit: void, unit, discrete, disjoint sums, lists, subset, lift, Π-types, Σ-types, finite partial maps, and lattices; a number of these are described in some detail in [DHA09]. Here we explain another generator, similar in some ways to the bijection DSA covered above but more general:

- *Section–retraction.* Suppose we have a DSA $(B, \oplus_B)$. A function $h : B \rightarrow B$ is a *join homomorphism* when:

$$b_1 \oplus_B b_2 = b_3 \quad \rightarrow \quad h(b_1) \oplus h(b_2) = h(b_3) \qquad \textit{(xxi)}$$

  That is, joining is preserved by h. Now suppose we have a set A and a section–retraction pair: two functions $f : A \rightarrow B$ and $g : B \rightarrow A$ such that $g \circ f$ is the identity function on A; note that in any section–retraction pair f is automatically injective while g is automatically surjective. Suppose further that $f \circ g : B \rightarrow B$ is a join homomorphism. Define the *section–retraction DSA* $(A, \oplus_{\langle f,g\rangle})$ by setting:

$$a_1 \oplus_{\langle f,g\rangle} a_2 = a_3 \quad \equiv \quad f(a_1) \oplus_B f(a_2) = f(a_3)$$

  In other words, we take the separation structure induced on the preimage of f. Axioms (d), (g), and (i) follow directly from the injectivity of f and the underlying axioms on $\oplus_B$. Axiom (e) is even simpler and is direct from the commutativity of $\oplus_B$. The associativity (f) and units (h) axioms are tougher; both require that $g \circ f$ is the identity, $f \circ g$ is a join homomorphism, and the underlying axioms on $\oplus_B$.

  The significance of the section–retraction generator is that it will be just what is needed to handle the unsquash–squash pair constructed by indirection theory.

6 Mixing Separation and Approximation

Once we have defined the separation structure on a set of worlds, we are nearly ready to define the operators of separation logic. However, to interface with the approximation features of the logic, we need some additional axioms which ensure that separation and approximation can play well together in the same sandbox (see figure 1). These four axioms have the flavor of commuting diagrams; we require that the approximation relation and separation "slide around" each other cleanly. (There are a total of six possible cases, but two are subsumed by commutativity). These axioms let us prove the heredity of the operators of separation logic and to show certain useful results about the commutativity of approximation operators with separation operators.

Now we can give the definitions of the standard operators of separation logic.

$$\text{Empty:} \quad w \models \mathsf{emp} \equiv \mathsf{identity}\ w \qquad \textit{(xxii)}$$

$$\text{Separation:} \quad w \models P * Q \equiv \begin{array}{l} \exists w_1, w_2.\ (w_1 \oplus w_2 = w) \wedge \\ \quad (w_1 \models P) \wedge (w_2 \models Q) \end{array} \qquad \textit{(xxiii)}$$

$$\text{Seplication:} \quad w_1 \models P \twoheadrightarrow Q \equiv \begin{array}{l} \forall w_1', w_2, w.\ (w_1 \leadsto^* w_1') \rightarrow (w_1' \oplus w_2 = w) \\ \quad \rightarrow (w_2 \models P) \rightarrow (w \models Q) \end{array} \qquad \textit{(xxiv)}$$

$$(w_1 \oplus w_2 = w_3) \to (w_1 \leadsto w_1') \to \\ \exists w_2', w_3'.\ (w_1' \oplus w_2' = w_3') \wedge (w_2 \leadsto w_2') \wedge (w_3 \leadsto w_3')$$

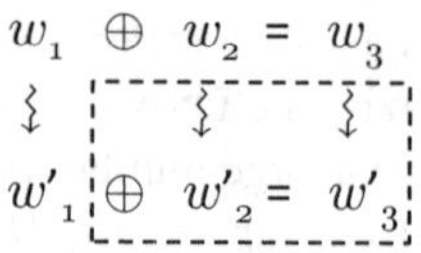

(j)

$$(w_1 \oplus w_2 = w_3) \to (w_3 \leadsto w_3') \to \\ \exists w_1', w_2'.\ (w_1' \oplus w_2' = w_3') \wedge (w_1 \leadsto w_1') \wedge (w_2 \leadsto w_2')$$

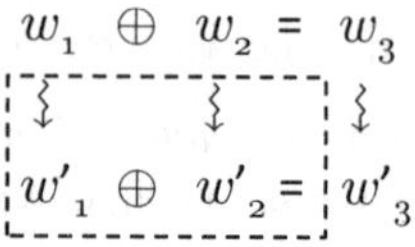

(k)

$$(w_1' \oplus w_2' = w_3') \to (w_1 \leadsto w_1') \to \\ \exists w_1, w_2.\ (w_1 \oplus w_2 = w_3) \wedge (w_2 \leadsto w_2') \wedge (w_3 \leadsto w_3')$$

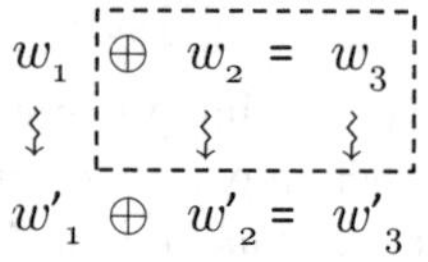

(l)

$$(w_1' \oplus w_2' = w_3') \to (w_3 \leadsto w_3') \to \\ \exists w_1, w_2.\ (w_1 \oplus w_2 = w_3) \wedge (w_1 \leadsto w_1') \wedge (w_2 \leadsto w_2')$$

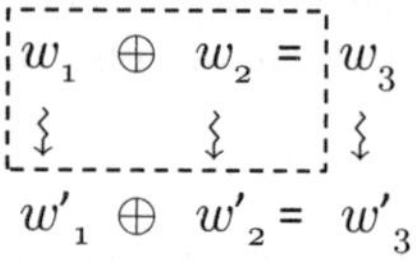

(m)

Fig. 1. Axioms for Mixing Separation and Approximation

The assertion emp and the separating conjunction $*$ can be shown hereditary by using axioms (j) and (k) . Notice that the definition of seplication explicitly quantifies over all more approximate worlds, just as does the definition of implication, making it immediately hereditary from the definition. Just as with implication, the semantics takes on an intuitionistic flavor, but in general works exactly as expected.

With these definitions stated, we can easily prove the standard inference rules of separation logic and various equalities among formulae. Note equations (20) and (21); these elegant equations are the result of our insistence that approximation and separation interact smoothly. Their proofs make essential use of axioms (l) and (m).

Commutativity:	$P * Q$	$=$	$Q * P$	(16)
Associativity:	$(P * Q) * R$	$=$	$P * (Q * R)$	(17)
Identity:	$\mathsf{emp} * P$	$=$	P	(18)
Seplication adjoint:	$(P * Q) \vdash R$	$=$	$P \vdash (Q \mathrel{-\!\!*} R)$	(19)
Approx sepconjunction:	$\rhd(P * Q)$	$=$	$(\rhd P * \rhd Q)$	(20)
Approx seplication:	$\rhd(P \mathrel{-\!\!*} Q)$	$=$	$(\rhd P \mathrel{-\!\!*} \rhd Q)$	(21)
Split sepconjunction:	$(P \vdash Q)$	$\to$	$(R \vdash S) \to (P * R) \vdash (Q * S)$	(22)
Cut seplication:	$(P \vdash Q \mathrel{-\!\!*} R)$	$\to$	$(S \vdash Q) \to (P * S) \vdash R$	(23)

In addition to the standard operators of separation logic, we can define three substructural modalities. First, we say that w_1 is a *substate* of w_2, written $w_1 \preceq w_2$, when

$$w_1 \preceq w_2 \quad \equiv \quad \exists w'.\ w_1 \oplus w' = w_2 \qquad (xxv)$$

Informally, w_1 is a smaller state than w_2 because you can add w' to w_1 to get w_2; it corresponds to the *substate* relation with respect to the separation structure. Second, we say that w_1 and w_2 are *orthogonal*, written $w_1 \sharp w_2$, when

$$w_1 \sharp w_2 \quad \equiv \quad \exists w'.\ w_1 \oplus w_2 = w' \tag{xxvi}$$

Two states are orthogonal when they are compatible in the sense that they can join together. Finally, w_1 and w_2 are *substructurally comparable*, written $w_1 \overset{\oplus}{\sim} w_2$, when

$$w_1 \overset{\oplus}{\sim} w_2 \quad \equiv \quad \exists w.\ (w_1 \sharp w) \wedge (w_2 \sharp w) \tag{xxvii}$$

Two worlds are substructurally comparable when there exists some world (typically an identity) that is orthogonal to both of them. We can consider the elements of a DSA as being divided into equivalence classes where there is one class for each unit, and every element with the same unit is in the class. Then $\overset{\oplus}{\sim}$ ranges over all the elements in the same equivalence class.

All of these substructural relations are valid modalities according to the definition from §3. The validity proofs are direct consequence of axioms from Figure 1.

$$\{\preceq, \sharp, \overset{\oplus}{\sim}\} \subsetneq \mathbb{M} \tag{24}$$

A further consequence is that our substructural modalities are all fashionable:

$$(w_1 \preceq w_2) \vee (w_1 \sharp w_2) \vee (w_1 \overset{\oplus}{\sim} w_2) \quad \rightarrow \quad w_1 \sim w_2 \tag{25}$$

We often find it convenient to express substructural ideas using modalities like these. For example, consider the diamond form of the substate relation; $\Diamond_{\preceq} P$ holds exactly when some substate of the current state satisfies P. In other words, adding $\Diamond_{\preceq}$ makes a predicate invariant under state expansion.[1] A little manipulation shows that:

$$\Diamond_{\preceq} P \quad = \quad P * \top. \tag{26}$$

7 Separation Logics over Knots

An important use case (indeed, our motivating use case) for combining approximation with separation are the "knots" of indirection theory. We can quite easily demonstrate that knots satisfy the approximation axioms using the interface provided by indirection theory. However, to define a separation structure on knots, we need to define an appropriate join relation and prove the DSA axioms. The knots provided to clients are *opaque*, which means the client cannot examine the details of the construction. However, the client has provided the critical functor F describing the internal structure of unsquashed knots. We require the client to define a separation structure over F which we then use to induce a separation structure over knots.

We proceed in stages. First we must make the set $\mathbb{N} \times F(\mathbb{P})$ into a DSA. We will require that the client of indirection theory demonstrate that F is a functor on DSAs,

[1] Such predicates were called *intuitionistic* in Reynolds' work on separation logic [Rey02].

$$x' \oplus f(y) = f(z) \;\rightarrow$$
$$\exists x, y_0.\; x \oplus y_0 = z \wedge f(x) = x' \wedge f(y_0) = f(y)$$

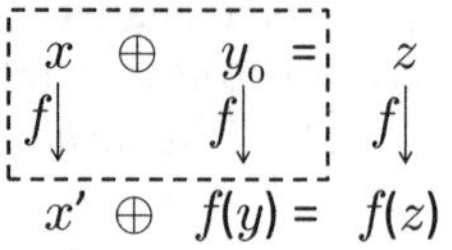

(n)

$$f(x) \oplus f(y) = z' \;\rightarrow$$
$$\exists y_0, z.\; x \oplus y_0 = z \wedge f(y_0) = f(y) \wedge f(z) = z'$$

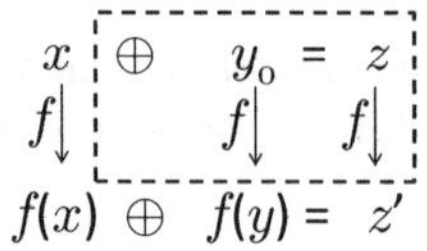

(o)

Fig. 2. Left and right unmappings

i.e., whenever X is a DSA, then $F(X)$ is also a DSA. Furthermore, we require that whenever $f : X \rightarrow Y$ is a join homomorphism, then $\mathsf{fmap}\ f : F(X) \rightarrow F(Y)$ must also be a join homomorphism. Now we use our generators to construct the DSA $(\mathbb{N} \times F(\mathbb{P}), \oplus_{(\mathbb{N}_=)\times(F(\mathbb{P}_=))})$: that is, we pair up a discrete DSA on $\mathbb{N}$ with the DSA generated by applying F to the discrete DSA on $\mathbb{P}$.

We will use the section–retraction generator to induce a DSA for the set $A \equiv K$ from the above DSA for $B \equiv \mathbb{N} \times F(\mathbb{P})$. Indirection theory gives us the section–retraction pair $(\mathsf{unsquash}, \mathsf{squash})$. It is easy to show that $\mathsf{unsquash} \circ \mathsf{squash}$ is a join homomorphism on B, completing the construction of the DSA for K.

We have two of the ingredients needed for a logic over knots with both separation and approximation. We have the approximation structure and we have a DSA. However, in order to complete the picture we need to prove the distributive axioms from §6.

The two "forward" axioms (j) and (k) follow easily from the assumption that F is a functor on DSAs. The "backward" axioms (l) and (m), however, are more involved. Proving these axioms appears to require additional technical restrictions on the functor F, having to do with "unmapping." The precise statement of these technical requirements is given in Figure 2 and is rather involved. However, proving that particular functors F have this property is usually easy.

Suppose one has a function $f : A \rightarrow B$ where A and B are DSAs. We say that f has *left unmappings* when it satisfies axiom (14) and *right unmappings* when it satisfies (15). We say a functor F *preserves unmappings* if, whenever f is a join homomorphism with left (right) unmappings, then $\mathsf{fmap}\ f$ has left (right) unmappings.

The existence of unmappings means that f has a weak kind of invertability property, and the preservation of unmappings means that when such a weakly invertable function is applied with fmap, the resulting function is itself weakly invertable.

As with approximation and DSAs, we can show that many standard constructions (when considered as functors) have the property of preserving unmappings. For example, products, disjoint sums, functions and lists all preserve unmappings.

If F preserves unmappings, then we can prove the "unapproximation" axioms (12) and (13) for knots. The key is to note that the approx function has left and right unmappings, and then lift the unmappings through the functor F using (14) and (15). The unmappings of $\mathsf{fmap}\ f$ then provide the required witnesses for axioms (12) and (13).

We now have all the pieces necessary to build a separation logic with approximation over the knots of indirection theory. In the final accounting, the client must provide, in addition to the data necessary for indirection theory itself, a proof that F is a functor on DSAs, and an easy technical proof about the preservation of unmappings. From this basic data, a rich logic of separation and approximation is automatically built.

8 Conclusion

We have presented a method for constructing powerful assertion logics using a Kripke semantics over a set of *worlds*. We have given axiomatic interfaces that worlds must satisfy in order to support higher-order stores in the step-indexing style, and to support substrucural features in the style of separation logic. These two features interact in non-trivial ways, and we have further shown how to get an elegant and well-behaved logic by requiring the approximation and separation relations to commute with one another. Finally, we have shown throughout the paper how to construct models of these axiomatic interfaces that support a variety of interesting programming language domains. The proofs and constructions that appear in this paper have been mechanized in Coq and are freely available as part of the Mechanized Semantic Library [ADH10].

Acknowledgements. Aquinas Hobor is supported by a Lee Kuan Yew Postdoctoral Fellowship. Robert Dockins and Andrew W. Appel are supported in part by NSF grant CNS-0910448 and AFOSR grant FA9550-09-1-0138.

References

[ADH10] Appel, A., Dockins, R., Hobor, A.: Mechanized Semantic Library (2009-2010), `http://msl.cs.princeton.edu`

[Ahm04] Ahmed, A.J.: Semantics of Types for Mutable State. PhD thesis, Princeton University, Princeton, NJ, Tech Report TR-713-04 (November 2004)

[AMRV07] Appel, A.W., Melliès, P.-A., Richards, C.D., Vouillon, J.: A very modal model of a modern, major, general type system. In: Proc. 34th Annual Symposium on Principles of Programming Languages (POPL 2007), pp. 109–122 (January 2007)

[COY07] Calcagno, C., O'Hearn, P.W., Yang, H.: Local action and abstract separation logic. In: LICS 2007: Proceedings of the 22nd Annual IEEE Symposium on Logic in Computer Science, pp. 366–378 (2007)

[DAB09] Dreyer, D., Ahmed, A., Birkedal, L.: Logical step-indexed logical relations. In: Proceedings 24th Annual IEEE Symposium on Logic in Computer Science, LICS 2009 (2009)

[DAH08] Dockins, R., Appel, A.W., Hobor, A.: Multimodal separation logic for reasoning about operational semantics. In: 24th Conference on the Mathematical Foundations of Programming Semantics (MFPS XXIV). Springer Electronic Notes in Theoretical Computer Science (ENTCS), pp. 5–20 (2008)

[DH10] Dockins, R., Hobor, A.: A theory of termination via indirection (July 2010) (under submission)

[DHA09] Dockins, R., Hobor, A., Appel, A.W.: A fresh look at separation algebras and share accounting. In: Hu, Z. (ed.) APLAS 2009. LNCS, vol. 5904, pp. 161–177. Springer, Heidelberg (2009) (to appear)

[HAZ08] Hobor, A., Appel, A.W., Nardelli, F.Z.: Oracle semantics for concurrent separation logic. In: Drossopoulou, S. (ed.) ESOP 2008. LNCS, vol. 4960, pp. 353–367. Springer, Heidelberg (2008)

[HDA10] Hobor, A., Dockins, R., Appel, A.W.: A theory of indirection via approximation. In: Proc. 37th Annual ACM Symposium on Principles of Programming Languages (POPL 2010), pp. 171–185 (January 2010)

[Hob08] Hobor, A.: Oracle Semanatics. PhD thesis, Princeton University, Princeton, NJ (November 2008)

[Ler06] Leroy, X.: Formal certification of a compiler back-end, or: programming a compiler with a proof assistant. In: POPL 2006, pp. 42–54 (2006)

[Nip02] Nipkow, T.: Hoare logics for recursive procedures and unbounded nondeterminism. In: Bradfield, J.C. (ed.) CSL 2002 and EACSL 2002. LNCS, vol. 2471, pp. 155–182. Springer, Heidelberg (2002)

[Res00] Restall, G.: An Introduction to Substructural Logics. Routledge, London (2000)

[Rey02] Reynolds, J.: Separation logic: A logic for shared mutable data structures. In: LICS 2002: IEEE Symposium on Logic in Computer Science, pp. 55–74 (July 2002)

[Ric10] Richards, C.D.: The Approximation Modality in Models of Higher-Order Types. PhD thesis, Princeton University, Princeton, NJ (June 2010)

Author Index

Printing: Mercedes-Druck, Berlin
Binding: Stein+Lehmann, Berlin